AF607823

THE VALLEY OF THE TRENT

Edited by EDWIN C. GUILLET

The Trent system of lakes, rivers, and canals occupies a considerable part of the counties of Hastings, Durham, Northumberland, Peterborough, Haliburton, and Victoria, in the province of Ontario. This volume of documents, records, and early writings covers the discovery and settlement of the valley, development and decline of the lumber trade, the Trent Canal and community life, and is abundantly illustrated in gravure and line from source materials. *The Times Literary Supplement* says of this first volume that it "raises high hopes of an important contribution to Canadian social and economic history." *British Book News* says that the "excerpts from manuscripts, newspapers, old and rare books and pamphlets, with the excellent contemporary illustrations, give a vivid and valuable account of early life in this interesting area."

EDWIN C. GUILLET is a distinguished Canadian historian, particularly noted for his volumes on the social and local history of Ontario. Included in his other publications are *Early Life in Upper Canada, The Great Migration, Lives and Times of the Patriots, Pioneer Arts and Crafts, Pioneer Days in Upper Canada, The Pioneer Farmer and Backwoodsman, Pioneer Inns and Taverns, Pioneer Travel, The Story of Canadian Roads,* and *Pioneer Settlements in Upper Canada.*

ONTARIO SERIES

I

THE VALLEY OF THE TRENT

EDITED, WITH AN INTRODUCTION
AND NOTES BY

EDWIN C. GUILLET

THE CHAMPLAIN SOCIETY
FOR THE GOVERNMENT OF ONTARIO
UNIVERSITY OF TORONTO PRESS

1957

All rights reserved

Printed in Great Britain

ISBN 978-0-8020-1072-8 (*cloth*)
ISBN 978-1-4875-9938-6 (*paper*)

Reprinted 2017

TO

GEORGE M. DOUGLAS

EXPLORER—ANTIQUARIAN—GOOD COMPANION

FOREWORD

> "I did not realize that the old grave that stood among the brambles at the foot of our farm was history."
>
> —STEPHEN LEACOCK

ALL TOO MANY of us, as Stephen Leacock has so well expressed it, are unaware of the great wealth of history that lies in the records of our past. As one decade and generation succeeds another, the gap between us and our forebears widens and the opportunity for collecting and preserving these records greatly diminishes.

It is very heartening to see the growing interest in our history that is being shown by the people and various communities of our young country. We are now developing a sense of history. An increasing number of our people are being made deeply conscious of the absorbing history of this Province and Nation. Steps have also been taken to expand the facilities available in our public archives. It is, however, true that many of these records exist only in manuscript form and are not readily accessible to the people. Many old records in private homes and in business offices are being inadvertently destroyed or lost.

It seemed proper, therefore, that the Government of Ontario should undertake to preserve in printed form, available to the interested public and to historians, a representative selection of the more interesting and significant records of the past, covering particularly those regions and periods in which historical research has not yet been extensive. To facilitate this, the Champlain Society was invited to undertake the preparation and publication of a series of documentary volumes on the early history of Ontario.

For over half a century, the Champlain Society has been engaged in publishing volumes of documents in the broader fields of Canadian history, and it has earned for itself an international reputation. It, therefore, is especially well qualified to undertake the preparation of this series, toward which the Government of Ontario will contribute the cost of publication and editorial expenses. There will be no diminution in the regular work of the Champlain Society. What is gained is an entirely new Ontario-assisted series which we would not otherwise have.

It is not intended that these volumes should deal with interpretive phases of history; rather they will represent a collection of basic historical facts, documentary in nature. It is hoped that interesting and important documents and records, including those pertaining to what is now Ontario during the French régime, will be available from within the Province itself. No doubt similar records are in existence in our sister Province of Quebec and overseas. If so, they can be copied and made available in these documentary volumes. From them historians and others may reach their own individual interpretations and draw their own conclusions.

Separate volumes are in the course of preparation on several geographic regions. Since in most cases, the early history of a locality tended to develop in its own way in accordance with the special conditions facing the pioneer families, the series, in the main, will cover the years from the early part of the seventeenth century into the days of settlement. But it is not bound by fixed dates, as in some areas the work of exploration and pioneer development began later than in others. Thus the development of some parts of the Province goes back well into the French régime, while in others it is not significant until the nineteenth century.

The first volume, *The Valley of the Trent*, is edited by Mr. Edwin C. Guillet, who is well known for his books on the pioneer history of Ontario. Mr. Guillet has an intimate knowledge of the Trent Valley, and through his associations and experience has been able to secure for his volume many valuable documents and illustrations.

In addition to Mr. Guillet's work, volumes on Fort Frontenac under the French régime, on Kingston from the English Conquest to the War of 1812, and on the Windsor area in the seventeenth and eighteenth centuries are all well under way and will appear in due course.

Under the general guidance of the officers of the Champlain Society, the editor of each volume is responsible for the selection of material. In each case, he will provide an introduction for the purpose of placing the documents in their proper perspective and assisting the reader to understand their significance. Any opinions expressed in these volumes are, of course, those of the editors. The reader of this Ontario-assisted series will not find in them a history of the conventional sort, but rather a collection of primary sources. Nevertheless, they should prove extremely valuable as a source of information and make for interesting reading in themselves.

The volumes of this "Ontario Series" in the Champlain Society format will be available to its individual members and also to students and the public through the university and public libraries holding memberships. In addition, arrangements have been made with the Ontario Historical Society for the distribution of a special issue. It is therefore hoped that each volume will be easily accessible to the public either through the libraries or private subscription. In the carrying out of this project, the co-operation of the Champlain Society is gratefully acknowledged.

LESLIE M. FROST
Prime Minister of Ontario

January 1, 1957

PREFACE

THE PREPARATION of an historical work, however much it may be a labour of love, is always to a large degree a co-operative effort; and it is usually true that the contributions of others add comprehensiveness and richness of detail, particularly when the volume concerns local history. I am indebted primarily to the Honourable Leslie Frost, Prime Minister of Ontario, and to the Champlain Society, joint sponsors of the series of which this is the initial volume. Dr. W. Kaye Lamb, Dominion Archivist and President of the Champlain Society, has taken a personal interest in the volume in both capacities; and both he and the Society's General Editor, Professor J. B. Conacher, have improved its content by critical comment and suggestion. Dr. George Spragge, Ontario Provincial Archivist, and Mr. D. F. McOuat, his capable and co-operative assistant,[1] have not only made available many documents which might otherwise have been missed, but have shortened the process of assembling these by providing facilities for photostating and typing.

Many other sources have supplemented these two large archival collections. With the assistance of my wife it was possible to locate and transcribe a number of rare items relative to the Trent region in the Library of the British Museum, the Cambridge University Library, and the Mitchell Collection in Glasgow. A good deal of general research has been done in the Canadian collections of the Toronto Public Library, the Legislative Library of Ontario, the University of Toronto Library, and the Library of Parliament in Ottawa. To the librarians and their staffs in these libraries my thanks are extended.

I should like to acknowledge the assistance of Mr. R. M. Lewis of the Ontario Department of Planning and Development, who is responsible for the excellent index of documents in the Ontario Parliament Buildings and related offices which made possible the location of items in various collections. The staff of the Surveys and Maps Division in the East Block gave me valuable assistance in making these available.

Mr. William Graff, Librarian of North York Township, who was

[1]Mr. McOuat is now Secretary of the Archaeological and Historic Sites Board of Ontario.

Librarian in Peterborough when research for this volume began, extended many courtesies when I consulted the invaluable Peter Robinson Collection of documents in that Library.

Not only co-operation but inspiration has come over a period of many years from Mr. George M. Douglas, of "Northcote", near Lakefield, to whom this volume is dedicated. His antiquarian interests and his photography render his contribution to this volume pre-eminent. Similarly outstanding has been the assistance of Mrs. Helen Fowlds Marryat of Hastings, long prominent in the historical field in Peterborough County, who has been enthusiastic and untiring in her contributions to the volume. She generously gives credit to many others along the Trent River, as follows: Mrs. George McCubbin, Warkworth; Lieutenant-Colonel F. E. Birdsall and Mrs. Gilbert Elmhurst, Birdsall; Miss Louisa V. Fowlds, Toronto; Miss Ivy Eggleton, Belleville; Miss Lilian Benor and Mr. C. W. Reycraft, Campbellford; Mr. C. S. Chard, Stirling; Mr. Percy Lancaster, Havelock; Mr. James Humphries, ex-Warden of Peterborough County; Miss M. E. Blacklock, Meadowvale; and Mrs. William Brooks and Messrs. Howard Fairman, Raymond McGuire, J. L. Doherty, and William Armstrong, all of Hastings.

One of the greatest contributors to the illustrations reproduced in this volume is Miss Phyllis Denne of Bridgenorth, who greatly enriched the book by making available a large number of historical negatives assembled many years ago by her father, the late T. H. G. Denne.[1] The Trustees of the National Maritime Museum, Greenwich, England, have permitted the reproduction of two paintings of sailing-ships contemporary with those used to transport the Peter Robinson emigrants across the Atlantic. Mr. Alen McCombie, Toronto, made available one of his paintings of Cameron Lake, and the Sigmund Samuel Canadiana Gallery, Toronto, a water-colour of Cramahe (Colborne) by James Pattison Cockburn. Miss Sheila Boyd, Bobcaygeon, grand-daughter of Mossom Boyd, who was long one of the best known lumbermen and industrialists of the Trent Valley, provided some early water-colours of that village. Items from both the writings of the Langtons and the sketches of Anne Langton are reproduced by courtesy of the Langton family, of the Fenelon Falls Public Library, and of the Macmillan Company of Canada and Clarke, Irwin & Company, the publishers respectively of the journals and letters of John Langton and his sister. Miss Florence Atwood, Lakefield, provided portraits of her grandfather and grandmother, Thomas and Catharine Traill, the former

[1]See Introduction, pp. lvii and lviii.

not previously reproduced; and Mrs. Robert Scully, Toronto, made available a rare portrait of her grandmother, the poet Rhoda Anne Page of Cobourg. Mrs. Kathleen Sibbald Lloyd of Cobourg, whose husband was a great-grandson of Captain Charles Rubidge, provided an early oil portrait of him not previously reproduced. For information about the Trent Canal I am indebted to Mr. A. L. Killaly, Peterborough, who was long its Superintendent, and whose grandfather was Minister of Public Works in the canal's early years.

My thanks are extended to two members of the staff of the Royal Ontario Museum. Mr. Kenneth E. Kidd, Curator of Ethnology, provided a valuable account of Indian remains along the Trent, as well as photographs; and Mr. James L. Baillie of the Department of Ornithology lent negatives of the Fothergill paintings in the Museum, interesting landscapes made in 1819 of the Port Hope-Rice Lake region.

To Mrs. Helen Marryat, Hastings, from whom I received numerous manuscript and printed materials, photographs and maps, I am indebted as well for the inclusion in this volume of several water-colours of the Trent region by the Reverend M. A. Farrar, a pupil of J. M. W. Turner, the English landscape artist. It has just come to my notice that another English artist of the same period has left work closely related to the Valley of the Trent. He is Edwin Whitefield (*b.* 1816), who came to America in his youth and won fame for his views of towns and scenes in the United States and Canada. About the middle of the century he was in Ontario; and during an itinerary from lakes Simcoe and Couchiching to the Rideau Canal and Kingston he made many sketches of scenes along the Trent system, including Peterborough, the Yankee Bonnet Rapids two miles below on the Otonabee, the steamer *Otonabee* wooding up in that neighbourhood, and a variety of others between Chemong and Rice lakes. His original sketchbook was sold in November 1956 by Goodspeed's Book Shop, Boston, to Mr. Walter Wallace, 922 Madison Avenue, New York City.[1]

The interpretation of Indian place-names has recently become more difficult because of the lack of experts in that field in museums. My thanks are due to Mr. John Huden, Burlington, Vermont, and Mr. Stephen Laurent, Intervale, New Hampshire, without whose assistance many Indian names of lakes and rivers would have gone without explanation.

[1]For a description of the sketchbook see *The Month at Goodspeed's*, Vol. XXVIII, Nos. 1–2, pp. 13–14. The booklet was brought to my attention through the courtesy of John Gray, President of the Macmillan Company of Canada.

I am indebted also to two literary experts who were good enough to read critically some portions of the poetical productions of two writers of the Rice Lake district in whom I have for many years been particularly interested. Professor R. L. McDougall of University College and Dr. E. J. Pratt, Professor *Emeritus* of Victoria University, favourably commented upon, respectively, John Copway's *The Ojibway Conquest* and certain of Rhoda Anne Page's poems, and the inclusion of these items at considerable length in these pages is the result.

For information and suggestions my appreciation is also extended to the following: Dr. W. Stewart Wallace, Librarian *Emeritus* of the University of Toronto; Dr. T. R. Millman, Archivist of Wycliffe College; Mrs. Margery Pewtress, Cobourg; Mr. Robert Porter, Peterborough Public Library; Mr. Stuart Ryan, Port Hope; Professor G. H. Needler, Toronto; Mr. William Colgate, Toronto; Mr. William Dennison, Toronto; and Mr. J. A. Edmison, Assistant to the Principal, Queen's University. My thanks are due to Mr. F. H. H. Lowe, Ninette, Manitoba, for portraits by Paul Kane of Mr. and Mrs. F. S. Clench, who were Mr. Lowe's grandparents and the parents of Kane's wife; and to various descendants of the Weller, Traill, Payne, Caddy, Dunford, Moodie, Ruttan, Batten, Rubidge, Strickland, McCauley, Hayward, Stewart, Matthews, Young, and Langton families who were prominent in the early history of the Valley of the Trent.

My wife, who continues to endure graciously my preoccupation in historical research, has assisted in many ways in the preparation of this volume; and my sons James Edwin and George Robert have aided in the photographic work.

E. C. G.

Toronto
January 1, 1957

Addendum

Please note the following alteration for the caption of illustration No. 51 facing page 359.

(51) COUNCIL AND OFFICIALS, PETERBOROUGH COUNTY, 1863

Rear Row: Robert Ritchie, Reeve of Snowdon; George Clark, Reeve of Douro; James A. Hall, Sheriff; John J. Hall, Clerk of Division Court; William Gainor, Reeve of Minden and Stanhope; Stephen P. Morton, Jailer.

Second Row: P. M. Grover, Reeve of Asphodel; Evans Ingram, Reeve of Otonabee; Peter Pearce, Reeve of Belmont and Methuen (in Warden's gown); R. D. Rodgers, Reeve of Ashburnham (in front of Warden); Francis Crowe, Reeve of Dummer; John Walton, Reeve of Smith; John Galvin, Deputy Reeve of Smith.

Front Row, Left to Right: Edgecumbe Pearce, County Clerk; Cornelius Sullivan, Reeve of Ennismore; George Lockie, Reeve of Monaghan; Christopher Burton, Auditor; Walter Sheridan, Treasurer; James Foley, Auditor; Andrew Nelson, Deputy Reeve of Otonabee; R. E. Birdsall, Deputy Reeve of Asphodel; Charles Perry, Mayor of Peterborough.

(The above names are found in faint pencil on the back of a copy of the photograph in the possession of J. B. Pearce, Norwood, grandson of Peter Pearce, the Warden.)

CONTENTS

IV. Settlement: The Peter Robinson Emigration, 1825

V. TRANSPORTATION: THE TRENT CANAL

VI. General Transportation

VII. Industry: Lumbering

VIII. Community Life: Land Boards, Quarter Sessions, Political Life

IX. Community Life: Religion

X. Community Life: Education

ILLUSTRATIONS

Plates

Maps

Between pages 182 and 183

Text-Figures

INTRODUCTION

THE TRENT system of lakes, rivers, and canals occupies a considerable part of the counties of Hastings, Durham, Northumberland, Peterborough, Haliburton, and Victoria. The first settlement in "the back townships"—as the entire region in the rear of the first tiers of townships along Lake Ontario was usually called—was in the year 1818 in Smith Township; and soon afterwards the potentialities of the trade in lumber were being eagerly explored. With the establishment of the first mills, and with the use of the first steamboats very shortly afterwards, came alterations in water levels and channels of communication; and all these developments in the Trent watershed were soon included in "the Trent Canal"—a long-term, spasmodic, and controversial project which continued until recent times. In 1912, when a survey of the region was made under the direction of the Commission of Conservation, it was estimated that the Dominion Government had spent "some ten million dollars on this canal and watershed, building dams at some forty lakes to regulate the waterflow," even though the government had never secured control of the watersheds which form the source of the system. The vast and unfortunate errors made in the spirit of pioneering and in the name of free enterprise had long since laid waste the greater part of the region. The *Survey* puts it this way:

> The slopes, once for the most part covered with valuable pine and hardwood forest, had been cut over. A large area, the pinery in particular, had been repeatedly subjected to fires and rendered liable to eventual total destruction. . . . A short inspection trip made it clear that these conditions presented a problem of peculiar and particular interest; . . . a problem meriting the development of some plan for its solution.[1]

The geological structure of the region, although an attraction to early settlers, was destined to be, in consequence of the mismanagement of the timber resources, a chief reason for the disastrous failure of the northerly sections as agricultural land. The eminent geologist, Dr. A. P. Coleman, summed up the situation as follows:

[1]See *Trent Watershed Survey: a Reconnaissance by C. D. Howe, Ph.D., and J. H. White, B.A., B.Sc.F., with an Introductory Discussion by B. E. Fernow, LL.D.* (Toronto, 1913), p. 1.

The combination of kames (hills of sand and gravel with boulders) with pure sand deposits, through which rise occasional hills of the harder Archaean rocks, makes a region entirely unsuited for agriculture, and useful only for forest growth. The result of glacial action north of the Palaeozoic rocks has been the formation of poor soils deficient in lime and often also in clayey constituents, except for the occasional lime-stone or shale and clay deposits.[1]

When the lumber industry was at its height it was unnecessary for settlers to live by agriculture alone, or even in part; but as the vicious exploitation of the timber resources proceeded, followed by bush-fires and the erosion of soil no longer held on the rocks by the roots of trees, agriculture became unprofitable because most of the good earth was washed into lake and river. The absence of all safeguards in early lumbering under the licence system had the inevitable result, as the *Survey* makes clear:

The sequence of this mismanagement is everywhere the same. The removal either of the best or of all timber, without disposing of the débris, leaves a slash which is invariably subject to fire; after this a loss of interest takes place on the part of the licensee and, what is worse, on the part of the government. Nature then attempts to reproduce the forest, and this is followed by a repetition of the fires, which kill the seed trees and seedlings of the better kinds. The ground is then re-covered by aspen and birch for a time; but, through repeated con-flagrations, it is finally rendered useless for any productive purpose. A similar sequence takes place in connection with the small-farm portions: at first, through the home market made by the lumbermen, a fair living may be made by the occupant; gradually this market vanishes and the soil becomes worked out; the surface wears away, the rocks are exposed, and the people are left destitute and miserable. . . . At the present time [1912] the pine timber, at least, is practically gone from this watershed; . . . finally the bare-rock condition or man-made desert is the result. At present only the beginnings of these conditions can be seen here and there, yet in the three townships of Methuen, Anstruther, and Burleigh alone nearly 150,000 acres of such desert exist.[2]

Although the half century since 1912 has seen a little reforesta-tion, a good deal of mining, and a great development of the region as a vacation paradise and the resort of hunters and fishermen, there has probably been a further deterioration of the land from the point of view of agriculture. In general, it has been abandoned

[1]Quoted in *Trent Watershed Survey*, pp. 9–10.
[2]*Trent Watershed Survey*, pp. 5 and 4.

to summer resorts, except where minerals have been found in quantities sufficient for commercial exploitation.

The chief headwaters of the Trent system lie in the central part of Haliburton County and consist of some 130,000 acres of water surface; and another 100,000 acres are added by nine other basins, comprising, in order of size, the Gull River, the Burnt River, the Mississauga, Jack's Creek, Eels Creek, Deer Bay Creek, Nogies[1] Creek, Buckhorn Creek, and Squaw River. The total water area of the Trent Canal and its feeders is estimated at nearly three hundred square miles.

The Trent Canal project, for a century developed in a slow and irrational fashion, has been subjected, according to the *Survey*, "to precisely the same kind of mismanagement as the territory through which it passes";[2] and the natural result has been public criticism and ridicule which the original idea did not deserve. Even a generation ago the canal's usefulness for local freight had practically ceased, and its value was largely restricted to facilities for water-power and pleasure craft.[3]

Apart from political considerations, the development of the Trent system was delayed, both early and late, by hopes of other routes and other types of transport. A great deal of research might be expended upon early maps and surveys without positive result; for the course of waterways has often been altered, and the general lack of names or of consistency in their use makes identification uncertain. An example of this confusion, and of the search for alternative routes, is afforded by Alexander Sherriff's "Topographical Notices of the Country lying between the Mouth of the Rideau and Penetanguishene on Lake Huron." He refers to the Muskoka River and lakes as named after a Mississauga chief; but only the traders used the name, the Indians employing another. From the southern branch of that river, wrote Sherriff, "canoes may pass to the Trent or Lake Simcoe." Travelling *viâ* the Severn, he was twelve days returning from Penetang to Lac des Allumettes.

[1]Chief Nogie (or "Captain Nogy" as John Langton knew him) is said to have discovered a lead mine near the creek, and to have gone there alone from time to time to replenish the supply for his tribesmen's muzzle-loaders. Jealous of his secret, he is said to have unwittingly killed his own son when he found he was being followed.

[2]*Trent Watershed Survey*, p. 2.

[3]The Peterborough region is probably best known because of its Lift Lock, a Trent Canal development inaugurated in 1904. The meetings of the American Canoe Association at Stoney Lake in 1883 and 1887 also drew attention to it; and the "Peterborough canoe" has long been famous.

The going was "not expeditious, the men being obliged to pass twice over the portages, and it being often very difficult to get our three fathomed canoe through the uncleared tracks."[1] He counted forty-five portages, the longest three-quarters of a mile, and he noted that many of them would need widening, and the rivers cleared of trees and driftwood, to enable the route to be covered in four or five days. The interpretation of such records is most difficult, however, and no one could trace the routes with certainty. These unsatisfactory experiences were several times repeated in the search for the best routes of travel.

The scope of this volume is not slavishly restricted to the geographical boundaries of the Trent watershed, which extends on either side of the system of lakes and rivers from the highlands above Balsam Lake to Trenton and Belleville. We omit, for several reasons, all reference to the Bay of Quinte and Belleville, as well as to most of Hastings County and to numerous outlying townships in various parts of the region. On the other hand Cobourg and Port Hope are included in some measure, for they were ports of entry and administrative and commercial centres of much of the region in the early period, and supplied many enterprising settlers and industrialists who were prominent in its development. The period under review is generally that prior to Confederation, but there are also references to post-Confederation settlement and development of several of the more northerly townships, including those which subsequently became part of the County of Haliburton.

A nation's history is basically the history of its innumerable communities and localities; and the national historian is always indebted to those who have investigated and recorded the local scene. Records—the heritage of the past which enables subsequent generations to understand how their ancestors lived and worked—have been preserved in Ontario only in part, and often more by accident than design. Some parts of the province have been fortunate, both in the amount of records available and in the assiduity with which competent historians have made use of them. Especially in recent times, university theses have advanced our knowledge of some localities; but still more valuable are the few local histories written within a generation of earliest settlement, at a time when many pioneers in the true sense of the word were still alive. The Peterborough district is among the more fortunate in both these respects; but there is another reason even more important which

[1]*Transactions*, Literary and Historical Society of Quebec, Vol. II, 1831, pp. 243–309.

makes the region's recorded history perhaps the richest and most informative in Ontario. This is the fact that many of the early residents, attracted to "the back lakes" largely by aesthetic considerations, were highly literate and lucid both in talking and writing about their experiences; and we consequently have for the region a body of literature that is approached nowhere else either in quantity or quality. The works of "the literary Stricklands"—Samuel Strickland, Susanna Moodie, and Catharine[1] Traill—are the best known; but we have letters, emigrant guidebooks, journals, accounts of pioneering, essays, and verse by John and Anne Langton, Frances Stewart, J. W. Dunbar Moodie, Rhoda Anne Page, Charles and Frederick Rubidge,[2] George Arundel Hill, Thomas Poole, and Thomas Need—to mention only the more prolific writers. There were plenty of cultured settlers[3] who did not write books, of course, and many others less cultured who were at least equally valuable in settlement, business, and public spirit; but the literary works of those named above provide a firm basis of source materials for a history of the Valley of the Trent.

"Old times" in the region have been investigated in recent years by several capable historians and newspapermen, among whom

[1]The name is often misspelled, the Toronto Public Library and many others using "Catherine" in their records; but Mrs. Traill herself never spelled her name other than "Catharine."

[2]In addition to his work in settling the Peter Robinson immigrants of 1825, Captain Charles Rubidge opened the Keene Road in the eighteen-thirties, and was responsible for the arrangements for a second emigration of Irish in 1839. These emigrants, totalling one hundred and eighty-three, were mainly from Colonel Wyndham's estates in Clare and Limerick, and were located in the rear concessions. Frederick Rubidge, half-brother of Charles, was a surveyor, poet, and leader in amateur dramatics in the eighteen-thirties.

[3]John Langton described Peterborough in the eighteen-thirties as "a very pretty, picturesque, thriving village, . . . with near thirty genteel families within visiting distance"; and he attended Bachelors' Balls there in evening dress, observing, "I certainly never expected on coming to Canada that I should be one of the Bachelors who gave a ball to between eighty and ninety, and meet with two of the best waltzers I ever figured with." (Langton, *Early Days in Upper Canada* (Toronto, 1926), pp. 21 and 82, respectively.) When Patrick Shirreff visited the village in 1833 he disliked the "mean houses," but noted that Peterborough's population included "a number of military and naval half-pay officers of Britain," and that the society of the place had the reputation of being "the most brilliant and polished in Canada." (Shirreff, *A Tour through North America* (Edinburgh, 1835), p. 123.) But there were others who visited the village and were "at a loss to see what was the great inducement" to settle in the region. When he enquired if there were many "good practical farmers" in the neighbourhood, William Hutton was answered in the negative, "the principal settlers around it being half-pay officers and others who generally consider not whether the locality they fix upon is likely to be profitable, but whether it be beautiful and likely to contribute to their pleasures." (Letter of William Hutton, dated at Belleville, June 20, 1834, in *The British Farmer's Magazine*, April, 1835, p. 104.)

may be mentioned Watson Kirkconnell, Helen Marryat, Howard Pammett, and F. H. Dobbin; but it is not our purpose here to compile an exhaustive bibliography of primary or secondary sources for the region's history, but rather to name only some of the earlier outstanding compilations. Of these, Dr. Thomas Poole's *A Sketch of the Early Settlement and Subsequent Progress of the Town of Peterborough, and of Each Township in the County of Peterborough* (Peterborough, 1867) is one of the earliest and most valuable of Canadian local histories. In 1941 a short *Completion of Sketch . . . , 1867–1941*, purported to bring Dr. Poole's work up to date. *The History of the County of Peterborough, Ontario; Containing a History of the County; History of Haliburton County; their Townships, Towns, Schools, Churches, etc.; General and Local Statistics; Biographical Sketches, . . .* (Toronto, 1884) is the work of C. Pelham Mulvany, Charles M. Ryan, and Charles R. Stewart, and it contains much of great value that could not be recovered now, however intense the research. Among other publications more or less contemporary with settlement is the valuable *Directory of the United Counties of Peterborough & Victoria for 1858. . . .* (Peterborough, 1858), and Thomas White's *An Exhibit of the Progress, Position, and Resources of the County of Peterboro', Canada West, Based upon the Census of 1861; together with a Statement of the Trade of the Town of Peterborough* (Peterborough, 1861), which contains much of historical value. A later survey, the 1944 *Report on the Ganaraska Watershed*, edited by A. H. Richardson for the Dominion and Ontario governments, contains a good deal of authentic historical material, some of which relates to the more southerly parts of the Trent Valley. Of prime importance to the history of the Trent Canal, of course, are the *Journals* and *Appendices* of the Legislative Assembly of Upper Canada and the various *Reports* of its history and improvements as at Confederation, 1867, when it was transferred to Dominion Government control.

Victoria County is rather deficient in source materials in comparison with its neighbour Peterborough, but Watson Kirkconnell's *Victoria County Centennial History* (Lindsay, 1921) is a scholarly and intensive study of the region; and if he had incorporated such pictorial materials as could then have been assembled it would have been still more valuable. Included in it is a painstaking summary of pioneer survival in the county,[1] as well as geological and Indian data seldom assembled by the local historian.

[1]See Chapter XV, "Research into Pioneer Survival," pp. 218–27.

Of the notable literary figures of the district, perhaps the most outstanding were the Stricklands of Reydon Hall, Suffolk, three of whom were early Trent Valley settlers. They came of a commercial family of which the father, Thomas Strickland, was so interested in the encouragement of literary pursuits that six out of the eight of his children who grew to maturity became well-known writers. Though their connection with the nobility was remote—if not non-existent—the family gloried in their alleged pedigree and assiduously nurtured it in an England noted for social caste and snobbery.[1] One daughter, Catharine Parr, was named after a possible progenitor, Katharine Parr, sixth wife of Henry VIII. A cogent reason for fame did exist, however, for Agnes and Eliza produced their *Queens of England* from arduous and painstaking research at a time when access to documents was seldom permitted. Agnes, particularly, felt throughout her life that by this work her family was identified with the whole pageant of English history.

The literary productions of the Canadian Stricklands are mentioned in various parts of this volume. Catharine, a clever essayist, made a name for herself as a lover of nature in a day when most people trampled and destroyed it with enthusiasm.[2] Susanna, something of a philosopher, became equally widely known for her books *Roughing It in the Bush* (London, 1852), and *Life in the Clearings versus the Bush* (London, 1853), in which she appears as a bitter satirist of her fellow-settlers, and no doubt with very good reason. She mellowed, however, with the years, and later admitted that the world—at least the Canadian pioneer world—did not owe aristocratic immigrants a living; and that the best settlers were those who exerted themselves and chopped a competence out of the forest, and did not assume that they were conferring a benefit upon Upper Canada merely by removing to it. The Stricklands, however, and many others like them, are to be credited with setting literary and cultural standards and raising the general tone of life in "the backwoods."[3]

Samuel Strickland (1804–1867), who merits extended notice here, came to Upper Canada in 1825, seven years earlier than his talented sisters. He first resided with a family friend, Colonel Black

[1]See Una Pope-Hennessy, *Agnes Strickland, Biographer of the Queens of England. 1786–1874* (London, 1940), *passim* and particularly p. 7. Eliza Strickland collaborated in the series.

[2]See below, Section XI, No. 7, and Section XII, No. 6, for Mrs. Traill's writings.

[3]See below, Section XI, No. 11, and Section XII, No. 5, for Mrs. Moodie's writings.

of Darlington Mills (now Bowmanville). Always highly susceptible to female charms, Strickland lost no time in marrying a daughter of the family, observing at the time that "the torch of wedded love" burned particularly brightly in Canada.

In May 1826 he removed to Otonabee Township, where he had purchased two hundred acres of land near Scott's Plains (Peterborough). His wife remained with her parents, and he learned of her death in childbirth while he was walking to "the front" from Peterborough. Within a short time he married Mary Reid, daughter of a settler in neighbouring Douro. In 1828 he became a superintendent of the Canada Company and spent some years in the "Huron Tract." In 1831 he was back in Peterborough, where he exchanged his Otonabee land for a lot in Douro, and became the founder of Lakefield, where he lived successively in a log shanty, a frame house, and a large stone mansion. A militia officer and an "uncompromising Conservative," he was successful as lumberman and farmer. In the latter capacity a substantial income and a great deal of labour later came from the pupils of his farm-school, for at that time young Englishmen paid large sums for such instruction as they received in Canadian backwoods life.[1] Strickland is best known from his two-volume *Twenty-Seven Years in Canada West* (London, 1853), but it is uncertain how much of the writing is his and how much that of his sister Agnes, whose name appeared on the title-page as editor, probably with an eye to increasing the book's sale. In any event the book, which contains a good deal of valuable material on pioneering, is often marred by sentimentality and gushing effusiveness. Not only his first wife died in childbirth, "snatched away in the bright morning of her existence with the rapturous feelings of maternity just budding into life" (as he put it); but so did his second wife when bearing her fourteenth child. Perhaps both of them had at the time some feelings other than "rapturous." A third wife, middle-aged, accompanied him back from a second trip to England in 1855. Probably some pupils for his farm-school accompanied him also. Certainly his school became at this time more prominent in the life of Lakefield and district.[2]

[1]Excerpts from Charles Weld's and Horton Rhys's accounts of visits to Samuel Strickland give further details. See below, Nos. 13 and 15 of Section XI. No. 14 of the same section is a short selection from the farm-pupils' newspaper, and is accompanied by a satirical sketch.

[2]In later years, and particularly in the Muskoka District, the farm-pupil business was an undisguised "racket." See Roger Vardon [*pseud.*, F. M. Dela-Fosse], *English Bloods* (Ottawa, 1930), and Volume III of Guillet, "Famous Canadian Trials," which describes the notorious Birchall murder case where the victim Benwell was deluded into the belief that he was to be a farm-pupil.

"The gallant Major," as his pupils often facetiously called him in "The Kachewanoonka Herald," the manuscript newspaper which they wrote and circulated for several years, was widely known in the region and in municipal life; and when he died on January 11, 1867, the local press referred to him as "one of our old Pioneers, . . . who as the type of a true Englishman in manly appearance, in cordial manner, in kindly and hospitable feeling, could scarcely be surpassed."

Archibald Lampman owes to the Trent region the inspiration he must have received from the years of boyhood he spent amid the beauties of Gore's Landing, Rice Lake. Isabella Valancy Crawford removed to Lakefield in 1866 when she was fifteen, and lived there until the late 'seventies. But apart from these more notable writers, a large number of others achieved something more than a local reputation. Neil Wilson, an early teacher in Percy and Asphodel, was the author of *Rescued in Time*, which was widely circulated in Sunday School libraries in the eighteen-nineties. In the Montreal *Literary Garland* and the *Maple Leaf*, and in the Moodies' short-lived *Victoria Magazine*, appears a good deal of fugitive verse and prose, some of it anonymous, from the pens of inhabitants of the Trent region, most of them already mentioned.[1] Dr. Samuel P. Ford of Peterborough and Norwood wrote a considerable amount of poetry, most of which appeared first in the *Waverley Magazine*, Boston. James McCarroll, a teacher and newspaperman, lived in the district for some years and contributed verse widely to the press and literary periodicals. Michael Ryan's verse is found in the *Literary Garland* and in *Barker's Canadian Monthly Magazine*. William McDonnell of Lindsay wrote two long narrative poems and several novels, and also composed both words and music for a three-act opera, "The Fisherman's Daughter." James Wicks Dunsford of the Bobcaygeon district wrote lengthy verse and an historical novel, "The State Messengers" (*Peterborough Gazette*, 1845–46). George Coventry of Cobourg and Caroline Hayward, who resided near Port Hope, added to the somewhat uninspired and uninspiring verse of the day. *The Poems of William Telford* (Peterborough, 1887) is the production of a resident of Smith

[1]Valuable biographical material on the Stricklands and Stewarts, to which is added a short account of Thomas Need and John Langton, may be found in print in G. H. Needler, *Otonabee Pioneers* (Toronto, 1953); but a larger coverage of the literary people of the region is in typescript and manuscript in E. C. Guillet, "Canadian Literary Pioneers" and "Early Canadian Literature," copies of which are in the Library of Parliament, Ottawa, the University of Toronto Library, the Legislative Library of Ontario, and the Toronto Public Library.

Township, whose Scottish neighbours hoped they recognized in him another Burns—or at least a Hogg or Fergusson. In general, these versifiers and poetasters may be graded as fair, bad, and worse—in which last category must be included the *Leisure Hour Musings* (Peterborough, 1874?) of Alexander Graham of Otonabee Township.

There is, however, a work of lasting interest which we include in this volume as one of the most remarkable literary items relating to the region. This is a poem entitled *The Ojibway Conquest*, by George Copway, or Kah-ge-ga-gah-bowh, a Rice Lake Indian. Trained by early Methodists as a missionary, he became a writer on Indian life and history, travelled in Europe, and was a friend of Longfellow. Though there is no proof of the opinion, it would appear probable that Longfellow aided him in the production of his epic poem, for Copway called upon him in February 1849, a year previous to its publication; and the two men were together on at least four or five other occasions.[1] Be this as it may, *The Ojibway Conquest* is a notable piece of composition which should no longer remain unknown and unappreciated.

The place-names of a district shed considerable light on its origins. Names given by the Indians to portages and trails have survived in the region. Among these are Coboconk, a contraction of Quash-qua-ge-conk—"where the gulls meet"; Bobcaygeon,[2] a corruption of Bob-cajewon-unk—"the shallow rapids"; and Omemee, named from a sub-tribe of the Missisaugas, the Pigeons, who are commemorated also in Pigeon Lake and Pigeon Creek.

Chewett's map of 1789, Collins's of 1790, Rubidge's of 1836, and others contain Indian names of lakes, rivers, and portages of which we have with difficulty obtained interpretations,[3] as follows:

Saggettewedgewam (Trent River)—"river hard to travel"

[1]See Samuel Longfellow, *Life of Henry Wadsworth Longfellow* (Boston, 1886), journal of February 26, 1849, *et seq.*

[2]Billy McKeough (or McCue) was early on the site as an Indian trader; Thomas Need was the founder of the village; and James McConnell built the first frame house and opened it as a tavern—the Travellers' Home. Lieutenant-Governor Sir John Colborne christened the place Rokeby in 1834, but fortunately the name was not perpetuated.

[3]A generation ago there were a few experts in the Algonquin and related tongues in the chief museums of Canada and the United States, but the field has apparently been abdicated. The National Museum of Canada and the Royal Ontario Museum have no interpreters of these languages. Almost all the interpretations herewith are contained in letters from John Huden, Burlington, Vermont, to whom the Museum of the American Indian, New York, referred our queries, and from Stephen Laurent of Intervale, New Hampshire.

Cheboutequion (Stoney Lake)—"big long rocky water"
Wabuscommough (Chemong or Mud Lake)—"lake of earth"
Annlequion Checom (Sturgeon Lake)—"good long pike to eat"
Yawbaskkaokawk (Scugog River)—"here hemlock bark is cut"
Ouskebawkning (Talbot Portage)—"green leaf place where we leave the river"
Squaknegossippi (Indian River)—"trout-spearing place"
Koshkahabogamog (Kasshabog or Kosh Lake, east of Stoney) —"lake of many bays";

a variant, Kashagawigamog, in Haliburton, is similarly interpreted "long and winding waters." Apparently the Indians were fond of the name, for another variant, Koshkibogamog, was given to a lake of many bays in Barrie Township, about a hundred miles northwest of Kingston.

A number of place-names in the region are from members of the British nobility, such as, for example, Burleigh, Ennismore, and Methuen. Smith Township commemorates Surveyor-General the Honourable D. W. Smith, and Asphodel appropriately recalls the trilliums that early settlers found there in abundance. Smaller localities had sometimes a name with a romantic connotation. Lovesick Lake, for example, was at first considered a part of Deer Bay, or called the Burleigh Rapids or Chutes; but when an Indian, Richard Fawn, was jilted by an Irish girl, Katharine O'Donohue, he decided to end his days in dejection on an island in the lake. He did not carry out his resolve, and lived to pay court to other girls, but the name "Lovesick" was nevertheless applied to the lake.[1]

The names of the first settlers in innumerable localities were used in early nomenclature, and many of them, such as Gore's Landing, Dunsford, Reaboro, Healey's Falls, Thurstonia, Crooks' Rapids, and Downeyville, to mention but a few, persist to the present.[2] Crowe's Landing on Stoney Lake recalls Francis Crowe (1808–1877), the first reeve of Dummer Township, an office he held for seventeen years. Across the lake is Mount Julian in Burleigh, originally called Julien's[3] Landing after a Frenchman who

[1]Strickland, *Twenty-Seven Years in Canada West*, Vol. II, pp. 233–4.

[2]Some early settlers were sometimes given curious appellations. Patrick Connel, who came to Ops Township in 1825, was commonly called "King Connel." His grave is still pointed out on his one-time farm, lot 7, Concession II. Humphrey Finlay and his wife, who came to Emily Township in 1820, were known locally as "King and Queen of Emily."

[3]With a very distinct French pronunciation, roughly "Jooliaw."

was probably an Indian trader. Purdy's Mills (Lindsay)[1] was called after William Purdy, who arrived in 1828. Peterborough, of course, was named after the Honourable Peter Robinson.[2] Still other names are due to the whim of minor officials at York; and an occasional one recalls sentimental associations of early settlers with the Old Land. For instance, Aros, the Scottish birthplace of Charles McInnis, an early postmaster on the north side of the Balsam Lake end of the Talbot Portage, was the name he gave the post office. The Aros post office was actually the front room of Admiral VanSittart's log mansion, long the curiosity of Bexley Township. In addition to numerous names of early settlers and mill-owners, there are along the Trent River many English names, such as Warkworth; while Frankford was named by Sir Francis Bond Head after himself, probably on the occasion of a visit.

The experiences of individuals are often lost in historical generalizations, and it is therefore the intention here to reproduce from the rarer sources a selection of those characteristic of the region, and of pioneering in general. In some districts a particular choice of location led to a settler's home being widely known. Robert Clifford, the third settler to find his way to North Burleigh, in 1862, is a case in point:

> . . . believing in the good old Scripture adage that the house founded upon a rock would stand the storms of life, [he] determined to test the truth of the maxim. He accordingly selected lot 24, concession 14, a few rods west of the Burleigh Road, a spot of ground which rises at an elevation of 100 feet, for a foundation of a house which is a huge granite rock, the white glittering surface of which has been polished by

[1]Lindsay was the name of one of the surveyors assisting John Huston in the survey of the town site in 1834, lots 20 and 21 of Concession IV having been reserved for the purpose in McDonell's survey of Ops Township in 1825. Lindsay was accidentally shot in the leg, and his death resulted from infection. He was buried on the river-bank, and Huston's plans gave his name to the incipient town. Lindsay was a community of 1200 inhabitants in 1861, when it was laid waste by a fire on July 5. In an hour, many wealthy people were rendered penniless and a hundred buildings consumed, most of them on Kent Street; but a wider street and improved buildings took their place.

[2]The name replaced "Scott's Mills" in 1827. In 1850 Peterborough was incorporated as a town. Several accounts are extant of the visit of the Prince of Wales to Peterborough in 1860, among them a good one in Poole, *op. cit.*, pp. 73–80. It had then been incorporated for ten years, but in the following year, when its population was 3841, three disastrous fires devastated much of the town. There is as yet no book on the history of the city of Peterborough, even though, in addition to all the other source materials, the collection of newspaper files in the Public Library is exceptionally large.

the suns and storms of many a century. At a distance it has the resemblance of a snowbank, and has been admired by every traveller who passes over the Government road.[1]

Many settlers—and not only the aristocrats—were enthralled by the opportunities for fishing and hunting, sports which only a few could enjoy in the Old Land except by poaching. Strickland, writing in the early 'fifties, said that "Parties are now made yearly every October to Stony Lake, Deer Bay, or the River Trent. . . . This is one of the great charms of a Canadian life." He had seventeen deer hanging in his barn at one time, and he and two of his sons caught, near Burleigh Falls, during one morning in October 1849, salmon trout, lunge, and bass totalling 473 pounds.[2] The *Canadian Handbook & Tourists' Guide* (1867) says that many Cobourg gentlemen had private shooting boxes on Rice Lake.[3] Typical of the early settlers was Washington Coones (son-in-law of Robert Clifford, mentioned above) who

from a boy was always fond of hunting, and when quite young, by chance, one day got hold of a rifle which was offered him for sale, and with the 'cuteness of a boy asked for a trial of the gun, which was allowed him; on the same day he went out and killed three fine deer, which amply paid for his investment. At last he had gained his long-felt wish to own a gun of his own, and from that day to this he has been a most zealous hunter, killing bears, wolves, and deer in abundance. Few hunters in northern Peterborough to-day can equal him, either in woodcraft or in drawing a bead on a head of game.[4]

Life in many a rear township was often crude in the extreme, even before actual degeneration set in from sheer isolation and the inability to make a living. Examples could be quoted of log shanties without furniture or heat, the occupants lacking even a few crusts of bread; of church collections with nothing put on the plate—from complete lack of funds; of illness and death from inability to procure a doctor or give any kind of remedy. Drunkenness often caused lapses even in what primitive civilization there was. In 1864 a New Year's Eve dance and "spree" at Buck's Hotel, Minden,

[1]Mulvany *et al.*, *op. cit.*, p. 719.

[2]Strickland, *op. cit.*, Vol. I, p. 179, and Vol. II, p. 238.

[3]An account of Cobourg is given on pp. 124–7 of the *Guide*.

[4]Mulvany, p. 721. A map of Burleigh Township issued by the Department of Crown Lands, Ottawa, May 7, 1866, shows Benjamin Coones's name on lot 8 of Concession X (Surveys Office, East Block of the Ontario Parliament Buildings).

went on for four days and five nights. Corson's Siding, in Bexley, was, according to Watson Kirkconnell, long called "Hell's Half Acre." He says that Gooderham and Worts owned a timber limit adjacent, and hired Corson, a lake captain, to ship cordwood to Toronto, and adds:

For the winter's cut of cordwood he [Corson] would import a gang of lake sailors from Toronto. The latter would bring with them an abundance of whiskey and an auxiliary corps of prostitutes, and the limits were so aflame with drunkenness and hot uncleanness that the siding was known throughout the north country as "Hell's Half Acre."[1]

Yet there were many worthy people who sought to relieve suffering without a thought of payment for their courage and sacrifice. There were circuit-riding clergymen, saddle-bag doctors, and self-sacrificing mid-wives. We mention on page xlvi of this introduction the services of Mrs. Robinson of Smith Township, and there was also Elizabeth Clague, whose obituary notice in a Peterborough newspaper, without date but probably of 1894, expresses public appreciation of her life and work—and incidentally gives us an interesting picture of her husband, a retired sailor and primitive artist who was long a character in Dummer Township:

The "Family Doctor" Gone
Death of Mrs. J. Clague, of North Dummer, One of the Best Known Persons in the Township—Sketch of Her Life.

The "family doctor" of North Dummer—Mrs. Elizabeth Clague—a lady esteemed for her amiable, kind, and hospitable disposition, and one known throughout the county for these unfailing qualities, died at her home, about three miles from McCracken's Landing, on Monday May 21st. Many a person had been enabled to leave a bed of sickness through the untiring efforts of Mrs. Clague, who was known throughout the district as "the family doctor". The deceased was born in Wales 76 years ago and married Mr. John Clague, her now bereaved husband. Mr. Clague was a sailor and for many years endured the difficulties of ocean life, the last vessel on which he was employed being the "Sir Walter Raleigh." For some years afterwards he sailed on Lake Ontario, and then he decided to purchase a farm, but he was so fond of the water that he would not make a deal unless there was a body of water in the vicinity. After some exploring he found a satisfactory place on the shores of Stony Lake in North Dummer, and still resides there. Mr. Clague is an enthusiastic mariner, which is well shown by the singular

[1]Kirkconnell, *Victoria County*, pp. 78-9.

device he has arranged on his property. On the roof of his barn a fort, which he terms "Fort Royal," has been carefully arranged with mechanical skill. It faces the lake. In this small but striking representation a figure of a marine officer scanning the water looms forth. This arrangement old Mr. Clague takes unmistakable pride in. As an artist Mr. Clague also is very enthusiastic. Many a summer tourist has registered in the art gallery register at Mr. Clague's and viewed the numerous paintings in the quaint little gallery. In Mrs. Clague the campers and residents of the northern section of the county have lost a staunch friend, the Methodist church a good woman, and the surviving husband and adopted daughter a loving wife and kind mother. The sympathy of a host of friends will go out to the bereaved ones in their sad loss.[1]

Accompanying, or sometimes preceding settlement, was the thoughtless exploitation of the vast timber lands. One can almost see it being done from Samuel Strickland's vivid description: "Three hundred axes will waken the slumbering echoes of the rocky glen and wood-crowned height where the foot of the white man never trod before," he writes, and notes with obvious enthusiasm that Gilmour and Company were about to lay waste "the noble pine forests of Burleigh and Methuen."[2] Strickland's sons Roland and George were subsequently head of a lumber firm which controlled two and one-half townships of timber limits and had mills at Lakefield and Lake Simcoe with an annual output of ten million feet of lumber and 300,000 feet of squared timber. E. Phelan, Mulvany tells us, "piloted the first timber that ever came to Peterborough, receiving for his services $16 per day. He run the river for many years."[3] French-Canadian log-drivers were soon imported into the district, and in 1866 the mills of the county sawed 50,650,000 feet of lumber for export. It was a stirring life on lake and river, for masts and squared timber were frequently driven all the way from Balsam Lake to Quebec.[4]

[1]This is a copy of a press clipping in the small hotel at Mount Julian, Stoney Lake, where a panel of Clague's paintings on wood is preserved. In the summer cottage of the Editor of this volume, on Stoney Lake, are many pine-board paintings from the interior of old "Fort Royal." A few other paintings are in the homes of neighbours of the old Clague home in Dummer Township. See portraits of the Clagues and an example of his work, plate-figures 39–41. The Clague register mentioned in the obituary notice has not been located but may have been preserved among the family connection of Mr. and Mrs. Ab Dunford, the adopted daughter and her husband.

[2]Strickland, Vol. II, p. 226.

[3]Mulvany, p. 579.

[4]See below, Section VII, Nos. 8, 9, and 10.

Flour-milling did not develop as quickly as saw-milling. The earliest settlers—if not reduced to chewing corn for their children, as were those in Smith Township—had to make long journeys to primitive mills, at first as far as Port Hope or Cobourg. As in other early settlements, hollowed tree-stumps were often used as "plumping-mills" until something better was available. A small mill was established by Adam Scott, at Scott's Plains (Peterborough) in 1821. His biography is given by C. P. Mulvany as follows:

Adam Scott, the first settler on the present site of the Town of Peterborough, was born in Edinburgh, Scotland, in 1796, and was a millwright by trade. In 1812 he left England for America and settled in Delaware County, New York State; he remained there for about six years, working at his trade. While there he married a daughter of J. Mann, of Yorkshire, England, by whom he had three sons and three daughters. In 1818 he came to Canada and, locating at Port Hope, worked at his trade and built a saw-mill. When he came out from Scotland he had about $4,000. He lost nearly all of this in building, by contract, a mill at Cobourg for old Squire Henry. In the spring of 1820 he came to what is now Peterborough, the site of which was then covered with a dense growth of huckleberry bushes interspersed with a few pines. The first thing he erected was a small log shanty, 18 by 20 feet, which he covered with black ash bark. Then he put up a saw and grist mill, which was of the most primitive kind. The saw was an "up and down" saw, and the millstones were taken from a neighbouring quarry. The few settlers who had located in Smith Township, two years before, gave the place the name of "Scott's Plains." His daughter Jeanette was the first person born in what is now Peterborough; this was in 1820. Adam Scott removed from "Scott's Plains" in 1827, having lost all his property through getting in debt with John Brown of Port Hope, and located on the Hagerman farm, one mile east of Port Hope, where he resided for two years. He then removed to the Township of Cavan, where he followed his trade. He died February 7th, 1838. Adam Scott was an immensely strong man. He stood 6 feet 4 inches in his stocking feet and weighed 260 pounds, which was nearly all muscle. With perfect ease he could shoulder a barrel of salt or cider. In a previous part of this History there is an incident recorded of his having carried a heavy millcrank from Peterborough to Port Hope to be repaired. His wife died at "Scott's Plains" in 1825, of the fever and cholera which then prevailed among the Peter Robinson immigrants. He was asked by Hon. Peter Robinson to accept the immigration agency but he declined. He owned twelve acres of land surrounding his [mill], and was frequently urged to purchase more, but he declined, thinking that the place would never amount to anything. He often crossed the River Otonabee in the summer season on stilts to reach his oxen, which were pastured where the village of Ashburnham now is. One of Adam Scott's sons, also named Adam Scott, who was born at Port Hope, December 21st, 1818, is now living in the Village of Millbrook, where he follows his father's trade; he has lived in Millbrook for four years. He has filled the office of Reeve of Manvers and Cavan for several years. On March 6th, 1840, he was married to a daughter of James Holmes of Cavan.[1]

Until Jacob Bromwell's mill was erected in Smith Township the only choice was between Scott's and an apology for a mill on Galloway's Creek in Cavan. As settlement proceeded, a grist mill was usually quickly established. There were often makeshifts, however, such as, for example, Brummill's Mill on the Otonabee, which was called the "pocket mill" because of its small size. Grain was often taken to mill in bags tied to a crotched stick, with a pair of oxen hauling the load.

The progress of settlement in the Trent region is illustrated by some of the documents which follow in this volume. It is my intention here to mention interesting features of the story to be found in other source materials. The growth of settlements was usually very gradual. In 1825 only three log houses occupied twenty miles of territory along the south shore of Rice Lake, and one of them was the tavern of David Tidy, known as "a very respectable Scotchman", who was the founder of Gore's Landing,[2] then called Tidy's Tavern. To the east of Rice Lake, in Seymour Township, there grew up in the early eighteen-thirties a settlement of military and naval officers, for it was one of a number of townships in which they were encouraged to locate. Major Campbell was the Government's agent, and M. S. Cassan describes in his journal his experiences in approaching and settling there.[3] Sir Richard

[1]Mulvany, pp. 589–91. "Squire" Henry of Cobourg, whose mills Scott erected at great loss to himself, was a nephew of Alexander Henry, fur-trader and explorer. Before settling in Cobourg he had spent twenty-five years in the Western trade, once being reduced to chewing leather aprons and shoes to avoid starvation. Adam Scott operated a distillery of low reputation in connection with his mill, where "unrectified" whiskey was supplied to the few settlers who would drink it, and to the Indians.

[2]Named after Captain Thomas Sinclair Gore, who owned 265 acres along the Rice Lake shore in 1840. He died in 1858.

[3]See *Transaction* 22, Women's Canadian Historical Society of Toronto, 1921–22.

Bonnycastle's impressions of the region during settlement are found in one of the documents in this volume.[1]

Although surveyed in the early 'twenties, it was not until 1860–1861 that the pushing of a so-called road into wild and rocky Burleigh Township first made settlement possible. The name "Burleigh Road Settlement" was applied, however, not only to Burleigh but to Chandos, Anstruther, and Monmouth (in Haliburton), all of them for purposes of administration part of the Township of Dummer until 1865. Indicative of the general hardship experienced in this region is that of Cornelius Maher, who removed from Douro to lot 5, Concession VIII, of Chandos in 1862. At first he was "the happy possessor of a horse, which he used for logging; but it was drowned in a beaver meadow, and he had to 'hand-log' for two years until he could afford to get another."[2]

The problem of the scarcity of cows in these settlements was solved by an ingenious—and profitable—scheme evolved by James Lickley[3] of Burleigh Township, who had saved a few hundred dollars capital and who certainly did not lack a spirit of enterprise. He developed a system of lending cows to settlers. Each cow was to be returned after three years, together with the first calf; but if it were killed by lightning or the falling of a green tree Lickley assumed the loss. The idea proved profitable, for Lickley became something of a capitalist and had leisure to be a hunter, according to Mulvany:

Mr. Lickley's flocks and herds have increased to such an extent that he is at the present time the largest owner in the county, notwithstanding he has annually sold a large number. His herd numbers 160 head besides a large flock of sheep, scattered over an area from Young's Point to the Provisional County of Haliburton, the value of which would exceed several thousand dollars. If by any chance he meets a stray cow in the road he never throws a stone at her for fear she may belong to his herd. He is strictly temperate, honest, accurate in all his dealings, and shares the confidence of his employers to the greatest degree. During the long sixteen years of his residence in Northern Peterborough he has indulged in that life-long cherished sport, hunting the wild part-

[1]See below, Section XI, No. 12.

[2]Mulvany, p. 743.

[3]Lickley's mother was left a widow on arrival in Canada in 1823 when her husband was drowned in the harbour of Quebec. In 1834 she died in Montreal during the second great "cholera year", and twelve-year-old James worked at various trades and in the fishing industry for many years, finally removing to Peterborough County in 1862. Obtaining employment on the Burleigh Road, he helped to chop and clear the portion from Burleigh Falls to the twenty-first mile-post, half a mile north of Apsley.

ridge, duck, and doe. He is often seen with his gun and dog, scaling the rocky heights or by the water's edge of some lake or pebbled brook in quest of fish or game. When the shades of evening gather round he retires to his humble log cabin laden with the proceeds of the day's hunt, and after placing his trusty rifle in its accustomed place over the door, prepares, with his own hand, his repast of partridge, venison, or other game, while his faithful dog, his only companion, sits by his side and patiently waits his share of the spoils. Mr. Lickley never married, the object of his admiration having died, and in obedience to the love he cherished for her memory never transferred his affections to another.[1]

Biographical material is particularly rich and informative for this region. The following examples are given as characteristic. Giles Stone,[2] generally recognized as the first settler in Burleigh, 1861 (though the census of 1850 shows forty-five inhabitants), purchased his hundred acres at eighty cents per acre. His father, William, had two hundred acres on the shore of Cedar Lake, and died there in 1869 at the age of eighty-four. Giles helped in building five miles of the Burleigh Road, and in 1862 the township's second post office, Haultain, was opened on his property. Daniel Couch was located on lot 39, Concession V, of Anstruther, where he had the first blacksmith shop north of Stoney Lake. His son Moses located on the south shore of Loon Lake, on lots 7 and 8 in Concession VII of Chandos. Samuel Edgar, whose wife was in 1862 the first white woman to enter Chandos, paid $14 to have a barrel of flour brought forty-three miles from Peterborough. Billings Kilborne entered the township in the same year and built a shanty; and in 1863 he took his family in to his ninety-six acres, before a tree had been cut or even the road blazed.[3]

The pre-emigration experiences of many families place them in categories now famous in history, though sad and depressing in their own day. Exemplifying this group are the Burts of Burleigh and Chandos townships. Ephraim Burt, of lot 7, Concession III, of Chandos, might well have been one of the "Tolpuddle Martyrs", for he belonged to a family of agricultural labourers in Dorsetshire. Mulvany tells his story:

As an instance of the struggle of the average English agricultural

[1]Mulvany, pp. 722–5.

[2]A grandson of Giles Stone (1756–1846) of Northumberland County, and an example of the many who removed from "the front" to "the back townships" to seek their fortunes.

[3]This paragraph is based upon the biographies in Mulvany, pp. 728, 735, 736, and 740–1.

labourer, it may be here mentioned that Mr. Burt had worked year after year, early and late, in Dorsetshire, for the sum of six shillings sterling per week, and "found himself" out of that! In 1838 Mr. Burt married. It may be imagined that with a young and increasing family, in a country where labour commands the pittance of six shillings per week, it was almost a life-and-death struggle to keep the wolf from the door. But when his son Charles grew up sufficiently to assist his father, they, together, by working over-time and practicing the most rigid economy, saved over three hundred dollars in money, and came to Canada in June 1862. . . .

Having decided to settle in Burleigh, they carried their entire store of this world's goods on their backs from Peterborough, in addition to a food supply, the latter being renewed from time to time in the same manner till land was cleared and the new clearing gave forth a crop. This journey required several days of hard tramping at that time, varied by night bivouacs in the forest or open field. . . . Without following Mr. Burt's varied and trying experiences, suffice to say that he subsequently removed to Chandos, . . . where he now resides in comfort and independence after passing a lifetime of rugged experiences in a battle against poverty and unpropitious fortune.[1]

A result of isolation in the early days was the growth of revivalist sects and camp-meetings. Well-known at these were Thomas Robinson and his wife, who hewed out a home in the wilderness in 1820, settling on lot 15, Concession VIII of Smith Township. They were old-time Methodists, widely recognized as fine singers, and, we are informed:

were the leaders in prayer and song at the good old-fashioned orthodox backwoods meetings. Mrs. Robinson was also a celebrated physician and midwife, doing all, however, without remuneration or reward save what a clear conscience and delight in doing good to her fellows ever carried to her heart. It was quite a common thing for her to go distances of thirty miles on horseback in the night, through storms and forbidding forests, across rivers and morasses, to render aid to the sick; and many of the most sturdy yeomanry of Peterborough and Victoria Counties were ushered into being under Mrs. Robinson's care.[2]

Organized religious life slowly penetrated into the rear settlements. Members of the Church of England were frequently aided

[1]Mulvany, p. 733. See also the memorial volume *The Book of the Martyrs of Tolpuddle, 1834–1934*. Five of the six "martyrs" subsequently emigrated to Ontario and are buried near London.

[2]Mulvany, pp. 580–1.

by well-to-do friends in the Old Land when they sought to establish parish churches in the New; but self-denying missionaries provided that church's first contact with many settlers in the Trent Valley. In Seymour Township members of the Church of England were numerous and influential, but the greater number of them became Methodists from the lack of Anglican facilities for worship. When Christ Church was founded in Campbellford it was the only Church of England in Seymour, and the MacHenry family provided a log house for the clergyman; but at that time the Methodists had eight churches in Seymour.[1] The Langtons describe in some detail the establishment of the Church of England in the Sturgeon Lake region. The erection of the church at Fenelon Falls was due to the Langtons and the Dunsfords, and also to James Wallis, a man who established grist and saw mills there and greatly developed the settlement.

The Roman Catholic Church sent its priests into the wilderness, wherever parishioners were settled. Patrick Scott, founder of the Scott Settlement in Chandos Township, joined with Michael O'Brien in the eighteen-sixties in erecting on lot 8, Concession XII, the only Roman Catholic church in the township. Fathers O'Connel, Lynch, and Keating were the earliest priests to minister to the parish. We have, however, no detailed records of early Roman Catholic penetration into the Valley of the Trent.

The cheapness and potency of badly made whiskey created many a problem in this as in other regions. But temperance societies were soon diligent in every district; and although the peace-loving and sober were often disturbed by the riotous and drunken, the worst conditions were gradually alleviated. This was sometimes effected—as in Ennismore village—by raising the tavern's licence to $600 or more, with the result that the township's inhabitants were to a large extent deprived of strong drink. The disgraceful riots on the Twelfth of July, and other occasions of Catholic-Protestant feuds, were always aggravated, if not caused, by the superabundance of whiskey at twenty-five cents a gallon—or less. Some localities established a reputation for sobriety which was considered an inducement to settlers. Among these was Harvey Township, which long granted no liquor licences.

The settlement of Haliburton, occurring as it did in the late 'fifties and early 'sixties, was quite different from that of the longer-

[1]See Women's Canadian Historical Society of Toronto, *Transaction* No. 24, 1923–24. For accounts of the ministrations of Methodist and Church of England clergy, see Section IX, Nos. 2 and 3, below.

settled regions to the south. Stanhope Township received some of the first settlers. Isaac Hunter arrived in 1855, and G. A. Mason at "The Point" in Boskung (or Bushkonk) in 1859. These and other old sailors, with their strange history and yarns, gave a special flavour to the Lake Onishkonk region. Haliburton village was just bush land in the early 'sixties, but by 1865 the forest began to disappear from the chief street, and some twenty acres was at least partially cleared. C. R. Stewart, Manager of the Canadian Land Company and the first settler on Head Lake, became a well-known figure in the settlement, and his son had a store in the village. Adam Garrett later purchased the store, and ran a boarding-house as well. Samuel Picket opened a tavern. Settlers within a radius of fifty miles came to Haliburton village to buy and sell, to go on a spree, and perchance to attend church. C. R. Stewart at first brought in the mail in a punt twice a week; but postal services were more frequent—and the population greater—when the Victoria Railway pushed into the region as far as Haliburton village, in the years 1874 to 1878. Stewart also erected a small wooden church sixteen feet by twenty-four, and the first services were read by Surveyor Miles. There was soon a larger edifice designed by John Belcher of Peterborough, to which the widow of Judge Haliburton (author of *Sam Slick* and a director of the Land Company) contributed an organ. Before that, Dr. Peake, newly arrived from England, led the choir with an accordeon mounted on a frame and run with a treadle. His repertoire consisted of two tunes—"The Evening Hymn" and "March of the Men of Harlech," but both were utilized in as effective a manner as possible and to the satisfaction of all.

Soon after the formation of Haliburton County in 1874 a rush to Western Canada and the United States began, and about a thousand settlers left for Dakota, Manitoba, and the North-West Territories. The more well-to-do simply abandoned their farm settlements, selling only their livestock to pay their way westward. The loss of population was only temporary; but many of the new-comers found conditions harsh, and they soon degenerated to such an extent that some of them had to be induced by government aid to move to more favoured lands. "A far-reaching policy for the management of this region," reports the *Trent Watershed Survey* of 1912 with reference to those who occupied farms unfit for sustaining civilized conditions, "must include a plan for the removal of this *degenerating* population."[1] Hardly ten per cent of the thirty-five townships included in the survey had, after half a century, been

[1]*Trent Watershed Survey*, p. 5.

cleared for farm purposes. The population of this district in the first decade of the century had decreased fifteen per cent, or three times as much as the rural population of the whole province. The *Survey* traces the pattern for us:

Time and again, following a spur road it would be found ending in a remote pocket of soil which had once been ferreted out as good farm land, but which had, after all, been finally abandoned. Along the earlier colonization highways one finds long stretches unsettled to-day and with no signs of any former occupation beyond the mute testimony of neat piles of stones or occasional ornamental or fruit trees. There is not a single township but has its quota of such examples. . . . Often these abandoned farms are among the best in the settlement, but their owners could not continue getting a mere subsistence despite their best efforts. Instances were met where the owner had simply left his farm, often with buildings above the average, unable to find a purchaser.[1]

The townships to the south of the lakes of the Trent system, usually good agricultural land, were omitted from the *Survey*. Of the others, the five in Hastings County—Lake, Faraday, Limerick, Tudor, and Wollaston—had twice as many abandoned farms listed for sale in 1912 as had ten townships in Haliburton, and three times as many as had six townships in Peterborough. The total for the three counties was one hundred and ninety-four farms comprising 18,085 acres, and they were offered for sale for three years' back taxes aggregating $3,178.29, or at the rate of less than six cents per acre per year. The presence of mental and physical defectives and the general social degeneracy in some of these regions were all part of a wasted human asset; and the whole situation, according to the *Survey*, "is but another example of past misguided or rather *unguided* occupancy of townships which should never have been thrown open for settlement, and of the lack of appreciation by Government of its obvious duties."[2]

Early transportation and communication in the Trent Valley was primitive. Each district slowly developed its roads, ferries, bridges, and steamships from makeshift beginnings. A few examples, proceeding from "the front" to "the backwoods", will indicate the general trend. The Port Hope-Rice Lake portage trail dates from Indian days, but the route followed by the earliest settlers was usually northward from Cobourg to Claverton (Gore's

[1] *Ibid.*, p. 95.
[2] *Ibid.*, p. 97.

Landing) or Sully (Harwood), on Rice Lake, whence water transport was available across the lake and up the Otonabee. In the early 'thirties a steamboat was running over the route, a service that was shortly extended to Healey's Falls on the Trent; and the Cleghorn and Weller stage-lines continued the communication to Cobourg.

Though possibly not the first over the route northward from Port Hope, Barnabas Bletcher's stage-line was an early and well-known one. Bletcher's Tavern was three miles north of Port Hope, the nucleus of a small settlement later called Dale. In the 'forties Bletcher's son-in-law, Thomas Eastland, became proprietor and extended the stage-line. Eastland continued the carriage of mail to Bobcaygeon, Chemong Lake, and Lakefield; and in the 'sixties on over the Burleigh Road to Apsley and Cheddar, sixty miles from Peterborough.

The first post office in Burleigh Township was called Burleigh, a settlement four miles south of Apsley which has long been abandoned and is now hardly a memory. Later post offices were established at Haultain and at John Holmes's Hotel at Burleigh Falls. In a period when isolation was hard to bear, the rural postman was a popular if overworked official, and he was everywhere a welcome visitor. The first post office in Asphodel Township, writes C. P. Mulvany,

> was kept by Thomas Walker on his farm near what is now the village of Westwood; it was opened about 1837–38. The second was that opened at Norwood by James Foley. The first mail carrier was a man named Joseph Hunter, who lived in Peterborough and who, as an old settler still living says, "was an Irishman and a Quaker"—truly an odd combination. He used to carry the mail, which was certainly not very bulky, on horseback once a week from Peterborough to Walker's farm and to Foley's, thence south across the Trent to Warkworth in Northumberland County.[1]

During the cholera epidemic of 1832 some regions went for months without mail. This was particularly trying to families separated because of the exigencies of pioneering. Joseph Ford, a Wiltshire weaver, left his wife with friends in Prescott while he went on to Peterborough to seek work at his trade. Finding no demand for weavers of fine broadcloth, he hired out to "log up." Hearing nothing from him, his wife became anxious and borrowed money to proceed to Peterborough. Mulvany tells the story:

[1]Mulvany, p. 412.

By chance he happened [to be] at the dock when the little steamer which carried her from Rice Lake hove in sight—an event which was looked upon as a happy omen of the future. By dint of unremitting toil Mr. Ford soon saved sufficient money to purchase a loom for himself, and with this he worked early and late for many years in his struggle — hard, but successful in the end—to rear and educate a family of five sons and two daughters.[1]

Tavern-keepers provided an essential service by "putting up" travellers and incoming settlers as they laboriously made their way into the rear townships. Peter Phelan had the first tavern in Burleigh, three miles south of Apsley, in the early 'sixties. The details we have about McCauley's Hotel, midway between Burleigh Falls and Apsley, may be taken as typical. Erected in 1863 by Edward Sanderson (better known as "Britannia Ned") who fought with the Union forces in the American Civil War, it was a log structure of one and one-half storeys in which Sanderson's daughter Sarah Jane was born—the first white child in the township. Mulvany describes it thus:

In the early days of the settlement this house often gave shelter to as many as sixty persons in a single night, the proprietor having to sit up all night to keep a fire going to warm his guests. Eight miles west and six miles east of the Burleigh Road at this point the country is entirely uninhabited and is a "wolf range," so called on account of the numerous bands of wolves that roam through the unbroken forests, making night hideous with their howlings; while along the road to the north for several miles the land is rough and mountainous, sparsley covered with dry pines which tower away up into the heavens like so many ship masts. Thousands of these dry trees meet the eyes, reminding one of approaching the harbours of Portsmouth or Liverpool. . . . Brown's Falls, a short distance north, situated upon Eels Creek,[2] is crossed by a bridge about one hundred feet in length. The spot is pointed out as being the place where a man named Henry Brown went over the falls some years ago and miraculously came out alive. The road at this point is extremely crooked, now dipping down into the deepest hollows and now rising over the tops of the highest hills. Farther on up the creek are the remains of a log structure, 10 by 12 feet, one storey high, erected in 1862 by Christopher White, one of the early settlers in Bur-

[1] *Ibid.*, pp. 540–1.

[2] Eels was a brother of "Handsome Jack" Cow, an Indian chief of the region. At certain seasons there are eels in the creek.

leigh. It contained but one door, in which were bored several auger holes for windows.[1]

The ancient carrying-places were not infrequently surveyed into settlers' roads, as for example the Ganaraska trail, the Communication Road between the Otonabee and Chemong Lake, and the Talbot Portage between Lake Simcoe and Balsam Lake. The early settlers in the Talbot River region, in following the portage trail, were often delayed at the Grass River, where a punt was kept to provide ferryage. If the punt was on the wrong side, the traveller had to wait until someone came along from the other direction; and tradition has it that one wayfarer waited two weeks. The terrain along the river banks was all beaver meadow, and there were no trees from which a raft could have been made as a substitute for the ferry.

The lack of bridges at strategic points was often disconcerting to neighbouring settlers on opposite sides of bodies of water. In northern districts particularly, the bridges on colonization roads were burned out at least once a year. Where the traffic warranted it, a ferry service was set up, especially at places where spring ice-floes washed out the bridges. After several failures to bridge Mud (Chemong) and Pigeon lakes, the District Council in 1844 granted £26 "for the purpose of building a scow and ferry boats on Mud Lake, to ply from Galt's Landing in Ennismore to Edmison's Landing in Smith."[2] Three commissioners were appointed to control the ferry and obtain a ferryman, and the tolls were:

Span of horses and waggon, 15d.
One horse, with or without waggon, 6d.
Yoke of oxen and vehicle, 9d.
Horned cattle, 3d. a head.
Pigs and calves, 2d. a head.
Passengers, 3d. each.

Floating bridges subsequently built on both lakes were landmarks of the region until modern times, when motor roads around the lakes made them unnecessary.

Nowhere in Canada was there more enthusiasm for railroads than in the villages of Cobourg and Port Hope, rivals for the Trent Valley trade. As early as 1831 Frederick Rubidge was busy surveying and map-making for a railway from Cobourg to Rice Lake, and the original charter for the line was dated March 6,

[1]Mulvany, p. 441. The township map of 1866 shows Robert McCauley's name on lots 5 and 6 of Concession IX.

[2]Poole, *Peterborough*, p. 188.

1834. The Rebellion of 1837 and subsequent repercussions, however, dampened the enthusiasm for these plans; and the early charter lapsed from non-fulfilment of the terms relating to the sale of stock. The Guarantee Act of 1849 inaugurated an era of railway-building in the Canadas; and the citizens of Cobourg obtained a new charter in 1852, with the ambitious plan of bridging Rice Lake and proceeding to Peterborough—whose town council was probably wise in refusing financial support to the scheme, though willing enough to accept any benefits that might accrue. The citizens of Port Hope were not much behind in railway plans to tap the country near Lindsay, Peterborough, and Beaverton; and their railway was at least untroubled by the Rice Lake problem which eventually ended all hope of success for the Cobourg line. The attempt of that line to bridge the lake on insecure piers might have been avoided by filling, for the average depth over the route from Harwood to the Indian Village was a mere seventeen feet; but the power of the ice of winter and the high water of spring combined to make the use of piers impossible, and the line was abandoned before it was well under way.[1]

A curious plan for railway-building is deserving of mention here because it touches upon the western part of the Trent Valley. It is the proposal of Sir John Smythe of Toronto, "a man *supra grammaticam*, and one possessed of a genius above commas", as Dr. Henry Scadding described him.[2] Smythe's great hobby was a railway to the Pacific, in connection with which he brought out a lithographed map. Dr. Scadding gives the following description of the project:

> In a tract of his on the subject of this railway, he provides, in the case of war with the United States, for steam communication between London in England and China and the East Indies, by 'a branch to run on the north side of the township of Cavan and on the south side of Balsam Lake'. "I propose this," he says, "to run in the rear of Lake Huron and in the rear of Lake Superior, twenty miles in the interior of the country of the Lake aforesaid; to unite with the railroad from Lake Superior to Winnipeg, at the south-west main trading-post of the North-West Company."[3]

[1]Guillet, *Cobourg, 1798–1948* (Oshawa, 1948), pp. 71–99.

[2]Scadding, *Toronto of Old* (Toronto, 1873), p. 177.

[3]*Ibid.* No doubt the value of this project was greatly enhanced in the eyes of *hoi polloi* by the signature at the end of "Sir John Smythe, Baronet and Royal Engineer, Canadian Poet, LL.D., and Moral Philosopher." Dated September 26, 1845, a copy of this peculiar production is bound with other printed matter of Smythe's in the Toronto Public Library.

It is probably unnecessary to mention that many a modern stream in the Trent Valley bears little relation to its appearance or potentialities in the days of early settlement. The River Ganaraska, which flows into Lake Ontario at Port Hope, is not, of course, in the Valley of the Trent, though it bears considerable relation to it because of the portage route from its mouth to Rice Lake. Ganaraske (or Ganaraské, as the French sometimes spelled it) was an Iroquois village so named from the prevalence of salmon there—"at the spawning-place."[1] The destruction of this river valley has been investigated and described scientifically in *The Ganaraska Watershed*, a work to which reference has earlier been made.

A much smaller stream, Shelter Valley Creek which empties into Lake Ontario about ten miles east of Cobourg, exemplifies in a small way the waste of natural resources so evident almost everywhere in the Trent Valley and its environs on a much greater scale. At one time considered by travellers an exceptionally beautiful stream, the Shelter Valley Creek supported a dozen saw mills, grist mills, wool factories, carding mills, and pump factories. It was a favoured spot to fish for trout, and they are still caught, though in decreasing numbers. Its banks were then well wooded, and soaked up with ease the rainfall and the melting snow of spring, while its mill-dams regulated the flow. But when large-scale production by electric power drove out the smaller operators and the remaining forest was cleared, the banks were left to cattle and sheep who ate off not only the grass but also such small saplings as sprang up. The thin topsoil washed into the lake, the neglected mill-dams broke away, and flash floods ravaged the stream-bed until it is now a sorry sight, full of boulders, broken fences, and refuse—a skeleton of its former beauty and usefulness.[2]

Introductory comments to the various sections of this volume

[1]Similarly Kentsio, an Iroquois village on Rice Lake, is interpreted to mean "abounding in fish." Until the eighteen-twenties, and in some regions later, sea-salmon ran up into Lake Ontario and up the streams emptying into it. An early writer says that many hundreds of barrels of salmon were taken from the Trent every autumn, and that fish of ten to twenty pounds "may be purchased of the Indians at one shilling each, or for a gill of whiskey, a cake of bread, or the like trifle." (M. Smith, *A Geographical View of the British Possessions in North America* (Baltimore, 1814), pp. 29 and 20). The building of dams and other obstructions and the sawdust and other refuse from mills are believed to have ended the salmon-run.

[2]The Toronto *Globe and Mail* of April 27, 1956, uses Shelter Valley as an example of erosion and waste of natural resources.

give reasons for documents' inclusion; but a few remarks here will provide the general political setting. The Conservatives of Upper Canada arrogated to themselves a monopoly of loyalty to the Crown, and those who challenged them were made to appear as rebels. Sir John Beverley Robinson and his brother the Honourable Peter Robinson, an Executive and Legislative Councillor, were members of the "Family Compact," and Peter Robinson, of course, is mentioned frequently in this volume. This small group, as A. R. M. Lower puts it, "managed to keep the good things to themselves"; and he points out that as Commissioner of Crown Lands, Peter Robinson was found short in his accounts and resigned, although his brother undertook to make good the deficit.[1] Among the documents in this volume are several relating to the court case arising from a tavern brawl which clearly shows that while cheers for Sir John Beverley Robinson or Bishop Strachan were in order, it was obviously most unpalatable, if not a seditious offence, to shout "Hurrah for Mackenzie and Papineau!"[2] This particular incident, of course, is understandable, occurring as it did near the time of the abortive Rebellion of 1837; but Upper Canada, prior to the coming of Durham and Elgin, was in no sense a democracy. As the books of the Stricklands, the Langtons, Mrs. Stewart, and Thomas Need show, aristocratic notions were increasingly unpopular among the settlers along the Trent, as in other parts of Upper Canada.

The sources of the documents reproduced in this volume are given in some detail in the introductions to the various Sections. In general, we may say here that the Public Archives of Canada is the source of a large number of documents—some sixteen inches of them if measured in bulk—found under the general head of correspondence and complaints relative to the Trent Canal. Search in the Upper Canada Sundries led to the location of a number of early letters on various aspects of life in the region; and individual items are from other sections of the Archives. Many of the maps reproduced in this volume are also from the Public Archives, as are numerous illustrations and portraits.

The Peter Robinson documents in the Peterborough Public Library form a group perhaps unparalleled in value outside the great archival collections. That they should have been carefully saved, and have survived the exigencies of life, is a pleasing cir-

[1]Lower, *Colony to Nation* (Toronto, 1946), p. 229.
[2]See Section VIII, No. 6 (c), below, pp. 297–300.

cumstance amid so much carelessness and so many unnecessary losses to which documentary, as well as printed, materials are frequently subjected.

The Ontario Bureau of Archives has been searched particularly for surveyors' reports and records of a similar nature. A great deal is available there, in the Department of Planning and Development, and in the Surveys and Maps office of the East Wing of the Ontario Parliament Buildings; and the few documents reproduced here must be taken as representative of a vast collection of surveys, correspondence, lists of early settlers, records of Courts of Quarter Sessions, and a variety of other material of interest to historians. Numerous items, documentary and illustrative, have come from individuals, and these, as well as those from the public collections, are acknowledged in the Preface.

Every effort has been made to include in this volume illustrations and maps calculated to equal the documents in comprehensiveness and human interest. A considerable proportion of them have been located only recently, and by far the greater number are reproduced for the first time. The illustrative material falls into four main divisions: maps, documents, portraits, and sketches or photographic representations of scenes of the past.

The maps have been chosen for several distinct purposes. The earliest indicate a defective knowledge of the Trent system, but are of particular value for their Indian or French place-names and, in some instances, for the carrying-places they show. Later maps, sections of which are reproduced, show township boundaries, early settlements, and Trent Canal developments. Several of these maps are reproduced for the first time.

The documents selected for illustrative purposes are from the Peter Robinson Papers and from the archival collections, as well as a few from other sources. All of them have some special value or interest, though consideration, of course, had to be given to their readability when reduced in size. As the Peter Robinson documents have not previously been printed, it has been thought worth while to reproduce an adequate selection representative of the more characteristic items.

The portraits and sketches were selected for this volume from a wide choice, for the Trent Valley is comparatively rich in the quantity and quality of art contemporary with its settlement. Among others, we have the work of Anne Langton, Charles Fothergill, Edward Caddy, the Reverend M. A. Farrar, and Caroline

Hayward, who was the mother of Alfred and Gerald Hayward, painters respectively of flowers and miniatures.[1] Anne Langton's paintings and sketches provide for the Sturgeon Lake-Fenelon Falls region pictorial representations of the conditions of early settlement in that part of Victoria County, a region which is otherwise not rich in illustrative material.[2] Paul Kane, the painter of the Indians of the Canadian West, lived for most of a year in Cobourg, and the Editor of this volume has recently located six portraits in oil of local people, almost certainly done by him at that time, which we now reproduce.[3] Kane married a Cobourg artist in her own right—Harriet Clench, daughter of F. S. Clench, one of the best of the early cabinetmakers[4]—and although most of her work does not seem to have survived, we reproduce in this volume an example of her flower-sketches.

A one-time mayor of Peterborough, the late T. H. G. Denne, should be accorded the appreciation of posterity for having assembled a fine collection of historical illustrations, the presence of which in the Peterborough Public Library makes all the difference between poverty and riches. Within its limits, the collection compares favorably with that of John Ross Robertson in the Toronto

[1]Their parents, Captain Alfred and Caroline Hayward, lived at "Ravenscourt," between Cobourg and Port Hope, and at Rice Lake. Marmaduke Matthews, a Toronto artist, encouraged the talent of the Haywards long before they became world famous. Gerald Hayward's grave is at Gore's Landing. Edith, the wife of Alfred, was also an artist of sensitivity, and painted many landscapes of the Cobourg-Rice Lake district.

[2]The Langton family has given a collection of her work to the Fenelon Falls Public Library.

[3]In an obituary notice entitled "Paul Kane, the Canadian Artist" (*The Canadian Journal of Science, Literature, and History*, Vol. XIII, 1873, pp. 66–72), Sir Daniel Wilson wrote: "His first scene of artistic labour, after leaving Toronto, was Cobourg, where portraits of Sheriff and Mrs. Conger, her sister Mrs. Perry, Sheriff Ruttan, and others of his early patrons, were executed." With this start I was able to locate Sheriff Conger's portrait in the Peterborough Public Library, and Sheriff Ruttan's in the home of his great-grandson, Colonel Charles Ruttan, of Toronto; and those of William Weller and his wife and of Kane's parents-in-law, the Clenches, in possession of their descendants. A comparison of the technique and colours of these portraits with those of the Kane collection in the Royal Ontario Museum adds to the weight of evidence, and Mr. Kenneth Kidd, Curator of Ethnology, considers them to be Kane's work. It is probable that other portraits will be located in Canada, as well as in the United States, for Kane, aided by his Cobourg earnings, engaged in portrait work for many years prior to his journey to the Canadian West where he made his Indian paintings.

[4]The Editor of this volume has in his home a desk built in the spring of 1845 by F. S. Clench for his own use. It is made of Brazilian flame walnut and bird's-eye maple, and is of fine craftsmanship. The pride of its maker is particularly evident in two small secret cabinets with red-leather covers made to look like books and entitled "The Works of F. S. Clench."

Public Library, and is particularly valuable because of the fact that, although in many parts of the province the Tremaine series of illustrated maps and the Belden historical atlases have added a good deal of useful illustration to the record of the past, the counties of Peterborough, Victoria, and Haliburton were, unfortunately, not included in either series.

The manuscript documents reproduced in this volume appear exactly as they are in the originals; but where errors in spelling might be taken as printer's errors, the Editor has inserted *sic* in square brackets. Printed materials of an official nature are reprinted here as in the originals, with two exceptions: obvious printer's errors have been corrected, and occasional usages such as periods after column headings have been modernized. In privately printed materials it has been assumed that the inordinate use of commas—often excessive to the point of unreadability a century ago—is due to the printer, not the author, and such commas have been omitted; but errors in spelling and construction have in no instance been altered. The documents have been selected to illustrate as many facets as possible of early life in the Valley of the Trent, and they speak eloquently for themselves. Of the great wealth of available material, much of value and interest has had to be omitted, and other documents have been in some cases abridged. The core of the volume is formed by those documents which relate to the Peter Robinson emigration and to the Trent Canal; but the literary and artistic productions of the inhabitants have been included in the belief that these best exemplify their spirit and culture. By introductory notes and footnotes, and by this Introduction, the Editor has endeavoured to elucidate these varied materials and to weld them into a composite whole that will serve to commemorate in some measure the valiant pioneers of a notable region.

EDWIN C. GUILLET

THE VALLEY OF THE TRENT

I. DISCOVERY OF THE TRENT VALLEY, AND ITS NATIVE INHABITANTS

In September 1615 Samuel de Champlain was at the northern outlet of Lake Simcoe, preparing to accompany his Huron allies on an expedition against the Iroquois. His account of the journey is not sufficiently definite to indicate with certainty whether all the carrying-places were used to save time; or whether, on the other hand, the Indians were pleased to show him all their best hunting-grounds, and avoided short-cuts. A notable recent discovery in France is Champlain's map of 1616,[1] but we reproduce here his later map of 1632, upon which the Huron country and the Valley of the Trent are more clearly delineated, although of course far from accurate.

Not only are Indian remains extensive in this region, but recent discoveries have aroused public interest and set off several scientific expeditions. In 1954 employees of the American Nepheline Company discovered rock carvings, or petroglyphs, four miles north-west of the eastern end of Stoney Lake. The following estimate and interpretation of this and various other important Indian remains along the Trent has been prepared for this volume by Kenneth E. Kidd, Curator of the Ethnology Division, Royal Ontario Museum:

Since man first became aware of its existence several thousands of years ago, the Trent Valley has been a major traffic artery between upper Lake Huron or Georgian Bay and the eastern end of Lake Ontario. The lakes and rivers which lie within it, beginning with Balsam Lake, continuing with Sturgeon Lake, Chemong Lake, the Otonabee River, and Rice Lake, and ending with the Trent River, provided relatively easy passage, in modern times made more easy by the construction of canals. Besides the facility which these lakes and rivers afforded for easy travel in aboriginal times, the land in which they lay was highly desirable, and its more northerly limits must have provided excellent hunting and fishing for all Indian tribes; while the lower or southerly portions were well suited to the horticultural methods of the later sedentary peoples. Remains of Indian occupation are exceptionally abundant in the northern parts of Simcoe and Victoria Counties, as well as around

[1]This map has been printed in *Imago Mundi*, Vol. XI, facing page 85.

the Bay of Quinte where the Trent System disembogues; and in the intervening territory some of the most unusual manifestations of aboriginal occupation in the Province of Ontario are to be found.

The first of these which may be described here is a group of rock carvings located about four miles northwest of the eastern end of Stoney Lake, in Burleigh Township, Peterborough County. More precisely they are on the east side of Jack's Creek and about two miles south of a small body of water called McGinnis Lake. Rock carvings, or "petroglyphs" to use the technical term, are widely distributed in both northern and southern America, and a few are known in Ontario, but no others of equal extent have so far been reported from this province.[1]

The carvings in question were made upon an oblong outcropping of crystalline limestone, a hundred and thirty feet long and a hundred and two feet wide, situated almost at the very edge of the Laurentian Shield. This soft but beautiful rock afforded the makers an ideal location upon which to engrave their carvings, of which there are approximately one hundred; the exact number depends largely upon the spectator, for some are so indistinct as to be disregarded by one but to strike another as quite obvious. The work is so shallow as to be visible to most people only in cross lighting, unless blackened in, and was probably done by a process of pecking or crushing the base rock with another stone.

The figures include an assortment of designs, the meanings of some of which are obvious enough, such as birds, a turtle, and manlike creatures; the intentions of the makers with regard to many of the others is far from clear. Triangular outlines might equally well signify coniferous trees or a certain form of arrow point. Some of the anthropomorphic figures, with heads resembling a sun with rays of light shooting out from them, may represent deities.

Many of the carvings already described correspond in greater or lesser degree to some of the symbols used by the historic Ojibwa in their birchbark scrolls which were used in secret societies of that tribe. Other carvings are sufficiently different to suggest that they may have been done by another people; such, for instance, as the very realistic bear tracks. Unfortunately, this point is at present as obscure as all other matters connected with the site; dates, the tribe or tribes responsible, and the meanings, are all quite unknown. It is likely, however, that the makers were an Algonkian people or peoples, that the carvings antedate the arrival of the white man, and that they had some religious significance.

[1]Paul W. Sweetman, director of the provincial expedition to the site of the petroglyphs in July 1954, has described them in detail, as well as the investigation of the site of a prehistoric Iroquoian village five miles to the south-east, on the Quackenbush farm, lot 29, Concession xii, Dummer Township. See "A preliminary report on the Peterborough petroglyphs," *Ontario History*, xlvii (1955, no. 3).

The second prehistoric site situated in the Trent Valley is that known as the "Serpent Mound" on Rice Lake. In actuality it is but the most spectacular of a number of similar remains in the area, for kindred structures exist—or did exist a half century ago—on east Sugar Island, Cameron's Point, and at the mouth of the Otonabee River on the north shore of Rice Lake. In the light of what information is extant concerning them, and in default of excavation, it seems reasonable to believe that they all were the product of one culture. Beyond any doubt, this was an Indian culture—the belief that the "mound builders" were members of some non-Indian race is quite unfounded—and possibly the Hopewell. Excavations now under way at the Serpent Mounds will clear up cultural affiliations once and for all.

The so-called Hopewellians, who are believed on current evidence to have flourished about two thousand years ago and whose most spectacular manifestations include the biggest "serpent mound" known, developed in Ohio. They were an agricultural people who cultivated maize, beans, and squash, smoked tobacco, wove cloth for garments, and, benefiting from a far-flung commerce, made liberal and highly artistic use of such exotic materials as obsidian from the foothills of the Rockies, fresh-water pearls from the Mississippi, shells from the Gulf of Mexico, and mica and copper from Isle Royal. The objects made from these substances have given the culture a pre-eminent position on artistic grounds so far as aboriginal North America is concerned. At present the Rice Lake Indians are believed to have belonged to this Hopewell Culture.

The group referred to as the "serpent mounds" represents the coordinated efforts of a large number of people, probably working over a period of years or decades. The visible remains include a large serpentine mound approximately a hundred and eighty-five feet long and twenty feet wide, lying east and west on a fairly high ridge about two hundred feet north of the waters of Rice Lake, on a seventy-acre promontory. In close proximity to this main mound are at least five others, one of which, lying immediately east of the "serpent", is popularly referred to as the "egg".

Less obvious remains include a village area where domestic refuse lies many inches deep, and very considerable deposits of clam shells. While it is entirely possible that the village remains are those of the builders of the mounds, there is reason to suspect that the shell heaps pertain to a much earlier people; which suggests that this part of the Trent Valley has been a favoured haunt of Indians from very ancient times indeed. The mounds already referred to as occupying scattered locations elsewhere on Rice Lake are believed to belong to the same manifestation as the "Serpent Mound" group.

Any discussion of the occupation of the valley would be incomplete without mention of the later inhabitants, the Iroquois and the Algonkians. The former are known from the extensive remains to be found in north Victoria County and from scattered sites elsewhere, notably around the Bay of Quinte. The Algonkians are later arrivals who apparently came in the eighteenth century. One branch of these, the Mississauga, still inhabit the area, and the well-known Indian missionaries, Peter Jones and Peter Jacobs, were both members of that tribe.[1]

No. 1 in this Section is Champlain's account of his journey of 1615. No. 2 is a short narrative of a visit to an ossuary discovered in Manvers Township in 1839; and while it is probably not of outstanding importance, the find may well lead to further excavations in that locality, and it is included here for that reason. The third item is a valuable statement of the traditional Indian history, as recorded in 1904.

There is much valuable information available as to more recent history of the Indian inhabitants of the region, their manners and customs, and their relations with the invading white man. With the one exception of his plying them with whiskey in the fur-trade, particularly at early trading depôts like Smith's Creek, settler and merchant appear, in general, to have had decent relations with the original proprietors of the region.

The remaining items in this Section, Nos. 4, 5, and 6, are accounts, by three people who had the best opportunity to know, of Indian life in the period of first settlement or immediately thereafter; and they present a reliable and generally pleasing record.

1. Excerpt from Champlain's Journal of his Journey with the Hurons, 1615

[*Samuel de Champlain,* Works, *Champlain Society edition, H. P. Biggar, General Editor; Volume III, translated and edited by H. H. Langton and W. F. Ganong, pp. 58–62*]

. . . They set out on the eighth of the said month, and on the tenth following there was a sharp white frost. We continued our course toward the enemy and made some five to six leagues through these lakes[2] and

[1]As was also George Copway, missionary and author of a number of books on his race, and of the epic poem *The Ojibway Conquest*, reprinted in this volume, Section xii, No. 8.

[2]Here the editors list "Cranberry, Balsam, and Cameron" lakes; but G. H. Needler, with considerable plausibility, suggests that Couchiching and Simcoe are intended (see *Ontario History*, 1949, p. 201).

thence the savages carried their canoes over land about ten leagues, and we came upon another lake from six to seven leagues in length and three in breadth. From here issues a river which makes its discharge into the great lake of the Onondagas.[1] Having crossed this lake we passed a rapid and followed the course of the said river, downstream continually, some sixty-four leagues, to what is the entrance of the said lake of the Onondagas, and on our way we portaged round five rapids, some from four to five leagues in length. We also passed through several lakes of very considerable size,[2] as is likewise the said river which passes through them, and which abounds greatly in good fish. It is certain that all this country is very fine and of pleasing character. Along the shores one would think the trees had been planted for ornament in most places. Moreover all these regions in time past were inhabited by savages, who have since been compelled to abandon them out of fear of their enemies. Vines and walnut-trees grow there in great quantity. Grapes here come to maturity, but there remains always a very pungent acidity which one feels in the throat after eating many of them. This proceeds from lack of cultivation. The cleared portion of these regions is quite pleasant. Hunting deer and bear is common here, and for the sake of the experience we had a hunt and captured quite a good number as we journeyed down. To do this four or five hundred savages placed themselves in line in the woods, until they reached certain points which jut out into the river; then marching in their order with bow and arrow in their hands, shouting and making a great noise to frighten the animals, they keep on until they come to the end of the point. In this way all the animals that are between the point and the hunters are compelled to throw themselves into the water, unless they pass through the line at the mercy of the arrows which are shot at them by the hunters. Meanwhile the savages posted in the canoes, ranged on purpose along the edge of the shore, easily draw near the stags and other animals, hunted and harried and very terrified. Then the hunters kill them easily with sword blades fastened to the end of a stick like a half-pike, and in this way they do their hunting, as also in like manner on the islands, where there is much game. I took a peculiar pleasure in watching them hunt in this manner, noting

[1]Lake Ontario.

[2]The editors here list, with some omissions and one bad error, the lakes through which they believe the expedition passed; the error is "Buckbarn" for "Buckhorn." The present editor takes the view that no finality is possible in the interpretation of Champlain's narrative when there were well-travelled carrying-places which may or may not have been followed, depending on whether the Indians' anxiety to get on with the invasion of the Iroquois country triumphed over their feeling of pride in showing Champlain the best and most beautiful of their hunting-grounds—the Stoney Lake section between Chemong Lake and the Otonabee—which could be cut off by a six-mile portage.

their skill. Many animals were killed by arquebus-shots, at which they were greatly astonished: but it unfortunately happened that in aiming at a stag, a savage came inadvertently in the line of fire and was wounded by a shot, having no idea of such a thing, as may be supposed. At this a great clamour arose among them, which nevertheless subsided upon the gift of some presents to the wounded man, which is the ordinary method of allaying and ending quarrels; in case the wounded man dies, the presents and gifts are made to his relations. As to game, it is in great abundance in its season. There are also many cranes as white as swans, and other kinds of birds, resembling those of France.

We went by short stages as far as the shores of the lake of the Onondagas, hunting continually, as is mentioned above, and when we reached it, we crossed it at one end, that pointing eastward, which is the entrance to the great river Saint Lawrence, in latitude forty-three degrees, and in this crossing are five very large islands. We paddled some fourteen leagues in order to cross to the south side of the lake, towards the enemy's country. . . .

2. Indian Burial Pit, Manvers Township

[*Letter of "J.H.,"* Cobourg Star, *June 19, 1839*]

Having learned that a number of Indian skeletons had been accidently discovered in the Township of Manvers, curiosity induced me to accompany two friends in Cavan on a visit to the spot.

On the apex of a conical hill of considerable height, covered with hard timber of ordinary size, we discovered a pit about 14 or 15 feet in diameter, surrounded by a circular embankment formed by earth thrown out at the time of the interment; on the west side was a gap of width sufficient to admit two persons passing abreast.

The mass of bones was slightly covered with black mould and large flat stones, and about 3 feet below the top of the embankment. From the centre of the pit grew a basswood tree, which on being half cut through and its concentric rings counted, proved to be 130 years old. A Beech growing on the top of the embankment, similarly cut, showed 150 rings or years. Forty or fifty skulls and a heap of other bones had been exhumed previous to our arrival.

Anxious to ascertain the depth, we directed the pit at one part to be dug to the bottom and found it about 8 feet from the top of the bank. We estimated that one-fourth of the area had been dug, and finding it yielded at least 150 skulls, inferred that 500 or 600 bodies had been deposited. The skulls and larger bones in the upper strata were sound and perfect, those in the lower, as might be expected, more decayed.

In the conformation of the skulls a remarkable uniformity prevailed: the facial angle close—forehead narrow—posterior part wide and heavy—the occipital protuberance large—and the cheek bones wide and high; many of them indicated great age, but the majority were those of subjects between 18 and 30; in stature they did not appear to exceed the average of Europeans.

Notwithstanding the strictest search, only two or three bones of a child were found, and none which could be decidedly pronounced female. Two skulls were picked up, apparently injured during life. . . . It is worthy of remark that the teeth left (and in a great proportion the set was complete) were perfectly sound and free from caries during life.

No relics of warlike weapons or ornaments were found. It was evident that the bodies had originally formed a mound above the surface, and had been protected from the depredations of animals by large stones. No lake or river of any size within several miles of the spot, which appears to have been selected for its abrupt elevations. On reviewing the appearances of this vast and sequestered Charnal house we ventured to conjecture that they had fallen in a battle fought in the vicinity and been conveyed to that place for interment, thrown in promiscuously, and probably in a state of nudity. The date cannot be far, if any, short of two centuries ago. But if any of your correspondents better versed in the history of aboriginal antiquities can throw any light on the probable origin of this remarkable grave, it would be especially gratifying to the hundreds who have been led by curiosity to visit it.[1]

3. The Coming of the Mississagas*

Prepared by J. Hampden Burnham, Esq., Peterborough
[*Ontario Historical Society*, Papers and Records, *1905*]

Paudash, son of Paudash, son of Cheneebeesh, son of Gemoaghpenassee, to the Ontario Historical Society:

I, Robert Paudash, with my son Johnson Paudash, am desirous of putting on record for the first time the solemn tradition of the Missis-

[1]A list of Indian camp and village sites in Victoria County, compiled after extensive research by George E. Laidlaw of Victoria Road, is given in Watson Kirkconnell, *Victoria County Centennial History* (Lindsay, 1921), pp. 124–6 and 133. In his reminiscences Henry Lye (1834–1926) of Hastings, referring to the eastern end of Rice Lake, says: "Cameron's Point had many evidences of Indian occupancy and hostile encounters; a sort of embankment had been constructed on its shore from the mouth of the Ouse River into the bay now known as Birdsall's Bay; remnants of clay pottery were abundant and there were large piles of mussel or clam shells in or near the water." (The Lye MSS. are in possession of Mrs. Helen Marryat, Hastings, and Mrs. Gilbert Elmhurst, Birdsall).

*Read by Lieut.-Col. H. C. Rogers, President of the Peterborough Historical Society, before the Ontario Historical Society, at Windsor, June 2, 1904.

sagas respecting their present place of settlement in Ontario, and the migration which led them thither. No word of what I am about to say has come from reading, or in any other way than from the mouth of Paudash, my father, who died, aged seventy-five, in the year 1893, the last hereditary chief of the tribe of Mississagas, situated at Rice Lake, and from the mouth of Cheneebeesh, my grandfather, who died in 1869, at the age of 104, the last Sachem, or Head Chief, of all the Mississagas, who in turn had learned, according to the Indian custom, what Gemoaghpenassee, his father, had heard from *his* father, and so on. I am glad for the sake of the memory of the Mississagas, who were always loyal to the great King, to hear of this revival of interest in the Mississagas, who do not appear in history or in the records of this country as much as they deserve from the importance of their deeds in war, and of their efforts to preserve peace and good-will towards the great King. In the first place, as you would know, the Algonkins, who include the Mississagas, inhabited the great northern portion of this continent, excepting the small part which the Iroquois, their deadly enemies, inhabited on the southern shore of the Lake Ontario; while far to the south dwelt the Muskokees. The Mississagas were so named because they settled on a river on the north shore of Lake Huron, about seventy miles from Sault Ste. Marie, the word Mississaga meaning river; but they were Shawnees, part of the great Ojibwa tribe, of which the word Chippeway is a corruption. In what is now the Ohio Valley, the Shawnees dwelt in peace and power till such time as their sachems became disturbed and divided by party strife. One party thereupon went north through the country of the Michigans, and crossed into Canada, at Boweeting, now known as Sault Ste. Marie, settling down on the north shore of Lake Huron. Not many years after the arrival of the Mississagas, the Iroquois, represented by their chief tribe, the Mohawks, came north across the Lake Ontario and massacred the Hurons, possessing themselves of their hunting-grounds. Coming into contact with the Mississagas, the Mohawks massacred small parties of them, and endeavored to drive them off. It being a matter of life and death to the Mississagas, they held a great council of war, and decided to attack the Mohawks, and, if possible, to drive them away. A party of Mohawks was entrenched at an island in lower Georgian Bay, afterwards known as Pequahkoondebaminis, or the Island of Skulls. The Mississagas surrounded and made great slaughter of them, the island taking its name from this circumstance. The remainder of the Mohawks were compelled to retreat eventually, but being a fierce and warlike tribe they resisted stubbornly. The Mississagas then advanced up what is now the Severn River to Shunyung, or Lake Simcoe, stopping at Machickning, which means Fish Fence, at the narrows between Lake Simcoe and Lake Couchiching, in order to get a supply of food. Parts of the fence remain to this day. There they received reinforcements, and making preparations for a campaign, divided into two parties. The main body proceeded along the portage, now called Portage Road, to Balsam Lake; the other party went south to Toronto. After various skirmishes the Mohawks continued their retreat down the valley of the Otonabee, or Trent, to where they were settled in numerous villages along the River Otonabee, and on Rice Lake. They made their first real stand at Nogojiwanong, which was the original name of the town of Peterborough, meaning the place at the end of the rapids; Katchewanook, above the present village of Lakefield, meaning the beginning of the rapids. A sharp skirmish took place here upon what is now known as Cemetery Point, the Mohawks being worsted and retreating farther down the river, making, however, a determined stand at the mouth of the river, while the Mississagas encamped at Onigon, now known as Campbelltown; the word Onigon meaning in Mississaga, 'the pulling-up of stakes', because the Mississagas, coming too closely upon the entrenched Mohawks, as they found when they had made their encampment, pulled up their stakes and retreated farther up the river. After great preparation, an attack was made by the Mississagas, both by land and water, and the Mohawks were driven, after a battle, in which no less than one thousand warriors were slain, down Rice Lake to what is now known as Roche's Point. Great quantities of bones and flint arrow-heads are found at the site of this battle, even to this day. At Roche's Point there was a Mohawk village, in front of the former site of which is a mound in the shape of a serpent, and having four smaller mounds about its head and body in the forms of turtles. These mounds are a pictorial representation of Mohawk totems placed there by the Mississagas in memory of the occurrence and of the Mohawks. It has been supposed by some to mean more than this, but my father has so stated it.

The Mohawks fought well, but the Mississagas were just as good. An attack having been made upon this village the Mohawks were compelled once more to retreat. The Mohawks then fled to Quegeeging, or Cameron's Point, at the foot of Rice Lake, where great numbers of weapons and bones have since been found, and were again fiercely attacked by the Mississagas, who compelled them to beat a further retreat down the river to Onigaming, the famous carrying-place, where the Murray Canal now is, being the portage across from Lake Ontario into the Bay of Quinte, and from there into their own country. The Mississagas rested at Onigaming, and waited for the detachment from Toronto to join them. Before pursuing the main body of the Mohawks further after the attack at Cameron's Point, a party of the Mississagas went up country to a lake called Chuncall,* in Madoc, north of Trenton, where a party of Mohawks dwelt, and wiped them out. The lake being small, the fish fed on human flesh, and became very savage, so much so that the Indians came to hold them in dread.

It being known that the Iroquois would never rest until they should return and attack the Mississagas, and, perhaps, at a disadvantage to the Mississagas, the latter decided to advance against the Mohawks and the Iroquois generally, beyond the Great Lake. They came upon them at their fort on the Mohawk River, and laid siege to it. After a long time the Mohawks, who resisted with great bravery, sent out two old men to see if peace could not be made, it being a pity that two brave enemies should fight till both were upon the point of extermination. It was evident, however, that there could be no certainty of peace for the future, since the Iroquois, as well as the Mississagas' children, would surely take up the quarrel and continue it. It was decided by treaty, therefore, that the children of the Mohawk and Mississaga warriors should be given and taken in intermarriage, and in this way peace was assured for the future. The Mississagas then returned, and seeing that the land conquered by them from the Mohawks, who had dispossessed the Hurons, was full of game and an excellent hunting-ground, they came down from Lake Huron and settled permanently in the valley of the Otonabee, or Trent, and along the St. Lawrence, as far east as Brockville. They thus extended from Lake Huron to Brockville, in the east, and in the west, where the Credit Indians live, a tribe of the same race, from Toronto to Lake Erie. The British Government subsequently recognized the claims of the Mississagas to this country, and the eastern bands were gathered together at Nanabojou, or Hiawatha,** on Rice Lake; at Chemong, near Peterborough; and at Scugog, near Port Perry. Hiawatha is not Mississaga, the Mississaga name for Rice Lake being Pamadusgodayong, meaning Lake of Plains, from the fact that when the Mississagas first came down to the mouth of the river, the southern shore of Rice Lake opposite appeared to be flat since it had been cleared of forest, being the corn-fields of the Mohawks. Chemong is a corruption of Oskigimong, and refers to the boat*** shape of the lake. Scugog means shallow water.

After the great war of the American Revolution, the Mohawks, who had been allies of the British, and for that reason had had to leave the

*Hog Lake, or Moira Lake, is in Huntingdon, near the south end of Madoc township. Perhaps this is the lake referred to.

**Nanbojou, Manabuzhoo, or Nanaboozhoo, is an Algonkin word. Hiawatha is of Iroquois origin.

***Boat? Chemong is usually interpreted as "canoe".

United States, came over to Canada and asked the Mississagas to allow them to settle at Grand River and the Bay of Quinte. The British Government bought both reservations for the Mohawks from their allies—the Mississagas—and settled them there as they desired.

In closing my remarks I would like to call your attention to the Indians at Moose Point on Georgian Bay. Last winter my son and I were at Parry Sound, where we met some of the Indians dwelling at Moose Point, who had war medals but no land or annuity. These Indians are the descendants of those who came with Tecumseh, and afterwards did not dare go back. I am sure that if their case was presented to the Government they would get either land or annuity like ourselves.

I solemnly declare this to be the tradition of the Mississagas, as given me by word of mouth by my father, Paudash, and by my grandfather Cheneebeesh.

Declared before me at Peterborough, this 28th day of May, 1904.	(Sd.) CHIEF ROBT. PAUDASH, Chief of the Mississagas at Pamadusgodoyong.
(Sd.) HAMPDEN BURNHAM, A Commissioner, etc.	Also (Sd.) JOHNSON PAUDASH.[1]

Note.—While it would be obviously improper to impute anything like a want of faith in the sincerity of Chief Paudash in the foregoing declaration, it would be misleading not to point out to the reader that the Otonabee Serpent Mound is, most undoubtedly, the work of a people who occupied the soil long before the coming of the Mississagas. We have to thank the Chief, nevertheless, for his courtesy in communicating to Mr. Burnham the story of the belief as it is entertained by the Mississagas of to-day. Chief Paudash is the very worthy and intelligent head of the Mississaga Band now residing at Hiawatha, on Rice Lake.—D. B.

4. A Settler's Impressions of the Indians

[*Catharine P. Traill,* The Backwoods of Canada: Being Letters from the Wife of an Emigrant Officer, Illustrative of the Domestic Economy of British America (*London, 1836*), *pp. 162–70*]

The Indians are very successful in their duck-shooting: they fill a canoe with green boughs so that it resembles a sort of floating island; beneath the cover of these boughs they remain concealed, and are en-

[1]A rather disappointing M.A. thesis, that of Jean E. Harstone, 1914, in the University of Toronto Library, has yet a few items of value. Entitled "The Early History of the County and Town of Peterborough and of Lakefield and Rice Lake," it describes historical records of the district as "meagre"(!). Included in the thesis is Mosang Paudash's long and bloody narrative of the feud between Chief Bald Eagle's Ojebwas on the north shore of Rice Lake and Chief Black Snake's Mohawks on the south shore.

abled by this device to approach much nearer than they otherwise could do to the wary birds. The same plan is often adopted by our own sportsmen with great success.

A family of Indians have pitched their tents very near us. On one of the islands in our lake we can distinguish the thin blue smoke of their wood fires, rising among the trees, from our front window, or curling over the bosom of the waters.

The squaws have been several times to see me; sometimes from curiosity, sometimes with the view of bartering their baskets, mats, ducks, or venison, for pork, flour, potatoes, or articles of wearing-apparel. Sometimes their object is to borrow 'kettle to cook', which they are very punctual in returning.

Once a squaw came to borrow a washing-tub, but not understanding her language I could not for some time discover the object of her solicitude; at last she took up a corner of her blanket, and pointing to some soap began rubbing it between her hands, imitated the action of washing, then laughed, and pointed to a tub; she then held up two fingers, to intimate it was for two days she needed the loan.

These people appear of gentle and amiable dispositions; and, as far as our experience goes, they are very honest. Once, indeed, the old hunter, Peter, obtained from me some bread, for which he promised to give a pair of ducks; but, when the time came for payment and I demanded my ducks, he looked gloomy and replied with characteristic brevity, 'No duck—Chippewa (meaning S———,[1] this being the name they have affectionately given him) gone up lake with canoe—no canoe —duck by-and-by.' By-and-by is a favourite expression of the Indians, signifying an indefinite point of time; may be it means to-morrow, or a week, or month, or it may be a year, or even more. They rarely give you a direct promise.

As it is not wise to let any one cheat you if you can prevent it, I coldly declined any further overtures to bartering with the Indians until my ducks made their appearance.

Some time afterwards I received one duck by the hands of Maquin, a sort of Indian Flibberty-gibbet: this lad is a hunchbacked dwarf, very shrewd, but a perfect imp; his delight seems to be tormenting the brown babies in the wigwam or teazing the meek deer-hounds. He speaks English very fluently, and writes tolerably for an Indian boy; he usually accompanies the women in their visits and acts as their interpreter,

[1]Her brother, Samuel Strickland, who was himself *persona grata* with the Indians. See his descriptions of them, relative to both those in the vicinity of Goderich and in the Trent Valley, in his *Twenty-Seven Years in Canada West* (London, 1853), Vol. II, pp. 32–53 and 90–108. See also, relative to Thomas Need and the Indians, Section XI, No. 9, pp. 387–92, below.

grinning with mischievous glee at his mother's bad English and my perplexity at not being able to understand her signs. In spite of his extreme deformity he seemed to possess no inconsiderable share of vanity, gazing with great satisfaction at his face in the looking-glass. When I asked his name he replied, 'Indian name Maquin, but English name 'Mister Walker', very good man'; this was the person he was called after.

These Indians are scrupulous in their observance of the Sabbath, and show great reluctance to having any dealings in the way of trading or pursuing their usual avocations of hunting or fishing on that day.[1]

The young Indians are very expert in the use of a long bow, with wooden arrows, rather heavy and blunt at the end. Maquin said he could shoot ducks and small birds with his arrows; but I should think they were not calculated to reach objects at any great distance, as they appeared very heavy.

'Tis sweet to hear the Indians singing their hymns of a Sunday night; their rich soft voices rising in the still evening air. I have often listened to this little choir praising the Lord's name in the simplicity and fervour of their hearts, and have felt it was a reproach that these poor half-civilized wanderers should alone be found to gather together to give glory to God in the wilderness.

I was much pleased with the simple piety of our friend the hunter Peter's squaw, a stout, swarthy matron, of most amiable expression. We were taking our tea when she softly opened the door and looked in; an encouraging smile induced her to enter, and depositing a brown papouse (Indian for baby or little child) on the ground, she gazed round with curiosity and delight in her eyes. We offered her some tea and bread, motioning to her to take a vacant seat beside the table. She seemed pleased by the invitation, and drawing her little one to her knee, poured some tea into a saucer and gave it to the child to drink. She ate very moderately, and when she had finished, rose, and, wrapping her face in the folds of her blanket, bent down her head on her breast in the attitude of prayer. This little act of devotion was performed

[1]Much was done to civilize the Indians, particularly by the Wesleyan Methodist Society. A good summary of the Indian settlements at Alderville (Alnwick Township) and Grape Island (Bay of Quinte) is given in W. H. Smith's *Canadian Gazetteer* (Toronto, 1846), p. 2. Training in the management of farms and vocational education of various types were included. The indenture for the lease of Grape Island is given in George F. Playter, *The History of Methodism in Canada* (Toronto, 1862), pp. 293–4, while Methodist religious and educational work among the Indians there and at Lake Scugog, Mud (Chemong) Lake, and Rice Lake are described *passim*, and particularly pp. 274–8, 287–8, 305–13, and 356–60. In 1856 the cornerstone of an industrial schoolhouse was laid at Alderville, and a description of the ceremony is given in the *Cobourg Star*, June 14, 1848. The Sons of Temperance was reorganized there in 1856 (*Cobourg Star*, September 17, 1856).

without the slightest appearance of pharisaical display, but in singleness and simplicity of heart. She then thanked us with a face beaming with smiles and good humour; and taking little Rachel by the hands, threw her over her shoulder with a peculiar sleight that I feared would dislocate the tender thing's arms, but the papouse seemed well satisfied with this mode of treatment.

In long journeys the children are placed in upright baskets of a peculiar form, which are fastened round the necks of the mothers by straps of deer-skin; but the *young* infant is swathed to a sort of flat cradle, secured with flexible hoops, to prevent it from falling out. To these machines they are strapped, so as to be unable to move a limb. Much finery is often displayed in the outer covering and the bandages that confine the papouse.

There is a sling attached to this cradle that passes over the squaw's neck, the back of the babe being placed to the back of the mother, and its face outward. The first thing a squaw does on entering a house is to release herself from her burden, and stick it up against the wall or chair, chest, or any thing that will support it, where the passive prisoner stands, looking not unlike a mummy in its case. I have seen the picture of the Virgin and Child in some of the old illuminated missals, not unlike the figure of a papouse in its swaddling-clothes.

The squaws are most affectionate to their little ones. Gentleness and good humour appear distinguishing traits in the tempers of the female Indians; whether this be natural to their characters in the savage state, or the softening effects of Christianity, I cannot determine. Certainly in no instance does the Christian religion appear more lovely than when, untainted by the doubts and infidelity of modern sceptics, it is displayed in the conduct of the reclaimed Indian breaking down the strong-holds of idolatry and natural evil and bringing forth the fruits of holiness and morality. They may be said to receive the truths of the Gospel as little children, with simplicity of heart and unclouded faith.

The squaws are very ingenious in many of their handiworks. We find their birch-bark baskets very convenient for a number of purposes. My bread-basket, knife-tray, sugar-basket are all of this humble material. When ornamented and wrought in patterns with dyed quills, I can assure you they are by no means inelegant. They manufacture vessels of birch-bark so well that they will serve for many useful household purposes, such as holding water, milk, broth, or any other liquid; they are sewn or rather stitched together with the tough roots of the tamarack or larch, or else with strips of cedar-bark. They also weave very useful sorts of baskets from the inner rind of the bass-wood and white ash. Some of these baskets, of a coarse kind, are made use of for gathering up potatoes, Indian corn, or turnips; the settlers finding them very good substitutes for the osier baskets used for such purposes in the old country.

The Indians are acquainted with a variety of dyes, with which they stain the more elegant fancy-baskets and porcupine-quills. Our parlour is ornamented with several very pretty specimens of their ingenuity in this way, which answer the purpose of note and letter-cases, flower-stands, and work-baskets.

They appear to value the useful rather more highly than the merely ornamental articles that you may exhibit to them. They are very shrewd and close in all their bargains, and exhibit a surprising degree of caution in their dealings. The men are much less difficult to trade with than the women; they display a singular pertinacity in some instances. If they have fixed their mind on any one article they will come to you day after day, refusing any other you may offer to their notice. One of the squaws fell in love with a gay chintz dressing-gown belonging to my husband, and though I resolutely refused to part with it, all the squaws in the wigwam by turns came to look at 'gown', which they pronounced with their peculiarly plaintive tone of voice; and when I said 'no gown to sell', they uttered a melancholy exclamation of regret and went away.

They will seldom make any article you want on purpose for you. If you express a desire to have baskets of a particular pattern that they do not happen to have ready made by them they give you the usual vague reply of 'by-and-by'. If the goods you offer them in exchange for theirs do not answer their expectations they give a sullen and dogged look or reply, '*Car-car*' (no, no), or '*Carwinni*', which is a still more forcible negative. But when the bargain pleases them they signify their approbation by several affirmative nods of the head and a note not much unlike a grunt; the ducks, fish, venison, or baskets are placed beside you, and the articles of exchange transferred to the folds of their capacious blankets or deposited in a sort of rushen wallets not unlike those straw baskets in which English carpenters carry their tools.

The women imitate the dresses of the whites, and are rather skilful in converting their purchases. Many of the young girls can sew very neatly. I often give them bits of silk and velvet and braid, for which they appear very thankful. . . .

5. Three Years among the Ojibways, 1857–1860

[*Emma Jeffers Graham, in* Transactions of the Women's Canadian Historical Society of Toronto, *1916–17*]

It was on an afternoon in June, 1857, that the Peterborough train, after crossing Rice Lake, stopped at the station of Hiawatha, where our small party of travellers from Montreal alighted. The station itself was only a shack, one end of which was devoted to the sale of groceries. It was kept by Mr. Waters, who was not only a station master and a grocer but also a pillar in the little mission church.

My father, Rev. Wellington Jeffers, had been pastor for several years of St. James Methodist Church, Montreal, and had suffered a severe nervous breakdown. At his own request he had been assigned to a mission where the outdoors life might prove beneficial. On leaving the train my father was surrounded by members of his flock, nearly all of them being of the Ojibway tribe. The women wore plain cotton gowns, neatly made, and simple straw hats, while the men were garbed in woollen shirts and trousers, with red scarfs tied around the waists. They also wore plain wide-brimmed hats of coarse straw. This conventional attire was highly disappointing to my brothers, James and Wellington, who had been looking forward to a community of fierce, dark-skinned braves who might at any moment decide to go upon the war path. The Indians bent with courtesy and grave decorum before my father, who was a man of commanding height, and seemed to be impressed by his greeting. The women, on the contrary, laughed joyously at the stature of my stepmother, who was but five feet in height, and took a great interest in my baby stepsister, Helen, whom they insisted on carrying in their arms through the village street.

There was neither carriage nor horse to carry us to the Mission House, for the reason that there were no vehicles in the village except a light waggon belonging to Mr. Waters and a veritable 'one hoss shay' owned by one of the Indians. So we proceeded along the street of the little settlement, my father and the chief, Paudaush, leading the way. The Indian women, who were child-like and merry in manner, surrounded my step-mother, while I, who was twelve years old, walked hand-in-hand with my brother, Wellington. We were both rather nervous, as we associated Indians with tomahawks and spears; but we arrived in safety at the cabin of Mr. Gervase Smith, who was an Indian of a superior order, having a house 'like white folks', as the villagers said when speaking of him. Here a delicious dinner awaited us of fish, wild rice, and other dainties served on shining dishes, while the polished cutlery might have adorned a city table. The wild rice was a dish of which we became very fond, as it seemed to have a sweetness and richness lacking in the lighter variety.

The little mission church, to which we were taken after this meal, seemed very small in comparison with the St. James Church in Montreal, which was then considered one of the largest Protestant churches in Canada. At the side of the church was a small gate which opened into the lane which led to the Mission House. To this we were escorted and duly welcomed. It was a good-sized modern house, painted a dark red, with a large garden which was fenced with pickets. Behind the church and just beyond the garden was the burying ground, which was held sacred by the Indians, no lawless or profane person being allowed burial there. It was a beautiful and picturesque spot. But who shall describe the lake—which was girdled by woods and hills and dotted with verdant islands? To the right of Hiawatha, high on the banks, nestled Gore's Landing, and away to the left, over which the setting sun rested in glory, was the important mission of Alnwick.

It was a simple yet not uneventful life which we lived among those friendly folk, and the life in the open air soon restored my father's shattered health. One of the things I learned was the art of fishing. My father bought a punt and in this we would sit for hours with our lines quivering and jerking, and we usually went home with the basket full of sunfish, white fish, and perhaps a maskinonge. It was there that one had every opportunity to study the art of cooking fish, and it proved a most useful accomplishment. In the autumn the Indians went out in their boats to the rice fields and there they carefully gathered in the grain. The process was a simple one: the Indian possessed himself of two shingles, and with these scraped the rice from the stalks into the boat. When the rice was all gathered in, it was poured into large wooden pans where the Indians shelled it by trampling it (with new moccasins on their feet). The peculiar flavour of the wild rice was remarked by all of us, and we soon came to regard the white rice as tasteless.

In 1859 the Great Comet appeared, causing much interesting discussion in scientific circles. Religious fanatics were sure that the end of the world was very near, and talked constantly of the various signs and wonders which assured them that the Last Day was at hand. I remember going out into our wood-yard one evening and seating myself on a log, prepared to watch the progress of the comet. As I looked at the great star with a tail which swept across half the heavens, my faith in the prophecies of direful happenings grew strong. I had brought from my father's study a copy of Pollock's 'Course of Time', as a help to interpret the doings of our celestial visitor. But the descriptions of the Last Day, as imagined by that writer, were so alarmingly vivid that I sprang from the log and ran back to the study with Pollock's 'Course of Time', pushing it down behind the larger books so that I might never see it again. The Indians, who had great reverence for the mysterious, looked upon the coming and passing of the great star with profound awe. Some of them believed that the Great Manitou was angry with the world and intended to destroy it. They asked many questions of my father, who held very calming views of the 'Second Coming' and who did his best to keep the members of his flock from becoming hysterical.

In their religious feeling these Indians were simple and sincere. The missionary meeting was a great annual event, and the young men and girls were trained to sing the old hymns and anthems. I do not think I have heard sweeter music than their singing of 'O'er the gloomy hills of darkness' or 'Hark the herald angels sing!' One Sunday my father asked me if I thought I could teach a class of young women in the Sunday School. I was only twelve years old but I said I would try. So every Sunday afternoon I knelt on the seat of a pew in the little church and told the most interesting Bible stories I knew to a class of about twenty young women. When they became excited over any incident in the story they would give loud cries like miniature war whoops, and finally became so noisy that my father questioned me as to the matter of my teaching. He told me not to tell them exciting stories, as we were disturbing the school; but when the war whoops lessened I felt that I had not been a success.

When the hunting season arrived there was a great stir in the village, every able-bodied man, woman, and child preparing for the fray. The Indians depended largely on their success in hunting for their support during the winter months. When they returned from the hunting-ground, laden with the spoils of victory, they feasted until they became ill with various humors caused by alternate over-eating and starvation. Forethought was almost an impossibility for many of them. They have learned much in the last fifty years, however, and the improved physique of the Indian is due to greater care in matters of diet.

On the first day of October two Indians came to the Mission House to tell my father that the day had come when the men filled the yard with wood for the winter. Of course we had to provide entertainment for our benefactors; so there was a hurried conference in the kitchen. We had to prepare large quantities of all kinds of food—a huge roast of venison, a boiled ham, a bushel of vegetables, and a vast number of pies. We were very tired at night, but our wood-yard was packed with many cords of good hickory and several cords of pine for kindling. We always found them honourable, and even noble, in their business dealings. Would that the same could invariably be said of the white man's dealings with his Indian brother!

Becoming dissatisfied with the small yearly grant which was given them by the Government, the different tribes in Canada decided to hold a Council of protest and appeal, and it was held in Hiawatha. Intense excitement was created in the village when it was known that the Great

Chiefs were coming to hold a pow-wow. The Council Hall was decorated with boughs and brilliant hangings, and the chiefs sat in Oriental fashion as they palavered. One day, during the Council, two stalwart braves in red garb and feathers, with tomahawks in their belts, came to the Mission House and asked that my elder brother, who was a handsome and extremely fair lad, should come to their afternoon session, as they decided to give him an Indian name. He went with them, greatly delighted by the honour paid him. On his return he related to us how they bade him sit by them and smoke the peace pipe—which he did rather reluctantly, not having as yet learned to enjoy such a rite. I am sorry that I cannot recall the syllables of the Indian name, but it meant the 'Rising Sun'. I am glad to say that the Government heeded the request of these 'wards' and increased their grants, both in money and land.

The mission was frequently visited, especially in the summer, by friends who were delighted with the picturesque scenery. Among the most welcome guests were Mr. John Dougall, the Editor of the 'Montreal Witness', and professors from Victoria College.

My father used to go to Peterborough frequently to purchase dry goods or household supplies. One day he brought home a book entitled 'Roughing it in the Bush', which he thought was a remarkable production. After reading every word of it I said to him: 'Why, she just writes about everyday life. I know people like those she tells about'. My father replied: 'That is what makes it literature'. My father became a friend of the author, Mrs. Moodie, and after the family moved to Belleville and my father was also living in that city they had many talks on old times in Canada. I was visiting my father in Belleville years ago, when one morning, in the course of a walk, we met an old lady who was evidently going to market. My father bowed so profoundly that I asked him about the lady who had just passed us. 'One of the ablest women in Canada', he said warmly. This was none other than Mrs. Moodie, a member of the famous Strickland family and grandmother of the late Mary Agnes Fitzgibbon, who, with Mrs. Curzon, founded the Women's Historical Society of Toronto and who will ever be kept in grateful memory.

An incident which shows the complications of our quiet existence at Hiawatha may be related. Our charwoman was of Irish parentage but was the wife of Daniel Cow, a rather riotous Indian who once came to shoot my father, declaring that the missionary was an idle citizen. Biddy Cow came to my father one day to ask that her son be baptized on the following Sunday. On being questioned about the name to be given the baby, she said that it was to be named after my father and therefore would be known as Wellington Jeffers Cow. Now my father shrank from such an honour in connection with that prosaic name. So he became a diplomat and suggested that Dr. Wood, who was the Superintendent of Missions, should share the honour, and thus it came about that the little Wellington Wood Cow received his name and grew up to be a stalwart Irish-Indian and a good Canadian too.

Sometimes the greatest enemy of the Indian was the clever and unscrupulous half-breed, who, in some cases, seemed to unite the vices of the two races. Such a one used to swoop down on Hiawatha at intervals and exercise a mysterious fascination over the younger Indians, who were sadly led astray owing to his evil influence. Then the older Indians would take their guns and search for this destroyer of the village peace, who was so fleet-footed and cunning that he easily avoided them. I saw this Evil Genius of Hiawatha one Sunday morning, for he did not hesitate to come to the mission church to seek his prey. He was a handsome creature in a dark desperate fashion, and I remember that my small brother whispered to me: 'He lookth like a pirate'.

The next morning the village was roused by the news that half-a-dozen of the young people of Hiawatha had been lured away from their homes by this rascal and had spent the night in one of the hidden drinking places which the half-breed frequented. One of the finest old Indians in the church came to my father with the tears rolling down his dark cheeks and cried: 'Oh, my meenister, he stole my little girl—my papoose—she sit on my knee and sing hymns and be a good little girl. But he take her and I kill him'. But he did not kill him, for when the searchers reached an old barn which stood in a deep wood about a mile from the village, the tempter had made his escape and only his victims were found lying in a drunken stupor. A few months later the half-breed was found in the same old barn, lying wasted by the disease then called 'consumption'. The old woman who found him took him to her little cabin and nursed him to the end. Before he died he said to her one day: 'I see I very wicked. But no one ever taught me—no mother—father very bad white man—sorry!' However, the Indians would not bury him in the sacred mound by the mission church, and the body was carried far into the woods where it was given a resting-place under a maple tree—and the grave was long regarded with terror as an evil spot.

In 1860 my father was appointed editor of the 'Christian Guardian' and we left the little mission for Toronto. I have always remembered with affection the simple people among whom we lived for a very happy three years by one of Ontario's loveliest lakes.

6. Indian History in Methuen Township[1]

[*C. Pelham Mulvany* et al., History of the County of Peterborough . . . (*Toronto, 1884*), *pp. 218–22*]

In the north-west corner of the Township of Methuen and about eight miles north-east of Stony Lake, with which it is connected by Jack's Creek, is a lake the real and common name of which is Jack's Lake, although on one map, at least, it is called White Lake. It derived its name from Handsome Jack, an Indian chief, who claimed all the streams and lands in this locality as his fishing and hunting grounds. He was considered the handsomest man among the Chippewas, then commanded by ' Cap.' Paudash, of Rice Lake; he stood six feet four inches in height and weighed fully 250 pounds. He belonged to the Cow family, and among the whites was known as Jack Cow. Stony Lake, Loon Lake in the Township of Chandos, and all the streams south of Loon Lake were claimed by him as his inherited property. He was most tenacious of his rights, and would invariabiy destroy all the traps of white-men he found set on his streams. But he would allow the pale face to hunt for deer and partridge or to fish in the streams, so long as no furs were taken.

Handsome Jack usually lived in a birch-bark wigwam, which he moved from place to place as circumstances required. Although he never missed an opportunity of rather greedily asserting his right to his streams and hunting grounds he, nevertheless, was very hospitable to those who were friendly with him. He would often invite the whites to his wigwam and would order his squaw to prepare a good meal of rice, beaver, and partridge boiled with a little pounded corn. This was 'Te Pake', a hodgepodge mixture, somewhat akin to an Irish stew. The hospitable Indian would sit by and apparently enjoy seeing the white man eat at his fireside. When the repast was finished he would light his pipe and relate thrilling scenes of his wild life in hunting the bear, wolf, deer, and other animals with which the woods were alive.

Handsome Jack was the father of two lovely girls named 'Baby Cow' and 'Polly Cow', both of whom inherited their father's extreme beauty and perfect symmetry of form. The latter grew up a most beautiful maiden; her soft-tinted complexion, heightened by the rose-hued blossom of health, and her long black hair reaching nearly to the ground, rendered her an object of envy to other dusky damsels. She possessed a fine voice, and on many a moonlight night have the pine-crowned

[1]This item is of special interest in that Mr. Mulvany personally interviewed numerous inhabitants of the region in the lifetime of many of the first settlers.

islands of Stony Lake re-echoed the sweet melody of her quaint and weird native songs, the faint ripple of the waters keeping time as she paddled her canoe beneath the shadows of the overhanging boughs or out on the open lake in the splendour of the full moon. She was the ever-worshipped idol of her father and of many others, who were alarmed when, at the age of sixteen years, she grew ill of a fever. The best efforts of the 'medicine men' were futile to stay the ravages of the disease, and Handsome Jack was inconsolable. So died the beautiful Polly Cow on an evening when the setting sun shot golden shafts through the frost-bitten leaves that fluttered in the autumn wind. The old Indian chief was heart-broken. He was determined that his darling daughter should sleep in a fitting grave, and accordingly repaired to one, the most southern, of the three islands at the point where the waters of Clear Lake run into Katchewanooka—the Water of Many Rapids. On this island, about ten feet from the water's edge, he dug the grave with his own hands and walled it up with stones. Then, placing the body in a birch-bark coffin, he paddled it down the lake in his canoe and buried it in the grave he had prepared beneath a balsam tree, which is still standing to mark the lonely grave of Handsome Jack's daughter. The disconsolate father then cleared away the trees and brushwood between the grave and the water's edge so that the dead girl's spirit could wander there daily for water, as was the Indian belief. Night after night did the sad-hearted chief watch by the grave, until he joined his daughter in the Happy Hunting Grounds in 1835. Since the occurrence of this touching incident these islands have been called the Polly Cow Islands. They are only about half a mile below the small village of Young's Point, and can be easily visited by the tourist or others who would like to stand under the balsam tree that shades Polly Cow's grave. A few years ago some young Englishmen who were residing in the neighbourhood arranged a plan to steal the remains of the lovely Indian maiden and send them to England as a curiosity, together with the story of her marvellous beauty, her death and burial; but happily the act of vandalism was frustrated. The squaw of Handsome Jack survived him many years, and married an Indian named Snow-storm. . . .

The northern portion of the County of Peterborough contains chains of small lakes nearly one hundred in number. Some of these possess names of historic character, being the names of Indian chiefs by whom they were claimed, with the land surrounding them, for hunting and fishing purposes. The first worthy of mention is Eels Lake, located in the north-east corner of the Township of Anstruther. It derives its name from 'Eels', a subordinate chief of the Chippewas. Its outlet is Eels River, a deep and swift-running stream of much importance for milling and log-floating purposes which flows directly south for about forty miles until it enters Stony Lake about seven miles east of Burleigh Falls. 'Eels' was a brother of 'Handsome Jack'. In the Township of Methuen, to the south-east of Jack's Lake, is Bottle Lake, so-called from the resemblance of its shape to that of a bottle. It empties itself into Kashabogamog Lake, also in Methuen Township. 'Kashabogamog' means 'lake of many passages', and like all Indian names is particularly appropriate. Its shape resembles very much a hand with wide outstretched fingers, each finger being a long and narrow piece of water. Some years ago a wealthy young Englishman named Falaasa met his death by drowning in this lake. This chain of lakes, together with Clear Lake three miles eastward, was formerly owned by John and Moses Taunchay, two Indian brothers, who held it and the surrounding land for many years as hunting and fishing grounds. Massossaga and Kitcheoum Lakes, in the southern portion of Township of Cavendish, on the east side of the Buckhorn Road, were at one time the hunting and fishing grounds of a Chemong Lake Indian named Isaac Irons, whose squaw was a sister of Handsome Jack.

Loon Lake, situated in the centre of the Township of Chandos, is a beautiful lake of very irregular shape, having no less than twelve distinct bays. The water is from twelve to twenty-five feet in depth and is very clear and cool, its supply being principally derived from springs. It was originally called, by the Indians, Mongosogan; but when the white man reached it, after making his way through the forests that lay between it and civilization, it received its present name out of respect to the thousands of loons that annually repaired to these waters about the first of June for the purpose of rearing their young.

II. PREPARATIONS FOR SETTLEMENT

THE SURVEYS in this Section will serve as examples of a large number that are available. Footnotes have been inserted in No. 3, John Smith's excellent and interesting survey of the entire Newcastle District, particularly to indicate the modern equivalent of Indian place-names. Richard Birdsall, whose reports are not among those included here, was among the more prominent early land surveyors in the region, having laid out, under the direction of Zacheus Burnham, the Peterborough townsite in 1825, and parts of various townships earlier and later. Frances Stewart describes the process in Douro in one of her 1823 letters[1]:

. . . one very wet day I saw two men walk past my window; one had a blanket about his shoulders, a pair of snowshoes in his hands, and a small fur cap. The other was dressed in ragged sailor's clothes. I took the foremost for an Indian as they generally wear blankets about them, but to our surprise we found this was Mr. Birdsall, a very smart young Englishman who is surveyor of the township in this district, and his assistant; they had five other men with them as chain-bearers, etc. I found that they had all been living in the woods for the months of March and April, which accounted for the ragged and weatherbeaten appearance of the whole party.

1. Surveying the Newcastle District Boundary, 1804

[*Archives of Ontario, Crown Land Papers, 72 (5)*]

Diary of Division Line between the Home & Newcastle Districts

Stegman—1804—Diary from the 13th of August to the 31st Inclusive, 1804.

Monday August the 13the 1804. Returned Diary and Field Notes in the Surveyor General's Office.

Tuesday the 14the. Waited on the Honorable the Executive Council.

Wednesday the 15the. Received Instructions for the Survey of the Division Line between the Home and Newcastle Districts and prepared for the same.

Thursday August the 16. Engaged men and provisions for the Survey.

Friday the 17the. Left York and went 18 miles.

[1]*Our Forest Home* (2nd ed., Montreal, 1902), p. 36. Birdsall, born in 1799 in England, died suddenly at Graham's Tavern (now Bailieboro) in 1851.

Saturday the 18the. Went 20 miles.
Sunday the 19the. Arived at the Boundary Line.
Monday the 20the. Went to the 9the Concession of Whitby.
Tuesday the 21st. Began to open the Division Line and run three Miles.
Wednesday the 22nd. Continued the aforesaid Line three Miles.
Thursday the 23rd. Finished the said Line and came to Lake Beobescugog at 5 O'Clock P.M.
Friday Augnst the 24the. Sealed the Lake Beobescugog and the Large Bay by intersection.
Saturday the 25the. Finished the Survey and returned to Dundas Street.
Sunday the 26the. Went to Tuffins' Creek.
Monday the 27the. Arived at York 5 O'Clock P.M.
Tuesday the 28the. Maid out the pay list and Discharged the party.
Wednesday the 29the. Protracted the Survey and returned a Plan of the same in the Surveyor General's Office.
Thursday the 30the. Maid out the Accounts for the Surveyor General's Office from the 1st of July, to the 31st of August.
Friday the 31st of August. Finished the Accounts and a Plan for His Honore the Chief Justice.

I Certify this to be a True Diary—John Stegmann, Dy Surveyor

2. Survey of Burleigh and Harvey Townships

(*a*) Letter of Andrew Miller explaining delay, July 18, 1823

[*Letters Received, Ontario Department of Lands and Forests*]

Dundas, 18: July 1823.—

Sir,

Having been informed a few days since by Colonel Nelles that the returns of the Survey of Burleigh and Harvey were wanted

I would beg leave to inform you that I have them both nearly completed, also that of the Gore between Emily and Mud Lake; I shall be able to deliver them in the space of six or eight days—I would also beg leave to state that I should have had these finished and delivered sooner but on account of the small Traverse yet to be done.—This on account of the great depth of Snow in the Winter, and the height of the Water this spring, was not practicable to be done sooner than now; I shall proceed immediately down and complete it, it will require but a few days.—We commenced running the first line, last Spring on the 20: June, and after that, Salmon Trout Lake, which bound Burleigh all on the South, fell five feet or more, so that large bays, and inundated Swamps or Marshes on its borders became entirely dry and passable

To
Thos Ridout Esqr
Surveyor General

I am Sir &c &c
(sgd) Andrew Miller
D.P.S.

(*b*) REPORT OF ANDREW MILLER, SEPTEMBER 29, 1823

[*Survey Reports, Ontario Department of Lands and Forests*]

To Thomas Ridout Esquire Surveyor Gen[l]
Of Upper Canada &c &c &c

Sir,

Having completed the survey of the Townships of Burleigh & Harvey in the District of New-Castle, together with a Gore of Emily lying on the west of Mud Lake, I have the honor herewith to transmit the Plans and field Notes of the same—

I would beg leave to remark concerning the said Townships of Burleigh & Harvey in general, that they are an extremely rough and rugged tract of Country; comprising but very little if any land, that in the strict sense of the word may be called good tillable land. The Waters and Lakes however bounding them on the south and west are large and fine; abounding with numerous kinds of large fish, and wild fowl, always producing large crops of wild rice, and affording, with the interruption of 4 rapids of a few rods each a good navigation for schooners and boats. The numerous and strong indications of Ore together with the frequent waterfalls, intimate that this Country may become of vast use to the government as a mining Country—

As it respects the Township of Burleigh in particular, I would remark, that there are four species of land or surface pertaining thereto—

First—large tracts of open rocky, barren pine plains, very thinly timbered, with little shrubbery or underwood, and interspersed with numerous small alder and tamarack swamps, cranberry marshes and broken sloughs,—

Second—Large tracts of hilly, ridgey, and in some places mountainous country, very rocky, steep, and precipitous. Hills thinly timbered with Hemlock and Pine some small stinted Oaks, and an almost impenetrable growth of young poplars and birches, about the size of large Sugar Canes, filling every foot of vacancy between the rocks. This hilly tract abounds in small lakes of from 30 to 100 and 200 chains in circumference, lying between the high and steep hills. These Lakes abound in beaver and wild fowl, and doubtless with fish. They are in the fine hunting grounds of the Massisiguas——

Third—Considerable tracts of level surface covered with a flat limestone rock. This is most curious and frequently extends for miles. The rock contains large seems from 6 to 10 inches wide, and frequently from 5 to 110 feet deep perpendicular. This rock is usually covered with a little leaves and rubbish and in most places an inch or two of earth—This tract is timbered quite well with Beech Maple Ash &c.

Fourth—A streak of from 2. to 4. lots wide and through several concessions, where the surface is bending in moderate swells and the stones appear to be broken or smaller and Limestone chiefly also, and completely filling the ground—This is also timbered with Beech, Maple, & Ash, the soil a grey loam——The Pine plains lie in the East and South east part of the Township, the rocky ridges are all the northern half—The lime rock in the western or S. Western corner, And the limestone swells in the southern part and the southwest——

The Complexion of the Township of Harvey is much the same as that of Burleigh only less of the pine plains, more of the flat lime rock, and as you approach Pigeon Lake on the west the Country becomes less rocky and in the Concession adjoining the lake and south of big island a few lots may be useful for cultivation but are still stony. This remark may also extend for a small distance down the river but with less propriety. Thus it fully appears a rough country. The rocks in general except the limestone land appear to be silicious and no doubt will be valuable for mill stones. We also found on breaking them specks of lead ore in places and by the large black seems appearing to run through many of them one would judge there was black lead. These seems contain large fleaks of isinglass and a substance by rubing which your fingers are blackened—I saw a piece of black lead near the size of an egg which was cut from some of the rocks by an indian, also a piece near the same size which marked like red chalk and resembled it exactly. This was brought also by the indians——

I have the honor to be
with much respect
York Sep[t]. 29th 1823— Your Most Obedient
And very Humble Servant
Andrew Miller Dep. Prov. Sur.

N.B. I learnt from the reports of the Indians that something like twenty miles back from the rear of Harvey the land became good—

3. General Account of the Newcastle District, 1827

[*Andrew Picken*, The Canadas (*London, 1832*), *pp. 153–166*]

MINUTES. Inspection of the Newcastle District made by Mr. John Smith, Junr., Deputy Pro. Surveyor, at the request of Mr. Galt.

On entering the Newcastle district the traveller cannot but be surprised that the only mode of crossing the river Trent is by a scow in summer and on the ice in winter, which, at certain seasons, is not without danger. A regular ferry is kept here, which pays the nominal rent of 10£ currency to the Provincial Government; the tolls are at the rate of threepence-halfpenny for every foot passenger, and eightpence for man and horse. Notwithstanding the great proportion of passage is taken by the steam-boats, the tolls at the ferry, for the season, amount to upwards of 150£ currency. As the travelling in the four winter at least equals that of the eight summer months, were a bridge erected and a moderate toll imposed, the proceeds would not only meet the interest but soon repay the principal; after which they might be applied to the improvement of the road (Dundas Street), which for ten miles to the westward is in a bad state. The only objection I have heard urged against a bridge is that the ice floating down with the spring floods would endanger it. I am assured, however, by old residents that the ice banks before it reaches the mouth of the river, and that it does not drift off into the bay of Quinté, but honeycombs and sinks. A tolerable road, on the line of which the land is generally inferior, skirts the bay of Quinté from the Trent to the Carrying Place, about five miles distant; at this point it branches to the westward until it join Dundas Street, and eastward into the county of Prince Edward. At the Carrying Place the steam-boats are met by the York stage.

At the first settlement of the country the only mode of communication to the settlements above was by boats which crossed from the head of the bay of Quinté by this portage (about 1 mile) to the lake Ontario, and thence coasted its shores; hence the name of the Carrying Place. The portage is laid out on either side in building lots. On the lake side flat rock is met with, while on the side next the bay of Quinté is a high sand-bank which extends some distance to the westward. On either hand the land differs materially, and to the west is very low and swampy. At one point the waters of lake Ontario and the bay are separated only by two miles of low wet land. It would appear that, at some period, there has been an open communication. There is a small village at the Carrying Place, with an Episcopal church, at which, for some years, a resident missionary has officiated. In this neighbourhood the Canada Company holds no lands, unless at Presqu'ile bay, which have been already inspected.

Proceeded direct to Cobourg, and thence to Peterborough by the route of the Rice lake.

The situation of Cobourg is healthy and pleasant. It stands immediately on the shore of lake Ontario, on lots 16 and 17 in concession B of Hamilton. In 1812 it had only one house; it now contains upwards of 40 houses, an Episcopal church, a Methodist chapel, 2 good inns, 4 stores, several distilleries, an extensive grist-mill, and the population may be estimated at about 350 souls. The trade of Cobourg is increasing rapidly, more through the spirit and enterprise of its merchants than its natural advantages. In alluding to its deficiency in the latter respect, the want of a harbour, and the break in its communication with the back country caused by the Rice lake, are particularly meant. It is, however, to be observed that the formation of a harbour is now proposed, as will be seen by the accompanying minutes, and that the Rice lake, by means of the extensive streams which pour into it, along which settlements are forming, promises to become the channel of a great addition to its inland trade.

The following has been mentioned to me as the present state of the trade of Cobourg, viz.:

EXPORTS.			IMPORTS.		
5000	barrels of	Flour.	200	tons of	Merchandize.
500	do.	Pork.	600	barrels of	Salt.
150	do.	Potash.	250	do.	bulk of Foreign Goods, &c.
200	do.	Sundries, such as Lard, Beef, Butter, Whiskey, &c.			

The adjoining townships are of a fertile soil. An excellent road leads from Cobourg through the centre of the township of Hamilton to the Rice lake. A large sum (I believe 600£ currency), borrowed from the bank of Upper Canada on the responsibility of the magistrate of the division, has been judiciously expended on this road in the course of the summer. It is expected that the amount of taxes in absentee lands, which is to be levied next year, will meet the expenditure. On both sides of the road the Canada Company holds lands, in general of a good soil; those nearest to Cobourg being the most eligible for immediate sale. It is now proposed to open a branch road from this to meet the Cavan road near the head of the Rice lake. The line selected will serve those lots belonging to the Company which lie in the 6th and 7th concessions of Hamilton, from the 20th lot westward.

The soil of Hamilton is generally a sandy loam. On the western part of the township it is clayey. Very extensive ridges border the Rice lake, which from their being bare of timber are called the Rice Lake Plains. The soil is a mixture of sand and clay in various proportions, according to the elevation: on the high-lands sand prevails, and *vice versa*. The whole is, in general, capable of cultivation; but from a want of wood and water, it is said, would answer best for sheep-walks. In most parts the plough could at once be used. The large grants held by absentees in

Hamilton have prevented the settlements extending beyond the fourth concession, excepting on the western boundary and a few on the Rice lake.

The following sale has come to my knowledge. *viz.*:

Edward Ellis and Co., of London, by their Agents Forsyth and Richardson, of Montreal, to David Sidey, No. 16 in 5 con. Hamilton, 200 acres at 15s. per acre; 25£ down, and the rest in 5 annual instalments with interest. The sale was made in the course of the summer; the lot is good, and on the Cobourg road.

The townships of Monaghan and Otanabee,[1] which are divided by the Otanabee river, form the northern shores of the Rice lake. Otanabee, though it has an excellent soil in general (loam upon clay), has been but very partially settled. This is mainly to be attributed to its distance from, and difficulty of access to, market. These objections are now removed; the roads on all sides being improved, and grist and saw mills built in the township (lot 13 on 6th concession), as also at Peterborough. From the Cobourg road a ferry is established across the Rice lake, whence a road runs from Banister's Landing northerly, until it branches on 13th lot between 10th and 11th concessions; eastward, through a settlement to the mills, and thence to Asphodel; and northerly, with scattering settlements on the line to Peterboro'. There are numerous swamps in the township, and sandy plains skirt the Rice lake shore. The settlers in Otanabee are chiefly from the lowlands; the rest are highlanders and a few English. The road through Otanabee to Peterborough is improving.

The town-lot of Peterborough is in the north-east angle of the township of Monaghan. It is laid out in half acres, the streets nearly at right angles with the river; park lots of nine acres each are reserved near the town. The patent fee on each is 8£ provincial currency, and office fees and agency will increase it 15s. or 20s. more.

The settlement commenced in 1825, at which time it formed the depôt of the emigration under the Hon. P. Robinson. The situation is most favourable, being on an elevated sandy plain watered by a fine creek, which discharges into the river below the town. The country round is fertile, and there is great waterpower on the town-plot, on which mills are now being built by the government. These mills are on an extensive scale, being calculated to pack 40 barrels of flour; and the saw-mill to cut 3000 feet of boards per diem.

A very substantial frame bridge has been thrown across the Otanabee

[1]From the persistence with which "Otanabee" is used in early records it would appear to have been the original spelling.

river at this place. There are now upwards of twenty buildings in Peterborough, including one store which does an extensive business, and another now being built. There is a medical practitioner and two clergymen resident here (Episcopalian and Roman Catholic), and a school to which the government allows a liberal aid.

The township of Smith is a peninsula formed by the Mud[1] or shallow lakes which divide it from Ennismore and Harvey, and the Otanabee river, which separates it from Douro. The soil is a loam; in the north-east angle it is rocky. The settlement was commenced, about nine years ago, by a small body of Cumberland miners, who were located by government on either side of the Indian portage from the Otanabee river to Mud lake. This is about seven miles over, and the road is tolerably good. To these emigrants, on depositing a sum of money, I believe in the proportion of 10£ to each head of a family, a free passage was afforded; the money was returned when their settlement had been completed.

These settlers are now independent farmers, although at first several had their own exertions alone to depend upon.

The principle of a deposit, in all cases where aid is given to emigrants, is well worthy consideration. It is a guarantee for their good intentions, a guard against a fickle disposition, and a reserved fund in the time of need for the emigrant. Since the period spoken of, many emigrants from the north of Ireland, and more lately from the south, have settled in Smith. It is in general well settled to the 7th concession, and on Mud lake to the 11th concession. Canada Company lands, within this range, are the most eligible for immediate sale. Several families, under the superintendence of Mr. Robinson, have been located as far back as the 12th and 13th concessions. The lakes and other waters bordering on Smith abound with the maskinonjee and bass, and Clear lake (between Douro and Smith) with salmon trout to the weight of 30 lb. and 40 lb. The canal, which has been spoken of between the bay of Quinté and lake Simcoe, it is supposed will cross the peninsula near the base. Several of the miners informed me that, being in search of a salt-spring, they had discovered on the 27th, in 10th concession, Smith, C. C., a spring which in smell and taste resembled that of Gollsland.

The townships of Douro, Emily, and Ennismore, or the Gore of Emily, have for the most part been settled by the emigrants of 1825.

The soil of Douro is calcareous; there are large swamps scattered through the township; the best lands are at a distance from the waters, and particularly on the eastern boundary; and the most eligible lots for

[1]Later named Shemong (Chemong).

sale are those approximating to Peterborough. Mr. Robinson's emigrants are located on the front third of the township; the rest has been located by militiamen chiefly, scarce one of whom has performed the settlement duties required. The lands will, of course, revert to the crown, and, as the localities are daily improving, will no doubt be speedily settled. The settlers are exerting themselves in opening roads.

The township of Dummer, which lies to the eastward of Douro, resembles it in soil. The front is generally good, the rear rocky. There is no settlement in this township as yet; the most eligible lots for immediate sale are those on the front. A large creek called the Squaw-kone-gaw, takes its rise in a small lake within fifty or sixty rods of a bay of the large lake[1] on the Otanabee river. They are separated by a rocky ridge, at the highest not more than six or seven feet above the level of either lake, and as the rocks rise abruptly on either side, a ravine is formed, down which part of the waters of the Otanabee find a passage in the spring flood. Were it at any time to become an object (for the sake of mills, &c.), by throwing a dam across the Otanabee river at 25th in 4th concession of Douro, a certain supply of water might be at all times diverted down the Squaw-kone-gaw; and this again might be regulated by a sluice-dam on the ravine, which it is believed is on 30th lot in 6th concession, Dummer, C. C.

This very extraordinary connexion of waters is met with in other parts of the province. I would instance the Salmon river and the Moira, which leave the same lake in Sheffield; and the Gananoqui and Cataraqui creeks, which flow from the same lakes on the line of the Rideau canal.

The township of Ennismore, or Gore of Emily, is generally of an excellent soil, loam upon clay. A large proportion is taken up by reserves and surveyor's land, the remainder by emigrants of 1825, chiefly from Kerry, and who are doing well. The nearest mills are at Peterborough.

Emily is settled, through a few of the first concessions, by emigrants from the north of Ireland, thence to the rear by those of 1825. The roads are yet new but improving; in the latest settlements but partially opened. The soil is generally good, sandy loams in the hills, on the flats and in the valleys clayey loam; the township is for the most part level, and has numerous swamps, especially towards the rear and on the line of Pigeon creek, which traverses the township. Beaver meadows are frequent in this, and are also met with in the other townships in this range:

[1]This is Stoney Lake, then usually called Salmon Trout Lake. Squaw-kone-gaw, or Squaknegossipi Creek, is the Indian name for Indian River.

they are very serviceable to the new settler. There are two good saw-mill sites in this township; one reserved by government on south half 18th and 19th in 8th concession; a second on 6th in 10th concession. A small grist-mill is being built on 19th in 4th concession. It is probable, however, that, excepting for the home use of settlers, the produce will be generally taken to Peterborough, from the excellent mills there and other conveniences. To that place a road has been opened, and the magistrates of Hamilton[1] having lately granted 30£ to aid the inhabitants, it will soon be improved. By the line of Pigeon creek the settlers in Emily may pass by water to Mud lake, within seven or eight miles (by a good road) of Peterborough, and by this route many of Mr. Robinson's emigrants and their provisions were conveyed.

There is such an advantageous line of water communication in that direction that the whole produce of the back country may be expected to pass by Peterborough; hence all lands in the situation relatively favourable may be considered the most valuable. Ops is one of the finest townships in this part of the country; the soil is loam upon clay; it is, in general, level: the north-east angle of the township has extensive swamps. The Scugog river, a very fine stream navigable for boats, traverses the township, by means of which settlers may proceed to Mud lake, with only one portage of one quarter mile, at what is called the Pau-boo-kaije-wenum[2] rapid. At one place in the township the river is very rapid, and, having a descent of from twelve to fourteen feet, would afford an excellent mill site. In a southern direction, by the Scugog lake from which the river issues, water communication may be had in spring and fall through the townships of Cartwright and Reach, within seventeen or eighteen miles of the Big Bay, in Whitby, on lake Ontario. The township was actually surveyed in 1825, and thrown open for location on the principle of actual settlement. Many locations were made, but it is to be feared that, from the want of roads and mills, the conditions of settlement will in very few instances be performed. There has been much said against the system of demanding fees on grants of land in this province, which would have never found utterance had a proportion been expended in opening roads, building mills, &c. Such improvements would ensure a more speedy and satisfactory settlement than any penal conditions annexed to grants of land.

A waggon road has been opened for about nine years from Port Hope, following the boundary line between Hope and Hamilton, Cavan and Monaghan, to Emily and Smith. The line of road is broken by ridges

[1]The township, of course.
[2]Apparently the Indian name for Bobcaygeon Falls.

and swamps, at which places much labour will be required to make it good. It is at all times passable.

Cavan was first settled in 1817. At this time scarce a lot remains unlocated (except reserves); the soil is generally good, sandy loam upon the west; on the east inclined to clay; in the front rather light. Those lots next Monaghan are the most eligible for immediate sale. The township is well watered and possesses numerous sites for saw-mills. There is already built, and at work, 1 grist and saw-mill on E. ½ 12th in 4th con.; 1 grist mill on 10th in 4th con.; and another on 14th in 9th con. There are 5 stores and 2 distilleries in the township. The mills are used for the home consumption only, the surplus wheat being sent to market at Port Hope. The majority of the inhabitants of Cavan are from the north of Ireland, the remainder English and from the south of Ireland. The first, it is believed, are Presbyterians, but attend the Episcopal service in the absence of a clergyman of their own.

The Episcopal church stands on 12th in 10th con.; a missionary has been resident from the first settlement of the township. There are six schools scattered through the township, with from twenty-five to forty scholars each. The clearings are large and in good order; frame barns are numerous, but the dwellings are yet of logs.

Monaghan was settled at the same time as Cavan, chiefly by English. The soil is loam upon clay. The township is generally well settled, with the exception of some large grants on the 13th con., and on the Rice lake. It is well watered, but without mill sites except at Peterborough. In this, as in all the adjoining townships, the timber for the most part remains uninjured; the roads are yet new, but the inhabitants are making exertions to improve them. There are two families in this township whose exertions and success deserve mention. Both came out with limited means about eight years since.

The Rutherfords, from Jedburgh in Scotland, had, in 1826, about fifty head of horned cattle, besides grain and meadow land.

. . . Smithson, from Yorkshire, raises, upon the average, sixty acres of wheat every year.

JOHN SMITH, Jun.,
Dep. Pro. Surveyor.

Cobourg, 14th Dec., 1827.

4. Inspection of Seymour Township, 1832

[*Excerpt from Archives of Ontario, Crown Land Papers, Inspection Reports, Seymour Township 1832, 25 (29)*]

INSPECTION AND VALUATION OF THE TOWNSHIP OF SEYMOUR IN THE NEWCASTLE DISTRICT BY SAML. S. WILMOT DY. SURVEYOR IN 1832

No. of Lots	Con.	No. of Acres	By whom occupied	Impt.	Quality of Soil	Description of Timber[1]	Value per Acre	General Remarks
1	2	200	not occupied	none	thin soil	All Pine [? ?] Oa Pine Iron[d] M	15/	Woods Creek crosses this lot good flats near Percy Settlement uneven in rear
2	2	200	do do	"	thin soil in rear	Ma E Bd O P Bd	15/	Woods Creek crosses this lot good Flats not [?] Road Crosses to Percy
3	2	200	do do	"	Poor land	Pine & Oak plum	10/	Woods Creek crosses this lot over flown by Adam H Meyers Mill dam not [?] populous
4	2	200	A. H. Meyers	50	do do	do do	—	Sawmill, framed House Barn & out houses Road down the Trent not populous
5	2	200	do do	50	Island & R. Trent	M, P, O, E, Bd	—	This lot includes the River and valuable Island poor Roads, not populous

[1]Apparently the abbreviations in this column are: Oa or O for oak, Ir[d] or Iron[d] for ironwood, Ma for maple, E or El for elm, Bd or Bas for basswood, P for poplar, A or A[b] for ash, and B[h] for birch.

4 *(cont'd)*

No. of Lots	Con.	No. of Acres	By whom occupied	Impt.	Quality of Soil	Description of Timber	Value per Acre	General Remarks
6	2	200	do do	none	do do do	do do	—	Do do do do
7	2	200	not occupied	"	this soil [thin]	do do	10/	a part of this lot is in the River Trent, no Roads, not populous
8	2	200	do do	"	do do	Pine & Oak plum	10/	Thick with under wood, no water nor Roads, natural Meadow in rear
9	2	200	do do	"	do do	do do	10/	Thick with underwood natural Meadow in rear and brook partially
10	2	200	not occupied	none	Good Land	M. Bd, E, B, [?] Ir[d]	12/6	2 brook from the North some pine Wind full
11	2	200	do do	"	do do	do do	13/9	a spring brook East side from the N.E.
12	2	200	do do	"	do do	do do	13/9	a Creek cross this north of line
13	2	200	do do	"	do do	do do	13/9	a brook in rear, Burned ridge in front
14	2	200	do do	"	do do	do do	13/9	no water disernable, brook from N.E. on rear part

15	2	200	do do	"	do do	do do	13/9	Brook 15^{L} wide good living water, from the north
16	2	200	Samuel Dank	6	thin soil	O and pine	12/6	no water in front but suppose the om on N° 15 cross is this lot, 4° E. of Road
17	2	200	not occupied	none	do do	do do	12/6	no water on the line
18	2	200	do do	"	Good land	Ma, Bd, El, Bl [?] Ir^{d}	12/6	Brook from the north
19	2	200	do do	"	do do	do do	12/6	Brook from N.W., and edge of the bank of the lost Channel of the Trent
20	2	200	do do	"	do do	do do	11/	no water on the line, flat land to the South
21	2	200	do do	"	do do	do do	12/6	Brook from the north
22	2	200	do do	"	do Wet land	do A & ash	12/6	no water on line spring brook in the rear
23	2	200	do do	"	Not rich land	do do do	12/6	no water in front brook in rear
24	2	200	not occupied	none	Not rich land	Ma, Bd, El, Bl ? A & ash	11/	no water in front Poor land in rear, burnt over
25	2	200	George Clute	30	do do	do do	12/6	Squires Creek 1° wide Crosses this lot north of the line near Rawdon Settlement

4 *(cont'd)*

No. of Lots	Con.	No. of Acres	By whom occupied	Impt.	Quality of Soil	Description of Timber	Value per Acre	General Remarks
26	2	200	Hezekiah Herd	30	do do	do do	13/9	Squires Creek 1 wide crosses this lot SW joins the Settlement in Rawdon
1	3	200	not occupied	none	Sandy loam	M, Oa, P, B & El	10/	Creek from the NW no Road nor Settlement near this
2	3	200	do do	"	Good land	M, Oa, P & Bd	8/9	no water on the line, brook in rear
3	3	200	do do	"	do do	do do	7/6	uneven and grown up with under wood
4	3	200	do do	"	Plains	Oak & pine	8/9	Creek from the North
5	3	200	A H Meyers	"	High land	do do		Creek crosses this lot and SEL terminates in the River Trent
6	3	200	not occupied	"	Sand loam & Stone	M E B As & pin	10/	River Trent and Island cross this lot
7	3	200	do do	"	Wet & ridges	M, Bd, E & Ash	10/	In the River Trent and Island
8	3	200	do do	"	do do	do do	9/	Wet with natural Meadow
9	3	200	do do	"	thin Soil & wet	do do	9/	natural meadow and brook part of the season

10	3	200	not occupied	none	Good land	M Bd, E, Bl & [?] Iron^{d}	11/	no water on the line, uneven
11	3	200	do do	"	do do	do do	11/	do do do
12	3	200	do do	"	do do	do do	12/6	Brook from the north East
13	3	200	do do	"	do do	do do	12/6	small brook from the north front and rear
14	3	200	do do	"	thin Soil	M, E, Bl & Ash	9/	no water on the line
15	3	200	William Loake	10	do do	do do	10/	small brook from the north East
16	3	200	not occupied	6	good land	M Bd E Br & [?] Iron^{d}	10/	no water on the line, about 6° East of Center Road to post Nos. 15 & 16.
17	3	200	in from occupied rear not occupied	none	do do	do do	11/	no water on the line, uneven land Brook in rear
18	3	200	do do	"	do do	do do	10/	High ridge and Windfall timber
19	3	200	do do	"	do do	do do	12/6	a good living Spring brook from the North
20	3	200	do do	"	do do	do do	11/	no water on the line
21	3	200	do do	"	do do	do do	12/6	Spring brook from the north front and rear
22	3	200	do do	"	do do	do do	12/6	do do do do

4 *(cont'd)*

No. of Lots	Con.	No. of Acres	By whom occupied	Impt.	Quality of Soil	Description of Timber	Value per Acre	General Remarks
23	3	200	do do	"	do do	do do	12/6	Brook from N & Crosses the NEL and a brook in the rear
24	3	200	William Twick	10	do do	do do	—	Saw Mill on a living [?] Cold Creek
25	3	200	Andrew Althouse	20	Good land	M Bd E Br & [?]	13/9	Cold Creek crosses this lot, Road in front Populous in Rawdon to the E
26	3	200	William Thrasher	30	do do	do do	13/9	Squires Creek crosses from the NE near the Center of lot
1	4	200	not occupied	none	Sandy Loam	Oa, M, P & Bd	9/	High land no water
2	4	200	do do	"	do do	do do	10/	spring brook from the north
3	4	200	do do	"	do do	do do	9/	Ridge of high land
4	4	200	do do	"	do do	do do	10/	spring brook from North at a Road and Shanty of A. H. Meyers
5	4	200	do do	"	do do	do do	11/	High land, brook back in the lot
6	4	200	do do	"	do do	do do	12/	a living brook 10 links wide from the north

7	4	200	do	do	"	thin soil	M P Popler E F	10/	This lot terminates on an Island across a branch of the Trent
8	4	200	do	do	"	Islands & Rover	M, E, B, B, [?] Iron^{d}	15/	This lot crosses 2 Islands and River Tnt probible a mill site
9	4	200	do	do	"	Sandy loam & Stone	do & pine	12/6	brook of water a part of the Year
10	4	200	do	do	"	Good land	do do do	12/6	no water on the line near the River Trent and R. C. Welkins Saw Mill
11	4	200	not occupied		none	Good land	M, E, B, B, Iron^{d} & pine	12/6	small spring from the north in the rear
12	4	200	do	do	"	do do	do & Ash Ced	11/	Brook from the north and swamp and spring in the rear
13	4	200	do	do	"	do do	do do do	10/	no water in front
14	4	200	do	do	"	very stony	M, Oa, Iron^{d} & Elm	9/	very high ridge of land and stone, no water on the line
15	4	200	do	do	"	do do	do do	11/	Descending to Road and 5° East to post Nos. 15 & 16, spring brook on rear
16	4	200	do	do	"	Good land	M, B^{d}, El, B^{r} & pine	12/6	Brook from the north, and Windfall timber with bushes

4 *(cont'd)*

No. of Lots	Con.	No. of Acres	By whom occupied	Impt.	Quality of Soil	Description of Timber	Value per Acre	General Remarks
17	4	200	do do	"	Windfall	M, B, E, Ir[d] & oak	12/	Thick with underwood & Windfall timber
18	4	200	do do	"	do Good land	do do & pine	12/6	do do brook from the north in rear
19	4	200	do do	"	do do	do do	12/6	a very cold living brook from north and flats
20	4	200	do do	"	do do	do do	12/6	old Windfall timber and good land, a spring brook north end
21	4	200	do do	"	do do	do do	12/6	Small spring brook from the north
22	4	200	do do	"	do do	do do	10/	no water in front nor rear
23	4	200	James Hubble	5	do do	do do	12/6	Cold Creek cross this lot through the lot from the north & a backing spring
24	4	200	not occupied	none	Windfall & good land	M B E Ir[d] Oak & pine	12/6	Brook in rear
25	4	200	Samuel Hubble	6	do do	do do	12/6	do do
26	4	200	not occupied	none	do do	do do	12/6	a good living spring brook in rear and runs upon 25

1	5	200	not occupied	none	Sandy Soil	M, E, B, Windfal	8/	High dry ridge burned over, and thick with bushes 5 ch west of new lines
2	5	200	do do	"	do & Stone	M O Bas E & pine	8/	High dry ridge ascending Lumber cut off by A. H. Meyers
3	5	200	do do	"	do do	do do	8/	Lumber cut by A. H. Meyers probable a brook near the center which [?] No. 6
4	5	200	do do	"	do do	do do	10/	Lumber cut by A. H. Meyers Creek in center good Lumber Road
5	5	200	do do	"	do do	do do	11/	Creek in center of the lot 3/4 mile to R. C. Wilkins Mill
6	5	200	Baker R – & Brother	12	Good Land	M, El, B^{d}, O & pine	12/6	a living brook passes through this lot from N.W. ½ in to Wilkins Mill
7	5	200	not occupied	none	Wet & Swamp	M C^{r} Ash E Iron^{d}	10/	Poor thin soil no water on line, one lot to the Mills
8	5	200	R. C. Wilkins	30	thin soil & stone	do do	"	Mill site sold to R. C. Wilkins at the lower falls on the River Trent
9	5	200	do do	5	do do	M, E, Iro^{d}, P & E^{d}	"	Mill site sold to R. C. Wilkins River Trent diagonally from NW to SE

4 *(cont'd)*

No. of Lots	Con.	No. of Acres	By whom occupied	Impt.	Quality of Soil	Description of Timber	Value per Acre	General Remarks
10	5	200	not occupied	none	Sandy loam	do do do	10/	High land no water on the line
11	5	200	not occupied	"	do GL do Clay	do do do	11/	Small spring from the north
12	5	200	do do	"	do " do "	do do do	12/6	Spring in a Cedar & ash ravine from north
13	5	200	do do	"	do " do "	do do do	10/	uneven no water on the line
14	5	200	do do	"	do " do "	do do do	11/	no water on the line
15	5	200	do do	"	do " do "	do do do	11/	small spring brook at the SEL to post Nos 15 & 16 and Road
16	5	200	do do	"	do " do "	M, E, B^{d}, B^{b}, & Iro^{d}	12/6	a brook from the N.E and a spring brook in rear
17	5	200	do do	"	G Land	do do	11/	uneven land no water on the line but probable in the center from the
18	5	200	not occupied	none	G Land	M, E, B^{d}, B^{h} & Iro^{d}	12/6	a brook from the N.E. partial and spring on the rear

19	5	200	do do	"	do do	do do	11/	good ash & Elm flats on West side, no water on the line
20	5	200	do do	"	do do	do do	12/6	a spring brook from the North East
21	5	200	do do	"	do do	do do	11/	no water on the line
22	5	200	occupied	2	do do	do do	12/6	no water on the line
23	5	200	occupied	"	do do	do do & pine	12/6	no water on the line
								It is probable those lots is watered by Creek No. 24
24	5	200	ditto	3	do do	do do	12/6	Creek from the north west about 40 Links wide
25	5	200	Andrew Emery	2	do do	do do	12/6	a branch of the above Creek waters this lot to the north
26	5		not occupied	"	do do	do do	13/	a good living spring brook from N.W.

. . . .

Sam[1] Wilmot
Dy Surveyor

5. Survey for the Town of Lindsay, 1834

[*Archives of Ontario, Crown Land Papers, Diaries & Field Notes, 72(2)*]

LINDSAY J HUSTON 1834

Diary whilst employed in Surveying the Town Plot in the Township of Ops ending in July 1833.[1]

Received from Samuel Proudfoot Hurd Esquire Surveyor General of the Province of Upper Canada—Instructions to Survey a Town Plot in the Township of Ops bearing date the 23rd of May 1833.—

1833

June 20th	Thursday left home to commence the Survey called upon Alexander McDonell Esq. at Peterboro for further instructions. got to Cottingham in Emily the same day
" 21	Friday employed William English and Thomas Laidly got near to the Town Plot in Ops the same day
" 22	Saturday employed James McGuire and James Ried for the day only set all hands to build a shanty on the Town Plot to sleep and cook in.
" 23	Sunday did no work
" 24	Monday I attended the sale of the improvements of the highways in Ops — being one of the Commissioners my men to have no pay this day but I had to find them —
" 25	Tuesday Surveyed.
" 26	Wednesday Do
" 27	Thursday dismissed Thomas Laidly, consulted Mr. Logie and Mr. Purdy who advised me to go to Peterboro and inform A. McDonell Esq. of the bad quality of the land I did so and Mr. McDonell directed me to return and go on and Survey — —
" 28	Got back to Cottingham in Emily. —
" 29	Saturday Engaged Isaac English both William English and Isaac English to have pay this day
" 30	Sunday — — —
July 1	Monday engaged James McGuire and James Ried again and also John McCarter —
" 2	Tuesday Surveyed
" 3	Wednesday Do
" 4	Thursday Surveyed engaged William Rich —
" 5	Friday Survey'd rain —
" 6	Saturday Survey'd John McCarter quit the employment.
" 7	Sunday — — —
" 8	Monday engaged Michael Sheels Survey'd —
" 9	Surveyed — rain
" 10	Wednesday Do dismissed William Rich —

[1]In June 1846 John K. Roche surveyed "the Park Lots adjacent to the Town Plot of Lindsay" (Archives of Ontario, Crown Land Papers, Diaries and Field Notes, 72 (6)).

" 11 Thursday Surveyed Isaac English left the employment
" 12 Friday Surveyed
" 13 Saturday Surveyed rain dismissed Michael Sheals
" 14 Sunday —
" 15 Monday Surveyed and finished dismissed all hands
" 16 Tuesday got to Peterboro At distant periods spent 4 days in writing my field book mapping and making out my returns

NewCastle District

To Wit

John Huston

Esquire of the Township of Cavan in the said district Deputy Surveyor maketh oath and saith that the annexed Diary is just and true to the best of his knowledge and belief.

J. Huston

Sworn before me this
31st day of May 1834.
R. Henry J.P.

III. SETTLEMENT AND PIONEER LIFE

THE CHARACTERISTICS of general settlement and early life in the region are exemplified in this Section. Several plans for settlement, some of them abortive, are included. To obtain action in promised surveys or grants, petitions were often necessary, as in No. 3. Pioneer conditions in some of the earliest settlements are well described in Nos. 2 and 7. No. 5, a letter of Admiral Van-Sittart relative to his proposed settlement in Bexley Township near Balsam Lake, opens up an intriguing episode in pioneering about which comparatively little is known. No. 9 is an interesting document relative to settlement at the mouth of the Trent (Trent Port or Trenton). Nos. 11 and 12 illustrate conditions of settlement in the northern townships just prior to Confederation, 1867, which is the limit of the period under review in this volume. It has been considered preferable for purposes of comparison to keep the excerpts from the prose writings of early settlers largely in one place (Section XI), and a great deal of valuable material on settlement and pioneer experiences is consequently to be found in that Section.

1. Early Plans for Settlement

(*a*) CHARLES FOTHERGILL PLANS A SETTLEMENT NEAR RICE LAKE, 1817

[Public Archives of Canada, Upper Canada Sundries, 1817]

May it please your Excellency

I trust your Excellency will pardon my accompanying the enclosed with a request for the honor of an interview in which I might further explain the views I have ventured to entertain, along with a few gentlemen of my acquaintance shortly expected from England, in respect of a settlement to be made in Upper Canada—

—I have taken the liberty of enclosing the copies of two letters addressed by myself to Henry Goulburne Esq[r], with their answers, in order that your Excellency might perceive, in some measure the nature & extent of my designs—and that my wishes extend somewhat beyond the limits of those grants which I have understood are usually made to mere, ordinary, farmers—

—On my arrival at Quebec, and my having the honor of an interview

Township of Hamilton June 5th 1797

Dear Sir

I take the Liberty to inform you that we have thirty Seven actual Settlers in the Township of Hamilton and a number more in the Township that have taken Lots but have not got on yet I am Expected to be at york in a few days and Shall Return the Settlers Names and Number of Lots they improve.

I am Sir your most Obed.t Servant

Elias Jones Jun.r
one of the proprietors agents

The Honourable
David Wm Smith
Acting Surveyor General

Archives of Ontario

LETTER OF ELIAS JONES TO THE HONOURABLE D. W. SMITH, 1797

with his Excellency Sir John C. Sherbrooke—after explaining the nature of my views—he returned the letter addressed to him by the Secretary of State at home—with a desire that I would give it to your Excellency, & with an assurance that, from your Excellency's indulgence & liberality, I might hope for everything for which I had expressed a desire—Being an entire stranger to your Excellency I can have no claims to urge for any particular indulgence or attention—I can only declare my hopes & in soliciting an opportunity further to explain them entreat your pardon for the manner, perhaps irregular—in which I have ventured thus to introduce myself—

I have the honor to subscribe myself,

With the highest Consideration & respect,
Your Excellency's
Most obed[t] & very humble Serv[t]—
Charles Fothergill

Jordan's
The York Hotel
Monday Morning
March 10th
1817

(*b*) FOTHERGILL'S PLAN, 1817

[*Public Archives of Canada, Upper Canada Sundries, 1817*]

May it please your Excellency

Encouraged by the kindness and condescension with which your Excellency listened to my proposal for the formation of a new settlement upon the Rice-Lake, and the readiness with which I was furnished with the means of procuring Major Wilmot's assistance—I hasten to lay before your Excellency the result of my further enquiries, & to solicit an opportunity of explaining it more fully.

—I had the misfortune to pass the Dpy Surveyor on the road, & to lose his personal assistance;— but, having procured a man well acquainted with the country and with the lines of the new Township, so far at least as they are run out, I have been enabled, after going over the ground, to ascertain all that is necessary—It appears that the new Township will not touch upon the Rice-Lake, but that it will leave a large broken front to the Eastward extending to that Lake—This tract will be probably about 8 miles long, by a breadth of from half a mile to 3—4—or even 5, miles in extent—in which space is comprehended a district of land admirably well calculated for the kind of settlement I wish, on behalf of myself and friends, to form—

I am perfectly well satisfied with its advantages, and have only to pray that it may be speedily reclaimed—There is already one broken Township on the opposite side of the Lake; this tract, forming another of nearly equal extent—will fill up a gap in the chain of settlement, and round off the cultivated lands in that quarter as far as the Indian possessions;—it will form a valuable back country productive of advantages to the front Townships, & water-communication to the Colony at large, of the first importance—The out-let to this back country will be by Smith's Creek, where an excellent harbour for schooners & small craft might be formed at no very considerable expense—and I think, by means of the kind of population I hope to see there, a considerable commerce in various kinds of valuable produce, might in a short time be carried on——I have already taken some steps towards the improvement of this out-let which, together with some other particulars connected with an extended plan of settlement, I am desirous of stating to your Excellency—more fully than can be done in a note—when I can have the honour of another interview—

With the sanction, and under the kind auspices of your Excellency I trust that much may be done by a few ardent, enterprising, minds acting upon a body of chosen settlers in so fine a country—Full of this hope, and with lively feelings of gratitude, mingled with those of the highest Consideration & respect, I have the honour to subscribe myself

Your Excellency's
most obed[t] & very humble servt
Charles Fothergill[1]

The York Hotel—March 29th

[1]The authority on Charles Fothergill (1782–1840) is James L. Baillie of the Royal Ontario Museum (see *Canadian Historical Review*, Vol. XXV; December 1944, pp. 376–96). Fothergill, among many other activities, was the author of *A Sketch of the Present State of Canada* (York, 1822), and other essays. He was associated with Adam Scott in the erection of the grist and saw mill at the Little Lake mouth of Jackson Park Creek. His plans to settle friends in Monaghan do not appear to have matured, but he was prominent in various business enterprises. He knew the Indians well and kept a shooting lodge at the mouth of the Otonabee. In the Legislative Assembly and in his newspaper he became increasingly critical of the government and was dismissed as King's Printer. He was a noted naturalist, and his manuscript journals on birds are a prized possession of the Royal Ontario Museum. His interest in the Indians led him to intercede in behalf of an Indian boy convicted of shooting a play-fellow (see Charles Fothergill to Sir Peregrine Maitland, from Blair's Tavern, Clarke Township, September 26, 1820, Upper Canada Sundries, Public Archives of Canada; and with reference to Adam Scott, founder of Peterborough, see the Introduction, pp. xlii, xliii).

2. PETERBOROUGH COUNTY'S FIRST SETTLERS, 1818

THE TOWNSHIP OF SMITH

[*Thomas W. Poole,*[1] A Sketch of the Early Settlement and Subsequent Progress of the Town of Peterborough, and of Each Township in the County of Peterborough (*Peterborough, 1867*), *pp. 123–7*]

The survey of the township of Smith was just completed in 1818 when a number of colonists who had sailed that year from Cumberland, in England, found their way to that township for the purpose of forming a settlement. There was as yet no semblance of road through the almost unbroken forest from Port Hope, and they accordingly chose the route by way of Rice Lake and the Otonabee river. On arriving at Smith the first thing done was to erect a temporary log house on the first lot west of the communication road, which is a small triangular piece of ground just outside of the present limits of the Town of Peterborough. Here they lived in common until, by mutual assistance, small houses or shanties were erected on their several lots, to which they then removed.

The names of those first settlers who comprised this group were William Dixon and his family of five sons, Joseph Lee and his sons John and George; Robert Millburn, Robert Walton, John Walton (not the late Reeve and no relative), Walton Wilson, Thomas W. Millburn, John Smith and his son Joseph Smith. These were commonly spoken of collectively as 'the colony' settlers, to distinguish them from others of an early period.

The following were also among the early pioneers, having settled in the township during the same season (1818) and but a little while later than those already named: John Harvey, Ralph Bickerton, Alexander Morrison, Jacob Bromwell, Robert Nicholson, James Mann and his son James, Thos. Lockhart, and John Yates. Among those from one to three years later were Walter McKibbon, Samuel McKibbon, William Tully, Thomas Robinson, Isaac Nicholson, Silas Pearson, Joseph Walton and sons, the eldest of which was the late Reeve of Smith; Matthew

[1]Dr. Thomas Poole (1831–1905), a medical graduate of Victoria University, Cobourg, who was born in 1831, served the Newcastle District in several capacities other than that of doctor in Asphodel Township, Lindsay, and Peterborough. He was for some time editor of the *Peterborough Weekly Review*, Superintendent of Schools for Asphodel, and the author of a history of the County which is one of the earliest and most valuable of Canada's local histories. The two great subjects of controversy in the period were politics and religion, but he dealt with restraint about both of them and produced a well-balanced volume based upon authentic records, and information from the earliest settlers, many of whom were still alive when he wrote. We have been unable to locate a photograph of Dr. Poole.

and Richard Bell, John Edmison, Ephraim Jackson and sons, and Thomas Millburn.

These names constitute the roll of honour among the early settlers of Smith—men who, by their courage in penetrating the forest and their example in enduring and finally overcoming its difficulties and hardships, laid the foundation of a fine settlement, in connection with which it is but fitting that their names should be remembered as those of practical patriots whose deeds remain, and the fruit of whose earnestness and industry it is to be hoped their children will long enjoy.

The first requisite to procure land in those days was to take the oath of allegiance, on which a certificate was issued as evidence of the fact. A location ticket for the lot sought was then granted, for which a small fee was charged. Owing to the wild and unsettled state of the township when the first of these were issued, 'the colony' or first settlers were not required to make any other payment than this mere nominal one: but in later years a fee of $25 was charged to others on the issuing of their deed. Before a full title to the land was procured an affidavit made by two persons, setting forth that the settlement duties were performed and a house at least 18 by 20 feet in size erected, had to be presented at the land office, which for some years rendered a second journey to Toronto a matter of necessity. The performance of the settlement duties was not so rigidly exacted in this township as in Otonabee, in connection with which they will be more clearly described.

The first settlers in Smith encountered difficulties and privations of which we, in after times, can have but a faint conception. Unaccustomed as many of them were to the new scenes in which they found themselves placed, with scant provisions and separated by long wastes of wood and water from their fellow-kind, their situation, with their wives and little ones, must have been at times appalling; and by less indomitable spirits would have been relinquished in despair. Looking back upon it now, in the light of their present prosperity, what have they not achieved! Such brave men are the true patriots, whose names deserve to be handed down in the annals of our history to future generations.

During the first few years great difficulties were often felt in procuring the necessary provisions with which to support life. These had to be brought all the way from Port Hope or Cobourg in the most laborious manner and in the total absence of even the most ordinary roads, the only guide being the 'blaze' upon the trees through the interminable forest in which they seemed entombed. Under these circumstances it is not to be wondered at that whole families were often for weeks without tasting bread, and that the herbs and succulent roots of the rich woods were often called into requisition to lengthen out their scanty fare.

Late in the autumn, during one of these critical junctures, a number of the younger men of the settlement started in company for Port Hope to bring in a supply of provisions, of which their families began to be sorely in need. The journey was made by way of the Otonabee river and Rice Lake, and on their way back to their expectant households they encamped on an island in Rice Lake. The season was already advanced, and a keen frost setting in, what was their surprise and mortification to find themselves next morning hemmed in by an icy barrier which stretched away in the distance and blocked up the mouth of the river through which their course lay. Imagine their impatience at being thus delayed, well knowing that during their absence their loved ones were living on short allowance, and their children vainly stretching out their hands for bread. On the next day the ice had become sufficiently firm to support them, and they proceeded on their way over its glassy surface, dragging their canoe with their provisions behind them. This is but a sample of the difficulties of which those early years furnish many examples.

Not even after their first small clearings were made and they began to sow and reap their tiny harvests was their condition greatly improved. How they watched the wheat as it grew, and tasted of the pulpy grain as it hardened and matured in the kernel! But there was no mill, and their utmost ingenuity could not convert it into the bread for which they longed with all the force of early relish. In this dilemma the stumps of trees, or some of the larger logs, were hollowed out into pot-shaped cavities, in which a huge mallet was made to fall to crush the grain, the process being aided by the spring of a sapling bent over for that purpose, or the unwieldy lever still used for raising the bucket in farm wells. Wheat was boiled, roasted, and as a food for children was even chewed by their parents, besides being thus pounded, in order to convert it into food.

The more robust and vigorous, indeed, not unfrequently shouldered a bag of wheat and carried it through the woods of Monaghan, Cavan, and Hope to Smith's Creek, as Port Hope was then called, returning with it ground, to the great joy of the household. On such journeys it was usual to take along a supply of potatoes to be eaten on the way, a sufficiency being concealed beneath some friendly root or convenient wind-fall at about midway of the distance to be used on the way home.

A little later an apology for a mill was erected on Galloway's Creek, in Cavan, and a now leading and wealthy farmer in Smith informs us that after the family were two weeks without flour he, then a young man, took the oxen and the sleigh and wended his way through the woods to Galloway's. Winter was setting in, and he found the mill silent and the water wheel frozen and immovable. Determined to have the flour, he set to work with a will, but after chopping away the ice and spending nearly all night in clearing obstructions, a few rounds was the utmost the machine could be urged to go, and he had to trudge back weary and disappointed.

About the year 1821 the little mill erected by Mr. Adam Scott, on the bank of the Otonabee at Peterborough, and which has been already described, was set in motion, and, imperfect though it was, it must nevertheless have been a great boon to settlers so situated.

A small grist mill was erected by Jacob Bromwell, one of the early settlers in Smith, which came into operation just before the mill erected by the Government in 1827. Bromwell's mill was a frame structure erected at the mouth of a small creek which enters the Otonabee river just below Mr. Snyder's saw mill. In point of size and usefulness it was about on a par with Adam Scott's; and was but a brief time in use, the erection of the larger mill referred to having superseded the necessity for both of these lesser structures.

A deputation from the early settlers in Smith waited upon His Excellency, Sir Peregrine Maitland, to express the disadvantages under which they labored; but as reference has already been made to the incidents of that occasion they need not be repeated here. With the erection of the grist mill at Peterborough by the Government a new era dawned upon the settlers in this as well as the adjacent townships, and thenceforward their prosperity and success were fully assured.

The present excellent roads in Smith were only brought to their present perfection after long years of successive improvement and the outlay of large sums of money. In 1831 a writer in the Cobourg *Star* described the communication road as scarcely passable for ox teams, and filled with boulders, stumps, and other obstructions. In 1832 £100 was granted by the U.C. Legislature to improve this road, and further sums in later years.

3. The Settlement of Otonabee Township

(*a*) petition of settlers, 1819

[*Public Archives of Canada, Upper Canada Sundries, 1819*]

Hamilton, Newcastle District,
12 Nov[r], 1819.

Sir,

I am desired by the Subscribers of the included Petition to forward it to you, and to request that you will be pleased to lay it before His

Excellency the Lieut. Governor. For His Excellency's information there is a List subjoined of all the Families who have signed the Petition.

Hoping that it will meet His Excellency's approbation and concurrence, and that you will be pleased to communicate the same, I beg leave to subscribe myself

Sir,
your most obd^t^ hble Servt.
Thomas Carr.[1]

Edward M^c^Mahon esquire
Acting Secretary &c.

To His Excellency Sir Peregrine Maitland, Knight, Commander of the Most Honorable Military Order of the Bath, Lieutenant Governor of the Province of Upper Canada, Major General commanding His Majesty's Forces therein, &c. &c.; the Petition of the undersigned Emigrants humbly sheweth,

That your Excellency's Petitioners are Emigrants from different parts of Great Britain, and arrived in the Township of Hamilton during the last summer, with an intention to settle in its neighbourhood.

That, having understood that a tract of Land, situated on the north side of the Rice Lake, and lying upon the Ottonabie river, was shortly to be surveyed to form a new Township for the location of Settlers in general, your Petitioners, thinking it an eligible situation, and preferring it to more remote Townships, have waited, with considerable inconvenience and expence, for the completion of its survey, in order to procure their Lands in it.

That your Petitioners are now informed, by respectable authorities that it is the intention of Your Excellency to reserve the said Township exclusively for naval Officers and Seamen.

That many of your Petitioners, having nearly exhausted their small funds, and having no prospect of obtaining steady employment during the winter, will be put to great inconvenience and hardships, unless Your Excellency will be pleased to grant them Lands, which they may be advantageously employed in clearing and preparing for a spring crop.

Your Petitioners therefore most humbly entreat, that Your Excellency will be pleased to allow them, together with persons belonging to the Navy, to participate [in] the advantages offered by the said Township, as a Settlement towards which their hopes and their wishes have been steadily directed, by allowing them to obtain their Grants of Land there, as soon as it shall be in a state of readiness to receive them. And Your Petitioners as in duty bound, shall ever pray, &c.

[1]See Section XII, No. 2, for a biographical note.

Thomas Plews
Wm Cosgrave
James Lowes
John Lacy's X mark
Andrew Carr
Thos Scott
William Bateson
William Bateson jun^{r}
Thomas Bateson
John McNie
Geo. Clark
Ambrose Male
Henry Lindsay
Robert Ferguson
Andrew Nelson
for himself and John and
William Nelson
John Blezard
Rich Dale
Thos Carr
Henry Adamson
William Watson
Thomas Autard

John Plews
William Neads
George Wilson
George Greenbank's X mark
William Howson
William Howson for George Howson
Thos Robertson
James Hunter
Thomas Nelson
John O'Bryan
Wm. Fleming
Ralph Davidson
Anthony Blezard
John McIntosh
Ja^{s} Radcliffe
John Betty
Alexander Noble
Peter Robertson
James McCarthey
James Robertson
John Hutchison
John Ainlay
John Barnet

May it please Your Excellency,

We the undersigned Commissioners of the Land-board, and Magistrates of the District of Newcastle, do certify that the circumstances stated in the foregoing Petition are, according to the best of our Knowledge, correct; and we humbly recommend the Petitioners to Your Excellency's attention and favour, as persons of sober and industrious habits.

Zacheus Burnham J.P.
H. Ruttan J.P.
R Henry J.P.

D M G Rogers.
Walter Boswell.
Elias Jones.
T Ward.

Settlers' Names, and the number of their respective Families

	Men	Women	Chdn & Young Persons	Total
John Lacy	1	1	7	9
William Needs	1	1	5	7
John Nelson	1	1	5	7
George Wilson	1	1	5	7

Thomas Robertson	1	1	5	7
Andrew Carr	1	1	5	7
Ambrose Male	1	1	5	7
John Blezard	1		5	6
John McIntosh	1	1	4	6
Richard Dale	1	1	4	6
Thomas Autard	1	1	4	6
Henry Lindsay	1	1	3	5
James Randolph	1	1	3	5
Anthony Blezard	1	1	3	5
William Watson	1	1	3	5
John Henly	1	1	3	5
Thomas Plews	1	1	2	4
William Howson	1		2	3
William Fleming	1		2	3
William Bateson	1	1	1	3
William Bateson	1	1	1	3
Thomas Carr	1		2	3
John Yates	1	1	1	3
George Howson	1			1
James Hunter	1			1
Thomas Bateson	1			1
John McNie	1			1
Andrew Nelson	1			1
William Nelson	1			1
John O'Bryan	1			1
Robert Ferguson	1			1
Thomas Nelson	1			1
Alexander Noble	1			1
John Plews	1			1
James Laws	1			1
George Clark	1			1
George Greenbank	1			1
Ralph Davidson	1			1
John Betty	1			1
Thomas Scott	1			1
James McCarthy	1			1
Henry Adamson	1			1
John Barnet	1			1
Peter Robertson	1			1
James Robertson	1			1
John Hutchinson	1			1
William Cosgrave	1			1
Total	47	19	80	140

(*b*) LETTER OF MARCUS F. WHITEHEAD, INQUIRING ON BEHALF OF SETTLERS, 1819

[*Public Archives of Canada, Upper Canada Sundries, 1819*]

Hope 3rd Decembr 1819

Major Hillier,

Sir,

A wish to satisfy the constant inquiries of the Settlers, (as well as Motives of interest) induces me to beg the favor of you, to inform me whether you are acquainted with His Excellency the Lieut. Governor's intentions, with regard to the disposal of the Township of Land, now Surveying at the Rice Lake. Reports say, that it is intended for the *Navy* only, while the Majority of the Gentlemen, of the Land Board assure me that it will be open for all descriptions of Settlers. therefore I am quite unable to give the Emigrants any determined satisfaction on the subject.

I would also beg the favor of you, to request Mr Baby to oblige me with some particular instructions, as to my duty as Collector. I feel myself rather awkwardly situated, being quite unacquainted with the particulars of the office, the statute not being sufficiently explicit—

In the mean time please to inform me, what was the amt of Cash paid by Mr Geo. Boulton to Mr Mc Mahon for the papers.

May I beg you to pardon the trouble I have given you? And believe

Me Sir,

Your Most Obedient Humble Servt–

Marcus F. Whitehead.

(*c*) LETTER OF CHARLES RUBIDGE, 1820

[*Public Archives of Canada, Upper Canada Sundries, 1820*]

Hamilton, District of Newcastle.
22 January 1820

Sir/

I am this day informed by letter from the Surveyor General that your Excellency will not confirm my location of Lot No 12 in the eleventh concession of Otonabee as Your Excellency had made a previous promise of it to Mr Charles Jones who has now a location Ticket for it.—in presuming to address you I do so convinced of your determination to do justice to every one, and certain that this deprivation must have arisen from some misrepresentation.—Allow me briefly to state to your Excellency that I have served twenty one years in the Navy to the satisfaction of every Officer I have ever Sailed under, that I came out to settle in this Country at a heavy expense, having a Wife and four Children and after waiting for the location of the grant allowed me by His Majesty for seven Months, being restricted by Your Excellency to a particular tract of land said to be reserved for the Navy. I attended at York and among others located the lot before mentioned which location your Excellency was pleased to approve of. and by the authority of an order in Council a location Ticket was given me of it—after so great a lapse of time when I am effectually prevented from the same advantage of choice given to other settlers to have part of my location, and in my first settlement with a young Family the most valuable part of it granted to another I feel convinced you will take into your favorable consideration, and if your Excellency will be pleased to direct reference to be made to the old diagram you will perceive this lot was reserved by an order in Council for Captain Spilsbury (prior to my order in favor of Mr Jones.) who gave it up to accomodate me in consideration of my Family.—allow me to add Mr. Jones had his choice in any Township whereas I was restricted to this alone.—I have the Honor to remain with all possible respect.

To/
His Excellency
Major General Sir Peregrin Maitland
W.C.B.—&c—&c—&c—

Your Excellencys
Most Obedient
Humble Servant
Charles Rubidge
Lieut. R.N.

4. Petition for a Militia Commission in the Rice Lake District, 1820

[*Public Archives of Canada, Upper Canada Sundries, 1820*]

The Memorial of James Furzer Elliot
Humbly sheweth

that your memorialists father Henry Elliot served twenty one Years in his Majestys Royal Marines and is now from Ill health contracted in the service on the half pay of that corps—

That your memorialist through the intent of Lord Forbes has the honour of having his name on the Duke of Yorks list for these some years past for a commission but the peace intervening prevented his having his wishes realized.

Your memorialist seeing no hopes of obtaining a commission was induced to come out to Canada as a settler and being desirous of serving his King in some degree hopes Your Excellency will honour him with a commission in the Militia for one of the new Townships settling at the Rice Lake, his claims are—

His fathers services in various climates for the before named period, a brother of his fathers, Capt. in the 28 Regt. Killed at S[t] Christophers, the loss of four out of five Uncles by the maternal side in his Majestys service all in active employ, his Grandfather and all his family for many generations being employed in either Army or Navy his two elder brothers served one thirteen and the other ten years in his Majestys Royal Marines the elder severely wounded.

Your memorialist humbly hopes your Excellency will take his case into consideration and comply with his wishes, should it not interfere with your other arrangements, and your memorialist will ever study to deserve Your Excellencys kindness and has the honour to subscribe himself

Your Excellencys
Most ob[t] humble Servant
James Furzer Elliot

Brookdale
Hamilton Jany. 7th 1820

5. Admiral VanSittart and Bexley Township, 1826

[*Archives of Ontario, C.L.P. General Correspondence of the C.C.L.*]

Woodstock 13th September 1826.

Sir

I have the honor to acknowledge the receipt of your letter of the 17th ulto; & beg to offer, as an apology for my not answering earlier that my son who was employed by me to make the purchase of the lands in Bexley, was at the time on the way to that place.

The terms on which I purchased the land in the township of Bexley *appear* not to have been complied with:—this appearance, however, originated in a permission given by the late Commissioner of Crown-lands, to delay indefinitely completing the purchase. The motives, amongst others, urged upon the late Commissioner to warrant the delay were drawn from the politically unsettled state of the Province at that time (or immediately succeeding it) & further from the prospect, sanctioned by a vote of the House of Assembly of a great & speedy reduction in the price of land in new Townships.

It is now my wish to pay the first Instalments on lots amounting to about three thousand acres, which my son will point out (not however definitely declining the remainder should the purchase be allowed to continue open for me); & I shall, of course, opportunity serving, be equally anxious with His Excellency the Lieutenant Governor to further "the actual settlement of that part of the Province."—

I have the Honor to be
Sir
Your obedient Servant
Henry VanSittart.[1]

The Honble R. B. Sullivan
& & &

6. Alexander McDonell[2] to Peter Robinson, 1829

[*Archives of Ontario, Crown Land Papers, Correspondence of the S.G. and C.C.L., McDonell to Robinson, August 16, 1829*]

Peterboro 16th August 1829

My dear Sir

Hearing yesterday morning in Ops that a number of settlers had arrived at Cobourg, I hastened to this place to make some arrangements to get them round at once to Cotnums with the Scow, but met

[1]The Admiral, a cousin of Baron Bexley, was the first settler in the township, through which passes the ancient Indian carrying-place from Lake Le Clie (Simcoe) to Balsam Lake. He was granted 1000 acres on the shore of West Bay, and came in with ox-waggons, chopping away logs and trees along the old trail which had seen a succession of Jesuits and *coureurs-de-bois* from Champlain onwards. The stone chimneys of an eighteenth-century trading-post of three buildings stood in this locality until the eighteen-seventies. "The old admiral [says Watson Kirkconnell in his *Victoria County Centennial History* (Lindsay, 1921), pp. 75–6] was not without character. Even in his wilderness home he insisted on dressing for formal dinner every evening and was never without his champagne. He was twice married. His second wife was Miss Stephenson, the daughter of one of his own servants, and to her he left the entire Balsam Lake estate. In later times, about 1871, the property passed into the hands of the late George Laidlaw, 'the Laird of Bexley', who named it 'The Fort Ranch'. The name does not refer to any fort on the premises, but to the customary question of a frequent guest, the late Hon. Rupert Wells, who, as the times were hard and money tight, would ask his host on each visit if he were still 'holding the fort.' One of his sons, Colonel George E. Laidlaw, now occupies the estate." (See also footnote to No. 2 of Section I.) John Langton, a contemporary of VanSittart and settled not far off, refers to the Admiral's son coming to the 24,000 acres his father had purchased, accompanied by the Reverend William Bettridge. VanSittart agreed to bring out thirty families of settlers the following summer, and his manager, Rebridge, was to go to Britain to conduct them thither. VanSittart's original settlement, at Woodstock, is described as "a log house of many additions, extending over the ground in all directions and looking, it was said, more like an African village than a house; but inside it was full of *objets d'art* from Italy." (*Early Days in Upper Canada: the Letters of John Langton*, p. xxxiii *inter alia.*)

[2]Colonel Alexander McDonell (1786–1861). In 1825 he aided in locating the Irish immigration, and he was subsequently Immigration and Crown Land Agent. In 1834 and 1836 he was elected to the Legislative Assembly; and he served in both the War of 1812 and the Rebellion of 1837.

Six heads of Families within a few Miles of this last Evening on their way out, they will reach my place today where I shall join them this Evening,—I am favoured with M[r] Buchanans list of Families from M[r] Bethune, which gives an account of Seven others not yet arrived but hourly expected at Cobourg—they are all from Scotland, two other families from the same place took possession of their Shanties on friday, it was my intention to send you a return of the locations already made, but shall now defer it until I shall have settled the late additions to our Settlement—As there is every appearance of a regular Succession of Emigrants to this quarter for a time, I intend contracting for the making of twenty or thirty Shanties immediately, as I keep but two Axemen (Canadians) who build a Shanty in three day's, from the manner these men have of making the roof, with small slips of basswood bark, bound together with poles, I have as yet heard no complaints from inconvenience by leaks—

From the men yesterday I received several letters, yours respecting Peter Morrison is among them, I have at present no recollection of having seen any person of that name, or of having received the letter of which he was to have been the bearer, I shall however examine the file of letters this Evening on my return to Ops—Two persons only I believe have left the Township without Settling who came to it with that view, Clyto [?] and Perry who were to return in the fall—

I am
My dear Sir
very faithfully Yours

Honble P Robinson A M[c]Donell

7. Emigrants from Frome, Somersetshire, to Dummer Township, 1831

In 1945 Ivan Grant, a Canadian soldier, visited Frome, in Somerset, to inquire about the emigration to Canada in 1831 of his ancestors William and Jane Grant. As a result a pamphlet was edited by J. O. Lewis and printed in Frome in June of that year, entitled *Letters from Poor Persons who Emigrated to Canada from the Parish of Frome in the County of Somerset.*[1] Herewith are two of the letters, both from settlers in Dummer Township, introduced by material on the means by which the 1831 emigration was effected, the send-off by the inhabitants of the parish, and the em-

[1]A copy of this rare pamphlet is in the possession of the Editor, to whom it was given by Adelaide Batten McGiffin and Caroline Grant Farrill, descendants of the Dummer Township pioneers who wrote the two letters reproduced herewith.

barkation. The following introductory material is stated in the pamphlet to have been taken from 'Tom Bunn's book . . . a Frome philanthropist.':

In the year 1830 about seventy persons went to North America from the neighbouring parish of Corsley, and were provided on their arrival with a small sum of money, and then left to Providence and their own discretion. Letters continued to be received from these persons, and from other settlers in North America, during the last year and the present, all of which, without an exception, gave a favourable account of the welcome and kindness with which they were received; the encouragement given to their industry; their good wages and plentiful support; and the easy terms on which an industrious labourer might acquire land and independence. These letters, which are too numerous to be quoted here, gradually removed the apprehension, which was at first entertained, of the consequences of landing poor families on a foreign shore without previously making a provision for their support.

At a meeting held the fifteenth of February last, of the Committee for the Relief and Employment of the Poor, the Right Honourable the Earl of Cork in the chair, after hearing evidence on the subject of emigration, it was ordered that notice be given on Sunday next of a parish meeting to be held on Thursday, to consider and decide on raising a moderate sum of money by poor rates for the purpose of assisting proper persons and their families, now receiving relief, to emigrate from this country to Canada. At this meeting an agricultural labourer who had gone to Canada at his own expense, had obtained there good wages and maintenance, and good treatment, and who had returned to fetch his wife and family, was examined in person. At the subsequent parish meeting £300 were voted for the assistance of families receiving parish relief only. It appeared that the sum paid for the maintenance of a family for less than two years would remove them to North America, never to be again burthensome to the parish; and the advantage of the poor in that country would be much superior to any which could be expected here. The three hundred pounds voted by the parish was increased by one hundred pounds given by the Most Honourable the Marquis of Bath; fifty pounds by the Earl of Cork; thirty pounds by the Messrs. Sheppard; and other smaller subscriptions. As soon as it was known that assistance would be given, about two hundred persons, including their families, gave in their names as volunteers. From these were selected thirteen heads of families, thirteen married women, four young men under twenty, twenty-seven daughters, and twenty-eight sons, going with their parents, in all eighty-five. No influence was used. Every emigrant who attended was requested to say whether he went of his own choice and freewill, and every one replied that he went entirely of his own free choice. There was an anxiety to be permitted to go. At different meetings of the committee, it was ordered that those who emigrated should be allowed one pound each for the heads of families, and their respective wives; one pound each for tools; one pound for any single person; ten shillings for each child; ten shillings for clothing; that they be conveyed in carriages; that they leave Frome on Monday night, the 21st of March instant; and embark, and sleep on board, Tuesday night. That their passage and provisions be paid for to Quebec, and a further passage to Montreal. That the allowances in money should be paid them after the voyage. Berths were previously secured on board the Airthry Castle, belonging to Messrs. Sheppard and Salmon, respectable merchants of Bristol.

No sooner was the decision known than all hands were at work to provide necessaries and conveniences for the poor who were to depart, and never to return. Ladies who had large families employed themselves, their children, and servants. The ladies of the Charitable Society, the numerous children of the National School, the forty girls at the Asylum, and many others, were busily engaged. Clothes, bedding, tools, and almost numberless articles were provided, without adhering to the limit of expense. Every emigrant had his separate bag and parcel, well filled, and carefully packed. All the travellers were invited to the house of the Minister of Christ Church, where they received Bibles and other religious books. On the Saturday the rites of Baptism, without fees, were administered to many of the children who were to cross the ocean, at the parish church. Many attended at Christ Church on the Sunday previous to their departure, and heard a discourse, purposely prepared for them, well adapted to their situation and their future prospects. Precautions were taken that Divine Service should be performed on Sundays during the passage.

One of the emigrants, to whom a gentleman had given a sovereign by mistake for a shilling, was so honest as to bring it back to him. In the night of the 21st instant eighty-five men, women, and children, with their baggage, set out in seven carriages, preceded by a band of music. Three proper persons accompanied them to preserve order and attend their wants. They embarked the next evening. The captain of the vessel appeared humane and attentive to all who were placed under his care. Necessary medicines were provided. Towards night the little children began to enquire when they were to go home? perfectly unconscious that they were never to see their homes again! One of them is said to have had an attachment at Frome. Her sister, it is reported, was averse to the water, and fainted when she came on board. Influenced by these circumstances, the parents sold part of the things given them, and returned with their family to Frome where they were received as unwelcome visitors, having prevented others from going who would gladly have taken their place. On the 23rd instant a gentleman went on board. He said it was not a pleasing sight. Their hearts seemed full, and the women were in tears at the thought of parting for ever from their native country. A lady went the next day, for the kind purpose of distributing useful gifts for the children. She said they were then more cheerful. Farmer Beauchamp, who accompanied them from Frome, proceeded a few miles on the voyage, and said that when he returned they were cheerful, and sent grateful remembrances to the friends they had left.

We have a description of the arrival of these emigrants in Canada, for William Lyon Mackenzie visited the ship when she docked in April 1831 at Quebec:

One forenoon I went on board the ship Airthy Castle, from Bristol, immediately after her arrival. The passengers were in number 254, all in the hold or steerage; all English, from about Bristol, Bath, Frome, Warminster, Maiden Bradley, etc. I went below, and truly it was a curious sight. About 200 human beings, male and female; young, old, and middle-aged; talking, singing, laughing, crying, eating, drinking, shaving, washing; some naked in bed, and others dressing to go on shore; handsome young women (perhaps some), and ugly old men, married and single; religious and irreligious. Here a grave matron chanting selections from the last edition of the last new hymn book; there a brawny ploughboy 'pouring forth the sweet melody of Robin Adair'. These settlers were poor, but in general they were fine-looking people, and such as I was glad to see come to America. . . . It is my opinion that few among them will forget being cooped up below deck for four weeks in a moveable bed-room, with 250 such fellow-lodgers as I have endeavoured to describe.[1]

Two letters in the collection are from settlers in the Township of Dummer. The first is from William and Jane Grant to their parents, the second from Levi Payne to his parents.

1

Dummer, September 6th, 1831.

Dear Father and Mother,

This comes with our kind love to you; I hope you are well; myself and the children are well, but William has got the ague, he has had it

[1]Mackenzie, *Sketches of Canada and the United States* (Toronto, 1833), pp. 179–80.

these five weeks; it has been a very wet Spring and a great many have the ague this season. But for all this we do not wish ourselves in Frome again. I suppose you would like to know how we live, since William is not able to work; we landed in Quebec the 21st April, then went by a steam packet to Montreal, 180 miles. I cannot tell the distance from one place to another, you have heard of the river St. Laurence, which is about one hundred and thirty miles long, we do go up there by the Dummer[1] boats, a tedious way to Prescot, then to Kingston (tell William Gregory we saw Robert Davis, he is well, he made us welcome) then we went to Little York to the Governor of the Upper Province, who lives there; now we had no longer to maintain ourselves we had our provisions found us and our passage paid back to Oberne,[2] seventy miles down the river, again from there to Peterborough. William gave in his discharge there, which entitles him to one hundred acres of land, which we are now in possession of, we have forty-nine pounds of flour and seven pounds of pork every week for a twelve month, and axes to chop with, (the old Country axes are no good here) great numbers of emigrants have come out this Summer, you would be surprised to see them, they are all provided for the same as we are, only those that are not soldiers have to pay £20 for the land in six years. We are eighteen miles from Peterborough, the pork and flour is brought out in casks. By the blessing of the Almighty, we expect to do well; we thought to sow two acres of fall wheat, but William's having the ague we shall not be able to sow any before Spring, then, please God, we think to sow two acres of wheat, one acre of potatoes, half an acre of corn, peas, garden, etc. I suppose you think this too much to be true; I have not told you one word that is not true. We have to chop down the timber, put it in piles, and burn it, if you had it in England you would grudge burning it, fine, clean-grown timber. Sugar-maple here is fine and high, (that is what the Corsey[3] man meant by the sugar bush). We have here a whole mass of woods, no one knows the bounds of it in England. If England, Ireland, and Scotland were to come out, they could not inhabit it. It was said before we came out, that it was going to be stopped, as so many were coming, but don't you believe it, they are all glad to see us come, Government pays for all, never a township filled so fast as Dummer, a house almost on every hundred acres. Every one here makes his own sugar, he makes a hole in the maple-tree at fall when the sap goes back, and in spring when it rises, then boils it and it makes beauti-

[1]Durham boats were large flat-bottomed craft used to carry freight and passengers up the St. Lawrence.

[2]Presumably Cobourg.

[3]Corsley.

ful sugar; they make their own soap and their own candles. There are people here, who came out as poor as we did, who have now their cows and oxen, sheep, pigs, etc., in short, every thing heart can wish for. A great many Irish came out this summer, but they would sooner see English and Scotch. Shoes are dear here; there is no clothing business carried on; all iron tools are very dear, axes from 10s. to 12s. each. We have a methodist preacher amongst us, and a gentleman from——— twenty-five miles off, comes once a fortnight. As for money, we shall have but little yet, till our crops come round to have something to sell. Clothes are dear; if any of the party come out next spring, let them buy as much as they can, and let them beware, that the people all up the country, will cheat them in every way they can. A man that has a family, will do better than one without, for every child that can carry a stick is of use. The summer has been much like the summers in England, we do not know what the winter will be. We have our houses built of wood, not for want of stone, but masons; we have plenty of limestone; these are now settled places; Government pays for all our houses. Let any one see the letter that wishes it, they may take it for a truth. A man from Bradley is come back, it was too hard work for him, he will give it a bad name, don't believe him, his name is T—r. I forgot to tell you that William was lost, when he went to see the land, two days and two nights, I never expected to see him again, twelve men went in search of him, almost all his clothes were torn off, such a figure I never saw!

Your affectionate Son and Daughter,
WILLIAM & JANE GRANT.

Direct to us, 3, 20 Lot, near Peterborough, in the Township of Dummer, Upper Canada.

2

Dummer, October 13, 1831.

Dear Father and Mother,

I write these few lines to let you know how we are getting on; we have one hundred acres of good land, and about seven acres of beaver meads on the land. Give my love to my father-in-law and brother-in-law, and my wife's love to her father and brother, and tell them that we are doing well, it was a good thing for us that we came here, we never wanted for neither bread and meat since we left home. When I got on my land I had one sovereign and twelve shillings left, but have more than one, two, or three now, and if I had not been ill I should have had near twenty pounds now, I was ill for nine weeks in the fever and ague, I should have had 5s. a day all the time; George can get 2s. 6d. a day and his keep; men get 4s. a day and their board, or 5s. a day and no board, in the summer; I have got two acres and a half of wheat this fall, and I shall sow about three acres of spring wheat next spring, besides other grain, if please God. The weather is near the same here as at home, if any difference, rather more thunder; the days are two hours and a half shorter here in the summer, and two hours and a half longer in the winter; the people tell us the frost goes into the ground about eight inches in the black peat land, but in the red land it goes in a foot or more some winters; the snow was not eight inches deep all last winter; all kinds of seed will grow here; please to send me a little early cabbage seed, a little white stone turnip seed, a little onion seed, a little carrot seed, and a few pig-berries. Please to tell my brother John to send over a pair of truck-axles, and make them strong; give my love to brother John and all the family; brother John you may do well here, blacksmiths and carpenters that can make carts and waggons, may get money as fast as any farmer in England; you can get your timber for nothing, I will give you as much timber as you can use in twenty years, if you come, 500 tons a week of fine deals and elm, or sugar timber; one tree shall measure forty yards in the body, without finding a knot or branch on it; a gun will not carry to the top of the deals. When we cut or burn one of them down, you can hear the fall of it for a mile, some of them is five yards round, and by the fall they break off in three or four pieces; sometimes we have a great many patriges [partridges] here, and a great many deer, woodcocks, snipes, ducks, geese, foxes, beavers, bears, and a few wolves. For killing a wolf we get £1 5s., we take the head to the governor and receive the money. We have all kinds of fish; George has caught 5s. worth in an afternoon; pigeons are beyond number, and hares not a great many; I have seen no pheasant yet; the price of things here is dearer than it is in some places; flour 6 pounds for one shilling; beef and mutton from 3d. to 4d. per pound; pork, from 4d. to 6d. per pound; sugar and soap, 8d. per pound; butter, 8d. per pound; candles, 1s. per pound; wheat, 5s. per bushel; brandy, 1s. 3d. per pot; rum, 10d. per pot; whiskey, 7½d. per pot at the still house, if you take a gallon, 2s. 9d.; cider, 6d. per gallon; beer, at the brew-house, 16d. per gallon. Cloth is as cheap or cheaper than it is at home; we can buy good blue cloth for 8s. 6d. per yard; kerseymere for 4s. per yard; a man's pair of half-boots, 15s.; shoes, 10s. 6d. per pair. Thomas Smith had a pair of half-boots made last week for 15s., good strong boots. The price of potatoes, 1s. 3d. per bushel; the best red ones, 1s. 6d. per bushel. Please to tell my brother John to give John Singer's love to his mother, and his wife's love, and James Sanders and his wife's love to them. John Singer's wife got a son a month old, they are all well and in health. So now with my love to my dear father and mother, brother and sister, brother-in-law and sisters-in-law, and my wife's love to every one of you all; my children's love to their grandfathers and grandmothers, uncles and aunts. David and Mary is at service under one roof, in families living in two adjoining houses, they got their washing, clothing, and keep, with 15s. per month for the winter, they like their places much, both families are English people. Father, there is a family coming from Chapmanslade, at spring, the man lives close by me, Henry Snelgrove, you can send the seeds by them, and the truck axles and letters; one of my brother's can go to the house, it is one field from the public house towards the Black Dog, tell the man's wife he is very well; he is in my house two or three times every day. Give my love to James Gold, Robert Butcher, and John Doman; if you like to come, you can get £3 per month, with your board, washing, mending, and lodgings anywhere. Give my love to John Whatley, and tell him I wanted him very bad one day, for I shot a deer and was not able to carry it home myself; I got it up at my back but I fell down with it, and I could not take it up again; I went to a farm house and got a man to help me, and the farmer dressed it for me, I gave him one quarter of it. I went home with the head, skin, heart, and liver, and next morning Joseph Edwards, myself, and George, my son, went and got it home. I got the skin for William Smith, of Deverill; I shall send it as soon as I can, give my love to him and his wife; give my love to Mrs. Goddard, and tell her we are all well; she should not want for game if she was here. Give my love to all my friends at Warminster and Crockerton; so I must conclude with my love to my father. When you write to me, direct to Levi Payne, in the township of Dummer, near Peterborough, in Upper Canada, in the second Concession, on the 18th lot of land. Send me word how things are going on, trade and other things, and whether you have work or not.

LEVI PAYNE.[1]

[1]The two letters are from the pamphlet, pages 5–6 and 10–12, respectively. These descriptions of the arrangements for removal to Canada, the departure, the arrival at Quebec, and the reaction to settlement form a remarkable sequence seldom found in the history of emigration. See E. C. Guillet, *The Great Migration* (New York, 1937) for conditions of travel and experiences in the arduous sailing-ship period; and Poole, *Early Settlement of Peterborough*, pp. 169–75, for a description of pioneering experiences in Dummer as given to Dr. Poole by those concerned.

8. Choosing Land in Upper Canada

[*This letter, in a subsequent undated edition* of The Emigrant's Guide . . . Containing . . . Letters from Emigrants *(1832), was copied from item 10470 aa. 19 in the Library of the British Museum. Numerous references in the letter suggest that it was written by J. W. Dunbar Moodie*]

Extracts of a letter from a Half-pay Officer settled in the Newcastle District, Upper Canada, to his Friend in London, dated 24th November, 1833.

. . . . . I have had much conversation regarding the former state of the colony with the older settlers, and they all agree in stating that, until within the last four or five years, they were obliged to take goods in exchange for their wheat, etc., from the merchant; now, however the case is totally altered, and MONEY can be readily obtained for most articles of *farm produce*. When the farmer happens to be in their debt, however, as *at home*, they frequently compel him to take goods in part payment, and allow a smaller price for their grain. . . .

Yesterday I completed a purchase for you of 227 acres of land, viz., 127 acres in Hamilton, about four miles to the eastward of Cobourg, and 100 acres in Haldimand, about nine miles east from Cobourg and two miles and a half from the village of Grafton, near the shore of the Lake. The first mentioned place is to cost £600 currency, and the last mentioned £300, in all £900 currency, or, at the present rate of exchange, about £760 sterling. Each of these places contains about 70 acres of cleared land, free from stumps, and has small orchards of apple-trees, log houses, barns, etc. My bargain with Mr. C., the seller, is that if you are not pleased with your purchase he will take back the land, and will return the price in two years, with 10 per cent. per annum for the use of the money. . . . I shall now give you some account of my own proceedings since I wrote last, and detail my *future prospects*, in which I feel assured you will lend me your assistance, which I am determined to merit by the manner in which I shall conduct any commissions I may receive. Some time ago, by the death of a relation, I came in for a legacy, which enabled me to make some most desirable purchases of land at a sale of Government lands; I bought 200 acres of wild land in Douro, adjoining part of my grant which I had taken up in that township. As none of the neighbours who knew the land would oppose me I got it at 20s. per acre, and immediately after the sale I was offered £2 per acre by a land speculator. I have contracted for clearing twenty acres and building a log-house there, where I intend to fix my future residence. I have sold my farm here for £200 and 800 acres of wild land, which is worth at least £400 more, in all £600, being better than double what my farm here cost a year ago. You will say *this is pretty well*; but I have been favoured by the circumstance alluded to. I now come to my future plans, in which I think you can materially assist me without incurring any kind of responsibility. I propose in conjunction with my brother-in-law, to undertake an agency business for investing money in *improved lands* for capitalists in England who may honour us with commissions for that purpose. My plan is shortly as follows; to make no purchases *until a good tenant is found*, who will pay a rent of from 6 to 8 per cent. on the price of the land for any term of years not exceeding twenty-one years. The price of the lands would not be payable until the purchase was effected, and clear titles made out and duly registered. We propose charging three per cent. on all transactions, with travelling expenses, which last would not be great. It would obviously be our interest, and we should make a point of managing the business in the most economical manner for the parties employing us. My brother-in-law has been several years employed by the Canada Company in locating settlers, etc., etc., and from his experience as a farmer is well qualified to form a correct judgement of the soil and situation of the lands, etc. As I have formerly stated, *wild lands* rise much more rapidly in value than improved lands, when judiciously chosen; but their ultimate rise in value, though certain, proceeds at a different rate, according to circumstances in different situations.

Of course if employed to make purchases of wild lands, which is not a part of our immediate plan, we would require to examine the lands particularly, which would be attended with considerable difficulty from want of roads, &c., and a greater expense than in the first case. I should feel particularly obliged by your mentioning our proposal to any of your friends who might wish to purchase land in Canada (that is to say in the neighbouring districts as regards Cobourg). I should state that, in *the first instance*, I would undertake to invest £5000 in land paying from 6 to 8 per cent in rent in the immediate neighbourhood of Cobourg, Port Hope, &c., &c.; our future proceedings must be determined by circumstances. The society in the neighbourhood of your farms is much better than where I am. By-the-bye I should mention that though one of the farms is called 127 acres in the deed, it is supposed actually to contain about 150 acres. I trust my arrangements will give you satisfaction, and

I am, &c., &c.,

N.B. During last winter one house in Cobourg paid £4000 in *cash* for the article of wheat alone.

9. Settlement at the Mouth of the Trent, 1834

[*Archives of Ontario, Crown Land Papers, General Correspondence of Surveyor General, 15 January, 1834*]

Commissioner of Crown Lands Office
York 15th Janry 1834.

Sir

I have the honour herewith to enclose you an application addressed to me by Mr. Sheldon Hawley and others residing at and near the mouth of the River Trent in which they beg that the portion of the Clergy Reserve remaining at the disposal of the Government, and containing about 40 Acres may be surveyed and laid out into Town lots and offered for sale in the usual manner.

As I fully concur with the Petitioners that great advantage would be derived by the establishment of a Town I beg to recommend their application to the favorable consideration of the Lieut. Governor and to request that the Surveyor General may be authorised to make the survey required.

I have the honour to be Sir

Your most obedient
Humble Servant
Peter Robinson

Sanctioned

Col. Rowan

J. C. [John Colborne]

To the Honble Peter Robinson
Commissioner of Crown Lands
&c &c &c

York

Sir,

We the undersigned residing at and near the mouth of the River Trent beg to remind you that there are at present, specially reserved by the Government, about one hundred acres of land in the township of Murray immediately adjoining the West Bank of the said River at its mouth; that about 12 acres of the said Reserve have recently been granted to the English Episcopal Church, the Roman Catholic Church, and for the erection of a school house in this township,—the Residue still remaining in a wild state and unappropriated.

As in our opinion the increasing wealth of this township and the neighbouring country stand in need of a village, and the mouth of this River is a situation particularly favoured by nature for that purpose,—we humbly beg leave to represent that the improvement of this part of the Province would be greatly accelerated was all the reserved land, above alluded to, surveyed and sold in town lots on the usual conditions of building that such lots are when sold by the authority of the Commissioner of Crown Lands. We beg also to suggest that a sufficient spot of ground, in such part of the above reserved land as may appear best adapted for the purpose, be set apart in order to enable the Inhabitants of this township and others to hold weekly markets thereon, together with Quarterly or Annual Fairs on such days and under such Regulations as His Excellency the Lieut[t] Governor may think proper to sanction.

We cannot help reminding you, Sir, altho' we deem it almost superfluous, in addressing a Gentleman who has always been so favourable to the General improvement of the Country as you have been, that the establishment of markets is a measure which invariably stimulates the industry of the poorer class of Agricultural Settlers.—at the same time that it affords great convenience and facilities in the disposal of their goods to the Merchant, the Storekeeper and the Mechanic.

We, therefore, beg you will be pleased to take our request into your serious consideration; and that you will be pleased to cause the Survey and sale of the above mentioned land to be carried into execution with as little delay as possible,—as we feel, with regret, that this portion of the Province is far behind other situations less favoured by nature, from the want of that patronage which the Government of this country has always been ready to extend, when the wants of any portion of its subjects are respectfully made known to it.

We have further to request that you will, if necessary, make the subject of our present application known to His Excellency the Lieut[t] Governor, and that you will be pleased to point out to him the great advantages that would be derived to all those living in this neighbourhood by a compliance with the request of those who have the honour to address you—We have the honour to be,

Sir,
Your Most obedient,
Humble Servants

River Trent
13th January 1834

Sheldon Hawley	Robt. Potts
John Grier	M. D. Curran
J. Brooks Crowe	Jacob Ford
William Robertson	Denis Macaulay
John N. Murphy	

10. Immigrants to the Newcastle District *viâ* Port Hope, 1836

[*Accounts and Papers, 1837: The Annual Report of A. C. Buchanan, Acting Chief Agent for Emigration to Canada, December 12, 1836*]

Letters from Landed Proprietors in England, with Answers thereto.

Beachamwell, Norfolk, 10th May 1836

Sir,

I had the satisfaction of learning from your letter to my friend, Mr. Daniel Gurney, the report which he had received from you of the success of the emigrants from this parish, whom I had ventured to recommend to you last year, and who sailed from Lynn by the brig "Shannon." The accounts received here by the relations of the parties themselves have excited such a desire to remove to Canada among the labouring people, that I have resolved to assist four families and two young men with means of emigrating, and have selected persons who, as able and dexterous labourers in husbandry, are well qualified to expect success in that line, and one youth, brought up a tailor, with probably talents enough to be useful in those parts. I have not invited my tenants to undertake any of the expenses attending this expedition, so that this not being exactly a parish measure, I again, by the advice of Mr. Pinnock, of the Colonial department, address all these people to you, soliciting your kindest interest in their behalf and aid to forward the whole of them to Port Hope, on Lake Ontario. I enclose you one of the office forms, filled up with the names of the party, amounting (including an infant) to 23 individuals, with the signatures of such of the men as were able to write.

On account of this undertaking I send you enclosed a remittance of 80£. sterling, to be paid to you by the Quebec Branch of the Montreal Bank, together with the addition of the current exchange; which sum of 80£. sterling I paid into the hands of Messrs. Thomas, Wilson & Co., of Warnford-Court, London.

The Schedule annexed to this letter points out in detail the apportionment of the above sum to the purposes of expediting the emigrants by the conveyances to Lake Ontario, and the sums to be paid to them in coin by the King's Receiver of Upper Canada to each family or individual, with the sums appointed to be received by the people, and which cannot be invaded or touched on their journey in any way. I hope these people will find themselves set down in Upper Canada under very advantageous circumstances. They will all have a little money in their pockets; I do not know what they may have of their own, by sale of their furniture etc., but I have given to the captain 12 half-sovereigns in gold to be distributed among them, according to instructions, as soon as they shall be quite clear of the Channel; and they will also, I believe, get some present of money from the farmers they have worked for, as well as hops etc., from me.

I should hope that the Spicer family, who are steady people, with four able persons among them, may, with the sum of money appointed for them to receive, and under your directions, be able to settle very advantageously.

I shall be glad to learn of the arrival of the "Penelope", with those emigrants in good health, and be very gratified for the services and kindness which you will bestow upon them.

I remain, etc.
(signed) John Motteaux

To A. C. Buchanan, Esq., etc., Quebec.

Beachamwell and Strangham emigrants by the "Penelope" from Lynn:

					£	S.	d.
Above 14 years—	Spicers - - -	5					
"	Reeves - - -	2					
"	John Furbys -	2					
"	Henry Furbys -	2					
"	Cornwall - -	1					
"	Moorcroft - -	1					
		13	@	1/11/6	20	9	6
Under 14 years—	Spicers - - -	4					
"	Infant - - -	–					
"	Reeves - - -	3					
"	John Furbys -	1					
"	Henry Furbys -	1					
		9	@	-/16/-	7	4	-
				less	27	13	6

To be paid in coin on the parties landing at Port Hope by the hands of his Majesty's Receiver, Upper Canada.

To William Spicer, self and family	£20
" William Reeves, for ditto - -	10
" John Furbys, for ditto - - -	6

To Henry Furbys, for ditto - - -	6	
" C. Cornwall - - - - - - -	2	
" William Moorcroft - - - -	2	46 — —
To meet any contingencies, and the residue if any to be divided		6 6 6
		£80 — —

If any death occurs previous to the distribution, the portion to go to the remainder of the family

(signed) John Motteaux.

Beachamwell, 10th May 1836.

The above sums are to be paid, together with all benefit arising from the course of exchange.

11. Settlement of the Northern Townships of the Trent Valley[1]

[*Public Archives of Canada, Parsonage Letters*]

Dysart Feby 29, 64

My dear Charles

Not having received any answers to letters written in July and September last to yourself Mrs Phillips and Mrs Bonwick we can only conclude they were never receiv'd as we have not even had a paper or any intelligence whatever In the first I inform'd you that we had a fine voyage out in 14 days and had arriv'd at Port Hope a very beautiful little Town on Lake Ontario *all* in good health, distant 437 miles from Quebec I also inform'd you that employment was very scarce Trade being almost at a stand still on account of the war in the States, In the

[1]The settlement of parts of Haliburton, and of many other outlying townships in the region, was largely in the post-Confederation period and consequently outside the scope of this volume. But many of the first settlers—including numerous children of the pioneers in the older and more southerly townships—found their way northward in the eighteen-fifties and -sixties. The letter quoted above describes experiences in Dysart Township which may be taken as typical. Dysart was part of Peterborough County until 1874 when Haliburton County was formed. Among the most remarkable early settlers of Haliburton was Thomas Mason of Boskung, Stanhope Township, whose experiences in various parts of the Empire, and in Haliburton after 1860, are vividly described in "The Patriarch of Boskung: the Strange Life History of a Venerable Canadian", by Watson Kirkconnell (*Minden Echo*, July 21, 1922). To obtain supplies Mason rowed or carried a punt 63 miles to Fenelon Falls, negotiating eight portages, one of them almost three miles long. In spite of all sorts of misfortunes and hardships—even more than ordinarily fell to the lot of the pioneer backwoodsman—Mason was still active at the age of 93, when his experiences were recorded.

next I inform'd you that not being able tò get any employment—Myself and Henry where about to start for the Backwoods we travelled 100 miles out the last 40 miles entirely through the woods the Land Company had the stands [torn] I took one of their lots and commenc'd Chopping when after clearing an acre I was informed I had been clearing on another man's ground after staying 6 weeks I return'd to Port Hope and not being able to do better we all started again for the Back Woods The Railway bringing us to Lindsay 40 miles the first day then by steamer the next day 20 miles to Bobcageon the remaining 40 I can scarcely describe for if any Road was ever made purposely to upset the Passengers the Bobcageon must be the one I am happy to say we arriv'd safely without any accident on the 3d day of October. I then commenc'd working for the Company and looking out for another Lot We had to build a Log House and come into it at Christmas when the Cold was so intense that the cups and saucers froze hard together whilst we where drinking our tea and a pail of water standing by the fire side would be frozen solid during the night I have had my fingers frozen whilst out chopping and this is nothing uncommon for fingers and toes should be well wrap'd up but people do not wrap up their bodies in great coats in this country as they do in England except when travelling for with the most intence frost we have the most beautiful sunshine and no rain, but it would be impossible to live in this country without fires in the night as it is quite common for the breath to be frozen on the Blankets But with all these drawbacks and a few others which I have not mentioned we are *all* much pleas'd with the general features of the Country. During the time we have been here we have had a greater number of fine days than I ever remember to have seen during the same time in England If you where to see the children you would believe them to be really happy altho they have been without shoes all the winter and our fare has been of the plainest description it has rarely ever varied from Bread Pork Potatoes and Tea without butter sugar or milk I only know of one milch cow and one horse in the whole 10 Townships consisting of 250 thousand acres When we came out here there where only four or five settlers or squatters in all, there are now nearly twenty besides a good many Lots taken by parties waiting for the melting of the snows which it is said will take place in about six weeks from this time. Henry is doing well working for himself being assistant cook to a gang of men who are cutting roads through the forests where he has been the last four months he looks fat and well If you have not received any of our Letters and I fear you have not for a young man out here who came from Manchester has written to his friends eight letters and they have wrote to say they have not had one of them you must have thought we had gone to some unknown Region and forgotten you altogether But *not so* we left too many really kind friends in England ever to forget them or the assistance we received in our greatest necessity and I hope you will give our kindest regards to as many as you can and take all the trouble you can to inform them of what I now state more especially our old neighbours and friends East and West I hope you will see Abraham and give my love to him and tell him to write a line also write yourself and let us know how you are both getting on I should like to give you a full discription of this Country but I can hardly find time for having only little Everett and Fred to assist me My time is all taken up I shall have to travel 26 miles through the snow to post these letters as I mean to have no mistake this time we are often oblig'd to trust to Indians Trappers and others going out to the front to sell their skins they are safe enough until they get hold of the Wiskey when they can no more be trusted than a mad dog We have plenty of other wild animals such as bears, Wolves, Beavers, Otters, Fishers, Martins, Minks and Muskrats and Wild Cats and a great many more that I cannot remember the names of The Deer are also numerous a very splendid Animal something of the Elk breed many of them weigh 200 Pounds each but the only animal the Hunters fear is the Wild Cat some of them measure 6 feet in length and have claws the length of a man's finger are a sort of Leopard and the Hunters say they always attack with their claws more than the teeth I am happy to say these animals are not numerous in these parts I have many a time regretted I had not even an old musket for the skins of many of these animals fetch a deal of money out at the front more even than they do in England The Lot I have taken contains 134 acres it is call'd the old Indian Portage which means *Road* leading the nearest way from the Kahshagawigamog Lake, the Indian name for long and crooked, to the Burnt River also a noble stream of water I should think no country in the world contains more numerous and beautiful Lakes than this one I have just mention'd if situate in England whould be called Virginia water the first our Shanty I mean House is in a most beautiful bay which command a view for several miles up the wildest part the scenery of which I cannot possibly describe even at this time of year, the country is very mountainous and cover'd with hard wood the number and size of the Trees would almost astonish you The soil is most prolific and the springs are very numerous, I must now conclude for the present and hope you will write as soon as you receive this and send me papers if it is only something suitable for the children for they are a long way from any school We all desire our kindest Love and regards to you and all of you and believe me to be your affectionate Father

A. Parsonage

12. Report on the Bobcaygeon Road Settlement, 1863

[*Archives of Ontario, Crown Land Papers, 62 (12), Reports on 'Locations' on Bobcaygeon Road*]

Minden January 10th 1863

To the Honorable Wm. McDougall

Sir

I have the honor to submit the following being my first report of the Free Grants on the Northern Section of the Bobcaygeon Road to Jany 1, 1863.

This Section of the road has only been opened dureing the past year, therefore any report will be found meagre as to the quantity of land under cultivation altho I think the general improvement will be found equal to most other roads, in the same space of time. The settlers wholely consist of persons who have been for a considerable time in the Country. Not one Emigrant family has reached my Agency for the last year.

The Number of Free grants located and nearly all occupied up to this time is 64, the great distance that they are North makes it rather inconveniant to be reached with wagons the Nothern part of the road not being quite finished, but now that we have snow, parties who have taken up their Lots are begining to arive.

The Most Notherly Settler is where the road crosses the Muscoca River about 70 Miles North of Bobcaygeon, at this place the land is very good and a large track of it being Beach and Maple with but little Stone. 9 Miles South the road crosses a narrows of the Lake of Bays, or more commonly called Trading Lake, here a good Settlement has commensed and here alls is a track of excellent Land to a large extent. In the lake fish abound, deer and other game is plentiful, which the new settlers find of great service.

The settlers generaly have wished to locate at the farther part of the road for at some future day they will be nearer an outlet for their produce by the way of Georgian bay or Parreys Sound, the distance about 45 Miles.

A Saw Mill will be erected this season on the Muscoca River, which place is well situated for a Grist and Saw Mill this will be a place of some importance.

The Country is unusually healthy free from Fever and Ague and other diseases incidental to a new Country.

The Nationality of the Free Grant Settlers may thus be classed vis

Irish	25	families
Canadian	26	"
English	11	"
U. States	2	"
	—	
	64	

No of Acres cleared 72

The quantity of Land cleared is small As I mentioned previously, the settlers have been on their Lots only a fiew months others are now taking possession of their Grants.

The Nothern part of the road is still unfinished, much to the inconvenience of the settlers

I have the honor to be Sir
Your Obedient Servent
George G. Burwell
Free Grant Agent
North Bobcaygeon

IV. SETTLEMENT: THE PETER ROBINSON EMIGRATION, 1825

AMONG the most remarkable documentary records to be preserved outside of our great archival collections is that of the Peter Robinson emigration from the south of Ireland to Peterborough County in 1825. The material is so complete that hardly an angle or episode in the state-conducted emigration—from petitions to be included, to reaction to settlement, and even to the state of the settlement many years later—is without documentary commentary.[1] The late Thomas A. S. Hay, for many years City Engineer of Peterborough, kept as a sort of personal treasure a tin box full of the documents, and upon his death they found their way to the museum in the Peterborough Public Library, probably through the interest of the late F. R. Yokome, editor of the *Examiner* and co-worker with Mr. Hay. F. H. Dobbin, writing in *Our Old Home Town* (Toronto, 1943, p. 47), says that the box remained unopened "until a short time ago." The editor of this volume worked upon the material in 1953–54 and reported upon its value, and as a result the Archives of Ontario made a photostatic copy of all of it. The selections which follow give a well-rounded picture of a notable experiment in large-scale emigration.

1. Handbill Announcing the Emigration[2]

EMIGRATION TO
CANADA

MEMORANDUM of the terms on which the Government has agreed to convey a limited number of Settlers from Ireland to Upper-Canada, under the superintendance of *Mr. Robinson* and to locate them upon lands in that Province; and also of the conditions upon which lands shall be granted.

Such Emigrants as the *Superintendant* shall accept, shall be con-

[1]The collection includes as well ship lists and other materials relative to the earlier Irish emigration of 1823 to the Lanark region in the old District of Bathurst. This emigration was also under the direction of the Honourable Peter Robinson.

[2]Probably posted widely in the south of Ireland, this item from the Collection would appear from a hand-written notation to have been in Cork. Some 50,000 people are said to have made application as a result.

Emigration to
CANADA.

MEMORANDUM of the terms on which the Government has agreed to convey a limited number of Settlers from Ireland to Upper-Canada, under the superintendance of *Mr. Robinson* and to locate them upon lands in that Province; and also of the conditions upon which lands shall be granted.

Such Emigrants as the *Superintendant* shall accept, shall be conveyed from the place of embarkation in Ireland, to their lands in *Upper-Canada*, wholly at the public charge, and provisions shall be furnished them during their voyage, and for one whole year after their location upon their respective lots.

Such Farming Utensils as are absolutely necessary to a new *Settler shall also* be found for each head of a FAMILY, or person receiving a grant of Land.

No Person above the Age of 45 *Years* shall be conveyed to Upper-Canada, at the Public Expence, unless under particular circumstances, in the discretion of the *Superintendant*, and no person above that age shall receive a grant of Land *on his arrival in the Colony*.

Every Male above 18 years of age and not exceeding 45 years to whom a certificate shall have been given by the *Superintendant* that he was accepted by him as an Emigrant Settler to receive lands in Upper Canada, shall on his arrival receive a location ticket, or order for 70 Acres of land in such part of the Province as the Lieutenant Governor or Person administering the Government shall assign, And in order that such emigrants as shall be industrious and prudent may have an opportunity of extending their possessions and providing for the respectable maintainance of their Children, an additional tract of 30 acres, adjoining every such Grant of 70 acres, shall be reserved by the Crown ungranted for the space of *ten years* after the location of the lot of 70 acres, to afford an opportunity to the proprietor of such larger tract of purchasing the same within the period, by paying the moderate sum of £10 *Sterling*.

The order or location ticket for 70 acres to be given to the Emigrant upon his arrival shall express certain duties of Settlement, and cultivation, the same in proportion as are required by the Government to be performed on lands granted in Upper Canada to other Settlers and the period to be allowed for the performance of such duties shall be also expressed in the order.

So soon as the settlement duties shall have been performed the party may obtain his Patent on paying the expence of [illegible] which is [illegible] not exceed £[illegible] Sterling [illegible]

Each tract of 70 Acres so granted shall be subject to the payment of an Annual quit Rent to the Crown of two pence per acre to be paid half Yearly in such manner, and subject to such penalties and forfeitures, in the case of failure, as shall be expressed in the Patent, and the same quit Rent shall be charged also upon the grants of 30 Acres. It shall however in every case be in the option of the Proprietor to redeem the quit Rent at any time on paying of *Twenty Years* purchase and with respect to the original location of Seventy Acres, no quit Rent shall be chargeable until 5 Years have expired from the time of the location.

As it is intended that all Persons who shall be thus assisted by the Government in removing to Upper-Canada shall become actual Settlers in the Province it is necessary it should be clearly understood, that if the conditions of cultivation and improvement to be specified in the location ticket, shall not be performed within the period prescribed, or if the person locating any lot under the present system shall before receiving his Patent for the same, withdraw from Upper-Canada, and remain absent for the space of Six Months without sufficient cause to be allowed by the Lieutenant Governor of the Province, the Land so assigned to such Person may be given to another Applicant.

Fermoy, Printed by Thomas Lindsey, King's Street opposite Abbey-Street

Peter Robinson Papers, Peterborough Public Library

EMIGRATION PLACARD, IRELAND, 1825

veyed from the place of embarkation in Ireland, to their lands in *Upper Canada*, wholly at the public charge, and provisions shall be furnished them during their voyage, and for one whole year after their location upon their respective lots.

Such Farming Utensils as are absolutely necessary to a new *Settler shall also* be found for each head of a *FAMILY*, or person receiving a grant of Land.

No Person above the Age of 45 *Years* shall be conveyed to Upper-Canada, at the Public Expence, unless under particular circumstances, in the discretion of the *Superintendant*, and no person above that age shall receive a grant of Land *on his arrival in the Colony*.

Every Male above 18 years of age and not exceeding 45 years to whom a certificate shall have been given by the *Superintendant* that he was accepted by him as an Emigrant Settler to receive lands in Upper Canada, shall on his arrival receive a location ticket, or order for 70 Acres of land in such part of the Province as the Lieutenant Governor or Person administering the Government shall assign, And in order that such emigrants as shall be industrious and prudent may have an opportunity of extending their possessions and providing for the respectable maintainance of their Children, an additional tract of 30 acres, adjoining every such Grant of 70 acres, to afford an opportunity to the proprietor of such larger tract of purchasing the same within the period, by paying the moderate sum of £10 *Sterling*.

The order or location ticket for 70 acres to be given to the Emigrant upon his arrival shall express certain duties of Settlement, and cultivation, the same in proportion as are required by the Government to be performed on lands granted in Upper Canada to other Settlers and the period to be allowed for the performance of such duties shall be also expressed in the order.

So soon as the settlement duties shall have been performed the party may obtain his Patent on paying the expence of preparing the same, which it is supposed will not exceed £2 10s. Sterling on each grant.

Each tract of 70 Acres so granted shall be subject to the payment of an Annual quit Rent to the Crown of two pence per acre to be paid half Yearly in such manner, and subject to such penalties and forfeitures, in the case of failure, as shall be expressed in the Patent, and the same quit Rent shall be charged also upon the grants of 30 Acres. It shall however in every case be in the option of the Proprietor to redeem the quit Rent at any time on paying of *Twenty Years* purchase and with respect to the original location of Seventy Acres, no quit Rent shall be chargeable until 5 Years have expired from the time of the location.

As it is intended that all Persons who shall be thus assisted by the

Government in removing to Upper-Canada shall become actual Settlers in the Province it is necessary it should be clearly understood, that if the conditions of cultivation and improvement to be specified in the location ticket, shall not be performed within the period prescribed, or if the person locating any lot under the present system shall before receiving his Patent for the same, withdraw from Upper-Canada, and remain absent for the space of Six Months without sufficient cause to be allowed by the Lieutenant Governor of the Province, the Land so assigned to such Person may be given to another Applicant.

Fermoy: Printed by Thomas Lindsey, King's Street opposite Abbey-Street

2. Petitions for Inclusion in the Emigration[1]

Aprill 28th 1825

To Peter Robinson Esqr

The Humble Petition of Michael Sullivan most submissively Sheweth —that Petitr nearly twelve months ago removed from a distant part of the Country to the Cove of Cork in order to be ready for Emigration to Upper Canada at the first opportunity—Petitr is a Stout healthy man has three young fellows Sons of a promising appearance Petitr and his Sons have been brought up to the Cultivation of the Land his wife also is a healthy woman & so is a Girl a Daughter of his Petitr humbly implores your Honor to tak him & his family into your Consideration he and his Boys are willing to go to the remotest Part of the Globe that they Could get a Piece of Land to Cultivate—Petitr Can produce excellent testimonials of Moral Character if required Petitr relies on your Honors humanity and will as in Duty Bound for ever

Pray

Newmarket on Fergus.
April 16th 1825.

Sir,

I beg leave to inform you, that I have written to you in July 1823, to request that my family would then be taken out to Canada, but found by the very polite reply with which Mr Ingram had the goodness

[1] See "The Assisted Irish Emigration to Upper Canada under Peter Robinson in 1825, including the Founding of the City of Peterborough and the Settlement of the Surrounding Townships," an M.A. thesis, Queen's University, 1934, by H. T. Pammett. Its historical value is lessened by an unnecessarily exaggerated bias against Robinson and the early aristocratic settlers in the region, but it contains a great deal of collateral material relative to conditions in Ireland and many other aspects of the Emigration.

County of Tipperary } We the undersigned Magistrates
to wit } Know the Bearer Jeremiah Boland
a Native Inhabitant of the City of
Cashel for a long period of years – He
has a wife and four Children their ages 18. 14. 7 and 5 years
The said Jeremiah Boland being inclined to go out to that part
of His Majesty's Dominions called Canada in North America
and having applied to us for a testimonial of Character – We
feel no hesitation in recommending him as an honest well
conducted and loyal man to the Governor General and the
other officers at the head of His Majesty's Government
in that part of His Majesty's Dominions referred to above
and We also think him well qualified to become a Settler
as he understands the tillage and Culture of Land –

To all whom these presents may concern Greeting &c. &c. &c.

At Cashel under the Corporation Seal of said City this 5th May 1825

Weldon Jordan
Depy Mayor

Henry Jordan
Town Clerk of Cashel

[illegible] Magistrate

Peter Robinson Papers, Peterborough Public Library

TESTIMONIAL OF CHARACTER FOR JEREMIAH BOLAND

to favor me, that you had sailed a few days previous to my application. I hope it is not now too late to address you on this subject, when the present benevolent Government contemplates the relief of some of the unfortunate sufferers of this country, by encouraging emigration. I have a Wife and Eight Children, four Sons and as many Daughters, rising gradually from 11 to 21 years of age; the Bearer, whom I send to wait on you, is my eldest son, they are all well educated and industrious, and I can procure the most satisfactory Documents of Character. I beg you will have the kindness to acquaint me with the latest period that is fixed for the Second Division of the Emigrants to sail, and if they will be allowed to take any Domestics or articles of furniture.

I have the honor to be, Sir,
your very obedient Servant
John Burke.

Sir

Having called at Mr Roberts and not meeting you there I beg leave most respectfully to request you will have the goodness to forward an answer to my Father as soon after the receipt of this as may be your convenience. I have shewn Mr Ingram's letter to Mr Roberts to whom I will take the liberty of referring you as to its contents, and have the honor to be Sir

Your most obedient
Humble Servant
Edm^d Burke.

The Humble Address of William Croak
Milthrea Parrish of Buttevant Reduced Farmer

Humbly Sheweth he (Addressor) Intered his name and Eight Children and wife 4 Boys and 4 Girls the youngest of which is 12 years of age in Ballygibblen last August for Immigration to Upper Canada and now on your Hon^rs Arrival Disposed of his potaties and Furniture and reduced himself to a State of Beggary as the regestry where addressor was Intered has been lost in Ballygibblen Addressor now has no refuge under Heaven but relying on your Hon^rs Goodness and Humane Character which Adorns the Country that Gave Your Hon^r birth for which Addressor and poor Family will Fervently pray your Temperal and Etternal welfar for life as in duty bound—

Sir

I take the liberty of recommending the bearer Marg^t Groves a widow with two sons and a daughter who are anxious to proceed to America to joint a part of the Family who have already gone and are settled there. The woman is a Native of the County of Wicklow and bears an Excellent Character. She has been All her life accustomed to Agricultural business and her Family is one of the better order of Irish Tenantry. Indeed I may recommend her and the Family she takes with her as persons who came within the description of those intended to be tempted by the measure of Emigrating to Canada and under these Circumstances I am induced to trouble you with a line in favour of a Family who have been always considered people of excellent Character and Conduct.

I am Sir
Your mo[t] Ob[t] Serv[t]
Tho[s] Otho Travers
E[t] Ind Co Recruiting Depart
Cork 27th Apr[l] 1825

Worthy Sir
the humble pettition of James Walsh humbly sheweth that he is a Poor man of a Young helpless Charge really Famishing for want of work his Name is on the Books with Lord Mount Cashels in Kilworth these two months two goe to uper Canada and he hopes Your Honor will take him in to your humane Consideration and give him a letter to Captain Robinson or to any of the Lords as he can Produce the Best of Caracters from the Rev[d] Thom[s] Barks and Father Foran it is the greatest act of Charity Ever was done to take him and his young helpless Charge out of misery

And he in Duty Bound
Will for Ever Pray
James Walsh

Sir I Beg leave to represent y[r] honour that I the returned Emigrant for upper Canada N[o] 166 am fully satisfied to Embark for the same with the exception of My Children Being not in array to Bear any of the frigids Nor am I provided With any farming utensils and in fine I Am not able to Defray my Expence to the Beach Sir I am anxious to know whether I am to be Provided with any of the above

Honoured S[ir]
I remain y[rs] Unexceptionably
Peter Fane

I certify that I have long known Francis Young—He is a man of most industrious sober habits & great mechanical ingenuity and having a numerous family—consisting of 7 Sons from the age of 7 to 20—and 2 daughters—I think him a person fully deserving of any encouragement which the Government may wish to offer to emigrants—

Dated at Newport
June 21 William See
1823 Curate of Newport

I am acquainted with the bearer margret St Leger alias Markaham, from her infancy, and intimately in my parish these eight years past, and from my knoledge of her, I consider her to be an honest, virtuos, & wel conducted young woman, who is respectably connected in the County of Clare, She is now determined to go to her her husband, to Canada in America, where he is there two years past. I recomend her most earnestly to the Care of Captain Robertson & the passengers of the vessel in which she is sail

Six mile Bridge County of Clare
Ireland April 25 1825— Cornelius Clune
Parish Priest

To Captain Robinson—

The Petition of Henry Molony of Six Mile Bridge in the County of Clare Labourer—

Humbly Sheweth

That your Honor's Petitioner has made Application to you in Cork on or about the 1st of July 1823 for a Passage to America at which time you were ready to sail—

That your Honor then informed Petr that, as Petr had not his family with him in Cork, nor Could not reach there before the Vessel would sail. Your Honor kindly advised Petr to return home, and the same opportunity wd offer the Spring following but your Honor did not come to Cork at that time—

That Petr was obliged to sell the Chief part of his effects to defray his travelling expenses then and now, and must remain in a most deplorable condition if Your Honor does not give him and family a Passage this time—

That as Petr is a Labouring man, as you may perceive by the Certificate herewith handed you, and placing a full reliance on the promise your Honor made him in July 1823 He therefore humbly hopes your Honor will grant him a Passage, and Petr will Pray—

Six Mile Bridge 14th March 1825—

Please your Honour

The humble petition of James Condon—

Most humbly and respectfully sheweth That petitioner held a small farm from the Earl of Kingston, and was dispossessed thereof last November, in consequence of the smallness of his Lot, as his Lordship would not allow small Lots to be let on his Estate in future That his Lordship promised petitioner at that time to recommend him and family to your Honour at your next arival in this Town. And that there was no occasion to have petitioner's name inserted on the List. Please your Honour petitioner has three Boys in his family. humbly hopes your Honour will take him into Consideration—

And petitioner as in Duty bound
will always pray for your
Honour's welfare.

No. 57— NOT TRANSFERABLE.

Ireland, April 15th 1825

Doneraile County of Cork

THESE are to Certify, that the undermentioned Persons, of the Parish of Churchtown in the County of Cork, Ireland, have been received by me, as Emigrant Settlers, to be conveyed to Upper Canada, and placed upon their Lands, at the Expense of His Majesty's Government.

Recommended by Lord Doneraile

NAME.	AGE.	
John Hartnett	46	Head of the Family. Ordnance [illegible]
Catherine	40	Wife.
Margaret	23	Children
Eliza	21	Children
John	19	Children
Maurice	17	Children
Mary	14	Children
Michael	13	Children
Honora	12	Children
Timothy	8	Children
Catherine	6	Children
Joanna	3	Children

{ Superintendent of Emigration from the South of Ireland to Canada.

Peter Robinson Papers, Peterborough Public Library

CERTIFICATE OF ACCEPTANCE, ROBINSON EMIGRATION

3. The Passengers on the Transport *Resolution*[1]

A return of IRISH EMIGRANTS proceeding to CANADA, to be settled at the Expense of His Majesty's Government, under the superintendence of Mr. PETER ROBINSON, Embarked at COVE on Board of the Resolution Transport, Captain Anthony Ward, Master for Passage, to QUEBEC.

G. H. Reade Esq[r] Surgeon in charge.

Cove of Cork, 5th May 1825.

[1]Two similar lists, one apparently for the Captain and one for the Surgeon, are found for each ship. The other ships and their quota of passengers are as follows: *Fortitude*, 282; *Star*, 214; *Regulus*, 157; *Amity*, 147; *Albion*, 191; *Elizabeth*, 210; *John Barry*, 253; and *Brunswick*, 343. The *Brunswick*, apparently the largest, is the only one that the editor has seen mentioned elsewhere, Edward Talbot referring to his passage on her in 1818 and to the same captain, Robert Blake. See Guillet, *The Great Migration: the Atlantic Crossing by Sailing-Ship since 1770* (New York, 1937), *passim*; and *Pioneer Inns and Taverns* (Toronto, 1956), Vol. II, p. 42. In this table six columns detailing sex and age have been deleted, as the information is apparent in the columns 'Names' and 'Age'.

A RETURN of IRISH EMIGRANTS proceeding to *Canada*, to be settled at the Expense of His Majesty's Government, under the superintendence of Mr. Peter Robinson, Embarked at *Cove*, on Board of the Elizabeth Transport, Donald Morison — — — Master, for Passage to *Quebec*.

Mr. Pierce Power R.N. Surgeon in charge.

COVE OF CORK, 18th May — — — 1825.

45	Men,		Included in the Males & Females above 14
31	Women,		
	Males, above 14	84	
	——— under 14	40	
	Females, above 14	56	
	——— under 14	30	
	Total....	Total.... 210	

No. of Heads of Families	Names.	Age.	Occupation.	Men.	Women.	Males above 14	Males under 14	Females above 14	Females under 14	Former Residence.	REMARKS.
1	John Nagle	40	Reduced Farmer	1		1				Jullins Cork	282 R. O. Howell Esq.
	Catherine - - -	40			1			1			
	Catherine -	24			1			1			
	Patrick - -	19				1					
	Mary - - -	16						1			
2	Timothy Buckley	34	Farmer	1		1				Rhincullen Cork	67 Lord Doneraile
	Julia - - -	30						1			
	Timothy - - -	14				1					
	Catherine -	9							1		
	Margaret - -	6							1		
	Margaret - -	17						1			Sister
3	William Brennan	44	Reduced Farmer	1		1				Poole Cork	120 Lord Ennismore
	Mary - - -	40			1			1			
	Dan - - -	21		1		1					
	George - - -	17				1					
	Catherine - -	18						1			
	Frank - - -	15				1					
	Mary -	13							1		
	Carried over			4	3	8	0	7	3		

Peter Robinson Papers, Peterborough Public Library

FIRST PAGE OF THE LIST OF PASSENGERS ON THE *ELIZABETH*, 1825

40 Men		Included in the Males
38 Women		and Females above 14
Males above	14	61
under	14	61
Females above	14	58
under	14	47
Total	Total	227

Heads of Families	Names	Age	Occupation	Former Residence	Remarks
1	Patrick Kearney	36	Farmer		
	Catherine	30		Castle Lyon	
	Denis	10		Cork	Lord
	James	8			Ennismore
	Mary	5			130
	Patrick	1			
2	Richd Andrews	42	Shoemaker		Earl of
	Susanna	38		Brigown	Kingston
	Jeremiah	16		Cork	32
	Ellen	12			
	Elisa	10			
	William	7			
	Frances	3			
3	John O Dogherty	37	Farmer	Brigown	Earl of
	Ellen	26		Cork	Kingston
	Anne	15			40
	Judith	5			
	Kitty	12			
	John	2			
	Mary	26			Sister to John
4	William Torpy	54	Farmer		
	Mary	40			
	Thomas	22			
	Michael	21			
	Mary	19			9
	Kitty	18			
	Honora	15			
	John	13			
	Elisabeth	10			
	Bridget	6			
5	Robin Walsh	38	Farmer		
	May Walsh	38			Earl of
	John	17			Kingston
	Thomas	15			1
	Judith	14			
	Johanna	9			
	Robert	4		Brigown	
	Michael	3		Cork	
6	David Magner	32	Farmer		
	Mary	32		Kilworth	Lord
	John	15		Cork	Mountcashel
	Catherine	11			84

Heads of Families	Names	Age	Occupation	Former Residence	Remarks
	David	9			
	Mary	4			
7	William Hogan	30	Sawyer	Mitchelstown	
	Alice	34		Cork	Earl of
	Thomas	9			Kingston
	Frances	7			35
	Mary	4			
	Ellen	1			
8	John McKoy	27	Labouror	Doneraile	Lord
	Catherine	24		Cork	Doneraile
	Ellen	7			52
	James	5			
	Catherine	2			
9	William Cleary	45	Farmer		
	Mary	40			
	Timothy	20			38
	Mary	15			
	Johanna	12			
	William	10			
	Catherine	3			
10	William Williams	20	Farmer		
	Michael	19			37
	Elisa	22			
11	John Quinlan	35	Labouror		
	Margaret	28		Affam	
	Michael	12		Waterford	Lord
	James	10			Mountchasel
	Mary	8			99
	Catherine	6			
	Nancy	1			
12	Bryan Walsh	35	Farmer	Temple Ling	
	Mary	32		Tipperary	Earl of
	Edmond	6			Kingston
	Mary	3			8
	Patk	2			
13	John McCraith	37	Farmer	Brigown	Earl of
	Mary	34		Cork	Kingston
	Ellen	14			17
	John	12			
	Daniel	10			
	Mary	8			
	Catherine	4			
14	John Lane	23	Farmer } Left	Castle Lyons	
	Mary	24	at	Cork	Lord
	Patrick	1	Lachine		Mountchashel
15	Thoms. McCraith	35	Farmer		94
	Margaret	28			
	Redmond	3			30
	Catherine Nevile	18			Sister
16	Mary Mahony	50			Mother
	William	26	Farmer		Head of Famy
	Michl	24		Brigown	

Heads of Families	Names	Age	Occupation	Former Residence	Remarks
	Ellen	23		Cork	Earl of
	Honora	20			Kingston
17	Thomas Carey	43	Farmer &		39
	Esther	41	Slater		
	Anne	21			
	Samuel	19		Farrahy	Lord
	Sarah	15		Cork	Ennismore
	Richard	13			129
	Thomas	11			
	Esther	9			
	John	7			
	Robert	2			
18	John Cranly	30	Farmer	Donesky	Lord
	Margaret	25		Tipperary	Ennismore
	John	1			126
19	Patrick Brien	30	Farmer		
	Honora	30			
	William	9			13
	Anne	6			
	John	4			
	David	1			
	Elizabeth Carrol	17			Sister in law
20	John Fleming	66	Reduced Farmer		
	Edmond Allen	39			
	Bridget Allen	38			
	John	19			2
	William	17			
	Mary	14			
	Edmond	7			
	Robert	5			
	Bridget	3			
	Bridget Johnson	11			Granddaugh
21	John Condon	30	Nailor		
	Sarah	24		Mitchelstown	
	Martin	7		Cork	
	Henry	6			Earl of
	James	1			Kingston
22	Henry Couche	41	Shoemaker		11
	Susanna	32			
	Susanna	19			
	Christopher	17			
	Henry	15		Mitchelstown	
	Mary	12		Cork	Earl of
	Anne	9			Kingston
	Jane	3			24
23	Thomas Condon	42	Farmer		
	Margaret	40		Kilworth	
	James	21		Cork	Lord
	Bartholomew	16			Ennismore
	Patrick	14			132
	Ellen	10			
	John	8			

Heads of Families	Names	Age	Occupation	Former Residence	Remarks
	Mary	5			
	Thomas	1			
24	Nancy Purcell	40			
	Thomas	24	Reduced	Church Town	Capt
	Elisa	22	Farmer	Cork	Roberts
	Patrick	17			185
	Margaret	15			
	John	14			
	Daniel	13			
	Mary	10			
25	William Barrett	35	Farmer		
	Johanna	35		Kilworth	Lord
	John	13		Cork	Mountchasel
	Mary	11			102
	William	9			
	Norah	7			
	Johana	4			
	Edmond	1			
26	Patk O Donnle	40	Farmer	Brigown	Earl of
	Martha	35		Cork	Kingston
	Edmond	25			16
	Catherine	20			
	Ellen	15			
	Patrick	14			
	Jane	11			
	Mary	8			
27	John Armstrong	32	Farmer	Mitchelstown	
	Elisa	30	Reduced	Cork	
	Mary	15			Earl of
	Samuel	16			Kingston
	Francis	9			232
	Thomas	8			
	Wheeler	7			
	Robert	3			
	Charles	1			
28	William Wall	48	Farmer	Mitchelstown	
	Mary	36		Cork	
	Anne	19			Earl of
	Mary	16			Kingston
	William	14			19
	Thomas	12			
29	Mauce Brien	37	Farmer		
	Mary	33			22
	Morgan	17			
	Honora	13			
	John	11			
	Thomas	7			
	William	4			
	Margaret	1			
30	Denis O Brien	35	Cooper	Mitchelstown	
	Bridget	26		Cork	Earl of
	James	5			Kingston

Heads of Families	Names	Age	Occupation	Former Residence	Remarks[1]
	Johanna	4			29
31	Michail O Brien	33	Farmer	Brigown	
	Gilliam	28		Cork	Earl of
	Mary Brien	12			Kingston
	John	8			23
	Elisa	6			
	Michael	4			
32	Patrick Clancy	40	Farmer	Kilworth	Lord
	Mary	33		Cork	Mountcasel
	Thomas	12			90
	Denis	10			
	Maurice	8			
	Daniel	4			
	Patrick	2			
33	James McCarthy	35	Farmer	Glandelane	
	Mary	34		Cork	Lord
	James	9			Mountcasel
	Thomas	6			85
	John	4			
	Mary	2			
34	Florence Driscoll	32	Farmer	Castle Lyons	
	Mary	26		Cork	Lord
	Denis	6			Ennismore
	Margaret	3			135
35	George Byrnes	25	Farmer	Brigown	
	Kitty	20		Cork	Earl of
	Patrick	4			34
					Kingston

4. Surgeons' Lists and Comments

(*a*) A list of the emigrants embarked on board the *Albion* in May 1825 for a passage to Quebec

[*Compiled by John Thomson, Surgeon R.N.*]

Number of Families	Number of Ticket	Name	Age	Remarks
1	60	James Daly	30	An excellent man worthy of
		Ellen	26	encouragement
		Patrick	21	
		Mary	2	
2	45	Thomas Stack	40	A good industrious man
		Mary	44	
		Honora	20	

[1]The columns are totalled at the end of the document as follows: Men 40, Women 38, Males above 14 61, Males under 14 61, Females above 14 58, Females under 14 47.

No. of Families	No. of Ticket	Name	Ages	Remarks
		Richard	16	
		Maurice	13	
		Thomas	10	
		Mary	6	
		Johanna	4	died on the 30th of May
3	46	James Barry	38	A decent family
		Bridget	37	
		Margaret	16	
		Bridget	14	
		Catherine	7	
		John	5	
		Ellen	2	
4	53	Michael Sullivan	28	
		Judith	26	Understands Midwifery
		Catherine	7	
		Michael	5	
		Mary	2	
5	55	Dan[l] Shea	34	Quiet but indolent, the wife
		Catherine	32	industrious
		Mary	14	
		Daniel	12	
		Jeremiah	9	
		Nancy	2	
6	125	Daniel Burgess	44	A plausible & I suspect a designing
		Avice	44	character
		William	23	A good young man, a cooper by trade
		Emanuel	22	Suspicious
		Sabina	21	
		Elizabeth	20	
		Mary Anne	19	
		Henry	18	
		Daniel	15	
		Avice	10	
7	59	Patrick Healy	35	Industrious & very quiet
		Eliza	36	
		Mary	19	
		Thomas	17	
		John	15	
		Judith	13	
		Ellen	11	
		Eliza	9	
		Margaret	2	
8	140	Patrick Lynam	22	Deserted at La Chine
		Ellen	21	Deserted at La Chine
9	146	Daniel Connor	33	A decent family
		Bridget	26	
		Judith	16	
		Margaret	14	
		James	12	
		Ellen	8	
		Bridget	5	
10	61	Timothy Sweeny	34	Very indolent

No. of Families	No. of Ticket	Name	Age	Remarks
		Johanna	30	
		Honora	11	
		Mary	9	
		Catherine	4	died on the 7th of June
11	136	John Clancy	30	A well behaved man
		Eliza	30	
		Ellen	16	
		William	11	
		John	5	
		Johanna	3	
12	183	John Collins	40	rather dirty & of an unhappy temper
		Johanna	40	
		Michael	20	
		Timothy	18	
		John	16	
		Catherine	14	
		Edmund	12	
		James	8	
		Bridget	3	
		Maurice	1	
13	138	Mary Keefe	48	very decent & quiet
		Mary	17	
		John	15	
14	69	Bartholomew Lingane	36	A quiet family
		Ellen	18	
		Mary	16	
		Jeremiah	13	
		David	12	
		Patrick	10	
		Eliza	6	died on the 23rd of May
		Margaret	3	died on the 13th of June
		Edmund	26	
15	63	James Keefe	38	tidy, but I fear not fit for hard work
		Ann	29	
		Catherine	18	
		James	17	
		Ellen	13	
		Eliza	12	
		Timothy	9	
		Mary Anne	5	
16	134	John Brien	40	well behaved
		Margaret	40	
		Thomas	15	
		Ellen	12	
		Catherine	9	
		Johanna	1	
17	170	William Ryan	30	well behaved
		Catherine	30	
		Michael	13	
		William	5	
		Ellen	3	
18	161	William Reily	35	well behaved
		Elizabeth	30	
		Thomas	13	

No. of Families	No. of Ticket	Name	Age	Remarks
		Joseph	11	
		John	8	
		Mary	4	
		Jeremiah	2	
		Johanna	1	died on the 13th of May
19	151	Daniel Sheehan	40	An industrious family
		Ellen	39	
		Mary	21	
		Elizabeth	17	
		Daniel	15	
		Patrick	10	
		Judith	9	
		Daniel	1	
20	121	David Nagle	37	well behaved
		Juliana	30	
		Richards	16	
		Ellen	13	
		John	10	
		Garret	7	
		Margaret	5	
		Patrick	15	found on board after we sailed, but not victualled at sea
21	87	Michael Sweeny	37	A very decent, good family
		Margaret	32	
		John	16	
		Richard	13	
		Mary	9	
		Catherine	5	
		Denis	1	
22	74	John Sheehan	39	An industrious good family
		Bridget	36	
		Cornelius	21	hard working good young men
		Timothy	18	
		Patrick	14	
		Michael	8	
		John	6	
		Mary	16	
23	76	William McDonald	34	Well behaved
		Mary	32	
		John	16	
		William	14	
		Alexander	11	
		Charles	8	
		Patrick	5	
		Michael	3	
24	62	Patrick Lynch	32	hard working tho' poor
		Deborah	30	
		Mary	14	
		Catherine	12	
		James	10	
		Eliza	8	
		Ellen	6	
		Thomas	3	
		Deborah		Born at La Chine

No. of Families	No. of Ticket	Name	Age	Remarks
25	267	James Sheneck	31	tolerable
		Johanna	28	
		Mary	2	discharged to the Star
		Mary		born on the 12th June
26	48	John Regan	32	rather dirty
		Nory	30	
		Abigail alias		
		William	16	victualled as a female
		Mary	6	
27	179	Michael Lowes	44	An excellent family, worthy of
		Sarah	42	favor
		Michael	28	
		Richard	24	
		Dorothy	20	
28	194	George Lowes	40	A most worthy man, wife very
		Hannah	32	industrious, he is brother to
		Zachariah	20	the above and wish to be to-
		Rebecca	8	gether, they are Protestants
		George	6	
29	301	Jeremiah Connor	35	rather dirty, but I hope will be
		Mary	30	industrious
		Margaret	9	
		Jeremiah	7	
		Johanna	3	
		Daniel		Born on the 3rd of June
30	104	Michael Kenny	30	hard working family
		Mary	32	
		James	28	
		Margaret	20	
		John	5	

Abstract of the foregoing List

	Males above 14	Females above 14	Children	Total
Embarked at the Cove of Cork	56	52	83	191
Discharged at the Cove of Cork	"	"	1	
On board at the time of sailing	56	52	82	190
Found on board when at sea	1	"	"	
Born on board			2	
	57	52	84	193
Died on board			5	
Arrived at Quebec	57	52	79	188

John Thomson Surgeon R.N.
and Superintendent

	Males above 14	Females above 14	Children	Total
Arrived at La Chine	57	52	79	188
Born at La Chine	"	"	1	
	57	52	80	
Deserted at La Chine	1	1	"	
Arrived at Prescott	56	51	80	187

(*b*) A LIST OF IRISH EMIGRANTS EMBARKED IN THE SHIP *John Barry*
W[m] BURNIE SURGEON

Names	General Remarks &c.
John Lane	A good Family. Instrumental in saving the Ship when on Shore, thereby avoiding additional expence and delay. Son Cottrel in a quarrel with an Indian of the Boat, brought on by himself, about the Tarpaulin, cut the Boatman in several places on the right arm, and was himself hurt. As a compensation and to prevent more serious consequences I gave a note on Com[er] Finlay for 11. Dollars which I must pay on my return.
Hen[y] Maloney	Youngest child died at the Cascades on passage up the River. Buried at the Cedars.
Ja[s] Slattery	A quiet Family. Youngest child died at Lachine.
Pa[t] Ryan	(A good Man. Instrumental in saving the Ship &c. &c. (Brothers Tim[y] & John very troublesome Ch[rts]
Mich[l] Dahill	A Protestant Family
Tim[y] Callaghan	A quiet Family. A child born in the John Barry.
Pat. Twomy	A willing, hard-working, good man
Tho[s] Shea	A quiet Family. Youngest Child died in Gulph St.Lawrence
Cor[ns] M[c]Auliffe	A quiet family
John Daly	(A good, industrious, obliging and willing Family. (Himself by trade a Cooper.
John Callaghan	
Rich[d] Sullivan	(A very good, quiet, willing & industrious Family deserving (every attention & encouragement
Ed[ard] Gillman	Himself a very good man. Has a large Family of Daughters
Ja[s] Hurly	
Rich[d] Walsh	
Tho[s] Hennessy	
John Blackwell	A very excellent Family, Protestants, of good and industrious Daughters. Was instrumental in saving the Ship &c. Brought out a Lad from Cork, engaged to serve him 3 years who has, to his great loss, left him on some frivolous excuse. Deserves every encouragement. Has behaved wholly to my satisfaction.
John Sullivan	A very good Family, of kind and industrious Daughters. Fully satisfied with their behaviour.

Names	General Remarks &c.
Corn[s] Sullivan	A very good and willing Family, chiefly grown up, behaved well on the Passage
Tho[s] Groves	A very excellent Family, Protestants, The Mother a worthy kind woman. Boys very willing and attentive. Affraid of her neighbours and has suffered ill, from some on account of religion. Has two daughters M[d] in Ramsay, whom she is anxious to join. She is very diserving every indulgence
John Walsh	A very excellent Family, acquainted with gardening. Has behaved himself well and deserves every encouragement and recommendation, wrought hard at the Pumps.
Francis Young	A very excellent Family, willing, industrious, and obliging in every respect, have behaved in the most examplary manner, and deserve every attention and encouragement. Instrumental in saving the Ship.
W[m] Foley	A very excellent Family, of quiet and willing lads, have behaved to my entire satisfaction. Has two sons at Godmanchester, whom he is anxious to join, provided he can have his land and allowances.
Martin O. Brien	A quiet Man, Youngest child died at P[t] Bersiamitis
D[d] Hogan	An old Soldier, wrought hard and behaved well on passage Acting as cook—Has since committed himself
Jer[h] Boland	
Ja[s] Condon	A very good, quiet, industrious & willing Family
Pat. Baragy	Assisted in cutting up and dividing provisions on passage
John Kelehar	Shannon!!! An excellent and willing man, and deserving every recommendation and encouragement from his good conduct, with which I am fully satisfied in every particular. Assisted the 3[d] Mate with the provisions and took care of the dogs on the Passage.
Tho[s] Casey	A very good Family—behaved well on passage
Tim[y] Regan	Came on board sickly, Took Fever on 2[d] June Died at Quebec Hospital. Wife took sick shortly after, produced a child in the 8th month. Convalescent at Quebec—hurried off to Lachine. Arrived on Saturday evening. Took dangerously sick, on Sunday and died at 12 on Tuesday—Child died and was buried at Kingston. Two Boys and Two girls—very fine Children are left orphans. I left 8 Dollars belonging to them in M[r] Reades charge—Their chest by some mistake has been left at Quebec
Tim[y] Leary	
D[d] Owens	Wife a lying mischief making woman
Ja[s] Mahony	A quiet Family. All very sickly
Dan[l] Malony	A very excellent Family, Behaved intirely to my satisfaction during the passage. Was instrumental in saving the Ship &c.

Names	General Remarks &c.
	and deserves every recommendation and attention from his general good conduct
D[d] Nagle	Behaved well on passage. Story being known thinks himself in danger among present neighbours.

5. Letters and Notes concerning the Ascent of St. Lawrence

(*a*) Surgeon Power of the *Elizabeth* to Peter Robinson

Prescott U Canada 21st July
1825

Sir

I deem it my duty to state to you that on the Emigrants under my charge landing at Montreal the 4th Instant—while busily employed in seeing them placed on the Carts with the baggage—James Lee and family Six in N[o.] deserted taking with him his bedding. I could not attend at the time neither had I means to prevent him—but on arriving at La Chiene I instituted an inquiry into the business and found that an Idea pretty generally prevailed that they Could do such an act with impunity. Not wishing to allow so erronious an Opinion to continue and also to deter others from following Lee's example I took two of the people who witnessed the theft before the authorities at Montreal and having attended two days Informations were lodged against the delinquent he was arrested and sent to Jail but afterwards admitted to bail for what in England is deemed felony—Altho this was strictly speaking nothing but my duty yet as it was attended with some additional expence (which together with small sums supplied from time to time to the women who had sick children and no means of providing refreshments) amounts I find to about Twenty dollars—

Should the service on which I was employed admit of its being reimbursed I will feel much obliged by your doing so. if not the intention of this Letter will be fulfilled by putting you in possession of the fact of the man's desertion

I have the Honor
to be
Sir your Most Obedient
Serv[t]
C. Power Surgeon

To P. Robinson Esq[r]) R. N. in Charge of Emigrants
&c &c &c) for Ship Elizabeth

P.S. Jeremiah Dwyer is bound in recognizance to prosecute at the next assizes holden at Montreal I believe in August.

(*b*) LETTER TO DR. READ,[1] PRESCOTT

Prescott 9th July 1825

Sir—

We have to request that you will be pleased to use your endeavours to procure a supply of fresh provisions for the Irish Emigrants just landed here under our superintendence—which their state of exhaustion & general health so much require—

We are Sir
your Ob. Servants
(Signed) Brian McMorris Surgeon R.N.
Superintending Ship Star.
James W. Ternan Surgeon R.N.
Superintending Ship Amity
Mathew Burnside Surgeon R.N.
Superintending Ship Regulus

To
Doctor Read
&c &c &c

(*c*) ACCOUNT FOR MEDICAL ATTENDANCE

Prescott 22nd January 1826

The Honble Peter Robinson
Dr to W. J. Scott[2]

		£	S	D
1825	To Strict Attendance upon the Sick Irish Emigrants from 26th of July to 19th August at 10 shillings per diem........	12	—	—
"	Attendance and Medicine to Mrs Buckley from 19th to 30th August........	1	5	—
"	Attending all night and Delivering Mrs Connel with Medicine subsequently........	1		
		£14	5	—

(*d*) LETTER RECOMMENDING WILLIAM FITZGERALD

Prescott July 1825

My Dear Sir

This will be handed to you by Wm Fitzgerald who came with me in the Amity & in whose welfare I feel a very great interest.

If any extra advantages be reserved for rectitude of conduct & strict probity they cannot be bestowed upon a more worthy person nor can any thing give me more satisfaction than to find that this making you acquainted with his worth should be productive of advantage to him.

Believe me Dr Sir
Very truly yours
James W. Ternan

P. Robinson Esqr
&c &c &c

[1]G. H. Reade, Surgeon of the *Resolution*, and subsequently doctor to the immigrants in Peterborough.

[2]Dr. William James Scott, born in 1793, died at Prescott on October 14, 1875.

(*e*) JAMES W. TERNAN, SURGEON ON THE *Amity*, TO PETER ROBINSON

Kingston 19th July 1825

My Dear Sir—

To this I beg to annex a list of Emigrants who came with me in the Amity with their respective characters which may in some degree guide you until confirmed by your own acquaintance with them—.

Thos Callaghan—quiet well behaved & Slothful
John Gordon—he and all his family highly deserving and well-conducted
Dennis Shanahan—an honest well-disposed man
John Galvin—as honest well disposed & industrious a young fellow as ever left his Country
Dennis Kearny—an honest well meaning creature
Michl Costello—a good honest man with a good family
Wm Oakly—a man of excellent principle & will be found to deserve encouragement
John Stark—has a very good family—himself imprudent
John Leary—an honest creature & a very deserving family
Patk Crowly—a quiet well disposed man
David Conry—was generally well behaved but consider him a stubborn turbulent character
Thos Hallahan—a well disposed man & a good family
Owen McCarthy—a good industrious man & a very well conducted family
Thos Murry—a well disposed honest indolent man
Michl Buckly—has a very honest well conducted family for whose sake I could wish him well-conducted
Wm Fitzgerald—a man of gentlemanlike behaviour & good principle—to be trusted
Rich English—a Slothful well-behaved man
John Twomy—an honest well disposed fellow
Danl Scully—a quiet industrious man
Bartw Sullivan—an insolent turbulent fellow
John Kennelly—an honest well disposed industrious creature
Jno Lancaster—a useful smart active well-conducted man with a decent family—

James W Ternan
Surgeon Royl Navy
Superintending Ship Amity

(*f*) JAMES W. TERNAN TO PETER ROBINSON

Kingston 1st August 1825

Dear Sir—

I beg leave to add my request to those of my Brother Officers who came to Canada in the Superintendence of Irish Emigrants, that you will have the kindness to arrange for the payment to us of a Colonial allowance usual in the Transport Service together with the travelling expences incurred from our arrival in the country. Indisposition prevents my having the pleasure of waiting on you but as one or more of the Officers concerned will have that pleasure I hope to be favored with your reply by their return—or else directed to me at "S. Garwood's Esqr R. N. Dockyard".

On my arrival here I had the pleasure of meeting your Brother who took with him your two dogs in excellent condition & as promising as ever visited Canada. Much of their good state they owe to a man (In Lancaster) who came out with me in the Amity to whom I gave a note of recommendation to you—To other deserving men I also gave recommendations which I hope you.[ll] give your kind attention to—In a private letter I gave an outline of the Characters of those who came with me & I cannot avoid the mention of the man Mich.[l] Buckly so highly recommended by the Mayor of Cork as one of the most infamous characters with regard to whose family D.[r] Reade has made some arrangements the necessity of which you.[ll] soon discover—Altho' it may be surely called supererrogation I cannot withold the charitable advice of the immediate removal of the Emigrants from this place—Their encampment is unhealthy & fever increases rapidly—I have to return my warmest thanks for your kind letters of introduction—not having visited York I had not the pleasure of delivering to the Att[y] Gen[l]—M[r] Price of Quebec I left well & should you have any commands to him I shall gladly be the bearer and am Dear Sir very sincerely yours

James W. Ternan

(*g*) RECOMMENDATION OF DAVID HOGAN

I have known the bearer David Hogan private in the 48 Regiment and on his passage from New South Wales— His conduct was correct & his character excellent, and I do believe him to be a good and honest man—

Kingston 7th August 1825

James W. Ternan
Surgeon Royal Navy
Superintendent of Emigrants

(*h*) RECOMMENDATION OF JOHN DOODY

John Doody a Butcher conducted himself with propriety on the passage and as I understand a good tradesman and well conversant with the cutting part of his trade

Prescott
5 July—1825

F. Connin
Surgeon R.N.

(*i*) NOTES CONCERNING EMIGRANTS ON THE *Fortitude*

Memo. of some of the Fortitudes Irish Emigrants

James Cotter) Bad and Dangerous characters &
Pat[k] Lehay) fit for any mischief
Mich. Elligott) Insolent
W[m] O'Halloran) Ruffians

I could not point out any others as with the above exceptions I had no reason to complain of the conduct of any between Cork & Quebec

Flaherty the bearer of this served as cook to the Emigrants on the passage out and conducted himself in every respect well

Fortitude
at Quebec
15 June 1825

F. Connin
Surgeon in
Charge

(*j*) EMIGRANT RIOT AT L'ISLE DE PERREAU

Memo

Friday 24 June 1825, about 9 P.M. arrived at L'ilse de Perreau found the boats that had arrived before us in terrible confusion landed with difficulty and discovered that some of the Emigrants had broken the door & windows of a house and severely cut two men in the head with stones, the clock was also broken dressed the wounded men & ordered the boats on for fear of more mischief. Originated in a dispute about boiling a kettle. Sunday 26 Mr Simson of Coteau endeavoured to discover the offenders the Sons of Cotter & Casey without doubt concerned as they were wounded. The damage estimated at ten pounds on our arrival at prescott Mr Reade dismissed Cotter and Casey they came out in the Fortitude but suspicion attaches also to the Henny's of the Albion.

John Thomson Surgeon R. N.

6. PETER ROBINSON'S DESCRIPTION OF THE ARRIVAL OF THE SETTLERS

[*Public Archives of Canada, Q 343 pt. 2, pages 263–4*]

Cobourg.
6th Octr 1825.

My Dear Brother

I leave this in a few minutes for Smith—The emigrants are all at the Depot[1] at the head of the Otonabee River, with the exception of a few invalids.—I send Major Hillier a return of the deaths that have occurred since their arrival in Prescott

[1]"The arrival of the poor immigrants from Ireland has given us some variety," wrote Frances Stewart. "They are encamped on the 'plains', a place about two and a half miles off. Their huts look very odd, being made with poles standing up, boughs or branches of trees interwoven, and mud plastered over this. They live in these till log shanties are ready for their families in Douro. These huts already cause the 'plains' to be called a village. . . . Dr. Reade has come as the emigrants' doctor, and his wife, the first lady who has settled here. The Doctor is liked among the poor Irish, he is a very humane, hospitable, friendly little man. The poor creatures suffered a good deal, and many died." (*Our Forest Home* (Toronto, 1889), p. 47).

Men Women & children	N°
from 14 years upwards	28
Children under 14 including	
those just born	37
	65 Total

by this you see that the mortality has not been so great for the numbers, & the uncommon unhealthy season.—I had a letter from Major Hillier in which he mentions that Birdsall had been instructed to call on me to consult as to the survey of the Town plot at the head of the Otonabee River, and I expect soon to see him—By the Bye why not call the Town *Wilmot Horton*[1] it is the prettiest place I ever saw the plain is very extensive & has just trees enough for ornament.

It is impossible to forsee what difficulties I may get into with such a party as I have so remote from any force sufficient to quell a riot. As yet I am obeyed, and I exact the strictest obedience but there are many idle rascals from Ireland frequently exciting our people to mischief and leading them astray.—Such advises do much mischief however I am determined to carry a high hand at the Depot, & the first man that troubles me shall be imprisoned & kept there, until I get advice—

A Mr Hearn a Catholic priest is now at the Depot he seems quiet enough but from what he said last Sunday at Mass I fear he wants discretion—He publicly told the—Ems. that Mr Crowley had no authority to come among them—The latter had spent some days with us & gained much, the affections of the people, and appears a very proper person—As soon as the Bishop arrives he must see to this.—

Love to Em. God bless you

P. Robinson

J.B.R.

[written in margin] Tell Mr Crowley he will hear from me next post.

7. Other Letters Relative to the Settlement

(a) JOHN STRACHAN TO R. W. HORTON

[*Public Archives of Canada, Q 343 pt. 3, pages 551–3*]

19 Bury Street St. James's
5 July 1826

Dear Sir,

In returning Mr Robinson's statement I beg leave to remark, that it mentions 120 families to be actually on their lands, and 62 missing. making up 182 heads of families which were located in 1824.

[1]Author of *Ireland and Canada*, London, 1839.

In accounting for these 62 it is stated, that 8 are dead,—but their children or relatives will certainly claim the lands assigned them, which are indeed secured to them by a special law of the Province.

As to these eight therefore the object of Gov[t] is obtained—a family has been sent from Ireland, or if the dead persons have no families, their heirs will come out to claim the property, and thus the same lot may produce a double emigration.—

Nine are said to have gone to the United States—but it does not follow that they are lost to the Province.—the probability is, that they have gone to work on the Canals and public works to gain money to enable them to purchase cattle, which is quite usual, and that in a short time they will all return—This is the case with hundreds of Emigrants—They leave their lands for different periods from 3 to 24 months according as they are successful. But should such persons not return, which I conceive to be improbable (as it is their interest to return) the lots assigned them, being now in an improved settlement, will sell for more than it cost Gov[t] to bring the first Locatees out.

Of the thirty two heads of families still remaining in Canada it appears to me of very little consequence to His Majesty's Gov[t]. whether they have continued on their original Locations or not—Some may have joined other Irish Settlements of which there are several in the Province from having friends and relations or liking the lands better, for these poor people are kind to each other.

Many of them are doubtless employed on the Welland Canal earning money to purchase live stock, and will either return to their first location, or purchase lands in another part of the Colony. Others again are employed in getting out timber from the woods, & rafting it to Quebec, an employment which often commands great wages—such will come back at the end of the season—One has returned to Ireland and may be considered the only loss—So that in my opinion 181 out of 182 are satisfactorily accounted for—I remain

Dear Sir

Rob[t] W. Horton Esq. M.P.

Yours sincerely

John Strachan.

(*b*) THOMAS A. STEWART TO THE REVEREND JAMES CROWLY

[*Evidence before Select Committee on Emigration from the United Kingdom, 1826*]

Copy of a Letter to the Rev. Mr. Crowly, a Roman Catholic Clergyman, from Mr. Stewart, a Magistrate and a very respectable gentleman residing in the midst of the Irish Emigrants:

Douro, January 20, 1826.

Dear Sir, I beg to transmit the following Statement:

Some days ago I perused a paragraph in the 'Colonial Advocate' relating to Mr. Robinson's Emigrants, stating that 30 had left this in one night and gone to the United States, and that the rest were inclined to go also; this I conceive to be entirely false and without foundation. I am here living in the very midst of them, from 20 to 30 pass my door almost every day; I visit the camp every week, and at all times I take an opportunity of conversing with them on their affairs. I have always found them satisfied and happy. Some of them have told me with tears in their eyes that they never knew what happiness was until now. In general they are making great exertions in clearing land, and the exertions have astonished many of the old settlers. I conceive that this is in general owing to the great care Mr. Robinson has shown to their complaints and studying their wants. Not one complaint has there been against them by any of the old settlers, and it is the general opinion that where so large a body of people are brought together none could conduct themselves better. When we heard of their coming among us we did not like the idea, and immediately began to think it necessary to put bolts and bars on our doors and windows; all these fears have vanished. These fears I must acknowledge were in consequence of stories that were circulated before their arrival in this part, which have all turned out to be equally *false* with those of the 'Colonial Advocate'. Mr. Robinson has also been particularly fortunate in his choice in the medical department, as the care, humanity, and great attention shown by Dr. Reade could not be exceeded. I could say much more, but the fact will speak for itself.

Thomas Alexander Stewart.[1]

To the Rev. Mr. Crowly.

8. Sir Peregrine Maitland to Earl Bathurst, 1826

[*Public Archives of Canada, Q340, pt. 2, pages 412–18*]

Upper Canada,
York, 31st March 1826.

My Lord

I have the Honor to inform Your Lordship that, during the last and present months, I visited those parts of the Country in which the Emi-

[1]See biographical notes on Frances and Thomas Stewart, Section XI, Nos. 1 and 2.

grants from the South of Ireland, sent out by the Government in 1823 and 1825, have been settled by the Superintendant.[1]

Of those brought out in 1825, whom I first saw, I have much pleasure, in stating to Your Lordship that every evidence was afforded to me which the appearance, the conduct and the declarations of the Emigrants themselves could furnish, that they have escaped[2] all that benefit from the change in their situations which they could possibly have expected; and which the Government, with the kindest intentions towards them, could have desired.

I transmit herewith the official return of Mr Robinson, shewing the distribution of the whole number brought out; and when it is considered that the season in which they arrived was one of the most unhealthy, throughout these Provinces, that has been for some years experienced, the deaths which have occurred will not appear numerous; nor indeed could they be so regarded, under the circumstances, at any time—One family, and one only it will be seen has removed to the United States; and they had, I understand, the inducement of relations residing in that Country.

All are now located on lands, with which they have every reason to be satisfied; the progress made by many of them in clearing their farms, was witnessed by myself, and not without surprise; and the example of the Emigrants who preceded them, their own evident emulation, and the opinion of the Inhabitants of the Country who have observed their progress, all confirm me in the conviction, that, with the aid so benevolently afforded them, they may become, and that they are in every way likely to become, very useful Settlers in the Province; and to support themselves and their families in a state of comfort, to which they could scarcely have expected to attain.

Not one complaint has hitherto been made of their conduct, they were unavoidably detained at different points of their route, in populous parts of the Country, Where they might have indulged a disposition to riot, and to such outrages as very frequently occur, when a large number of such are assembled in a place in which they are strangers.

Your Lordship will perceive, in most of the addresses which were presented to me in the course of my journey through the Eastern parts of the Province, and which accompany my despatch to Your Lordship No 15., that the Inhabitants of the Country bear ample testimony to the good conduct of these Emigrants, and speak with much gratitude of the liberal policy of His Majesty's Government, in providing for their Settlement in Upper Canada.

[1]In one of her letters Frances Stewart gives a whimsical account of the visit to Peterborough. See *Our Forest Home* (2nd ed., Montreal. 1902), pp. 50–3.
[2]Probably a copyist's error for the word *experienced*.

As they are now on their lands, very much dispersed, and industriously occupied; having properties to improve, and families whom they can certainly support by their labor, I can see no reason for apprehending that they will not become speedily identified with the other classes of our population, and continue to live in the same peaceable obedience to the laws, which they have to this time exhibited. I am indeed fully persuaded that Your Lordship may congratulate yourself on the complete fulfilment of the most favorable expectations that could have been indulged, with regard to these people, and that the result of the measure, so far as it has proceeded, offers, in its effects here, every encouragement to its continuance.

With respect to the Emigrants of 1825, I cannot perceive that difference of religion has occasioned, or is likely to occasion, any disagreable occurrences among themselves, or between them and the other settlers. On the contrary, though they are in general Roman Catholics, they are kindly received by the Irish Protestants settled in the adjoining Township, and I trust nothing will occur to interrupt their friendly intercourse.

After having visited these Emigrants in their Settlements in the District of Newcastle, near the Rice Lake, I proceeded, accompanied by Mr Robinson the Superintendant, to the District of Bathurst, to learn the state of those who had come out in 1823; and I was pleased to find, that the only doubt I have felt, with respect to the measure, and which regarded its details, was groundless; for these people, from whom the assistance of Government Rations was withdrawn at the end of the year, are certainly not in a state of suffering, but, on the contrary, have advanced, judging from those whom I promiscuously visited, to a degree of comfort with which they have reason to be, and evidently are, entirely satisfied. Mr Robinson had been prevented by the unremitting attention which the other 2000 settlers required, and by the necessity of his constant presence with them, from paying an earlier visit to those of 1823 since his arrival from England; but the accounts which he received, on this occasion, were of the most gratifying description. He has directed a minute return to be made, from actual personal visitation at the house of every one of the settlers of 1823, which will soon be completed, and which will exhibit to Your Lordship, at one view, the progress they have made in cultivating their lands, acquiring stock &c. It will shew also what number of them are actually residing upon their lands, and what degree of truth there is in the report which has reached Your Lordship, of more than one half of them, having withdrawn to the United States. There were among these Emigrants some young unmarried men, of whom some were turbulent characters; and having taken an active part in the disturbance, which unfortunately occurred two years ago between them and the Scots Settlers, they happily found it prudent to leave the Country.

The general conduct of the Settlers, I am happy to be able to inform Your Lordship, is in every respect satisfactory. The affray of April 1824, the causes and progress of which[1] I reported fully, to Your Lordship at the time, does not appear to have left any unfriendly feeling behind it, and the Magistrates of the District publicly assured me, as Your Lordship will perceive in their address, that these settlers are, equally with the other Inhabitants, an industrious contented, and peaceable population.

Mr Robinson himself can best inform Your Lordship, by what methods that good understanding, industry, and rapid advancement, so very conspicuous in both his settlements have been promoted, I found the Emigrants forward and unanimous in expressing a most grateful sense of the unwearied attention personally given by him to their wants and interests. Most probably the prevalence of this sense contributed in a very material degree, to the complete success which the experiment has had; and when I consider the great numbers and peculiar spirit of the people, who have been so happily provided for, and how many local difficulties have been overcome in carrying the measure into effect, I cannot but feel, that the selection of the Superintendant has been most fortunate; and that the manner in which Mr Robinson has performed the Service committed to him by Your Lordship, is justly entitled to the highest commendation.

I make these remarks, not so much from a sense of Justice to Mr Robinson, who is sufficiently known to Your Lordship, as to impress upon Your Lordship the consideration, that the result, as it respects the condition, and conduct of the Emigrants, and their feelings towards the Government, might have been very different, under other circumstances; and that it cannot be safely anticipated, that future experiments, which may be differently conducted, may not be attended with very different consequences.

I have the Honor to be,
My Lord
Your Lordship's
Most Obedient
Humble Servant,
P. Maitland.

[1]See Andrew Haydon, *Pioneer Sketches in the District of Bathurst* (Toronto, 1925), pp. 143-61.

9. The Honourable Peter Robinson's Report, 1827

4th May 1827.

Sir.——

I have the honor to report for the information of Lord Goderich, that having been appointed to select and take charge of a limited number of Emigrants from the South of Ireland, and settle them in the Province of Upper Canada, I left London on the 8th April 1825, and reached Mitchelstown in the County of Cork, on the 12th. From this date to the 23rd day of May, I was employed in selecting persons agreeably to my instructions, superintending their embarkation, and discharging the different Ships employed in their transportation.

To choose about two thousand individuals out of fifty thousand who were anxious to emigrate, was found a very difficult and in many cases, an ungrateful task;—and altho I was assisted in the most zealous and friendly manner by the Noblemen, Magistrates and respectable Gentlemen of the Baronies from which they were taken, the utmost vigilance became necessary to prevent imposition.

In making my selection, I gave each man (head of a family) after being approved, a Certificate, and retained a duplicate, a method which I found on trial, to be a much better plan, than merely keeping a register of their names in a book. In a few instances, persons holding these Certificates sold them to others, who were perhaps, still more desirous of emigrating, and whose families nearly corresponded in age, and number to their own; but I believe, in no instance, did the deception succeed.

The Surgeon of each Transport had orders to report as soon as he had received his complement of Settlers on board, on which I proceeded to the Ship and mustered them all on the Main-deck—the Hatches were then closed except one, when in the presence of the Surgeon and Master, I took the Original Certificates which had been given over by the head of each family to the Surgeon, at the time of his embarkation, and from these after comparing them with the duplicates in my own possession, I called over the names of each individual belonging to the different families, and made them pass before me, and when I was satisfied they were of the age and description given in by the Father, and that no imposition had been practised, they were sent between decks.

In chosing [*sic*] the Emigrants the instructions that they should be small Farmers, able to make good Settlers, and without the means of supporting themselves in Ireland, were scrupulously adhered to.

In one particular I was induced to deviate, in a few instances, which was in admitting a very small number above the age of forty five. They are however, farmers of superior intelligence and character to the other Emigrants, and appear from their experience in agriculture, and their greater practical knowledge, capable of giving a good example to the other Settlers, and of contributing essentially to the making of this second experiment still more creditable than the first.

My anxiety to produce this desirable result, and the intelligence manifested by the persons in question, and the good characters which they produced, will, I hope, be deemed a sufficient excuse for this deviation in a very few instances.

Nor is it irrelevant to remark that aged Men and Women, when carefully selected, are of great service by their influence and advice, in keeping up order, temperance and kindliness among the Settlers, and in repressing discontent, insobriety and contention.

It was of great importance to me, that in selecting the persons deemed most proper to emigrate, I was assisted by the neighbouring Noblemen, Magistrates, and Gentry, because notwithstanding every precaution, murmurs were heard, and accusations were made.

These were the more difficult to remove or answer, because they seldom descended to particular cases, but were so conducted as to produce a general impression, if not contradicted, that the Emigrants selected, wore the exterior appearance, at least of having been exempted from that Distress which their removal from the Country was intended to remedy; and consequently that they were not of the description of persons whom it was the intention of Parliament to relieve.

It was fortunate that these things came to my ears before I left Ireland, as it afforded me an opportunity of submitting my instructions to several Gentlemen of the first respectability and honor, who could not be supposed in any way interested, and who had an opportunity by personal inspection, and inquiry to ascertain how far these instructions had governed my conduct.

I therefore applied to the Mayor of Cork and Sir Anthony Perrier, to accompany me on board of the Ships, Fortitude, Resolution, Albion, and Brunswick, then at Cove, and ready for Sea, that by the most minute investigation, they might ascertain how far the Settlers on board of these Ships corresponded with the description of persons whom I was instructed to Select. Their Certificate I beg leave to annex: Nor was this all, so deeply did I feel my responsibility that I invited Mr Horace Townsend and Mr Callaghan, to examine the Emigrants after they were all on board, and to assist me in re detecting any imposition which might have been practiced upon me, in order that even at that late period, the object of such imposition might be discovered and punished.

I was the more anxious to procure the assistance of these two Gentlemen, because I had been given to understand that they entertained a very unfavourable opinion of the mode of selection, and in particular imagined, that the recommendation of the Noblemen, Magistrates, and Gentry, to whom I had been particularly referred, had been confined to their own Tenantry.

The result was the most satisfactory; every suspicion was removed, and the approbation of the Gentlemen above noticed, given with the utmost sincerity and good will, to the faithfulness of my selection.

I beg to add the testimony of the Magistrates attending the Petty Sessions at Cecilstown, County of Cork.

"We hereby, Certify, that on Mr Robinson's arrival in this Country, in the year 1823, the people of our neighbourhood were disinclined to accompany him to Canada, appearing to doubt the advantages held out by the Government, to persons willing to emigrate to that Country being realized, on their arrival; and it was with great difficulty, the Gentlemen in whom they had confidence, could induce them to believe, that no deception was intended.

"That since that time their minds have undergone a total change, in consequence, as we conceive, of the favourable accounts that have been received from the Settlers of 1823. And that on Mr Robinson's recent arrival in this country, the applications were so very numerous that it became a matter of great difficulty to make a selection from amongst them, claims and qualifications being so nearly balanced.

"That no persons however, were approved of, but such as were recommended by the written or personal applications of the respectable Gentlemen from whose Neighbourhood they came, and were of the description we understood from Mr Robinson it was the intention of Government to prefer, such as the Inhabitants of the disturbed Districts, and farmers and others in reduced circumstances, unable to obtain an honest livelihood at home, or to pay their passage to Canada."

Before quitting this part of my subject, I feel also great pleasure in adding the testimony of thirty of the most respectable Gentlemen in the County of Cork, to the success of the former emigration, and the effect which it had produced on the population generally.

They also recommended one hundred families from their populous district, all of whom were totally without the means of subsistance but of those I could only take a very few.

"We the undersigned Magistrates Clergy, and principal Inhabitants of the Parishes of Passage, Monkstown, Shanabally, Barnaheely and Carrigline, beg leave to call your humane attention to the alarming state of our numerous labouring Classes in these extremely poor and populous parishes.

"We have tried various expedients by voluntary contributions, and through the aid of Collections at Charity Sermons, to mitigate the distress which so awfully exists in this part of the County of Cork, and in the Vicinity of the City on the verge of the Harbour. Various causes have arisen to create this peculiar distress, especially the number of idle hands who congregated from all parts, and who were thrown out of Employment by the stoppage of the great works on the fortifications of Spike-Island, and the completion of the Naval and Ordnance Works at Haulbowlin and Rocky Islands.

"Superadded to this, there are nearly two thousand Acres of Land unleased and untilled in a great measure, and consequently unproductive, close to the Town of Passage, and the Village of Monkstown. Poverty induced Fever—fever numerous deaths of heads of families, which have thrown numbers of Widows and Orphans on the bounty of the benevolent, who feel in this neighbourhood all the evils of absenteeship. You have Sir, reduced what was deemed theory in 1823, to practice, through your Skill, ability, and zeal, and your knowledge of Canada.

"You have removed the prejudices which ignorance produced against Emigration to that Colony, by the successful experiment already tried.

"We are of opinion, that about one hundred heads of families in this Barony, would gladly avail themselves of the bounty of Parliament to proceed under your directions to the proposed locations. We therefore hope that you will be pleased to take measures to relieve this District, from a portion of our unfortunate Population, who have no honest means of subsistence in the absence of productive Employment."

The whole number of Emigrants embarked amounted to 2024, in nine Transports as follows:

Fortitude.	Thomas Lewis, Master,	
	Mr Francis Connin, R.N. Surgeon.	
61 Men	Males, above 14	89
48 Women	do. under "	56
Sailed 10th May.	Females, above 14	75
	do. under "	62
	Total	282

Resolution.	Anthony Ward, Master.	
	Mr G. H. Reade, Surgeon.	
40 Men	Males, above 14	61
38 Women	do. under "	61
Sailed 10th May.	Females, above 14	58
	Do. under "	47
	Total	227
Albion.	John Mills, Master,	
	Mr Jno Thomson, R.N. Surgeon.	
37 Men	Males, above 14	56
31 Women	Do, under "	39
Sailed 11th May.	Females, above 14	52
	do under "	44
	Total	191
Brunswick.	Robert Blake, Master.	
	Mr Jno Tarn, R.N. Surgeon.	
63 Men	Males, above 14	108
58 Women	do. under "	76
Sailed 11th May.	Females, above 14	92
	do. under "	67
	Total	343
Star.	Joseph Becket, Master.	
	Mr Ninian McMorris, R.N. Surgeon.	
35 Men	Males, under 14	67
32 Women	do. under "	48
Sailed 13th May.	Females, above 14	55
	do, under "	44
	Total	214
Amity.	Wm Arrowsmith, Master.	
	Mr James W. Ternan, R.N. Surgeon.	
27 Men	Males, above 14	47
24 Women	do. under "	40
Sailed 16th May.	Females, above 14	42
	do. under "	18
	Total	147

Regulus.	George Dixon, Master.	
	Mr Mathew Burnside, R.N. Surgeon.	
29 Men	Males, above 14	52
25 Women	do. under "	39
	Females, above 14	36
Sailed 10th May	do. under "	30
	Total	157
Elizabeth.	Donald Morrison, Master.	
	Mr Pierce Power, R.N. Surgeon.	
45 Men	Males, above 14	84
31 Women	do. under "	40
	Females, above 14	56
Sailed 18. May	do. under "	30
	Total	210
John Barry.	Peter Roche, Master.	
	Mr W. Burnie, R.N. Surgeon.	
48 Men	Males, under 14	88
38 Women	do. under "	60
	Females, above 14	58
Sailed 25 May.	do under "	47
	Total	253

Having seen all the Emigrants embarked, and under weigh, I found it requisite to return to London to make the necessary pecuniary arrangements. Accordingly I left Cork on the 24th, and arrived in London on the 27th May, and having made such arrangements as were deemed sufficient, I got to Liverpool on the 8th, and sailed in the Panthea for New York, on the 9th of June.

The passage was unusually long, and I did not reach Niagara till the 28th July. Here, I learned that the Transports conveying the Emigrants had all arrived, having had very short passages, not any of them except the John Barry, having had more than 31 days. The greater number of the Settlers had been actually forwarded to Kingston, where they were encamped in Tents by order of His Excellency Sir Peregrine Maitland, and were anxiously waiting my arrival.

I likewise understood, that some of them were suffering from fever and Ague, occasioned by the excessive heat of the Season—the Thermometer having stood at 100 in the Shade, within the last ten days.

Having delivered Lord Bathursts dispatches to His Excellency Sir

Peregrine Maitland, and received the warmest assurances of support, in forwarding the Settlement of the Emigrants, as had indeed been strongly manifested in the measure which has been already adopted by His Excellency, in setting apart for their reception, the Townships in the rear of the Rice Lake, which consist of as fine land as there is in the Province.

Leaving Niagara on the 30th of July, I proceeded to York, and procured without delay, from the Surveyor General all the information in his possession, relative to the land which I was about to Settle.

On the third of August I arrived at Cobourg in a Waggon, a distance of 70 miles from York, and altho' I felt impatient to proceed to Kingston to see the Settlers, yet, on consideration, I thought I should forward my object more, by viewing the lands on which they were to be located, ascertaining the means of Communication, and the proper place for the depot of Stores and provisions. Instead therefore of going forward to Kingston, I went back into the interior, to ascertain these respective objects.

Having employed Mr McDonell, an intelligent and respectable young Man, well acquainted with the Country, as my Guide—I explored the different rivers and avenues of access, to the lands allotted for the Emigrants, and was highly gratified in discovering greater facilities of communication than I had anticipated, and that the tract was in every respect, highly eligible. I found that we could get our Provisions and Stores forwarded half the distance by Water, and that there was a central situation at the head of the Otanabee River highly convenient for a Depot.

Having spent six days in exploring the Woods, and satisfied myself as to the quality and situation of the land, I joined the Emigrants at Kingston. Here I found them as comfortable as could be reasonably expected—some of them suffering from fever and Ague,[1] owing to the intense heat of the Weather, tho' not in a greater proportion than the Inhabitants of the Province generally.

Every thing possible had been done for their benefit by His Excellency Sir Peregrine Maitland. He had appointed Colonel Burke, Deputy Superintendent, who was in charge at Kingston, on my arrival, and Dr Reade the Surgeon had been left at Prescott, to forward the Settlers who still remained behind.

On the 11th August I embarked five hundred on board of a Steamboat and landed them the next day at Cobourg on Lake Ontario, a distance of 100 miles—the remainder of the Settlers were brought up in the same manner, the boat making a trip each Week.

Our route from Cobourg to Smith, at the head of the Otanabee

[1]There were three hundred ill with these diseases, and thirty-three of the immigrants died.

River, lay through a Country, as yet, very thinly inhabited. The Road leading from Lake Ontario, to the Rice Lake, (12 Miles) hardly passable—and the Otanabee river, in many places, very rapid, and the Water much lower than it had been for many Years.

The first thing I did was to repair the road, so that loaded Waggons might pass; and in this Work I received every assistance from the Magistrates of the district, who gave me fifty pounds from the district funds and this Sum, together with the labour of our people, enabled me to improve the road in ten days so much, that our provisions and baggage could be sent across with ease and three large boats were transported on Wheels, from Lake Ontario, to the Rice Lake.

The Otanabee River is navigable for twenty four miles, altho' in many places it is very rapid, and at this Season there was not water sufficient to float a boat of the ordinary size over some of the Shoals. To remedy this difficulty, I had a boat constructed of such dimensions as I thought might best answer, to ascend the Rapids, and had her completed in eight days, so much depended upon the success of this experiment, that I felt great anxiety until the trial was made, and I cannot express the happiness I felt at finding that nothing could more fully have answered our purpose, and that this Boat sixty feet in length, carrying an immense burden, could be more easily worked up the Stream, than one of half the size, carrying comparatively nothing.

Now that I had opened the way to the Depot at the head of the river, there was no other difficulty to surmount than that which arose from the prevailing Sickness, the ague and fever, which at this time was as common among the old Settlers as ourselves.

The first party I ascended the River with, consisted of twenty men of the Country hired as axe men, and thirty of the healthiest of the Settlers: not one of these men escaped the ague and fever, and two died. This circumstance affords abundant proof that the Settlers were much better off, encamped in the open Country during the greatest heat of the Weather, where they were not only less liable to contract disease, but were also exempt from being tormented by the flies, which swarm in the Woods during the Summer months.

The location of the Immigrants by far the most troublesome and labourious part of the service, was completed before the Winter commenced, and I had a small log House built for each head of a family on their respective lots where they reside; and it gives me much pleasure to be enabled to assure you that they have been obedient and well conducted, and that they have cleared and cultivated as great a proportion of their land as could be expected, as will appear by the annexed return.

Their letters to their friends in Ireland, will sufficiently prove how far they are satisfied with their present condition,[1] and it will be easy

[1]See No. 11 for their address to Sir Peregrine Maitland in 1826.

for me to furnish you with such abundant evidence of their actual residence and industry as will fully satisfy you of their happy and prosperous condition.

With regard to myself, I shall only remark, that from the commencement of my appointment, I have felt the utmost anxiety for the success of the measure, and have not only devoted my whole time and thoughts to its progress and happy accomplishment, but (besides exploring the Country) I have resided constantly with the Emigrants in the Woods, from the 15th August 1825, to March 1827, and a greater part of that time under Canvass.

I embrace with pleasure, this opportunity of acknowledging my obligations to Colonel Burke the deputy Superintendent, and Mr Reade the Surgeon, for their able and zealous assistance, for altho' they suffered as well as myself, from the unusual heat and sickness of the Season, they were, nevertheless, most assiduous in the discharge of their duty.

After all, the general summary annexed of the actual state of the Settlers, their improvements, Cattle, and produce, will furnish his Lordship with more favourable and pleasing evidence than any thing I can say of the inestimable benefit conferred upon them, by their removal to Canada, and of the unquestionable success of this second experiment.

I have the honor to be
Sir,—
Your most obedient
Humble Servant.

Return of the Irish Emigrants of 1825,
up to the 24th November 1826.[1]

Distribution	Men	Women	Children	Total
Settled in the Newcastle district,	655	530	674	1,859
do. in the Bathurst, do......	20	19	28	67
Remained with friends in Lower Canada........	14	5	11	30
do, with do, at Kingston.........	2	"	"	2
Absent at Cobourg...............	1	1	3	5
Died at Sea, and in Canada.......	51	18	76	145
	743	573	792	2,108

Embarked at the Cove of Cork, total 2,024.
Born at Sea, 15, in Canada, 54....... 69
Joined in Canada.................. 15
2,108.

[1]Based upon the 2024 emigrants who embarked at Cork, the cost of this notable experiment in mass migration under state control and at state expense was £21 5s. per head.

Actual state of the Settlement, on the 24th November 1826.

General Summary

No.	Townships	No. of locations	No. of acres cleared	Produce raised this year: Potatoes bushels	Turnips bushels	Indian Corn bushels	Bushels Wheat sown this fall	Maple Sugar made in Spring	Purchased by themselves: Oxen	Cows	Hogs
1	Douro	60	245⅓	8251	4175	1777	80¾	1159	11	18	22
2	Smith	34	113¼	4800	1550	637	40¾	889	6	7	21
3	Otanabee	51	186	10500	4250	1395	38	1419	4	13	11
4	Emily	142	351⅓	22200	7700	3442	44⅓	2880	6	10	47
5	Ennismore	67	195	8900	3000	1042⅓	44⅓	1330	4	9	10
6	Asphodel	36	173	9150	2850	1733	86	1345	2	8	32
7	Marmora	6	35	1198	548	207	2	45	5	4	7
8	Ops	7	12	800	100	"	2	"	"	"	2
9	Ramsey	5	39	800	750	120	16		2	4	8
10	Goulbourn	4	18	600	500	10	2			3	1
11	Huntley	3	18⅓	600	200	75	7			4	5
	Total	415	1,386¼	67,799	25,623	10,438⅓	363⅓	9,067	40	80	166

10. Address to Sir Peregrine Maitland on his Visit to Peterborough, 1826

[*Presented on behalf of the immigrants by Patrick Barragan, a school-teacher, this interesting and characteristically Irish address is printed in the* Appendix to the Report of the Select Committee of the British Parliament . . ., *1826, p. 299*]

To His Excellency Sir Peregrine Maitland, &c., &c.,

We, the Irish Emigrants recently brought out by Colonel Robinson to this country, feel grateful to our gracious good King, and to His Majesty's worthy, good, and humane government for all they have, and we hope yet intend, to do for us.

We also are well pleased, and entertain the best wishes for, our Worthy Chief Mr. Robinson for all he has done for us[1]; and we are fully sensible that his fine and humane feelings will not permit him to leave anything undone that may forward our welfare.

Please Your Excellency, we are totally at a loss for words adequate to express the thanks and gratitude we owe Doctor Reade for his active, skillful, and unremitting care, &c., of us. We are likewise thankful to, and well pleased with, the officers placed over us.

Please Your Excellency, we agree very well, and are pleased with the proceedings of the old settlers amongst us, as it is in the interest of us all to do the same. And should an enemy have the presumption ever to invade this portion of His Majesty's dominions, Your Excellency will find that we, when called upon to face and expel the common foe, will to a man follow our brave commanders; not an Irish soul shall stay behind; and if we have no better weapons in our hands, mow them down with our Irish shillelahs.

Please Your Excellency, we labor under a heavy grievance, which we confidently hope Your Excellency will redress, and then we will be completely happy, viz:—the want of clergymen to administer to us the comforts of our Holy Religion, and good school-masters to instruct our children.

We now beg leave to retire, wishing Your Excellency long life, good health, and every success.

GOD SAVE THE KING

[1]If corroboration were needed it is afforded by John Richards, sent out by the British Government to investigate the success of the emigrations of 1823 and 1825. "I was two or three days at Peterborough," he wrote, "during which time perhaps thirty or forty settlers, and some with their families, came in to see Mr. Robinson, and the manner in which they met him was quite affecting; it was more to bless him as a benefactor than to receive him as a visitor." (Sir R. W. Horton, *Ireland and Canada* (London, 1839), p. 36.)

11. Progress of the Robinson Settlers by 1847

[Papers Relative to Emigration to Canada, *pp. 10–11*]

(No. 137.)

Copy of a DESPATCH from Earl *Grey* to Governor-general the Right Honourable the Earl of *Elgin*.

Downing-street, 18 November 1847.

My Lord,

Referring to your Lordship's despatch, No. 82, of the 26th of August last, enclosing a return of the assessed value of certain townships in the Newcastle District, in Western Canada, settled by pauper emigrants from Ireland between the years 1825 and 1828, for the purpose of being laid before Parliament, I have to inform your Lordship that I gather, from two Reports of a Select Committee of the House of Commons on Emigration, dated on the 26th May 1826, and 29th June 1827, that 2,024 Irish pauper emigrants, embarked from Cork in the year 1825 for Upper Canada, under the superintendence of Mr. Peter Robinson; that of this number 621 men, 512 women, and 745 children were located on the Newcastle District, and that the total expense of the conveyance of these emigrants from Ireland to Canada, and of their settlement at Newcastle, including their sustenance up to the period at which their first crops enabled them to provide for themselves, was 43,145 *l.*, no portion of which appears to have been repaid by the settlers.

I have now to request that your Lordship will ascertain and report to me, whether the townships, of which the assessed value is contained in your despatch, No. 82, are the townships on which these Irish pauper emigrants were settled, and if not, that you will furnish me with any information which it may be in your power to obtain respecting the formation of these settlements.

I have, &c.
(signed) *Grey*

(No. 30.)

Copy of a DESPATCH from Governor-general the Right Honourable the Earl of *Elgin* to Earl *Grey*

Government House, Montreal, 15 March 1848.
(Received 10 April 1848.)

My Lord,

With reference to your Lordship's Despatch, No. 137, of the 18th November, calling for further information respecting the settlements formed in the year 1826 by emigrants from Ireland, under the superintendence of Mr. Robinson, I have the honour to communicate such additional particulars as it has been in my power to collect from the scanty records remaining in the public offices here, relating to those settlements, and from inquiries which I have instituted on the spot.

Enclosed is a return of the number of acres granted to Mr. Robinson's emigrant's in each township, and returns in detail showing the present condition of every lot so granted, that is to say, the number of acres in each lot (generally 100,) the number of acres now cleared and under cultivation, the number of souls, houses, cattle, &c., on each lot. From these details it will be sufficiently apparent, that none of these townships were settled exclusively by the emigrants of 1826. Since that period the remaining lands have continued to be taken up by voluntary settlement, and the present condition of these townships may be gathered from the following Table, compiled from the best information that can be obtained.

FROM whence did you emigrate to Upper-Canada, and when?	Co Wexford in 1825
What was your trade or occupation at home? And what were your circumstances when you embarked?	a farmer I had about £20
DID you come out independently of any public assistance?	I did
IF you were assisted by the public, what assistance was given you, and under whose superintendence were you?	
HAD you any money when you came out, and how much?	£20
WHAT are your present circumstances, as to house and other buildings, lands cleared and fenced, and farming stock?	a House and Barn 3 Cows 3 head of Cattle 3 Pigs
WHAT family had you with you when you embarked?	Wife and three Children
DID any of your family die on the passage to Quebec; and, if so, how many?	None
WHAT family have you now?	Wife and five Children
Have any died since you landed at Quebec; and, if so, how many?	
WHAT state of health were they in during the last year?	Very Good

Peter Robinson Papers, Peterborough Public Library

QUESTIONNAIRE ISSUED IN 1828 (*a*)

To what value had you produce or live stock to dispose of in the last year, above what you required for your family?	7 Bushels of Grain
On what kind of provisions does your family usually subsist?	pork flour Meat Milk Butter and potatos
Are you pleased with your situation in Upper-Canada?	
Have your comfort and happiness been increased by coming to Upper-Canada?	the are
Would you advise any of your friends in the Country you left, whose situation there is the same as yours was, to come out to Upper Canada upon the same terms that you did?	I Would
Suppose the government had furnished you and your family with a passage out, paid your expenses to your lands, given you 100 acres free of expense, provisions for a year, and the necessary farming utensils, and that this was done upon the condition that you should repay the sum advanced by annual instalments, beginning to pay at the end of years, after you had been settled, and paying pounds in each year after, until the whole was paid up, would it have been in your power to make those payments?	it Would
Knowing Upper Canada as you do now, would you think it advisable for a head of a family in Ireland, who is now poor, and without employment, to accept of such terms?	I Sertenly would
Would it be better for him to receive from government, after landing in Quebec, £60, or whatever may be necessary for taking himself and his family to his land, finding him provisions for a year, and farming utensils, upon the condition of his repaying to the government, the amount so advanced to him, either in money or the produce of his land, or to be merely landed at Quebec, and afterwards to depend upon his own exertions for establishing himself and family?	I think it would be Better to take the provisions utensils &c and to repay Government

d
11 June. 1828

Joseph Dogherty

Peter Robinson Papers, Peterborough Public Library

QUESTIONNAIRE ISSUED IN 1828 (*b*)

——	Present Number of Acres settled in the Township. Total	Number of Acres settled by Mr. Robinson's Emigrants.	Present Number of Inhabitants.	Present Assessed Value of Rateable Property.
				£.
Douro - -	25,740	6,000	1,194	14,751
Smith - -	33,410	3,000	1,989	26,828
Otonabee - -	48,138	5,200	2,689	36,307
Ennismore- -	8,090	6,600	463	4,169
Asphodel - -	22,013	3,600	870	14,022
Emily - -	35,899	13,800	2,341	20,667
Ops - - -	33,831	610	1,855	20,972

It must be observed, that in the year 1826, when Mr. Robinson brought out the Irish emigrants, the above townships were all wilderness lands, in the rear of the Newcastle District, and far removed from the settled tracts. They now form part of the District of Colbourne which has the flourishing town of Peterborough for its chief town, a town first laid out in the same year of 1826.

I have, &c.

(signed) *Elgin & Kincardine*

Enclosure 1, in No. 4.

No. 1.—Return of the Number of Acres in each of the under-mentioned Townships of *Upper Canada*, located by Emigrants from the South of *Ireland*, under the superintendence of the late Honourable *Peter Robinson*, in the year 1826; also exhibiting the Number of Acres in the said Townships respectively, for which Patents have since issued.

Townships	Number of Acres Located	Number of Acres Patented.
Douro- - - - -	6,000	5,2000
Smith - - - - -	3,000	2,300
Otonabee - - - -	5,200	5,050
Ennismore - - - -	6,600	4,600
Emily - - - - -	13,800	12,200
Asphodel - - - -	3,600	1,800
Ops - - - - -	610	300
Total Located - -	38,810	
Total Patented - -	- - -	31,450

Of the unpatented lands, the parties concerned are from time to time proving their claims, and applying for patents; the decease of the locatees in some instances rendering it necessary to prove before the Heir and Devisee Commission their claims.

A very small proportion of the lots have been resumed in consequence of the locatees abandoning their lands.

V. TRANSPORTATION: THE TRENT CANAL

THIS SECTION and that upon the Peter Robinson emigration of 1825, containing as they do so many documents previously unpublished, form the core of this volume. Wide research has unearthed a great deal of value on the Trent lakes and rivers, apart altogether from the more obvious printed reports of surveys, notably those of N. H. Baird. After Champlain was taken by the Hurons over the route in 1615, not much use was made of it for two centuries. But in 1785, and from time to time thereafter, maps, reports, and surveys were made so that the Government could decide whether the Toronto Portage was a better means to reach Lake Simcoe than was the Trent system, or whether there were not alternative routes to the north or east of the Trent lakes which might be preferable to either of the others as a connecting link with the Ottawa River or Lake Ontario. The decision in favour of the Toronto Carrying-Place shelved all thought of the Trent until the arrival of the first settlers along "the front" in the seventeen-nineties and in the Trent Valley a quarter century later. The exploitation of the timber resources then attracted men of enterprise and capital, and it was only a matter of time before the Trent Canal was under way, though the slow, intermittent development which characterised it throughout resulted in its being outmoded and of little value long before completion. The Frobisher letter (No. 1), and its accompanying map, indicate that but little of an exact nature was known of the Trent waterway in 1785. The Collins Map of 1790 (No. 2) is of special value for its careful delineation of the four main carrying-places connected with the route. No. 3, Lieutenant Catty's survey of a possible alternative route to the north, discouraged further efforts in that direction. John William Bannister's rather visionary and impracticable plans for canal construction (No. 4) are of interest, especially because of his early prominence as a settler on the shores of Rice Lake. N. H. Baird's surveys of the eighteen-thirties, Nos. 7 and 8, are, of course, of pre-eminent importance, but the piecemeal construction was unworthy both of his survey and of the need as it existed in the eyes of his contemporaries—as exemplified in No. 10. Nos. 11 and 12 indicate the mass of correspondence, largely in the Public Archives of Canada, that remains to testify to the ramifications of the Trent development;

and No. 13 is an historical statement of what had been accomplished when the Federal Government took over the canal at the time of Confederation.

1. Benjamin Frobisher Describes the Trent Route, 1785

[*Public Archives of Canada, C.O. 42, Volume 47*]

Montreal 2nd May 1785.

Sir

. . . Since I had the Honor to receive Your letter of the 10th March, I have made every enquiry in my power, not only in Town but in different parts of the Country, respecting the practibility of a Communication from Lake Ontario to Lake Huron, and am sorry to say, all my endeavours to acquire some knowledge of it are far from being satisfactory.

I have seen several persons who have gone from hence to Lake Huron by the carrying place of Toronto, but have only met with one who set out from the Bay of Kentie, and that so far back as the year 1761, and the knowledge he seems to have of the Country he travelled thro' I consider as very imperfect, I have however laid it down, in the inclosed Sketch, more to shew that there is such a Road, than any opinion I have of its being Correct—I am told the Lands from the Bay of Kentie, to Lake la Clie abound with good Wood, and are generally fit for Cultivation, there are several Villages of the Mississagues on different parts of that Road, who raise Indian Corn, and other grain, and whose friendship it will be necessary to Cultivate, if upon survey it should be found practicable but if I may rely on information, there is very little probability of establishing in that quarter a Communication for Boats or Large Canoes, on account of the Water being generally very shallow between the different Lakes, except in the Spring, and even then, it is described to me, as being insufficient for large Canoes, not to mention the Carrying Places, which are Six or Seven in Number to reach Lake la Clie, and I am told two of them are near three leagues in length; I am however informed that to the distance of the Rice or the *Folle avoine*[1] Lake from the Bay of Kentie, there is plenty of Water for Boats of any Burthen—From all these circumstances as related to me, I judge a Communication that way without paying any regard to the Carrying Places, to be from the want of Water totally impracticable, however as I believe there is no Man in the Country capable of giving any certain

[1]Literally translated "wild oats." As wild rice much resembles oats during growth, "the Lake of Wild Oats" is almost as appropriate as "the Rice Lake."

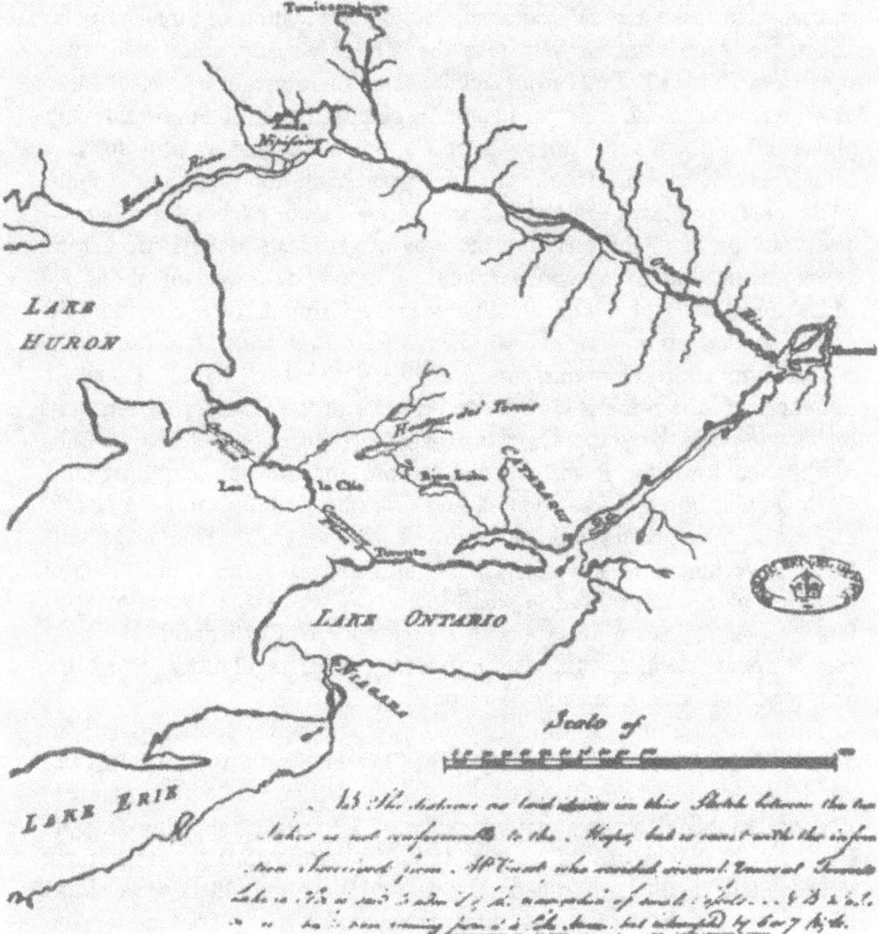

Public Archives of Canada

FROBISHER MAP OF 1785
Three alternative routes to the west are shown

information about it, I think a Project that holds out so many advantages to the Province at large ought not to be relinquished, until it is found upon Survey, to be as represented really impracticable and should that be the Case, the next object that offers to Introduce a Communication between the two Lakes is the Carrying place of Toronto which from the Ontario side to Lake Huron is a direct line, is no more than 100 Miles, and by Water it does not exceed 160—That is Toronto 45 Miles, Lake La Clie 37, thence to Lake Huron over Land 18, or by the River as laid down in the inclosed sketch about 70.

I am told Lake LaClie will admit of the Navigation of small vessels, and there is no want of Water in the Rivers already mentioned, that runs from it, into Lake Huron, but it seems there are in it several Falls of Water, which with other obstructions occasions Six or Seven carrying places, all of them short ones—large Canoes have gone up and down it at different times, but am told it is not practicable for Boats untill some of the carrying places are levelled so as to get them over upon rollers—To avoid this river there is no other way of getting to Lake Huron from Lake LaClie, but by a road overland as before described of about 18 Miles some parts of which are low Marshy Grounds of a considerable extent so that embrasing every object for the purpose of Establishing a sure and short Communication between the two Lakes, I am of opinion from the present knowledge we have of the Country, it can only be Accomplished by the Carrying place of Toronto to Lake LaClie, and thence down the River to Lake Huron, and tho' the length of land Carriage will be very great, yet as it is in a fine Country, and the Lands as I am told exceeding good, it would require very little encouragement from Government to have it Settled; and provided the Lands on the Carrying place are granted in small lots and not in large Tracts to opulent Proprietors, we may expect in a high state of Cultivation, in which case, Carriages will not be wanting under proper regulations, to Insure at a moderate rate a speedy Transport.

These Sir are my Sentiments, until we are better informed of the nature of the Communication from the Bay of Kentie to Lake LaClie, and let what will be the Event of that Survey, I conceive there is a necessity for Establishing the Carrying place of Toronto as speedily as possible, as in the course of a very few Years the Settlers, from their vicinity, and facility of Transport to Lake Huron, would be in a situation to supply the Provisions that are wanted by the Traders for the Northern Countries, which under the most precarious circumstances, such as the failure of Crops &c they have hitherto been obliged to procure from Detroit, and should the United States be put in possession of the Posts, their Situation will be stil more precarious, the Americans will have it in their power to injure or Ruin, every Man from this part of the Province who depends on receiving Provisions from that Settlement, from which and other reasons needless to ennumerate, I submit to Your Honor the propriety of encouraging Farmers to take up lands on the North Side of Lake Huron, at such places as will admit of Cultivation, particularly in the Two Tessalone, all of which Collectively will facilitate the procuring of Provisions, and give the Traders from hence a manifest Superiority over their American Neighbours. On the other hand we must also consider the advantages that would arrise from

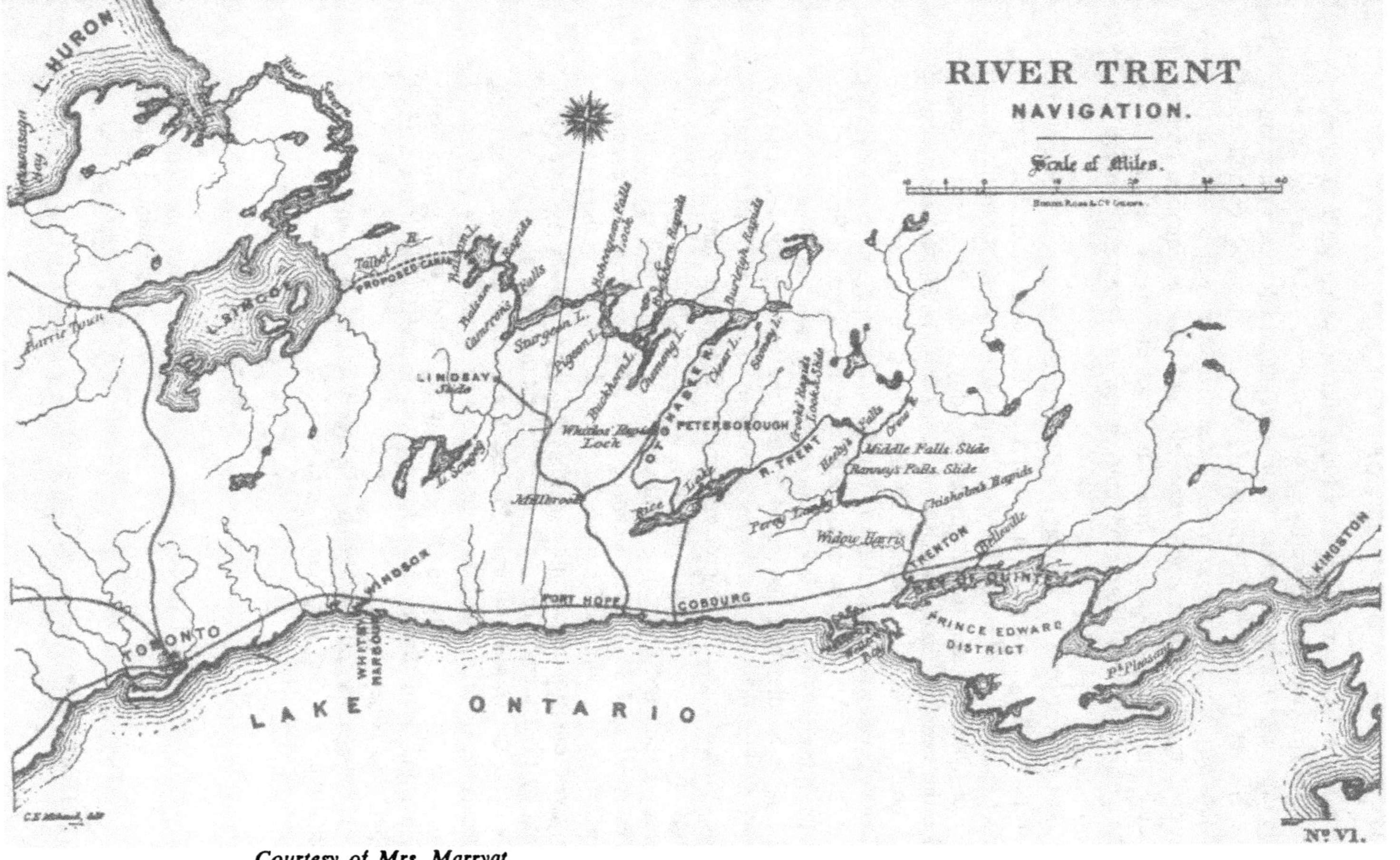

Courtesy of Mrs. Marryat

NAVIGATION OF THE TRENT
(*General Report of the Commission of Public Works*, 1867)

so ready a Communication with Lake Huron, which while it extends, and adds strength and Security to our Frontier, (If I may be allowed the expression) with the other Settlements afford effectual Protection to the Natives between the Two Lakes, who are Mississagues and some Tribes of Chippawas, from whom I conceive there will be no difficulty in making the purchase, more especially as I believe their best hunting Lands are at some distance from the Tract that would be chosen for the purpose of establishing an entercourse of Transport between the two Lakes.

The present road by the Ottawa River, & the communication now in prospect will not Admit of a comparison with each other. The first is most eminently dangerous for the Transport of Goods, from the Number of Cataracts, and the length and rapidity of the River, not to mention the carrying Places, which from hence to Lake Huron, are upwards of Forty in Number, over which the Canadians carry the Goods, & Canoes occasionally, and it is to their dexterity alone and the knowledge they have of the management of Canoes in this particular Branch of the Inland business, that so few accidents happen, whereas Boats of about the same burthen, are navigated by half the number of Men, and for their Service they are always to be had on more easy Terms than for the other, as it requires a greater degree of Experience, and which nothing can give them but that of being constantly employed in that business—I shall not pretend to estimate the difference of Expence in the Transport, as I do not see it can be done with any degree of exactness until the other Communication is Established, however in the mean time to give Your Honor some idea of what it may be, I must Acquaint You, that by the Ottawa River, it is generally estimated at about twenty Per Cent on the Canoes assorted for the Trade, but in Cases of sending Provisions or other Articles of little value here, the Freight to Michilimakimac on every Package of One hundred pounds in weight is about Fifty, and from that to Sixty Livres, and to the Grand Portage from Eighty to Ninety.—

If these hints and the Sketch I inclose you can be of any Service, I shall think my Self very happy in having laid them before You.

I have the Honor to be
Most respectfully
Sir

Your obedient and
most humble Servant

(Sign'd) Benj^m Frobisher

The Honble Henry Hamilton Esqr

2. The Collins Map of 1790

[Manuscript Notes RE *the Portages along the Trent, in "A Plan of the District of Nassau in the Province of Quebec, Compiled in the Surveyor-General's Office Pursuant to an Order in Council of the 22nd day of February, 1790, and dated Quebec this 1st day of October 1790." It is signed by Samuel Holland, Surveyor-General, and John Collins, Deputy Surveyor-General. The copy in the Surveys office of the Department of Lands and Forests, Ontario Parliament Buildings, appears to be the original, as the other two known copies are without the Notes. The two notes on the Toronto Carrying Place are omitted here]*[1]

(1) *Northerly Part of the Trent (Healey's Falls)*:
'This fall is twelve feet high the Hill you ascend at landing is on a level with the top of the Fall, the Carrying Place across is twenty five Chains in length, the road is good and you embark on a level with the Water.—'

(2) *A Short Distance South (Middle Falls)*:
'This Fall six feet high, the Hill at landing is twelve Feet, the Carrying place across the Point, is twenty Chains, and the road is level and good to where you embark.—'

(3) *A Short Distance further South (Ranney's Falls)*:
'A Beautiful Fall of fifteen feet high, the bank at Landing is three feet, the Carrying place on the opposite side is agreeable to the dotted line being forty Chains in length, and a good level road to where you embark, you then descend a Hill of twenty feet,.—'

(4) *At the Point later called Percy Landing (Percy Boom)*:
'A: A Salt Spring discharges into this River, Three Gallons of the Water makes one Gallon of Salt, the Natives make great Quantities of it.—'

(5) *The Portage*[2] *from Percy Landing to the Upper Trent near the East End of Rice Lake*:
'A B Carrying Place of eight Miles and Seventy six Chains through and [*sic*] Excellent Country for making a road, Should this Communication be Established by opening this Road, you shorten the distance thirteen Miles and avoid three Falls, as laid down on the Plan on the opposite side.—' [*i.e.*, numbers 1, 2, and 3 above.]

[1]They are given, though with several errors in transcription, in Percy J. Robinson's scholarly *Toronto during the French Régime* (Toronto, 1933), pp. 198 and 204.

[2]No efforts have been made to trace accurately the route of this Indian carrying-place, which was no doubt followed by Champlain in 1615. But Mrs. Helen Marryat is actively investigating clues in the region, such as Indian campsites, burial grounds, and other evidences of a well-travelled route in times past; such research, however, is complicated by extensive changes in the height and course of the Trent due to timber shutes, mill-dams, and locks.

(6) *The Ganaraska*[1] *Carrying Place* (*Port Hope to Rice Lake near Bewdley*):

'N O. Carrying Place from Lake Ontario to the Rice Lake is is [*sic*] eleven Miles and ten Chains, through an excellent Country for making a road, the first four Miles the land is very good, the remaining part is high Sandy land.—This road might be made Compleat for fifty Pounds Currency. If this Communication should be made use of it will be Necessary to have a Post at N, and another at O, in order to forward the Transport.—'

(7) *The Chemong Portage from the site of Peterborough* (*Little Lake*) *to Lake Wabuscommoug* (*Chemong*):[2]

'C D Carrying Place of Six Miles four Chains and one Perch, through a very good Country for making a road by opening this Communication you shorten the distance twenty Miles, you avoid three Carrying Places, and a great number of Rapids of very Strong Water, many so very shoal that in the fall of the Year you have great dificulties to pass with light Canoes.—'

[1]Another Indian name for Port Hope–Cochingomink–signifies "the commencement of the carrying-place." The Collins Map of 1790 shows the carrying-place west of the River Ganaraska (later called Smith's Creek), while a Port Hope historian says that it began on the east side and continued through blazed trees, "a direct and most convenient route from Smith's Creek to Sackville's Creek, at which point the Indians were accustomed to launch their canoes. Its course lay to the eastward of the present gravel road, sometimes running as far as a mile away. As the woods have been gradually cleared away all traces of this old road have been obliterated." (W. Arnot Craick, *Port Hope Historical Sketches* (Port Hope, 1901), p. 44). The Collins Map gives the length of the portage as eleven miles and ten chains. Stuart Ryan of Port Hope, an authority on the town's history, says that natural features suggest that the carrying-place commenced on the west side of the mouth of the river, crossed it just below the present Art School, and continued along the east bank to a point near Dale, probably along or near the present Cavan Street, the first settlers' line of communication with the north. Mr. Ryan believes the name Cochingomink erroneous, and that the proper name of the Indian village at the mouth of the Ganaraska was Pemetascutiang or Pemetash Wationg, among numerous variants, a name apparently brought down from Rice Lake (Letter to the Editor, March 7, 1956).

[2]The following table gives the Indian and English names of the chief lakes and rivers of the Trent system under three main heads, from east to west:

Chewett's Map of 1789	*Collins' Map of 1790*	*Later Maps*
Saggettewedgewam River	(not named)	Trent River
Rice Lake	Rice Lake	Rice Lake
Lake Cheboutequion	Lake Cheboutequion	Salmon Trout, Rock, or Stoney Lake
Lake Wabuscommough	Lake Wabuscommoug	Mud or Chemong Lake
Lake Annlequion Checom	Lake Annleequionchecom	Sturgeon Lake

Other units of the system, such as the Otonabee River, Lovesick Lake, Buckhorn,

Collins map of 1790, Surveys Department, Ontario Parliament Buildings

THE PETERBOROUGH-CHEMONG PORTAGE

Annleequionchecom is Sturgeon Lake, *Cheboutequion* is Stoney Lake, and *Wabuscommoug* is Chemong Lake

---

Cameron, and Balsam Lakes, are not named on the early maps. A variant of the Indian name for the Trent is "Saggettaweddaw," and the Indians are known to have called Rice Lake "Pemedashcoutayang" ("Lake of the Burning Plains"). "Shemong" is Indian for "canoe," and "Otonabee" is interpreted "Waters running swiftly, flashing brightly." Salmon Trout Lake was subsequently given two names: Clear Lake for the southern and westerly parts, and Stoney Lake for that portion east of Boschink Narrows, earlier called "Boshing," interpreted "spattered with many islands." See Introduction, pp. xxxvi and xxxvii.

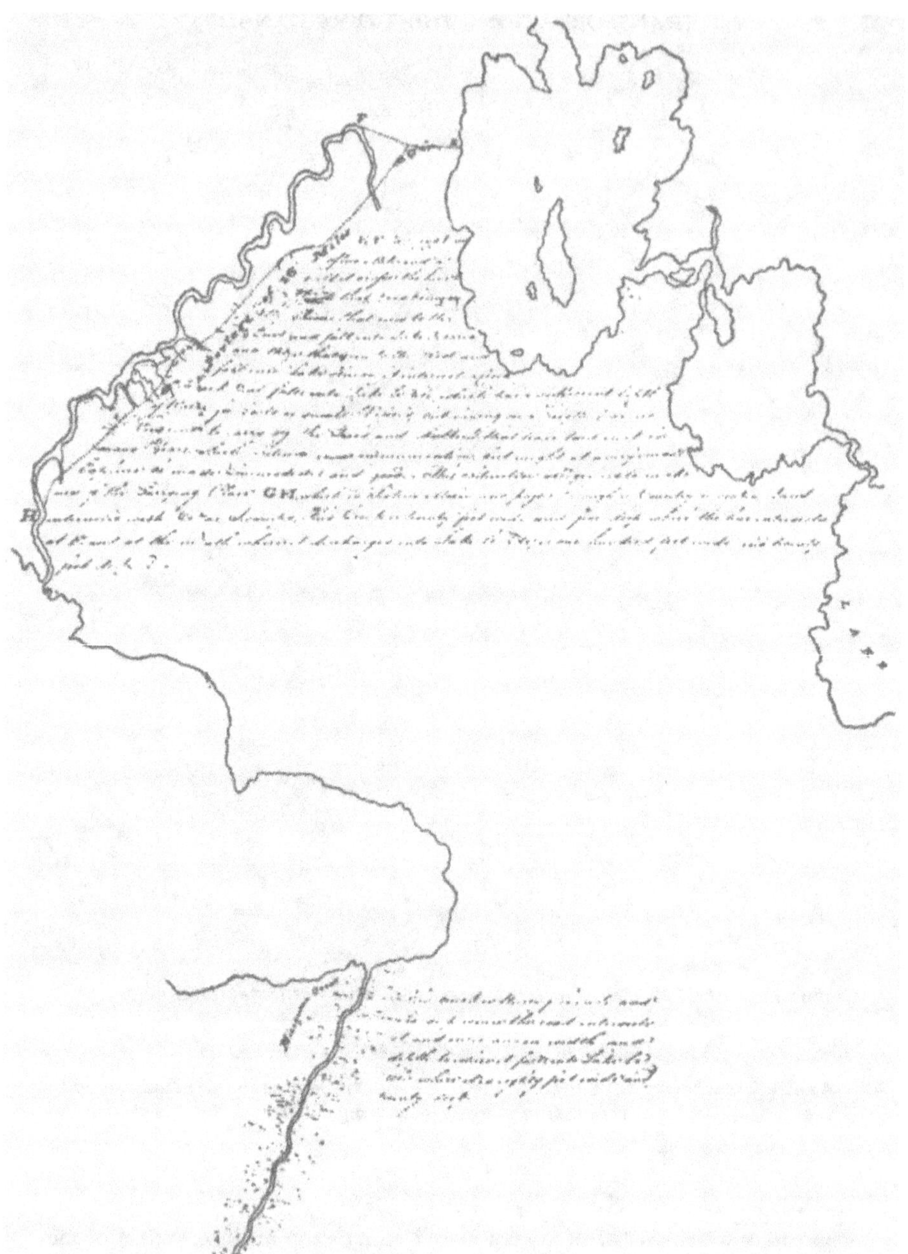

Collins map of 1790

THE TALBOT PORTAGE

Ouskebawkning ("green leaf place where we leave the river") connected Lakes Simcoe and Balsam. The lower inscription describes the upper part of the Toronto carrying-place, which followed a creek to Lake Simcoe—variously known in the French period as *lac aux Claies, lac Le* (or *La*) *Clie*, and Lake Toronto

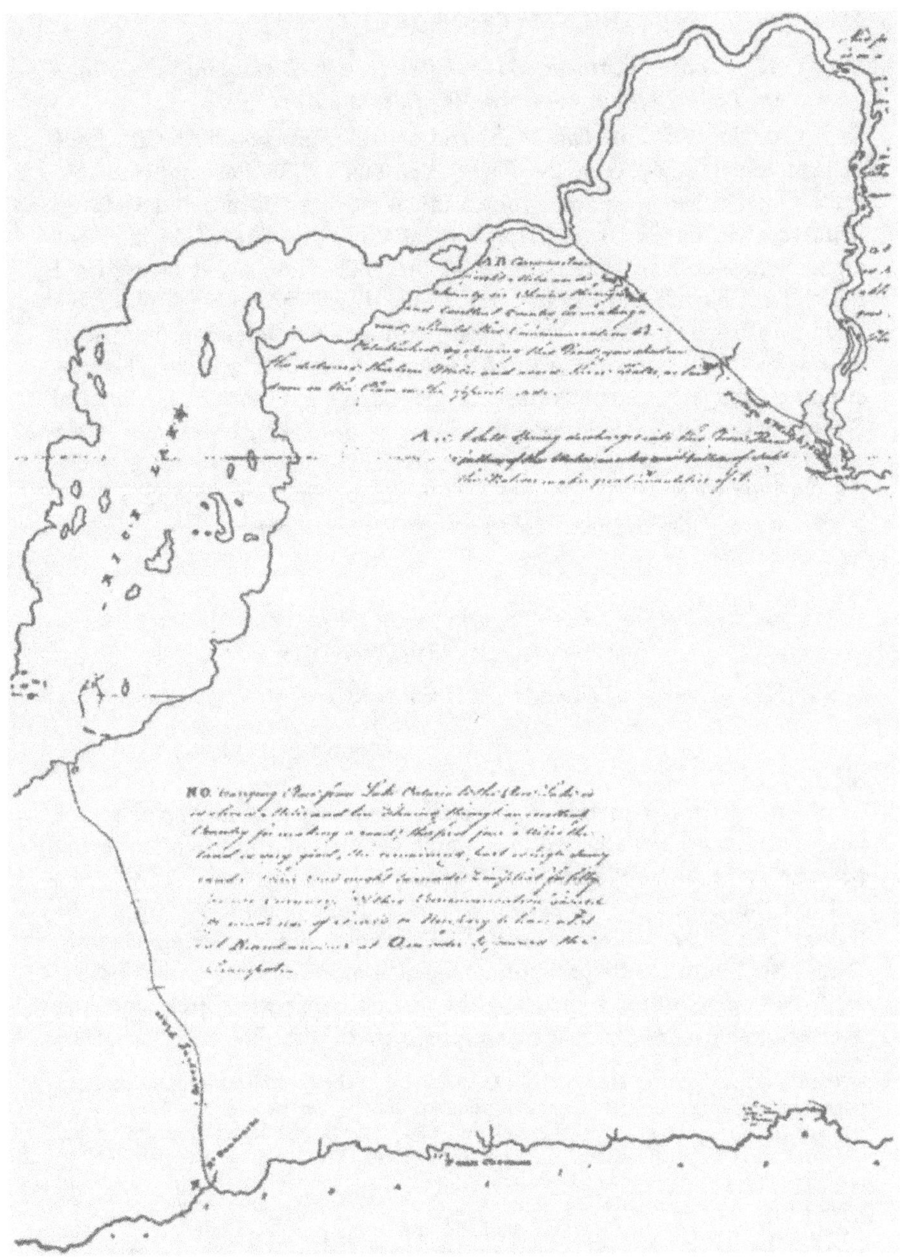

Collins map of 1790

THE GANARASKA AND TRENT PORTAGES

These Indian carrying-places led to Rice Lake, called by the French *Folle Avoine* ("wild oats"), and known to the Indians as *Pamadusgodoyong* or *Pemedash-coutayang*, because of the plains on the southern shore

(8) *The Talbot Portage*[1] *of 16 miles from "Champlain's Landing" on Lake Le Clie (Simcoe) to Balsam Lake*:

'E F Carrying Place of two Miles and a half it crosses the heigth [*sic*] of land that lays between the Rivers that run to the East and fall into Lake Ontario and those that run to the West and fall into Lake Huron it intersects a Creek Creek [*sic*] that falls into Lake le Cle, which has a sufficient Depth of Water for Boats or small Vessels, but laying on a heigth [*sic*] has no Current to carry off the Trees and Rubbish that have laid in it for many Years, which obstruct the Communication, but might at a very small Expence be made Commodious and good.—This obstruction obliges us to make use of the Carrying Place G H, which is Sixteen Miles, and passes through a Country of broken Land intersected with Cedar Swamps, This Creek is twenty feet wide and five deep, where the line intersects at F. and at the mouth where it discharges into Lake le Cle, is one hundred feet wide and twenty feet deep.—'

3. Lieutenant J. P. Catty's Survey of a Route between Lake Simcoe and the Ottawa, 1819

[*Public Archives of Canada, Public Works I, Vol. 9, pp. 25–30*]

Montreal 1st October 1819

Sir

I have the honor to report to your Excellency that in pursuance of your instructions I proceeded to examine the course of the Waters laying between Lake Simcoe and the Otawa–

I left the Lake by a River which I have every reason to suppose the Talbot river, but which I cannot determine without seeing Captain Owens Survey of it. We had not ascended it more than two miles before we found our Course impeded by the Stream being completely choaked by trees fallen across it—We here commenced the first carrying Place

[1]Some years ago the Honourable Leslie Frost, Prime Minister of Ontario, engaged in research upon this ancient road, probably the province's oldest. With the aid of early maps and surveys, later road surveys passing over parts of the old trail, and Superintendent A. L. Killaly of the Trent Canal, he was able to establish that the present road, the carrying-place on the Collins Map, and Champlain's trail are essentially the same. On the Collins Map are shown the Grass River, half a dozen smaller streams, and low swampy places along the route. In 1834–35, when J. Smith surveyed it, the road was so closely defined that a more recent road following it was surveyed into French-style lots with narrow frontage and great depth. It was apparently intended that these lots should be occupied by Indians as a Reserve, and one Cottingham of Omemee was given the contract to erect thirty houses for "Christian Indians" at Indian Point, the heathen apparently being left to fend for themselves. The Prime Minister has in mind a suitable historical marker for this road.

of about twelve miles through a flat Country very finely timbered and the land to all appearance of the first quality We now and then came upon the river and found the Channel narrower and Shallow, not more than two feet water in deepest Parts. The River, however, rises two feet at least in the Spring which would make this part navigable for Batteaux were it cleared of the timber. At the end of this Portage the River widens into a fine deep Stream with about twelve feet Water on an average, which continues for about five miles when the River again becomes Shallow and unavigable even for Canoes wherever there is deep water it so narrow that there appears scarce room for a Batteau to pass—The bed of the river about ten miles higher up is entirely dry and the Water passes under ground for about half a mile, and there Seems but little appearance of any Channel for boats, even when the Water is highest—From this place to the first Carrying Place to the Lakes the river is navigable though very much choaked by fallen trees. The land on each side is low but of good quality—The course of the river about S S W. the carrying place to the first Lake is about four miles in length over very fine land but hilly—This neck or ridge of Land appears to form the divisions between the head of the waters which fall into Lake Simcoe and those which take their course towards Lake Ontario in the direction of Kingston. The first Lake is about seven or eight miles in length, the Banks rocky and Producing little else but Pine timber. On the Eastern side it discharges itself by a small river into another Lake which I understand communicates with some river falling into Lake Ontario near the Bay of Quinte. We left it by the North east end and ascended a fine broad and deep Stream for about seven miles into a chain of small narrow Lakes which communicate with each other by separate streams—

From the Second to the third Lake the navigation is interupted by four separate falls of about twelve feet each, and after passing the third Lake, we were generally obliged to carry from one to the other as the Streams which joined them were so filled with trees as to prevent our taking up the Canoes—The Lakes are ten in number the two last very shallow and the land in the neighbourhood of the last connecting Stream nearly all low land and Swamp——The whole distance from the first to the last Lake is about ninety miles. The land has uniformly the same appearance on the banks of these Lakes viz. high rocky and Barren but I observed whenever we left the immediate Vicinity of the Lake and advanced into the interior the land appeared to improve—At the south east end of the last Lake is a river which runs in the direction of and discharges itself near Kingston. We here commenced a Portage of about four miles over very high but fine Land. This ridge divides the Waters falling into Lake Ontario from those falling into the Otawa. Our Course had hitherto been from N.N.E. to N. E. The Lake to which we carried the Canoes is about five miles in length and in appearance Shallower than any of the others—We left it by a fine broad and deep Stream running in an Easterly direction through a flat and low Country rather marshy—We went down the river about sixteen miles without interuption to a large Swampy Lake very Shallow which is the commencement of a Chain of Lakes about ten miles in length the remainder are however deep and have much the same appearance as those already passed. At the East End of the Lakes, is a fall of about thirty feet with rapids for about half a mile below. These lead to a fine river with low sandy Banks and on an average about six feet water. The Stream is here and there blocked up by trees but we proceeded about thirty three miles with little interuption, we here came to some strong Rapids about half a mile in length, which were succeeded by about Eight miles of Smooth water—The River here makes a circuit of seven or eight miles and becomes very rapid with three separate falls. The carrying place across is not more than one mile and over very fine Land. We then proceeded about forty miles with little interuption down to the river's junction with the Madaswasca which takes place in a large plain bounded on every side by High Land—

The Madaswasca comes into this Plain from the South. About Six miles below, the rapids commence which occasioned us to make small carrying places for about One mile when the river is again navigable for six or seven miles—We then arrived at a succession of rapids for about sixty miles over ledges of rock—The river here enters a very fine Lake with high banks and finely timbered with beech, Elm, and Maple—The Lake itself is about Seven or eight miles in extent. Immediately upon leaving the Lake the river assumes its former appearance and becomes a continued Strong rapid with falls of four or five feet here and there, for about forty five miles when it falls into the Otawa about eight miles above the rapids and falls of the Chat.—

From this sketch of our cursory passage through the Country your Excellency will perceive that the only part which offers any encouragement to the hope of establishing a batteau communication is the first chain of Lakes and the river which falls into the Madawasca, and even this presents many obstacles, as the Communications from Lake to Lake are generally very bad and would require great labour to render them passable for light Boats. Should these difficulties be overcome, some other communication than by the Madawasca must be found as its whole course is almost an uninterupted Rapid, when the water is low, Scarce affording enough to float Canoes in Safety over the Rocks, when high, rising to such a degree and flowing with such rapidity as to preclude the possibility of taking up Batteaux and much more of bringing them down—

The Talbot River may be navigable in the Spring, when the waters are high but is so shallow in the fall as scarcely to afford Water enough for a Canal. The Land I have reason to believe is good in every part except in the immediate Vicinity of the Lakes and Rivers—

These, Sir, are the Principal Observations I have been able to make during my Journey through the Country which has been much more tedious and less Satisfactory than might have been expected from the first accounts I received

I have the honor to be
Your Excellency's
Most obedient humble Servt
(Signed) J. P. Catty
Lt R^{l} Eng^{s}

4. J. W. Bannister[1] Suggests Means of Building the Canal

(*a*) THE FIRST PLAN, A LOTTERY

[*Public Archives of Canada, Upper Canada Sundries, J. W. Bannister to the Lieutenant-Governor.*]

Rice Lake, Upper Canada
15th Decr 1820

May it please Your Excellency,

My Location happening to be on the Rice Lake Settlement, the absolute want of a Communication, thence to the Bay of Quinte, of necessity occurred to me in the strongest Light. During my residence here, I have been particular in exploring and inquiring, so as to enable myself to form a reasonable opinion of this matter.

I have been informed, that Surveys from Lake Simcoe to the Bay of

[1]The Introduction to the fourth edition of his pamphlet contains the following outline of his life: "The writer of the Pamphlet now reprinted was brought up in the navy; and by hard service from nine to nineteen years of age acquired the reputation of being a daring officer and a skilful seaman. After considerable experiences in civil affairs, and especially in agriculture, at the peace in 1819 he visited Canada, where he obtained several thousand acres of land. He was subsequently called to the English bar, intending to settle in Canada; but in August, 1829, died Chief Justice of Sierra Leone. In Africa he was remarkable for the same earnest desire to promote good public objects, and for the same right feelings, in all respects, which had ever distinguished him. A memoir of his short but active life may be found in the *New Monthly Magazine* for December, 1829." Bannister's original lot appears to have been 800 acres granted in November 1820 in the rear of Bannister's Landing (Hiawatha Indian Village).

Quinte have been made, by fit and able Men; consequently, any observations from me, as to their local capability will be superfluous, and it only remains to submit to Your Excellency, a mode to raise the money, for this purpose, to carry the proposed work into effect.

A Government Lottery, under every consideration that I have given to the subject, appears to me, to be the *only probable* method, to collect so large a sum, as the contemplated work will require.

I trust that your Excellency will do me the justice to believe, that I far, from approve of this species of gambling and that I have not hastily submitted it to your Excellency; No, the seeming otherwise impracticability of raising so much money, except by being assisted from Home; The paramount necessity for the Country in general (independent of its Local advantages) of the inland navigation being begun; The gigantic strides daily making by our aspiring and republican neighbour, in this Valuable power; and "tho' last not least," the present overwhelming petty Lotteries, Raffles, and other sorts of gambling, which may be more effectively put down by the more respectable Classes, preferring a Legal Lottery to illegal gambling; are the strong inducements which have forced me thus to intrude myself upon Your Excellency,

I have now to conclude with every sentiment of respect for Your Excellency; and to

Subscribe myself,
Your Excellency's
Most humble servant
John William Bannister.

(*b*) THE SECOND PLAN, TO COMBINE SETTLEMENT AND A CANAL

[*John William Bannister*, Sketches of Plans for Settling in Upper Canada a Portion of the Unemployed Labourers of Great Britain and Ireland (*London, 1821*). *At least four editions of this pamphlet appeared. The following excerpts are from the fourth, entitled On Emigration to Upper Canada, by the Late John William Bannister, Esq. Rice Lake, Upper Canada* (London, 1831)]

. . . A sketch of the second plan follows, by which a party can be settled in Canada without burthening the mother-country to a larger amount than the *expense of conveying them from Europe to their places* of destination.

It will doubtless be in remembrance of many persons in the province that a plan was agitated in 1820 relative to making a canal from the

Rice Lake to the head of the Bay of Quinté by the means of a subscription of the *produce* of the country to defray the expense, and that subscription entitling the contributors to proportionate shares in the canal: it may also be well remembered how readily the views of the proposer were entered into by the richer and poorer classes of the district of Newcastle, the district in which the then proposed canal was to have been cut, as well as by many of the inhabitants higher up the country; let us then see how we can connect this plan of opening a canal by the above means of defraying the expense with that of settling six thousand men, women, and children in comfort in the neighbouring country.

We will divide the party into three divisions of two thousand each, to be sent out to the river Trent, which connects the Rice Lake with the Bay of Quinté, in three successive springs. On the arrival of the first two thousand let those who are capable of labouring, immediately to be put to fitting work at the proposed canal, instead of proceeding forthwith to their location. Provisions, clothing, lodging, medical assistance, and certain instruction for the children will be provided by preliminary arrangements to be hereafter noticed. The second spring will bring the next division, and the course of the ensuing year will be as the former; the arrival of the third two thousand will be the commencement of new and pleasant occupations to the first division; *they* will now be permitted to have so much time to visit the lands appointed (during which they will be allowed provisions, etc.) for location, in order to fix upon a lot; to put up their 'tshantees'; as also afterwards to put up their houses, to clear five acres of land for a spring crop, together with the use of a pair of oxen for a given time to perform the 'logging'; again, they must have partial allowances whilst preparing for the autumn season and finishing the settlement duties, together with some assistance during the following winter. On the opening of the fourth spring perfect freedom begins to dawn: we must now (for the last time) supply our friends (according to the number of their *helpless* children) with a few other necessaries, the deeds of their land *free of any expense*, and then leave them to the protection of their Maker, the laws of their adopted country, and their own industry. . . .*

*Should the patrons of a system for colonising upon the above principles perceive, at or before this period, that the result may be convenience to the mother country, advantage to the province, and happiness to the settlers, it can be continued to many succeeding bodies of two thousand persons, inasmuch as after the completion of the work from the Bay of Quinté to the Rice Lake, there will be no obstacle to proceeding thence to the carrying place in the township of Smith, and forward through the shallow Lakes to the boundaries of the Canadas.

5. Tenders Asked for Works on Proposed Trent Canal, 1833

[Cobourg Star and Newcastle Commercial and General Advertiser, *April 3, 1833*]

Internal Navigation of the Newcastle District

Notice is hereby give[n] that the undersigned Commissioners will receive Tenders until the first day of June next, to be opened at the Superintendent's Office, *Peterborough*, from such persons as are willing to contract for the performance of the following work, viz:—

First.—To construct a Lock at the Bobcaygeon Falls, on the outlet between Sturgeon and Pigeon Lakes, of about 28 feet in width by 120 feet in length.

Second.—To construct a Lock of same dimensions at Purdy's Mill, on the Scugog River in the Township of Ops.

Third.—To clear the Channel of the Otonabee River at Dangerfield, Robinson's Island, and Yankey Bonnet Shallows, not less than 66 feet in width and of sufficient depth to admit Steamers drawing 4 feet water to pass at the lowest water.

Fourth.—To deepen the principal entrance to the Otonabee River from Rice Lake.

Fifth.—To erect Piers and deepen the Channel of the Otonabee from the head of Whitelas' Rapid[1] to the little Lake near Peterborough.

Sixth.—To clear out and make navigable for Boats, Cavan Creek from the mouth on the Otonabee to Taggest's Mill, in Cavan.

Further information may be obtained by applying to *J. G. Bethune*, Cobourg, or *Thomas Need*, Peterborough, after the 10th day of May next, by which time the Commissioners will have had the whole intended improvements surveyed and reported upon by a practical Engineer.

Persons tendering to erect the two Locks above mentioned must produce satisfactory references that they have knowledge of that kind of work, otherwise their tenders will not be noticed.

No contract will be entered into without two sufficient Sureties for the due performance of the work.

Jas. G. Bethune — A. McDonell
B. Brown — Thos. Need
John Hall — J. Huston

Peterborough, March 1833.

[1]William and George Whitla were owners of land near the rapids after 1828. Samuel Strickland wrote in 1851 that the lock and dam at Whitla's Rapids were the best-constructed in the county. (*Twenty-Seven Years in Canada West* (London, 1853), Vol. II, p. 228).

TO

EXPERIENCED CONTRACTORS,

FOR THE

Improvement of the Navigation of the

RIVER TRENT,

NEWCASTLE DISTRICT.

SEALED TENDERS

Will be received for the execution of the whole, or a portion, of the undermentioned Works, (for the due performance of which good and sufficient security will be required) till Tuesday, the 16th of October next.

Plans and Specifications of the works may be seen, after the 1st of October next, at the Office of *Sheldon Hawley, Esq.*, Trent Port, or of *G. S. Boulton, Esq.*, Cobourg; and necessary information had, on application to N. H. Baird, Esq., *Civil Engineer.*

Tenders to be addressed (*post paid*) to Sheldon Hawley, *Esq.*, *Trent Port*, and marked,

"*Tenders for the Improvement of the River Trent.*"

ON SECTION 1st.

A Dam, Stone Lock and excavation at Meyers' Island, Mouth of the River Trent, and a Dam at Widow Harris's.

ON SECTION 2d.

Stone Lock, Excavation and Dam at Chisholm's Rapids.

Cobourg, Sept. 18, 1837.

[STAR OFFICE, COBOURG.]

Public Archives of Canada

ADVERTISEMENT FOR TENDERS, 1837

6. Progress in Transportation

[Cobourg Star, *July 31, 1833*]

Steam-Boat Notice

Internal Navigation of the Newcastle District, via Cobourg

The Steam-boat PEMEDASH,[1] Captain Cleghorn, plies daily between the town of Peterborough and Sully on the Rice Lake, every day as follows:—

Leaves Peterboro' for Sully every morning (Sundays excepted) at 8 o'clock—leaves Sully every afternoon and arrives at Peterborough early the same evenings.

STAGES in connection with the above Boat leave the *Steam-Boat Hotel* at Cobourg every morning (Sundays excepted) at 8 o'clock, for the conveyance of passengers—and from 5 to 10 heavy waggons leave the Cobourg Harbor Ware-house every morning (Sundays excepted) at half-past six, for the conveyance of merchandise and luggage directed to Peterboro' or any other part of the interior.

A large and secure Ware-house has been erected at the landing at Peterboro', where Goods and Luggage will be stored free of expense.

The STEAM BOAT STURGEON, Captain Nichols, is now receiving her Engine at the village of Bridgenorth, Lake Chemong, and will be ready in a few weeks to ply between Bridgenorth and the Bobcaygean falls through Chemong, Buckhorn, and Pigeon Lakes, calling at several intermediate places, of which due notice will be given. A large sum of money is now expending on the communication road between Peterborough and Bridgenorth, a distance of only 6 miles, which will render it equal to any in the Province.

Persons arriving at Cobourg will obtain every information by applying to Mr. T. Evans, at the Office of the Harbor Company, or at the office of the undersigned.

J. G. Bethune.

Cobourg, 20th July, 1833.[2]

[1]An abbreviation of "Pemedashcoutayang," "the Lake of the Burning Plains," the name arising from intentional burning of the south shore of the lake by the Indians to increase the growth of deer-grass as a feeding-ground for game. A highly laudatory letter describing the "enchanting" scenery of Rice Lake is in the *Cobourg Star* of June 18, 1833.

[2]The *Cobourg Star* of September 4, 1833, contains an account of a public meeting to further the work then in progress along the Trent system. Those mentioned as taking a prominent part in the proceedings are Robert Reid, Thomas V. Tupper, Dr. John Hutchinson, Cheseman Moe, John Hall, J. B. Ferguson, Walter McFarlane, John R. Benson, Major Logie, John Huston, Charles Rubidge, Ephraim Sandford, and Thomas Murphy. Almost all of these were inhabitants of Peterborough. The meeting was held in the King's Arms Hotel, Peterborough,

7. Initial Survey for the Trent River Section of the Canal, 1833

[Journal of the House of Assembly of Upper Canada, *1833–34*]

November, 1833

REPORT

To His Excellency SIR JOHN COLBORNE, Knight, Commander of the Most Honorable Military Order of the Bath, Lieutenant Governor of the Province of Upper Canada, Major General Commanding His Majesty's Forces therein, &c. &c. &c., on the practicability of rendering the River Trent navigable from its mouth or confluence with the Bay of Quinte to Rice Lake.

By N. H. BAIRD,
Civil Engineer,
M.I.C.E.L.

In obedience to Your Excellency's commands, transmitted to me by Lieutenant Colonel Rowan, Civil Secretary, in his communication, bearing date 19th March last, as well as subsequent correspondence, I proceeded upon the 7th day of September last to the mouth of the Trent (the state of the waters preventing an earlier inspection,) for the purpose of attending to the import of my instructions, viz: To survey and estimate the expense of rendering that River navigable for Steam Boats drawing five feet water, with Locks of commensurate dimensions, 134 feet in length by 33 feet in the clear, the result of which examination, survey and levels, I have the honor now to lay before your Excellency.

Before coming to a conclusion, as to the mode most likely to be attended with expediency in rendering the River navigable, I conceived it necessary, first, to traverse and explore the whole course of the River, its banks and contiguous ravines, the result of which determined the principle upon which I should proceed to estimate the difficulties to be overcome, and taking into account the great quantity of water in the River (nearly the second in the Province in point of discharge) the effects which such might have on the construction of the different works required, connected with the vast accumulation of anchor ice along the

---

and it adjourned to meet again on September 18th. A long letter signed by "C. K." describes improvements in the region (*Cobourg Star*, October 9, 1833), and in the same issue it is announced that N. H. Baird is actively surveying the Trent for the proposed canal. Further letters by "C. K." occur in succeeding issues of the *Cobourg Star*.

banks and shallows, and from the very great facility afforded, from the favourable nature of the banks, as illustrated by the several sections accompanying, the principle of damming the River, would seem, under all circumstances, to be the preferable mode of overcoming the several obstructions, and upon which principle I shall proceed to point out to Your Excellency the manner in which I would propose surmounting the obstacles to such a grand and available stream.

It will, however, in the first place be necessary, in order that Your Excellency may have a comprehensive view of the subject, to enumerate, in as condensed a form as may be consistent with the extent of the undertaking, the several obstructions to the navigation of the River, from its mouth to the Rice Lake, and may be classed under the following general sections, viz:

feet in. 1st. The Rapids, commonly called the nine mile rapids,
116 5 9 extending from a mile above the mouth to navigable water
at the Widow Harris', rising in all 116 feet.

2d. After passing along a fine navigable sheet of water,
8 7 8 available at present for moderate sized craft, for 6 miles,
the Little, or Chisholm's Rapids, present themselves in extent 1100 yards, and rising 8 7 8 feet to Chisholm's Sawmill, which leads to a still finer sheet of navigable water, with a moderate current, not less than 12½ miles to the Percy Landing,[1] at which place the 3d Section commences, in extent 12½ miles to Crow Bay, and rising 150 feet—
150 5 3 with the exception of a small sheet or pond opposite to
Major Campbell's new settlement in Seymour,[2] the whole of this Section consists of a series of rapids interrupted only by big Falls, Chutes, &c.

From the foot of Crow Bay (along the bay) the water is of sufficient depth for 1½ miles until reaching the foot

[1]Percy Landing, which was also known as Beatty's Landing from a man who kept boats there, is near Meyersburg, where Colonel Myers kept a shop. Percy Landing is now called Percy Boom. Numerous officers were early settled below Beatty's.

[2]Seymour Township is one of several in the province that were originally opened for the settlement of military and naval officers. Major Campbell was in charge as Government Agent, and the town of Campbellford was named in his honour. "At the two principal bends of the river [Trent]," wrote John Langton in 1833, the same year as Baird's Report, "there are two cities, Cambleton and Howard; the one consisting of a shanty, and the other of a loghouse without windows." Subsequently he reverses the order of their achievement as settlements, but there is little difference. (*Early Days in Upper Canada*, pp. 6 and 21). Soon afterwards there was a tavern near Campbell's house, and a ferry (and later a bridge) opposite, so the settlement was for a time called Seymour Bridge.

of the rapids from Heeley's Falls in extent 1½ miles, at which point, commonly called the Forks, being at the confluence of the Crow River with the Trent, commence the next series of obstacles, the 4th in rotation which embraces
72 9 5 Heeley's Falls, extending as stated 1½ miles where commences the Long Reach, navigable for 13½ miles with the exception of three shallows* or rifts which as will after-
*4 2 0 wards be detailed, may be easily overcome, to the foot of Crooks' Rapids[1] immediately below Asphodel bridge, six miles from Rice Lake; at this point the 5th and last general section occurs, in extent about ½ a mile and rising 7 ft. 9 in.

Natural rise		
	7 9 0	
Increase	0 5 0	0 5
	8 2 0	8 2

which overcome brings the navigation into the head or summit pond of Rice Lake, making from the mouth of the River at the Bay of Quinte, a total rise independent of the natural current along the several navigable portions, which of course I wave,

		Ft.	In.
	of	360	8 5-10
rifts		4	3 5-10
		365	0 0

in a distance of 61 miles, and which I would propose to overcome by the following operations; and in detailing which, with reference to the plans and sections, I trust I may succeed in laying the matter in as clear a light before your Excellency as the subject will admit.

With reference to the abstract of obstruction to be overcome, the 1st. or nine mile rapids present the most formidable, the natural rise to widow Harris' at the then lowest pitch of water being 116 feet 5 inches 9-10ths.

These being a continued succession of rapids, cascades, chutes and

[1]The Honourable James Crooks first bought land along the Trent in 1810. He built a mill in 1835, and sold out to Henry Fowlds in 1851. For a time "Fowlds' Rapids" replaced the earlier name. His steamship, the *Forest City*, was launched on September 11, 1858, and during her inaugural trip on the Trent Mr. Fowlds was tendered an address, eulogizing his public spirit, by a large number of Asphodel-Percy residents (See the *Cobourg Star*, September 22, 1858).

shallows, until reaching the small pond of still water near the Highlands over O'Connor's Tavern, I propose surmounting by the construction of Dams and Locks, with the requisite excavation for the foundations and entrances, as shewn on the sections, placing the Lock No. 1 first or entrance Lock in the now dry channel at the head of Myers' Island, and taking advantage of the present channel between the island and main shore, as a line of ingress, as shewn on the detailed plan. The navigation keeping the channel of the River,* until reaching below Robinson's Mills, at which point marked on the plan, a collateral cut will be required for a short distance into the still water at O'Connor's, which being raised eight feet, will sufficiently drown the Highland Rapids to throw the requisite depth into another collateral cut, as shewn on the detailed plan, along a meadow, chiefly through rock excavation, upon which I propose to have Lock No. XIII. of 9 feet lift, which will carry the communication into the navigable sheet above Widow Harris's house, at which point the Wing Dam, as shewn, will be required to raise the water sufficiently to insure the necessary draft of water over the shallows above Lewis Bush's, and before coming to the foot of the little or Chisholm's Rapids, at which place the second Section commences, and which, although of no continuance, and the rise apparently trifling, being only 8 7 8, yet presents considerable difficulty, and which may be overcome with most advantage by one lock of 10 feet lift, the difference from the natural rise (8 7 8) occasioned by raising the long reach above, and by 1100 yards of excavation through lime stone rock, of a nature easy of excavation, and of suitable material for the lock, &c. as the rate per estimate will shew. This Section will cost £13814 7 6, and bring the navigation into what I shall (for distinction) call the *Percy Reach*, extending 12½ miles to Percy Landing, the waters of which, however, will require to be raised, as shewn on the Sections, 1 foot 4 inches 2 by the construction of a Dam at the head of Chisholm's Rapids, on the Table Rock, in order to afford a sufficiency of water to the rocky shallows opposite to the Government place, from the head of Long Island upwards; and will cost, as per estimate, £400 0 0 Halifax Currency, and ensure a perfect navigation to the foot of Section 3d or Percy Landing, which place is by nature calculated for the reception of any number of vessels, from its extended Bay (Trent Lake) and the secreting coves issuing from it.

From this point to Crow Bay (termination of Section 3d) a distance of 12½ miles, the river does not, upon the whole, afford such opportunities of improvement by damming, particularly the first 1½ mile. From Percy Landing at Point A. (being the deepest and most con-

*By 9 Dams & 12 Locks.

venient spot for leaving the river) the navigation must follow a collateral cut along the West shore in suitable excavation, until reaching Myers's Mill pond, as shewn on the plan, rising 23 ft. 8, 8, by 2 Locks of 12 & 13, 7 and from which, until reaching Wilkins' Mills, a distance of 2⅜ miles, the river, from the fortunate circumstance of being divided by a long island, extending from Percy Landing, offers every facility that could be wished, as the whole of the water can be turned down the back or main channel during the excavations from the bed of the river, which must be lowered at the different points, as shewn on the Section, to save raising the dams to an inconvenient height, and consequent embankments, the banks for the greater part (to the head of Long Island) being rather low—then from Myers' mill the navigation will be carried to the foot of the Big Falls or Wilkins' Mills by 2 Locks, 2 Dams, and the different excavation from the bed of the river.

From the waters immediately below the Falls, which are of sufficient depth, and only require to be deadened by the Dam, head of Long Island, the line of navigation must leave the river until reaching the Table Rock rapids above the Falls, or to Wilkins' boom, a distance of 1430 yards, for which purpose, as favourable an opportunity presents as could well be conceived, along a natural hollow or ravine, coursing by the rear of Mr. Wilkins' house and leading nearly to the point where it is intended to rejoin the river: at this place three combined and two detached Locks will be required to carry the navigation over the Big Falls, their contributary rapids and table rock chute, into the river above the boom, making a rise of 39 ft. 11. in. chiefly through favourable excavation.

From hence to Crow Bay the river presents every opportunity for improvement with the exception of the Crow Bay or middle rapids, at which point a collateral cut from No. XXVII. at the foot of these rapids to No. XXIX. foot of Crow Bay, will be required with 3 Locks, through rock excavation of well bedded limestone; from the Boom to this point (XXVII.) requiring (comprehending the still water at Major Campbell's) 2 Locks and 3 Dams, the whole rise being 58 ft. 5 in. 3 from Wilkins' Boom to Crow Bay, with the increased head on the Bay necessary to cover a table rock to the requisite depth.—This Section from Percy Landing will cost £113,714 13 4, which brings the line to the Forks at the foot of Heeley's rapids, where commences Section No. 4. which rising 72 ft. 9 in. 5 in a distance of 1½ miles, I propose surmounting by 8 Locks 3 Dams and 220 yards of excavation, as shewn on the section for this place, in the following manner, viz:—At or near the Forks, by the construction of 3 Dams 14, 13 & 13 feet in height by 180 feet in width with 3 Locks of 9 ft. 6 in. 8 ft. 8 ft. lift, which will back the water into what may be termed Entrance Bay, at the foot of Heeley's Falls, from which point in a direct line to the summit water of the *Long-Reach*, a ravine leads, in every respect calculated to assist in overcoming the difficulties on this important station, and which may be accomplished by the construction of one detached, three combined, and one regulating Lock, making a total rise with the increase of head on summit level of 76 ft. 11 in. 5 pts requisite as afterwards will be shewn, and will cost in all £32,892 2 5 bringing the navigation into the 14 Mile Reach, on which however there exists three different impediments to more than 18 inches draft of water, and which are tinged on the general plan amounting in all to 4 ft. 2 in. perpendicular rise, which, together with the complement of water required over the Upper Shallow (say 3 feet) make a total of 7 ft. 2 in. The surmounting these, I had in contemplation to accomplish by part excavation, and to have towed up Craft by a Machine suitable for the purpose, but after taking into account the comparative trifling damages which would arise, from raising the level of the Long Reach, and the facility of doing so at Heeley's Falls, the adoption of the latter measure, would seem the more advisable, and which is intended to be effected by a dam across the table rock at the summit of Heeley's Falls of 13 feet in height and 320 in length, at an expense of £750 which at the same time will effect a material saving in the rock excavation, from the summit level, head of the Falls, to the guard Lock, and which being wholly rock, will more than compensate for the construction of the Dam. To last Section, the 5th, the navigation is now brought by the last named dam, backing the water to Crooks' rapids, where a similar obstruction to the rapids at Chisholm's occurs; the natural rise being 8 ft. 2 in. and the rapids running over a continuation of table rock, with at the time of inspection only 9 inches water, and at lowest water nearly dry.

To overcome these, as well as to ensure a sufficiency of water over the rocky shallows between Asphodel Bridge and Rice Lake, I should propose the construction of a dam across the river below the rapids, at a convenient site, which shall be of sufficient height to throw 5 feet water over the now lowest portion of the table rock, on which there is above the Mill, 1 ft. 4 in., and from which, excavating a few beds, say to 2 feet in depth for a short distance, will leave a permanent increase of level at and above Asphodel Bridge of from 1 ft. 8 in. to 2 feet, sufficient, I believe, to cover the rocky shallows above, and which in consequence, will raise the general summit level of Rice Lake, allowing for difference of current from the Lake to Asphodel Bridge, at least 1 ft. 8 in. above the lowest water, which would, I presume, be attended with no serious inconvenience but probably a benefit.

	£	s.	d.
	7062	9	10
Thus may the different obstructions to the free navigation of the River Trent be overcome and rendered available for the passage of Steam Vessels drawing 5 feet water, 110 feet over all by 32 feet beam, viz. by Section 1st. from the mouth to the Widow Harris', 9 miles, rise 116 5 9, by the construction of 13 locks, 9 dams, and two collateral cuts, 1st. 432 yards in length, 2d. 770 yards in length.			
Section 2.—From Widow Harris' to head of Chisholm Rapids, about 6 miles, rise 8 ft. 7 in. 8 by a wing dam at widow Harris' to drown the shallow above Lewis Bush's, and by one lock and 1100 yd. rock excavation at Chisholm's.	63683	3	10½
	13814	7	6
Section 3.—From Chisholm's to Crow Bay, including Percy Reach, by a dam at Chisholm's to cover the shallows at the Government place, by 2 locks and 1½ miles of excavation to Myers' Mills, 2 locks, 2 dams, and excavation from the bed of the river to Wilkins' Mills or Big Falls—thence 3 combined and one detached lock and a guard lock, with ¾ mile excavation to Wilkins' Boom, thence to Crow Bay by a dam across the river above the Boom with 5 detached locks, with their respective excavations from the bottom of the river with a collateral cut from 27 into Crow Bay, 1100 yards.	113714	13	4
Section 4.—From the foot of Crow Bay, by a dam across one of the outlet channels to cover the table rock sufficiently—to the forks or foot of Heeley's Rapids by 3 dams and 3 locks to Entrance Bay (foot of Heeley's Falls) and by one detached, 3 combined, and 1 guard lock with their excavations and cut of 220 yards through chiefly limestone rock to the summit of the Long Reach.	32892	2	5
Section 5.—From Heeley's Falls to Rice Lake, by the construction of a dam at the head of Heeley's Falls to drown the three interven-			

ing rifts 4 2 3 0 or shallow above, and to back sufficient water into the lock at Crooks' Mill, by the construction of one lock and dam there, to cover the rocky shoals above together with considerable rock excavation above, and under water.		6420	9	0
	Con.	642	0	10
		£7062	9	10

Including for Lock Houses £1320 0 0

All which may be accomplished for the sum of £233447 6 11½ H. C'y. in 4 years from commencement.

Having thus endeavored to lay before Your Excellency what occurs to me, after two months of constant investigation, the mode by which the River Trent may be rendered navigable; it may perhaps, not be out of place should I endeavour to lay before Your Excellency a few of the advantages likely to accrue from the fulfillment of such a measure, not only to the country immediately contiguous, but to regions beyond, thereby relieving them from the land locked predicament in which they now are and must remain, unless relieved by some such expedient.

To the country immediately bordering on the river, the advantages are too apparent, from the harrassing inconvenience experienced in dragging every species of commodity and provisions required for the many wants of new settlements through, perhaps, the worst of roads in the Province, and obviate the many heart-rending scenes of endurance, scarcely to be credited but by an eye witness.

To Government, the benefit must come more immediately home, in the increase in value of the many thousands of acres on, and contiguous to its banks and contributory lakes and streams which, on all hands, (and by people much more conversant with the true estimation than I can be) is admitted, must rise at least 100 per cent, the moment these operations shall commence.

The facility for the transport of Lumber from the waters above, and from the different manufacturing establishments now existing, and which must soon double, will form a very prominent feature in the advantages likely to follow. The Tolls upon which will be cheerfully paid, and that dangerous business of "driving the river" to the destruction of much valuable property, and loss of human life among the "wicked" Rapids, obviated, and have no doubt, from all the information I have been able to collect, will, the first year, yield £6,000.

To this add the still more incalculable benefit this Province would derive from the Marmora iron works being set in operation, which being situated on Crow River, (which in conjunction with the Trent I also inspected) only nine miles from where the line of communication passes in Crow Bay, a fine navigable stream with the exception of three ranges of rapids, each of which admit of easy improvement, and which

I have reason to believe would be commenced so soon as the prosecution of the Trent should be decided upon.

From these works the Falls would also be considerable.

To new settlements to the North, and round the Rice Lake, Ottanabee River, and Lakes beyond, what an incalculable benefit would accrue from the improvement in contemplation; necessitated now to drag from Lake Ontario all the many wants for their infant settlements at exhorbitant rates, over a hill and dale road to Rice Lake, there shipped on board of a Steam Boat for Peterboro' established nearly two years ago by an enterprising individual (J. G. Bethune, Esquire, of Cobourg) there unloaded and conveyed again nine miles by land into another Steamer, (belonging to the same individual) thence by various portages to their different destinations. When the Trent shall be rendered navigable, the Settler and Merchant may have their goods shipped under their own eye at Montreal wharf, pass along the Lachine, Ottawa River, and Canals at Carrillion, Chute Aux-Blondeau and Grenville, along the Rideau Canal, up the Bay of Quinte, along the Trent navigation, Rice Lake and to Peterboro' without ever once being disturbed after leaving the Montreal wharf, to say nothing of the diminution in freight, which must, as a matter of course follow—and on the other hand it requires no stretch of imagination to anticipate all those settlements in a few years contributing materially towards the export Trade, and that Wheat, Pot Ash, Staves, &c must be re-shipped as return Cargoes.

Another, and by no means the least, consideration, to induce the *early* adoption of such a splendid scheme and rational measure, should be the consideration of the fact, that the navigation carried into Rice Lake is, comparatively speaking, the communication carried into Lake Huron, as appears evident from all the information I have been able to collect, (not having visited those quarters) as to the obstructions existing between Peterboro' and Lake Huron, and which, although not coming within the immediate sphere of my instructions, I have the honor to submit for your Excellency's information, as collected from my intelligent guide, John Harris (an Indian Trader.)

1st. From the Otonabee River to Mud Lake, excavation 7 miles.

2d. Thence into Chemong, Buck, Pigeon and Sturgeon Lakes, rapids 1 mile.

3rd. Into Cameron's lake, rapids ½ mile.

4th. Into Balsam lake, rapids 1 mile.

From thence to Lake Simcoe, 18 miles by land, making the total canaling from Rice Lake to Lake Simcoe, 27½ miles, then into Lake Huron down the Severn (I believe the difference of level is somewhere about 70 feet.)

Taking all these into consideration, connected with the immediate local advantages which must, as a matter of course, follow the improvements now in contemplation; the key to all those regions beyond, and viewed in connexion with the Ottawa and Rideau navigation already in operation, and those in contemplation by the back of the Island of Montreal, the grand desideratum of an internal water communication from the Atlantic or Gulph of St. Lawrence to Lake Huron, ought certainly to have some weight in interesting the Mother Country in furthering such an undertaking; that is, if the Provincial funds should not be adequate within the 4 years of execution, (which, however, is somewhat out of my sphere) but I believe I may safely assert, without the fear of contradiction, that there is not a landholder between the Trent's mouth and Lake Simcoe but would cheerfully submit to an annual tax on his lands during the execution of the works, to assist in defraying the expense; and if such a measure were properly digested and arranged, I have little doubt but as an alternative it would meet the general feeling of the District, and tend to facilitate the undertaking.

From the preconceived magnitude of the undertaking, the short time from necessity available to accomplish the whole during the lowest pitch of water, and to enable me to give my exclusive attention to the levels and localities of the river, I found it indispensable to engage the services of a Provincial Surveyor (Mr. Rubidge of the Newcastle District) in whom I found, throughout the whole of the arduous duty, much perseverence and attention, and in the necessity of which engagement, I trust your Excellency may concur.

In submitting the foregoing as the result of your Excellency's commands, I trust I may have succeeded in laying the matter before Your Excellency in a comprehensive light.

I have the honor to be,
Your Excellency's
Most obedient and
Very humble Servant,
N. H. BAIRD,
Civil Engineer,
M.I.C.E.L.

MONTREAL, 28th Nov. 1833.

Amount of estimate for locks of substantial rough Masonry as per detailed estimate with wooden dams,	£233447	6	11½
Locks, 134 x 33 x 5 feet water.			
Estimate for locks of dimensions similar to the Lachine Canal	195300	10	0
E.E. Difference,	£ 38146	16	11½

8. Initial Survey for the Trent Canal, Rice Lake to Lake Simcoe

[*Appendix to the Journal of the House of Assembly of Upper Canada, 1836*]

NO. 12.

REPORT

On the most eligible route for a Canal between Lake Simcoe and the Rice Lake, and on the practicability and expense of connecting these waters—by order of His Excellency Sir John Colborne, K.C.B. &c. &c. &c.

BY N. H. BAIRD, Civil Engineer, M.I.C.E.L.
December, 1835

REPORT

To His Excellency SIR JOHN COLBORNE, K.C.B. Lieutenant Governor of the Province of Upper Canada, and Major General commanding His Majesty's Forces, &c. &c. &c. on the most eligible route for a Canal between Lake Simcoe and the Rice Lake, and on the practicability and probable expense of connecting these Lakes.

BY N. H. BAIRD
Civil Engineer,
& M.I.C.E.L.

MAY IT PLEASE YOUR EXCELLENCY,

THAT in accordance with your Excellency's commands, conveyed to me in Lieutenant Colonel Rowan's communications of the 29th May and 6th June last, and in the spirit of the particular instructions conveyed in the latter, in conformity with the Address of the House of Assembly of date 16th April last, viz:—"To examine the most elig-"ible route for a Canal between Lake Simcoe and the Rice Lake, by a "series of running levels, and to report to your Excellency, for the "information of the House at its next Session, respecting the practic-"ability and expense of connecting these Lakes."

I have, in consequence, the honor to state for your Excellency's information, that upon the 18th day of June last, having completed my preliminary arrangements, in providing proper assistance and canoes, in which I found more difficulty than I anticipated, and having engaged the services of Mr. F. P. Rubige, Deputy Provincial Surveyor, for the surveying department, I proceeded to the inspection and examination of the country between Rice Lake and Lake Simcoe, conceiving it more in order to follow up the route from the Bay of Quinte, as detailed in my former report to your Excellency on the proposed improvements on the River Trent, in 1833, than to reverse, and commence from Lake Simcoe—the result of which inspection, levels, survey, &c. I shall endeavour, with as much perspicuity and brevity as the nature of the important subject will admit, to lay before your Excellency, assuming, although not expressed in my instructions, or in the Address from the House, the same scale of navigation as that reported on for the improvement of the Trent, viz. for locks 134 x 33 x 5 feet water as the data upon which to proceed; accordingly commencing from Rice Lake, into which the navigation must be understood as made available by the requisite operations formerly reported and estimated, and for perspicuity and reference sake shall divide the whole route into five sections, commencing from the Rice Lake, thus:

				Miles
Section	1st.	From	Rice Lake to Peterborough,	$21\frac{22}{80}$
"	2nd.	"	Peterborough to outlet of Clear Lake	$14\frac{34}{80}$
"	3rd.	"	Outlet of Clear Lake to Bobcaygean lock and rapids	$31\frac{40}{80}$
"	4th.	"	Bobcaygean to Balsam Lake Portage	$26\frac{24}{80}$
"	5th.	"	Balsam Lake to Lake Simcoe	$16\frac{40}{80}$
			Making in all,	110 miles

With reference to section No. 1, the first obstacle presenting itself is the bar at the outlet of the Otanabee River, over which, in some seasons, at lowest summer water, there is not more than eighteen inches; from this point of difficulty to within half a mile of Peterboro', or at Whitlaw's Rapids, a distance of 21 miles, the river presents a fine available stream for moderate sized steamers, with the exception of three trifling obstructions, as shewn in the accompanying plan and section, viz. Danger Field, Robinson's Island, and Yankee Bonnet Shoals,[1] over which, at lowest summer water, 18 inches will be the utmost, and would not even have reached that but for the exertions made last summer, or summer before, in removing the round bolders from the channel, and placing them in heaps or piles, out of the fair way, by a grant (I understand) from the Provincial Parliament, laid out under Commissioners appointed for the purpose, and which in so far as such partial improve-

[1]See Mrs. Traill's explanation of the name on p. 371 below.

ments go, appears to have been a benefit to the navigation. The next obstruction, in rotation, is the Whitlaw's Rapids, a pitch of about 2 feet 9 inches (2–9;) at this point considerable expense has been incurred, in clearing the bottom from bolders and in forming buttresses therewith to contract and deepen the bed of the river, and which seems to have so far succeeded; but, at the same time, the benefit seems to have been counteracted on the other hand by the increase of current, which, as a matter of course, the contracting the channel has had the effect of creating, although not so great as to prevent the steamer *Northumberland*, a twin boat of particular construction, and drawing very little water (say 2–6,) laid on that route by individual enterprise, to surmount at a moderate pitch of water, when she readily gains the extent of the navigation of the Otanabee River in its present state, in the basin immediately below the town, and at the foot of the 9 mile rapids, having surmounted with ease a small ripple of a few inches difference of level, at the narrows between the Little Lake and upper bay. Thus terminating the first section of difficulties on the route, viz. the bar at the mouth of the river, Danger Field, Robinson's, and Yankee Bonnet Shoals, with Whitlaw's rapid, and small rapid above, making in all, from Rice Lake to Peterboro', a difference of level of 4 feet 6 inches.

The next and more serious obstruction to the navigation of the Otanabee River, presents itself prominently in a series of uninterrupted rapids and chutes from Peterboro' Bay to above Herriot's mill, in Douro, and into the now dead water of Katchiwannoe Lake, a distance of 9½ miles,[1] and rising no less than 147–6 feet odd, on which portion of section 2nd are situated, above Peterboro' bridge, Hall's mills, built for the use of the settlement by Government some years ago, taking the water from the river above the mill by a very long aqueduct, and by the construction of a dam across the river, as shewn upon the accompanying detailed plans, having a head and fall of 12–7 8/10 feet. This dam has the effect of sending the water as far back as point A on the plan—from thence to the tail water of Stevenson's saw mill, the river preserves its general character of rapids and swift water, and generally deep, say from 3 to 4 feet; above this point is situated Mr. Stevenson's mill dam, of rude construction, but it is presumed sufficient for all the purposes required, making a head and fall of 2–7 feet, and throwing the water as far back as point B on the plan—from which to the next

[1]These Nine-Mile Rapids, so different from the present navigation, form another cogent reason for believing that Champlain's Indian expedition of 1615 avoided the long and arduous route *viâ* Stoney Lake by using the Chemong carrying-place; but if they did enter Stoney Lake, a shorter route to Rice Lake would be by the Indian River, though it would be then, as it is now, very shallow in many places.

artificial obstruction to the river, the same characteristic of rapid and chute prevails, until reaching Lee's mill-dam and works, at which place a dam, on somewhat more substantial form and principle of construction, affords a command of 13–1 2/10 feet of head and fall, and backs the water, with the exception of a slight current, as far as point C, at the foot of Mr. Reid's clearance; from the mill pond, it is worthy of remark, that the water has been conducted scientifically by the late Mr. Lees along an expensive and well constructed canal to his mill, as shewn on the plan, and being somewhat through rock, must have cost a considerable amount—this work will be more particularly referred to when treating of the improvement.

From point C. on the plan, or from the head of Lee's mill pond, the river presents one continued series of rapids and chutes until reaching the dead water of Katchiwannoe Lake. The general character of the banks, high and rocky, and well bedded, affording excellent materials for lockage, &c. being of a good compact limestone.

From the detailed plan accompanying, from actual survey, a more correct idea may be formed of the general character of the river than any attempt at description could convey, while at the same time the longitudinal section shews the continued rise, with the general depths of water, as found at the time of inspection.

From the foot of Herriot's rapids (on which an excellent saw mill is in operation, and a grist mill in progress of being erected) 8 feet–10–3 of rise carries into the mill pond dead water, upheld at that level, say 142 ft.–3–5 above Peterboro' Bay, by a short substantial dam, as shewn on the plan and section, and backing the water over the former rapids into Katchiuwannoe Lake, at the lower extremity of which a shoal presents itself, an obstruction to the requisite navigable qualities, but of short duration. Next in order, and the only obstruction to the navigation on the 2nd section, is the rapids at and opposite Young's house and mill, and the artificial obstruction of a dam thrown roughly across the river by Mr. Young, for the use of a very complete common principled grist mill, made to drive two runs of stones, with a total head and fall of only 3 feet, and during the particular period of my inspection, had only 24 inches, and affords an instance of what *properly* applied power may produce, with a due regard to economy of water. By the accompanying plan it will be seen the enterprising proprietor has spared no pains in the construction of an aqueduct, &c. through a stony stratum to gain his end; as to the expediency or propriety of his throwing a dam across the river at the particular spot he has, will afterwards be considered in this report, although it would appear to have materially benefited the navigation into the outlet of Clear Lake, by drowning the rapids thereon and giving sufficiency of water over them, thus terminating the second general section of the route.

The next portion (forming the 3rd section) extends from Young's rapids to Bobcaygean, a distance of 31½ miles, rising 38–4 feet, and taking in its course Clear and Stoney Lakes, Peninsula Falls, Deer Bay, and Burleigh Chutes, and Buckhorn's rapids or Hall's mill, with the navigation of Buckhorn and Pigeon Lakes, with their shallows, &c.

Then to resume at Young's mill rapid, the navigation, in consequence of the dam already constructed, is complete, with the exception of 3 in place of 5 feet water on the outlet of Clear Lake, until reaching the Peninsula Falls, through the rather intricate navigation of Clear Lake, among its rocky islands and sunken rocks, and along the splendid navigation of Stoney Lake, until reaching the head thereof, in the spacious basin into which the Falls disgorge themselves with boisterous rapidity from the several ragged and iron-bound outlets. To surmount the obstacle at this point (rise 25–8 3/10) seemed at first, and even on mature reflection and inspection, to be a work of somewhat of a serious nature, from the particular quality of the obstructions in the several openings and outlets and ravines of which the mass of adament obstruction is composed, when after much search, a small channel, emitting the least quantity of water of the whole, afforded an opportunity of carrying the navigation over an ascent of 25–8–3, and into the water connecting with Deer Bay, and at which point the dreaded iron-bound nature of the rock turned out to be the finest *workable* granite—the only instance of the real granite, in any quantity, which has come within my observation in either of the Provinces, with the exception of Buckhorn rapids, where it also exists; by the general plan the position of the lockage can be seen—conceiving it unnecessary, so long as I had a correct section of the ravine, to have a detailed plan of the whole, particularly as such could not be properly done till winter, from the very intricate and insulated nature of the several islands, bluff points, &c. Having gained the waters of the bay above, the next obstruction occurs at the outlet of Deer Bay, as shewn on the plan, where a rise of 2–2 6/10 presents itself in a smart wicked chute or jump, in a short distance, but affords an excellent opportunity for improvement in the well-protected bay below, and advantageous ravine and low ground adjoining. Having overcome this obstacle, a small chute again interrupts the navigation, of 18 inches, as shewn on the longitudinal sections of the route, until reaching Buckhorn rapids, on which are situated Hall's mills, (and which point forms a particular feature in the line of communication, as commanding and regulating the whole surfaces of Buckhorn, Chemong, and Pigeon Lakes, up to Bobcaygean, 15½ miles,) at which place a difference of level occurs of 8–2 6/10, to be overcome, as afterwards described—and carry the navigation to Bobcaygean rapids and locks, thus terminating the 3rd sectional division of the route, from which to Balsam Lake Portage, a distance of 26¼ miles, and rising 34 feet, the 4th section extends, comprehending the rapids and works at Bobcaygean, the shallows from thence to Sturgeon Lake, the works at Cameron's Falls and Balsam Rapids, and which present the following obstructions, namely—at Bobcaygean a rise of 5 ft. 5 in. 4 pts. and a continuation of rapid of considerable extent, together with shallows, until reaching the outlet of Sturgeon Lake, and which has been attempted to be surmounted by the construction of a lock and a dam at considerable expense, by a Provincial grant, but which has not as yet been available, by some unaccountable oversight in three circumstances, from the *level* of the lower sill being equal to that of the lowest water in Pigeon Lake, in place of being the requisite Canal water depth below the same, say 3 feet for these purposes—from the dams above not being sufficient to retain a sufficient head of water over the shallows above, and lastly, from the loose and open nature of the cut from the above to the lock, not retaining the water for want of proper means being used in the construction, allowing the water to escape in the many crevices and open chasms which the nature of the ground presents, thereby rendering the works at this place entirely useless, without an adequate outlay to remedy the evil.

The next and most serious obstruction to the navigation on this section occurs at Cameron's Falls, up to which point, after overcoming the difficulties at and above Bobcaygean, a most excellent line of navigation, in deep waters of Sturgeon Lake presents itself, when a rise of 24–10 2/10 occurs, from the waters of the deep navigable inlet from Sturgeon Lake to the foot of Cameron's Falls, into the still water of Cameron's Lake,[1] rendering the adoption of two locks and guard lock at a most convenient site, as shewn on the plan, necessary. None who have ever witnessed the scenery of Niagara Falls but must at once have the impression forced on their minds of a resemblance in miniature, in Cameron's Falls—the approach from Sturgeon Lake, between the high rocky banks, in their perpendicular grandeur, until instantaneously the Fall presents itself in the same horse-shoe form, with a curtain similarly

[1]Named after Duncan Cameron, Provincial Secretary of Upper Canada, 1817–1838, the original grantee of lot 23, Concession x, which included the falls. The modern name, Fenelon Falls, recalls François de Salignac de Fénelon, explorer and Sulpician missionary, who spent the winter of 1669–70 at the Seneca village of Ganatsekwyagon ("opening in sand cliffs") to the east of Rivière Rouge and Frenchman's Bay. The latter name commemorates the event—the first recorded residence of a white man in the vicinity of Toronto.

arranged, affording behind it, trom one shore to the other, a promenade. A commencement has beer made by the enterprising proprietor, on an extensive scale, indicative of the rise and progress of a place of importance, and which, doubtless, its central situation must insure; in addition to a saw-mill, preparations are making for the erection of a grist and other mills. An inn of unusual extent and accommodation for a new country, has just been completed, together with the proprietor's own and several other houses, store, &c. forms quite a village in a wilderness.

Leaving Cameron's Falls, the route continues somewhat shallow up the river, (until reaching Cameron's Lake, which is in general very deep,) but which, by the operations at Cameron's Falls, will readily be overcome, and thus carry the navigation over the shallows, foot of the Balsam Rapids, opposite the head of the Fork Island, and at which place the rapids may be *said* to commence, and although rising only 2 ft. 8 in. into Balsam Lake, present a very protracted and serious interruption, (compared to what the first impression did import,) as shewn in the detailed plan and section accompanying, and this accomplished, carries the navigation into Balsam Lake, 227 2/10 ft. above the Rice Lake, and the summit level of the communication from the Bay of Quinte to Lake Simcoe and Huron, 592 ft. above the Bay of Quinte, and 118 ft. 6 in. above Lake Simcoe. The surface of Balsam Lake I purpose holding permanently near high water mark, for the purpose of giving sufficient water over the bar at the outlet of the Lake, head of Balsam rapids, as also to afford better access to the shore at the Portage, or the point where the cut of junction with the Talbot is intended to leave, besides saving many thousand pounds in excavation—thus terminating the 4th section, and commencing the 5th and last to Lake Simcoe—descending 118 ft. 5 3/10 in. in a total distance to the Lake of 16½ miles, or to the point of junction with the Talbot, discharging itself into Lake Simcoe, 13¾ miles.

In attempting a description of the obstructions on the section, I may commence by remarking generally that they are two-fold:—in the Talbot River, on the one hand, in its course holding out one line for consideration, in contra-distinction to carrying a continuous navigation over a most favourable country of 13¾ miles, until intersecting the Talbot River in its more developed character for navigation, within 2¾ miles of Lake Simcoe, and in either affording sufficient scope for the duties of the Engineer.

The Talbot River in its southern branch, taking its rise in a swamp to the west of Balsam Lake, continues winding in a very narrow and serpentine course for about 3 miles, until reaching the Forks or junction with the north branch, at which point the river assumes a respectable navigable appearance for batteaux, and continues so, but in a very serpentine course, until reaching the Long Portage and head of the Lost Channel, and continuation of Dry-bedded River, where the water finds its way under ground, and makes out "to day" again at about a mile below, from which the river continues as formerly described until reaching the Crooked or Wicked Rapids, of about half a mile in extent, along which we had great difficulty to float the canoes, with the baggage and provisions out, which brings the river into what may be called the commencement of the navigable portion, having at this point, by three successive rapids, descended about 55 ft. From this point to the Summer Portage, on the plains, or near the head of the next rapids and flood wood interruptions, the river preserves a navigable character, being from 70 to 100 ft. in width, and from 4 to 5 ft. in depth, with the exception of a small interruption, about 4½ miles from the Portage, of rocks and gravel in form of a shoal and rapid, which might easily be overcome.

From this point (the Summer Portage) the rapids commence, and continue, interspersed with short stretches of still water and jambs of flood wood, until reaching the termination of any thing like serious interruption at point T. on the plan, from which, downwards, may be reckoned the really available portion of the Talbot River for improvement, and which, from the detailed plan accompanying, made out from actual survey, at much inconvenience to the party, will appear to be of a nature somewhat doubtful in its present state—the *radii* of the survey being such as to render the ready navigation by the description of craft intended to be used on this inland communication at least difficult, although the elbows may be materially relieved of their acuteness, from which point until reaching Lake Simcoe no material difficulty occurs, with the exception of flood wood, but what lockage will easily overcome.

Having reached the mouths of the river along 8, 10, 18, and 20 ft. water for the last 3 or 4 miles, as shewn in the plan, the progress into the lake is impeded by the existence of a gravelly and sandy bar of considerable extent into the lake, as per plan and section, affording at low water not more than 2 ft. 6 in. in the fair way, but which can be removed and permanently secured against filling up by the construction of piers properly thrown out.

Of the capabilities of the Talbot, from its confluence with Lake Simcoe to the commencement of the rapids, there can be but one opinion, although that is in some degree shackled from the very circuitous nature of its course, making, for instance, a distance by following the river, of 30 miles to Balsam Lake, whereas by a direct line from the present Indian Landing, or rather from a more convenient basin one-eighth of a mile above, the distance would be reduced to 16½ miles, thereby not only avoiding many inconvenient turns, as shewn in the plan, but shortening the distance greatly, say 3½ miles.

Having thus endeavoured to lay before your Excellency the difficulties and obstructions to be overcome, in order to render what I conceive, after mature deliberation, the most eligible route for a water communication available to connect Lake Simcoe with Rice Lake; I shall, in order as they occur, suggest such operations as I consider will be required to accomplish the end in view.

But prior to entering into the details of the route proposed for adoption, it may not be out of place to remark, that in gaining the extremity of the 1st or lower section, viz. Peterborough Bay, the attention was naturally called to look around for an outlet—appearances indicating that the navigable qualities at that point ceased. When my attention was naturally drawn towards the ultimate object of my search—the direction of the head waters—Chemong or Mud Lake naturally attracted attention; however forbidding its appearance in the present state at low water, through which a canoe can be paddled but with difficulty, and the general report as to its inadequacy to any thing like navigable purposes, nevertheless, I resolved on trial, and steering my course in that direction, following a natural ravine and apparently low ground, leaving the bay at the convenient basin, as shewn on the plan, and passing through chiefly the unlocated town lots of Peterboro'—crossing the communication road at Mr. Dixon's gate, and thence bending northward in easy curvature through convenient ground, until reaching by easy ascent the height of land between Peterboro' and Chemong Lake, in the shortest feasible route between the two waters which afterwards, contrary to my expectation, on applying the level, I found not to exceed 50 feet above Chemong Lake, thereby offering a *probability* of the internal or cross-the-country line, being worthy of attention; still as the Otanabee, in its circuit, had to form the criterion of competition, I resolved not to abandon it without an examination, particularly as the land route did not hold out any very flattering inducement to at once adopt it; however, when on the ground, and as the country afforded an excellent oportunity of ascertaining the gross difference of level, and at the same time afforded data for a sectional view of the country for whatever purposes its capabilities afterwards might be deemed susceptible, I instituted a set of levels across from Chemong or Mud Lake to Peterboro' Bay, and found I had the quantity of 189 ft. of difference of level or lockage to contend with, and of course to be encountered, in the several obstructions in the Otanabee, in its elbow course, a difference of level, which somewhat staggered my confidence, being led to believe that the difference (of level) was inconsiderable, as stated in my report on the Trent: but having soon thereafter an opportunity of proving those levels by a series from Chemong Lake, down through Buckhorn and Peninsula Falls, and down the long rapids of the Otanabee to Peterboro', putting the matter beyond all doubt, which led to the idea (taking into account the probability of a proportionate increase on the several remaining sections of the route from the original conjectures on the subject) of addressing the Interim Report, which I had the honor of handing your Excellency personally, and thereon receiving your Excellency's further instructions, which the importance and consideration of the subject required.

I would further remark, that in consequence of the tenor of my instructions, and from circumstances occurring since the issuing of the address, and in obedience to your Excellency's commands, originating from such circumstances, viz.—"The reputed eligibility of a route "existing to connect these waters by way of Stoney Lake, with Belmont, "Ball, and Crow Lakes, and thence with the Rideau Canal head waters "on the Crow River,"—

In consequence, and with the view of leaving no room to doubt as to the most eligible, I inspected the reputed route, in a most arduous and unsatisfactory exploration of that country, in its iron bound coasts and islands, continued rapids and vexatious portages, over hill and dale —occupying myself and part of my hands nine days, serving only fully to establish the impossibility of finding a practicable route in that direction for a canal communication.

From Crow Lake, which I reached by the several continuous rapids and blind portages described by way of Belmont and Ball Lakes, and finding no prospect of reaching the head waters of the Rideau from either of those points, although from the cursory knowledge I have of the direction of the Rideau's head waters, I had all along been convinced of the probability of finding a choice of communication from thence to the upper lakes, although at much sacrifice of lockage, but not in the direction reported to your Excellency; I reached the Marmora Iron Works, and from thence descended the Crow River, and from thence by Heely's Falls, on the Trent—fixing beyond doubt, that the Otanabee was the most probable, and in all likelihood, the *only* practicable route for the object in view.

Having thus described the endeavors to establish the most eligible route, I now come to lay before Your Excellency the operations required on the different sections to render them available for navigation, commencing in rotation, as formerly, from Rice Lake; and under section 1, occur, the Bar at the mouth of the River, the Shallows of Dangersfield, Robinson's Island, and Yankee Bonnet,[1] and which I would propose surmounting by such additional height to the dam at Asphodel bridge, (proposed as necessary for the improvement of that portion of the Trent) as will maintain Rice Lake *permanently* at or near high water mark, and which from the slight difference of level from Rice Lake to Whitlaw's Rapids, (about 2 ft. 9 in.) can easily be done; at the same time, I would recommend the closing up the centre channel of the mouth of the Otanabee, with the view of assisting either of the others, in having a clear passage, and preventing the formation of an additional bar, which would be apt to form, if not artificially prevented, and which the formation of piers will ensure.

In raising the waters of Rice Lake a decided general advantage will arise to the surrounding country, in rendering the whole comparatively healthy, and insure, at a trifling expenditure, an available navigation to Peterboro', at all times, by the simple adoption of a dam and lock at Whitlaw's Rapids, which is the next obstruction on this section, thereby throwing back water over the Little Lake, sufficient to drown the ripple at the Narrows between the lake and bay, and throw sufficient water into No. 1 lock of the collateral cut from Entrance Bay; thus carrying the navigation from Asphodel Bridge to Peterboro', 40 miles, at an expense of, per estimate, £4,246. 19s. a very inconsiderable amount indeed, when compared to the advantages to be derived, the enumeration of the whole of which I do not consider comes within the immediate sphere of this report.

Section 2nd.—From Peterboro' to Clear Lake, 14½ miles, and rising 147 feet, with a continuation of rapid for 9 miles, until reaching Herriot's mill pond in Katchiuwannoe Lake, and thereafter the rapids at Young's mill, of short duration.

To overcome these, (the most serious obstruction on the whole route) there can be but one opinion, pointed out in the extreme facilities the river affords in its universally high and well defined banks, and the convenience afforded for the construction of dams at suitable distances, to render the intermediate spaces available, the practicability of which system has been so *amply* tested on the Rideau communication, that leaves not a doubt as to the applicability in the present instance, while the existence of tolerably sized dams at present, proves the facility with which such can be constructed where required. But although I should recommend the system as generally applicable to the nine mile rapids, yet, as will be seen by the accompanying detailed and minute plans, I propose leaving the river at the Little Bay, immediately contiguous to

[1]For Mrs. Traill's explanation of the name see p. 375.

the store-house, and making part of the present marsh and Bay, a receiving basin, and carrying the navigation inland through the town of Peterboro', as nearly parallel with the streets as now laid out as possible, along favourable low ground, and well suited to lockage—bounded by the natural mound or bank on the western side—bending its course round to the plain lots, until reaching the natural ravine at R, to which point the levels naturally lead, as shewn on the accompanying plan and section, until reaching the river at S, and into the dead water from Hall's mill-dam, or from the termination of the mound referred to, to carry on a continued navigation to the summit line of Lee's mill-pond, for which the ground is favourable; and as this would appear in the meantime to be more eligible, it may be deemed sufficient to estimate on this line, leaving the adoption as a matter of expediency hereafter, when the works may go into operation.

I would, therefore, propose for the present, the continuation of the cut to Lee's mill-pond, by which all the mill operations will be left undisturbed, and the wicked chain of rapids avoided.

Having gained the mill-pond by a collateral cut of 2½ miles, with 5 locks, making 56 ft. lift, and the necessary bridges, &c. for the accommodation of the public, the dam and lock system will come into good play, until reaching the foot of Herriot's rapids—by the several locks, dams and excavations, as shewn on the plan and section, from which a collateral cut of one-eighth of a mile will be necessary to carry the line past the mill and rapids, and avoid interfering with the operations thereof, which are likely to become extensive, and secure a more convenient and ready mode of passing this particular spot of difficulty, than by following the river and then by raising and strengthening the present dam, a sufficiency of water can be backed up, with no inconvenience to the adjoining lands, to the foot of Young's rapids—covering the small rapids at the outlet of Katchewannoe Lake, and throwing sufficient water into the lock of 3 ft. lift at Young's, as shewn on the plan and section—from which to the waters of Clear Lake, a short cut of 70 yards in length, averaging 6 ft. deep, through a gravelly section, will carry the navigation (and completing section 2nd) from Peterboro' to Clear Lake, 14¼ miles, and rising 146–10 plus 3 2/10–150 ft. and at an estimated expense of £66,524 14s. 1d.

Section 3rd—From Young's to Bobcaygean, including in its course, through Clear and Stoney Lakes, the Peninsula Falls, Burleigh Chutes, Deer Bay, Buckhorn Rapids, and the navigation of Buckhorn and Pigeon Lakes.

Having gained the waters of Clear Lake, the only operation required to complete the navigation to Peninsula Falls will be a properly constructed dam, to raise the waters of Clear and Stoney Lakes 2 ft. above their present heights, so as to give sufficiency over the outlet of the lakes at lowest summer water, which cannot in any way interfere with adjoining lands, the general character of Clear and Stoney Lakes being rocky and barren shores, and in general very abrupt. The Peninsula Falls, gross rise of 25–8 3/10, I propose surmounting by 3 locks and extended wing walls, with the requisite guard lock at the head or summit to regulate the spring floods. From this point the navigation continues through Deer Bay, until reaching Burleigh Rapids, a pitch of 2 ft. 2 in. at which place a most favourable opportunity presents to surmount, what otherwise would have been attended with trouble and expense, in the placing of a lock in the neck of a Peninsula, as shewn upon the general plan, with the necessary excavation, &c. which will carry the navigation, by the construction of a dam at this place over the little chute to Buckhorn Lake extremity, of rock excavation, as also in the raising of the present or the construction of an additional dam, sufficient to deaden the rapids and swift water above, and throw sufficient additional head in Buckhorn, Chemong and Pigeon Lakes, so as to retain those waters at high water mark, and thereby insure a constant, safe navigation to Bobcaygean Rapids, where terminates section 3rd, in a distance of 31½ miles, ascending 38 ft. 4 in. at an expense of £21,102 2s. 5d.

Section 4th—From Bobcaygean to Balsam Portage (to Lake Simcoe.,) 26¼ miles,—

Will require the re-construction of the lock at Bobcaygean, the lower sill being placed, as already stated, at least 3 ft. too high, besides the dimensions of the lock chamber being too contracted for the present contemplated scale, being only 28 ft. in the clear; the cut from the lock head to the bay above will require considerable enlargement and deepening, so as to admit of being properly secured by lining, &c. to prevent the escape of the water through the open fissures of the loose rock, as provided for in detailed estimate; the re-constructions and increased height to the present dam, with the addition of a smaller one, between the upper island and main land, as shewn upon the plan, with the view of giving a sufficiency of wall over the long continued shallows in the river above to Sturgeon Lake—which gained, gives a splendid navigation for any sized craft to Cameron's Falls, and to the very foot thereof, where a most favourable opportunity occurs for lockage into Cameron's Lake, or rather the river leading to said lake, as shewn on detailed plan and section of that place, surmounting the difference of level of 24/10 2/10, by two locks advantageously located on the brink of the rocky bank, with the addition of a guard lock and excavation into the river or mill-pond above—in a distance of only 265 yards, and averaging 6 ft. cutting, passing between the hotel and saw-mill.

Before leaving the extended and fine navigable water of Sturgeon Lake, it may not be out of place to refer your Excellency simply to the fact of the existence of one of the most favourable opportunities ever presented to open up the same extent of country, by so very little assistance from art, as the waters of Scugog River and Lake afford, passing in the course from Sturgeon Lake, from the south-west angle of Fenelon, through the whole of Ops (40 miles in extent, interrupted only by the rapids at Purdy's mill), touching on Manvers, watering the whole of Cartwright, and part of Reach, at the upper extremity of the lake, and even extending its ramificated contributory branches, rendered partially available (and which little local enterprise would make perfectly so,) into Mariposa, Brock, and Whitby, and as a matter of course not confining its spreading influence to these alone, but enabling an available communication being opened up from the safe and convenient Bay of Windsor (where it is now in contemplation to construct a harbour) by a railroad, or a good macadamized road, *for the present*, from which point the head of the extended navigation seems to be distant only 18 miles, and which, as already shewn on the particular report on that subject, can be rendered available by the simple operation of one dam and lock below the present site of Purdy's mill, and at an expense not exceeding £2500, (under *proper* management)—thereby affording an immediate relief to those rapidly settling Districts—at a trifling outlay, until the through main channel of communication should be opened up, and then affording a permanent local benefit to the Townships immediately bordering on the Scugog River and Lake, as also on the contributaries, the Non-can and Cross Creeks.

To resume my sectional description of the main line:—Having gained by the operations stated, the summit of Cameron's Lake, as the river above the dam, particularly at the outlet into Cameron's Lake, at low water, does not exceed 18 inches, it will be necessary that the dam now existing, and which is one of the most substantial and creditable pieces of workmanship I have seen in the Province, should be raised from 2 to 3 ft. to assist in giving sufficiency of water over the bar at the mouth of the river, where some rock excavation will also be necessary; but if the banks will bear it, and I have no doubt but they will, even a greater increase would be advantageous, not only in the saving of rock excavations at this point (under water) but in materially assisting operations at the foot of Balsam Rapids, which point the navigation reaches easily through the deep Cameron's Lake, and up either of the channels of the river, communicating with Balsam Rapids and Lake, where operations of considerable magnitude, compared to the trifling difference of level, will be requisite to connect with Balsam Lake, in the construction of a lock of 3 ft. lift—and a continuous excavation, chiefly through rock, for 450 yards to the river above, at point B, where a dam will also be required to throw sufficient water over the bar and into Portage Bay—on the summit level of the chain of communications, from the Bay of Quinte to Lakes Simcoe and Huron, making a distance of section 4th of 26¼ miles, and rising 34 ft. at an expenditure of £25,546 16s. 2d. Currency, being a total difference of level above Rice Lake, with the increased head on Balsam Lake of 227 ft.; above the Bay of Quinte,—592 ft.—assuming Balsam Lake to be 3 ft. above July mark, and 118–6 ditto above Lake Simcoe, and assuming Lake Huron, as shewn on the map, 594 ft. above the sea, would seem to leave a difference of level between Lakes Simcoe and Huron of 110 ft. odd, say 110 ft. 6 in.

Next comes the last sectional division of the route No. 5, and one, as already stated, upon which there is sufficient scope for the Engineer's duties—not in point of any very untoward difficulties to be surmounted, but in the proper selection of the most eligible route from Balsam Lake to Lake Simcoe, between which there is a difference of level of 118–5–3 in the present state of the waters, an amount far beyond what was anticipated, and which, consequently, suggested the strictest investigation into the merits of the two probable routes already spoken of, viz. to follow, as much as may be available, the course of the Talbot River from its source downwards—or to adopt an eligible line for a more continuous navigation from Balsam to Lake Simcoe, and for which latter the face of the country affords (with the exception of a trifling rise near Balsam Lake) an opportunity equalled only in one instance in the course of my observation in either Province, and in that for a more limited distance (viz. on the line for a continuous Canal from Lake St. Francis to Lake St. Louis, which runs through the Seigniory of Beauharnois, and which I estimated last year for the Honourable Edward Ellice, in contra-distinction to the other side of the river—the expense being much less.) Still, how-much-soever I might be disposed to avail of such facility for continuous navigation by a cut to Lake Simcoe direct, yet there are circumstances sufficiently urgent to give the preference to a *medium* between the two, and which, I have no doubt, will present the most eligible for adoption, as in tracing the Talbot River from its commencement in the great swamp near Balsam Lake to Lake Simcoe, in all its freaks of serpentine curvature, which I did in the month of June, when the water was very low, as well as in the months of October and November—I fully came to the opinion that to follow the Talbot higher up (as for the sake of description I would beg leave to reverse the order and commence from Lake Simcoe,) thus the commencement of the rapids, at McQuaig's rapids or house, as marked Q on the accompanying detailed plan, made from actual survey, with the view of ascertaining the real nature of the river, would not only be exposing the works to much tardiness of execution from the limited period in which operations could be carried on among a continuation of rapids, but at the same time, when done, would add much to the length of the communication—the direct line with the point of junction with Balsam Lake being only 13¾ miles in extent—and although I should certainly look forward ultimately to carry the navigation to this point, or into the Simcoe Portage reach—yet, in the mean time, I would suggest the propriety of leaving the Talbot either at the convenient and commodious basin, as shewn on the plan at D, 1¾ miles above the mouth, &c. or above the termination of the lately constructed road from Balsam Lake—and from the said basin, or point T, to carry an inland cut to Balsam Lake, as per line delineated *red* on the plan, with the necessary 12 locks of, in all, 116 feet lift, as thereon shewn, or as may afterwards be found more convenient to locate; for which, as already stated, the section of the country is most favourable, with the exception of considerable rock excavation in bedded limestone on leaving Balsam Lake, which, however, will meet well the purposes of lock building, of which there will require to be in all the inland cut 12 locks, (of different feet lift each) besides on the Talbot River, between Lake Simcoe and Talbot basin, of nominal feet lift, with the requisite continuous excavation, culverts, bridges, &c. together with the necessary operations at the mouth of the river, in the removal of the bar and by the construction of *piers*, to prevent its again forming; thus overcoming the obstruction in this section, by an inland continuous cut from Balsam Lake to Talbot River at T, of 13¾ miles, with 12 locks thrown at suitable distances, as shewn on the plan and sections, by one lock on the Talbot River, if found necessary, and the construction of the necessary works at the mouth of the river, in all 16½ miles; descending 121-1 3/10 feet by lockage, or 118-5 7/10 natural difference of level, at an expenditure of £121,212 18s. 1d. Currency.

For the sake of perspicuity, I beg leave to annex a recapitulation of the whole for your Excellency's information, which at one view will shew the abstract of operations required, amounting in all to the sum of £262,067 16s. 4d. and for which I consider these works may be constructed in a permanent, substantial, and workmanlike manner, and under a similar specification as intended for the Trent works, viz.—"Of good substantial hammer-dressed masonry, with ashler hollow quoins, corners, and coping, wooden sills, &c. &c."—Thus opening up an *uninterrupted* water communication from the Bay of Quinte to Lake Simcoe, a distance of *about* 195 miles, and 706–4 feet of lockage, for the sum of £495,515 *odd*, Currency, including the Trent estimate, which amounts to £233,447 6s. 11½d. Currency.

RECAPITULATION

Sec.	Description of Route	Miles		Rise		Dms	Loc.	Amount		
				ft.	in.			£	s	d
No. 1	From Rice Lake to Peterborough, including the bar at the mouth of the Otanabee, Danger's Field, Robinson's & Yankee Bonnet Shallows, Whitlaw's Rapids, &c.	21	$\frac{22}{80}$	4	6	2	1	4,246	19	0
				3 lock.						
2	From Peterborough to Clear Lake, including the nine mile Rapids, Herriott's Rapids, Katchiwannoe Lake, & Young's Rapids	14	$\frac{34}{80}$	147	6	6	14	66,524	14	1
3	From Young's outlet of Clear Lake to Bobcaygean, including Clear and Stoney Lakes, Peninsula Falls, Burleigh Chutes, Buckhorn's Rapids, Buckhorn's Lake, Chemong and Pigeon Lakes	31	$\frac{40}{80}$	38	4	2	5	21,102	2	5
4	From Bobcaygean to Cameron's Falls and Balsam Lake Portage, including Sturgeon Lake, with Bobcaygean Rapids, Shallows above Rapids, Dams there—Dam at or below mouth of Little Bobcaygean, navigation of Sturgeon Lake, Cameron's Falls & Shallows, Cameron's Lake, Balsam Rapids and Balsam Lake,	26	$\frac{24}{80}$	34	0	3	5	22,546	16	2

Sec.	Description of Route	Miles	Rise	Dms	Loc.	Amount
5	From Balsam Lake to Lake Simcoe, including collateral cut to Talbot River, Locks thereon, clearing of Flood Wood, and piers at the mouth of Talbot Harbour,	16	118 Fall of Collateral Cut. 5–3		12	121,212 18 1
	Amounting to					£235,643 9 10
	Lock-Masters houses, &c					2,600 0 0
						£238,243 9 10
	To which add contingencies & management &c. 10 per Cent					23,824 6 6
	Total amount of Estimate,					£262,067 16 4

N. H. BAIRD,
Civil Engineer,
M.I.C.E.L.

December, 1835.

Having now, for your Excellency's information, submitted the result of my labours, and of a more protracted survey than I had anticipated, arising from circumstances which oftentimes give rise to, and create more difficulties in the progress of the Engineer's operations than the real difficulties presented, namely, the different supposed routes which offer themselves to consideration, as imagined eligible, through the different sections of country in which they occur, and pressed upon the attention as the best, or as in many instances, the *only* practicable route——thereby diverting the attention and occupying that time which would have been more advantageously directed to the natural course of the communication, but which, from the circumstance of a doubt existing or possibility thereof, leaves no alternative but to follow out such, if in any way feasible; and under such impression, I was led to make the tour of the back line of Lakes, Rapids and Portages, from Stoney to Crow Lake, which, as already stated, serves but to confirm the prior opinion of improbability, as also in examining the lay of the country, through the different Townships of Eldon and Fenelon, as directed in your Excellency's detailed instructions, per Lieutenant Colonel Rowan's communication of date 16th June last, particularly the portions bordering on, and in the proximity rather of Lake Simcoe and Sturgeon Lake; but soon ascertaining that such a route must entail with it, not only a very material increase in distance, but at the same time an increase in lockage, and without any certain supply of water from a summit level, the country rising gradually towards that course from the Talbot valley (certainly the lowest ground in that section of country) until again falling into the Scugog—and having followed that fine river and more extended lake navigation to its head, and ascertaining, geographically speaking, that that route, although apparently feasible towards Lake Simcoe, would be entirely too circuitous.

After due consideration of the matter in all its bearings, and weighing the merits of the junction with Lake Simcoe, through the Scugog route, which must have been down the valley of the Little Talbot to Beavertown, a stream by no means bearing comparison with its greater rival of the same name, independent of the want of accommodation for shipping, except at a very great outlay of money, and by the *Scugog Lake* route, following either the North-Cross-Creek route, 7 miles above Purdy's mill, into the centre of Mariposa, where the height of land occurs—or continuing up the Lake, take the Noncan River or Creek at the north-west angle of Cartwright, and crossing the south-west angle of Mariposa, gain the height of land in Brock, and from thence descend into Lake Simcoe, down the Black River Valley, which holds out no particular inducement or accommodation for lake craft, which at times will be hard enough pressed to find shelter, all independent of the geographical objection in point of distance—not only in a local view, from Sturgeon Lake to Lake Simcoe, but in following up the ulterior object of continuing the chain of communication with Lake Huron—all of which will be avoided, and the grand object of the most direct and least expensive mode of connecting these waters obtained by the Balsam Lake route; and the Talbot River, as now estimated, besides having the double advantage of bearing out the general character of the whole line as an *internal* communication, opening up a widely extended and valuable country, and one which promises, ere long, to be second to no proportionate space of inland country in the Province, in point of capabilities of improvement, productions and opportunities for enterprise.

For the general line of communication and its connection with the adjacent and surrounding country, and shewing that the line as now surveyed and estimated is not only the most direct that can be found, but the one most calculated to develop the resources of the fertile and valuable country through which it passes, I would beg to refer your Excellency to the accompanying general plan which I have had compiled (by Mr. F. P. Rubige, D.P.S.) to shew the whole line at one view, with the different works proposed to render the whole navigable, by which it will be seen that from the Bay of Quinte to Lake Huron, the general direction of the communication maintains a pretty straight course—that assuming the section from Lake Simcoe to Huron as practicable, and which I extremely regret was not in my power, on account of the advanced state of the season, to have examined, as stated by your Excellency as desirable, when I last had the honour of an interview, and with which intention I did proceed to the Narrows of Lake Simcoe, from the Talbot River, when the difficulty of procuring a proper canoe and crew, and accommodation proper for the excursion, (having left my canoe, &c. at the Talbot, to complete some measurements, under an assistant,) added to the apprehension, which afterwards turned out to be well founded, of being frozen up in some of my operations below, resolved me (then the 5th of November,) to abandon the task; but still I had the satisfaction of gleaning a considerable deal of information from the kindness of an individual in Orillia, who is much interested in the furtherance of the grand object—and in the perusal of a Report, drawn up by an Officer of Engineers, on the state of the Severn River, and which, from the *general* description therein given, would appear to be not more sectionally objectionable for improvement, than what has been met with on the lower sections of the route—the difference of level, as already stated, being about 110 ft.

I would also state that I had, at the same time, an opportunity of gaining information as to the projected route (by a Mr. Boyde,) from Shingle Bay, but which from the general principle, as I understood the description, nearly double the lockage would have to be encountered, than by a gradual descent; besides, judging from past observation and experience, and studying the course of nature in her multiplied arrangements, it ever appears that the lowest pass between any two sections of country is generally, if not always indicated by the greatest discharge of water—although, as a matter of course, and one in all cases not to be avoided, the route may be somewhat circuitous. I would, therefore, be disposed to hazard the opinion, that either by the Severn or Nottawasaga Rivers must be the line of communication, unless the latter be intercepted from Lake Simcoe by a considerable height of land, which I have not had an opportunity of examining; in support of which hypothesis, and which I consider by no means problematical, I would refer, as an example, to the country lying between Peterboro' and Chemong Lake, around which the River Otanabee, the main outlet from these waters down the Trent, &c. makes such a circuitous bend of no less than 23 miles—that having traversed the country between these points in all directions, for the purpose of endeavouring to find a practicable over-land route, and actually running levels of the most probable, I found the lowest ridge of land to be 49 ft. 4 8/10 above the waters of Chemong and Pigeon Lakes, diminishing proportionately, on approaching the outlet, and *vice versa*. I might quote many other instances, which have come within my observation, to strengthen the hypothesis, that the country between Lakes Simcoe and Huron may have a similar sectional character—unless some convulsion of nature may have interfered in the general arrangement.

Having thus attempted to lay before your Excellency the result of a very minute and detailed examination of the country lying between Rice Lake and Lake Simcoe, with the lakes and waters thereon, and of a series of running and detached levels, as in terms of your Excellency's instructions, and in pointing out what I conceive to be the most eligible line for connecting those lakes, I should now proceed to point out the prospective benefits likely to arise from the adoption and execution of such a measure, but for which task I really do feel an inadequacy to do the subject the justice its importance demands, whether considered in a political or commercial point of view: but as such is generally expected from, or to wind up, an Engineer's Report—particularly if such should refer to operations proposed through any new (and scientifically unknown) country, as the route I have just had the honour to examine—I shall use my best endeavours to comply with the task.

As the great object of Internal Improvement through any country, is to afford the means of cheap and expeditious transport for the resources thereof, and to afford the opportunity of connecting the most distant points of fertility and scenes of industry and enterprise with their respective marts, it follows that the shortest and most available route for such an object must be the *sine-qua-non-data* upon which to start—and which, with a due regard to the local interests at the same time through which such a line of communication may pass, for the development of the resources of wealth and enterprise, in which every section abounds, have been the regulating principles in the selections made, and which I flatter myself will be found unequalled in any other, in a geographical point of view, viz. the affording a thorough communication for the produce of the Western countries bordering on Lakes Simcoe, Huron and Michigan—particularly Illinois, Indiana, Michigan and Huron Territories, and partially Ohio—all rising rapidly into the first scale of commercial importance, in their rich productions, now pouring down the rapids of Detroit and St. Clair, from and across those immense inland seas into Lakes Erie and Ontario, and by the famed speculation of the Erie Canal, which was at first, and for long, considered to be so chimerical an undertaking; but now demanding, from the consequent development of those fertile regions, increased dimensions—still, however, subject to the inconvenience of such very hazardous circumnavigation, as a single glance at the map of the Province and adjoining States will demonstrate, and which every season affords fresh instances of the melancholy occurrences, in the many shipwrecks and loss of life and property in consequence, must point out as an ulterior object to be gained, that the tide of the Western trade, at least a great proportion thereof, would naturally find its way by the safer, more expeditious and certain route, the Georgian Bay, and from thence down through the now proposed line of communication, by Lake Simcoe, the waters of the Newcastle District, and the Bay of Quinte, thereby saving, as already observed, not only the very perilous circumnavigation of Lakes Huron, Erie and Ontario, but absolutely shortening the route the inconceivable distance of 261 miles.

Having reached the Bay of Quinte at the conflux of the splendid River Trent, so very susceptible of improvement, as shewn by the detailed Report I had the honour to address to your Excellency in 1833, the transit from thence to our own mart becomes a matter of ease and safety, either by the St. Lawrence or by the present available and certain navigation of the Rideau and Ottawa Canals, now in active operation, and, for our neighbours, affording an opportunity of transit and communication with New York market through the Upper Gap to Oswego—at which point the Erie Canal touches in its course—but as the St. Lawrence and Rideau must be allowed to be the natural outlet for Upper Canada, the proposed improvements, as a matter of course, should be contemplated in connection with these outlets, particularly the most practicable and available for general purposes of commerce, although when the gigantic improvements on the St. Lawrence are completed, she must stand unrivalled in the annals of internal navigation in point of magnitude of construction—and which, of course, is intended to draw the Western trade in that channel, which the intended improvements from the Bay of Quinte to Lake Huron *must insure*.

To the local advantages which, from the extent of country traversed, may with propriety be called *national*, it would almost be presumptuous to set limits, and in which I conceive I am borne out in the retrospective glance of the rapid strides now making towards settlement and development—I may say, from the Bay of Quinte to Lake Huron, under the most untoward and inconvenient circumstances a young country could expect to progress—land-locked with the worst of roads, where such exist, and equally so, with the present state of the river and lakes in their several insurmountable rapids, to any description of craft but the fragile bark canoe, and that only in descending—the improvement of which latter would unquestionably unfold the resources in a ratio I should be at a loss to name, was such an outlet afforded.

To agriculture, the great stand-by of any country, I would add the immense increase in the article of lumber, of all descriptions, now car-

c Archives of Canada

A SECTION OF CHAMPLAIN'S MAP OF 1632
The Trent system is shown above Lac St. Louis (Lake Ontario)

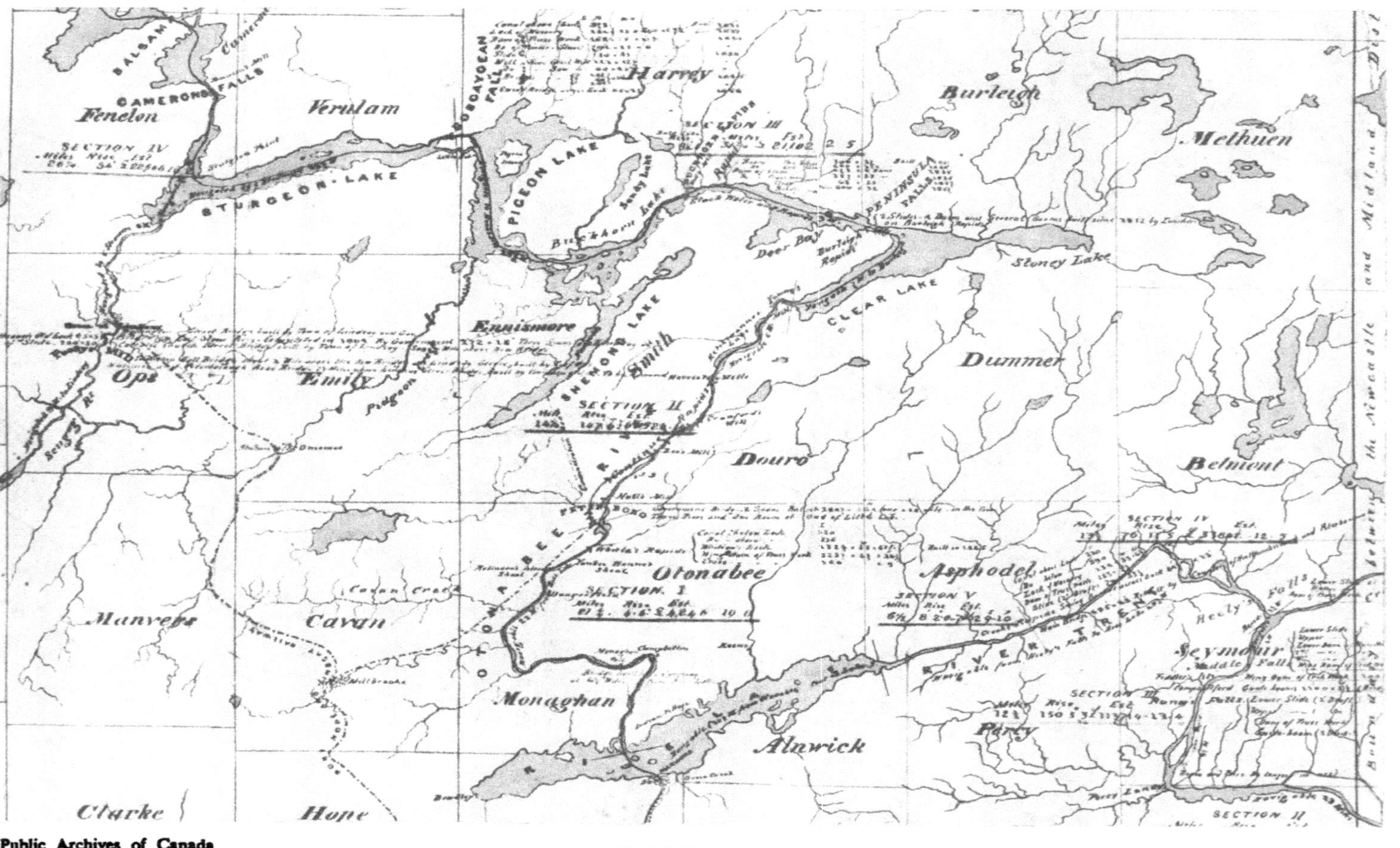

Public Archives of Canada

THE TRENT VALLEY, 1836

From a map of the Inland Water Communications from Lake Huron to the Bay of Quinte

Public Archives of Canada

THE OLD NEWCASTLE DISTRICT
From Chewett's Map of Upper Canada, 1826

ried on to a very limited extent (by a few of those enterprising, hardy speculators, with which the country so copiously abounds,) particularly in the article of staves, for which abundance of the finest oak exists, untouched and unvisited but by the Indian—affording, with an outlet, unlimited scope for individual enterprise throughout the whole line of communication, to say nothing of the vast importance in point of settlement of those fine Districts, bordering on and adjacent to the several extensive lakes, and which have of late drawn the attention of wealth and enterprise to their shores.

Of the benefit to be derived from the opening of the Trent above, it may be conceived superfluous to again refer, having been discussed in my former report on that river and its contributaries—and would but briefly again refer to the importance of having an outlet for the wares of the Marmora Iron Works, so much required in a new country, and which may be viewed in a political or national, as well as commercial light.

To sum up these cursory observations I would merely call your Excellency's attention to the different Townships through which the communication is intended to pass in its course through the Home and Midland Districts, in number no less than *nineteen*, immediately bordering on the waters of the communications, besides bringing into play as many more, with all their agricultural and commercial resources, with their respective already populous settlements, as sufficient guarantee, independent of the great *through* communication object, which, as a matter of course, must positively insure an ample return to the Province of the outlay required—really of secondary consideration to the object to be gained—and to the Home Government, in the ready settlement of those vast tracts of fine lands throughout the Province, now *inaccessible*, an ample return for any interest which the Mother Country might be induced to take in such a national undertaking—were it only with the limited view of enhancing the value of Crown Lands, but particularly, I should say, in rendering fully available the great outlays on the Ottawa and Rideau Canals, of which the contemplated communication may now be said to be a *continuation.*

I would further remark—and perhaps it may be presumptuous in me so doing, but I feel as if I owed it as a duty to the land of my adoption, as well as within the sphere of my instructions—that if we intend to maintain our commercial importance in the scale of nations, and preserve for ourselves an *independent* port of entry for the Canadas, something must be done, and that immediately, to secure such; and nothing, it is believed, will tend so much towards such a desirable object, as an early commencement of this internal work, which not only does more immediately interest all Upper Canada in promoting, by any means, and at all hazards, but not less interested is Lower Canada—which should consider the cause as intimately and more immediately connected with *her* existence, as the outlet not only for *all* our exports, but as a natural reciprocating consequence, the imports into these Provinces. On this subject our enterprising neighbours on the other side are wide awake, and who make no hesitation in their different reports and remarks on their further proposed communications, which have of late engaged their attention—and about some of which they seem in good earnest to make frequent allusion to the contemporary rival to all their projected lines to market—"*The back waters of the Newcastle District and the River Trent.*" Shewing distinctly the importance *they* attach to such a direct line from the *far* west—as likely to anticipate, if put in execution, their best exertions; but unless we be more active in the cause than we have hitherto shewn any disposition to be, I fear we shall be anticipated by their well known prompt and energetic measures, and that those natural facilities of communication may lay dormant, and the surrounding country and resources with it—and that the year now ensuing will go far to decide the question, I believe, is generally admitted on all hands, "whether we give up the cream of our resources, the Carry- "ing Trade, to a foreign power, thereby rendering all our immense "expenditure, as well as the bonus of the Mother Country, more an "injury than a benefit to the Province."

I would further remark, for your Excellency's information, that whilst on the importance of the most prompt and energetic measures being used to open up the grand internal communication, so nearly and intimately connected with the vital interests of these Provinces, that as much of the intrinsic importance in the opening up such a communication, having so many rival competitors, however-so-much in embryo, will depend upon an *early* commencement (as an earnest of the intentions of the Provincial Government) and expeditious execution, for the reasons I have endeavoured to assign, and which might be multiplied beyond the limits of this report the expediency of adopting such measures and system in execution, as would as early as possible secure the results contemplated, and on which subject I would beg to refer your Excellency to the interim report I had the honor of submitting some months ago, (30th September) suggesting the expediency, for reasons therein assigned, of, in the first place, constructing with all expedition such works along the whole line of communication, as might at the smallest expense, (as per estimate of respective sections which I have all along purposely kept detached) open up the greatest extent of navigation, or in other words, the least expensive sections along the line, such as on the River Trent—the dam only at Widow Harris'—the operations at Chisholm's rapids—the dam above Heeley's falls, and works at Asphodel Bridge or Crooks' rapids—thereby opening up the navigation from Widow Harris' (9 miles above the Bay of Quinte) to Percy Landing, 21 miles, and again from Heeley's Falls to Peterboro', by the construction of the small dam and lock of 3 feet lift at Whitlaw's rapids, half a mile below Peterboro', and again on the present section from Peterboro' to Lake Simcoe, or more properly from Rice Lake to Lake Simcoe, by the construction of the dam at Buckhorn rapids, sufficient to maintain Chemong Lake at or about high water mark—by the water at Bobcaygean, Cameron's Falls, and Balsam Rapids to Balsam Portage, with the proposed works on and at the mouth of the Talbot River—leaving the intermediate more expensive, but short sections, from the mouth of the Trent to Widow Harris', 9 miles; from Percy Landing to head of Heeley's Falls, 11 miles; again from Peterboro' to Chemong Lake, 8 miles, in place of 30 miles, as per river and lakes as stated; and lastly, from Balsam Lake Portage to the basin on the Talbot River—to be railwayed *in the mean time*, for which it is rather remarkable, the whole of the ground of these intermediate sections affords the most favorable opportunity for construction that can be imagined or wished for, any descent that is being in the proper direction, and easy of formation.

As an *expedient* only do I venture to suggest to your Excellency's consideration, the adoption; at the same time I am perfectly convinced that the plan will meet with some local opposition, in the apprehension of its practical utility, superseding probably the necessity of (for some years) carrying the through water communication into operation, which would better suit for the transport of heavy lumber; but which objection I should be desirous of removing, by the construction at the most difficult falls, of *slides*, which cost comparatively little, and much *better* suit the purpose for heavy lumber, than lockage; the intermediate railroad system (without transhipment) serving every purpose of the transport of staves down—and the requisite outfittings for lumber establishments upwards—and for a general carrying trade, equally answering every purpose, until its increase should be such as to warrant the putting the whole in full operation.

By this mode of adoption, the communication would be three years earlier opened up than in waiting for the completion of the whole—an immense saving in the *interest* of expenditure effected, such as would go far towards the formation of such expedients; and when the trade and traffic of the country should require, or when it might be found necessary to carry the grand scheme into effect, I am satisfied, from the experience I have had in conducting such heavy works in the interior of a *new* country, that the facilities which such means of transport of materials &c. would afford, would compensate for the execution, taking credit for the raw material, and when it might be deemed necessary (if ever) to remove them, particularly applicable to the inland sections; in consequence, this latter argument would not bear so strong upon the 9 mile section of the Trent.

With the view of doing away with the only, at least the chief objection to the expedient system—the idea of frequent transhipment, I would propose that long and substantial steamers, of particular construction, should regularly ply to and from, on the intermediate extensive water communication, viz. from Widow Harris' to Percy Landing, 21 miles.

From Heeley's Falls to Peterboro', about .... 55 miles
From Chemong Lake to Balsam Lake Portage .... 40 "
From Talbot River to the Narrows, or Kempenfeldt Bay, as the case may be, ... 22 "

And so arranged as to admit of the train of cars being transported at once, with their loadings, direct either from Lake Huron or Lake Simcoe, as the case may be, and which I am satisfied can be done in such a way as to be practically useful, and serve well the present, and until such time as it may be deemed proper to put the lockage system in execution, the prospective wants of the country; and for the purpose of enabling your Excellency to form an opinion on the merits of the plan, I annex an approximate estimate of the opening up the whole route from the Bay of Quinte to Lake Simcoe and Lake Huron, on the combined system, by which it would appear the whole may be accomplished for the sum of £195,565 6s. 6d. currency, somewhat more than I formerly hazarded to your Excellency in my interim report, and may be completed in two and a half years from date of commencement.

Having endeavoured to set before your Excellency the advantages likely to arise to these Provinces and the Mother Country from the *early* opening up of the communications now under review, in a commercial and political point of view, in so far as consistent with the limits of this Report, I should consider the task but half performed, did I not in some degree refer to the *incalculable* facilities which, in a military point of view, would, as a natural consequence, follow the completion of such a work as connecting the Bay of Quinte with Lake Huron, or in reality, the Atlantic with the far West—completing the chain of communication (so generously commenced and so far completed and practically useful to the country) from the Atlantic to Michigan and Sault St. Marie, by the works of the Carrillon, Chute au

Blondeau, and Grenville Canals on the Ottawa River, and thence by the Rideau to Lake Ontario, an internal navigation of immense extent, say 1214 miles—but by the present circumnavigation already referred to, 1475—difference 261 miles, in rounding the Upper Canada Peninsula by the River and Lake St. Clair, and by a lockage of apparently only 33 ft. at Sault St. Marie, carry the navigation into Lake Superior and regions beyond, at little additional expense—thus admitting of the transport of stores to the most distant portions of the Province, with the greatest ease, certainty, and expedition, and in which point of view I would particularly call your Excellency's attention to the combined system *in point of despatch*—having not the smallest doubt but the passage from the Bay of Quinte to Penetanguishine could be accomplished, on the combined system, in 30 hours—or even less.

Having thus completed the result of the examination, levels, &c. of the country between Rice Lake and Lake Simcoe, as in terms of your Excellency's instructions, and in accordance with the spirit of the Address of the House of Assembly, of the important undertaking with which I have had the honour to be entrusted,—I beg leave to submit the whole for your Excellency's information, trusting that I have fully complied with your Excellency's intentions, and that if in any instance I may have exceeded my limits, that such has been dictated from a sense of the particular predicament in which our common interest seems placed; demanding that some active measures be adopted to save our best interests from passing into other hands, and diverting the Trade of the far West from its natural outlet, and which a cursory view of the general map will amply demonstrate.

I have the honour to remain,
With much respect,
Your Excellency's
Most obedient, humble Servant,

N. H. BAIRD,
December, 1835. CIVIL ENGINEER, & M.I.C.E., LONDON.

ABSTRACT ESTIMATE

Of the Expense of effecting a Communication from the Bay of Quinte to Lakes Simcoe and Huron, via. the Trent and Back Waters of the Newcastle District, on the combined principle as referred to in the foregoing Report.

					Currency £	s	d
From	the Bay of Quinte to Widow Harris'....................	9 miles	Per	Rail-road	17,500	0	0
"	Widow Harris' to Percy Landing....................	21	"	" Navigation	14,114	7	6
"	Percy Landing to Head of Heeley Falls................	11	"	" Rail-road	12,000	0	0
"	Heeley Falls to Peterborough Basin.......................	55	"	" Navigation	21,359	8	10
"	Peterborough to Chemong Lake......................	8	"	" Rail-road	15,000	0	0
"	Chemong Lake to Balsam Lake......................	40	"	" Navigation	33,362	17	4
"	Balsam Lake to Talbot River	13¾	"	" Rail-road	27,000	0	0
"	thence along River to Lake Simcoe...............	2½	"	" Navigation	7,450	0	0
"	across Lake Simcoe to Narrows	22	"	" Navigation			
"	Narrows to Lake Huron say..	15	"	" Rail-road	30,000	0	0
	Making in all..				£177,786	13	8
	To which add for contingencies, management, &c...........				17,778	12	10
	Making a total of...................................				£195,565	6	6

N. H. BAIRD
Civil Engineer,
M.I.C.E.L.

MEMORANDA OF LOCKAGE

One Lock .... at Whitlaw's Rapids.
Five do .... at Peterboro', and to Lee's Mill-pond.
Six do .... from Lees to Herriott's.
One do .... at Herriott's Mill.
One do .... at Young's do.
Three do .... at Peninsula Falls.
One do .... at Chute (Deer Bay).
One do .... at Buckhorn Rapid.
One do .... at Bobcaygean.
Three do .... at Cameron's Falls.
One do .... at Balsam Rapids.
Twelve do .... from Balsam Lake to Lake Simcoe.

In all 36 Locks, besides 2 Guard Locks 341 ft. 3 3/10 in. Lockage.

INTERIM REPORT

To His Excellency SIR JOHN COLBORNE, K.C.B. &c., suggesting the expediency of a combined system of Communications from the Bay of Quinte to Lake Huron,

By N. H. BAIRD, Civil Engineer.

30th Sept. 1835.

Cobourg, 30th Sept. 1835.

To COLONEL ROWAN,
Civil Secretary:

Sir,

At this stage of the survey of the water communication from Rice Lake to Lake Simcoe, in connexion with the River Trent improvements, and looking forward to the ultimate end in view, viz.—a communication between the Bay of Quinte and Lake Huron, I feel myself called upon to lay before you, for His Excellency's information, the result of my labours up to this time, in a condensed form, in case the result thereof might lead to other arrangements which might be more conveniently carried on now than at a future period.

On running the levels from the Otanabee River at Peterboro' to the head waters in Chemong and Pigeon Lakes, I found the difference to be much greater than was anticipated in my Report on the Trent improvements, as also the difference of level to Lake Simcoe, equally so, and which, for perspicuity, I shall now enumerate in order, viz.:

	ft.	in.	pts.
From Bay of Quinte to Rice Lake	365 ft.	0 in.	0 pts.
" Rice Lake to Peterboro'	4	6	0
" Otanabee River to head water Chemong Lake	189	9	7
Bobcaygeon Rapids	6	6	0
Cameron's Falls	26	8	0
Balsam Rapids	2	4	7
To Lake Simcoe, (descending)	118	5	3
Making difference of levels from the Rice Lake to Lake Simcoe	348	3	7
Lake Simcoe to Lake Huron, assuming the Lake 594 feet above the sea	110	0	0
Total lockage from the Bay of Quinte to Lake Huron	823 ft.	3 in.	7 pts.

Conceiving, from the very great extent of lockage, the sum unavoidably necessary to accomplish such, (on the most economical principle) and regarding the improvements now in progress and in agitation *everywhere*, to command the commerce of the Western Territory, and divert it from the natural outlet, (the Trent) it has occurred to me, and I am strongly impressed with the conviction, that a species of communication might be adopted, with advantage, between the Bay of Quinte and Lake Huron, to answer every purpose required, in the mean time, with the advantage of increase of speed to a considerable extent, and would propose for the expensive sections of the Trent, and along the line of communication to Lake Simcoe, to substitute Rail Roads, viz.:—

From the mouth of the Trent to Widow Harris'	9 miles
From Percy Landing to summit of Heely's Falls, about	11 "
From Peterboro' to Chemong and Pigeon Lakes	8 "
And from Balsam Lake to Talbot River	13¾ "
Or Lake Simcoe, direct	16½ "
Making in all, from the Bay of Quinte to Lake Simcoe, only	41 miles of Rail Road.

The communication to Lake Huron, from Kempenfeldt Bay, I am not in possession of sufficient data to say what proportion may be railwayed, but from the lockage being so heavy, I am disposed to think the combined principle may be equally applicable on that section.

The whole expense of opening up a direct communication from the Bay of Quinte to Lake Simcoe, on the combined system, will not exceed the sum of £195,565. 6s. 6d. and may be completed in three years.

By continuous lockage, £495,515. 3s. 3½d.

In the one case the passage of goods from the Bay of Quinte to Lake Simcoe may be accomplished with ease in twenty-four hours, whilst by the other three days would be required.

From the manner in which the arrangements can be effected, the wagons will pass directly, with their loads, from Lake Simcoe to the Bay of Quinte, and vice versa undisturbed, by steamers constructed for the purpose, to ply on the intermediate waters.

Having laid this cursory view of the subject before you, for His Excellency's consideration, feeling it a duty I owe to the Country, as well as in accordance with the spirit of the instructions I have in command from His Excellency, I shall be glad to be informed whether His Excellency would approve of the estimate of such a communication being made out, to lay before the House, in addition to the lockage estimate, or whether the latter should not be dispensed with in the mean time.

I must beg to be understood in recommending the combined system, that it cannot in any manner interfere with the through water communication, in any other than to materially lessen the estimate, when it might be carried into effect, in the construction of which a saving nearly equal to the expense of such intermediate rail roads would be effected.

Awaiting His Excellency's commands—
I have the honor to be,
Sir,
Your most obedient Servant,
N. H. BAIRD,
Civil Engineer.

9. Visit of Lieutenant-Governor Sir John Colborne to the Trent Lakes, 1834

[Cobourg Star, *October 8, 1834.*]

A friend in Peterboro has favored us with the following graphic account of His Excellency Sir John Colborne's late visit to that Town and neighborhood. We are much pleased to find Sir John has visited our back lakes, as he cannot fail of being impressed with the extraordinary advantages they offer to the country at large:

His Excellency Sir John Colborne, attended by two of his sons and his aids, Col. Rown and Capt. Philpotts, left Toronto on the 10th inst. on a tour of the back Townships and Lakes of the Newcastle District.

11th—Landing at Port Hope on the evening of the same day, His Excellency proceeded through Hope to Graham's Inn,[1] Cavan, and early next morning through Monaghan to Peterboro. The remainder of the day was spent in viewing this rapidly increasing and flourishing town and neighborhood. The beauty of the situation—an elevated plain on the banks of the Otonabee, studded with neat villas and more solid essentials to the wealth of a settlement—mills and machinery—added to the activity and enterprise which seemed to pervade the whole, appeared to afford much gratification to His Excellency.

12th—On Thursday His Excellency and suite, accompanied by the Hon. T. A. Stewart and Alexander M'Donell, Esq., Government Agent at Peterboro, proceeded under the guidance of the latter on the tour of the Lakes. After inspecting the Indian Village at Chemong Lake, there meeting the Indians, His Excellency and suite proceeded in canoes to the rapids at the foot of Buckhorn Lake. The improvements now being carried into execution by John Hall, Esq., late of Peterboro, will induce settlers to visit this hitherto isolated part. A stone dam is now

[1]Graham's Inn, Cavan, was in the present Bailieboro. In 1817 Michael Graham, then about seventy years old, emigrated to Canada from Fermanaugh, Ireland. He and his family settled on the present site of Bailieboro, of which he was the founder. His son Joseph established the inn referred to, and for many years the settlement continued to be called Joseph Graham's Tavern or Graham's.

being constructed, on which will be raised a bridge connecting the Townships of Harvey and Smith.

13th—Returning to the Indian Village, on the day following His Excellency proceeded by way of Pigeon Lake to the rapids at Bobcaygeon, and after viewing the public works passed the night at the hospitable dwelling of Thomas Need, Esq., on the shore of Sturgeon Lake. On the 14th the party proceeded through Sturgeon Lake, visiting the settlements on its banks, to Cameron Falls.

With the romantic beauty of the village site at the Falls His Excellency and the whole party were much pleased. It is scarcely too much to anticipate the not distant period when its claims in this respect will draw many a gay tourist to the spot. Of the natural advantages of the situation its proprietors, Messrs. Jamieson and Wallace, are preparing fully to avail themselves, having now in rapid course of execution extensive mills, a large substantial Building for a Hotel, &c.

On the 15th His Excellency proceeded through Cameron and Balsam Lakes to the Portage which leads from the latter to the Talbot river flowing into Lake Simcoe, and after examining the Portage as far as the Talbot returned to the Falls.

We have the high gratification of noticing the deep impression which the extraordinary capabilities of this chain of waters, their fine scenery, the extensive improvements on their shores, and the favorable character of the country appeared to make on His Excellency. We anticipate the best results from the visit with which our District has been favored, and the more so from the unwearied and vigilant attention of Sir John Colborne to everything which came under his notice.

We understand from good authority that very extended plans, tending to open the resources of this fine country, are under His Excellency's consideration, and we again congratulate the Inhabitants that their interests are in the hands of a Governor who permits no personal considerations of inconvenience or fatigue to interfere with his anxious desire to promote their welfare.

16th—From the Falls His Excellency returned by way of Harvey, visiting the farm of R. Madge, Esq., on Manetow Lake, where he passed the night and arrived at Peterboro on the following day.

17th—The party, under an escort of our yeomanry, cavalry, and many respectable gentlemen of the town and vicinity, took the route through the township of Otonabee to the Indian village on Rice Lake, where they were saluted with three rounds from the fusils of the Indians, under the command of their chief, Pawtawche. His Excellency then went on board the steamboat for Bewdley, from where he proceeded, we understand, direct by land to Toronto.

10. Report on Petition for an Inland Waterway in the District of Newcastle

[*Appendix 12 to the* Journal of the House of Assembly of Upper Canada, *1837*]

REPORT

Of Select Committee on Petition of T. A. Stewart, and others, of the District of Newcastle.

TO THE HONORABLE THE COMMONS HOUSE OF ASSEMBLY.

Your Committee, to whom was referred the Petition of T. A. Stewart, and others, for rendering navigable the inland waters of the District of Newcastle, beg leave to Report—

That your Committee have not had it in their power, from the great distance at which some of the witnesses reside, and the absence in Lower Canada of others, to lay before your Honorable House the evidence in detail upon the several facilities and advantages which would be likely to accrue to the Province in general, and to the District of Newcastle in particular, from the rendering navigable the waters of the River Trent. But they trust, that, from the circumstance of its having for several years engaged the attention of your Honorable House —from the Report of the Engineer, Mr. Baird—from the Reports of two Select Committees—and from the general knowledge which, they presume, most of the members of your Honorable House must have of the vast tract of good land, having this channel only for communication with the markets for their surplus produce and lumber—such statement would be entirely superfluous. They feel it, however, a duty which they owe to the country to lay before your Honorable House a plain statement of facts elicited from Mr. Baird, the Engineer, and Mr. Myres and Mr. Robertson, Mr. Manahan and Mr. M'Donell, all gentlemen of the first respectability, well acquainted with the local matters relating to this communication.

1st, There are now thirty settled Townships dependent on this line of communication for egress to market with their produce.

2nd, That in consequence of the expense necessarily incurred in taking their produce to market, it is not worth exceeding one half, on an average, as much as it is in the front Townships.

3d, That several gentlemen, of very considerable means, and some of large capital, (one of whom has expended, in the Township of Fenelon, 40 miles above the Rice Lake, upwards of £10,000,) have settled in those rear Townships, with the full impression that the Trent would be made navigable, and who, if it be not immediately commenced, must abandon it.

4th, That a number of the new settlers have, within the last twelve months, gone to look for labor in the United States.

5th, That in consequence of a land carriage through a new country, and bad roads, of 37 miles, the Marmora Iron Works, for the present, have been abandoned, and which, by opening the lower sections of the Trent, will be immediately put in operation, and £200,000 worth of iron supplied annually within the Province, which is now received from abroad; and it is submitted, that the propriety of opening these sections of the Trent, if for no other purpose than to insure a supply of iron within the Province for the contemplated Railroads, will to your Honorable House be too obvious to need any remarks from your Committee.

6th, That for the whole distance between the Rice Lake and Lake Simcoe, both sides of the said communication, including many large contributory streams, are almost a continued forest of white oak, pine, and other valuable timber, never yet entered upon by lumber-men, and which must remain locked up until this object be accomplished.

Your Committee forbear entering into the numerous and cogent reasonings which might be brought to bear upon this subject in a political point of view, but they cannot, in justice to your Honorable House, conceal their fears that in the event of the settlers now residing along the whole contemplated route being led to believe, by any measures which your Honorable House may adopt at this time, that the work which they have hitherto for several years looked upon as certain to be accomplished at no distant period is to be postponed or abandoned, the effect will be not only completely to paralyze their future exertions, and prevent accession to the population or capital from abroad, but will be the means of actually compelling them to seek another country and foreign employment, in order to ameliorate their condition.

Seven-eighths of the population in the new townships dependent upon, and interested in the navigation of these waters, are emigrants who have settled there within the last fifteen years, and the time has now arrived at which their consumption of British goods is increasing to a very great degree, to pay for which, as well as for the education of their large and increasing families, they are of course dependent wholly upon the produce of their land.

Your Committee beg leave, in further proof of the vast importance that the opening of this communication must be to the inhabitants in that section of the country, to draw the attention of your Honorable House to the important fact, that out of a population, which, according to the official returns, amounted in the year 1835 to 30,245 souls in the

Newcastle District, 15,756 are dependent upon and deeply interested in the opening of this communication. The front part of the townships bordering upon Lake Ontario only, containing a population not exceeding 14,489 souls, having a more convenient access to that lake.

Your Committee further beg leave to direct the attention of your Honorable House, in proof of the correctness of their opinion, that the tracts of country settled, and settling, contiguous to those waters, are not surpassed in Upper Canada for all those requisites which constitute a desirable location for new settlers, to the facts, that whilst the Province has increased her population from 107,980 to 346,165 in the last fifteen years, being a little more than 300 per cent., the Newcastle District in the same period has increased hers from 6,150 to 30,245 souls, being nearly 500 per cent.

Your Committee have documents and evidence from R. C. Wilkins and William Robertson, Esqs., two gentlemen who have been many years engaged in the lumber trade along the waters, and men of the most unimpeachable character for integrity, that if this work were now finished from the mouth of the Trent to the Rice Lake, the lumber alone which has been taken down for several years, on an average, in defiance of all risks and disadvantages, would at a moderate toll pay £8,000, or the interest of £133,000.

Your Committee therefore feel no hesitation in coming to the conclusion, if that data be correct, and of which they have no doubt, that the immediate increase of that trade, together with the produce from Peterboro' and the surrounding country, and the settlements extending from thence to the mouth of the Trent, a distance of 95 miles, to say nothing of the produce from the iron works, and the merchandize and stores which will ascend the river, will, as soon as the channel shall be completed, pay the interest of £237,694 5s. 11½d. being the estimate for the whole work from the Bay of Quinte to Peterboro'.

Your Committee cannot forbear to direct the attention of your Honorable House, to the further important fact, that the mouth of the River Trent is now, by the circuitous route of the Bay of Quinte, within ten hours' sail of Oswego and Rochester, in the State of New York, (and when the contemplated Canal, from the head of that Bay to Presqu'isle, shall be completed, within six hours,) where sawed pine lumber, such as boards and planks, are from sixteen to twenty dollars per thousand feet, while the same lumber can be delivered on board the vessels at any point, from the mouth of the Trent to Peterborough, a distance of near one hundred miles, abounding all the way with water power and pine timber, for one pound five shillings per thousand feet. This immense source of wealth, can never be made available, unless by means of this work.

In short, your Committee feel persuaded, that no public work hitherto undertaken in Upper Canada, holds out a more reasonable prospect of success, either as it regards the immediate interest and wealth of the people within that District, or that of the Province at large.

They, therefore, respectfully but earnestly recommend to your Honorable House, the adoption of the work, from the mouth of the Trent to Peterborough, ninety-five miles, estimated by the Engineer, to cost £237,694 5s. 11½d., and also the appropriation of the sum of £4850, to complete the navigation from Chemong Lake, in and through the settled Townships of Smith, Ennismore, Emily, Harvey, Verulam, and Fenelon, to Cameron's Falls, thirty-two miles on the route to Lake Simcoe, fourteen miles to Hall's Mills in Harvey, and forty miles up to the Scugog Lake and River, running in and through the settled Townships of Ops, Manvers, Cartwright, Reach, Brock, and Mariposa. Thus, for the last mentioned sum of £4850, a navigation of eighty-six miles, is laid open for steam boats.

The total sum then of £242,544 2s. 11½d. will be [for] a continuous steam boat navigation for the distance of one hundred and sixty miles, commencing at the Head of the Bay of Quinte—with the single exception of the Seven-mile Carrying Place, between Peterborough and Chemong Lake, over which there is a good road.

Your Committee are aware, that in consequence of the vast sum of money already laid out in public works, which have not yet been completed, or made available to the Province, it might not be considered advisable to raise the whole sum for the first year, and they, therefore, with a view to obviate this objection, as far as a sense of duty to the country will justify, recommend that, for the year 1837, there be granted the sum of £16,059 8s. 0d., for the upper sections, as follows:—

	£	s.	d.
From foot of Crooks Rapids to Rice Lake	£7812	9	0
River Otanabee & Whitelaw's Rapids	4246	19	0
Bobcaygean and Scugog	4000	0	0
	£16,059	8	0

And also the estimated sum for the two lower sections, being £77,507 11s. 4½d., to be payable the one half in the year 1837, and the other half in the year 1838.

All which is respectfully submitted.

H. RUTTAN,
Chairman.

Committee Room,
House of Assembly,
November 29, 1836.

11. Reports, Tenders, and Letters concerning the Trent Canal

(a) Report of Commissioners, Trent Canal, 1839

[*Public Archives of Canada, R.G.11, P.W. 5, Vol. 17*]

To His Excellency Sir George Arthur
K.C.H. Lieutenant Governor of the
Province of Upper Canada
&c &c &c

The Commissioners for the improvement of the navigation of the River Trent, beg leave to report:—

That in the discharge of their duties during the last year they have met with difficulties of a most serious and formidable character and such as they conceive they never should have experienced—That in the commencement of the work under their superintendence they were very careful not to enter into any contract without being fully aware that the amount necessary for such contract had been raised by Debenture and paid into the hands of the Receiver General for the purpose of the work.

Your Commissioners however regret to find that the greater part of the money so raised for that express object has been appropriated to other purposes and cannot now be obtained to meet the claims of Contractors on the works—Your Commissioners as they have formerly made known to Your Excellency entered into a contract with Messrs Barclay & Co for that section of the work at Chisholm Rapids and with Messrs Francis & Hay for that at the mouth of the Trent—The first mentioned Contractors have always conducted their work much to the satisfaction of the Commissioners and have advanced very near completion but Your Commissioners have been compelled in consequence of the difficulty of obtaining money from time to time to meet their engagements with the contractors and at length on being informed by Your Excellency that no more money could be obtained to acquaint the Contractors that they must make the work they had done secure and discontinue further operations as soon as possible. This of course was a disappointment to the contractors who now make a claim for damages and according to the Report of the Engineer may produce an ultimate loss to the Province of Upwards of £1500 Messrs Francis & Hay failed in their contract and abandoned their work but Your Commissioners believe that if they had been assured that their money would be paid to them regularly as the work proceeded Messrs Francis & Hay would not have abandoned the work and might have completed it—Your Commissioners consider they have paid these Contractors the

List of Amounts for Stone drawn from Dummer Quarry to Whitlas Rapids 1839

No	Names	£	s	d	No	Names	£	s	d
						Brought forward	262	3	6
1	J. Davey	1	4	1	27	Henry Best	4	6	9
2	T. Harper	37	19	.	28	Irving Brisbin	1	6	3
3	Edward Freeman	16	17	10	29	Charles Brisbin	3	13	9
4	Barnabas Fletcher	39	17	4	30	James Groome	4	9	3
5	John Yates	11	6	.	31	James McGroome	4	11	10
6	John Wilson	5	10	5	32	Peter Currill	3	3	7
7	Henry Crowe	5	1	11	33	Francis Sanderson	4	3	2
8	Michael Sullivan	7	7	2	34	Alexander Swinton	8	6	11
9	Jonathan Stevenson	12	6	2	35	A. B. Cowan	1	17	9
10	John Welch (1)	12	10	2	36	Robert Houston	-	9	2
11	John Welch (2)	6	16	4	37	Joseph Hoop	2	15	7
12	James Welch	8	18	5	38	H. Barclay & Co	4	6	1
13	John Walton	7	6	11	39	John Bone	-	18	5
14	Joseph Walton	4	13	4	40	Benjamin Runnels	1	8	3
15	Patrick McCarty	6	5	-	41	Thomas Beavis	1	7	6
16	Henry Cowan	14	1	.	42	William Best	5	11	6
17	Richard Hamblin	1	18	5	43	Thomas Bell	-	10	1
18	John Hall	5	5	4	44	William Elliott	3	3	9
19	Adam Hall	5	17	11	45	David Porter	-	9	9
20	James Bevard	6	15	9	46	John Tully	4	3	5
21	Patrick Sheehan	5	7	9	47	Henry Floyd	1	12	4
22	George Dixon	5	19	1	48	Thomas Hanlin	1	6	4
23	Samuel Dixon	-	18	11		Barnabas Fletcher	-	8	.
24	Thomas Rutherford	5	19	6		Edward Sloan	7	15	.
25	Benj. Fleming	23	18	8		oil and paint for marking	-	7	6
26	Patrick Leahy	2	17	1					
	Carried forward £	262	3	6		£	335	1	11

I certify the above to be correct
(signed) Thos. McNeil [illegible]
Overseer of Works

A True Copy
Charles [illegible]
Secy

N H Baird
Civil Engineer
28 Feb 1839

Public Archives of Canada

ACCOUNT FOR STONE DRAWN FROM DUMMER TO WHITLA'S RAPIDS, 1839

full amount of work done altho' they do not think so, and Messrs Barclay & Co have also been nearly paid for the work done.

The amount in the hands of the Commissioners is about £400 and will scarcely be sufficient to enable them to pay off the balance due Barclay & Co for the work actually done and the contingencies to the 1st of February at which time Your Commissioners have determined to discharge the Engineer and Secretary unless means can be obtained to proceed with the work—Your Commissioners have had a most unpleasant duty to perform in consequence of the circumstances hereinbefore detailed and regret that their services which have been altogether gratuitous should have failed to accomplish that good which the completion of the works in progress would have effected but which the want of Funds prevented—Your Commissioners have directed the Engineer employed to superintend the works to make a particular return and estimate of the work done and of the sums requisite to complete the Contracts as also a Statement of the probable loss to the public in case works are abandoned; This will probably occupy a few days and so soon as it is obtained it shall be transmitted to Your Excellency.

Toronto 7th December 1839—

(signed)	John S. Cartwright,
"	G. S. Boulton,
"	Charles Anderson
"	A. McDonell.

(*b*) TENDER OF B. BLETCHER[1] AND THOMAS HARPER

[*Public Archives of Canada, Trent Canal, R.G. 11, P.W. 5, Vol. 18*]

The undersigned Barnabas Bletcher of the Township of Hope and Thomas Harper of the Town of Peterboro hereby contract with The Honble Zacheus Burnham on behalf of the Commissioners for the Improvement of the Inland Waters of the Newcastle District to draw the Stone required for the Works at Whitla's Rapids from Dummer Quarry on the undermentioned terms—namely—

All Stone under Twenty five feet Cube Measurement—	at Eleven pence half penny per cubic foot
All Stone at or about Twenty five feet Cube Measurement	at one shilling and three pence per cubic foot

[1]The Bletchers were prominent operators of a stage-line northward from Port Hope, and for a time westward to Toronto. Dale, a small settlement three miles north of Port Hope, was long called Bletcher's Tavern.

the said Stone to be deposited in such places at or near the Works at Whitla's Rapids as may be directed by the person in Charge there— and they (the Contractors, further agree to draw the said Stone and deliver it on or before the tenth day of March 1841 the Weather permitting—
And further it is agreed that the said Contractors, if they require it, shall be paid Eighty per Cent on such portion of the Work they execute, at the end of Each Month from this date and the balance on Completion of the Contract

Executed at Cobourg
this Twenty fourth day
of December 1840
In presence of
Charles Green

Zacheus Burnham
B. Bletcher
Tho[s] Harper

(*c*) WILLIAM BOWEN TO THE HONOURABLE J. B. HARRISON

[*Public Archives of Canada, R.G. 11, P.W. 5, Vol. 19*]

Frankford 22nd April 1843

Sir

I have to acquaint you for the information of His Excellency the Governor General that a most Violent outrage was lately committed on the person of M[r] Noble Barry, while at Chisolm's rapids, one of the portions of the River Trent, now under improvement, and that other Violence both to persons and property have been committed at the same place.—In consequence of the information which I received I issued a warrant against two persons implicated in the disgraceful and riotous proceedings and entrusted the execution of it to two Constables —The Constables have returned and declared their inability to execute the warrant; and further that on applying to the person in charge of the works, he declared his willingness that the persons should be given up but that if the Constables attempted an arrest it would be one which might endanger their lives, and that if their lives were saved it would be at the risk of his own—The Constables have since been informed that a party of eight men armed followed them from the rapids with Violent intentions against them; fortunately the Constables crossed the river on their return instead of Keeping the road, which probably saved them from Violence if any was intended against them—at the same time with the warrant I caused some persons residing at the rapids and Known

TO CONTRACTORS.

SEALED TENDERS will be received at the Office of Mr. Thomas McGrath, Superintendant of the Trent Works, (Brophy's Hotel, Frankfort,) until *Monday, the 6th February next*, for the supply of the Material for the undermentioned Works.

HEELEY FALLS DAM.

From 500 to 700 Cords heavy *Cobble* or *Rubble-Stone*, about 20,000 Cubic feet White Pine, and about 6,000 cubic feet of White Oak Lumber.

The Stones to be regularly corded, and delivered at such dates in the interim from now until the 1st of next September, as will ensure, from time to time, a supply of such quantities, as may be required in construction of the work. The Lumber to be *well dressed, straight*, without *bad knot* or *shake*; of sizes accordant to a specification to be furnished to the persons whose Tenders are accepted; to be delivered before the 1st of June, and together with the stone, in such place in the vicinity of the Falls, as may be pointed out by the Superintendant.

For Harris Rapids Dam.

From 1,200 to 1,500 Cords Stone, about 46,000 cubic feet White Pine, and about 13,000 cubic feet White Oak Lumber. To be delivered at such place near the site of the Dam, as may suit the Superintendant; and in such manner, of such description, and at such times as named of the material for Heely Dam.

For Lock Gates,

AT CHISHOLM'S RAPIDS.

About 2,000 cubic feet White Oak, of the *best description, entirely free of fault*; dimensions to be specified the day of receiving Tenders, and to be delivered before the 1st day of next March.

The Tenders not to be for less than 50 cord stone, or 2,000 feet of Lumber; to be addressed to *Mr. Thomas McGrath, Superintendant Trent Works*; to specify the price in H. C'y. per Cord of Stone, and per thousand feet of Lumber, of the different kinds, and to particularize for what work.

PAYMENTS to be made monthly, during the time of the delivery of the materials, in proportion of two-thirds of the price of the accepted quantity; and each tender to bear the names of two sufficient persons, willing to become security for the fulfilment of the Contract.

By order

THOMAS McGRATH,
Sup'd't Trent Works.

Frankfort, 13th Jan. 1843.

Public Archives of Canada

ADVERTISEMENT FOR TENDERS, TRENT CANAL, 1843

Committed to be summoned to give their testimony—They have not yet made their appearance, and one of the Constables has informed me, that the parties expressed a perfect willingness to give their testimony but declared that they were afraid both of their lives and property to be cognizant of the assault on M[r] Barry and the Violence afterwards should it be known that they had any intention of bringing the evil doers to justice—

I feel confident that His Excellency will not Consent that such an infraction of the law should be committed with impunity, and that the civil authorities of the Country should thus be set at defiance—Not only are the offenders in the present instance allowed to escape, but offences of a more aggravated nature both against property and life will be attempted if the law is not enforced—In the mean time great dissatisfaction and discontent prevails that such atrocities should be committed and the offenders protected from the Civil Authorities by men employed on the public works of the Country but who would seem to be banded together and armed for the support of the disorderly and the discomfiture of the legal Authorities. As the case is Completely of a novel nature and as the force necessary to bring the offenders to justice is greater than any I have at my Command, I have to request the assistance of the Executive Government, and also that His Excellency the Governor General will be pleased to give me such further instructions for my guidance as he may consider the exigencies of this peculiar Case to require—

I have to request you will Convey to His Excellency my humble opinion that if the outrage at present Complained of be not promptly punished, and a stop in the first instance put to such Violence that the Consequences will be most serious; as the feeling in the Country is very much against the perpetrators of this outrage; and if the law is not found strong enough to Curb such Violence, I dread that recourse will be had to other and less satisfactory means to obtain redress—

I have the honor to be
Sir
Your Most obedient humble Servant

William Bowen

The Hon —
J. B. Harrison
Secretary
Canada West

(*d*) SAMUEL KEEFER TO T. A. BEGLY, 1845

[*Public Archives of Canada, R.G. 11, P.W. 5, Vol. 19*]

Board of Works.
Montreal 26th April 1845

Sir

In reference to Mr Wilsons letter of the 14th Inst. I beg leave to report.

That in my opinion it is desirable that Mr Wilson should make immediate preparations for commencing the slides at Buckhorn Dam and Burleigh Chute, by building shanties, and getting out timber for the works—In the mean time however he should make arrangements for building the pier which he intended placing at the foot of the Middle falls Slide on the East side of the River for the purpose of throwing more water over the Shoal—also to prepare a boom and cribs for it to rest against, to extend from the head of Ranneys falls slide to the opposite banks of the river, and booms to protect the Seymour Bridge from injury. These are to be ready for placing when the water is low enough to admit of it.

I agree with Mr Wilson as to the propriety of Booms being kept up by the Board at the foot of Crow Bay and at Percy Landing, even should it be necessary to charge for so doing, for hitherto the expense of keeping up a Boom at the latter place has fallen chiefly upon one or two individuals, and other lumberers have been benefited at their expense. I am in hopes, that after this year, these booms will not be required, as the slides will be so much improved, that cribs may run down all of them without breaking.

It appears not unreasonable that some allowance beyond the yearly stipend, shd be made to the persons in charge at Crooks and Chisholms Rapids.

There are some other works in the vicinity which, I conceive might be undertaken at once by Mr. Wilson—

1st Building the Bridge at Crooks Rapids with a swing Bridge over the Lock.

2d A Boom at Whitlas Lock.

The tenders obtained by Mr Lyons for these works, exceed his estimate, and are not from parties who can be depended upon.

3d Bridge at Buckhorn Dam.

There are tenders for this work, less than Mr Lyons Estimate, but for fear the giving a Contract Might interfere with the Works at the Slide, and at the repairs to the Dam, I am inclined to recommend that the whole be done by Mr Wilson.

If the B^d approves of these suggestions I can prepare plans and instructions such as will enable Mr Wilson to go on forthwith.

I have the honor to be
Sir
Your ob^t Ser^vt
Samuel Keefer
E B W

T. A. Begly
P.S.

I enclose the tenders referred to, together with Mr Lyons reports on the same. *S.K.*

(*e*) SAMUEL KEEFER TO T. A. BEGLY, 1846

[*Public Archives of Canada, R.G. 11, P.W. 5, Vol. 19.*]

Board of Works
Montreal 13^h January 1846

Sir

The Slides and other improvements upon the River Trent designed to facilitate the running down of lumber, having been fully completed last fall; it only remains that proper regulations for using them be adopted before spring, as without the enforcement of such there will be no possibility of maintaining the works against the irregularities that will follow. If the timber is not rafted in Crow Bay and sent down in cribs from thence through the slides, but is allowed to pass down in single pieces, beyond all question the Booms will be destroyed and the slides rendered useless.

To insure the proper working of the slides, I propose that Mr Wilson be further instructed to construct a retaining boom at the foot of Crow Bay the cost of which will be about £250, and that the person in charge of the slides be instructed by the proper authority to allow no timber to pass out of that Boom except in Cribs properly rafted for running the slides.

I have the honour to be
Sir
Your very ob^t Servt
Samuel Keefer
Eng^r B^d Works.

Thomas A. Begly Esqr.
Sec^y B^d Works
Montreal

P.S. Since writing the foregoing, I have seen the report of Mr. Davis in which he recommends another boom being thrown across the River at the Mouth of the Trent to insure also collection of the Slide dues. This I suppose would cost about £50, but before I would recommend the expenditure, I think it desirable to obtain from M[r] Davis his opinion as to the expediency of collecting the dues at Chisholms Slide the last one on the River, and so save the expense of making and maintaining a second Boom.

In the rest of his suggestions, I fully concur.

S. Keefer

(*f*) LETTER OF "A REFORMER" CHARGING VANDALISM

[*Public Archives of Canada, R.G. 11, P.W. 5, Vol. 17*]

River Trent—
24 January 1849

To the Honb[le]
Malcomb Cameron.
Commissioner of Public Works

Sir,

Permit me to lay before you a temporary inspection which I have lately made on the locks and Slides of the River Trent Navigation, Commencing at the Dam at W[d] Harrises which appears to be Shamefully neglected by those who now Superintend, and more particularly Chishelums rapids, Here the lock is stripped of its Chains and the iron Clamps and lead taken out from the Coping of the lock and carried off, and if not soon repaired Must inevitably go to decay, In the next place the Lock house and its out buildings are in a state of Delapidation having the windows broken &c Also the Carts and barrows left there have all nearly disappeared, as to the Slide it is equally in a State of ruin, the Stop logs of the Slides cut out last fall are not heeded the person in charge being drunk whenever he has an opportunity of doing so and the Superintendant M[r] Rayney is totally unfit for his Situation

I shall not at present get into a general detail of the River Trent as it is all ill attended to to the disgrace of those in Authority, and how long the Country will have to bear this is a tale yet to be told under the late administration things were better attended to, but now when the Country expects justice done to them by not neglecting this branch of improvement which cost them such an enormous Sums—Why not appoint a proper practical Superintendant A person Capable of Conducting the repairs of slides and Bridges and Locks &[c] Also doing all the Duty required as Slide Master, It is no more than Work for one

Competent Man, The Trent Bridge also requires a friendly hand as the butments are falling and ought to be immediately repaired while the ice is good

I have the Honor to remain
Your obt Servt
A Reformer

(*g*) JOHN LANGTON TO THE COMMISSIONER OF PUBLIC WORKS

[*Public Archives of Canada, Trent Canal, R.G. 11, P.W. 5, Vol. 19*]

Fenelon Falls Nov. 28 1850

Sir

On the 1st of October last I made an application on behalf of the County of Peterborough, that the sale of the Public works in this county, advertised for that day, might be postponed, in order to afford time for obtaining information as to the nature of the property to be sold—My request was complied with, but I have still been unable to ascertain what it is that the Government propose to sell—Mr Hall to whom you first referred me for information expressed himself unable to give any as to the nature of the property, & only a recollection of a conversation as to the terms proposed, upon which he requested us not to rely; Mr Benson, the Chairman of the Committee of the Council on County property, wrote to you at my request on Sept 24th with particulars of the information wanted, to which letter no reply has been received; & when I was in Toronto myself in October I was unable to get any explanation at your office in consequence of your absence—As it is impossible that the County Council can make any offer in total ignorance of what they are to offer for, I am compelled to apply to you again for information—

(1) In your note to me of Sept 5 you mention 'the locks, dams & water power at Whitla's, Bobcaygeon, Buckhorn & Lindsay' & particularly direct my attention to the water power—The printed advertisement however only mentions water power at Whitlas & does not mention Bobcaygeon at all—Are all the four works for sale, & is there water power at all or any except Whitla's?

(2) What (described) quantity of land adjoining the works will the Government convey to the purchasers at each or any of these places?

(3) Where the works & the land conveyed with them are surrounded by private property will the government convey a road to the purchasers?

(4) In the case of Bobcaygeon, Lindsay & Buckhorn, where private mills are already in operation, if any water power is sold, it is very essential that the right of water conveyed to the purchaser by the Government should be strictly defined—

(5) At Bobcaygeon, where there are islands in the dam, will these be conveyed also?

(6) At the same place the present Mill proprietor draws his water from the canal—May he open a new flume out of the canal at his pleasure; & would the Government secure to the purchasers any power to controul the consumption of water, or interference with the works? This would appear to be essential even if no water power is included—

(7) Under what limitations as to tolls would the purchaser be bound?

(8) What stipulation as to repairs will the Government insist upon? The government must be aware that at Bobcaygeon *repair* is equivalent to *reconstruction* & that the works at Whitla's & Lindsay have never been finished—

(9) Would the purchaser be authorized to construct slides where required & to charge tolls thereon?

(10) What are the terms of payment proposed?

In some of the above queries I have assumed that other water powers than that at Whitlas are proposed to be sold, though from the proviso in the schedule at the end of 9 Victoria C.37 I presume that not to be the case; but I am obliged to make the distinct enquiry as the inhabitants in the neighbourhood of Lindsay are exceedingly anxious to obtain a water power there, which they believe essential to the prosperity of the village—

As it is understood that at least two private companies, besides the Council are proposing to purchase part of the works, it is suggested that the Government should fix an upset price & dispose of the works by auction as has been done in other instances—

Trusting to receive an early reply, which, I may lay before the Council at its approaching session.

I have the honor to be
Your obedient servant

John Langton
Warden County Peterborough

To the Honourable
The Chief Commissioner of Public Works

(*h*) JAMES CUMMING TO THE HONOURABLE F. LEMIEUX

[*Public Archives of Canada, R.G. 11, P.W. 5, Vol. 19*]

Trenton, 27th April 1857

To the Honble F. Lemieux.
Chief Comnr Board of Works
Toronto

Sir

By an order in Council of February 1854 all the Slides and Dams, built by the Government, on the River Trent, was handed over to the management and Superintendance of Messrs Henry Fowlds, Elijah W. Meyers, Charles Perry, Donald Campbell, Charles Townsend and the writer, who being at that time all interested in Lumber coming down the River Trent, undertook the management of those Works, for the general good of all concerned. Up to last summer, our Authority in protecting these Works from intentional, and unintentional, injury and to if necessary, force the Collecting of slide dues, was not disputed by any.

During last Summer, our Manager of the Slides allowed a few parties to pass their Timber, taking their promise to pay, which parties, now refuse and say we cannot collect from them. Two or three parties during last summer, done intentional and unintentional injury to the Works; One was a Mr Casey, who cut a hole through one of the Dams, which resulted in an outlay, in repairs, this spring of about £300. Our Superintendant was instructed to, and did, call on Mr Casey forbidding him, at the time of cutting the Dam, and has since frequently, asked him, to repair the damage, or pay for repairing, Casey persisted in cutting through the Dam and has refused to make good the damage, setting the Commissioners at defiance.

During the past Winter, a Mr Harnden has built a Dam across the River, opposite to two of the most important Slides, which now raises the water over our Dam and Slides, rendering them unmanageable, and threatens to carry away the whole Works, and in any case materially injure them.

We are not aware that we are invested with any authority whatever, that gives us the power to act Legally in the protection of these Works, or in forcing the Collection of Tolls, intended to be collected for the purposes of Keeping the Slides Dams &c. in repair and in working order.

And we ask now, that you will please give us the necessary Authority, either to act in the name and under Authority of the Board of Works, or in some efficient way, such as is required generally and in such as I have referred to

I have the honor to be
Your most Ob^{t} Servt

James Cumming

12. Claims for Damages, Trent Canal

(*a*) statement of loss by james cunningham, 1843

[*Public Archives of Canada, R.G. 11, P.W. 5, Vol. 17*]

Williamstown March 8, 1843

Being requested by Wm Cottingham Esqr of Emily to state my candid opinion, relative to the damages which might be sustained by myself and other individuals in the Event of *raising the water* at *his Mills*, two feet six inches above what it was originally, or is at present—I do therefore give it as my honest conviction, that the loss which I would thereby sustain, would be firstly the preventing the building of Mills, on a lot of land owned by me in the Township of Ops, upon which lot it can be proved by many individuals, there is at present an excellent Mill cite, which alone is estimated to be worth the sum of £250,—Secondly a considerable portion of said lot of land, which would not be flooded by the construction of a dam on that lot, would be flooded and become useless by raising the water to the above height at Emily Mills.—this land would be worth about £25

Again the damages, which must certainly accrue to other settlers in that section of Ops would be considerable And as to the damages accrueing to those in Emily I am not prepared to give any opinion—given under my hand this 8th day of March as above

James Cunningham

(a copy)

James Cunningham of Emily (School Master) maketh oath and saith, that the above statements are true, and the opinions as there in Expressed are those which he sincerely entertains

James Cunningham

Sworn before me at Emily
this 8 day of March 1843
J.L.H. J.P.,

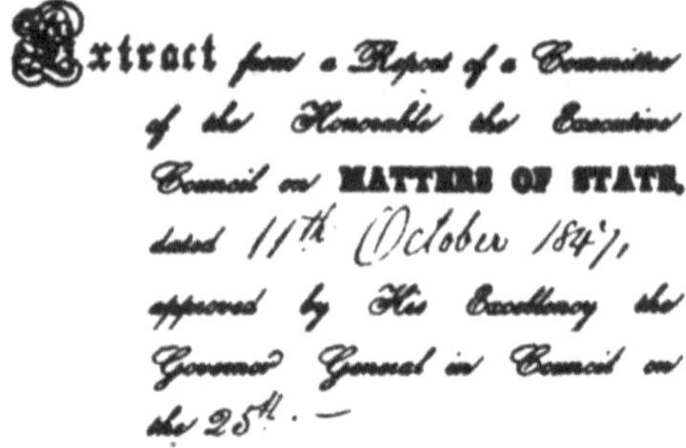
Extract from a Report of a Committee of the Honorable the Executive Council on MATTERS OF STATE, dated 11th October 1847, approved by His Excellency the Governor General in Council on the 25th. —

On the Letter of the Commissioners of Public Works, dated 7th October instant, for authority to pay to Mr Cottingham £339. 10. 0. due to him on an award of Arbitrators for damages sustained in the Colborne District.

An appropriation of £1500 was made by the Legislature two years ago to pay demands of this nature, and of that sum, more than sufficient remains to pay the amount due to Mr Cottingham. The Committee therefore humbly advise Your Excellency that the Commissioners of Public Works be authorized to pay Mr. Cottingham the sum awarded to him, vizt £339. 10/- from the abovementioned appropriation.

Certified.

Wm. H. Lee

To The Honourable
The Provincial Secretary
&c. &c. &c.

Public Archives of Canada

MINUTE OF THE EXECUTIVE COUNCIL, 1847

(*b*) MINUTE OF EXECUTIVE COUNCIL, 1845

[*Public Archives of Canada, Trent Canal, R.G. 11, P.W. 5, Vol. 19*]

EXTRACT from a Report of Committee of the Honorable the Executive Council, dated 31st December 1845.
approved by His Excellency the Administrator of the Government, in Council, on the same day.

On the Report of the Board of Works, dated 13th December Instant, recommending that an allowance be made to John White, who has been disabled from earning a livelyhood in consequence of a severe accident while on duty as the Board's foreman of Works at Ranney Falls;—

The Committee cannot advise Your Excellency to comply with the recommendation of the Board of Works.

Certified
E Parent

To
The Board of Works.

(*c*) PETITION OF THE WIDOW O'HARE

[*Public Archives of Canada, Trent Canal, R.G. 11, P.W. 5, Vol. 19*]

The Humble Petition of the Widow O'Hare Humbly Sheweth

That her husband Peter O'Hare was killed in June last by an accident while blasting rock at Chisholms Rapids station of the river Trent improvements then as now going on under the superintendance of Mr Thos McGrath, who she hopes will bear testimony to the good conduct of her late husband while employed on the works by him, as petitioner has no doubt Mr Baird will also do, who has known him to follow this Profession of Miner for the last eighteen or twenty Years, and to which he at last unhappily fell a victim.

Petitioner being a poor distressed woman advanced in Years with no other dependance for her future support than the assistance of God with that of the humane and charitable. She confidently hopes and humbly supplicates, that the Honourable Gentlemen who Compose the Board of Works will be graciously pleased to take her—Petitioner's most doleful case into their serious Consideration, that thro the benign deliberations of that Honourable body, petitioner may be saved from want and destitution to which she has hitherto been a stranger thro the indefatigable exertions of her late husband, And petitioner as in duty bound will ever pray.

(*d*) COMPLAINT OF WILLIAM WELLER *re* WHITLA'S DAM, 1847

[*Public Archives of Canada, R.G. 11, P.W. 5, Vol. 18*]

Cobourg March 8th 1847

Dear Sir

I have just arrived from Peterboro, and I find that the water is a going to be so high at the, Lock, that it will be very dangers going down in to the lock with the Steamers. it always has been dangerous, although last year we got through without much damage, if there was an other stick of timber put on part of the dam it would help it very much. If the board of Works are not disposed to do it I will do it, with your permission, as the agent for the board of works at Peterboro dont like to do it, or let me without authority. I am afraid if it is not done, I shall run the dam. or run against the gates and break them up, as it is we have to go into the Locke with full Steam an immidiate reply will much

Oblige
Your Obt
Servant
W. Weller[1]

Wm Robertson Esq
Montreal

(*e*) CLAIM OF J. RAINIE FOR DAMAGES

[*Public Archives of Canada, R.G. 11, P.W. 5, Vol. 17*]

The undersigned being one of the first settlers in the Township of Seymour and holding the offices of Town Clerk Surveyor, Assessor, & Collector, almost from the first settling of the Township; In the Township's infancy when we were without either grist or sawmill we applied to the Honbl R.C. Wilkins Through B.B. Ranney the Leases of Lot 8

[1]William Weller (1799–1863) was well known as a road contractor, stage-coach builder, and the operator of the Royal Mail Line of stages between Toronto and Montreal. He was a prominent resident of Cobourg for many years. In the winter of 1840 he transported the Governor-General (Mr. Poulett Thomson, later Lord Sydenham) from Toronto to Montreal in record time, but the number of hours is in dispute. The gold watch given to Weller, still a family heirloom, is said to bear as part of its inscription "35 hours and 40 minutes"; but the *Cornwall Observer* (as quoted in the *Cobourg Star* of February 26, 1840), very definitely states that the two stage-sleighs "left Toronto at six o'clock on Monday morning last, and arrived in Montreal at twenty minutes before eight o'clock on Tuesday evening," the elapsed time thus being 37 hours, 40 minutes. Weller was given £100 as well as the watch, and is said to have won a side bet of £1000 in addition. He himself drove the Governor-General's sleigh the entire distance, with changes of horses arranged ahead every fifteen miles.

and 9 in the 5th Concn of Seymour belonging to Mr Wilkins to erect Mill's for the use of the Township which he very generously consented to at a very considerable expence. I was at the time the Mill's was in operation in the habit of getting my wheat floured then to My Satisfaction and also boards from the saw mill and can testifie that up to the time that the Board of Works Commenced Making the Slides at the High Fall's on the said Mr Wilkins Property both Mill's were not only kept in good order and well attended but the settlers considered that they were under a great obligation to the Honbl R.C. Wilkins for so great a boon confered on them: I can also say that I consider the Mill privalidge entirely don away with; and as I have had some experience of the value of Mills in similar situations I am of of opinion that he could have rented them for at least Two Hundred & Sixty Pounds per annum Mr Wilkins has also sustained very heavy losses on his property with the People employed by the Board of Works using his Fences as fire wood leaving the Farm an open Common and also Cutting and carrying of his best and most valuable Timbers the whole was done with so Much impunity that it appeared to Me that Mr Wilkins had no Control ovver them to put a stop to it I Should Consider the Farm to have been worth at least Thirty Pounds per Annum & the balance of Timbers taken off his lands Five Hundred Pounds I had also almost forgot to say that the Board of Works pulled down his Saw Mill at least one Hundred Pounds given under My hand at Seymour this 15th Feby 1849

John Rainie

New Castle District } Personally appeared before me Saml Humphrye one of Her Majestys Justice of the Peace in and for the Said District John Rainie Esqr and being Sworn deposeth and saith that the above statement is true—Sworn before me at Seymour 10th Feby 1849

Samuel Humphries J.P. John Rainie

P.S. Since writing the above I have seen an Estimate made by Whelan Hauley J.P. Murphy & C. Bullocks Esquires and from the Knowledge I have of the Property I know and Consider that their Estimate is reasonable and fair. J. Rainie

(*f*) GEORGE B. HALL CLAIMS DAMAGES AT BUCKHORN, 1852

[*Public Archives of Canada, R.G. 11, P.W. 5, Vol. 20*]

To His Excellency The Right Honorable James, Earl of Elgin & Kincardine &c &c. Governor General of British North America, &c.

The Memorial of George Barker Hall, of the Town of Peterborough, respectfully sheweth:

That in the year 1836 the Commissioners for improving the navigation of the Inland Waters of the Newcastle District, took possession of the Dam at the Buckhorn Rapids and raised the same to such height as was necessary for their purposes.

That the said Dam (without the Waterpower,) was, by Act of Parliament, Vested in the Board of Works.

That neither the Commissioners or the Board of Works ever paid anything for the Dam so taken, or for the side dams and other works which had to be built in consequence of the raising of the Main Dam.

That your memorialist considering that the Dam (as a Government work,) would be preserved and maintained in repair did not press for the compensation to which he was entitled.

That the said Dam raises the waters of Buckhorn, Chemong and Pigeon Lakes on a shore of over 100 miles, And is indispensible to the navigation of the Lakes.

That in the month of May or June last the Gates and a large pier in the said Dam, with about 60 feet of the Government Bridge over the same, were destroyed by a party of lumbermen.*

That unless immediate steps are taken to repair the said Dam the water will be drained from the said Lakes, and the health of the Inhabitants of the surrounding County seriously affected.

That in view of the settlement of the County north of the County of Peterborough, the *Bridge* which has been partially destroyed, is of great importance as it is on the direct route to the interior And within ten miles of the unsurveyed lands.

That altho the damage which has been done will cause the stoppage of your Memorialists Mills, Yet as the Dam and Bridge are the property of the Government he has no immediate remedy, And cannot obtain any redress except by a difficult form of action in the Queens Bench against persons who are or may be worthless.

Your Memorialist therefore prays that, both on public and private grounds, the Dam and Bridge may be repaired as soon as possible. And that as lumbering is about to be carried on extensively in that part of the Country that for the sake of example Your Excellency will cause the parties offending in this case to be prosecuted and punished.

And Your Memorialist &c
Geo B. Hall[1]
3[d] August 1852

*Charles Townsend
John D. Macaulay
Mossom Boyd

[1]Hall was long the most prominent settler at the narrows of Buckhorn Lake, the front of the Township of Harvey, operating at Buckhorn Falls a fine sawmill

(*g*) PETITION OF GEORGE B. HALL FOR CANAL REPAIRS AT BUCKHORN

[*Public Archives of Canada, R.G. 11, P.W. 5, Vol. 20*]

To
His Excellency Sir Edmund Walker Head, Baronet, Governor General of British North America, &c &c &c

The memorial of George Barker Hall, of the Town and County of Peterborough, humbly sheweth:

That about 18 years ago the Government of Canada ordered the erection of a Dam and Bridge across the Buckhorn Rapids between the townships of Harvey and Smith.

That the Bridge was built upon and over the Dam, and that the two form one work.

That last year, so much of the Dam and Bridge as had been carried away (about one third) was repaired by the commissioners of the Board of Works.

That the remainder of the Bridge, (owing to the decay of the timbers,) is extremely unsafe, and the crossing is peculiarly dangerous, as the unrepaired portion of the Bridge is immediately over the worst part of the Rapids.

That the travel over the Bridge is comparatively large, it being the only means (the ice on Buckhorn Lake being unreliable) of ingress and egress for some hundreds of Lumbermen with their teams and supplies.

That in view of the contemplated settlement of the Townships of Harvey and Burleigh and the three townships now being surveyed, this Bridge is not only important but absolutely indispensible as it is the only place of communication for fifty miles, and is the connecting link between the existing and proposed Road to the New settlements.

---

and other industries. The Government pushed a road northward from Hall's Bridge (Buckhorn) in the 'sixties to facilitate settlement. About 1832 a group of "gentlemen" settlers, including the Wallis and Dennistoun families, were attracted by the scenery and hunting to the southwest corner of Harvey, near Pigeon and Sandy lakes. "The spot chosen by them," wrote Samuel Strickland, "was one of great natural beauty, but it possessed no other advantages except an abundance of game, which was no small inducement to them. They spent several thousand pounds in building fancy log houses and making large clearings which they had neither the ability nor the industry to cultivate. But even if they had possessed sufficient perseverance, their great distance from market, bad roads, want of knowledge of cropping after they had cleared the land, lack of bridges, and poor soil would have been a great drawback to the chance of effecting a prosperous settlement. In a few years not a settler remained of this little colony. Some stayed till their means were exhausted; others, more wise, purchased ready cleared farms in the settlements or followed some profession more congenial to their tastes or more suited to their abilities." (*Twenty-Seven Years in Canada West*, Vol. I, pp. 135–6.)

That your memorialist, if requisite, could obtain the signatures of a thousand petitioners praying for the repair of this Bridge, but, Your memorialist considers it unnecessary; being satisfied that upon the matter being brought to the notice of Your Excellency it will receive such attention as to Your Excellency it may seem to deserve.

That the Contractor with the Board of Works, being upon the spot the repairs could now be made much more economically than at any future time. Your Memorialist therefore prays that the subject may receive Your Excellencys favourable consideration.

And &c

10th February 1857. Geo. B. Hall

13. The Trent Canal at the Confederation of the Provinces, 1867

[General Report of the Commissioner of Public Works for the Year Ending 30th June, 1867, *pp. 70–79*]

(*a*) RIVER TRENT AND NEWCASTLE DISTRICT

The public Works on the River Trent, and on the inland waters of the Newcastle District, consist of certain locks and dams designed to improve the navigation of these waters; and of slides, dams, and booms made to facilitate the descent of timber.

In earlier times it was thought that a line of navigation might with advantage be opened between Lake Ontario and Lake Huron by means of the River Trent and the rivers and lakes of the Newcastle District, so as to afford accommodation to the local traffic and shorten the distance by water between Lake Ontario and the far West.

The Trent is a large river which discharges into the Bay of Quinté at a point about 67 miles above Kingston; and in passing from Lake Ontario to Lake Huron by this proposed route a vessel would ascend the River Trent, Rice Lake, the Otonabee River, Clear Lake, Buckhorn Lake, Chemong Lake, Pigeon Lake, Sturgeon Lake, Cameron's Lake, and Balsam Lake, which is the summit and has an elevation of 589½ feet above Lake Ontario; thence descending 118½, by a Canal and the Talbot River, to Lake Simcoe, and 124⅚ by the River Severn, it would enter the Georgian Bay (Lake Huron), 243⅓ feet below the summit level of Lake Balsam. Thus the total rise and fall between Lakes Ontario and Huron by this route would be 832⅔ feet.

This line of navigation, if ever completed, would be extremely crooked, for the actual distance in a straight line from the mouth of the Trent on Lake Ontario to the mouth of the Severn on Lake Huron

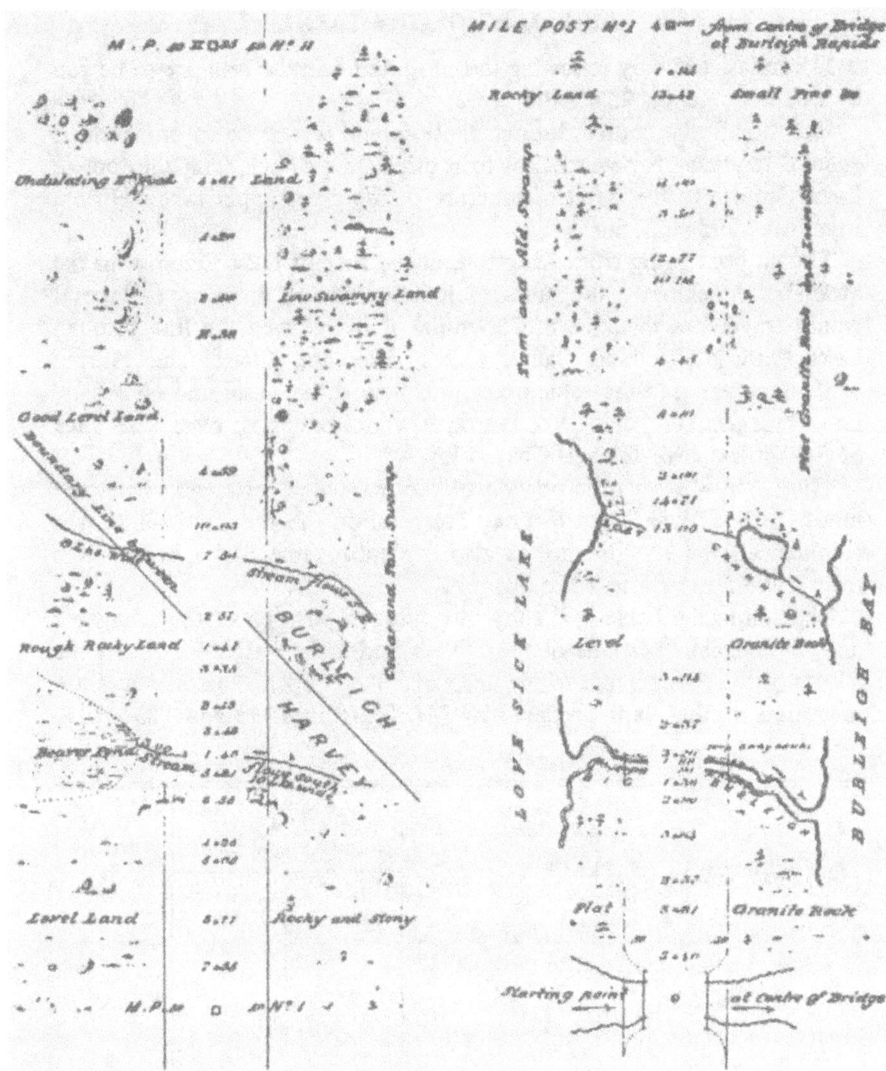

Archives of Ontario

FIELD NOTES OF BURLEIGH TOWNSHIP SURVEY

Undated picture-maps of J. W. Fitzgerald, the first two of a series, probably made in the decade 1850–1860

is 112 miles, while by following the proposed line the distance to be run by boats would be 235 miles.

But though the course through these inland waters be so crooked, its general tendency is nevertheless in a direct line drawn from the foot of Lake Ontario to the point of juncture of the great upper lakes, Huron, Michigan, and Superior.

Thus a boat going from Kingston, at the foot of Lake Ontario, to the Straits of Mackinaw (the point of junction of the three upper lakes), would traverse a distance of 785 miles if it followed the line through Lake Ontario, Welland Canal, Lakes Erie, Ste. Claire, and Huron; while if, in going to the same point, it followed the Trent and Newcastle line, Georgian Bay, and Lake Huron it would only pass over a distance of 567 miles. (See Diagram No. VI.)

The improvement of a portion of the main line, extending from the mouth of the River Trent to Lake Sturgeon on the proposed route, was commenced some years ago; as also the improvement of a branch line from Lake Sturgeon to Lake Scugog.

The following Table will show the relative position of the navigable and unnavigable portions of the Rivers and Lakes extending from the mouth of the River Trent to the head of Lake Scugog. The distances are measured on the plans prepared by Mr. Baird in 1835 and 1836.

NAMES OF PLACES.	Length of River and Lakes, in miles		Total distance in miles.
	Navigable.	Unnavigable.	
From the mouth of the Trent to the Foot of the Nine Mile Rapids....................	1	....	1
From the foot of the Nine Mile Rapids to the head of the same........................	....	8	9
From the head of Nine Mile Rapids to the foot of Canal at Chisholm's Rapids	6	....	15
The Canal at Chisholm's Rapids...........	⅓	....	15⅓
From the Canal at Chisholm's Rapids to Percy Landing.........................	13	....	28⅓
From Percy Landing to the foot of Crow Bay	....	9⅓	38
From foot of Crow Bay to junction of Crow and Trent Rivers.......................	3	....	41

From junction to the Lower Slide at Heely's Falls..........	....	1¼	42¼
Lower Slide and Upper Slide at Heely's Falls	....	½	42¾
From Upper Slide at Heely's Falls to Canal at Crooks' Rapids..........	11¾	....	54½
The Canal at Crooks' Rapids..........	½	....	54
From Canal at Crooks' Rapids to Canal at Whitlas' Rapids..........	38¼	....	92
The Canal at Whitlas' Rapids..........	½	....	93
From the Canal at Whitlas' Rapids to the head of Little Lake at Peterborough..........	1	....	94
From the head of Little Lake to the Slides and Dams at Buckhorn Rapids..........	12½	18½	125
Buckhorn Slide (sixty-five feet long)........			
From Slide and Dam at Buckhorn Rapids to Canal at Bobcaygean Rapids..........	15¾	....	140¾
The Canal at Bobcaygean Rapids..........	¼	....	141
From the Canal at Bobcaygean Rapids to the Slide at the Town of Lindsay (formerly Purdy's Mill on the River Scugog).......	20¼	....	161¼
The Slide at Lindsay..........	sixty-five	feet long.	
From the Slide at the Town of Lindsay to the head of Lake Scugog..........	28¾	....	190
Total..........	152¼	37¾	

For further details respecting rise of river and lakes above the Bay of Quinte—see Appendix No. 15, at page 122.

In 1827, on a petition from Mr. Stewart and others relative to the navigation of the waters of the Newcastle District, a Committee of the Lower House of the Legislature of Upper Canada reported that it was 'exceedingly desirable and important that those waters which constitute the chain of lakes and rivers which run in a south-easterly direction from the vicinity of Lake Simcoe, and which empty into the Bay of Quinté by the River Trent, should be examined and surveyed by competent persons with a view to ascertain how far they might be rendered navigable, and the probable expense attending the same.'

Nothing, however, appears to have been done before Feb., 1833, when a Bill was passed appointing Commissioners to receive plans and to execute the works necessary to the improvement of the inland waters of the Newcastle District, commencing at the mouth of the Otonabee River which discharges into Rice Lake and extending to Lake Scugog; and the Commissioners were authorized to raise a loan of £2,000 ($8,000) for this purpose.

This Commission obtained a design for a short canal at Bobcaygean, with a wooden lock. It was commenced in 1833 and completed in 1835. The length of the Canal was 973 feet, and the lock was 119½ feet long by 28 feet broad, with 4¾ feet water on the sills at low water and 7¼ feet at high water.

This lock permitted vessels navigating Lakes Chemong, Buckhorn, and Pigeon, which are on the same level, to ascend into Sturgeon Lake, and thence up the Scugog River as far as Lindsay.

It also appears that the Commissioners effected a slight clearing of the River Otonabee, below Peterborough.

Notwithstanding this commencement of the works by the Commissioners, it seems to have been well understood at the time that the small wooden lock thus executed was only a temporary expedient and that works on a much larger scale with stone locks and on a comprehensive plan, extending from Lake Ontario to Lake Huron, will be ultimately undertaken, for we find that, in 1833, the Lieutenant-Governor was pleased to instruct Mr. N. H. Baird to make a survey of the section extending from the mouth of the Trent to Rice Lake, and to estimate the cost of rendering these waters navigable for vessels drawing five feet, the locks to be 134 feet long by 33 feet broad.

Mr. Baird reported, in November of the same year (1833), that the distance from the mouth of the Trent to the foot of Rice Lake was 61 miles, and that the obstructions to navigation were as follows:—

1st., At the nine-mile Rapids,

2nd., At Chisholm's,

3rd., At a succession of Rapids and Falls between Percy Landing and Crow Bay, a distance of 12½ miles,

4th., At Heely's Falls,

5th., At Crooks' Rapids.

He proposed to overcome the Nine-mile Rapids by 13 locks, the Chisholm's by 1 lock, the 12½ miles of Rapids and Falls by 14 locks, Heely's Falls by 8 locks, and Crooks' Rapids by 1 lock,—forming a total of 37 locks, with 18 dams and 4¾ miles of side cuts, &c., the locks to be of stone; and the estimated cost of the whole works was £233,447 6s. 11½ ($933,789.39½).

The survey of the second section of the line was only commenced in 1835; when, in compliance with an Address from the House of Assembly dated April 16th, 1835, His Excellency, Sir John Colborne, appointed Mr. Baird 'to examine the most eligible route for a Canal between Rice Lake and Lake Simcoe'.

Mr. Baird did not recommend the cutting of a Canal throughout the whole distance, but he advised the formation of a Canal of 13¾ miles in length for the Talbot River section, and for the remainder of the line he advocated the damming of the rivers, so as to establish a succession of still water reaches connected by means of locks (a plan at the time successfully carried out on the Rideau).

Leaving Rice Lake, he proposed to ascend the Otonabee, Clear Lake, Buckhorn Lake, Chemong Lake, Pigeon Lake, Sturgeon Lake, Cameron Lake, and Balsam Lake—which is the summit; thence to descend into Lake Simcoe by means of a Canal and about 2¾ miles of the River Talbot.

He found that the distance from Rice Lake to Lake Simcoe was 109½ miles; and his Report divided the works into five sections, as follows:—

NAMES OF SECTIONS.	Distance in Miles.	Rise in Feet.	No. of Dams Required.	No. of Locks Required.
1. From Rice Lake to Peterborough	21 22/80	4½	2	1
2. From Peterborough to Clear Lake ..	14 34/80	147½	6	14
3. From Clear Lake to Bobcaygean	31 40/80	38½	2	5
4. From Bobcaygean to Balsam Lake ...	26 24/80	34	3	5
5. From Balsam Lake to Lake Simcoe	16 40/80	118½ (fall.)	....	12
Total	110	342⅝	13	37

For further details respecting the *Profile of the Inland Water Communication* proposed by N. H. Baird, from Rice Lake to Lake Simcoe, —and thence to Lake Huron—see Appendix No. 15, at page 129.

The total length of Canal required on these five subdivisions was about 17 miles.

Mr. Baird proposed stone locks, 134 x 33, with 5 feet of water on the sills, and estimated the cost of the whole at £262,067 16s. 4d. Halifax currency ($1,048,271.27).

It will thus be seen that Mr. Baird's estimate for a line of navigation from the mouth of the Trent to Lake Simcoe, with stone locks 134 feet long by 33 feet broad and 5 feet of water on the sills, was as follows:—

		$ cts.
For the divisions extending from the mouth of the Trent to Rice Lake	£233,447 6s. 11½d.,	(933,789 39½).
For the division extending from Rice Lake to Lake Simcoe	£262,067 16s. 4d.,	(1,048,271 27).
Total	£496,515 3s. 3½d.	($1,982,060 66½).

It was resolved that the works should be commenced forthwith; and to facilitate the working of the details they were put into two divisions:

1st. The River Trent.

2nd. The inland or back waters of the Newcastle District.

The first division comprised all the works from the mouth of the Trent to Heely's Falls.

The second extended from Heely's Falls, on the River Trent, to Lake Scugog.

In 1836 an Act of Parliament was passed, authorized a loan of £16,000 ($64,000), to be applied to the construction of works on the inland or back waters; and in 1837 a loan of £77,507 11s. 4½d. ($310,030.27) was authorized, to be appropriated to the River Trent works. In 1839 a further loan of £3,000 ($12,000) was authorized, to be applied to the inland division; thus forming, with the £16,000 ($64,000) previously authorized, a sum of £19,000 ($76,000) for the inland or back water section.

Two Boards of Commissioners were appointed by the Governor, one for each division, as provided by the Acts; and, under the auspices of these Commissioners, the works were commenced in 1837 with Mr. Baird as Engineer.

The works of the Trent division were commenced near the mouth of the Trent, at Myers' Island, and at Chisholm's Rapids. At Myers' Island they consisted of one dam and one lock; and at Chisholm's Rapids of one dam and one short canal with a single lock.

The engineer in charge of the works informed the Commissioners that the lock at Chisholm's could not be used without a dam at the head of the Nine-mile Rapids to retain the waters in the reach between Nine-mile Rapids and Chisholm's. The matter was considered, and it was decided to postpone the construction of this dam until after the completion of the lock at Chisholm's.

The dams at Myers' Island and at Chisholm's were to be of wood, and the locks of cut stone 134 x 33 feet, and with 5 feet of water on the sills.

On the commencement of the works, in 1837, the Receiver General laid aside the sum of £28,000 stg. ($136,266.66), which had been provided by the sale of Debentures, to be applied to the works on the River Trent division.

The value of the works under contract, with the proposed dam at the head of the Nine-mile Rapids together with contingencies, engineering expenses, &c., did not amount to more than £25,000 ($100,000).

The funds provided were therefore sufficient; but it appears that in 1838 and 1839, during a stringency in the money market, the sums which were to have been paid to the Commissioners were applied to other purposes; and moreover, that up to the end of the year 1841, when the Commissioners gave up their charge, the total amount that had been placed in their hands for the works was only £20,935 0s. 3d., Halifax c'y. ($83,740.05), as is shown by a Return to an Address of the House, dated 18th December, 1844.

The want of funds was a source of embarrassment to the Commissioners; and early in 1839 the contractors suspended operations.

At the date of the Union of the Provinces of Upper and Lower Canada the works at Myers' Island, which had then been abandoned for some time, consisted of two coffer dams, excavation of lock-pit, stone prepared for lock, timber for lock gates, and a permanent dam between the island and the main shore. The dam at the head of the Nine-mile Rapids (Widow Harris) had not been commenced.

At Chisholm's Rapids the dam was finished at the time of the union of the Provinces; while the slide, which was to be 100 feet in length, was only about half finished. The lock, however, was far advanced towards completion, and about two-thirds of the rock excavation were made.

On the inland or back water division the works had been commenced by the Commissioners early in the spring of 1837. The works undertaken were as follows:—

At Heely's Falls	1 dam.
" Crooks' Rapids	1 do. and 1 lock.
" Whitlas	1 do. and 1 do.
" Buckhorn	Enlargement of dam.
" Bobcaygean	1 new dam, and repairs to old lock.
" Purdy's Mills (now Lindsay)	1 dam and 1 lock.

The dams were to be of wood, filled with stone; the locks at Crooks' and Whitlas' to be of stone, and the dam at Purdy's mills of wood. All the new locks were to be 134 x 33 feet with 5 feet of water on the sills, as on the lower divisions.

Tenders were received for the execution of the works, within the appropriations that had been made; but their progress up to the period of the Union of the Provinces (1841) was slow, and often interrupted altogether, owing, it appears, to the limited advances made by the Receiver General to the Commissioners.

At the date of the Union the condition of the works on this division was as follows:—

At Heely's Falls: timber had been provided, but no part of the dam was commenced.

At Crooks' Rapids: the lock was nearly completed; the channels leading to the lock, above and below, had to be excavated, but the dam had been completed as early as 1838.

At Whitlas' Rapids: the site of the lock had been partly excavated by a contractor who abandoned the work in 1838, and partly by men hired by the day by the Commissioners. Stone for the lock and timber for the dam had been delivered on the ground, part of the stone being cut; but no works of construction had been commenced.

At Buckhorn: the old dam, which had been constructed by a private individual for milling purposes, had been raised sufficiently to give five feet of water on the sills of the locks at Bobcaygean before the autumn of 1840. At Bobcaygean the old lock had been thoroughly repaired and the dam reconstructed prior to the autumn of 1839.

At Purdy's Mills (now the Town of Lindsay): the site of the lock had been partly excavated, coffer dams made round the lock excavation, lumber for the dam and lock prepared and delivered on the ground, and the lock partly framed. This had all been done in the years 1837 and 1838. In 1839 the works were abandoned by the contractors.

The total expenditure previous to the Union, in February, 1841, on the two divisions, namely—the River Trent and the Inland and Backwater, was £44,398—($177,592), according to a Return made to the Legislative Assembly on the 27th July, 1847.

At the period of the Union of the Provinces these works were placed under the control of the Board of Works; and in a Memorandum to His Excellency the Governor General, dated August 12th, 1841, the Chairman of the Board reported that the intention of the original designers of this line of navigation was to establish a through line of communication which would accommodate the through trade between the Western States and the Sea-board, and also the local traffic of the Counties it traversed. As a through line he maintained that it could not be successful, owing to the great lockage required and the limited draft of water of the vessels which could be used on this route.

As an accommodation to the local traffic he stated that the route through its greater part, was extremely circuitous; assigning as an example that a farmer or merchant settled at the head of Rice Lake could, by passing over 12 or 14 miles of road, reach the harbors of Port Hope and Cobourg on Lake Ontario; whereas by following the Trent he would have to pass over a distance of 80 miles before he reached that lake.

He also stated that the probable cost of the works, when completed, would be from £800,000 ($3,200,000) to £900,000 ($3,600,000), and advised that the scheme of forming the through line should be abandoned, and, in lieu thereof, that the locks which had been commenced should be finished, and that slides to facilitate the descent of timber should be made.

An appropriation of £50,000 ($200,000) was asked from the House, to be applied to these works.

His Excellency having approved of these suggestions, the following works were authorized, and have since been executed:—

NINE-MILE RAPIDS

At the head of these Rapids a stone dam was erected in 1844.

CHISHOLM'S RAPIDS

The unfinished lock and slide were completed and ready for use in 1844.

PERCY LANDING

Piers and booms were constructed and placed at this station in 1844; but it having been found that the expense of maintaining this station was too great in proportion to the benefits it conferred, the works were allowed to decay. The piers were carried away by floods and have not since been replaced; a part of the boom was removed and fitted elsewhere, and another part has been lost.

RANNEY'S FALLS

At this station a dam was built in 1844; and a slide one thousand four hundred and ninety-two feet in length was completed in 1845. Necessary guide booms were also provided.

CAMPBELLFORD

Guide booms were placed here in 1844. A bridge was built in the same year, and has been placed under the control of the Township Council of Seymour.

FIDDLER'S ISLAND

A cross dam of some 12 feet in height, and a wing dam, were built here in 1848.

MIDDLE FALLS

Four dams and two slides were built here in 1844.

CROW BAY

At the foot of this Bay a retaining boom of some 2,600 feet in length is maintained.

HEELY'S FALLS

A dam and two slides were placed here in 1844.

CROOKS' RAPIDS

As already stated, the Commissioners of the Inland waters had completed the dam at this station in 1838, and had advanced far towards completing the lock and canal.

The Board of Works completed the lock and canal in 1844.

In 1845 a slide for timber was constructed, and a bridge of 485 feet in length was made over the river below the dam, with a swing bridge over the lock. This bridge is now under the control of the Counties of Northumberland and Peterborough.

WHITLAS' RAPIDS

The lock, dam, and canal commenced by the Inland Water Commissioners were finished in 1843.

LITTLE LAKE

Three piers and one boom were placed here in 1852.

PETERBOROUGH BRIDGE

This bridge is introduced here merely to show, at one glance, all the works in connection with these waters. It was built in 1847

BUCKHORN RAPIDS

It has been already stated that the Inland Waters Commission had built a dam at this station previous to the Union. A bridge on bents was built in 1845, and rebuilt in 1857. A slide with two feet draught of water, with booms, were made for this station in 1857, and additional booms in 1865.

BOBCAYGEAN

It has been stated that the Inland Waters Commission had before the Union built a dam and a wooden lock at this station. In 1857 the wooden lock was replaced by one of stone, and in 1858 two slides were built and a basin and two mill-races excavated.

Three sections of bridges were built over branches of the river opposite the lock in 1845, and have since (as before stated) been placed in charge of the local Township Municipalities. A swing bridge connecting with this line of bridges was placed over the lock in 1858.

LINDSAY (FORMERLY PURDY'S MILLS)

The wooden lock, as commenced by the Inland Commission, was completed in 1844, the lock was converted into a slide in 1859, and a bridge, consisting of three spans on cut stone abutments and piers, was opened in 1864.

In obedience to a request made by the Legislature the Chief Engineer of this Department, acting under the orders of the Commissioner of Public Works, caused an examination of the River Trent to be made between the Bay of Quinté and Rice Lake.

In his Report (22nd April, 1846) he reviewed the plan proposed by Mr. Baird in 1833, of building dams across the river at various points in its most rapid sections, so as to form it into a series of still water reaches which were to be connected by means of locks.

He objected to this scheme that dams would always interfere, more or less, with the passage of timber; that they were not durable, and were too liable to be damaged by floods; he suggested in lieu thereof the forming of three sections of canal, the first extending from near the mouth of the Trent to the head of the Nine-mile Rapids; the second from Percy's Landing to the foot of Crow Bay; and the third from Crow Bay to the head of Heely's Falls.

These three Canals, in connection with the locks at Chisholm's and Crooks' Rapids which were then completed, would have opened a line of navigation from the Bay of Quinté to Peterboro and the Otonabee.

He stated that the entire length of Canal required in the three sections proposed was about 18¼ miles, and that 29 locks were necessary.

He also stated that before a final opinion could be given further surveys were necessary, and that the probable cost of the works (if executed on the scale adopted for the locks at Chisholm's and Crook's Rapids) would be about £400,000 Halifax currency ($1,600,000).

In 1855 the Commissioner of Public Works reported that the cost of maintaining the slides, booms, and other works connected with the descent of timber on the Trent was much greater than the revenue they produced; he recommended that the said works should be placed in charge of a Committee or Company of persons interested in the lumber trade on the Trent, who had offered to assume their management. In accordance with this recommendation the works connected with navigation, such as locks, lock-houses, &c., remained under the direct control of the Department of Public Works; while the works connected with the descent of timber at Chisholm's Rapids, Ranney's Falls, Middle Falls, Heely's Falls, and Crooks' Rapids were handed over to the care of the Company.

The Company undertook to keep the slides, &c., in working order, but were not held to renew them when worn out. They were authorized to levy tolls on timber descending the river. At Chisholm's and at Crooks' Rapids the facilities for bringing down timber were not increased by the Government works; tolls were therefore not levied at either of these stations. But at Ranney's Falls, Middle Falls, and Heely's Falls the works had been constructed expressly for the safe descent of timber, and therefore tolls were collected at each of these stations.

Previous to December, 1866, the rate of toll was one dollar per crib for each of the 3 slides; but on the 8th December, 1866, an Order in Council was passed fixing the rate of tolls payable at each of the three stations just named at one cent for each log of 13 feet in length, and a proportionate sum on pieces of greater length; and for each crib of square timber one dollar.

The expenditure by the Department on these improvements since the Union in 1841 up to the 30th of June, 1867, as shown in Appendix No. 1, at page 3, is $492,486.31. Appendix No. 16, at page 130, shows the expenditure on the slides by the 'Trent Slides Company' from the spring of 1855 to 1st January, 1867.

In the public accounts the amount charged against the 'Improvements of the Trent' is $558,506.20.

For the expenditure on these works before and since the Union, from Government and other funds, see Appendix No. 70, at pages 486, 507 to 509, and 514 to 516.

The total cost of construction on these works since their commencement up to the 30th June, 1867, as shown by Appendix No. 70, amounts to $670,078.31, subdivided as follows, viz:

On Canals, &c., prior to the Union	$ 92,449.33	
Slides, &c., " " " "	85,142.67	$177,592.00
On Canals, &c., since the Union	216,921.98	
Slides, &c., " " "	228,347.05	
Roads, " " "	30,454.40	
Bridges, " " "	16,762.88	492,486.31
Total		$670,078.31

(*b*) REPORT OF SUPERINTENDENT G. W. RANNEY

[General Report of the Commissioners of Public Works for the Year Ending 30th June, 1867, *pp. 361–2*]

APPENDIX NO. 41

(No. 341.)

REPORT BY G. W. RANNEY,[1] SUPERINTENDENT DESCRIBING THE WORKS AND REPAIRS EXECUTED ON THE RIVER TRENT AND ITS TRIBUTARIES, DURING THE FISCAL YEAR ENDING 30th JUNE, 1867.

F. BRAUN, Esq. BELLEVILLE, 19th July, 1867.
Secretary, Public Works Dept., Ottawa.

Sir,—I have the honor, in compliance with the instructions contained in No. 62,924, dated 15th of June, to report to the Department the state, and cost of repairs, and additions to the works of the Inland Navigation of the Newcastle (or Trent) District, under my charge, for the past fiscal year ending 30th June, 1867.

WIDOW HARRIS'

The dam is in good order and has had no repairs for the past year.

CHISHOLM'S RAPIDS

The slide and booms are in good working order. The dam should be made more staunch by gravelling it for its preservation; waste weirs should be made, to waste the surplus water in the spring to keep the water at a more uniform level. The Canal and lock are not in use, therefore no repairs were required.

Application has been made to build a fish slide in the dam; salmon migrate in the river, and the dam obstructs the way.

The following works, next in order, are managed by a Committee in the lumbering trade, and maintained by the tolls levied on lumber passing down the river:—

Ranney Falls.—Slides, dam, and guide booms.

Campbellford.—Guide booms.

Fiddler's Island.—Wing dams.

Middle Falls.—Slides, dams and wing dams, and guide booms.

Crow Bay.—Retaining boom.

Heely Falls.—Dam, slides, and guide booms.

These works are in good working order. A considerable amount of

[1]George Ranney, a mill-owner, is commemorated by Ranney's Falls and by Ranney Street in Campbellford.

repairs have to be done to them yearly to replace the decayed parts. No changes have been made for several years.

At Heely Falls the still-water navigation commences. It is the lower end of the lower reach of still-water navigation on the line. The dam was not staunch, and allowed the water to decline below the level of intended navigable height. $400 was appropriated and expended in gravelling it; but the sum was insufficient to complete it satisfactorily. It would require $400 more. The navigation between Heely Falls and Crooks' Rapids is impeded by a ridge of boulders on flat rock bed at Stewart's Island, about a mile below Crooks' Lock. The same difficulty exists between Crooks' Lock and the foot of Rice Lake. The steamers now engaged drawing ore from the Marmora works have been fast on these rocks. A sum of $700 has been appropriated for the removal of the boulders, and the work will be commenced as soon as the water gets low enough.

CROOKS' RAPIDS

The works have been and are now under a state of repair and improvements for the accommodation of the newly existing traffic—that of the transportation of Marmora ore. The lock gates have been renewed; the guard walls repaired; frame guards built for guidance and protection of steamers along the banks; a new swing bridge over lock, and other necessary conveniences for the well working of the station, which have cost $3,730. There are still further improvements and repairs necessary.

Although these works have been a long time in existence, they were never worked, and, in a manner, not perfected, causing now more than ordinary putting to rights. Portions have gone to decay that have now to be renewed. The lock-house is untenantable and requires repairs; there is a strong leak under the lower mitre still that requires to be staunched; an engine-house built for the engine that was used to pump the lock.

As before stated, there exists the difficulty of an intricate channel between the boulders from the works to Rice Lake. The navigation to Whitlas from Rice Lake is good.

WHITLAS RAPIDS

The works are not in use for still-water navigation, and entirely out of repair.

LITTLE LAKE

The booms and piers are in good order.

National Maritime Museum, Greenwich R. Salmon

[1] THE *ANN* OFF BIRKENHEAD

National Maritime Museum, Greenwich T. Whitcombe

[2] THE *EALING GROVE*

The *Ann* and the *Ealing Grove* were ships of the type which carried the Peter Robinson Emigration to Canada in 1825; oil paintings reproduced by permission of the Trustees of the Museum

Courtesy Royal Ontario Museum

[3] SHELL GORGET

An ocean shell found in a mound on Sugar Island, Rice Lake, indicating Indian trade with tribes on the Atlantic coast

Photograph by David Brooks

[4] POTHOLE NEAR CEDAR LAKE

The belief in the locality is that the Indians made it for threshing wild rice

Courtesy Royal Ontario Museum

[5] AERIAL VIEW OF THE SERPENT MOUNDS, RICE LAKE

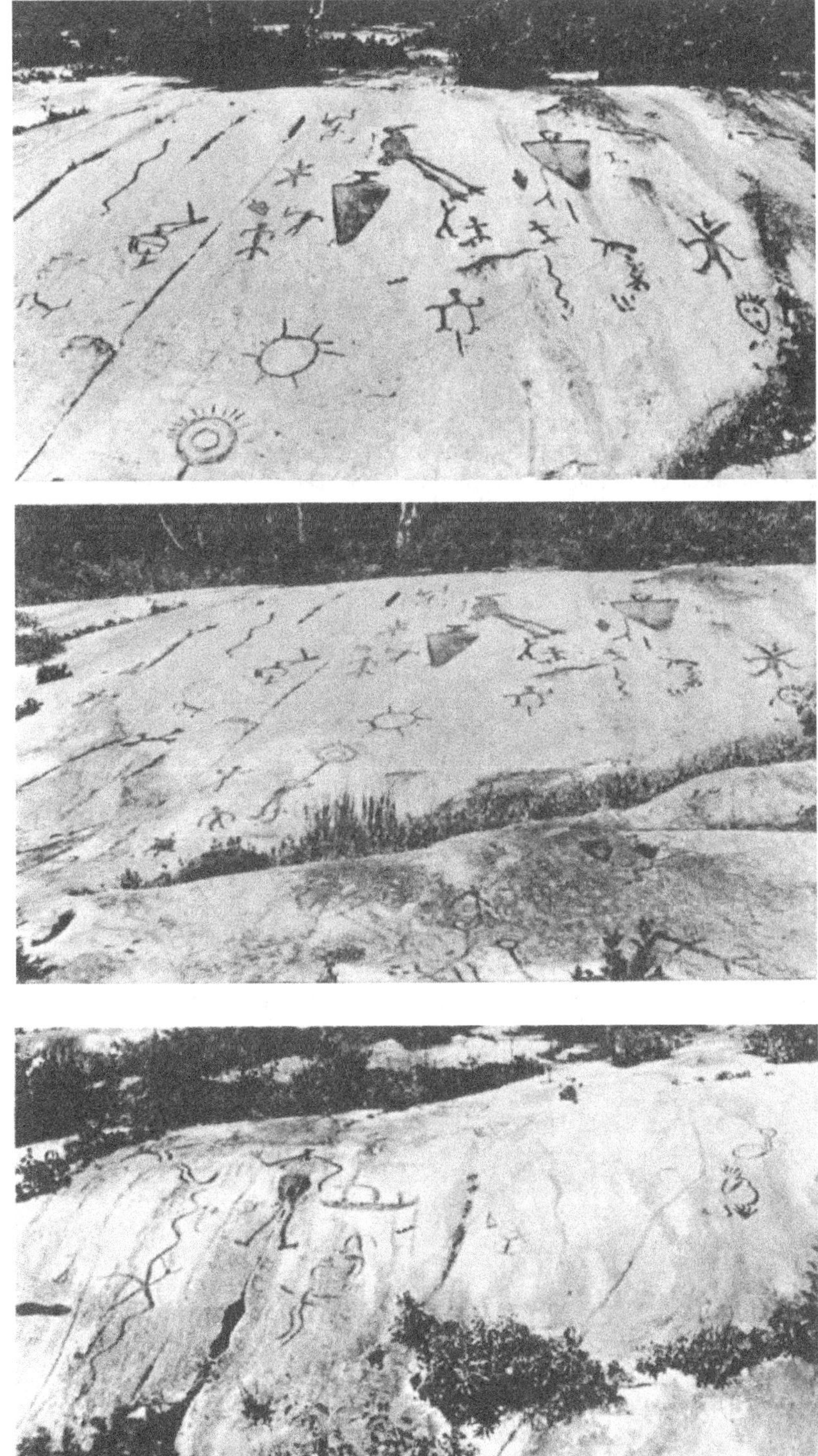

Sigmund Samuel Canadiana Gallery — James Pattison Cockburn

[9] JOSEPH KEELER'S TAVERN, CRAMAHE, 1829-30

Keeler, founder of Cramahe (Colborne), was prominent in settling and developing both front and rear townships

Public Archives of Canada — Lieut. Philip Bainbrigge

[10] COBOURG IN 1840

Old Victoria College is seen in the rear, and the Custom House at the left through which wagons were driven on to the pier

Peterborough Public Library — Attributed to Mrs. Caroline Hayward

[11] PORT HOPE IN THE EIGHTEEN-FORTIES

This fine lithograph has only recently been discovered

BUCKHORN

The works are in good order. An order for the two new boom piers to be built has been given, and will be put in soon: will cost about $100. Of late the boom has been carried away by lumbermen, which will have to be replaced or paid for by the parties.

At this station is another division between the lumber navigation and the still water navigation. The dam here maintains the level of Buckhorn, Chemong, and Pigeon Lakes, and sets the water back to the lock at Bobcaygean, a large sheet of water. In seasons of low water a division of the channel between the steamboat navigation and the lumberers is a matter of contention.

BOBCAYGEAN

The dams and slides are in good order.

The lock gates do not work well; one of the wicket gates is broken in the north upper gate, which involves the necessity of raising the gate above water or pumping the lock to repair it. The leak caused by that defect makes the lower gates work hard.

The water in the river being too high during the whole of last winter to undertake to raise the gates above it is why it was not repaired last winter. I believe it will be advisable to pump the lock chamber next winter to clean it out, and put all the gates in order. The swing bridge over the canal is worn out and should be repaired immediately, fearing it may drop into the Canal. Preparations are being made to repair it.

There are four steamers that ply through this lock daily.

The navigation to Lindsay from Bobcaygean is good except through the cuts on the Scugog River.

Piles and booms should be placed along the sides to guard off the stumps and trees. The direction is bad and the width narrow.

LINDSAY

The works are in good order. The slide is not very much used. A fish slide has been asked for at this station. A good deal of difficulty exists in keeping the level of the water above the dam uniform; conflicting interests are hard to satisfy, and it is rather difficult at all seasons to meet the exactness required by the different parties.

The navigation from Lindsay to Lake Scugog could be improved a good deal by removing trees and stumps from off the points and sharp turns, giving a greater width of river which is required in many places. The navigation has been very much impeded by Township Bridges across the river, with no provision made to pass them. They have been removed of late. At the foot of Scugog Lake the deepest channel is very crooked; eight buoys to mark the channel would be a very great improvement.

All of which are respectfully submitted.

I have the honor to be, Sir,
Your obedient servant,
G. W. RANNEY,[1]
Superintendent, Trent Works.

[1]A longer and more detailed but somewhat repetitious account of the Trent development at the time of Confederation is "Description of Works on the Trent . . . Report by G. W. Ranney" in *General Report of the Commissioner of Public Works for the Year Ending 30th June, 1867*, pp. 116-30. Included is an elaborate table of changes in water levels, of dams, slides, piers, booms, and other works; and in many instances the date of construction, cost, and other details are given.

VI. GENERAL TRANSPORTATION

THE NINE documents in this Section are illustrative of the numerous petitions, reports, agreements, and projects with respect to transportation that are to be found in every type of record of the times. Covering as they do roads, ferries, bridges, railroads, and plank roads, these items indicate the continual efforts that were made to improve travel conditions. The Rice Lake ferry, the subject of Nos. 1 and 2, was apparently inaugurated, though it was no doubt superseded by Captain Cleghorn's steamboat *Pemedash*, a schedule of the operation of which appears in the *Cobourg Star* of July 31, 1833. No. 4, the first report relative to the projected railway from Cobourg northward, is a rare item found in the Library of the British Museum upon a subject on which a book might be written. Nos. 6 and 9 typefy the innumerable petitions for improved transportation facilities; and Nos. 7 and 8 outline the plans for and construction of the plank road which temporarily replaced proceedings on the construction of the Cobourg-Rice Lake railway. In the late eighteen-fifties two railways northward were in operation, and No. 10 provides a summary of their early traffic.

1. RICE LAKE FERRY, 1820

[*Archives of Ontario, Crown Land Papers, 61 (11), Ferry Service Leases*]

In Council 13th December 1820,

Administration of Sir Peregrine Maitland K.C.B. Lieutenant-Governor. Ordered that John William Bannister, of the Township of Otonabie, in the District of Newcastle, Esquire, Lieutenant Royal Navy, Shall receive a Lease of the Ferry from Lot number sixteen in the ninth Concession of the Township of Hamilton, to any part of the Waters of the Rice Lake, and up and down the Rivers Otonabie and Trent, for the Term of five years—from the next Quarter day after this date, at the annual Rent of One Pound five Shillings Currency, the Rent to commence on the said Quarter day and to be paid annually—

The Lease to be always subject to such Rules and Regulations for Ferriage and attendance as the Justices of the said District of Newcastle in Sessions may adopt.

John Beikie
Confl Clk

To
The Attorney General

2. Petition for a Ferry at Rice Lake, 1827

[*Public Archives of Canada, Executive Council Papers, R.G. 1, E. 3, Vol. 28, pp. 71–4*]

We the undersigned beg leave to state that in consequence of no regular Ferry being kept on the Rice Lake, Persons arriving there, and wishing to cross, are often put to very great inconvenience and delay and subject to imposition from Persons taking advantage of their necessities.

We are therefore of opinion that the situation mentioned in the Petition of Aaron Elsworth is the one most proper for a Ferry upon the Lake and we have no hesitation in recommending him as a very suitable person to keep the same.

We are likewise of opinion that it is expedient that some land on each side of the Lake should be assigned to the Lessee of the Ferry.—

John Covert J.P.
W. Falkner J.P.
John Lester J.P.
Chas. Rubidge J.P.
David Smart J.P.
John Brown J.P.
J. Williams J.P.
Zacheus Burnham J.P.
Saml. S. Wilmot J.P.
Elias Jones J.P.
Walter Boswell J.P.
Richd. Hare J.P.
J. A. Keeler J.P.

To His Excellency Sir P. Maitland
K.C.B. &c &c &c

The Petition of Aaron Elsworth of the Township of Hamilton in the District of Newcastle.

Humbly represents—

That it would greatly promote the Public convenience in general &

particularly add to the prosperity of the Settlements— North of the Rice Lake, if a regular Ferry were established & properly conducted, across the Rice Lake connecting that line of Road leading from Cobourg to Peterboro'—

Your Petitioner further represents— that, in order to have the Ferry properly conducted, it is necessary that a Ferry-House be kept on each side of the Lake; & as the business of the Ferry, would, for some time to Come, afford but partial employment & small remuneration to the Persons keeping the same, it is desirable that a quantity of land suitable for cultivation be reserved for the use of the Ferry on each side of the Lake at, or convenient to, the Landing Place

Your Petitioner therefore humbly prays, that 100 acres of the Town reservation in Otonobee adjoining Capt. Chas. Anderson's East Line, and 15 acres of the North East corner of Lot No 10 in the 9th Concession of Hamilton may be reserved for the use of a Ferry—

And your petitioner further prays that the Ferry with the Lands reserved for its use, may be leased to him for the Period of 21 Years, and in duty Bound will ever pray—

Aaron Ellsworth

Cobourg April 13th 1827

Executive Council Office
York 8th June 1827

Notice is hereby given, by order of His Excellency the Lieutenant Governor in Council, that Sealed Tenders, Post paid, for Lease of the Ferry across the Rice Lake, in the Line of communication leading from Cobourg to Peterborough, for the term of seven years, from the first of August next, subject to such Rules and Regulations for Ferriage and attendance, as the Magistrates in General Quarter Sessions of the Peace may adopt, endorsed "Tender for Ferry"—will be received at this Office until the said first day of August, on which day the Lease will be adjudged to the Highest Bidder, who will be required to pay One Pound, twelve Shillings, and six Pence, Currency before the Patent issues, and to enter into the usual Security for the due payment of the Rent.

(Signed) John Small
Clerk Executive Council

3. "THE COMPLAINT OF THE TRENT BRIDGE"[1]

[*Thomas Carr in the* Cobourg Star, *May 10, 1831*]

To the Editor of the Cobourg Star and Newcastle General Advertiser.

Dear Mr. Editor,—

As complaints for real or fancied grievances are now the order of the day, I too must lift my feeble voice among my betters, and pour my sorrows into your ear—an ear which should be ever open to any information, suggestion, or complaint touching public property or prosperity.

Although I form a communication over the noblest river in this prosperous district—a river, which, at no distant period will, despite of the gay and haughty villages on its front, concentrate and pour into Lake Ontario all the wealth produced near its tributary streams—yet I have been unfortunate and neglected ever since the hour of my birth. Some indeed say that one of my misfortunes was born with me; and that, even during my very youth, I could never get one of my feet on the ground.

But my misfortunes have been brought upon me chiefly by an incorrigible, though perhaps a useful, race of mortals called LUMBER-JACKS, whom, however, I would name the Cossacks of Upper Canada, who, having been reared among the oaks and pines of the wild forest, have never been subjected to the salutary restraint of laws. The injuries which they have done me have been marked by wantonness and ingratitude; for to them have I been hitherto chiefly useful.

One night (I shall never forget it) a band of these foresters having reached the foot of the Rice Lake upon a raft, they secured, as they thought, their charge to the shore; and being all votaries of Bacchus and tormented with an incessant and unextinguishable thirst, they adjourned to a tavern to spend the night in the worship of the jolly god. Meantime the huge raft, being no partaker of their orgies, took its revenge by breaking from its moorings and (dreadful to relate) entered the TRENT without a pilot. What was my consternation, Mr. Editor, when the great mass of timber came floating on, like an island, or like the Kraken, that vast sea-monster, which was seen and described

[1]This bridge connected Asphodel and Percy townships and was built in 1827, after the previous one, built a year earlier, had been carried away by spring floods. The letter appearing on May 10, 1831, had apparently some effect, for in the 1832–33 sessions of the Legislative Assembly a grant of £300 was made towards its repair, and £100 further in 1834. See Section XII, No. 2, for a biographical note on Thomas Carr.

by the Danish Bishop of Pontoppidon. On it came, and right against my weak part it drove, giving it a lurch to leeward from which it has never recovered.

Another disaster, still more fatal, befell me in the spring of 1830. For you must know that these my bitter enemies, whose obdurate hearts no services of mine can nullify, purposely ran their rafts against me, and wishing me with the most cordial goodwill at the d——l. At the time just mentioned another raft, manned by a crew of dreadnoughts, either from negligence, drunkenness, or design, ran foul of one of my piers which, to my great grief and the detriment of his Majesty's loyal subjects, was either cut or carried away, leaving a monstrous chasm through which the Shannon, with all her studdin' sails set, might have chased the Chesapeake. For this damage no redress could be obtained; because, forsooth, there was either no law or none to prosecute.

But this, Mr. Editor, is by no means the sum total of my distresses. For the points of my piers and my legs or posts have been so chafed, rubbed, fretted, attrited, and shattered by the ice that unless they be speedily cased and protected they will soon fail me, and then there will be at once an end to my sufferings and existence.

It seems, and I am sorry to say it, that I have even false friends as well as open enemies. For, a subscription having been made lately to repair my shattered frame, a person, it has been said, engaged by contract to make me a new pier as good as the others; to lay my flooring with hewed or flatted timber, to straighten my obliquity, and to ease all the points of my piers and posts to secure them from further damage from ice.

But mark the manner in which I have been treated. The new pier is six feet too short and formed of timbers partly decayed; the flooring is composed of ugly poles; no casing has been done; and my obliquity remains the same.

Now as far as contracts are concerned, my case, Mr. Editor, is doubtful, for in this respect I must submit to such treatment as my neighbors receive. But might not our legislators, those guardians of public property and liberty, pass an act to protect me, and others exposed as I am, from wanton violence, and to place us under the custody of some persons—say the Surveyor of Roads, who might be amenable to punishment for neglect of duty.

By making my case known to the public, you may convince me, dear Mr. Editor, that I have at least one friend, and make me proud whenever you travel this way to convey you safely across the noble stream, over which stands the injured TRENT BRIDGE.

4. SURVEY FOR THE COBOURG RAIL ROAD COMPANY, 1835

[*A copy of* First Report of the Directors of the Cobourg Rail Road Company (Cobourg, 1835), *Library of the British Museum*]

In laying before the stockholders the Report of the Engineer on the completion of his Survey, the Directors deem it incumbent on them to furnish a detailed account of their progress, and to draw attention to some of the most striking points connected with the important work in which they are engaged.

Their first object being to obtain, with as much expedition as possible, such an estimate of the cost of the undertaking as could be relied on with security, they devoted their earliest attention in selecting an Engineer of known practical skill to accomplish that task. With this view, they opened a correspondence with gentlemen in the United States and other parts, from whom they deemed they might obtain the necessary information. Several Engineers in the former country, who were highly recommended, offered to undertake the work, but the Directors consider they exercised the trust confided to them with prudence, in preferring the services of a gentleman of acknowledged ability and high standing in the profession, in their own country; who, having been employed by the Government in the extensive surveys of the waters of this part of the Province, with which the contemplated Rail-road is so closely connected, might be considered as having some claim to their particular consideration.

The choice of the Engineer having been thus made,[1] and the terms of the Survey agreed on, they instructed him 'to ascertain the most eligible and least expensive route, for a railway from Cobourg to the Rice Lake, at that point which might be found most practicable, near the direct line of communication with the Otonabee River'. To aid him in this work, the Directors spared no pains in seeking all the information that could be obtained, respecting the nature of the country and its capabilities for the purposes required. Several of them, during the progress of the Survey, were nearly constantly employed in examining the country personally; and the Engineer acknowledges in his Report,

[1]N. H. Baird, who was also the original surveyor for the Trent Canal. He was assisted by Frederick P. Rubidge, Cobourg, a poet as well as a surveyor. (See Section XII, No. 1, for a biographical note and a selection from his verse.) The original charter of the Cobourg and Rice Lake Rail Road Company is dated March 6, 1834, and provided for a capital of £40,000 in shares of £10. Construction was to start within two years and be finished within eight. Indicative of the enthusiasm is the fact that £4650 was subscribed at a public meeting in Cobourg, the proceedings of which are detailed in the *Cobourg Star* of July 8, 1835.

A CHART,

SHEWING THE

INTERNAL NAVIGATION

OF THE

DISTRICT OF NEWCASTLE,

And the proposed improvements on the

OTONABEE RIVER.

Drawn by F. P. Rubidge, ... Engraved by T. Evans.

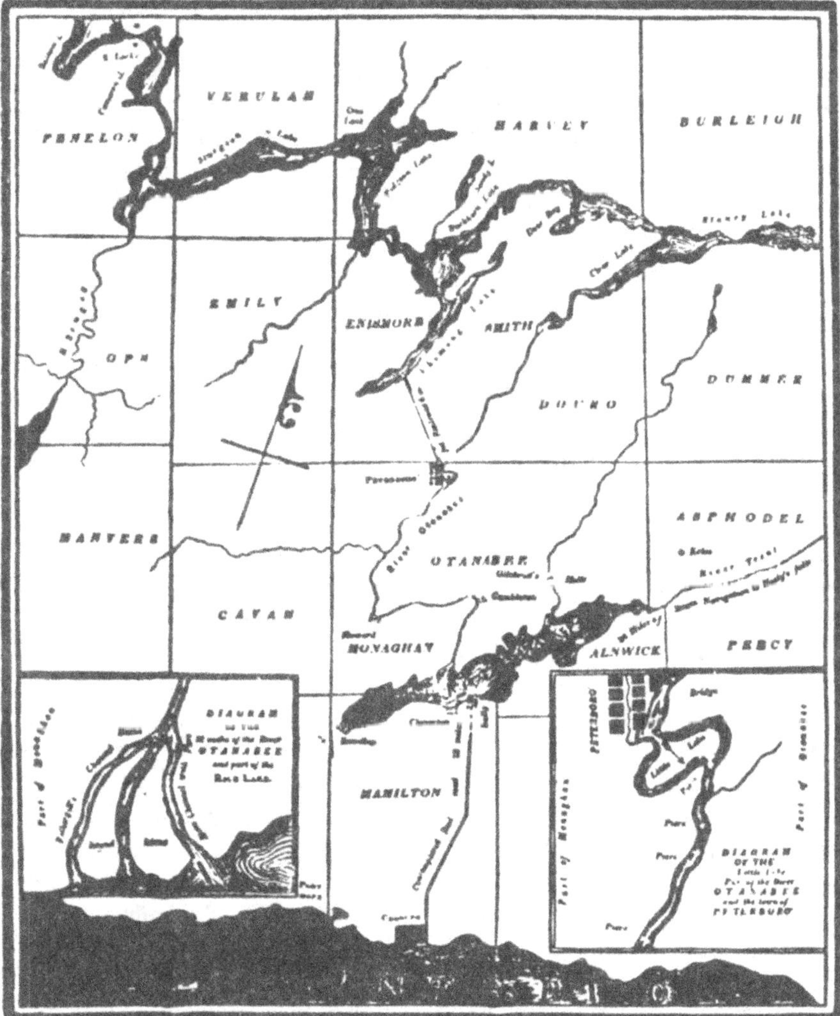

TABLE OF DISTANCES.

Cobourg to Rice Lake,	13 Miles,	Land Carriage.
Rice Lake to Peterborough,	25 "	by Steam boat.
Peterborough to Chemong Lake,	7 "	Land Carriage.
Chemong, through Smith, Ennismore, Harvey, Verulam Ops, Cartwright, and Fenelon,	81 "	by Steam boat.
Rice Lake to Heely's Fall in Seymour,	35 "	by Steam boat.

Bethune, Schedule of Real Estate . . . [1833]

NAVIGATION OF THE DISTRICT OF NEWCASTLE, 1833

that by their activity his labors were materially lessened, and much time was saved.

To meet the outlay necessarily incurred in this preliminary portion of the undertaking, the Directors thought proper to call in an instalment of 2½ per cent on the stock subscribed, which will pay a large portion of the expense of the Survey.

Until the estimate was completed, and the practicability of the work ascertained, it was determined not to solicit subscribers amongst those whose only object could be the investment of their capital with the expectation of a reasonable return; as it was deemed more just that the cost incurred in determining whether the work were practicable at a moderate outlay, and could therefore be profitably engaged in, should at first be met by individuals whose residence in the country, and particular interest in its prosperity, rendered the completion of the work, with them, an object of paramount importance.

It is with much satisfaction the Directors have it in their power to state, that the result of the Survey has been in every respect most favorable.

In the investigation of the country over which the road will have to pass, no essential difficulty has presented itself, and the estimate does not exceed the usual cost of works of a similar description. Although, upon an inspection of the plans, it will be found that in the progress of the road to the Rice Lake a considerable rise has to be overcome, yet, taking the nature of the trade of the country into consideration, it will not form any serious obstacle to the undertaking. On a comparison of the weight of the productions of the country which will have to descend this road to find their market with the supplies which are sent into the country in return, it will readily be conceded, by every person who has the slightest knowledge of the subject, that the former bears a proportion to the latter of at least *ten* to *one*; and consequently, if the road were perfectly level, ten times more power would be required to bring the produce of the back country to market, than would be necessary for the transport of merchandize to the interior. That which would, therefore, prove, under different circumstances, if not an insurmountable difficulty to the success of the work, at least a very considerable injury to it, from the nature of the trade for which the railway is to prove a medium, becomes a positive advantage.

The route at present contemplated, without reference to such improvements as may be fairly anticipated from more particular examination during the progress of the work, will permit the successful application of *animal* or locomotive power upon the whole line; the cost of which, ready for complete operation, is estimated at *Twenty-six thousand eight hundred and thirty-two pounds five shillings and three pence, for the grading of a double track,* and the completion of a single line of railway. A result, in the opinion of the Directors, most satisfactory, and as favorable as the most sanguine could have ventured to anticipate.

In consequence of the numerous suggestions to the Engineer, of probable improvements in the line, all which required particular investigation, the Survey has occupied more time than the Directors were led to anticipate. It was, however, deemed by them to be their particular duty to take care that the country should be thoroughly examined before the stock was brought fully into the market, in order that enterprising individuals, who embarked their capital in the undertaking, should have before them an estimate founded upon certain data.

The Survey being completed, and the expense carefully ascertained, the Directors have it now in their power, to invite Capitalists to invest their means in the work, with the confident assurance of a speedy and ample return.

If the cost of this work be considered with reference to the important objects to be effected by it, it will be found to bear a proportion more inconsiderable than most works of a similar nature. In the interior of this portion of the Province we have beautiful lakes and rivers, made navigable by nature for vessels of all descriptions, washing shores of nearly 200 miles of country, teeming with rich productions, and rapidly increasing in population. On the banks of these waters, towns and villages are erecting and rapidly rising into notice, while streams, fit for all purposes of machinery, pursue their course through the country in almost every direction. The only drawback to its prosperity, the only want, the supply of which would at once render it one of the most rich and populous sections of the New World, is an easy and ready access to market. When it is considered that this object can be fully effected, at a cost of only about £26,000, that this sum will at once open this splendid portion of country to the markets of the United States and Lower Canada, and through them give access even to the sea, no doubt can remain of the advantage of the investment now offered to the Public. If it be permitted to speculate upon the probable results, from the improvement of the magnificent rivers and lakes, which connect the Rice Lake with Lakes Simcoe and Huron, which at present engage so much the attention of the Government of this Province, it must be allowed not [to] be unreasonable to entertain the expectation, that a great portion of the produce of the Western Country would find its way to market over this rail-way. This view of the subject is particularly alluded to and supported in the report of the Engineer, and the fact that it would shorten the distance from the Western shores of Lake Michigan to the Southern shore of Lake Ontario, (say at Oswego,) nearly 300 miles, is amply sufficient to show that this opinion is not a mere chimera. It is unnecessary however to resort to this argument for the purpose of inducing conviction of the advantages of our undertaking, and the return likely to arise from it; the extent of trade with the rapidly improving country north of the Rice Lake, which this communication must demand, will surely warrant the outlay of the sum required, and the most sanguine hopes of an ample remuneration.[1]

A. Rubidge,
Secretary.

W. Boswell,
P. C. R. R. Co'.

5. Petition of Inhabitants of Fenelon and Verulam Townships for a Road, 1842

[*Public Archives of Canada, Public Works I, Vol. 46, March, 1842*]

Peterboro 31st March 42

F. C. Murdock Esqr
Chief Secretary &c. &c.
Kingston

Sir

I have the honor to enclose a petition from the Inhabitants of Fenelon & neighbourhood to his Excellency the Governor General praying his Excellency to take into consideration the expediency of completing the work commenced at Lindsay and constructing a Road from Scugog to Windsor[2] on Lake Ontario.

[1]This hope proved far from realization. As the years passed, the scope of the line was extended across Rice Lake by bridge, and on to Peterborough. The line was opened with great *éclat* in December 1854, but the initial enthusiasm soon faded, as did most of a capital investment of about $1,000,000. During the winters of 1855 and 1857 the railway bridge was squeezed out of position by ice. Communication across Rice Lake was cut for months, and was uncertain at best. "I was on the last train to cross the bridge," said William Burnet of Cobourg to the editor in 1931, "and it swayed so much that the passengers were afraid they would never reach Harwood." (See Edwin C. Guillet, *Cobourg, 1798–1948* (Oshawa, 1948), pp. 71–99, for an account of the history of the railroad, and of a walk over the old roadbed from Cobourg to Peterborough by the author and his sons on May 15 and 16, 1948.)

[2]An early name for Whitby. The reason for frequent petitions for roads is apparent from the hard conditions of early travel. An example from the central Trent Valley well illustrates the point. The *Peterborough Review* of December 23, 1864, mentions a project to bridge the narrows at Stoney Lake, presumably at Boshing (Boschink). The intention was to connect Dummer Township with the

I most cordially join in this Petition being well aware of the immense benefit the line of communication there proposed would be to a number of very fine Townships as well as Fenelon in which I am deeply interested being holder of a large tract of Land there and in Verulam the adjoining township. I was among the first that settled in Fenelon and have expended a large sum in improving it.

I have the honor to remain

Sir

Your Ob[t] Hum[l] Ser[t]
James Wallis

To His Excellency, The Right Honorable, Sir Charles Bagot, G.C.B. Governor General of British North America, &c. &c. &c.

The Humble Petition of the undersigned Inhabitants of the Townships of Fenelon and Verulam—

Sheweth

That your Petitioners, not without feeling of the most devoted Esteem & respect, beg leave to approach your Excellency with the subject of their Prayer—

That your Petitioners are Residents of that part of the Province which was until lately the rear of the District of Newcastle, now forming part of the new District of Colborne, in the fourth range of Townships from lake Ontario.

That your Petitioners were induced to become settlers in this remote, though fertile section of the country by the demonstration on the part of the Government of an intention to lay open a communication between it and the front Townships by means of the numerous lakes and rivers which intersect this portion of the Country, but the free navigation of which is at present obstructed by natural barriers— That the erection of a dock, to effect the above object, at the Town of Lindsay, was commenced, but all operation upon it has been long since suspended. That the lamentably imperfect roads which have been cut through the wilderness by the needy and thinly scattered pioneers of the forest are such as

Burleigh Colonization Road, at that time under construction, as may be seen from numerous items in that newspaper in the previous months. Work was begun in 1860, but the notorious "Burleigh rocks," and the frequent burning of the bridges, were difficulties hard to surmount, and the road was entirely impassable early in 1864. At that time, and earlier, it was a three-day trip from Peterborough to the region north of Stoney Lake. The first was by hired team to Young's Point, where a canoe or other boat could be engaged to carry freight and passengers to Julien's Landing (a sleigh would be used in winter); from Julien's travel continued by ox-team over what was at best a winter road, the trail often being more readily negotiated by "packing" the supplies on the shoulders of the travellers. (See Poole, *op. cit.*, pp. 208–11, for a contemporary account.)

can be traversed for only a short portion of the year, the husbandman being compelled to remain within the circumscribed limits of his home for the remainder—his grain & other produce during that time being comparatively valueless for want of an avenue by which he may transfer the same to market.

That such disadvantage naturally chills the ardour of enterprize, clogs the wheels of industry, and destroys the energy of the agriculturist —That it prevents an extensive and fertile region from being made to yield the immense stores it is capable of producing—That it prevents the useful Artisan and others from settling among us—since they are naturally led to other Countries where more favourable circumstances enable the Inhabitants to offer them a more abundant and a more certain subsistence.—

That your Petitioners beg most respectfully to call your Excellency's attention to this subject and humbly hope your Excellency will be pleased to take into consideration the expediency of completing the work commenced at Lindsay, in the Township of Ops, and of constructing a Plank or other road from the head of Scugog Lake to the Harbour of Windsor, by which the Inhabitants of this Portion of the Province will be immensely benefitted, and a wide and encouraging field will be opened to the in-coming stranger and the industrious yeoman of our Father Land.—

And your Petitioners, as in duty bound, will ever pray.

I. Fidler
Resident Clergyman of Fenelon
Robert Dennistoun
John Langton
Jno. Hore
Chas Hore
James McLaren
his
Willm x Crowley
mark
Drury Hutchinson
Richd Linehan
George Irwin
Pat. Power
his
Ja^{s} x Cook
mark
Andrew Mortimer

James Wallis
Geo H Sanders [?]
Geo^{e} Parker
his
Thos x Brady
mark
B. Beresford
William Jordon
Alex Umphrey
his
Thomas x Hooke
mark
John Bentley
Tanziy[?] Bentley
Wm Montgomery
his
John x Cook
mark

Arthur McConnell
James Walsh
James Bell
Alex. Bell
Samuel Walsh
Thomas Ellis
John Jordan
Augustus Sawers
William thornhill
John Power
Robt Brownlee
Horace umphrey

his
John x Duggan
mark
Frank Cochlan
Willm Allen
James Macculum
Wm Elliott
John Bell S^r^
John Bell J^r^
Robert Irwin
Henry Brassichant
William Jones
Alexander Dennistoun
David M^c^farland
William Dick
Robert Hamilton

6. Projected Plank Road, Cobourg to Rice Lake, 1842

[Public Archives of Canada, Public Works I, Vol. 51, Second Report of N. H. Baird, surveyor, on the several routes possible for a road from Rice Lake to Lake Ontario. This re-examination may have been due to a long letter of protest by Henry Ruttan in the previous February. Baird's first report was dated April 26, 1842]

'Memoranda on the Plank Road', October 3, 1842.

1. The Object to be effected by the proposed road, is to complete the Communications between the back country (the chief depot of which is Peterboro') and Lake Ontario in such a way as will give the inhabitants of that section of country a ready access and to the most advantageous market by this means to afford them some compensations for the want of the natural outlet by the River Trent which they have been led to expect would be improved by the Provincial Government but which I have understood the Board of Works are not at present prepared to recommend as it involves an expenditure of about £200,000

2^d^ The points to be connected are the Rice Lake and the best Market and shipping Port on Lake Ontario

3^d^ I do not conceive the question to be between *two* roads only—there are four roads which necessarily engaged my attention before recommending the one adopted by the Board of Works

The 1st Commencing opposite the mouth of the Ottonabee River and thence nearly direct south to Cobourg which was the main through fare to L Ontario when Steam Boats formerly plied upon Rice Lake

The 2[d] Commencing from the same point i e the mouth of the Ottonabee river to the head of the Rice Lake or near it, say the old Indian Landing, and thence direct to Cobourg about 17 miles that is 4¾ by water distance I take by the Lots allowing for angling across and 12¾ by Land

The 3[d] from the same point viz the mouth of the Ottonabee River to Pt Hope by the Head of the Lake 17 miles—viz about 6½ by water and 10½ by Land

		miles	ch
and the 4th by the road recommended	To Cobourg	15	31 —
	To Pt Hope	13	71 — i e
	from the Rice Lake —		

No detailed estimate has been made of the first mentioned route viz "from opposite the mouth of the Ottonabee River direct to Cobourg" as my Instructions confined me to "*at or near the head of Rice Lake*" as a starting point

The road recommended from the head of Rice Lake direct to Cobourg—I estimate it a sum not exceeding £11,000

The road at present travelled from the head of the Lake to Port Hope is impracticable for a plank road but with an entire deviation of 3 2/3

miles would cost about	£11,040 —
if planked to Cobourg —	3 250
making in all about	£15 290[1]

The road recommended will cost £11,166 2/ to the main road and including planking the main road between Cobourg & Pt Hope £4073— Making in all for the accommodation of the back Country in a choice of markets £15,239—

The road first mentioned in answer to Question N[r] 3 certainly would have great advantages in reference to the navigational *only* but would lose the object to be obtained by either of the other routes, of starting from a point where there is considerable travel and intercourse with the back Country and part by Land.

If the road were to be confined to one port only on Lake Ontario The second Road refered to is preferable in point of practicability & Expense to either of the others and would combine many advantages of a road to one point only besides giving facility of access to the District Towns—

No 3 or present travelled road presents great obstacles and obstructions for a plank road but has an advantage if the object be to reach one port only, in any other respect my opinion is, that the routes No 2 & 4 are both preferable to it—

[1]The error in addition is Baird's. In his MS. he wrote "£11, & 40."

And Your Petitioners as in duty bound, &c.

Dated at Cobourg this 12th day of December 1845.

Public Archives of Canada

PETITIONERS FOR THE PROMOTION OF THE COBOURG AND RICE LAKE PLANK ROAD AND FERRY COMPANY, 1845

The road recommended in my opinion combines for greater advantages than either of the others—I consider it of immense importance to the back country, that no step should be taken to give P^t^ Hope or Cobourg any advantage the one above the other; for the competition between these two places renders both markets far better than they otherwise would be—and the same competition by the plank road as recommended would lessen the expense of freight to come from the back Country at the lowest calculation 30 pr cent, and to adopt either of the other routes would at once have the effect to give the Port at which the road should terminate, so great an advantage, that it would necessarily have the effect to almost destroy the other as a market and would consequently by putting an end to competition maintain the cost of transport at nearly the present rates—

I have no hesitation in giving it again as my decided opinion that the middle road will accommodate a far greater number than either of the others, and that it is the only one that offers a fair promise of reasonable communication

N H Baird
Civil Engr

Kingston 3^d October
1842

7. Cobourg-Rice Lake Plank Road

[From the original, presented to the Manuscript Collection, Toronto Public Library, by Edwin C. Guillet]

Agreement between Josiah White et al and the Cobourg and Rice Lake Plank Road and Ferry Company. Dated 5th October, 1847.

Articles of Agreement had made and entered into at Cobourg this fifth day of october in the year of our Lord one thousand eight hundred and forty seven. Between Josiah White of Cobourg, Gentleman, Josiah Charles White of the same place, Miller, and John White of Alnwick, Saw Miller parties of the first part—and "The Cobourg and Rice Lake plank Road and Ferry Company" of the second part as follows

The said parties of the first part for the consideration hereinafter mentioned do hereby for themselves their Executors, Administrators and assigns—covenant promise and agree to and with the said parties of the second part their Successors and Assigns that they the said parties of the first part their Executors or Administrators shall and will at their own proper costs and charges make and deliver to the said parties of the second part and their Successors on the Shore at Gores Landing on or before the tenth day of May next properly piled up two hundred thousand feet of three inch plank in quality, good, sound, plumb measured, square edged and fit for the purpose of the road to be approved by the Engineers for the time being, sixteen feet or eight feet in length and scantling four by six inches sufficient to lay the plank upon forming two lines of Sills, And enough plank two by eight inches to lay one line as far as the plank will extend. And also on or before the fifteenth day of June next one hundred and fifty thousand feet of plank of like measurement and quality and subject to the same approval and scantling and two inch plank same as aforesaid sufficient to lay the said one hundred fifty thousand feet in manner aforesaid. And it is further agreed by and between the said parties that if the said parties of the first part shall be guilty of any neglect or delay in the delivery of the said plank or scantling or if the said plank do not answer the above description of Stuff and the said parties of the second part shall give or leave notice in writing of such neglect or delay at the place of abode of either of the said parties his Executors or Administrators that then and in such case it shall and may be lawful to and for the said parties of the second part or their Successors within the space of ten days after such notice given or left as aforesaid in case the said parties of the first part their Executors or Administrators shall not complete the delivery of the said Lumber at either of the said times aforesaid or in case any portion of it shall not be square edged sound and plumb measured as aforesaid required or if such portion as may not answer that described be not within the time aforesaid supplied in lieu of that, that may be cast to purchase from other persons willing to contract for the same, plank and scantling sufficient to complete the above contract of good sound plumb measured square-edged stuff fit for the Road And shall and may deduct and retain to themselves all such sum and sums of money and expenses as they shall pay or incur in supplying the said plank or Scantling

And the said parties of the second part do hereby for themselves their successors and Assigns covenant, promise and agree to and with the said parties of the first part their Executors, Administrators and assigns that they the said parties of the second part shall and will well and truly pay or cause to be paid unto the said parties of the first part their Executors, Administrators and Assigns the sum of twenty-five shillings per thousand feet (board measure) of plank when delivered as aforesaid. And for the Scantling twenty five shillings per thousand in manner following that is to say,

Immediately on delivery of the several quantities one half the value thereof and the remaining half due within six months after delivery as aforesaid.

And for the due performance and stipulations by them mutually entered into each of them the said parties of the first and second part by these presents do bind themselves unto the other of them in the penal sum of one hundred and fifty pounds of lawful money of Canada by way of liquidated damages. And lastly it is hereby convenanted and agreed by and between the said parties to these presents that if any dispute or difference shall happen to arise between them touching the said contract that then and in such case it shall be left to the determination and award of three indifferent persons or any two of them one to be named by the said parties of the first part their Executors Administrators or Assigns and the other by the said parties of the second part their Successors or Assigns and the third by the said two persons so to be named immediately after such dispute shall arise.

And the said parties hereto do hereby covenant promise and agree to and with each other that they the said parties shall and will severally stand to, abide, perform, and keep the award and determination of the said three persons or any two of them so as the same shall be made in writing under the hands and seals of the said Arbitrators within one calendar month next after such reference.

In Witness whereof the said parties of the first part have hereunto severally set their hands and seals. And the said Rice Lake Plank Road and ferry Company have hereunto affixed their corporate seal and caused to be put the hand of William Weller Esquire President thereof on the day and year first above written

Signed Sealed and
Delivered in presance of
John Beatty Jr.
Witness to first Signature
John Beatty Jr
Witness to all Signatures

Josiah White
Josiah C White
John White
Wm Weller President

Memorandum [on back] The Cobourg and Rice Lake Plank Road and Ferry Company of the one part and Josiah White, Josiah Charles White and John White, the parties within named of the second part do hereby mutually release and discharge each other from all liability and demands of what kind or nature soever upon or in respect of the within contract—and the said Parties of the second part hereby acknowledge payment in full of all monies due or payable to them by the said Company upon the within Contract Dated at Cobourg this Seventh day of July Anno Domini 1848[1]—

Signed Sealed and
Delivered in presence of
James Cockburn. Witness to
Execution by the President and
by Josiah and Josiah Cha[s]
White —

Wm Weller President
Josiah White
J C White

8. Transportation Petition from Inhabitants of Port Perry, 1857

[*Public Archives of Canada, Trent Canal, R.G. 11, P.W. 5, Vol. 19*]

Memorial for the Improvement of the Navigation between Port Perry and Fenelon Falls.

To the Honourable Francois Lemieux Chief Commissioner of Public Works of Canada &c &c &c

[1]"The Cobourg and Rice Lake Road is getting on famously. The whole line is now graded, and a portion of it planked. So good is the road at present that one team can with ease draw 14 bbls. of flour from Gore's Landing to the Cobourg wharf twice a day. We hope that our fair townswomen will make the Lords of creation drive them out to Rice Lake at least once a week during the summer. It will do all parties good to escape from the dust and dirt of the town to the green fields and pure air of the country." (*Cobourg Star*, May 17, 1848.) "A fine plank-road," wrote Samuel Strickland in 1851, "has been constructed from this

We your petitioners Inhabitants of the Village of Port Perry in the County of Ontario

Humbly Sheweth that they have sufered much in consequence of the Imperfect state of the Navigation between this place and Fenelon Falls during the past season that the Steamers plying between those two places and Lindsay could not perform their regular trips and portion of the season one of them was obliged to be confined to Sturgeon Lake thereby requiring transhipment at Lindsay of All through freight caused partialy by the lowness of the water and a bar across the river below the Lock at Lindsay, and the Imperfect condition of the Lock and dam at Lindsay Alowing the watter to escape and thereby lowering the watter in Scugog Lake. not only preventing the free and easy Navigation of the Lake, but a stopage of the Numerous Sawmills to the great damage of the owners at this place, your petitioners feel the great and urgent necesity of perfecting the Navigation of Scugog Lake and the river through to Sturgeon Lake by dredging out and straightening portions of the river and building of a new Dock at Lindsay is of great Importance to meet the growing wants of the Country, that the completion of these works in a good and substantial manner would not only be of great Importance to this section of the Country, but to the Townships lying North of Lindsay, and the construction of Locks at Fenelon Falls for Vesels to ascend would open up another new feature to the Country lying North and west of Fenelon Falls and bring into market a large portion of Government Lands which would be settled and Improved at once, Not taking into account the extensive Lumbering operations which would be carried on on those Lakes and rivers. Now lying in a state of Nature for the want of a proper communication with the frontier, and when completed, those lines of Navigable watters extending as they do far into the Interior would be of least Importance to every portion of the Country with in its Influence as well as a source of revenue to the public Treasury, whearas the present outlay and Imperfect state of the Navigation will only be comparitively of little or no benefit.

Your petitioners would most earnestly request that you would lay the matter before the Government and take such measures as desired advisable to apropriate a sufficient sum of Money for the completion of those works or as much as would be deemed prudent with a View to the completion of the whole and that the work should be commenced at as

---

place [Gore's Landing] to Cobourg, avoiding all the high hills. The stage time is an hour and a half between lake and lake." (*Twenty-Seven Years in Canada West*, (London, 1853), Vol. 1, p. 64.) A typescript on plank roads in Canada West, "Plank Roads: an Account of their History and Construction, together with Travellers' Descriptions of Journeys upon Them," by Edwin C. Guillet, may be found in the Library of Parliament, Ottawa, the Toronto Public Library, and the University of Toronto Library.

early a day as posible and as in duty bound your petitioners will ever pray

R Lund J.P.
Edward Major
Chas Payne
John W. Davis
Thos Paxton
Joseph Bigelow, P.M.
William Paxton
George Paxton
William King
William James Trounce
Robert Parker
David Rose
T Bigelow
John Buchanan
D. V. Daily
Jacob W. Straw
John A. Mason
William White
J D Foster
Robert Kelly
Daniel [?]
Aaron [?]
Jacob Burnham
George Snook
Philip Smith
B. G. Whittaker
Charles M. Martin
Benjamin Crandell
Levi Chatelle
John Platten
Thos Buchanan
Jabez Barns
W. S. Smith
Geo. M. Ewart
John Nott
John Addison
Chas Weightman
Jacob Corbman
Alonzo Sexton
J Smith
Joseph B. More
Henry R. Haskin
Gasper Bowen
John P Randall
Harvey Staley
Geo Everest
James B Lazier
James Squire
Andrew Lazier
William Nott
Cuff Buland
John Jeffery
Isaac Weeks
Allen J McNab
Jeremiah Centers
A. H. Doty
Samuel Platten
John Nichols
Willis W Cook
Jesse Ireland
J. C. Bowerman
W. D. Bowerman
A B Mc Donald
John Robert Hurst
Ira Whitney
Silas J. Haight
J W. Allison
John Bower
Solomon Mc vaigh
W. S. H. Smith
Thomas McMichael
Fred Vincent
Geo Goose
Alvan T. Corson
[? ?]
H. Phillips
Waren Norton
James Good
Wm Vincent
Joseph G. Schell

Wm Ross	Warren Schell
Wm S Sexton	Caleb Crandell
George Cain	George Crandell
James Morris	John [?]

9. Early Freight and Passenger Traffic *viâ* Railway

[Directory . . . of Peterborough and Victoria for 1858, *p. 68*]

THE COBOURG AND PETERBOROUGH RAILROAD

Lumber, Produce, &c., shipped by Cobourg and Peterborough Railroad from Peterborough, during the years 1855, 1856, and 1857.

Years	Lumber—feet.	Flour—barrels.	Wheat—bushels.	Wool—lbs.	Potash—barrels.	Lath—bundles.
1855	11,142,479	6539	23,255¾	38,519	43	4188
1856	15,946,158	19,095	56,862½	36,047	57	25,546
1857	13,365,503	9714	21,717	62,772	56	16,548

The inward freight over the Cobourg Road for the same years amounted to: 1855, $750,390: 1856, $968,349: and 1857, $888,933.

The number of passenger tickets sold at the Cobourg and Peterborough Railroad stations from 1st April, 1857, to 1st April, 1858, was as follows:

Cobourg to	Peterborough	6883	Peterborough to	Cobourg	5800
"	Baltimore	260	"	Baltimore	304
"	Braden's	200	"	Braden's	35
"	Harwood	1400	"	Harwood	480
"	I. Village	200	"	I. Village	643
"	Keene	500	"	Keene	754
"	Morgan's	100	"	Morgan's	132

Making a total received for passenger travel of $15,343.23.

PORT HOPE AND LINDSAY RAILROAD

The returns of freight over the road since it was opened were as follows: From 10th October, 1857, to March 31st, 1858:

881	Tons Merchandize	$3070
2023	" Heavy Freight	2810
5248	Barrels Flour	670
13,656	Bushels Wheat	670
450,000	Feet Lumber	611
24	Cords Firewood	24
	Unclassified	859
		9243
	Passengers, 4884	5834
	Total	$14,627

The gross receipts for April and May 1858 were $10,409.60.

VII. INDUSTRY: LUMBERING

THIS SECTION outlines the growth of industry, with special reference to the lumber trade. The early items indicate the common practice of stealing timber. Petitions for state aid in the building of mills, and for damages as a result of high water held back by dams, were not infrequent in the period. A particularly valuable list of early mills is contained in No. 11, and a summary of industrial development in the County of Peterborough in 1861 in No. 12. No. 13 is a very early attempt by workmen to regulate their hours of work; and the section is rounded out by three excellent accounts of the process of lumbering and of driving logs to Quebec.

1. PETITION FOR SAWMILL AND COMPLAINT OF ILLEGAL LIQUOR SALE, SEYMOUR TOWNSHIP, 1810

[*Public Archives of Canada, Upper Canada Sundries*]

Upper Canada.
York 29th March 1810.

Sir

M[r] Cumming & I have a wish of sawing some of the yellow Pine Timber which we have taken on the terms of our Contract, into Ship Plank, would His Excellency the Lieutenant Governor be pleased to grant us a License of occupation to build a Sawmill on the River Trent in the Township of Seymour.—There are many Trees which we have taken that fit for nothing else, and a vast number felled in 1808. which we could only take on the condition of being permitted to build a Saw Mill, that must otherwise be lost.

I take the liberty of mentioning for The information of His Excellency, that a worthless Yanky of the name of Truman Napping, has without authority set himself down in Seymour, where he has built a House & vends liquor in the most disorderly manner—He has constantly a gang of drunken vagabonds about him, of vagrant whites & Indians, constantly fighting among themselves and abusive to others. Napping, is himself a notorious bad character, and the greatest irregularities have been committed in his House—the abuse of the Government and Laws

—his removal would much contribute to the quiet and good order of that part of the Country—

Major Halton
&c &c &c

I have the honor to be
Sir
Your Most obedient
Humble Servant
Miles Macdonell

2. Sale of Stolen Timber, Seymour Township, 1821

[*Archives of Ontario, Crown Land Papers, Correspondence, Memoranda, and Reports on Lumbering*]

Hamilton 30th April 1821

Sir

I have the honor to inform you that I have made two Journeys to Seymour in compliance with your letter of the 8th Instant relating to the timber cut in that Township by persons unauthorised and have seized the Same—amounting to about Six thousand Pipe Staves—five thousand feet Square Oak timber, and four thousand West India Staves—The last mentioned Staves are of little value.—I have advertised the same to be sold on the Seventh day of May next—but from the bad prospect of the market of lumber this Year in consequence of the report of duty being placed on that article—and the scarcity of money—will (in all probability) render the sale of the lumber merely nominal.—I am informed that it has been represented to you that I bought the norway, cut in that Township last Year (by way of Speculation) which representation I am bound to say is totally void of fact—and dictated by a turbulent and vindictive spirit.—for, leaving the impropriety of such a transaction out of the question, I would not have taken the said norway timber, in the state that it was when sold, even as a present.

I think that I may venture to say that the late depredations committed in the Township of Seymour will be the last in that Township on the score of lumber.

I have the honor to be
Sir
Your Most Obedt
Humble Servant
John Spencer, Sheriff
N. District

Jno. B. Robinson Esqr
Atty-Genl
&c &c &c

3. Stolen Timber, Newcastle District, 1821

[*Archives of Ontario, Crown Land Papers, Correspondence, Memoranda, and Reports on Lumbering*]

A Report Shewing the names of trespassers on Lands belonging to the Crown in the District of Newcastle, as far as it can be ascertained together with their place of residence, quantity of timber Cut, description of the same, and where cut

Names of heads of parties	Places of residence Township	District	Quantity of timber	Description	Where cut	Names of procurers	Names of Men employed
Samuel Sherwood Jr and Ira Nichols	Murray / Belville	NewCastle / Midland	8000 feet	Squared Norway	Seymour	John Everet *of Belville*	Samuel Miller / Thomas Barns
Edward McConnel	Ameliasburg	Midland	4000 do	do	do	Jacob Germain *of Ameliasburgh*	——Churchill
David Johns	Murray	NewCastle	50000 do	do	do		John Clute
William Sweete	Belville	Midland	4500 do	do	do	Adam H. Meyers *of Murray*	Gilbert Beatys & Silas Smith
William Townsend & William Stone	Percy	NewCastle	8000 do	do	do		
Truman Nappin	Seymour	do	2000 do	do	do	Allan B. McDonell *of Glengary*	
William Townsend & William Stone	Percy	do	20	Spars	do		

To

John B. Robinson Esquire
Atty. Genl.

John Spencer Sheriff
NewCastle District

4. Sale of Stolen Timber, 1821

[*Archives of Ontario, Crown Land Papers, Correspondence, Memoranda, and Reports on Lumbering*]

Port Hope 1st May 1821

Dear Sir

The Sheriff of this District having seized a large quantity of Timber which has been cut on the Crown Lands, has given very general Notice of the Sale of it on the 7th Inst. Owing to the Belief that prevails of a Duty being intended to be laid on American Lumber, I think very few if any Bidders will be found—I therefore considered that it would not be improper in me to suggest to you the expediency of some persons being authorised to purchase the said Timber at a reasonable Rate for the Government which could then be very easily transported to Quebec. And this could be done rather advantageously, and at a moderate Expence, because the persons who have got out Lumber and intend going down with it would be very glad to attach a few more Cribs (as they are called) to their Rafts and thereby ensure to themselves Remuneration for their Journey which would have been made at all Events.—My Reason for making the above Observations is that I perceived a petition has very lately been laid before the Imperial Parlt, by some Merchants interested in the Lumber Trade of this Country, which may prevent the Enactment of the Law imposing Restrictions.

David Johns has a large Contract with the Navy for the delivery of Lumber at Kingston, and it is possible a great proportion of this now to be sold might be disposed of there, in Case of more being wanted—At any Rate I think Johns would be a safe hand to take Charge of it to Quebec. He is going to Quebec in a few weeks—In Case you approve of these Remarks you can submit them to the Govr but not otherwise.

Be so good as tell McAulay I recd his Letter and shall not neglect it's Contents—At present I know of no person in this District of the Name of Wm. Bullock—

I hope you are all well—

Believe me Dear Sir
Yr's very faithfully

G. S. Boulton

John B. Robinson Esq
Atty. Genl.
York

5. Return of Timber, Seymour Township, 1832

[Archives of Ontario, Crown Lands Papers, 84 (3)]

General Returns of Lumber Cut upon Crown Lands in the Township of Seymour Shewing the Quantity and Description Cut by authority and also by Trespassers an Account of which has been ascertained by David Campbell between the 1st of January and 31st of December 1832

Names of Lumberers	No. of pieces of Timber	White Oak Timber Cubic Feet	White Pine Timber Cubic feet	Red Pine Timber Cubic feet	Standard Staves No. of pieces	West India Staves No. of pieces	White Pine Standard Saw Logs	With or Without License	Aggregate	Description of Lumber	Rate of Timber Dues	Provincial Currency
Willard Ferguson*	78	1937				5790		With	*Recapitulation*			
Donald McKenzie	257	4455	5800	300	3000		404	Without	10,332	Cubic feet of White Oak Timber	@ 9½ per foot	64 11 6
Alexander Chisholm							799	With	62,059	Cubic feet White Pine Timber	½ " "	129 5 9

*Note—6201 feet White Pine Timber made under this License but found to be on private property and the amount paid to the owner.

5 (*cont'd*)

Benjamin Romney							3812	Do	936	Cubic feet Red Pine Timber	9 " "	3	18	-
Adam H. Myers	55	1565		636		20,072		Do	3,000	Pieces of Standard Staves	9 ? Stave	12	10	-
Anthony Monahan	544		51250					Do						
Amos Thrasher	26	675						Without	25,862	Pieces of West India Staves	½ "	26	18	9
William Zeosch							1100	With	7315	White Pine Standard Saw Logs	4 Log	121	18	4
Jonathan Phillips		842	1559					Do						
William Robertson		858	3450				1200	Do				£359	2	4
		10332	62059	936	3000	25862	7315							

Amounting to Three hundred and fifty nine Pounds two shillings and four pence Currency

Sworn before me at Cobourg this 23 day of April 1833.
N. Henry J.P.
W.

David Campbell Collector of dues on Crown Timber maketh oath and saith that this his account is just and true according to his knowledge and belief.
J. Campbell

6. Petition of William Purdy, Ops Township, and Report of A. McDonell, 1837

[*Archives of Ontario, Crown Land Papers, 62 (1), "Mill Sites"*]

To His Excellency Sir Francis Bond Head Knight commander of the Royal Hanoverian Guelphic order and of the Prussian Military order of Merit. Lieut. Governor of the Province of Upper Canada &c &c &c in Council

The Petition of William Purdy of the Township of Ops in the New-Castle District

Humbly Sheweth:

That your Petitioner in consideration of His building a grist and saw mill on the Scugog River on lots number 20, and 21. in the sixth concession of the said Township of Ops, which was expected to be and has been a great public convenience & accommodation but has required a very considerable investment of money and many privations by your Petitioner, received a grant of said lots and other lands amounting altogether to four hundred acres and the promise of being allowed to overflow so much of the lands bordering on the waters above the said mills as should be required for that purpose, in order to have a convenient & advantageous use of the mill: that the arrangements between the Government & your Petitioner were made with the Hon. Peter Robinson to whom your Petitioner would respectfully refer on the Subject: that your Petitioner is apprehensive that unless some order of your Excellency is made, some of the lands necessarily overflowed by your Petitioner's mill dam may be granted unconditionally: which would be not only inconsistent with the promise made to your Petitioner without which he would not have undertaken this enterprise but would also prevent your Petitioner from using his mill & would prove ruinous to your Petitioner.

Wherefore your Petitioner prays that your Excellency will be pleased to order that in any grants of such lands a licence to your Petitioner & his assigns to overflow them may be reserved, so far as may be required for the purposes aforesaid.

And as in duty bound will ever pray

Wm Purdy

Toronto 31st January 1837

With respect to the Petition of William Purdy I beg to state that the Mill Site therein alluded to was assigned to the Petitioner on condition of his building a good and sufficient Grist & Saw Mill, whereby the Settlement in that part of the Country would enjoy the benefit intended by the Government in consideration of such assignment; that from the confidence reposed in the Petitioners Knowledge in the erection of Mills in situations similar to that referred to in his petition, he was recommended by the Honble Peter Robinson as a suitable locatee for the Mill reservation; on which he has since built Mills in every respect adequate to the demand of the surrounding Country.—

I would also state that being in charge of the Settlement forming in the Township of Ops I was necessarily made acquainted with the understanding that existed between the Petitioner and the Government, and I have no Knowledge of any promise of indemnification as to the overflowing of any other lands than those on the Shores of the Skugog River in the immediate neighborhood of the Works, and then in the hands of Government and for which I believe no patents have issued without a protecting clause—All which is respectfully submitted.—

A. McDonell

Toronto 2nd February 1837

7. Petition of Charles Blue *et al.*, Eldon Township, 1838

[*Archives of Ontario, Crown Lands Papers, 62 (1), 'Mill Sites'*]

Unto His Excellency Sir George Arthur Lieutenant Governor &c &c of the Province of Upper Canada

The Petition of Charles Blue and other Inhabitants of the Township of Eldon in the NewCastle District

Humbly Sheweth

That we your humble & loyal subjects humbly request that our extreme case would be taken into your Excellency's consideration in rendering more or less aid to building a grist Mill in this Township which is a sequestered valey surrounded with great swamps and at the distance of twelve miles from the nighest Mill. providing a pair of millstones was granted we should be well pleased and would manage the rest of the Mill ourselves and your petitioners as in duty bound will ever pray

Eldon 13 July 1838	George Campbell	John McCallum
	Duncan Campbell	Neil Smith
Jas. McDonald	Arch[d] McArthur	Colin McLancy
Arch[d] McFadyen	Alex[r] McEachern	Aarichibald McCofer
Allan MacEachern	Farquhar McEachern	Archy McCafer
Donald Gunn	Neill McEachern	Donald McCofer
Arch[d] Campbell	Alex[r] McAlpin	John Well
David Logan	Gilbert McAlpen	Peter Smith

To

The Honble the Chairman and Members of the Board of Works

The Memorial of the undersigned, engaged in the Lumber Trade on the River Trent,

Sheweth:

That in the opinion of Your Memorialists, the Slides at present erected on the River Trent, having been constructed for facilitating the descent of Lumber down that River, are ineffective for the purpose intended, unless Booms be constructed below them for the safety of the timber after its descent

With the view therefore of giving facilities to the Lumber trade on the said River, and to enable Your Memorialists to give the Slides, as now amended, a fair trial, Your Memorialists humbly request that Your Honble Board will be pleased to give directions for the construction of good and substantial Booms, forthwith, at the following

Public Archives of Canada

TRENT RIVER LUMBERMEN PETITION THE BOARD OF WORKS, 1856 (*a*)

Courtesy Miss Phyllis Denne

[12] DRIVE OF LOGS, RICE LAKE, 1864
The cookery and stable in the foreground

Photograph by James Guillet

[13] BLUEBERRY RIDGES, MOUNTAIN LAKE, BURLEIGH TOWNSHIP
Typical of hundreds of square miles in the region

Canadian Illustrated News

[14] CUTTING THE KEY LOG IN A JAM
A hazardous operation in log-driving

The Ganaraska Watershed

[15] THE MULEY UP-AND-DOWN SAW
Commonly used before 1850

The Ganaraska Watershed

[16] SQUARING TIMBER

Virgin pine was very different from the modern product

Boyd Collection, Public Archives of Canada

[17] IN THE WOODS NEAR COBOCONK

Photograph by George M. Douglas, " Northcote "

[18] A DRIVE OF LOGS IN KATCHEWANOONK

Located below Young's Point, the home of George M. Douglas is in the background

Courtesy Miss Phyllis Denne

[19] THE *ECLIPSE* WITH BOOM OF LOGS, RICE LAKE, 1874

Boyd Collection, Public Archives of Canada

[20] RIVER-DRIVING

Archives of Ontario

[21] LOG-JAM, FENELON FALLS

Canadian Illustrated News B. Kroupa

[22] BLAIRTON IRON MINE, MARMORA, 1873

The ore was carried by boat to Harwood

Courtesy Miss Phyllis Denne

[23] RAILWAY TERMINUS AT HARWOOD

The railway carried the ore to Coburg

Canadian Illustrated News

[24] NORTH HASTINGS GOLD MINE, 1880

Canadian Illustrated News B. Kroupa

[25] WILLIAMS GOLD MINE, MARMORA, 1873

Developments in mining were in progress in this region as early as the eighteen-twenties

places, viz. Crow River, Crow Bay, Percy Landing Place and the mouth of the River Trent.

Your Memorialists beg to subscribe themselves.

Your most obedient
Humble Servants.

River Trent
18th Feby 1846.

Jacob Ford
Charles Clark
Benj.n Clark
Dun. Grant
Hugh McGowan

Robert C. Wilkins
Joseph Shuter
Benj.n Weller
David Smith
Donald Stewart
Joseph Errington

Public Archives of Canada

TRENT RIVER LUMBERMEN PETITION THE BOARD OF WORKS, 1856 (*b*)

Duncan MacEachern
Niel McFarlane
Edward Maden
Winn Mitchell
Robert Williamson
Malcolm McEachern
John McEachern
Donald Campbell
James Fresar
Donald McArthur
Hugh Campbell
John Brown
John Brown
Malcolm McArthur
Rodrick Grant
Alex^{r} Grant
Archibald McArter
John McInnes
John McIntyre
Peter Campbell
John Campbell
Alex^{r} Campbell
Archibald Campbell
Malcolm McEchnie
Dugal McGilhrie
Robart McKay
Alex^{r} Campbell
Duncan Campbell
John McArthur
John McAlpen
James McAlepen
Gilbart McAlpen
Duncan McIntyre
Angue McIntyre
Andrew McIntyre
Archibald McDugald
Donald McDugald
Andrew McPherson
Hector Grant
John Grant
Neil Smith
Donald Grant
James Ure
John Anderson
Donald Anderson
Alex^{r} Anderson
Alex^{r} McDonald
Edward Mather
Walter Pepper
Archd Sinclair
Angus McLeoud
Thos. Dunn
John Mahoney
James FitsSimans
Robt Ringland
John Ringland
Robt Ringland Junior
Donald McQuaige
Angus Fergeson
Alex^{r} Fergeson
Arch^{d} Stewart
John Stewart
D. Cameron
Duncan McCorquordale
Isacc Ferguson
Arch^{d} McIntyre
Archibald Jackson
Alex^{r} Currie
Archy McDiffe
Alex^{r} Ross
Duncan McCorquodale
John McCorquodale
James McLachlen
William McLachlen
Archibald Spenck
Archibald Currie
John Ray
Archd Ray
Colin Ray
Hugh MacEachern
Eachon MacEachern
Donald McFadyen
Gilbert Keith
John Smith
James Campbell

8. The Quebec Timber Trade

(a) EXCERPT FROM LETTER OF HENRY FOWLDS[1] TO HIS SON, 1851

[In the Possession of Mrs. Helen Marryat, Hastings]

Quebec 23^{d} June 51 Dear James

My five Drams got down in Safety Saturday afternoon the weather calm landed 12 drams in

[1]Henry Fowlds was born in 1790 in the Isle of Skye. In 1851 he purchased from the Honourable James Crooks 1171 acres of land at Crooks' Rapids, including the mill-site and water power. Long a successful lumberman and public-spirited citizen, he was the founder of the village of Hastings and gave it its name in 1852 in commemoration of Lady Flora Hastings of whom he had been a boyhood admirer. He died in 1872. Mrs. Marryat is his great-granddaughter.

Gilmours Booms containing three of Adam Earhearts gatherd timber and 9 drams of Charles Townsends Mine with 3 drams of Gilchrists was to have been left at Mr Walkers we ley far out in the tide water there being a large Otawa Raft between us and the loading Pears And finding that I was expected to bring the timber to the little River at any rate intel Sold I thought I might Save time in dooing so at once I could not bargain in Montreal with the Agent for the Lumber Merch^s^ left them £10 to put me in Paradis Boom and thought I should do better below but was mistaken every Boat is in the midst of their hearvest and was forced to go over to Point Levee to try the lumber merch^t^ again where She had gone to take in coal and agreed for £8 15s. on Sunday morning about light it blew heavey draging the Boat and tossing the timber much but they lost none And got in themselves freed from the Boat Today Monday I have got £250 and paid of the hands honestly and as I think fairly without any grumbling

Timber has been sold as high as 7^d^ pr foot from samples in Shiping order but measured off I cannot say what I will get perhaps 6½ and 10½ for Elm More has been gotten for a little larger av^g^ say 11^d^ Scott of Scott & Robb is after it would like to have it for 6^d^ perhaps 6½ but I have not had oppertunity of judging its value will try tomorrow

Henry needs £15 more than I sent him and must try and send it forthwith I wish he mey come with the first Tow in cribs lathed it is just as good and will sell much better And by all means steal ahead of the rest for which purpose has sent him 3 Sails which is absolutely needful. I rec^d^ Mr Crooks letter and accepted his preposal of 27th May with the proviso that the Board of Works allow the uce of the waste way for the purpose of obtaining their permission for that purpose I have wrote James Hall to try and refere theme to Mr Crooks for explination I ask £5000 to deliver 100,000 of hardwood 100,000 of pine and say 25000 1st & 2^d^ Deal next year in market F. Burstill says enquire at Henry who says he will take it into concederation as there is no haste Paradis & Anderson will shortley give me an answer I believe I shall get it from eather

I wrote Crooks that I would prefere his allowing the operation at Crooks to be suspended for the present as I wished Miller to finish the work begun as I should choose and by in the materials for that purpose myself. . . . Temperance goes hard. I drink only som cordial it is too cold for Spruce beer besides it disagrees with me as well as Soda water And drink something I must truely I am paying for nothing

Henderson had his timber better than last year loaded but the best of some of the Cribs is in the bottom. Still his taste is however much better than last years foreman & Henry speaks truth when he says he has no taste at all but crowded and careless loading will not sell a raft. . . . A Heavey Blow and storm of Rain has done much dammaige here on Sunday morning 2 rafts the property of an Otaway lumberman called has been wrecked to single pieces above Carush and others at Wood & Petries lying outside Boom has suffered And it has turned out very fortunate that care was taken of ours on Saturday night or we would nor could not have escaped. I will do all I can to hurry the Sales of what is here and get it imadiately measured And will not lost sight of Henry will write him imadiatley The Boilar for the Lake Steam Tug should be got upon the Novelly principle And the Engine ought to be had in the States with a moving cillender and ocetating valves which is caused by the motion of the cillender hanging as it does on pinions

Pipe-staves were invariably made from blue or white oak, while like the knobs of a cannon. . . .

Henry Fowlds

(*b*) FOWLDS'S OFFER TO DELIVER TIMBER IN QUEBEC, 1856(?)

[*In the possession of Mrs. Helen Marryat, Hastings*]

I hereby ofer Messrs Gilespie & Co^{y} of the City of Quebec to place in William Walkers Booms of that Ctiy *in* or before the Month of August next Square timber Spars of Red pine & White pine Masts to the Amount and value of Nine thousand pounds and over at the following valuations

White pine @ 6½^{d} pr foot
Red pine @ 7½ " " "
Elm timber @ 9^{d} " "

White pine girds over $\frac{18}{12}$ & Masts over *20* £15 each

and pay them 5 pr C^{t} for Sales and guarentee requiring them to give their letter of C^{r} to the Montreal or Comercial Bank to accept paper drawn on them by me payable by them maturity in Quebec to the amount of Five thousand pounds Currency drawn as follows

£1000 in Decr next
1000 in Jany next
1000 in Feby next
1000 in March next
1000 in May next £2000 coming due in June
£2000 coming due in July
1000 coming due in August

and to pay the raft hands on placing the raft £1000.

9. Taking Square Timber from Sturgeon Lake to Quebec, 1849

[*John Langton,*[1] Early Days in Upper Canada: Letters of John Langton *(Toronto, 1926), pp. 201–9*]

June 18th, 1849

Our lumber after all sorts of ups and downs, sometimes getting easily through bad places and being awfully detained at easy ones, has got to Peterborough at last, with the loss of only four sticks left behind and available for next year and one spoiled.[2] As an illustration of the uncertain freaks of the Goddess that presides over lumber I may mention that we had two bad sticks, a crooked one and an unsound one, which we meant to leave behind, but like the bottle imp we never could get rid of them. The crooked went over everything without touching and reached Peterborough where it lay exposed to public view, to our confusion and disgrace, one whole month before it was joined by its fellows. The unsound one formed the foundation of almost every jam in the river, and even after it was cut in two parts pertinaciously annoyed us all the way. My first estimate of the cost down to Peterborough was £2 or £2.5s per stick, but I do not think they have cost more than £1. 10s or £1. 15s at farthest. £1 more will certainly take them down to Quebec. What they will fetch there it is impossible to find out. Nobody will tell who knows, and very few know anything about that description of lum-

[1]Among the most capable and public-spirited pioneers in the Trent Valley was John Langton (1808–1894). Born in Lancashire of mercantile parents, he was educated at Pestalozzi's Institute in Switzerland and by private tutors. When poverty succeeded affluence in the family's fortunes, John Langton emigrated to Canada in 1833, soon after graduation from Cambridge. Four years later his father, his sister Anne, and several others of his family followed, and "Blythe Farm," on Sturgeon Lake near Fenelon Falls, became their home. In 1845 he married Lydia Dunsford, daughter of the Church of England incumbent. Prominent in the lumber business, Warden of the Colborne District, and subsequently a member of the Legislative Assembly, Langton was noted for his shrewd estimate of men and affairs, best exemplified, perhaps, by his astute opinion against Church of England monopoly of Clergy Reserves, in which controversy he fell foul of the clerical hierarchy, upon whose heads he let fall some caustic comments. He was appointed first Auditor of Public Accounts. At Confederation he became Auditor-General of Canada and was long an authority on public finance. His well-developed sense of humour is exemplified by his comment about the first six settlers on Sturgeon Lake, who made up in quality for their lack of numbers; for, as he put it, four of them "have been at an university, one at the military college at Woolwich, and the sixth, though boasting no such honours, has half a dozen silver spoons and a wife who plays the guitar." Langton died in Toronto on March 19, 1894.

[2]The *Peterborough Review* of June 17, 1864, states as a news item that one day's run down the Otonabee from Lakefield to Peterborough was 280 cribs, worked by 1150 men. A jam caused a three-hour delay, but there was no violence among the French-Canadian rivermen.

ber. I knew a raft last year of seventy, of which the twenty best sold for £8; and we hear on good authority that the owner was offered £5. 10s for the rest this spring. Now we have very few as bad as his best, and I have had pointed out one or two of ours which they say are worth £20 or £25. This looks well but per contra I learned from the manager of one of the larger lumbering firms at Quebec that the annual demand is only for about 2,000 pieces and that their house is concerned in about 1,500; but he adds that there is always a demand for such sticks as some of ours which he saw, and I don't think he saw our best.

10. Reminiscences of Robert Harrison, Asphodel Township

[*Peterborough* Daily Evening Review, *October 27, 1902*]

Being at this time engaged in various branches of the timber trade, our practice was to mulnette the square pine, load it, all that it would float, with pipe staves (which were then in good demand for the West India trade), take all down the river and sell out at the Trent, and in these respects our efforts were almost always crowned with success. These events took place in the thirties, and even then money was gaining a wider and better circulation; the pulse of Colonial life was making itself felt with fairly regular beat in the hearts and homes of families far removed from the centres of, perhaps more active, yet certainly not more forceful thought that inspired the leading minds of those communities that were rapidly and permanently lining the shores of the greater waters to the south.

In those early days the timber easily obtainable in Asphodel was of great size, and very much of it was of the finest quality. Let one or two instances in the experience of the narrator be here cited in illustration of the foregoing statement. Shortly after the erection of Walker's Mill we were engaged taking our saw-logs on the high sandy ridges a mile westward, known as 'Walker's Mountains', when from a pine tree little more than three feet in diameter at the ground we cut eleven twelve foot sawlogs; the top end of the top log was a foot in diameter, and showing but a few small knots. This was in 1832. On another occasion we took out a mast from Lot 15, con. 4, that measured one hundred and twenty feet in length, and had a diameter of forty-two inches at what was known as the 'first partner', which, in that instance, would be the distance of forty feet from the 'grub', one-third of the entire length. The largest piece of square timber ever taken out in Asphodel was cut on the west half of Lot 12, con. 3, by the men employed by Foley and Grover of Norwood. The stump of the tree, where cut, was seven feet six inches in diameter, and the piece contained by admeasurement nine hundred and sixty cubic feet of timber. Every man in the shanty, cook included, got on the piece and danced jigs, reels and hornpipes on its surface to the music of the fiddle for the two miles' distance between the shanty and the landing place at the forks of the Ouse. The hauling and landing of masts, while at times very laborious work on the men and horses, had, withal, a spice of real danger to the limbs and lives of both sufficiently great to make the work of the mast gang lively, exciting, and dashing; being ever surcharged with the spirit of daring amounting to fascination. To command twenty-two span of spirited, active, powerful horses hitched to a 'bridled' mast-sleigh to prevent the liability while crossing steep ridges to being 'jacked' as the mast broke over the hillcrests and rushed headlong towards the valley beneath, with teamsters mounted and every horse of the forty-four galloping for life at full speed; usually on a crooked road, frequently leaping the 'lead-chain' sideways to avoid being caught and thrown, is by no means the office of a sinecure, and has furnished the numberless experiences in the life of the narrator not easily either imagined or described. This much for the road; now for the landing. Delaney's was a splendid landing on the Trent, two miles below Hastings. A long but not too steep slope formed the north bank of the River Trent at this place. Winter was very rapidly becoming a thing of the past on the occasion in question. The ground was being laid bare of the fast-melting snow. The last monster pine was yet lying prone in the mast-road at the foot of a ridge where, at near one o'clock in the morning, the sleigh 'bridle' had given way, and the sleigh was 'jacked'. But this last mast of the season must be landed early next morning, for the ice at Delaney's was fast becoming honeycombed. Every horse and every available man was, at day-light next morning, called into requisition. The tacklings were all made ready, and mast rolled over and the 'jacked' sleigh turned right side up, and right end ahead once more. Soon the giant was loaded and again slowly moving, for the trusty forty-four men were obliged to test their firm muscle and rigid sinew to the utmost. The hill-top was gained; the hundreds of broad acres of clearing were passed, the brow of the long slope to Delaney's was at last reached. The sun was high in the noonday skies and shone with all the brilliancy and strength of his early April vigor. The flanks of the horses were heaving from long applied and strenuous exertion. A ten minutes' rest was taken, for the work had been heavy for the past few hours, and the giant had to be roused from his slumbers again, as teamsters bringing forward their peeled skids gave evidence of the effort yet to come before the monster would begin his head-long rush for the landing berth of his fellows. But, right there, the element of extreme danger lay shimmering in the sunbeams, and in the water-covered and honey-combed ice of that splendid river. Soon the skids were in position and everything made ready for a start. The preliminary order 'tighten up', then the command 'All together', were responded to very closely, yet very quietly, for the men seemed impressed with a sense of unusual danger from the ice beneath. All seemed, instinctively, to become silent, save for an occasional word of direction, soon changed to fiery urging to the far ahead lead to 'clear the way', as the occasional swish of the lead-chain on the icy slope or the clanking of the whittletrees against the heels of the horses indicated that the mast-sleigh with its ponderous load was coming with an ever-increasing momentum and carrying destruction to everything caught or overtaken in the descent. Urton Hill, my trusty lieutenant, had in the meantime daringly mounted the mast, immediately in rear of the chain, and was carrying a keen-edge six-pound blocking axe in his hands, which he used in lieu of a balancing pole. Every horse had soon reached the ice, and all were galloping at the top of their speed; the mast was well-nigh full length from the shore when the ice suddenly broke under the great strain, and mast, sleigh, and twelve span of the rear horses were in a moment, with their riders, floundering in the mass of broken ice and water. Ten span of the forward horses were yet on sound ice; there remained not a single moment to be lost, otherwise all might be lost with it. Instantly the command 'Cut the Mast Chain' was given, and Hill's axe swept down upon it like a flash, completely severing it at one blow. Then almost as quickly the order 'heavy on the lead' was followed by descending whips on the flanks of the horses that were still out of the water, and though not another word was spoken by anyone, each man and horse seemed to work instinctively, with a will; and in less time than is required to tell the story of their escape, men and horses were all safely standing on the unbroken ice, very little the worse of this their last adventure of the season before disbanding for our homes on the nearby farms. Blue and white oak, too, was frequently to be found with diameter at the stump of more than forty inches, and a height of sixty to seventy feet without a branch.

As the forest rapidly receded before the powerful, well-aimed blows of the woodsman's axe the industry of making pot and pearl ash was introduced in the neighborhood of the west branch of the Ouse by the late Henry Fowlds. Wheat, too, began to be extensively raised and prepared for market—not only at Cobourg but at Keene and other points of increasing interest. Prices for grain increased with the ever increasing demand; labor, by hand, became every year a little higher in price; farm hands eagerly taking up land and making homes for themselves;

flail-threshing became a tedious, expensive, and unsatisfactory method—largely owing to the fact that the chaff could not always be effectually removed from the grain. In the rank condition in which wheat usually grew in those days the flail left great quantities of chaff known as 'white-caps' and which was objected to by the wheat buyers.

Thus matters progressed until in the year 1843 George Ashe of Cold-springs in the township of Hamilton, county of Northumberland, introduced the first threshing-machine—an open cylinder—but it remained for the late James Fife, lot 12, con. 1, to be the first owner of a threshing-machine operated and owned in the township. James Fife, Donald Cameron, Hugh Christie, and myself were the first in the township to own and work the spring-tooth, hand-lift horse-rake, we each having purchased one of those horse-rakes on the same day of July in the year 1852. The first eliptic steel-spring carriage was brought into the township by the late Henry Fowlds, then of Westwood; it was a three-seated family carriage, seats all facing forward, capable of seating nine full-grown people, and apparently strongly enough built to successfully carry three times that number of full grown men of the average avoirdupois weight. This was in the year 1850, and at its first day's real service in the township Mr. and Mrs. Fowlds, Mr. Jas. Fowlds and his wife and two of their children, Miss Elizabeth Fowlds and Messrs. Harry and William Fowlds all rode quite comfortably to attend divine service, conducted by the newly-inducted minister, Rev. Francis Andrews, in Cameron's school house. Shortly after this Mr. Fowlds gave the deed of an acre of land and enough lumber to build the Presbyterian church, now standing on the south-west corner, lot 11, in the 2nd con. of the township of Asphodel. For a number of years, during the sixties, this church edifice was occupied by both the Presbyterians under the pastorate of the Rev. Francis Andrews, and the Church of England, under the pastorate of Rev. Michael Angelo Farrar. But, returning to more primitive times, the first religious services held in the township were conducted by a layman, the late John Cameron, at his home at Cameron's Point. The Indians had, some of them at least, been converted to Christianity about this time; but the precepts of the white man's religion not being always carried out by him in practice, the Indians did not always agree to be governed by it; and although all were nominally Christian, the late James Cameron has frequently told me of seeing the children of the forest performing acts of heavily beating their bare chests with their clenched fists, and with faces upturned towards the sun, indicating in these ways and by a sort of weird chant or dirge, that they were either lamenting the loss of their dead ones or engaged in solemn acts of Sun worship.

Be these things as they may, changed conditions of life, dwelling in houses instead of wigwams, the clearing up of the country, and the advance of civilization are clearly proving that the Indian is fast passing away and only at rare and long intervals are they now seen in the township.

While the work of clearing the land was necessarily slow and laborious yet it was not without many pleasing features both as regards the nature of the work itself—wholesome, though heavy—and the abundance of good cheer which usually accompanied its performance. The common practice among farmers in clearing their lands was to cut down the timber in fallows of from ten to twelve acres in extent. The underbrush was first cut, trimmed, and carefully laid in heaps, as far as possible lengthwise, especially if any considerable quantity of beech or birch timber grew upon the land, as the brush of these woods, also black oak and butternut, were difficult to burn when clearings were small and the seasons wet. All fallen timber, too, was cut in convenient lengths for logging, which was usually from sixteen to twenty feet, as the underbrushing progressed. A good chopper invariably followed the terms of an excellent, though unwritten law pertaining to land-clearing, which may be here briefly stated; that is to say, underbrush, which included all young trees of four inches and under at the ground, were to be cut at not more than three inches above the surface; all fallen timber except such as would make either pipe staves, square timber, saw logs, or fence rails, was to be cut into logging lengths as the underbrushing proceeded and an acre in extent of such chopping was, by common consent, allowed to be a fair day's work for a good axe-man.

Pipe-staves were invariably made from blue or white oak, while square timber and sawlogs were usually cut from white or yellow pine, it being the timber chiefly in demand as sawn lumber or square timber either for home use or frontier market. Fence-rails were made from all varieties of oak and pine, and from white and black ash, cherry, butternut, grey and rock elm, cedar, basswood, and even red beech, maple, and black birch were used for making fence rails when other more suitable timber could not be obtained in sufficient quantity, within the limits of the fallow to enclose it with a five-rail fence with locks and rider. Timber suitable for fence rails whether it were fallen timber or that which was cut down in chopping a fallow, was not cut into the ordinary twelve-foot rail lengths, or even cut off where the tree was of no further use for rails, for the very good reason that if so cut off the entire tree would in all probability be greatly damaged if not entirely destroyed by fire in the work of burning off the brush, usually done in

May or June. Land clearing was sometimes done by contract, but as a rule by the settlers themselves, and the chopping and logging was frequently done by 'bees' to which the men would collect for a radius of one to three or four miles. Five men formed a gang of loggers, one of them being a teamster in charge of his yoke of oxen. A fallow of ten acres was staked off into one acre parcels and when a teamster and a gang got their acre logged the day's work was by common consent, at an end with that gang. If, however, any gang should have fallen upon a piece of bad fortune in the way of an extra heavy 'through' as the acre parcels were called, his more fortunate comrades as a rule assisted him to a finish. Severe contests for who would have his 'through' completed first often occurred, yet owing to difficulties in timber or the nature of the ground in the various 'throughs' the best men and best oxen did not in all cases succeed in being first done. After the day's logging was over sports were usually engaged in, such as foot races, leaping, vaulting with the pole, and wrestling, and the Township of Asphodel produced in those days not a few rare champions in the line of athletic sports as well as in the safer and more permanent results obtained from clearing the land of timber and subsequent tillage of the soil. Severe contests would take place at barn raisings, not only as to which side would seal their victory and claim their laurels through their having their plate first in position and pinned down, but the contest would often be continued until nightfall in the matter of athletic sports. The personal experiences of the narrator in two or three instances in the above connection may be related here in evidence of the nature and extent of the feats sometimes performed at barn raisings. On the day of the raising the first frame barn on the Robert Humphries homestead the narrator was chosen captain on one side and victory was wrested from his opponents with long odds in placing the plates. The cheers of the victors were met by the vanquished with the retort that the victor's captain was too badly used up in his efforts to win success to be capable of engaging in the athletic sports that were to follow the erection of the frame. This was a challenge of no mean order in the estimation of one who has never yet been beaten by his fellows in athletic circles.

The gauntlet was no sooner flung down on this as on every other occasion than it was picked up by the narrator, as the victorious side as a matter of honor was bound to meet all challenges from any quarter whatever. At that time Mr. Humphries owned a span of handsome dappled grey horses that stood sixteen hands in height. This team had been used in hauling the timber to convenient places for the men to lift it and place it together in bents, and when the raising contest began the team of horses was left standing on a smooth, grassy plot a few rods distant. When the vanquished captain of the barn-raising called out his challenge in athletics it was instantly responded to by the narrator who, throwing off his round-about jacket, called out: 'Here, then, for a leader', and with a run of twenty feet in length cleared he landed safely on his feet on the furwithers of the dappled greys and other side, the feat being thus done on level ground. The narrator, in company with the late Robert Steele and others, frequently performed feats at barn-raisings of walking from opposite plates to the end rafter, there lock arms, make a right-about-face, and return to the starting point.

Feats of slack and tight rope walking, wrestling, vaulting with the pole, leaping, lifting heavy weights, etc., were the usual sports engaged in by the young men of those days, and few serious accidents of any kind attended their performance.

One good result that followed was to be found in the fact that to engage in such sports tended to draw the attention of the younger men from the use of ardent spirits and directed their minds and their physical energies into better channels.

11. Early Mills in Peterborough and Victoria Counties

[Directory of the United Counties of Peterborough and Victoria for 1858 . . . (*Peterborough, 1858*), *pp. 64–8*]

LIST OF SAW MILLS.

Seawright's Saw Mill: Thos. Seawright, Proprietor. Situated on outlet of Round Lake, Lot 19th, 6th Con., Belmont. 1 saw, cuts 4,000 feet per day.

Breakenridge Mill: Jehiel Breakenridge, Proprietor. Situated on same stream, Lot 18, in 5th Con., Belmont. 1 saw, cuts 4,000 feet per day. This mill also contains a run of stones for gristing.

Holcomb's Mills: John Holcomb, Proprietor. Situated on Lot 12 in 2nd Con., Belmont. 1 saw, cuts 2,000 feet per day.

Pearce's Mill: Peter Pearce, Proprietor. On Lot 6th, in 9th Con., Belmont. 1 saw, cuts 2,000 feet daily.

Holbrook's Mills: James Holbrook, Proprietor. On Lot 4th in the 8th Con., Belmont. 1 saw, cuts 3,000 feet per day.

Norwood Mills: P. M. Grover, Proprietor. In village of Norwood. 1 saw, cuts 4,000 feet per day.

Grover's Mills: P. M. Grover, Proprietor. About a mile from Norwood. 1 saw, cuts 4,000 feet per day.

Westwood Mill: Ewing & Roxborough, Proprietor. Village of Westwood. 1 saw, cuts 4,000 feet per day.

Ewing's Mills: R. D. Ewing, Proprietor. Lot ..... in 2nd Con., Asphodel. Patent circular saw and 1 upright saw, cuts 15,000 feet per day.

Hastings Mill: Messrs. Fowlds, Proprietor. Village of Hastings. 1 'yankee gang', 1 muley, and 1 circular saw. Cuts 14,000 feet per day.

Pyne's Saw Mill. Lot 19, 3rd con., Dummer. 1 saw, 2,000 feet a day.

Richie's Saw Mill. Lot 3, 3rd Con., Dummer. 1 saw, 2,000 feet a day.

Choate's Saw Mill: T. G. Choate, Proprietor, Warsaw. 1 saw, 3,000 feet a day.

Buck's Saw Mill. Lot 8, 9th Con., Dummer. 1 saw, 2,000 feet a day.

Carveth's Mill: S. Carveth, Proprietor. Lot 13, 2nd Con., Dummer. 1 saw, cuts 2,000 per day.

Ferrier's Saw Mill: Ferrier, Proprietor, Douro. Has not been working for some time.

Sawers' Saw Mill. A. Sawers, Proprietor. Douro. Has also been idle for some time.

Shaw's Mill. Village of Lakefield, Douro. This mill is not quite completed. It will be of about the same capacity as Snyder's Mill.

Nassau Mills. Charles Perry, Proprietor. This, which is the largest and most complete mill in the Counties, and one of the finest in the Province, is situated about three miles from Peterboro', in the Township of Smith. A challenge to cut against any other mill in the Province remains unanswered. It has 2 'yankee gangs', a 'slabber', 'stock gang', and an 'English gate', containing in all 130 saws, besides circulars for butting, cutting laths, &c. It has also a very ingenious machine for grinding slabs. This mill has cut 90,000 feet of lumber in 12 hours.

Perry's Mill. E. Perry & Co., Proprietor. Situated about two miles from Peterboro', in the Township of Douro. Contains 3 gangs and 1 span, in all 100 saws, besides circulars for edging, butting, cutting laths, &c. Averages when cutting about 60,000 feet in twenty-four hours.

Snyder's Mill: Wm. Snyder, Proprietor. About two miles from Peterboro', in Township of Smith. This mill is similar to the preceding one, and of about equal capacity.

Blythe Saw Mill, Jas. Bird, Proprietor. About a mile from Peterboro', in the Township of Smith. Contains 1 'yankee gang' and 1 'English gate', in all 36 saws, besides lathing machines, and circulars for butting, edging, &c. Capable of cutting 20,000 per day.

Dickson's Mill: S. Dickson, Proprietor. Situated in Peterboro' East. Is similarly fitted up and of same capacity as Bird's mill.

Ludgate's Mill: J. Ludgate, Proprietor. This mill is also situated in Peterboro' east, and is of same capacity as the two former.

Dickson's Steam Mill: S. Dickson, Proprietor. Situated on Little Lake, Peterboro' east. Contains one slabber, one gang, and one muley, besides lathing machines and circular saws for butting, edging, &c. Can cut 50,000 feet a day. It is driven by steam power.

Austin's Mill: J. H. Austin, Proprietor; situated near the Otonabee bridge, Peterboro' East, contains 1 circular and one 'English gate'. Can cut 15,000 feet per day.

Boswell's Mill: G. C. Boswell, Proprietor, Douro. Contains 1 gang and 1 muley, in all 31 upright saws, besides circulars for edging, butting, and lathing. Can cut 25,000 feet per day.

Allandale Mills: Thos. Short, Proprietor. Situated in Village of Allandale.

Contains a muley and circular saw, a shingle cutting machine, cutting from 40 to 60 a minute; a stave cutting machine, turning out 40 a minute; a circular saw for cutting lath; and a planing and groving machine. In the upper part of the building is a very convenient machine shop. The mill can cut 20,000 feet a day and is driven by steam and water power.

Burnham's Mill: M. Burnham, Proprietor, Keene. 1 saw, cuts 2,000 feet per day.

Kelly's Mill: S. S. Kelly, Proprietor, Bridgenorth. This mill is driven by steam power and cuts about 300,000 feet during the summer months.

Scott's Mills: Walter Scott, Proprietor. Situated about a mile beyond the village of Bridgenorth. This mill is also driven by steam power, and turns out about 500,000 feet during the summer months.

Boswell's Mill: W. Boswell, Proprietor, Monaghan. 1 saw, cuts 2,000 feet per day.

Omemee Mill: W. Cottingham, Proprietor. Situated in the Village of Omemee on Pigeon river. 1 saw, cuts 2,000 feet of lumber a day.

Bobcaygeon Mill: Mossom Boyd, Proprietor. Village of Bobcaygeon. Contains 1 'yankee gang' about 30 saws and 1 'gate', 2 saws, besides circulars for butting, edging, &c. Cuts 20,000 feet a day.

Sheriff's Mill: David Sheriff, Proprietor. Situated on Lot 5, 3rd Con., Verulam. 2 saws, cuts 5,000 feet a day.

Thurston's Mill: Jabez Thurston, Proprietor. Situated in Lot 6, 3rd Con., Verulam, 1 saw, cuts 800 feet a day.

Cambray Mill: Joseph Elliot, Proprietor. Situated in the village of Cambray. 1 saw, cuts 1,500 feet a day.

Lawrence Mill: Thos. Lawrence, Proprietor, Township of Fenelon. 1 saw, cuts 1,500 feet per day.

Bald Point Steam Mill: John Bowes, Proprictor. 1 saw, cuts 2,000 feet per day.

Logie's Saw Mill: Alexander Logie, Proprietor. Lot 24 in the 4th Con., Ops. 1 saw, cuts about 2,000 feet a day.

Lindsay Mills: McDermot & Walsh, Proprietors. Has 2 upright and 4 circular saws, capable of cutting about 20,000 feet a day.

Little Briton Mill: R. F. Whitesides, Proprietor. 1 saw, cuts about 2,000 feet a day.

Jacobs' Saw Mill: J. Jacobs, Proprietor. Lot 19 in 13th Con., Mariposa. 1 saw, cuts 2,000 feet a day.

FLOUR AND GRIST MILLS.

Westwood Mill: Messrs. Ewing and Roxborough, Proprietors, Village of Westwood. Two run of stones,—for gristing only.

Hastings' Mill: Messrs. Fowlds, Proprietors, Village of Hastings. Three run of stones,—250 bushels wheat daily.

Norwood Mill: P. M. Grover, Proprietor; occupied by L. P. Lewis. Two run stones,—200 bushels of wheat daily.

Burnham's Mill: M. Burnham, Proprietor, Keene. Three runs of stones,—250 bushels wheat daily.

Allandale Flour Mill: Thomas Short, Proprietor. This mill—an excellent stone structure—is fitted up with all the modern appliances for manufacturing merchantable flour. It has four run of stones and two bolts for country use. The building is also fitted up with an oatmeal mill, with kiln, &c., for preparing the oats. It is driven by water power; but a forty horse power engine has been placed in the building in case of failure of water. Besides the country work, from 6,000 to 8,000 barrels of flour are exported from the Allandale Mills.

Blythe Mills: Herst & Denne, Proprietors. Situated on Otonabee River, about a mile from the town of Peterborough. Three run of stones,—600 barrels of flour a week.

Otonabee Mill: R. D. Rogers, Proprietor. Situated in Peterborough East. A substantial stone building, four run of stones, manufactures 100 barrels of flour a day.

Hall's Mill: M. Martin, Proprietor. Situated on the Otonabee within the Peterborough limits. Three run of stones, manufacturing 80 barrels a day.

Peplow's Mill: E. Peplow, Lessee; James Wallis, Proprietor. Situated on the Otonabee, near the Market Square, Peterborough. Three run of stones, manufacturing 75 barrels a day.

Omemee Mill: W. Cottingham, Proprietor. Three run of stones,—250 bushels wheat per day.

Fair's Grist Mill: John Fair, Proprietor. Situated on Lot No. 2, 10th concession, Ops. Two run of stones,—grinds about 40 bushels a day.

Lindsay Mill: Robert Lang, Proprietor. This is an excellent stone building, newly fitted up with the most recent improvements for the manufacture of flour for exportation. It has four run of stones, and is capable of turning out about 100 barrels of flour per day.

Alma Mills: B. Cullis, Proprietor, lot 18 in 5th concession, Mariposa. Two run of stones, grinds about 75 barrels a day.

Mariposa Steam Mill: Taylor and Westwood, Proprietors, Oakwood. Four run of stones, capable of turning out 150 barrels of flour a day. The engine is 45 horse power.

12. Industries of Peterborough County, 1861

[*Thomas White*, An Exhibit of the Progress, Position, and Resources of the County of Peterboro', Canada West, Based upon the Census of 1861; together with a Statement of the Trade of the Town of Peterborough (*Peterborough, 1861?*), *p. 22*[1]]

These constitute the principal manufactures of the County of Peterboro', and they form a most important element in establishing its position and prospects. Recapitulating we find the following result:

[1]Preceding this summary are valuable details of the industries, pp. 17–22. The two oatmeal mills are also referred to in the 1852 census, so it is perhaps appropriate that the Quaker Oats Company of Canada has its headquarters in Peterborough. Among other valuable items in this small volume are a census by national origin, an abstract of the agricultural census for both 1852 and 1861, a short history of the Bobcaygeon Road and settlement along it, an account of the trade of the early town of Peterborough, and early surveys of a number of the rear townships.

	No.	Hands employed.	Annual Cost of labour.	Capital invested.	Value of Produce
Saw mills	37	637	167,280	361,748	609,330
Grist mills	12	28	12,732	149,082	367,000
Oatmeal mills	2	4	1,104	—	12,548
Carding mills and woolen factories	4	26	4,524	19,900	14,656
Foundries	5	54	16,944	45,900	56,075*
Tanneries	8	21	4,812	22,685	34,178
Breweries	3	12	2,940	10,400	13,490
Cooperage and stave factories	8	28	8,680	9,870	23,630
Carriage and wagon factories	6	44	12,528	11,500	31,390
Planing and shingle machines	9	34	11,976	7,100	11,100
Cabinet ware factories	4	18	5,844	8,400	14,712
Chair factory	1	2	600	—	1,500
Chandleries	2	7	1,680	5,500	15,000
Pottery	1	5	1,200	—	2,000
Axe factories	2	23	6,000	8,800	26,000
Square Timber		1,000	240,000	300,000	625,000
		1,939	$490,848	$960,885	1,857,609

*Three out of the five only included here.

13. Cobourg Mechanics Regulate Hours of Work[1]

[Cobourg Star, *July 13, 1836*]

Pursuant to notice, a meeting of the Mechanic's and Laborers of the village of Cobourg and vicinity assembled at the Common School House on Monday the eleventh inst., to take into consideration the present unsettled condition and existing usages practised by most Mechanics and Laborers in this place as respects the quantity of time required of most of the journeymen Mechanics and Laborers, in daily labour, and to adopt a specific time for a days labor.

[1]This is a very early evidence in Canada that workers were becoming aware that they were to a large extent masters of their own destiny. An excellent M.A. thesis by Dora E. Wattie, entitled "Cobourg 1784–1867" (University of Toronto, 1949), has a full bibliography and is an admirable account of the town's early history. This and the editor's *Cobourg, 1798–1948,* and his two long series; "Cobourg" (*Cobourg Sentinel-Star,* May 29, 1930, to July 28, 1932), and "Old Times in Cobourg and District" (*Sentinel-Star,* January 2, 1936, to February 6, 1947) provide for the old capital of the Newcastle District a very detailed coverage. Peterborough's history has been similarly described over many years in the *Peterborough Examiner* by Mrs. Helen Marryat, Howard T. Pammett, and others; and in 1941 Dr. Poole's *Early Settlement* . . . (1867) was in some measure brought up to date.

On motion, Mr. Wm. Bradbear was called to the Chair, and C. Pomery appointed Secretary.

On Motion, it was—*Resolved*—That the number of hours which we now work is nothing better than domestic Slavery, is altogether derogatory to the improvement of our moral and intellectual powers and progress in the arts and sciences, and is one of the chief causes of vice and ignorance.

Resolved 2—That our condition connectedly and individually in consequence of past and present usages has become a matter of indispensable consideration and concern; and we hold ourselves under a sacred obligation that we will not labour more than ten hours for a day's work.

Resolved 3d—That the following persons do form the Committee to draw up regulations to carry the said resolutions into effect: Messrs. John Helms, James Cannevan, William Pomery, James Pyne, Robert Creag, William Nicols, John S. Smith, Z. Sisson, James Burnett.[1]

Resolved 4th—That on Friday evening next at 8 o'clock we meet again at this place for the inspection of the regulations and the obtaining of signatures.

Resolved 5th—That the Editors of the COBOURG STAR and REFORMER be requested to insert the above proceedings.

After which it was moved that the Chairman do leave the Chair, and Mr. Helm take the same, when a vote of thanks was passed to the Chairman for his able conduct in the business of the evening.

W. BRADBEAR Chairman.
Signed. C. POMERY Secretary.

Cobourg, July 11, 1836.[2]

[1]In almost every instance the spelling of these names varies from that considered correct later, exact orthography being unusual in the period. That accuracy or consistency in the spelling of proper names was not a pioneer virtue is apparent from the following classic example from the record of a Court of Quarter Sessions: "John Hart, otherwise John Hait, who was appointed Constable for Pickering, appeared in Person and said that his name is John Hait and that he was Constable for Gwillimbury the last year under the name of John Heath, but whose real name is JOHN ALLAN HAIGHT, and therefore prayed to be discharged from his present appointment; and he is discharged accordingly." (Ontario Archives *Report*, 1932, under date of May 16, 1809.)

[2]In the *Cobourg Star* of July 27th appears a lengthy account of the second meeting. An amendment to the ten-hours resolution, to add 'for which we will take no store pay, but cash', was lost. The 'proper division of time' was then resolved to be, between March 20th and September 20th, from six a.m. to six p.m., with an hour off for breakfast between 7.30 and 8.30, and an hour for dinner between 12 and 1; and during the winter months, from 7 a.m. to 6 p.m., with breakfast before starting work, and dinner from 12 to 1. To this agreement all those present then affixed their signatures in the presence of one another, with the covenant to go into effect on July 18th.

VIII. COMMUNITY LIFE: LAND BOARDS, QUARTER SESSIONS, POLITICAL LIFE

THE SOCIAL controls under which civilized community life is possible are illustrated in this Section. No. 1 gives the names and lots of the earliest settlers in a "front" township, of interest here since many of the inhabitants along the Lake Ontario shore held important administrative offices both for the front and rear townships, and were concerned in developing the region. No. 2 contains the minutes of an early Court of Quarter Sessions. One of the earliest efforts to control the sale of liquor is shewn by the licencees listed in No. 3, a type of licensing that became increasingly extensive as the years passed, for a tavern was often the nucleus of settlement. No. 4, an item from proceedings of the Newcastle District Land Board, indicates that much of the settlement of rear townships was directed from Amherst, in the outskirts of Cobourg, which was the administrative centre of the District from the early years of the century, when the site of Cobourg was a cedar swamp with one or two log shanties. No. 5 describes the proceedings of a township meeting, accounts of which are rare. To illustrate politics and elections, with resulting riots, are the several items of No. 6.

1. First Settlers, Haldimand Township, 1796

[*Archives of Ontario, Crown Land Papers, 79 (5), Newcastle District*]

A List of the names of those who have taken Lots in the town of HOLDIMAN [Haldimand] with the Concession and the Number of the Lots anexed to each mans name 29 Oct.
[1796]
A. Greeley

Name	*Concession*	*No. of the lots*
Joseph Keeler	Con^n^ 1))	No. 1 & 2
	) Broken)	
	Con^n^ 2) front)	No. 1 & 2
	)	
George Garner	Con^n^ 1 B^n^ front)	No. 4
	)	
Timothy Silver	Ditto)	No. 6

Cramhae June the 27 1796

Sir—

I have this day arrived on Cramhae with a number of hands to begin the Settlement of Holderman and Cramhae and a Surveyor and hands also to run the Subdivision lines of Said Towns and if it is necessary that I Should wait upon your Excellency at the Present Session of the Honorable Council or your Excellency at any time Concerning the Said Towns I Should take it very kind that you would write to me as I Shall be on Said Towns Seeing to the Settlement of them I will attend with all readiness at any time when your Excellency Shall See fit I would also inform you that I have been Sick with the Ague and fever till very late which has kept me from Comeing forward earlier in the Spring I am Sir with great respect your Excellencys most obedient and very Humble Servant

Joseph Keeler

To his Excellency
John Graves Simcoe Esqr
&c &c &c

NB by reason of my Brothers Sickness and Mr Laphams they have employed me to see to the Surveying of Holderman Mr [illegible] expect in here every day —

Archives of Ontario

LETTER OF JOSEPH KEELER TO LIEUTENANT-GOVERNOR SIMCOE, 1796

The townships are Haldimand and Cramahe. Keeler furthered their settlement and development

Name	*Concession*	*No. of the lots*
Asa Burnham	Concession 1st)	No. 32
David Story	Ditto)	No. 33
Aaron Greeley	Ditto)	No. 29
John Stocker	Ditto)	No. 30
Solomon Spafford	Ditto)	No. 26 & 27
Peres Cooper	Ditto)	No. 22
Allen Brown	Ditto)	No. 23
Aaron Goodell	Ditto)	No. 24

The eight last above mentioned Names have their lots in the first Concession of the town with the Broken front, the three first in the 1st & 2d Concession of the Broken front.

John Richards	Con[n] 2[d] B[n] front	No. 14
Aaron White	Con[n] 1)Broken) Front Con[n] 2[d])	No. 12)) No. 13)
Christopher Hagerman	Con 1 B[n] Front	No. 10
Charles Cuningham	Con[n] 2[d] B. Front	No. 4
Abner Silver	Con[n] 1 B[n] Front	No. 7
Abner Spencer	Con[n] 2[d] B[n] Front	No. 7
Gershom Beech	Con[n] 1) Broken) Con[n] 2[d]) Front	No. 9
Jonathan D. Hurd	Con[n] 1st	No. 1
Benjamin Palmer	Ditto	No. 3
Isaac Weight	Ditto	No. 10
Benjamin Weight	Ditto	No. 7
Benjamin Weight Ju[r]	Ditto	No. 6
Arthur Youmans	Ditto	No. 9

Name	*Concession*	*No. of the lots*
Daniel Richards	Ditto	No. 14
Wm. Cuningham	Ditto	No. 4
Wm. Williams	B^{n} Front) Con^{n} 1st	No. 29 No. 29
David Lent	Con^{n} 2^{d}) Con^{n} 3^{d})	No. 35 No. 35
Wm. Williams ju^{r}	B. Front) Con^{n} 1)	No. 30 No. 30
Ebenezer Williams	Con^{n} 2^{d}) Con^{n} 3^{d})	No. 29 No. 29
Stephen Tuttle	Con^{n} 2^{d}) Con^{n} 3^{d})	No. 28 No. 28
John McDougle	Con^{n} 2) Con^{n} 3)	No. 34 No. 34
Isaac Lent	Con^{n} 1st	No. 35
James Williams	Con^{n} 2^{d}	No. 26
John Rogers	Con^{n} 2^{d}	No. 25

2. Court of Quarter Sessions, 1802

[*Archives of Ontario, Municipal Records, Minutes of Quarter Sessions, Newcastle District*]

At a General Quarter Sessions of the Peace held at Murray in and for the District of Newcastle the 12th day of October 1802.

Present Alexander Chisholm
and
Isaiah Hall Esquires

Read the Act for the administration of Justice in the District of Newcastle.

The Sheriff returned the following Grand Jury who were duly sworn Viz:

Foreman Joseph Keeler
Jacob Ferguson
Elias Jones
Asa Burnham
Richard Hare
David Ferguson
Joel Merriman
Benjamin Richardson

Jeremiah Scripture	Stephen Campbell
John Spencer	Alex[r] McDonald
Thomas Hinman	Matthew Gorlee
Ferdinand Grout	Oliver Campbell
Jonathan Greeley	William Carl.

Ordered that John Peters Esq. be appointed Treasurer for this present year.

Ordered that Thomas Gastin be appointed High Constable for this year.

Indictment)
)
The King) Defendant pleads not guilty and puts himself upon his
vs) country.
John Darling)

Jurors to try	Zadock Hurd	William Johnson	
Evidence for the King	Joel Halstead	John Campbell	
Abner Spencer)	Elisha Bristol	Obadiah	[blot]
)			
Thomas Hinman)	Allan McDonell	John	[blot]
David D. Verrian)	John Ward	Henry Frint	
)			
Obadiah Bennet)	Moses Hinman	Nathan Gould	

The Jury by their Foreman Moses Hinman say that the Prisoner is guilty. Fine set at seven dollars which he paid into Court.

At a General Quarter Sessions of the Peace held at Murray the 11th day of January 1803.

Present Alexander Chisholm)
)
John Bleecker) Esquires
)
Isaiah Hall)

Act for the Administration of Justice read

The Sheriff returned the following Grand Jury who were duly sworn Viz

Gaius Dean Foreman	John Kelly
Joseph Harris	Stephen Hare
Isacc Secor Jun[r]	Nathan Bradley
Asa Willer	Ebenezer Allen
Daniel Adams	Nathan Burnham
Robert C. Wilkins	Silas L. Lothrip
David H. Wyatt	David Turney Sen[r]
Moses Doolittle	Rufus Wells
Robinson Irish	Joel Parker
Benjamin Wait	

John Smith of Murray appears upon his recognizance and is bound to appear at the next Court of General goal delivery and Assizes to be held for this District

James Hendricks £100)	Viz	John Smith in £100
William Welch 50)		Timothy Porter)
)		&) 50 each
to give evidence)		Abram Simmons)

Christopher Hagermon appears upon his recognizance and is bound to appear at the next Assizes and General Goal delivery for this District Viz

Thomas Freeman £100	Christopher Hagerman/ in £100
Isace Hageman)	David Turney Senr and
Asa Callender)	Isace Hagerman in £50 each
) 25 each	
Stephen Sheldon)	
&)	
Amos Fuller)	

to appear & give evidence

At a General Quarter Sessions of the Peace for the District of Newcastle held at Murray the 12th day of April 1803

Present	Alexander Chisholm)	
	John Bleecker)	
	Timothy Thompson)	Esqrs
	Benjamin Richardson)	
	Elias Jones)	
	Joseph Keeler)	

The Commission of the Peace read.

The Sheriff returned the following Grand Jury

David Kerr
Francis Burnham
Isaiah Honeywell
Thomas Goheen
Noah Dean
Roger Wolcott
Joseph Purdey
Eldridge Stanton
George Ash
Ranna Perrin
Joshua Smades
Zacheus Burnham
Joel Culver
Asahel Jerome
Elipud Nickerson
John Carter

The Grand Jury do not find any indictments
Ordered that the following divisions be made for holding Courts of Requests
Townships of Murray, Cramahe & Piercy—together
do Haldimand and Hamilton — do
do Hope Clark and Darlington do

The Clerk of the Peace presented his account as follows.
No. 1 The District of Newcastle to D M G Rogers

To engrossing precept and sending to Sheriff 3 quart Sess	£3
" makeing up records of 3 quarter Sessions 50/ each	7 - 10
" Attending 3 quarter Sessions 30/ each	4 - 10 - 0
" paid for a Seal for the Quarter Sessions	1 - 5 - 0
" Allowance for Stationary for one year	2 - 6 - 8
	£18 " 11 " 8

E. E. Cramahe 12th April 1803

Ordered that the treasurer pay the said Account out of the Public monies belonging to the District.

The Sheriff presented his account as follows No. 2
The District of Newcastle to John Peters Dr 1803
April 12th To summoning three Juries and attending)
) $15-0-0
three Quarter Sessions)

Ordered that the treasurer pay the same out of the Public money.
Ordered by the Justices in quarter Sessions Assembled that one penny on the Pound shall be collected in this District for the year insuing.
Ordered that the Clerks in the different Townships do receive from the Treasurer the sum of ten Shillings for making the return of the inhabitants.
Ordered that the Town Clerk do receive the sum of sixpence for registering each mark.
Ordered that the Pound keeper take the sum of ninepence for impounding each Creature of whatever discription and the sum of ninepence pr. day for feeding each horse sixpence pr. day for feeding each Ox or cow and threepence pr. day for feeding each Hog Sheep or Young cattle
Ordered that the next General Quarter Sessions of the Peace be held at the House of Mr. Leonard Soapers in Hope

Thos. Gaston sworn High Constable sworn
Joseph Phillips Constable sworn
Nathl Herskill Constable Hope sworn
Edward Goodyear do Cramahe sworn
John Vaughn do Hamilton sworn
Elisha Alger Pathmaster & fence viewer Cramahe sworn
Jas Henderson Constable Cramahe sworn
Nathl Abbey do Hamilton sworn

The following persons were appointed Constables for the ensuing year Viz

William Kayton)
) for Murray
Simon Westfall)

Edward Goodyear)
) for Cramahe
James Henderson J[r])

John Eastman)
) for Haldimand
Joseph Phillips)

John Vaughn)
) for Hamilton
Nathaniel Abbey)

Rufus Wells)
) for Piercy
James I Merriam)

Nathaniel Herskill)
) for Hope
Ephraim Gifford)

Seth Hamlin)
) for the Townships of Clark and Darlington
Ebenezer Hartwell)
Thomas Gastin of Piercy High Constable
John Peters Esq[r] Treasurer

District of) The General Quarter Sessions of the Peace Holden at Hope in
)
Newcastle) and for the said District on the twelvth day of July in the Forty third year of the Reign of our Sovereign Lord George the third by the grace of God of the United Kingdom of Great Britain and Ireland King defender of the faith. Before Robert Baldwin, Timothy Thompson, Elias Jones, Leonard Soaper, Asa Burnham Benjamin Marsh and Richard Lovekin - - - - - Esquires Justices of our said sovereign Lord the King assigned to keep the peace in the said District and also to hear and determine divers felonies tresspasses and other misdemeanors in the said District commited. &c

The Sessions opened and the Commission of the Peace read.

The Sheriff returned the following Grand Jury

Roger Bates foreman
Silas Serjeant
John Burk
Roger Conate
William Marr
William Lovekin
John Hartwell
Samuel Cozens
Joshua Cozens
Shivers Cozens
Jacob Cozens
Adne Bates
Peletiah Soaper
Samuel Marsh
James Norris
James Hawkins
John Burn
Seth Soaper
Nathan Walton
Lotrip Smith
Seth Hamlin
Jesiar Burk
John Lovekins

The King) Indictment found

vs) Prisoner Pleads not guilty

James Stevens)

Jurors to try	August Barber	Major Evans
Evidence for the King	Norris Karr	James Burk
Joel Calver Junr	Luke Burk	William Borland
Amos Leach	Abel Conate	Eliflet Conate
For the Prisoner	Daniel Lighthart	Harry Facer
Jonathan Weedon	Jonathan Bedford Junr	Joseph Caldwell

The Jury by their foreman say that the Prisoner is guilty fine set at two Shillings and sixpence which he paid to the Sheriff.

Ordered by the Justices in General Quarter Sessions Assembled that three pounds be allowed to the crier for the year past and at the rate of three pounds Pr Annum for the Sessions to come until the April Sessions next.*

The Court broke up Thursday 14th July 1803

District of) At the General Quarter Sessions of the peace Holden at Murray
)
Newcastle) in and for the said District on the Eleventh day of October in the Forty third year of the Reign of our Sovereign Lord George the third by the grace of God of the united Kingdom of Great Britain and Ireland King, defender of the faith Before Timothy Thompson, Alexander Chisholm, Joseph Keelor, Leonard Soaper, John Bleecker, Asa Burnham, Asa Willer, Benjamin Marsh Esquires Justices of our said Sovereign Lord the King assigned to keep the peace and also to hear and determine divers felonies tresspasses and other misdeameanors in the said District Committed.

Commission of the peace read.

Grand Jury sworn

William Carl Foreman
Oliver Campbell
David Turney Senr
William Simson
John Dingman
Stephen Campbell
David H Wyatt
Moses Doolittle

Benjamin Wait
Bays M. Eddys
Silas L Lothrop
Abner Spencer
Thewn Hinman
Benjn Ewing
Elisha Jones

The grand Jury do not find any Bills

Be it remembered that, on the Eleventh day of october in the Forty third year of His Majesty's Reign At the General Quarter Sessions of the peace held at Murray in and for the District of Newcastle Before Alexander Chisholm John Bleecker Joseph Keelor Asa Burnham Leonard Soaper Benjamin Marsh

*Gave a Certificate for Octr and Jany Sessions 25th Apl 1805.

and Asa Willer Esquires Justices Assigned to keep the peace and also to hear and determine divers felonies tresspasses and other misdeameanors in the said District Committed. Daniel Adams Deputy Collector of the Port of Newcastle cometh before the aforesaid Justices and giveth them to understand and be informed that on the twelvth day of August now last past at the River Trent in the Township of Murray in the District of Newcastle, he did seize on one four handed Batteau and six Barrels of salt said to be the Property of Bass Chard on suspicion that it came from the United States of America and had not been entered at either of His Majesty's Customs Houses in this Province or that the duties on the same had been paid agreeable to Law. And the said Daniel Adams having made oath before John Bleecker Esq[r] one of His Majesty's Justices of the Peace in and for the district in which the said salt and Batteaux was seized that he believed the property abovementioned not to be of more value Than Twenty Pounds lawful money of this Province and the said Bass Chard being duly summoned before the said Justices appeareth and is present in order to make his defence against the said charge contained in the said information and having heard the same he the said Bass Chard is asked by the said Justices if he can say anything why he the said Bass Chard should not be convicted of the premises above charged upon him in form aforesaid. And because the said Bass Chard hath nothing to say nor can say anything in his own defence touching and concerning the premises aforesaid but doth of his own accord freely and voluntarily acknowledge and confess all and singular the said Premises to be true in manner and form as the same are charged upon him in the said information And because all and singular the premises being heard and fully understood by us the said Justices it manifestly appears to us that the said Bass Chard is guilty of the premises and according to the Statute in that case made is convicted and for his offence aforesaid hath forfeited the said Batteaux and the said six Barrels of Salt, to be sold by public auction and the monies arising from such sale to be distributed according to Law.

A Warrant to sell signed the 12th October 1803

Ordered that the next Court of Sessions do sit in Haldimand

District of) The General Quarter Sessions of the peace Holden at Haldimand
)
Newcastle) in and for the said District on the tenth day of January in the Forty fourth year of the Reign of our Sovereign Lord George the third by the grace of God of the United Kingdom of Great Britain and Ireland King defender of the faith Before Timothy Thompson, Joseph Keelor, Asa Miller Leonard Soper, Asa Burnham, Elias Jones and Benjamin Marsh Justices of our said Sovereign Lord the King Assigned to keep the Peace in the said District and also to hear and determine divers felonies tresspasses and other Misdemeanors in the said District committed

The Sessions opened and the Commission of the Peace read The Sheriff returned the following Grand Jury

Joel Merriman	Nathan Bradley
Joel Parker	Gaius Dean
John Spencer	Stephen Hare
Aaron Greeley	Nathan Burnham
Jonathan Greeley	Luther Hull

Ferdinand Grout	Francis Burnham
Robinson Irish	Christopher Winters
John Kelly	David Ferguson

The Court of Quarter Sessions 11th January 1804

The Grand Jury found the following indictments

The King) For an Assault and Battery
vs) A Bench warrant issued to take the Defendant.
Jeremiah Beaty)

The King
vs

Daniel Lighthart) For a Riot Assault and Battery
Francis Lighthart) Francis Lighthart is committed to the Custody of the
Rachel Lighthart) Sheriff and a Bench warrant issued to take Rach & Pheobe
Pheobe Lighthart) Lighthart.

Daniel Lighthart appears and is bound by the court in a Recognizance conditioned for his appearance at the next Court of Quarter Sessions to be held in and for this District Viz

Daniel Lighthart in fifty Pounds
Thoday Cowl &) In Twenty five Pounds each
Augustua Barber)

Isacc Smith, Lucy Smith by Isacc Smith, George Shanks, William Borland, and Norris Karr in the sum of Twenty five Pounds each conditioned for their appearance at the next court of Quarter Sessions to give evidence on the last mentioned Indictment.

The King) For Robbery from the person on the Highway Francis
vs) Lighthart being present in Court is committed to the
Francis Lighthart) Custody of the Sheriff, not procuring any Bail for his appearance at the Assizes. Isacc Smith, Lucy Smith (by Isacc Smith her husband) George Shanks, William Borland, and Norris Karr in the sum of Twenty five Pounds each conditioned for their Appearance at the next Assizes to be held in and for the District of Newcastle to give evidence on behalf of the King against the said Francis Lighthart.

Ordered that the next Court of General Quarter Sessions do sit in Haldimand.
The Sessions adjourned the 12th January 1804.

1st ANNUAL RETURN OF THE INHABITANTS OF THE DISTRICT OF NEWCASTLE for the year 1803

Townships	Men	Women	Children: Male above 16 yrs	Male under 16 yrs	Female above 16	Female under 16	Number in each Township
Murray	34	21	2	25	1	20	103
Cramahe	66	60	"	93	"	90	314
Haldimand	91	69	"	71	"	81	312
Hope	68	47	"	80	"	82	277
Piercy	22	22	9	45	2	27	127
Clark	16	6	"	6	"	11	39
Darlington	25	15	"	27	"	21	88
Total	322	240	11	352	3	332	1260

2 GENERAL ACCOUNT OF RATEABLE PROPERTY DISTRICT OF NEWCASTLE 1803

253 persons have the following property	Aggregate of each article	Amount of Valuation £	s	d	Amount of Rate £	s	d
Acres of uncultivated land	63661½	3183	1	6	13	5	1
Acres of cultivated land	3748½	3748	10	"	15	12	4½
Horse of 3 years and upwards	100	800	"	"	3	6	8
Oxen of 4 years and upwards	308	1232	"	"	5	2	8
Milch Cows	514	1542	"	"	6	8	6
Young horned cattle	252	252	"	"	1	1	"
Grist Mills having only one pair stones	2½	375	"	"	1	11	3
Saw Mills	6¼	616	13	4	2	11	4½

Houses in Town	1	40	"	"	"	3	4
Houses in the Country 2 fireplaces	21	840	"	"	3	10	"
Town Lots	1	10	"	"	"	"	10
Additional fireplaces	5	50	"	"	"	4	2
No. of swine of one year and upwards	231	115	10	"	"	9	7½
Merchant Shops	1	200	"	"	"	16	8
Taverns	2	200	"	"	"	16	8
Gallons contained in Stills	280	280	"	"	1	3	4
Total		£13484	14	10	£56	3	6½

3 (*a*). Newcastle District Liquor Licences, 1818–1819

[*Archives of Ontario. The following list is compiled from 'Schedule of Licences issued upon Stills, Innkeepers and Shop Keepers for the year commencing on the sixth day of January 1818 and ending the fifth day of January 1819 both days inclusive'. The list is signed by Elias Jones, Inspector for the District of Newcastle*]

Innkeepers:
Thomas Powers, Darlington
John Blair, Clark
John Hagerman, Hamilton
James Parker, Hope
Timothy Kittridge, Hamilton
John Grover, Haldimand
George Stephens, Darlington
Joseph A. Keeler, Cramahe
Benjamin Young, Murray
Thomas D. Sanford, Cramahe
David Johns, Murray
John Drum Smith, Murray
John Singleton, Murray
Samuel Potter, Hamilton
Schyler Hodge, Cramahe
Jacob Choat, Hope
John B. Bletcher, Murray
John Brown, Haldimand
Jeremiah Wood, Cramahe
Pelatiah Soper, Hope
Cyrus Marsh, Murray
Thomas M. Spalding, Haldimand
Joseph T. Losie, Haldimand
Thomas Hartwell, Hope

Shop Keepers
Monjeau & St. German, Hamilton
John David Smith, Hope
Charles Bigger, Murray
Charles Fothergill, Hope

Stills
Joseph Keeler, Cramahe
Alva Hewly, Hope (two stills)
Barnabas Bletcher, Hope
Eliakim Barnham, Haldimand (two stills)
Samuel Griffen, Hope
Henry Ruttan, Haldimand
David Johns, Murray

3 (*b*). Regulations for Innkeepers, 1818

[*Archives of Ontario, Municipal Records, Quarter Sessions, Newcastle District*]

Regulations

To be observed by the Innkeepers, in the District of New Castle, made at a General Sessions of the Peace for the said District, on Monday the 28th December 1818, in pursuance of the Statute in that case made and Provided.—

1st That no wines or Spirituous liquors shall be sold to any Inhabitant or Inhabitants of the respective Town or Townships for which such Inn is Licensed on the Sabbath Day, Travellers of all description excepted—

2d That no wines or Spirituous liquors shall be sold to any person or persons after Ten O'Clock at night—Travellers excepted.

3d That Gaming shall not be allowed on any occasion—

4th That no Innkeeper shall have less than Three decent Beds in his House for the accommodation of Travellers Solely.

5th That no profane Swearing, or immodest or disloyal songs or Tales shall be allowed on any pretence, and if an offender prove refractory, the Innkeeper shall take down his name and give information thereof to the nearest Justice of the Peace.

6th That every Innkeeper is to take particular notice, that the clause in a Provincial Statute respecting a Commodious yard be strictly complied with.

7th That every Innkeeper shall at all times provide proper attendance, particularly for Travellers Horses, Baggage &c—

By order of the Court
D. M. G. Rogers
Chs Js Jefrious

4. Proceedings of the Land Board in the District of Newcastle, 1819

[*Archives of Ontario, Crown Land Papers, Vol. 7 (4), pp. 3 to 5*]

At a meeting of the Land Board held at the court House in the Township of Hamilton, on the 2nd day of June 1819.

Present—David M. Rogers—Chairman
Elias Jones
Walter Boswell
John Burn &
Charles Fothergill, Esq'res } Members

No 1 Benjamin Purdy Junior, born in the Township of Hamilton in the District of Newcastle of the age of twenty one years, produced proof of his having done his duty during the late War, and having taken the Oath of Allegiance is permitted to Locate the South part of Lot No. 7 in the 3rd Concession of the Township of Smith.

2 Nathaniel Abbey born in the State of New York, aged Forty five years, came into this Province twenty one years ago, and having declared that he never drew any Land in this Province, and having produced proof that he did his duty during the late War, and having taken the Oath of Allegiance is allowed to locate the North part of Lot No 7 in the third Concession of the township of Smith.

3 John Bice born in Upper Canada, aged twenty two years, having produced proof that he has done his duty during the late War, and having taken the Oath of Allegiance is permitted to Locate the South half of Lot Number 6 in the second Concession of the Township of Smith.

4 John Parker born in the State of New York, aged twenty three years, has been in this Province Twenty-one years, and having done his duty during the late War and having taken the Oath of Allegiance is permitted to Locate the South half of Lot No 4 in the second Concession of the Township of Smith.

5 Michael Sammons of Hamilton, born in the State of New York, aged thirty years, been in this Province ten years, and having done his duty during the late War and taken the Oath of Allegiance is permitted to Locate the West side of Lot number Five in the third concession of the Township of Smith.

6 Michael Sweetman an Emigrant, born in Ireland, aged twenty three years, has been in this Province nearly two years, never drew any lands, having taken the Oath of Allegiance is allowed to Locate the East half of Lot No 5 in the 3rd Concession of the Township of Smith.

7 Richard Carrall born in Ireland, Aged 26 years came to this Province about two years ago, having taken the Oath of Allegiance, is allowed to locate the East half of Lot number three in the third Concession of the Township of Smith.

8 Patrick Toburn, aged twenty six years, born in Ireland been in this Province two years, having taken the Oath of Allegiance is allowed to Locate the West half of Lot number three in the third Concession of the Township of Smith.

9 Thomas Calvert aged twenty five years, born in Ireland, been in this Province one year, having taken the oath of Allegiance is allowed to Locate the North end of Lot number four in the second Concession of the Township of Smith.

10 William Andrews, aged twenty two years been in Ireland came into this Province a few days since, having taken the oath of Allegiance is allowed to Locate the East half of Lot number eight in the fourth Concession of the Township of Smith. [Cancelled]

11 James McConnell aged thirty nine years, born in Ireland, been in this Province but a few days, having a passport from the British Consul at New York, and having taken the oath of Allegiance, is allowed to Locate the South half of Lot number six in the fourth Concession of the Township of Smith. [Cancelled]

(Signed) D. M. Rogers
Charles Fothergill
Elias Jones
John Burn
Walter Boswell

5. Proceedings of Town Meeting, Percy Township, 1828

[*Archives of Ontario, Municipal Records Group, General Correspondence of Clerk of the Peace*]

Percey Jany 22nd 1828

Sir

This Serves to report to you your [sic] office that at a town meeting held at the house of Joseph Sparrow on Monday the 4 Instant for the Townships of Percey and Seymore the following appointments were made (viz) for the ensuing year

Names	Office
Jacob Cryderman Philip Waldron	Assessors
David Blair Junr	Collector
John Warner Orsemen Brunson Joshaua Birdsal Russell Merrill Jonathan Tripp John Boothe William Wilson William Robinson	Pathmasters
Comfort Curtice Archibald Wilcox Samuel Dingman	Pound Keepers
William Stone Elijah Walbridge	Town Wardens

All hogs excepting Boars over 25Ct Weight to be free commoners

No unruly horses or cattle to run at large

All fences to be four and a half feet high and four inches between rails

Sir

I beg leave to state that I have never before had business of this sort appointed for me to do concequently totally ignorant and unaware that it was incumbent on me to report the proceedings of town meeting at an earlier day and t'was only now that it was Suggested to me by a neighbour that I incurred a fine for not having done it Sooner I hope however that this will come to hand time enough to answer its purpose as I am always willing to do the duties enjoined me without paying fines

I am

Sir

respectfully

your Hbl Servt

Stephen Campbell

Town Clerk

6. Politics in the Eighteen-Thirties

(*a*) political riot in port hope, 1832

[Cobourg Star, *August 29, 1832*]

Another of those disgraceful scenes which have so frequently of late disturbed the peace of the neighboring village of Port Hope occurred there on the 18th instant, the particulars of which are most shameful. It seems that on that day a number of persons assembled together with banners, guns, swords, pistols, axes, and a drum, and paraded the streets, yelling and shouting like so many demons, and hissing and groaning at all whom they regarded as opponents. As to be expected, a row took place in the course of which a stone or some other weighty missile was thrown with brutal violence at Mr. John Crawford, which, striking him on the chest, inflicted a very serious and painful injury. The persons engaged in this outrage are represented as having been instigated to their lawless course by Mr. John Brown, the member for Durham, who is stated to have encouraged them, in person, by clapping of hands, etc. . . . One story is always good till another be heard, and therefore we strongly recommend our readers to suspend their judgment upon this matter till Mr. Brown's explanation shall enable them to form it correctly.

(*b*) NEWCASTLE DISTRICT ELECTION, 1834

[Cobourg Star, *October 8 and 15, 1834*]

Our election commenced on Monday last at Sully,[1] and never since we have lived in Cobourg do we remember an event which has occasioned such universal interest. The whole town, in fact, seems to be election mad. Horses, carriages, and wagons, each with their meed of voters, are rattling about in every direction, to or from the scene of action; while the warlike bugle and the banners of the different candidates, with the cheers of their friends, complete the spirit of the scene.

Jas. Gray Bethune, Esq., was the first candidate who addressed the electors. He spoke for upwards of two hours with a fluency and eloquence that astonished even his warmest friends. But it was when he came to refer to the immediate interests of the district of Newcastle that the sympathy and feelings of his auditors were most sensibly aroused.

Mr. McDonell next briefly addressed the electors, assuring them, should he obtain the honor of their selection, their welfare and interests should ever command his warmest advocacy and regard. (Cheers.)

Dr. Gilchrist, disclaiming any pretensions to oratory, requested permission to read his sentiments from a paper which had been prepared for the occasion; we earnestly hope not by the worthy Doctor himself!

Mr. Conger, the fourth and last candidate, next stepped forward and delivered a remarkably neat and pertinent address with great fluency and correctness; the leading character of which was Radical reform in

[1]Now Harwood, Rice Lake.

all its branches, and no Baneful Domination—but at the same time no separation—also voting by ballot, abolition of primogeniture act, election of the council, &c., but no republicanism!!!

The poll clerk, Mr. Crofton, being sworn, the electors now came forward to give their votes, which, as the reformers had mustered their chief strength and taken early possession of the field, while but a few of Messrs. Bethune and McDonell's friends had yet arrived, at first went rather against the latter. The very first vote given, however, augured well, being a plumper by Mr. John Heard for James Gray Bethune, Esq.! At the close of the poll the first day the numbers were Gilchrist 79, Conger 71, Bethune 59, and McDonell 52, showing a majority of 30 in favor of the reformers. The next day, however, told a different tale, after a hard day's polling the numbers being Bethune 177, McDonell 167, Gilchrist 127, and Conger 115, being 50 majority for the Constitutional side . . . At the close of the contest the numbers stood thus: Gilchrist 602, McDonell 598, Bethune 572, Conger 486.[1]

(c) REBELLION RIOT AT KEENE, OTONABEE TOWNSHIP, 1837

[*Archives of Ontario, Municipal Records Group, Quarter Sessions of the Newcastle District, Miscellaneous Papers*]

(1) *Evidence of John Blezard*

New Castle } Before the Honble T A Stewart, Ephraim Sanford &
To Wit } Robert Reid three of her Majestys Justices of the Peace for said District—appeared John Blizzard of Otanabee in said District Yeoman who being duly sworn saith That on Saturday the Malitia of Otanabee & Asphodel met to train, what he believes was last Saturday two Clocke 9th Instant he was present at the training and afterwards at Mrs Pattersons Tavern—he thinks he may have Hurra'd for the Queen & the Governor but he has not a distinct recollection—does not recollect any of the Neilsons Hurraying for Papineau & Mackenzie—

[1]The first two candidates were elected, though there was a fiery dispute over the closing of the poll at 3 p.m. on Saturday, the sixth day of the election. John Langton went down to Rice Lake for the 1836 election, camping a week on Spoke (Spook) Island and using "a large marquée which had served as a hospital tent during the [Irish] emigration of '25 and '26". Concerning the district as a whole during the election, in which the Reformers ("Yankees") were defeated by the Tories, he comments in his best whimsical style, "There was astonishingly little fighting," he wrote, "considering the number of wild Irishmen we brought down, but they were altogether too strong for the Yankees, who after giving their votes generally mounted their horses and made off; so for want of better game our Patlanders occasionally got up a snug fight amongst themselves, but though there were three or four *kilt* I did not hear of any very serious damage." (*Early Days in Upper Canada*, p. 170.)

but the evidence of William Thomas who has sworn that they did Hurra for Papineau & Mackenzie may be true And altho he has no distinct recollection of being knocked down & severely beaten by John Andrew & Robert Neilson yet he does not dispute the evidence of William Thomas who has sworn that they did—Witness had drank a considerable quantity of Beer that day and when he has drank freely his memory is bad—the morning after the affray Witness had a Black Eye and his face a good deal disfigured—

Sworn before us John Blezard Jr
at Peterborough
28 Decm^{r} 1837—
Thos A. Stewart J.P.
Edwd S. Hickson J.P.

(2) *Evidence of James Keeffe*

New Castle To Wit } Before Honble T A Stewart, Cheeseman Moe, Ephraim Sanford, Edwd S. Hickson & Robert Reid five of her Majestys Justices of the peace for s^{d} District appeared James Keefe of Otanabee in s^{d} District Yeoman who being duly sworn Witnesseth that he recollects the training of the Malitia on Saturday the 9th Instant was present in Mrs Pattersons when fighting took place—he had drank freely—John Blizzard was attacked by the Neilsons cannot say how many of them; Witness took part with John Blizzard as they belong to the same side being Tories—does not recollect any Hurrays in Mrs Pattersons to the best of his knowledge—there was some Hurraying in the Still House before they came into Mrs Pattersons but he cannot say whether it was for the Reformers or for Papineau or Mackenzie—He drank Whiskey in the Still House of Dr Gilchrist—he bought ½ Gallon from the Doctor and paid him for it One Shilling & sixpence—witness treated some of his acquaintances—

James Keeffe

Sworn before us at
Peterborough 28 Dec^{r}
1837 —
Thos A. Stewart J.P
Edwd S. Hickson J.P

(3) *Evidence of William Thomas*

New Castle To Wit Before us Honble T.A. Stewart Ephraim Sanford Edwd Hickson & Robert Reid Esqr four of her Majestys Justices of the Peace for said District—Appeared William Thomas

Labourer for the last two Months, a resident of Keane in the Township of Otanabee in said District who being duly sworn deposeth and saith That on or about last Saturday Week a meeting for training of the Malitia of Asphodel & Otanabee took place at Keane aforesaid—about four or five O Clock in the Ev^g deponent was present in Mrs Pattersons Tavern when a number of persons where drinking and generally the worse of liquor Politicks were talked of and different opinions given John Blizzard of Otanabee gave a Hurra for the Queen & the Governor. John Neilson. Andrew Neilson & Robert Neilson, with some other persons deponent does not know cried out Hurra for Mackenzie & Pappineau and the said Andrew Neilson attacked John Blizzard and was joined by his two Brothers John & Robert they knocked John Blizzard down and beat him severely—James Keith interferred in favour of John Blizzard and fought in favour of Blizzard against the Neilsons
Peterborough 28th December 1837

his
William X Thomas
mark

Sworn before us
Thos A. Stewart J.P)
Edwd S. Hickson J.P)

(4) *Conviction of Andrew Neilson*

New Castle } To Wit } Be it remembered that on the 28th day of December in the Year of our Lord 1837 at Peterborough in said District Andrew Neilson of Otanabee in s^d District was convicted before us Honble T. A. Stewart Edward S Hickson & Robert Reid Esq^rs three of Her Majestys Jus[t]ices of the Peace for said District for that he the said Andrew Neilson did on Saturday the 9th day of Decem^r Instant at the Tavern of Mrs Patterson in Otanabee aforesaid, with divers other persons, cause and provoke a serious Riot and Affray And did, then and there Commit a violent assault on John Blizzard of Otanabee aforesaid And we the said Justices do adjudge the said Andrew Neilson to forfeit and pay on or before the 14th day of February next the sum of Five Pounds Halifax Currency And also the sum of Three Pounds Five Shillings & Eleven pence Halifax Currency for Costs of Constable & Court—The said fine when recovered to be appropriated as the Law directs.

Given under our hands & Seals the day and Year first above written—

Thos A. Stewart J P
Edwd S. Hickson *J.P.*
R^t Reid

(5) *Sworn Statement of William Thomas*

New Castle } Before us Hon[ble] T.A. Stewart, Edward S Hickson &
To Wit } Robert Reid Esq[r] three of her Majestys Justices of the Peace for said District appeared William Thomas of Keane of Otonabee in said District who being duly sworn saith That the persons appearing before the Magistrates in Peterborough as John Neilson, Andrew Neilson & Robert Neilson of Otanabee aforesaid on the 28th day of Decem[r] last are not all the same persons who were guilty of the Riot and committed the Assault on John Blizzard as sworn to in his examination on 28 Decem[r] last but One of said persons Andrew Neilson was actively engaged on that occasion in shouting for Papineau & Mackenzie, causing the Riot and in assaulting and beating the aforesaid John Blizzard—The other two persons of the Name of Neilson he saw acting with Andrew Neilson on that occasion are not the same persons brought before the Magistrates

his
William X Thomas
mark

Sworn before us at—
Peterborough 5 Jan[y] 1838
Thos[s] A. Stewart J P
Edw[d] S. Hickson J.P
Witness
Charles Green

IX. COMMUNITY LIFE: RELIGION

A GREAT DEAL of historical value is found in the journals of Methodist and Church of England clergymen here presented. Particularly are they important for the details they give of early settlers in remote regions, but as examples of courage and intrepidity they hold a high place in the annals of pioneering. Though Father Edmund Burke kept a journal of his travels in Upper Canada in a supervisory capacity in the seventeen-nineties, nothing similar appears to have been written concerning the ministrations of early Roman Catholic priests in the Trent Valley. Occasional references are found indicating where the first log church in a township was erected, who gave the land, when and how the building was constructed, and which priest first ministered there, but nothing which might be taken as a narrative of the beginnings of the Roman Catholic Church in the region.

This section appropriately opens with the famous hymn composed by Joseph Medlicott Scriven near Rice Lake.

1. What a Friend We Have in Jesus![1]

BY JOSEPH SCRIVEN (1819–1886)

What a Friend we have in Jesus,
    All our Sins and griefs to bear!
What a privilege to carry
    Everything to God in prayer!
O what peace we often forfeit,
    O what needless pain we bear,
All because we do not carry
    Everything to God in prayer.

[1]This hymn, among the best-known and a favourite of millions, was written, probably in 1855, at the home of Scriven's friend James Sackville, who lived near Rice Lake. The music to which it is usually sung was composed in 1868 by Charles C. Converse (1832–1918), well-known editor of Methodist and Presbyterian hymnals. Joseph Scriven, a graduate of Trinity College, Dublin, and long a street preacher in Port Hope, is buried near Bewdley, Rice Lake. A small volume of his hymns was published in Peterborough, but more complete is James Cleland, *What a Friend We Have in Jesus, and Other Hymns by Joseph Scriven, with a Sketch of the Author* (Port Hope, 1895).

Have we trials and temptations?
Is there trouble anywhere?
We should never be discouraged;
Take it to the Lord in prayer.
Can we find a friend so faithful,
Who will all our sorrows share?
Jesus knows our every weakness;
Take it to the Lord in prayer.

Are we weak and heavy-laden,
Cumbered with a load of care?
Precious Saviour, still our refuge—
Take it to the Lord in prayer.
Do thy friends despise, forsake thee?
Take it to the Lord in prayer;
In his arms he'll take and shield thee;
Thou wilt find a solace there.

2. Experiences of a Methodist Circuit-Rider, 1824–1825

[The Life and Times of the Rev. Anson Green, D.D., Written by Himself . . . *(Toronto, 1877) pp. 48–59*]

[1824] MY FIRST CIRCUIT.—I had purchased the best young horse I could find in the township, got my saddle-bags, completed my travelling outfit, and was ready for my appointment. I had received no intimation from anyone to what circuit I would probably be sent; nor had I the slightest anxiety on the subject. Still, I had an impression that I would go to the Smith's Creek Circuit. And, sure enough, that was my place. When the Bishop had finished reading the appointments, the Presiding Elder came to me on the Conference floor and said, 'You are appointed to the Smith's Creek Circuit.' I thank you, said I; just where I expected to go. On the morning of September the 7th, in company with a pleasant young preacher by the name of Griffis, I mounted my beautiful steed, with saddle-bags and valise well filled, and started on my mission as a TRAVELLING PREACHER. As I left the house of my dear friends, Brother and Sister J. P. Williams, I could not but drop a tear. Their kindness to me and attentions to my wants, when I was a stranger in a strange land, I can never forget. They, with a goodly number of the young converts, gathered around us at the gate, wept as we mounted, blessed us as we started, and watched us anxiously until we were out of sight. The morning was lovely. Seldom has the sun shone upon a more charming day or a clearer sky. If this is an index to, and the precursor of, my day of ministerial toil, thought I, then surely I may look for a sunny noon and a cloudless evening. I have had many a struggle to bring my mind to a godly decision, but the struggle is now over. Christ says, 'You have not chosen me, but I have chosen you, and ordained you, that ye should go and bring forth fruit, and that your fruit should remain.' I have no selfish ends in view. I go at the call of God and his Church, only to bring forth *fruit that will remain.* And now, having fairly and prayerfully buckled on the armour, I am quite resolved never to cast it off until the war is over and the victory gained, or I receive an honourable discharge. Mr. Case has furnished me with written authority and directions, and given me his blessing. He has promised, if possible, to give me a year or two at Cazenovia, and I have sold a lot of land and placed my available funds on interest in view of such a contingency.

A charming ride of twenty-five miles brought us to the eastern limit of my circuit, where we found a sweet home with one of my circuit stewards, Chas. Biggar, Esq. The Carrying Place is about two miles long, and connects the Bay of Quinte with the lake. On Wednesday I had an appointment at Presque Isle, but Bro. Demorest, who was on his way to his circuit, kindly preached for me. He said many good things, with scarcely a motion of his body, or much emotion of soul. Thursday, the 9th, I PREACHED MY FIRST SERMON in our Church at Cramahe, now called Colborne, from 1 Peter 4:18. I did not venture into the pulpit but spoke from the chancel. I had tolerable liberty, but was not greatly encouraged. On Sunday preached at Haldimand Four Corners, from 'What will this babbler say?' I scarcely knew myself what he would say, but he tried to preach Jesus and the resurrection. In the evening, at the school-house at what is now called Grafton, from Romans 10:13. Had good liberty and was comforted.

Sunday, 19th. At Hawkins' school-house, in Hope, from Matthew 11:25; and in Cobourg in the evening, from Romans 5:2. Cobourg is the name of a small village of some 100 inhabitants. The Church of England has a young clergyman here by the name of McCaulay. He has a small Church, the only one in the village, while we preach in a school-house. There are two small stores here, several mechanics, and plenty of taverns. The court-house and its surroundings form a small villa, more than a mile distant. We have a good Church two miles north of the village, with a small log cabin near it which they call the parsonage. Here my colleague is to live, and this is really the head of the circuit. The Church is respectable; but oh, the parsonage! Thursday, the 25th, preached at Baltimore—Matt. 7:7. At Wm. Kelley's the next day—Psalms 40:2. A kind family and a good home. Sunday, the 26th. At the parsonage Church in the morning—Col. 3:4; and at Cobourg in the evening—Rom. 10:13. Thank God for such a day. Had much liberty in preaching, for God was our leader. How encouraging to get such 'showers of blessing'! Monday, Sept. 27th, start for the bush, a distance of twenty miles, over rough roads, with plenty of corduroy bridges. Stop at De Ells', and preach in a house just erected both for a church and a school-house. It had no windows, doors, nor floor, and yet we had plenty of light coming through the doorway, and between the logs with which it was built. Our position was as novel as it was awkward. The people sat upon the sleepers, with their feet dangling below, while I took another sleeper for my pulpit. It being my birthday I took a text in accordance with my feelings,—'The world passeth away, and the lust thereof, but he that doeth the will of God abideth forever.' Much of my time has run to waste. It pains me to reflect upon the little good I have done. May I be of some service in the future, and that quickly, for

'Our life is a dream; our time as a stream
Glides swiftly away,
And the fugitive moment refuses to stay'.

On the 28th September I started for the township of Smith, passing through where the town of Peterboro' now stands; but there was only one house there then, and that one down on the river's bank, quite out of my sight. My path was a winding Indian trail, where no wheel carriage had ever passed. I was obliged to jump my horse over logs, ride him through deep mud-holes and bridgeless streams, guided sometimes by marked trees. When I got a short distance beyond Peterboro' I entered a clearing with two or three log cabins in view. In one of these lived a godly old Yorkshire woman, who received me joyfully. Her house was covered with hollow logs, halved, and so arranged as to shelter its inmates from the rain and snow. The room was about fifteen by twenty feet in size, and it served for our kitchen, bed-room, parlour, dining-room, and church. Here I preached to a congregation of eight souls, and was happy. O how these people in the bush value the Gospel, and love the messengers who deliver it to them. On Wednesday returned to the town-line, and found my way to the house of Mr. Morrow, in Cavan, and preached to the best congregation I found in these woods. Here, too, I met with an intelligent Irish local preacher by the name of Blackstock. We had a good class-meeting, and rejoiced together. I was not surprised to learn that my predecessor, Brother Belton, had lost his way in these primeval forests. I was told that he took a wrong path one stormy day; but as night was coming on he fortunately met a man who knew him, and accosted him thus: 'Sure, and is this you, your riverence; pray, where are you going?' 'Oh, to hunt up the lost sheep,' says Mr. B. 'Indade, well, I am afraid the sheep stand a poor chance of being found tonight, since the shepherd himself is lost'! The poor preacher was six miles out of his way, but he was kindly guided to the little flock who were anxiously waiting for him. Thursday, preached at Mr. Sheckleton's, and on Friday at Mr. Thompson's, in Monaghan. This last appointment was not on my plan, but Mrs. Thompson had met me at my appointment on the town-line last Monday, and pressed me to take an appointment at her house, promising me a good congregation. I was glad I went. I found a sterling family, who were Wesleyans in England. The congregation were perched upon a loom, like a flock of pigeons on a tree. After preaching, Mrs. Thompson related to me the following most thrilling event in her own experience, showing how much good we may accomplish when our hearts are free to do it:

'In England', said she, 'we were members of class, and accustomed to hear preaching every week. When we came to these woods we were three years without seeing a minister. Hearing that one was to preach on the front, I travelled out fifteen miles on foot to hear him. My soul was filled with comfort, and I begged him to come to the bush and preach in our house, promising him that, if possible, every person in the township would be present to hear him. He consented. On the day appointed I gave our family their breakfast, and then went to every house and got a pledge that every man and woman would be present at the appointed hour. On my way home I saw the track of a horse in our field, and knowing that there was no horse in the settlement I thought it must be the horse of the man of God who had come to bring the Gospel to our forest. Is it possible, thought I, that after so long a famine for the bread of life, the time has come at last when we are to have the Gospel preached in our own humble cabin! The thought was overwhelming; tears came to my eyes, my heart throbbed with emotion, and I sank upon the earth and kissed the ground on which the horse had trod which brought the man of God to our township. I thought of former times in Yorkshire, and then and there renewed my covenant with God, pledging myself to do all I could to spread the Gospel through these forests.'

This good family prospered in everything; and thirteen years after this visit I had the pleasure of preaching in a comfortable church erected on their farm. This pious and devoted woman comforted me much, and encouraged me to greater diligence in acts of self-denial. I met one of her sons, now venerable in appearance, at the Peterboro' Conference. Hard, indeed, must be that heart which would not go any lengths, and make any sacrifice, to preach the Gospel to such a people! If Wesley was right when he directed us to go to those who need us most, then I was right in taking up this appointment, and I left one for my colleague. While riding back towards the front over rough roads and through gloomy forests I dismounted to relieve my horse a little and stretch my own limbs by walking, leaving my saddle-bags on the saddle. But the cunning beast proved treacherous—I had good cause to regret my kindness. I had left the bridle on his neck and was walking by his side, when he managed to get a few steps in advance. Having walked a couple of miles in this way, I began to feel weary, and asked my horse to stop; but he seemed to prefer walking alone, and resolved to keep out of my reach. When I walked fast, he increased his pace accordingly. When I ran he ran—then off came my bags, which I had to carry. This appeared to amuse him much, and no intreaty could induce him to wait for me. Is it possible, thought I, that I am doomed to walk and carry this burden, through this solitary wilderness, all the way to Cobourg. In my dejection and weariness a happy thought came into my mind. There is a long corduroy bridge about a mile ahead, and on that bridge I can outrun the cruel beast. The plan was laid and the conquest effected; but I learned that too much liberty was a bad thing for a horse, while there might be circumstances under which even these miserable log-bridges might be of service to a travelling preacher.

Sunday, the 3rd of October. Preached at Cramahe and at Presque Isle. Cramahe is a small village about the size of Cobourg, but it has a good Church, a better society, and a larger congregation. Hiram Merriman, a faithful undershepherd, is our leader here. He is very fond of a good, warm-hearted shout, and, when he feels well, he can bear his part in it with stunning effect. At Presque Isle we have a large log-house for worship, and an excellent class. James Lyons, Esq., M.P.P., is our leader, and an excellent leader he is. James Richardson, Esq., his brother-in-law, lives near him and is an able local preacher, but it is intimated that he is soon to take a circuit. On Monday preached at Sherwood's, and on Tuesday at the Carrying Place. Called on the Rev. Mr. Greer, a young Episcopal clergyman, who had just settled in this village. Wednesday, rode round the head of the Bay to the Trent, thence over to Mr. Young's (father to the Rev. Wm. Young), and preached from Proverbs 8:4. Wednesday, preached at Cold Creek to a few settlers, but no class. After a lonely ride to Percy Mills I preached to a small congregation, led a small class, and was entertained by the father of the Rev. Solomon Waldron, of our Conference. Friday, rode back through the woods towards the front, and preached in the house of a local preacher by the name of Joshua Webster—an intelligent man and good company. Sunday, 10th Oct. At Haldimand and Grafton preached on 'What will it profit a man if he gain the whole world and lose his soul?' A question, this, of infinite importance, but easily answered.

Monday, the 11th, at Bro. Waite's, back of Grafton. Saturday and Sunday, the 16th and 17th of October, heard Mr. Case at our Quarterly Meeting in Hamilton Church. He is a lovable man; mild as St. John, but firm as St. Paul. Not a great, but a good preacher. His sermons are not deep, but efficacious, and we love him, admire him, and pray for him. I received twenty-five cents travelling expenses, but no quarterage, as my colleague required all the money paid in to meet his moving expenses. We arranged for a *new* appointment at Mr. Bullock's neighbourhood, near the Carrying Place, and another at what is now called Newtonville, about twelve miles west of Port Hope—since become the head of a circuit. On the 4th of November I preached the first sermon ever delivered at Newtonville, in a log house owned by Mr. Soules, situated on the main road and on the west side of a high hill. I gave them a synopsis of our doctrines. One intelligent-looking gentleman eyed me closely, and seemed to be carefully weighing every sentence uttered. He thanked me for a doctrinal sermon, and invited me to visit him at his house, which I did; and this visit led to the following *case of conscience*: In accordance with Dr. Adam Clarke's 'Advice to Young Preachers', I had resolved to pray with every family I visited. I found this gentleman alone, and as he did not propose prayers I had not courage to do so myself, but left him alone in his musings. The cross was heavy, and I failed to bear it, though Jesus had said, 'Whosoever doth not *bear his cross* and come after me, cannot be my disciple'. As I rode away my conscience stung me severely—Is that the way you carry out your purposes? Is that all the courage you have to bear the cross for him who bore the cross for you? Then better leave this field to others and go home! I stopped my horse to return to the house; but this would appear absurd, hence I compromised the matter by promising to call on my next round and ask to have prayers with this gentleman. After this decision I rode on; but, alas! on my next visit to that place his house was empty. This gentleman had left the neighbourhood and I never saw him more! But his image is photographed indelibly upon my mind, and I can never forget that first breach of faith with myself. It is a dangerous thing to trifle with a good conscience. I was miserable in the extreme, and would have given much if I had never seen that man, or, having seen him, had done my duty. Our next appointment led me to Major Wilmott's—now Newcastle—preached in a school-house a little west of Salmon Creek. From this we went to

Mr. Butterworth's, in a back concession; and I left an appointment also, on the main road, at Mr. Wallbridge's house. Sunday, the 7th of November, preached at Hope school-house in the morning, and at Mr. J. Boyce's in the evening. Dined with Mr. Hawkins, and found good lodgings at Bro. Boyce's during the night. We had also a regular appointment at Mr. Farley's school-house. I have now preached in all the regular appointments, and find we have enough to do. We preach in twelve townships, have thirty-three appointments each for every twenty-eight days, lead all the classes after public service, preach funeral sermons, and attend as many prayer-meetings as possible. Our Circuit embraces all the country between Bowmanville and the Carrying Place, River Trent, and Mud Lake. It requires a ride of 400 miles to get round it, which we performed, winter and summer, on horseback. There are now twenty-four circuits within these limits. We had only two churches on the circuit which we could use for Quarterly meetings—one in Colborne, and one in Hamilton, near Cobourg—but we erected a small one in the village of Cobourg before Christmas. My colleague, the Rev. David Breakenridge, is kind and industrious, but, like myself, is a new recruit in the ministry. He is blessed with a charming wife. Her maiden name was Lawrence, but her mother was once the wife of the celebrated Philip Embury.

DEDICATION AT COBOURG.—On the 28th of November, I had the pleasure of opening our new church, erected on the corner of Division and Chapel streets. My text was from Zech. 14:6, 8. These 'living waters' were refreshing, and all were invited to drink freely. Very little ceremony was connected with church-openings in those days. Father Wilson was present and took part in the services; but, strange to say, he was not in my way at all. I had feared him greatly, but he removed that fear entirely during my second sermon at the Parsonage Church. He was living near that church, and I could not think of preaching in his presence. I, therefore, took the first opportunity to call on this venerable divine, and earnestly request him not to be present when I preached, as I had not been accustomed to preach before ministers and feared I might break down in the attempt. He said he knew how to sympathize with such feelings, and at once assured me he would not attend until I was an established preacher. I felt much relieved by this promise; but alas! he thought I was 'established' long before I thought so myself; and at my second appointment in that church, after the preliminaries were over and I stood up to read my text, I saw his venerable form enter the door. He had on short breeches, with silk stockings, knee-buckles, shoe-buckles, &c., and with his clerical garb and venerable locks he made a most formidable appearance. I was both surprised and frightened. Indeed, I trembled to that extent that I could scarcely hold my pocket Bible in my hand. I first thought of sitting down and calling upon him to preach, but dared not do it. I then placed both elbows upon the pulpit to steady my trembling nerves, and read, 'Unto you that fear my name shall the sun of righteousness arise with healing in his wings; and ye shall go forth and grow up as calves of the stall'. By the time I got through with my introduction I had lost sight of the old divine; my trembling ceased, and from that moment I had no more fear of Father Wilson.

FIRST SERMON AT PORT HOPE.—November 30th. This afternoon, by previous arrangement, I delivered what I was informed was the *first sermon* preached in Port Hope by a Wesleyan minister—it was certainly the first appointment in our circuit work there. I had a shoemaker's shop for my church, his shoe-bench for a pulpit, and six persons for a congregation. Port Hope is the largest village on the circuit. It is situated at the mouth of Smith's Creek, from which our circuit takes its name. It is full of enterprise and spirit, but so full of whisky and sin that it bears the name of 'Sodom'. My text was, 'Some have not the knowledge of God: I speak this to your shame'. The wedge is now entered, and, if we can manage to get a congregation, Sodom may yet be redeemed, and by divine aid we may hope to do some good there. December 1st, took up another new appointment at Mr. Herchel's, on the lake shore, some four or five miles west of Port Hope. December 8th. My colleague has also taken up an appointment at Mr. Purdy's, on the lake shore, in Cramahe, where I preached today. We have also arranged to preach at the Court-house, and at the school-house at Major Jones', half-way to Port Hope.

FATHER WILSON'S NARROW ESCAPE.—When in Cobourg last October I saw the beach, west of Division Street, covered with small white tents filled with Irish immigrants. The Hon. Peter Robinson had been home and brought out a shipload of these people, whom he landed here. There was no wharf in Cobourg then, and the landing was somewhat difficult. They were to be located in the bush beyond Rice Lake. Mr. R. has given his own name to the place, calling it PETERBOROUGH. These white tents presented a beautiful and attractive appearance. They stretched along on the sand beach lying between the lake and a forest of small cedars, which covered the worst part of the swampy ground east of Ham's mills. Among the newly-arrived were fourteen Protestant families; the remainder were Papists, with a priest at their head. Mr. W., being an Irishman himself, went and preached to his countrymen; but when the priest—who was absent at the time—returned, he was much displeased and told his flock that if that heretic came there again to preach they were 'to cool his zeal by throwing him into the lake'. The Protestants reported this to our brethren; and soon after the magistrate sent for the priest and asked him if the report was true. 'Certainly it is', said the priest. 'What right had that man to preach to my people in my absence?' 'Just as much right as you have, sir, if they wish to hear him. You are in a free country now, where the liberty of free speech is protected. You are therefore to go immediately and call the people together and tell them if Mr. W. comes there again they are to use him civilly; and I will hold you responsible for any mischief done him.' The priest very properly hastened to the camp, blew his horn, collected the people, and said to them, 'I perceive I have made a mistake. If Mr. Wilson comes here be sure you use him well, or I will hold you responsible for any mischief done him. Remember what I tell you.' I scarcely need to add that these immigrants were well taught in Gospel truth while they remained on the beach.

3. Church of England Missionaries

At a meeting of the Newcastle District Committee of the Society for Promoting Christian Knowledge, held at the Court House, Cobourg, on September 16, 1835, the following resolutions were adopted, and a subscription list was opened:

1. That Christians, when animated by the genuine principles of their religion, esteem it a privilege as well as a duty to promote the temporal, and especially the eternal, welfare of their brethren in the world; and that all institutions having for their object the spread of the truth as it is revealed in the Gospel possess an irresistible claim upon their benevolent aid and exertions.

2. That the many Protestant families throughout the District of Newcastle, who from remoteness of situation have no access to the regular ministrations of the word and ordinances, render highly expedient the appointment of a TRAVELLING MISSIONARY for the District of Newcastle, to be employed in disposing the services and consolations of the Gospel amongst the remote and unprovided settlers thereof.

In September 1836 the Bishop of Quebec met the views of this Association by appointing a minister to this important charge. The Reverend C. T. Wade, who had recently come to Canada, offered his services and was appointed travelling missionary in the Newcastle District, his duties commencing October 1, 1836. He was succeeded in 1838 by the Reverend W. F. S. Harper, and after an interval by the Reverend G. C. Street on July 1, 1839. If the general statement be true that Church of England clergymen in the pioneer period were inclined to expect a "living" rather than to travel widely in their parishes, the following letters of these itinerant missionaries indicate that their writers were among the more notable exceptions.[1]

(*a*) EXTRACTS FROM THE MISSIONARY JOURNAL OF THE REVEREND CHARLES TAYLOR WADE

[The Church,[2] *Cobourg, 1837–1838*]

Cobourg, Sept. 10, 1836.—Having arrived here this day by the Steam Boat 'Traveller' from Toronto, I lost no time in calling upon the Rev. A. N. Bethune, Rector of St. Peter's Church. To the advice and suggestions of this gentleman as to my proceedings I had been particularly recommended by our excellent and revered Diocesan, now no more, with whom, by a remarkable interposition of Providence, I was privileged to form an acquaintance at New York, as well as with the reverend gentleman already named, in the previous month. His Lordship had also directed me, as far as compatible with my extensive duties, to assist this devoted minister in the sphere of his multiplied and arduous duties. With this gentleman I have ever lived on terms of the most affectionate Christian friendship, and readily do I embrace the opportunity of expressing my obligations to him for every species of useful information respecting my mission, and for unvarying personal kindness since I have had the benefit of his acquaintance.

Sept. 11.—This day, by request of the Rector, I preached in St. Peter's Church and assisted in the administration of the Holy Communion, at which 60 persons were present. In the very interesting and attentive congregation of this town, numbering generally in the forenoon about 300, are strikingly evidenced the effects of a stated and faithful ministration of Gospel ordinances. In the afternoon we proceeded to Port Hope, the pastoral charge of which had, from peculiar circumstances, devolved upon Mr. Bethune. Here likewise I was privileged to address a respectable and attentive audience; and in the evening at 7 o'clock I officiated at the desk in St. Peter's, Cobourg.

[1]Some missionaries had worked east and west of the Newcastle District a few years previously. See W. J. D. Waddilove, *The Stewart Missions* (London, 1838).

[2]The Church of England publication, published in Cobourg from 1837 to 1846, and subsequently in Toronto and Hamilton until 1856. The name implies a view commonly held by members of the Church of England at the time—that the term "church" was not for nonconformists and dissenters.

Sept. 16.—The previous days having been employed in preparations for my missionary journey and in some occasional duty in aid of Mr. B., I proceeded on this day to the village of Colborne in the township of Cramahe. Here I was most hospitably received by B.Y. McKyes, Esq., whose amiable partner, long afflicted, it was my melancholy duty to visit. She has since 'entered into her rest'—that 'rest which remaineth for the people of God'. In the evening (Friday) I read prayers and preached in the school-house to an attentive congregation of about 50 persons, most of them, I believe, members of the Established Church and upon that occasion and many subsequent ones expressing a strong wish for stated services. Thus encouraged I gave notice for a sacramental service on the 9th proximo.

Sept. 17.—Proceeded through an interesting country to Percy, purposing to proceed to Seymour, whither notices of service for the 18th inst. had been forwarded. But on reaching Percy Landing I found that the bridge across the Trent was broken; and it being too late to return and take the other road, I decided on spending the night at Mr. Francis Beattie's, who, on this and many subsequent occasions, most kindly welcomed me. At a very short notice a congregation assembled in the evening, to whom I read prayers and expounded a portion of God's word, and had with many some pleasing conversation regarding the rites and ceremonies of our Church. I removed, through God's mercy, some objections which are often made to Baptism.

Sept. 18—On this sabbath morning proceeded to Seymour, and found that the Rev. W. F. S. Harper, Travelling Missionary in the Midland District, who had been requested by the Bishop to extend his visits to this place and to whose pastoral care it has since been committed, was preparing to officiate. Happy in the unexpected opportunity of becoming acquainted with a valued fellow-labourer, of whose zealous services in the adjoining District I had been informed, I assisted him at the desk and was gratified by finding 23 persons remain to partake of the Lord's Supper.

Having notified my intention of revisiting this township and administering the Sacrament on the 16th prox., I returned to the Landing and at Mr. Beattie's house read prayers and preached to a respectable congregation, who very anxiously pressed for another appointment.

Sept. 19.—Returning to Percy I rode some miles to see a sick woman. She proved an interesting example of the power of Divine grace and of the faithfulness of a covenant-keeping God to his promises. The seeds of scriptural knowledge had been sown in her mind in a Sunday School in Ireland under an excellent minister of Christ's Gospel; but the sense of her soul's best interests seemed for years to lie buried under the cares of this world and the pressure of outward circumstances, yet, in the hour of affliction true religion revived; that God whose 'word shall prosper in the thing whereto he sends it', gave her, from those early impressions, such 'joy and peace in believing' that there seems no doubt she is now 'pressing onward towards the prize of her high calling of God in Christ Jesus'. Having had frequent opportunities of visiting this woman since, I have found her always the same, a consistent, practical follower of the Master who has 'left us an example that we should follow his steps'.

In proceeding this day I have to place on record a merciful interposition of that God 'whose I am and whom I (labour to) serve': my horse taking fright, I was thrown forward out of the waggon, and almost miraculously escaped the wheels and the horse's feet. How needful it is to recognize the movements of His gracious hand 'in whom we live and move and have our being!' On reaching the house of James Platt, Esq., I was most hospitably welcomed. In this little circle I was pleased to discern the characteristic marks of genuine piety, as far at least as man can judge. Throughout the family its influence seemed to be felt; no ostentatious parade, no enthusiasm, but a fervent love to God in Christ, and love to man for his sake. It was my privilege on several occasions to be an inmate of this well-regulated household, and I think I never left the roof without finding myself edified, and, thanking God, took courage to proceed. In the evening I preached to a most attentive congregation of about 60 persons, of whom, however, but few were members of the Church.

Sept. 20.—My horse being from an accident unable to proceed, I was fortunate in finding a gentleman who took me in his wagon to Brighton, Mr. Solomon Hoff, with whom I had much interesting conversation on the 'things which pertain to the kingdom of God'. Stopping at the house of Mr. Stevens, in the 4th concession of Cramahe, near which is a place called the 'happy valley', I was much pressed to make an appointment, and promised, if God willed, to return soon and assist in directing their views to that which alone can constitute true happiness. Proceeding to Brighton where I had anticipated a numerous meeting, I found that a Baptist and Presbyterian minister were there holding services at the same time, and consequently the attendance on my services consisted of not more than 30 hearers.

I could not ascertain that there are many Churchmen in this place; it abounds in a variety of Dissenters of different denominations, yet not unfavourably disposed to hear 'the truth as it is in Jesus' from any minister. In this and the adjoining townships there are many of the sect called Christians, with whose tenets, as far as I have been able to discover, there seems much of infidelity connected. There are also many who are termed Disciples or Campbellites, in some points approaching to the creed of the Anti-poedobaptists. Such of them as I conversed with seemed not to entertain sound views of the Atonement in its scriptural fulness, nor did they appear to lay much stress on personal and practical holiness of heart and life, as the *certain evidence* of 'receiving the truth as it is in Jesus'.

Sept. 21.—Proceeded this day to Colborne, where, after visiting some Christian friends, I preached in the evening to a congregation of about 50 persons. On the following day (Thursday) I assisted my dear brother, the Rector of Cobourg, in a service at Grafton, where he addressed himself extemporaneously—his general custom in these week-day ministrations—to a most attentive congregation of about 40 persons. There are few villages which I have visited in which Church privileges are more duly estimated than in this; Mr. Barnham[1] and his family, and others in the neighbourhood, are ever ready to promote the interests of religion, and their example sets beneficially on the good cause.

Sept. 23.—Having returned to Cobourg, proceeded on the evening of this day, in company with Mr. Bethune, to a school-house about 4 miles distant, which partakes of his stated visits. An excellent congregation here waited to 'draw water with joy out of the wells of salvation'. The remainder of the evening was pleasantly and profitably spent in a Christian family, several members of which, under his ministrations, have ripened for and entered into their glorious rest; and to whose head, recently departed, an affecting allusion was made in the sermon preached on that occasion.

Sept. 24.—Rode out to a school-house in the 4th concession of Haldimand, which also partakes of the occasional visits of the pastor of Cobourg (who on this occasion baptised four persons), and where a good congregation had come together to 'hear the word of God'.

Sunday, Sept. 25, 1836.—Being obliged to remain a few days at Cobourg, I was strongly solicited by my friend and brother, the Rector of St. Peter's, to advocate the cause of the Christian Knowledge Society this day. But on account of my recent arrival in the country, not being sufficiently acquainted with its local details and operations, I felt obliged to decline the request; and the advocacy of the excellent Society consequently devolved upon himself. In St. Peter's in the forenoon, and in St. John's, Port Hope, in the afternoon, impressive sermons were preached and good collections made. In the desk, on both those oc-

[1]The Barnum house, a gem of colonial architecture, has been preserved by the Architectural Conservancy of Ontario.

casions, I assisted, and preached in the evening to a good congregation at Cobourg.

Sept. 26.—This day I had the gratification of attending the Annual Meeting of the Society for Promoting Christian Knowledge, which was followed by that of the Newcastle Branch of the Society for the Propagation of the Gospel amongst Destitute Settlers. The details presented were full of interest; and amongst the useful bequests of the former Society was a grant of books to the extent of £10 for distribution by myself in the remoter parts of my missionary sphere of duty.

Sept. 30.—This evening accompanied the Rev. A. N. Bethune to another scene of his week-day ministrations, in the 2d. concession of Hamilton, about 5 miles from Cobourg, where the congregation we met was highly respectable. In consequence of the falling of a portion of the boarded ceiling during the time of service—through the mercy of Providence none were injured—this service was subsequently transferred to another school-house somewhat nearer Cobourg but within reach of most of the persons who composed the congregation at that time.

October 2.—In order to enable my reverend brother at Cobourg to attend on this morning at Port Hope for the purpose of administering the Holy Sacrament, I had agreed to perform the forenoon service at St. Peter's. Here, however, I had the gratification of receiving the assistance of the Rev. John Bethune, Rector of Montreal, who had unexpectedly arrived on the preceding day; and in the evening we were favored with the like help from the Rev. E. J. Boswell of Carleton Place. In the afternoon of this day, at 3 P.M., I attended at Grafton, where a numerous and attentive congregation were present.

Sunday, October 9.—Having returned, on the previous day, from Toronto, where I had been present at a meeting of the clergy of the two Archdeaconries of this Province, I proceeded this morning to Colborne. The unfavourable state of the weather prevented the assemblage of the usual congregation, and the number of communicants was also few. In the afternoon I proceeded to Brighton; but owing to the feuds existing there between some of the different denominations, the windows of the school-house had been broken and the building otherwise so dismantled that it was impossible to officiate in it. I therefore resolved upon addressing myself to such as could be assembled in a room of the inn at which I was stopping; and I was gratified to find that in the course of half an hour a congregation of about 50 persons were collected, who gave attentive ear to the declaration of the 'counsel of God'.

October 10.—Proceeded this day to Percy to fulfill an engagement at Centreville. Having been hospitably entertained by Mr. Isaac Platt on the way, I proceeded in the evening to Mr. J. Platt's, with whose family I went to the school-house, where a crowded congregation awaited me. I may say in truth that the meetings in Percy were bright spots in my Missionary tour; and I think that future labourers in this District would view that township with more than common interest.

October 12.—Having arrived at Percy Landing, had a service which was well attended, Mr. Cassan kindly acting as a clerk on the occasion. Arriving at Seymour, was most kindly received by Mr. Ranney, to whose uniform attention and kindness my brother missionary of the Midland District has frequently alluded in his journal. In company with some members of his amiable family I visited a few of the neighbouring gentry, and returned to spend in their domestic circle an edifying and profitable evening.

October 14.—The preceding day being occupied in visiting several families in Seymour, I returned on this day to Percy (Benton). Here I was grieved to discover that some who professed themselves members of our venerable and apostolic Church were leading a course of life by no means consistent with their faith; with these I took occasion to converse in a friendly and affectionate manner and to reprove in the spirit of love; and I have reason to believe that, with the blessing of God, the solemn truths set before them were not without some due effect upon their souls.

October 15.—Rode into the country a few miles to see a woman bowed down under severe domestic afflictions; endeavoured to direct her mind to Jesus, the sinner's hope and only ground of comfort; read and prayed with her a considerable time; and before leaving had the satisfaction of seeing her much comforted. In the evening read prayers and preached at a school-house in the 2nd concession, where about 80 people were assembled. After service instructed several in the nature and privilege of Baptism and received three members into the Church by that ordinance.

Sunday, October 16.—This day proved the first of heavy and continued rain since I had entered upon my labour. Proceeded on to Seymour, about 10 miles, where I had made a sacramental appointment for this day. The congregation, from the scattered nature of the population, was necessarily small; and in the expectation of another opportunity at no distant date I deemed it expedient to postpone the administration of the Holy Communion. Three services, however, were performed on this day; and the auditory at each, though small, was attentive.

October 17.—Returning by Percy Mills I made a few calls according to promise, and think that some to whom I had spoken manifested improvement. Professing themselves to be 'convinced of sin', I directed them—with an endeavour to adapt my discourse to their respective characters—individually and collectively to the sinner's Advocate, to the 'Lamb of God that taketh away sin'. Amidst the outward obstacles of a heavy fall of snow and very bad roads I proceeded to Asphodel; and night overtaking me, I experienced a most kind and hospitable reception at Mr. R. Humphrey's. Before retiring to rest I was gratified in joining his family circle in reading the Holy Scriptures—each child furnished with his Bible and reading a passage in turn—and concluding these meditations upon the word of God with prayer.

November 4th, 1836.—Having completed my first and highly encouraging visit to the townships of Clarke and Darlington, I returned to Cramahe, where, after visiting a widow in her affliction, I proceeded to the 'happy valley' in the 4th concession. On this evening I met a considerable congregation and much attention; nor can I omit the tribute of my thankful recollection of the disinterested kindness of Mr. and Mrs. Stevens in that neighborhood. As I proceeded from hence to Percy, I distributed some Testaments and Tracts, furnished to me by the Christian Knowledge Society, which were most gratefully accepted.

Nov. 5.—Performed service this evening at Centreville in Percy, where I had the gratification of meeting a large assemblage; and at the conclusion of the public exercises had much conversation with persons anxious to be informed concerning the ritual, doctrines, and ministry of our venerated Church. I am persuaded that, under God's blessing, the mind being directed to these things, many prejudices and misconceptions will be removed; and the subject I would, with all deference, recommend to the consideration of those whom the Lord may appoint to succeed me in this interesting field of labour, as one possessing no small share of interest in the minds of the people.

Nov. 6.—This day, according to appointment, officiated in Seymour; and it being a bright and beautiful morning a large congregation was assembled, almost all of whom partook of the holy Sacrament. The congregation in the afternoon in another part of the township was not so encouraging; but various reasons were assigned for the comparative thinness of the attendance which seemed to remove all suspicion of an indifference to the privilege.

Nov. 7.—On this day, returning to Percy Mills, was hospitably received by Mr. Humphrey, brother to the gentleman to whom I was so much indebted for similar kindness in Asphodel. Here I received four children into the church by baptism, and had an opportunity of explaining some of the difficulties with which, in the minds of dissenters at least from our communion, the subject is often connected. In the evening read prayers and preached in a school-house to upwards of 60 people; and afterwards some of the neighbours assembled to whom I read and expounded a portion of God's word, engaging with them in familiar and kindly conversation on subjects which should be dear to every Christian's heart and hopes.

Nov. 11.—Having spent the three previous days in a species of pastoral intercourse with the inhabitants in the neighbourhood of Mr. Ranney's, I returned to Benton where I preached on this day to a very large and attentive congregation. Sudden and acute illness, though, as it providentially turned out, not lasting, coupled with the complete breaking up of the roads, compelled me to relinquish my proposed visit to Asphodel for the present at least, and I returned to Cobourg in order from thence to enter upon a more practicable sphere of duty.

Nov. 31.—This day assisted my friend and brother, the Rector of St. Peter's, both morning and evening, he himself having fulfilled the duty at Port Hope at 3 P.M. The following day I accompanied him to a funeral at the latter place, which peculiar circumstances rendered unusually large, the man having been unhappily killed by violence on the wharf.

Nov. 14.—Accompanied Mr. Bethune to a school house about 5 miles distant where a very large congregation united in the services of the church and gave earnest attention to the exposition of the revealed Word.

Nov. 17.—On this day the youngest son of the dear and valued friend just mentioned was received into the church by baptism; nor do we doubt that there were prayers offered up on that occasion which will be answered in the communication of spiritual blessings. It was my privilege to administer the sacred rite in the house of God and in the presence of numerous friends.

Nov. 18.—Mr. Bethune having left me in temporary charge of his parish while he proceeded to Cavan in order to induct into that Rectory the Rev. Samuel Armour, I repaired on this evening, in fulfilment of his engagements, to a school house about 4 miles to the westward of Cobourg, where I had the satisfaction of preaching to an excellent congregation; and on the following day I fulfilled a similar appointment in the 4th concession of Haldimand.

Nov. 20.—The duties of the Rector of Cobourg having this day devolved upon me, I preached at 11 A.M. in St. Peter's to a very numerous auditory; at 3 P.M. I delivered a funeral sermon at Port Hope, founded upon the circumstances alluded to above, when the church was crowded to overflowing; and again at 7 P.M., at Cobourg, assisted in the latter service by the Rev. J. Coghlan.

Nov. 23.—Being relieved from my temporary charge of the manifold duties of Cobourg, I proceeded on this day towards the northwestern parts of the Newcastle District. Spent this night at the hospitable abode of Mr. Joseph Graham, having previously officiated in a private dwelling in the vicinity where a considerable congregation was assembled, but less than would have attended had the notice been more generally circulated.

The following day I had the pleasure of becoming acquainted with a brother labourer, the Rev. Samuel Armour, whose praise as a zealous and indefatigable minister of the Gospel of Christ is well and widely known. From few have I experienced more kindness, and with few maintained more delightful Christian intercourse than with this respected minister and his amiable family.

Nov. 25.—Accompanied by Mr. Armour I proceeded this day to the house of Mr. Hughes in the 4th concession of Cavan, where a small but attentive assembly awaited our arrival; several had returned home, as the bad roads had delayed us considerably beyond the hour appointed. Upon this and every subsequent occasion I found Mr. Hughes, and the several branches of his family with whom I came in contact in various parts of the District, most friendly and obliging.

On the following day, accompanied by Mr. H., I proceeded to the 2d. concession of Emily, where, in a convenient school-house, I read prayers and preached to a tolerably good congregation. A 'raising-bee' in the neighborhood prevented many from attending: a species of friendly association which, whatever may be its value to the new settler, is generally accompanied by demoralizing effects.

Nov. 26.—Arrived this day in Williamstown, Emily, where I experienced a most kind welcome from Messrs. Cottingham and Josiah Hughes. In the evening read prayers and preached to a large and attentive audience.

In this township is a large Protestant population and many firm and attached adherents of our invaluable Church. A very anxious desire was expressed for the ministrations of a regular clergyman, a desire embodied shortly after in a numerously signed memorial to the Lord Bishop of Montreal; and a considerable sum was subscribed towards the erection of a church.

Nov. 27.—This day, in company with Messrs. Hughes and Cottingham, I proceeded in Ops, and found a large congregation awaiting my arrival in the second concession, at the house of Mr. Rae, a pious and excellent man. The state of the roads rendered it impossible to proceed to the fulfilment of an appointment made for me at Purdy's Mills, about 13 miles further; so that I returned in the hope of having a second service at Williamstown in Emily. The ground, however, having been preoccupied by Mr. Armstrong, of the Methodist connexion, with whom I had subsequently much interesting conversation, I returned to Cavan; and after a visit to Peterboro', when I formed my first acquaintance with its valuable Rector of whom I shall have occasion hereafter to speak much and often, I accompanied Mr. Armour, on

Dec. 2, to the fourth concession of Cavan, where I officiated to a numerous congregation. On the following day, being Sunday, I attended at Williamstown in Emily in the forenoon; and in a commodious room fitted up for divine worship by Mr. Cottingham I preached to upwards of 100 persons. In the afternoon I proceeded about five miles to another school house, where I found fully 150 persons assembled to join in the admirable prayers of our Church and to hear the word of God. Of this township it may truly be said that 'a great and effectual door is opened', and such circumstances may well animate our prayers to 'the Lord of the harvest that he would send forth more labourers into his harvest'. Having spent some days in visiting these parts and endeavouring to 'preach Jesus Christ from house to house', and finding that the impassable state of the roads rendered it expedient to direct my ministrations to the un-supplied townships in front, I returned on the 8th. instant to Cobourg. During this week I was introduced, by my reverend brother the Rector of this parish, to another most interesting and useful sphere of his labours, termed 'household, or cottage lectures', known better in England, I believe, by the latter term. On these occasions a portion of Scripture is familiarly expounded, and the exercise is concluded with prayer. From frequent participation in these devotional exercises I can bear my most unqualified testimony to their admirable and important effect; nothing, in short, can better second and establish the influence of those more public and solemn services which form the duties of the Sabbath day. The illustrations of Scripture or of Christian duty which are, on these occasions, given—from the familiar and conversational manner in which they are conveyed—have the best possible tendency in impressing with a clearer knowledge of Scripture truth, and in enforcing those practical duties which the profession of Christian faith so necessarily involves. That these Christian exercises are so appreciated by those for whose benefit they are designed is sufficiently manifest from the number and the deep attention of those who engage in them.

Dec. 11.—This day I assisted at St. Peter's Church both morning and evening, and officiated at Port Hope at 3 P.M., at which hour Mr. Bethune availed himself of my aid to attend at Grafton. On Wednesday the 14th walked with Mr. B. about five miles over frozen mud to fulfil an engagement at a school-house in Hamilton, where, notwithstanding the wretched roads and severe weather, we met a considerable congregation; and on the 16th I accompanied the same gentleman to a school-house in another direction under circumstances of roads and weather nearly as unfavourable.

Dec. 18.—This day, Mr. Bethune having volunteered with me an exchange of duties, I officiated twice in St. Peter's, Cobourg, as also at Port Hope, while he brought back most favorable accounts of gratifying attendance on three occasions of public worship in Darlington and Clark on the same day. On the previous day (Saturday) service was performed by me in the 4th concession of Haldimand.

Dec. 20.—Proceeded this day to Brighton, where, after a hospitable reception on the way by Mr. Goslee of Colborne, I officiated at a respectable farmer's of the name of Hubble, and was gratified by the attendance of a large congregation. On returning preached at Grafton on the evening of the 22d.; attended a funeral at Port Hope on the 24h., and officiated and administered the Holy Sacrament in the latter place on Christmas Day. The weather on this day was particularly unfavourable, so that the numbers both of the congregation and communicants was comparatively small; I returned and by request preached at Cobourg at 7 P.M.[1]

(*b*) MINISTRATIONS OF THE REVEREND W. S. F. HARPER

[The Church, *1838*]

. . . In the early part of the month of May having occasion to go down to Kingston, I officiated once or twice during my absence in that neighbourhood, as also at the Mohawk Mission, and Napanee for the Rev. G. Givins. On my return into Seymour I was enabled to carry my plans for the establishment of a Sunday-school on either side of the river into effect, and succeeded far beyond my expectation. A Sunday-school conducted by the Scotch Presbyterians (whose efforts in this particular demand the highest commendation) had been for some time in operation in Seymour-East, so that all that now remained to be done in this quarter, was to select some new teachers and take the whole under my own supervision. This then was readily accomplished, the Presbyterians cheerfully relinquishing their claims in my favour, and they together with many others volunteering their services as teachers. To the family of R. P. Boucher, Esq., and to Mr. Alex. Menzies (the Superintendent) I am much indebted for their ready concurrence and unremitted assiduity

[1]The Wade journal is concluded by less detailed material published in *The Church*, August 25, 1838, *et seq.* Meanwhile the Reverend W. F. S. Harper had written to *The Church* on April 27 of that year, outlining his ministrations in the district during 1837, which, omitting some general observations, is given in subsection (*b*).

in this labour of love. In Seymour-West a small school was also established under the superintendence of Mr. J. Tice, Jun., who in this as well as many other respects, proved himself a most valuable 'fellow-labourer with me in the Gospel'. To the family of B. B. Ranney, Esq., we were indebted for the use of the room, and also for one of our most useful and exemplary teachers. The attendance at these schools was necessarily very fluctuating, owing to the great distance many of the children had to come and the often almost impassable state of the roads; the same causes also prevented the schools being in operation during the winter months, or rather during the Spring and Fall of the year. The number of children who generally attended the school in Seymour-East averaged from thirty to forty, that in Seymour-West from fifteen to twenty. A day school, after much difficulty and through the unwearied exertions and generosity of Major Campbell, was also established about this time, which averaged in attendance from eighteen to twenty-five scholars; but from the same causes which operated against the Sunday schools it was frequently considerably under that number.

In the course of the following month (June) I made a Missionary excursion into the townships of Marmora, Madoc, Huntingdon, and Hungerford, performed Divine Service at several different places in each of them, and baptized six children. The attendance every where was good, and refreshing indeed was the manner in which these simple but well meaning people greeted my return among them. So rejoiced did many of them appear, and so anxious to improve the opportunity afforded them, that several accompanied me on foot to the different stations where duty called me, regardless of the toils of the way, the excessive heat, and the innumerable swarms of flies and mosquitoes which, in the back settlements, are at this particular season almost intolerable. Such little incidents as these surely more than repay the perplexities and toils to which the Missionary is naturally subjected, affording as they do a comfortable hope that he has not 'laboured in vain' but shall yet 'reap if he faint not'.

The persons of whom I speak were not *all* members of our Communion, but as in most other settlements were composed of various denominations. Many of them too, in the 'time of their ignorance', had, like others, been disposed to lift up their voice against our revered Establishment, her ministers and her ritual. Here then is one among many proofs which might be adduced, that the Church is only to be known to be revered, and to disarm that prejudice which alas! so many in this country have imbibed, in consequence of having her represented to them, by wilfully ignorant or ill-disposed persons, in a false and unhallowed light. What then have those to answer for who from their exalted situations should be the protectors and defenders of the Church, that is, as far as regards her temporalities, have suffered her so long to be deprived of her lawful rights; for to this is undoubtedly owing, in a great measure at least, the lamentable destitution which now prevails in every District throughout the Province. Had the original intention of Government been carried into effect, had the stream of Royal bounty been permitted to flow in its intended channel and a clergyman placed in every township as it became settled, the result would have been widely different both in a religious, moral, and political point of view from that which now unfortunately exists. The question, however, is not what *might* have been, but what is to be done to remedy the evil and to supply the wants of the destitute Settlers. Certainly no more effectual plan could have been devised than that adopted by the Society under whose auspices I have had the honor to be employed now nearly three years. . . .

In addition to the above mentioned tours I made several other excursions, during my sojourn in Seymour, into the adjoining Townships, baptized several children, and attended the funerals of several persons, on which occasions I invariably preached to large assemblies. On my return to Seymour in October I resumed my pastoral labours and was also engaged collecting subscriptions for fitting up the temporary buildings appropriated for public worship. In Seymour East a School-house, the frame of which had been put up some time previous, was completed and made to answer the purpose both of a school and temporary Church. In Seymour West we were indebted for the building and all the conveniences necessary to fit it for a Church—the stove alone excepted—to the kindness and generosity of B. B. Ranney, Esq., whose kindness and liberality has indeed upon all occasions been most unbounded.

Towards the end of December I again set out on a missionary excursion into the Midland District; but previous to my reaching Kingston had the misfortune to injure my horse so severely as to render him useless during the remainder of the season. Some time necessarily elapsed before I was enabled to procure another; which together with the almost impassable state of the roads and the very unsettled state of the country, in consequence of the unnatural Rebellion, prevented my giving that attention to missionary duty I was desirous of doing during the winter season, and indeed detained me much longer than I had intended from my home mission in Seymour.

I have the honor to remain,

Rev. Sir, your obedient servant,

W. F. STUART HARPER.

(c) THE REVEREND G. C. STREET'S TRAVELLING MISSION

[The Church, *October 19, 1839*, et seq.]

To the Editor of the Church.

Cobourg, 7th October, 1839.

Revd. and dear Sir,

As I have observed it to be the custom of our Travelling Missionaries to give an account of the most interesting particulars of their tours, through the medium of 'THE CHURCH', I have thought that it might not be unacceptable, nor perhaps altogether without its use, were I to follow their example and throw together in as small a compass as possible my recollections of such incidents connected with my last Missionary tour as have seemed to me the most likely to be of interest to your readers.

I left this on the afternoon of Saturday the 6th July, and arriving at Colborne the same evening, took up my quarters as usual at the residence of our hospitable friend Mr. Goslee. Having performed Divine Service the next morning to a good congregation in the village, I was on the point of starting for Percy when a severe storm came on, which detained me till 4 P.M. After travelling for the first hour and a half in the rain the weather cleared up, but owing to the state of the roads I was unable to reach my destination till half past 7 o'clock, and unfortunately just as the congregation which had assembled were dispersing. Mr. Platt, however, at whose house I was kindly received, called in a few of his neighbors, and I read a part of the evening service and a sermon. On the following morning I proceeded to Seymour, and after encountering another violent thunder storm reached it in time for Divine Service at 4 P.M. The congregation, owing to this interruption and the busy season of the year, was small, but the attention of the audience and the personal kindness of Mr. Ranni were very gratifying. Early on the 9th I left for Asphodel, returning through Percy; and after a long and tedious ride—having gone two or three miles out of my way—I arrived at Mr. Birdsall's, whose house is beautifully situated at the head of Rice Lake, commanding a view of that picturesque sheet of water for a distance of many miles. Mr. and Mrs. B. I regretted to find were absent, and my notice of service had in consequence not been circulated. At noon the next day I left for Otonabee, and arrived at Mr. Rubidge's in the course of the afternoon, and employed the greater part of the following day in riding through the neighbourhood, giving notice for a service on Friday. That morning set in with rain, and my congregation was consequently but small; although as it was, many walked a distance of three miles through the wet, and over muddy roads. There was much anxiety manifested in this neighbourhood for the regular ministrations of the Church; and I understood that a rear concession of this Township is settled almost exclusively with members of the Church of England, who have but very rarely indeed an opportunity of attending her services.

On the following day passing through Peterborough I proceeded to Cavan, and from thence early on Sunday morning I rode to Emily, a distance of 10 miles. At 11 o'clock I met the largest congregation that I have seen assemble in the back-woods, numbering, I should suppose, 250 persons. The school-house, although more spacious than those buildings usually are, was unable to contain the whole of the congregation, so that numbers were accomodated with seats on the outside round the open windows. After the services were concluded many of the congregation, several of whom came from the distance of seven miles, crowded round me to express their earnest desire for the settlement of a clergyman amongst them, and tears evinced their sincerity. A very good frame for a church with a tower had been erected and nearly roofed, and the residents were only waiting till there should appear a reasonable prospect of the appointment of a clergyman in order to complete the building. In the afternoon of the same day I rode to Ops, and preached to a tolerable congregation in a private house. Being kindly pressed by my very hospitable host Mr. Hughes, I remained in Emily till Wednesday morning, having no appointment in the mean time. On that day I proceeded to Peterborough, and reached it early in the afternoon in time to attend the meeting of the clergy at the Rev. C. T. Wade's. This and the following day were spent most pleasantly, and I trust profitably, with my clerical brethren.

On Friday morning, the 19th July, I left at an early hour for Fenelon Falls; and having travelled the first 12 miles in a waggon, embarked in a private four-oared boat and ascended the Lakes, arriving at our destination a little before midnight. The scenery through which we passed was often very beautiful, though extremely wild. On Sunday, although much indisposed from the fluctuations of the weather and exposure to the night air, I was, by the blessing of God, enabled to perform service and preach twice to a very good congregation. I also christened nine children and had an application for an adult baptism, but declined on finding after examination that the candidate did not evince a sufficient knowledge of the great truths of Christianity. The spirited proprietors of this flourishing spot have been the means of the erection of a log church, neatly fitted up with pulpit, reading desk, and communion table. The building is beautifully situated on the summit of a rising ground in their new village. A fund has also been raised in the mother country among the friends of the settlers in this neighbourhood, which will assist very materially in the support of a clergyman.

On Monday morning I left in a two-oared boat with a gentleman and lady who had come up the lake seven miles on Sunday morning to attend the services, and I was obliged to take shelter from a thunder storm under their roof, where we arrived just in time to escape it. As soon as the weather had cleared up I embarked again with my boatman, and about 5 P.M. arrived at Bobcaygean, where for the first time I performed the marriage ceremony. Starting with my boatman before sunrise the next morning, we arrived at the landing on Mud Lake about noon. From thence I walked 12 miles to Peterborough, and availed myself once more of the hospitality of the Rev. C. T. Wade. We left together the next morning, and had service in Otonabee at 11 o'clock. The day again proved, unfortunately, very wet and stormy; yet I proceeded in the evening to fulfil my engagement at Gilchrist's mills, but found that publicity had not been given to my notice, through the inadvertency of the party to whom I had entrusted its circulation. I subsequently experienced a similar disappointment, from the same cause, at Asphodel.

On Saturday I proceeded through Percy to Seymour, where I performed service on Sunday morning, and at Percy at 6 o'clock the same evening. Leaving early on Monday morning the 29th. inst., I returned once more to Cobourg, by the blessing of God in health and safety, having travelled in all, by land and water, upwards of 300 miles.

In some instances, in the remote settlements, I found a plan pursued which appears to have been attended with beneficial results. I allude to the practice of a layman reading the Church service and a printed sermon to his neighbours every Sunday. This I have found to have been the means of keeping alive a sense of religion in the backwoods, and of maintaining affection towards the Church and a desire for the regular ministrations of her clergy. It would be impossible for one who had not witnessed it to conceive adequately the spiritual destitution existing in those remote places; and while it is seldom relieved by any sound or regular ministration, Socinians, Mormons, and other teachers of false doctrines reap an abundant harvest.

It is impossible that a conscientious Christian having at heart, as he must have, the salvation of the souls of his fellow-creatures and the advancement of Christ's kingdom, could see what I have seen and remain unconvinced of the necessity for the recognition of Religion by a Government professedly Christian. The consideration of the means—obviously simple as circumstances would seem to render them—to be adopted I leave to others; but to the existence of the *absolute need* of

Courtesy Mrs. Marryat

[26] HENRY FOWLDS (1790-1872)

Founder of the village of Hastings

Courtesy Mrs. Marryat

[27] HON. JAMES CROOKS (1778-1860)

First landowner in Hastings district

Courtesy Mrs. Marryat

[28] DR. AMOS McCREA (1821-1886)

Early saddle-bag doctor of Keene

Courtesy Mrs. Helen (Fowlds) Marryat

[29] HEALEY'S FALLS, RIVER TRENT

Photograph by George M. Douglas

[30] FORD ON THE INDIAN RIVER, DUMMER TOWNSHIP

Courtesy Mrs. Marryat M. A. Farrar

[31] COTTON MILL, HASTINGS, 1863

Courtesy Mrs. Marryat M. A. Farrar

[32] HOMES OF HENRY FOWLDS AND HIS CHILDREN

Courtesy Mrs. Marryat M. A. Farrar

[33] LOOKING DOWN THE RIVER TRENT

The Reverend Michael A. Farrar (1813-1876) was the Church of England missionary in the region. The steamboat in two of the water-colours is the *Forest City*

Courtesy Royal Ontario Museum

Charles Fothergill

[34] PORT HOPE IN 1819

Courtesy Royal Ontario Museum

Charles Fothergill

[35] RICE LAKE IN 1819

Courtesy Miss Phyllis Denne

[36] SERGT. MAJ. McCRACKEN'S LOG HOUSE
Erected at McCracken's Landing, Stoney Lake, in 1832

Courtesy Royal Ontario Museum Charles Fothergill

[37] LOG HOUSES, RICE LAKE, 1819

Courtesy Mrs. Adelaide McGiffin

[38] LOG SCHOOLHOUSE, DUMMER TOWNSHIP
This house, earlier the Batten homestead, is remarkable for the large logs used in its construction

such a course, I bear my testimony, however feeble. We know that the blessed day will arrive when 'the kingdoms of this world shall become the kingdoms of our Lord, and his Christ; and He shall reign for ever', but this conviction should not lead man presumptuously to forgo the use of the most effectual means; and I confidently trust that we may yet see, where now there is but 'the voice of one crying in the wilderness', the prophecy amply fulfilled in its spiritual sense; 'The wilderness and the solitary place shall be glad for them; and the desert shall rejoice, and blossom as the rose'.

I remain, Rev. and dear Sir,
Yours very faithfully,
Geo. Charles Street,
Travelling Missionary.

(*d*) CONCLUSION OF THE REVEREND GEORGE C. STREET'S MISSION

[The Church, *February 1, 1840*]

To the Editor of the Church. Cobourg, 28th January, 1840.

Rev. and dear Sir,—Having made two missionary tours since the publication of my letter in October last, I now present a short sketch of them to the friends of the Church, through the medium of your valuable and interesting journal.

I left this on Thursday the 10th of October, and the same evening reached Cavan; and having availed myself of the wonted hospitality of the Rev. S. Armour, I proceeded on the following morning to Emily, where I had service at 3 P.M. On the following Sunday, according to appointment, I undertook the duties of the Rev. C. T. Wade at Peterborough, he having had occasion to make a journey to Quebec. In the afternoon of that day I also preached in Otonabie according to previous notice, a Methodist preacher having concluded his services to the same congregation but a few minutes before my arrival. This is an occurrence which must often happen, and results from the want of a system of stated services, which however I fear will be impracticable while the labourers in the vineyard are so deplorably few.

On Monday the 14th October I proceeded to Percy, and from thence to the Carrying-Place, where on the 16th and 17th I had the satisfaction of attending the Clerical Meeting held at the residence of the Rev. J. Grier.

On the following Friday I proceeded to Seymour, and on the succeeding Sunday preached to a large congregation at Mr. Rannie's in the morning, and officiated at Percy at 7 in the evening.

On Monday the 21st I proceeded to Mr. Birdsall's in Asphodel, and on Tuesday fulfilled an engagement which had been made for me at Keeler's Mills, a distance of 12 miles. Here I christened a child. On Wednesday I preached to a good congregation at Walker's Mills, and baptized four children. On the following day I had service at Gilchrist's Mills, and was again called on to christen a child. On the 26th I reached Emily, and the next day being Sunday preached in the village in the morning, and in the afternoon in Ops. Subsequently I spent two or three days in Peterborough, and on the 1st November rode to Lindsay, in Ops, where I preached at 3 P.M. I baptized this week six children in this township.

On Saturday, a boat having been sent for me from Fenelon Falls, I proceeded thither, and preached there twice on the following day.

Monday evening found me once more in Emily, and on the next evening I rode through a pitiless snow storm to Mr. Armour's which, although but a distance of ten miles, it took me between three and four hours to accomplish. The next day was equally unpropitious, and I had a very disagreeable ride of 34 miles, but arrived once more, by God's blessing, in good health, at Cobourg, having been absent about a month, and having travelled in that time nearly 400 miles.

Having remained at Cobourg for about three weeks—performing in the interval services at Colborne and Grafton, and otherwise assisting the Rector of the Parish—I left again on the 30th Nov. and preached at 10 o'clock the following morning, being Sunday, to a numerous congregation at a station about eleven miles on the Peterborough road. There are many families in this neighbourhood warmly attached to the Church, but it is seldom that they have an opportunity of attending her services. Previous to the assembling of the congregation I had an opportunity of briefly examining a very respectable Sunday-school which is steadily conducted here. I reached St. Paul's church in Cavan shortly after the commencement of afternoon services; and having preached for Mr. Armour I proceeded in company with him to his residence, and remaining till Wednesday, went on to Emily. As I had come out almost entirely upon a pioneering expedition, to explore townships hitherto unvisited by any of our Clergy, and to make stations for future appointments, I had no engagements this week, but made the most of my time by forwarding as far as I could the plans for the completion of the Church at this spot. On Thursday I rode round, accompanied by Mr. Hughes, to call on the members of the Building Committee, a meeting of which was called for Saturday. On the evening of that day the Rev. R. J. C. Taylor arrived from Peterborough, not having been aware that

I was in the neighbourhood; on the following morning I assisted him in the service at the village, and while he returned to Peterborough, officiating at a station about five miles on the road, I had divine service in Ops at 3 P.M. On Monday I rode to Mr. Ruttan's, in the latter township, where I was kindly received, and left an appointment for the 12th. Passing through Mariposa on the following day, I found myself in the evening in Brock, in the Home District, where I was hospitably received at the house of Major Thompson. From Mr. Cowan also, a neighbouring magistrate, I received kind attention, both now and the following week. I found that, according to the returns lately made of the comparative numbers belonging to different denominations, there were 554 members of our communion in this township; and yet it had not been visited by a clergyman for between two and three years.

On Wednesday evening I rode on into Eldon and was kindly entertained at the house of Mr. Ewing, Snow having fallen in great quantities and the ground being yet soft, my ride to Mr. Ruttan's was rendered very unpleasant, the mud reaching at times almost to the stirrups as I sat on horseback. However, I arrived in time to fulfil my appointment, and had the gratification of preaching to a large congregation. I also christened four children. I returned on Friday to Emily, and on Saturday attended a second meeting of the Building Committee, upon which occasion the contract for the completion of the church was given out. I preached on the following day at the village in the morning, and in the afternoon at Braden's on the Peterborough road. This was the first time of my officiating at this place, and I had much reason to be pleased with the number, attention, and respectability of my congregation. The members of the Church in this quarter are only waiting for the appointment of a resident minister in Emily in order to erect a suitable building for Divine worship. On Monday afternoon, having been provided with a sleigh by the kindness of Mr. Hughes, I commenced a second tour in the western townships in order to fulfil the appointments made the week previous. I preached on Tuesday evening in Mariposa to a large congregation, and christened two children. On the following day, accompanied by several members of Major Thompson's and Mr. Cowan's families, I proceeded to Mr. Vrooman's, situated almost in the centre of Brock. The roads were so unexpectedly bad that, although the hour appointed was 11 A.M., we did not arrive till half-past twelve; yet I found a very large congregation waiting with patience for my arrival. A petition to the Lord Bishop for a resident clergyman was put into my hands, with a request that I would give notice after service of its remaining at Mr. Vrooman's for signature. With this request I had much satisfaction in complying, and read it aloud to the congregation, upon which they came forward with much alacrity to add their names. I christened at this time nine children, and although I could not insist upon sponsors in every case, it will, I am sure, be gratifying to all well-wishers of the Church, and particularly to your correspondent C., to learn that those who did take that obligation upon them on this occasion were communicants. I will take this opportunity of stating that I exercise as much care as circumstances will permit with regard to the parents of the children, and as for the sponsors, am invariably in the habit of rejecting them unless they appear sensible of the solemn nature of the responsibility incurred. It must be evident to you that it is impossible, under the circumstances in which a Travelling Missionary is placed, to exercise as much care in this respect as resident ministers with a knowledge of their people are enabled to do.

My lengthened duties in Brock detained me till 3 P.M. and having at 6 o'clock an appointment in Eldon at a distance of 12 miles, I made the best of my way to that quarter, accompanied by Mr. Cowan, on horseback. Not knowing the exact situation of the spot where I was to officiate, we took the wrong road, and in consequence found upon reaching the school-house that about half of the congregation had left. I preached however to those who had remained, and found them grateful for the privilege of service afforded them. One female, whose attention I had observed to be rivetted to the service as it proceeded, came up upon its conclusion to the person who had led the responses, and, as he afterwards told me, took him by the hand and thanking him exclaimed, 'O Sir, I have been this evening in England again!' It must be indeed no small delight to those who have been, perhaps for years, debarred from listening to and joining in the exquisite prayers of our Liturgy, to have all their old associations revived in so calm and holy a manner. I could almost envy the poor woman her feelings as the recollections of her father-land came crowding on her mind. May I be allowed to digress a little longer in order to remind those who have constant facilities for attending the services of the sanctuary—so much so as almost to have forgotten the greatness of the privilege—that there are hundreds and even thousands of their brethren, scattered through the wilderness 'as sheep having no shepherd', who would rejoice to be even 'door-keepers in the house of the Lord'.

I neglected to mention in its proper place that a Sunday-School exists in Brock, numbering 50 children; and to which my attention was repeatedly and earnestly called, as they were destitute of books. I was requested to obtain a supply of the Church Catechisms for it, which

I promised to do. You will agree with me that it is highly creditable to the members of the Church in this neighbourhood to have kept alive, as they have done, a sense of their duties as Christians by providing for the religious instruction of the rising generation.

Arriving at Mr. Ruttan's on the 19th I preached again to a congregation of about 30; and drove to Emily on the following day. There I ministered private baptism to an infant and married a couple; after which I proceeded to Mr. Armour's. On Sunday I preached for him in the morning, and at St. Paul's church in the afternoon on my way home, while he undertook my Missionary duty in the township of Manvers.

Thus ended my third tour of 280 miles, which had proved to me highly interesting; and which, I devoutly trust, may not have been without a blessing to some immortal soul.

I take the opportunity once for all of acknowledging the great kindness which in every quarter was exercised towards me during my travels; and I am constrained to say that, whatever other apostolic precept may fall short of fulfilment in the backwoods, this one does not,—'Use hospitality one to another without grudging'.

Neither, while I bear testimony to the kindness of man, would I forbear to acknowledge thus publicly my gratitude to Almighty God, who has given and continued to me in all my wanderings health and strength and cheerfulness.

I hope it will not be trespassing on the limits of a letter to offer a suggestion before concluding, for the supply in part of the wants of the spiritually destitute. My plan is this:—to appoint stations as nearly equi-distant as possible from two, three, or more resident clergymen, as the opportunities may exist; and which shall be visited by each of them alternately, at stated intervals. For the sake of example, we will suppose that there is a settlement having one minister resident within eighteen, another within twenty, and another within thirty miles. They agree to have service there once a fortnight, so that, taking it alternately, each would be obliged to go once in six weeks only; and the benefits that would, by the blessing of God, result from such a plan, would far more than compensate for the additional labour. This, combined with a modification of the plan recommended by a recent correspondent in your paper (M.M.), might, and I feel confident, would be productive of the happiest results.

I remain, Rev. and dear Sir,
Ever yours faithfully,
Geo. C. Street.

X. COMMUNITY LIFE: EDUCATION

THIS SECTION exemplifies the attempt to provide educational facilities under the most adverse conditions. The first known letters relative to schools are here reproduced, together with inspectors' reports which outline the problems to be faced and how they were met. The public-spirited work of those who strove to advance education amid discouraging conditions of every type is here given recognition. An example of efforts to educate privately where public facilities were not available is No. 6, consisting of excerpts from the journal of Anne Langton, 1839.

1. LACK OF SCHOOLS IN THE NEWCASTLE DISTRICT, 1816

(*a*) LETTER OF ELIAS JONES

[*Public Archives of Canada, Educational Papers, U. C., R.G. 5 B 11, Vol. 2, No. 9*]

Hamilton[1] 30th August 1816.

Sir,

Your Letter of the 19th Instant Requesting a Report of the State of the Public School in the District of New Castle I have had the Honor to Receive, and in reply, beg leave to state for the information of His Excellency the Lieutenant Governor, that in consequence of the great difficulty, for these last Three Years in obtaining a Teacher adequate to the overseeing the Public School, and in consequence of the delinquency of the one last Recommended to His Excellency, there has been no Public School kept.—I have the Honor to be

Sir

Your obdt Hbl. Servt—

To Benjm Geale Esqr — Elias Jones Trustee

In absence of Mr — Actg Secy. — N Castle District School

McMahon.

[1]Hamilton was the early name for Cobourg, after the township in which it is situated.

(*b*) LETTER OF JOHN PETERS

[*Public Archives of Canada, Educational Papers U.C. R.G. 5, B11, Vol. 2, No. 13*]

Cramahé[1] Oct. 3d 1816.

Sir,

I had the honor to receive a letter from His Excellency the Lieut. Governors office the 15th Septr last, requiring a report of the public School in the District of Newcastle. There has been no public school in the District for several years at least since Mr Richard Carterel let it.—

A Mr Stoughton was recommended last Winter, and approved by His Excellency but now declines Teaching.

I have the honor to be
Sir
your most Obedient
Humble Servant

Jn Peters Trustee

To
Edward MacMahon Esqr
Actg Secretary &c. &c. &c.
York

2. SCHOOLS IN THE NEWCASTLE DISTRICT, 1818

[*Public Archives of Canada, Upper Canada Sundries*]

To His Honor Samuel Smith Esquire Administrator Administering the Government of the Province of Upper Canada—&c—&c—&c—

The Board of Education for the District of New Castle beg leave most Respectfully to report.—

That upon examining the Reports from the Trustees of the Common Schools in this District.—

[1]This was the original spelling, the name of Hector T. Cramahé, Administrator of the Government during Sir Guy Carleton's absence, 1770–4. The pronunciation of the name has similarly changed from "Crá-ma-hay" to "Crá-mee."

We find that there is at present Ten Schools Kept as the Law directs; in which Schools there is Two Hundred and fifty seven Scholars And by every appearance the Youth of this District seem to be very eager for Education under the fostering hand of our Benevolent Government.—

I have &c
(signed) John Burn
Secretary to the Board
of Education for the
New Castle District

Hope/
14th January 1818.

3. Report of the District Superintendent of Schools for 1844

[*Thomas Poole*, A Sketch of . . . the County of Peterborough, *pp. 55–6*]

To the Warden and Councillors of the Colborne District,

GENTLEMEN:

I beg to lay before you a report relating to the Common Schools of the Colborne District for the year 1844. I have visited all the schools during the past year, in operation at the time of my annual examination, except one in Verulam and Harvey, and one in Fenelon and Bexley. Circumstances have delayed my examination of these beyond the time prescribed. The character of the schools generally is satisfactory. It is to be regretted, however, that in many of the school districts, particularly those in the townships of Ops and North Monaghan, the school houses are so very bad, amounting in some instances to a state of actual discomfort and unhealthiness; but I have invariably urged upon the people the necessity of their improvement, and I have reason to believe that they fully agree with me therein, and that they will remedy the evil as soon as possible.

The attendance of children is good, averaging to each school about twenty-five, but I am sorry to see this number confined solely, or nearly so, to children of small age. Taking one school with another, there is a fair proportion of children who read and write.

In no instances in my recollection, with one or two exceptions, have I seen the English grammar in use; very seldom geography, and no history, except occasionally in a reading book. The bible I found in general use.

There is a great deficiency of books in very many of the schools.[1]

This, I was told, originated in the carelessness or poverty of the parents. I have, however, invariably urged upon them the necessity of supplying their children with proper books. The teachers frequently complain of this deficiency, and of their consequent inability to classify their scholars; which is prejudicial to their advancement.

I have reason to believe that the teachers rely more upon reason and common sense in their instruction, than upon the rod; and I have invariably urged upon them to do so. I have also had to suggest the benefit of allowing the children a short relaxation during school hours. I have also made it known that intemperance in any teacher will be regarded by me as a good cause for his immediate removal, and that cruelty towards his scholars will be promptly put down.

Upon the whole I may say that, although there is much room for improvement in many of the schools, still there is no real cause for complaint, and I am satisfied that they will continue gradually to prosper, and that the teachers will be improving. . . .

I may further state that I made an application some time ago to the Governor General for the free grant of a lot in the Town of Peterborough to Trustees, with the view of ultimately being able to build thereon a commodious school house, and establishing by private munificence a fund the interest from which would be sufficient to supply free tuition to all who might choose to avail themselves of it, and to have a good library in connection therewith; and I have intended, if my exertions had been successful, to have devoted the entire of my salary, as Superintendent, for that purpose. But His Excellency did not condescend to notice my petition, and so the matter for the present has ended.

I have the honor to be, &c,

E. BURNHAM,

County Superintendent of Schools for the Colborne District

Peterborough, February 11, 1845

[1]Books, as well as other elements in the lives of early teachers of the district, are described by Superintendent E. Burnham in "Schools in the Township of Emily in the Old Days," in J. George Hodgins, *The Establishment of Schools and Colleges in Ontario, 1792–1910* (Toronto, 1910), Vol. II, p. 140; and by W. Kerr's reminiscences (*ibid.*, pp. 107–8). Notable among early teachers in other townships was Daniel Sheehan. He was born in 1781, came to the district in the Peter Robinson emigration, and was still living in Douro in 1885. He taught school in Doûro and Otonabee townships from 1826 to 1846 and retired on a pension of $120 a year. Alexander Edmison, son of Thomas H. Edmison of Smith Township, kept a somewhat desultory journal during 1857–1858 while he was a teacher there. He found teaching "abominable", and lived in hopes of advancing himself to something better. The journal is in the possession of J. Alec. Edmison, Assistant to the Principal, Queen's University.

4. Superintendent Thomas Benson Explains his Resignation, 1851

[*Quoted in Poole*, A Sketch of the County of Peterborough, *pp. 56–8*]

To the Warden and Municipal Councillors of the County of Peterborough, in Council Assembled.[1]

GENTLEMEN:—The period having arrived when it becomes necessary that you should provide for the superintendence of the Common Schools of the county for the ensuing year, it is proper that I should inform you that I do not intend to offer myself as a candidate for the situation you did me the honor to confer upon me at the commencement of the past year.

If I here take occasion to refer to a few of the reasons which have induced me to come to this determination, it will be with the sole view of increasing the usefulness and efficiency of an office the faithful discharge of the duties of which may do more to promote the social and moral advancement of the rural population of this county than any other secular agency within your control. The first and most powerful motive which impels me to decline a reappointment to the office of superintendent of schools is the conviction that the amount of labour which the faithful discharge of its duties would entail upon the incumbent is more than any one person could possibly endure.

I trust it will be apparent that in alluding to the extent of this labor I do not seek to magnify my own exertions. I crave your attention to this point merely to shew that a change of the former system is necessary.

The distance which must be travelled over to complete one visit to each school section in this county would appear totally incredible to any one who had not taken some pains to reckon up the numerous journeys it occasions; one visit could not be nearly accomplished in a quarter of the year at an average rate of travelling of twenty miles a day. This rate, considering the state of most of the roads and the time which must be spent in properly examining a school, is greater than could possibly be maintained for a whole year. The extent of my correspondence during the past year has been much greater than any

[1]Dr. Poole comments as follows upon this report: "Thomas Benson, Esq., succeeded E. Burnham, Esq., in the office of County Superintendent, the salary being now raised to £130 per year. Mr. Benson was highly respected both for his intelligence and the urbanity of his manners. His was one of the many valuable lives lost in the terrible railroad disaster at the Desjardines Canal in 1857. He retained the office of County Superintendent only for one year. His letter of resignation is interesting as pourtraying the arduous duties of that office and the scant remuneration thus afforded for services so important." (*Ibid.*)

one anticipated. Upwards of six hundred communications have been received and nearly five hundred despatched. It is true that this will be in future greatly diminished, unless changes are made in the school law: but it will always be very considerable. The operation of a law but newly introduced entailed upon me the preparation of opinions and decisions which not infrequently required days of careful research, and much labor in furnishing numerous copies. I do not at all exaggerate when I state that the office work alone of my situation has consumed more time, and required more anxious exertion, than is devoted to some of the best paid offices in the country.

In the next place I find that my health is not equal to the task this office imposes. Frequent night journeys and change of quarters brought on a fit of illness which kept me from the performance of my duties for several weeks, every effort to resume my journeys bringing on a relapse.

But I should be recreant to the cause I profess to advocate if I allowed any cowardly apprehension of being misunderstood or misrepresented to prevent me from stating that the remuneration attached to the office under consideration is out of all proportion to the nature and importance of its duties, and to the value of such qualification as a superintendent should possess.

My personal expenses for the year, including travelling expenses, repairs, stationery, postage, and loss in the value of a horse worn down, have amounted to about seventy pounds, leaving only about sixty pounds as compensation for services which occupied the whole of my time to the exclusion of all other sources of income.

The conclusion I desire to draw from these statements is one to which I trust I may be permitted to call your attention without exposing myself to the imputation of officious interference with privileges and duties which are peculiarly committed to you by the law: it is this—that the interests of education will be promoted by a division of the county into at least two districts for school superintendence, and by fixing a rate of remuneration more justly proportioned to the value of the services and attainments called into exercise by its arduous duties and high requirements.

With regard to the condition and prospects of common school education in the county an improvement has taken place, and an impetus has been given to the desire for further advancement which must have become so apparent to each of you, gentlemen, in your several localities, as to leave no need to enlarge upon it here. Whether this improvement shall go on with a much needed and steadily increasing progress will greatly depend upon the appointments which the Council may now make to fill a situation the duties of which I feel that I have very imperfectly discharged.

I have the honor to be, Gentlemen,
Your most obedient humble servant,

(Signed) THOMAS BENSON,
Sup't. Schools Co. Peterboro'.

Peterborough, 28th January, 1852.

5. Report of Inspection of Schools in Asphodel Township by Dr. Thomas Poole, 1855

[Colborne Transcript and Castleton, Percy, Hastings, & Norwood Advertiser, *January 19, 1856*]

The examination of the Norwood Grammar and Common Schools was held on Wednesday, the 19th. inst. Your space and my time will not suffer any minute details. Suffice it to say that in the many and varied subjects in which the classes were examined they acquitted themselves most creditably, and reflected the highest honor upon the excellent teachers under whose care they have the good fortune to be placed. The existence of such a school is a boon of inestimable value to those residing in a remote section of the country, placing them, in an educational point of view, upon an equality with the more favored residents of the frontier townships. The new school-house, built of brick and resembling in size and appearance the Town-hall of Peterboro, is rapidly approaching completion; and from the increased accommodation thus provided, and a continuation of the valuable services of Mr. and Mrs. Daunt, we have reason to expect a still more auspicious future.

Here my remarks might close, and should do so were it not that the mind is led involuntarily to contrast the present efficient system of teaching with that which prevailed only a few years ago in our country schools. Many of your readers can call to mind the time when Walker's dictionary was placed in their hands, and they commenced the hopeless task of committing it to memory. Visions of the well-thumbed Mavor and the perpetual English reader, sandwiched with certain rude hieroglyphics, bedimmed by the falling tear and overshadowed by the awful birch, still haunt the minds of those who have survived those melancholy hours. What wonder that school was voted a gloomy place and learning a drudgery! But the scene has changed, and with far less labor and much greater efficiency we have learned—

'To pour the fresh instruction o'er the mind'.

We rejoice to know that the other branches, besides those of the willow, are now appreciated in our schools, and trust that the portrait of—

'The whining school-boy with his satchel
And shining morning face, creeping like snail
Unwillingly to school'—

will be found to be only a portrait of the past, and that its original will be very seldom seen in the future.

Norwood, Dec. 24, 1855. T. W. Poole, Local Superintendent, Asphodel.

6. Anne Langton's Private School, 1839

[*Anne Langton,*[1] A Gentlewoman in Upper Canada: the Journals of Anne Langton *(Toronto, 1950), pp. 89, 95–6, and 117*]

Wednesday, January 2 [1839].— . . . I had Menzies' two little girls for a lesson to-day. I have lately begun to teach them a little. They come for about an hour three times a week; as yet we are not at all perfect in our letters, and I sometimes feel that, unaccustomed as I am to teaching, I shall not accomplish much in my short schooling. But one good effect it appears to have, that they get a little more teaching at home. I hope this may continue, and then my own efforts will certainly not have been thrown away. My pupils are two very pretty little girls about five and seven, and sometimes recall to my mind the dear little girls at Seedley. . . .

Wednesday, January 16.—I had a new pupil today, a little girl of the Daniels about ten years old. I scarcely yet know what her attainments are, for she is dreadfully frightened, and though she appeared to know scarcely more than her letters at first, I shall not think it all my own doing if I find that she can read at the end of a fortnight. I hope she will get some good from me, however, for she has nearly two miles to come for her lesson. . . .

Tuesday, July 9— . . . My school assembled in the afternoon, but

[1]Anne Langton (1804?–1893), sister of John Langton, added greatly to the record of early life in the Trent Valley by her journal and her sketches. She was, in addition, a capable painter of miniatures and devoted to music. She returned to England for a time in 1846, but from 1850 until her death in 1893 she was a member of the household of John Langton. A number of her sketches are reproduced in this volume.

we all felt the weather. I was sleepy, and the children were languid. I had a new scholar, a girl of ten or twelve years of age, not yet perfect in her letters. And now I think my number is up. When more come on I must turn some of the old ones off, unless I can introduce the mutual instruction system, or, as I cannot well extend my school hours, the benefit to each individual must be necessarily diminished by an increase of numbers. At present if the amount of good gained in a lesson is not very great, at any rate they are put into the way of learning, and rendered capable of improving themselves.

XI. SELECTIONS FROM WRITINGS DESCRIPTIVE OF THE REGION

In one important respect the inhabitants of the old Newcastle District, comprising the present counties of Northumberland, Durham, Peterborough, Victoria, and Haliburton, are unique in Canada; for nowhere else were there so many men and women of intellect and taste who wrote prose and verse of a high standard, and produced works of art without which we would be much the poorer. The leaders in authorship were the three Stricklands, but numerous others produced essays and poems that were equal, if not superior, to theirs. These cultural efforts were highly appreciated among their contemporaries, as may be seen from the columns of the newspapers and periodicals of the day; but they have been in large measure unknown in our day both to critics and to the general public. Their value as part of our record of pioneering—apart altogether as a literary heritage—is inestimable, and it is fitting that selections from them should be reproduced in this volume. A few descriptions by visitors to the region are added for their historical value and human interest.

1. Frances Stewart (1794–1872)

Thomas and Frances Stewart, among the most cultured and public-spirited early settlers in the Newcastle District, emigrated to Upper Canada in 1822, owing, like many another, to reduced circumstances. They were accompanied by a brother-in-law, Robert Reid, and his family. They stayed in Cobourg while land grants were being arranged, and due to influence in British and Canadian official circles each family received a grant of 1200 acres of land in Douro Township, together with control for five years of further settlement in the district. They settled near one another on the Otonabee, just north of what was soon to become the village of Scott's Plains (Peterborough).

Frances Stewart's letters to England, published in *Our Forest Home* (Toronto, 1889), indicate her cultural interests, her love of nature, and a determined spirit that the exigencies of pioneer life could not dampen. She and Mrs. Catharine Traill were kindred spirits, and her ten children were taught to recognize the flowers and the trees. In 1831 her husband was appointed to the Legislative

Council, and he remained a member until his death in 1847. He appears in this volume in various capacities, but particularly as author of a letter sent to Captain Basil Hall and printed anonymously in his *Travels in North America in the Years 1827 and 1828* (Edinburgh, 1829). His talented wife died in 1872.

FRANCES STEWART'S NARRATIVE OF PIONEER EXPERIENCES

[*Poole*, A Sketch of . . . the County of Peterborough, *pp. 147–50*]

On the first day of June, 1822, we sailed from Quebec, accompanied by my brother-in-law and his family, which consisted of his wife, six daughters, and three sons. We came up the St. Lawrence from La Chine in *batteaux*, which was a very tedious mode of travelling. We reached Toronto (then called York) in August, and were detained there several weeks by illness. Meantime my husband and brother-in-law procured a grant of land in Douro and started to see it.

About the first of October we came to Cobourg, then a very small village. From thence my brother-in-law with some hired men proceeded direct to Douro to make an opening in the woods, my husband being prevented by illness from accompanying them. Two clearings were commenced about a mile from the boundary of the township of Otonabee. Early in November my sister-in-law and her children joined her husband in the backwoods. They took a large scow, or flat bottomed boat, from Rice Lake, which on the second evening reached the Little Lake. They landed on the point of land near where the village of Ashburnham is now situated, and from thence proceeded to their shanty about three miles from the landing.

My husband, myself, and three little children, with a maid-servant and a boy, were to come up on the return of the boat; but we were detained at Cobourg by the illness of one of our children, and therefore were obliged to wait for sleighing, to perform the journey by land through the townships of Hope, Cavan, and Monaghan.

At that time there were but few settlers in these townships; and on the second day we travelled nine or ten miles without seeing a house or clearing. At last we reached 'Scott's mill' (on the 12th of February, 1823, at 1 o'clock p.m.), then the only house in Peterborough. The Little Lake not being safe for teams to cross on the ice, we were obliged to walk over—our children and luggage being carried by our servants and some men who kindly assisted. The snow was then about two feet deep. Our ox-team and sleigh were in waiting on the other side, but by the time we had all reached the place daylight began to fail, which made our progress through the woods much more difficult; and the sleigh being loaded I was obliged to walk. Our lantern, unfortunately, got filled with snow, and our candle so wet that it would not light. So we proceeded slowly, and at last perceived a light before us and soon reached our log house. The light proceeded from a large wood fire, which rejoiced our hearts.

We found our house in a very unfinished state; the door had not been hung, nor were any partitions made. A large opening was left in the roof where the chimney was to have gone up, but the intense frost had stopped the mason-work when about half completed. Finding this rather cooled us, and we felt puzzled where to lay our sleeping children, as the floor was covered with a thick coating of ice and mortar. However, we soon discovered some shavings left by the shingle makers, which we spread on the ice and then laid on our mattrasses, and on these made a temporary 'shake-down' on which we cheerfully laid down, after a supper of tea, bread, butter, and pork. Being very weary we slept soundly; but in the morning, on looking up, I saw the stars through the aperture left for the chimney.

At this time my brother-in-law and his family lived in an open shanty about half a mile north of us, and from having their fire outside they were much annoyed by the smoke and sparks blowing in, which at night often set fire to their bedding.

By slow degrees these difficulties were surmounted; but we found new difficulties arising from the want of roads or some means of conveying our provisions from Cobourg, which was the nearest town. Mr. Bethune was then the only store-keeper there, and was also Postmaster. We sent to him when a fresh supply of provisions or other necessaries was required, and these were forwarded to us by way of Rice Lake, which proved a very tedious and expensive mode of conveyance, and the delay of our supplies sometimes drove us to most painful straits. In the autumn a sufficient store had to be procured in this way to last for five months, as our winters at that time set in about the end of October and seldom terminated until the middle or end of April. At one time, before we had any shoemakers near us, we sent an order to Cobourg for boots and shoes for both families, numbering about twenty persons of all ages, and after waiting a long time for them, we learned that they had been lost in crossing Rice Lake and could not be recovered. This was a serious loss, as they could not be replaced for some months, and in the meantime many were obliged to go barefooted.

Pea soup and pork was our principal food. Our bread was good when we could get good flour, or when the yeast was not frozen. Very often we had only rye meal, which was not disagreeable; but one season, not being able to procure flour or meal of any kind, we were obliged to use boiled wheat and corn, and were once reduced to bran cakes, which soon disagreed with us.

As our first Spring in the backwoods advanced I was delighted with the beauty and novelty of the scene around us. Our clearing[1] was opened to the river, which in those days rushed along with great rapidity and noise, carrying down large masses of ice from the lakes and waters above us. Since then the numerous dams have marred the natural beauty of the river; while the fine hemlocks and cedars which grew so beautifully along the bank were since cut down and have disappeared.

In the Autumn of our first year in Douro our youngest child, a sweet little girl of not quite two years old, was seized with dysentery. I was quite ignorant of the treatment of that disease and there was no doctor within reach—the nearest being Dr. Hutcheson, who then resided in Cavan, a good many miles distant. We had as yet no canoes on the river, and were often depending upon a chance visit of the Indians for a passage to the other side. One of our hired men, a faithful Highlander, seeing how very ill our darling was, volunteered to swim across the rapid stream and walk through the woods to the doctor, promising that, if I wrote the particulars, he would bring the necessary medicine. He started early in the morning of a cold October day, and returned about midnight, with some powders and a message that the doctor would come up on the following day. But no improvement followed, and the day was passed in great anxiety, for the doctor did not arrive. On the third day he came, having left home at the promised time but lost his way in the woods, and hence the delay. The next day she appeared more lively but refused to take the arrowroot and sago which I offered her. She asked for bread, and of this we had none fit to give her, having for some time been unable to procure good flour. It was a bitter trial not to have what she seemed to crave. The next day she fell into a stupor, and towards midnight her angel spirit passed away to the immortal land. A few weeks after this sad event she was replaced by another dear little daughter—the first white child born in Douro, who still lives and is a comfort and a blessing to her aged mother and a fine family of her own.

Ague did not make its appearance for some years. Between 1823 and 1825, when the Hon. Peter Robinson arrived with a large immigration,

[1]Many settlers retained in their memory as a place almost sacred the spot where they first encamped when they entered their lot. In his reminiscences Henry Lye of Hastings states that large trees in the shade of which the Fife, Cameron, and Macintosh families spent their first nights on their land were pointed out to him with evident pride.

we had many hardships and privations to endure, partly from a want of knowledge of the proper way of managing, and partly from the heavy expenses incurred on our first starting, by the exorbitant charges and high price of every kind of provisions and clothing, besides the great difficulty of procuring even the most necessary articles. But after the establishment of Peterborough all these difficulties gradually disappeared, and have now nearly faded from my memory.

F. S.

2. Thomas Stewart's Narrative

[*Hall*, Travels in North America . . ., *Vol. I, pp. 307–23*]

Douro in Upper Canada
21st April, 1828.

My Dear Sir,

As you were commissioned by Captain Hall to procure from me answers to some queries, I shall just give you a short sketch of the proceedings of my own family from the commencement. I shall declare the truth—but not the whole truth—as it would require volumes to contain all I could relate; and as you are partly aware of the difficulties we had to encounter, you will perceive there is no exaggeration.

After various dangers on the voyage out we reached Quebec in safety. Our party was very large, consisting of 21 persons; and wishing to use as much economy as possible, we engaged some births in the steerage of the steam-boat for Montreal, having a temporary division made to prevent our party from being annoyed by the common passengers. Two dollars a-head was the charge. Three children were charged for as one passenger. From La Chine, near Montreal, we proceeded in Batteaux up the river St. Lawrence. This was very pleasant for a day or two, but when continued for eight or nine it became tiresome. Sometimes we slept in haylofts, preferring the sweet fresh hay and cool air to the small close rooms in taverns, which abounded with bugs. Sometimes we lay on the grass near the river side, and though frequently wet through with dew, yet our party enjoyed good health. We arrived at Kingston, at the east end of Lake Ontario, on the night of the ninth day, and as all the houses were shut up, were obliged to remain in the boats till morning, when we engaged a schooner, and took our passage for York, the capital of Upper Canada. Lay two days waiting for a fair wind—weather oppressively hot.

At York we remained for six weeks, the greater part of which time my family was accommodated in the garrison by permission of the governor. During our stay at York we unpacked our boxes, and found our things much injured by the wet they received in the schooner. At the end of a month we received a carte blanche from the Governor in Council to pitch our tents in any township in which there was vacant land. I hired a waggon, and, accompanied by my brother-in-law and his son, and laying in a store of provisions sufficient for a week, we proceeded to Cobourg, delivered a few letters of introduction to some of the principal people there, and in company with a friend went to the Rice Lake, where he introduced us to the surveyor of the back township, who lives at the east end of the lake. This was the first time I had ever been in the house of a back-wood settler. The lady of the house was ill with the Lake fever, the little infant sick with ague, so that all the housekeeping devolved upon the man of the house, who milked the cows, cooked their meals, and attended the invalids, besides attending to all the business of the farms. This, I must confess, staggered me a little, particularly as I myself felt ill at the time; but I saw no appearance of dejection in him, and why should I allow fears to arise? The next morning a female was procured to attend the sick, and we proceeded 24 miles up the Otanabee River, to a place then called Scott's Plains, now Peterborough, where there was, and still is, a most wretched farm-house and tumbling down grist and saw-mill. My brother-in-law and three men, including the surveyor, crossed the river to spy the promised land, and walked to Douro, about three miles higher up the river. I was ill and not able to accompany them. When they returned they made a very favourable report, and literally brought a bunch of wild grapes.

We all then came back again, with the full determination to bring our families to Douro. I became very ill before I reached Cobourg, where I was confined to bed in a miserable tavern. I was visited by a gentleman who, in the most friendly and hospitable manner, insisted on my being removed to his house, where I remained dangerously ill for about three weeks. My brother-in-law, in the meantime, had returned to York for our two families, leaving his son to take care of me. In about ten days they reached Cobourg in a schooner, after having encountered a storm and having been nearly shipwrecked. The ladies and myself remained in lodgings at Cobourg, and my brother-in-law and his sons, along with some labourers, went to Douro, to begin operations where none but Indians or Indian traders had ever been before, and the party merely guessing where they were, as that township had not yet been surveyed. They cut a road from the landing-place opposite to Scott's Mills, three miles through thick woods, to the place they were to begin to build the house, for the strong current in the river prevented them from proceeding farther by water. With some difficulty they procured a yoke of oxen to hire in Smyth Town, and were obliged to swim them across the river.

After some time provisions began to run short, and two men were sent out to forage. After travelling for many miles they returned with one small pig, which lasted for only two days. No flour was to be had at the Mill, as the neighbourhood afforded no wheat. At this time 18 men were employed by my brother-in-law to saw the logs of our houses, and he was quite at a loss where to send for food. Fortunately I arrived that very evening with a supply of pork, pease, flour, and whisky; for if I had not come, all the men would have gone away and it would have been nearly impossible to collect them again, as they lived many miles from each other and from Douro. This collection of neighbours is called a Bee, and is the common custom to assist each other in any great piece of labour, such as building a house, logging, &c. The person who 'calls the bee' is expected to feed them well, and to return their work day for day. On my way up the river from Rice Lake I was obliged to sleep in the woods with a blanket rolled round me, and a large fire at my feet. Some Indians who were coming down the river came to us, and sold us some venison for a little whisky; we made them cook it for us, and also remain with us all night to keep on a good fire, as it was cold weather in November, and there was some snow on the ground.

I spent a day or two at Douro to see my house put up, as it was quite a new scene to me and is extremely interesting to see a small opening made in the forest, and with the trees cut down the walls of a house erected in a few hours; and when every thing has been prepared, a house may be finished and ready to be inhabited in two days. But this was not so with us; for, from the difficulty of procuring hands and materials so far back, we had many delays; in consequence of the severe frost setting in and the illness of the only mason in the country, the stone work of our chimneys was only half done.

I returned to Cobourg to bring out our families to the woods; but I found my wife very ill, and also one of our children, which delayed us for some months; but my sister and her family went out and took up their abode in what is called a shanty, which is merely a shed or hut made of logs and roofed with slabs hollowed out of logs to turn the wet, and was quite open at one side, and in front was a great log fire. They were obliged to live in this shanty the whole winter, as the frost prevented the mason from building the chimneys of their house: that winter we had much deeper snow than we have seen since we have been in Canada, being then 3½ feet deep; and I have seen the little children, from two years old and upwards, sitting round the fire, heavy snow falling all the time; yet both my brother-in-law and sister say they never knew their children so healthy or so lively as they then were.

On the 1st of March, 1823, they got into their house, having put up a stove: the thermometer often 30 below zero during this winter.

Upon the 10th of February, 1823, my family being once more in good travelling order, we departed from Cobourg, to the surprise of some of our friends who thought that our courage would have failed when the great plunge was actually to be taken. The first night we slept at a little tavern, and adopting the custom of woods-folk at once, we rolled ourselves in our blankets and lay down on the floor before a large fire. The next evening we reached Scott's Mills; had our luggage and children carried across the river; we were met on the other side with a sleigh and oxen to convey us to our new abode. Having arranged our bedding and the younger children on the sleigh, we proceeded; the snow nearly knee-deep, and for the last two miles in darkness; so that we were right glad to see the cheerful light of a good fire shining through our log-hut windows. Here my sister and most of her family met us to welcome us to the woods. Our house appeared large and wild, as, from the difficulty of procuring boards at the saw-mill, there was not a single partition in ours put up; even on the floors the boards were scarcely sufficient to prevent the children's feet from going through. When we set about to prepare our beds we found the floor covered above an inch thick with ice, of which we removed as much as we could with axes and spades, and then put a layer of chips and shavings, upon which we spread our mattresses and blankets; then having hung up some blankets at the doors, and also for partitions, we lay down to rest, being pretty well fatigued; and upon looking upwards from our beds we saw the sky through the roof; and have often, during the time we lay in that manner, amused ourselves watching the stars passing and others appearing.

The next morning I sent all hands to Scott's Mills for the remainder of our luggage, and my wife and I set out to go to see my sister. However, having occasion to return for something, I observed smoke issuing from many parts of the roof. As quickly as I could I went up the ladder, and found the upper part of the chimney and a great part of the roof on fire. No one was in the house except a maid-servant and three little children; fortunately the scaffolding had not been removed; I climbed up, and was just taking a pail of water from the girl when the scaffolding gave way and down I came. I with much difficulty scrambled up again and tore away the shingles which were on fire, and after some time and trouble succeeded in extinguishing the fire. This fire was caused by a dangerous method they have here of building chimneys with cross sticks, plastered with clay; but this had been built in severe frost, so that the clay did not adhere and the sticks caught fire.

Our time was now occupied in endeavouring to make ourselves comfortable, and we amused ourselves by looking forward to seeing some appearance of vegetation. This, however, did not occur until the beginning of May. In April we tried to make some sugar; but as we had nobody to tell us how to set about it we did not succeed at all. The place we boiled the sap was within one hundred yards of the house; but so close were the trees that I could not see the house; and it even appeared so long a walk there that I had my dinner carried to me, thinking it too far to return for it myself. This is a mistake which frequently occurs to new settlers; and I have often since laughed, as that very spot is now cleared and appears almost at the very door; and, although we are only 84 yards from the river, we were two months here before we could see it from the house. As soon, however, as the snow went off we commenced chopping to admit air and sun, and got ten acres ready for spring crops. It has occurred to us more than once, in the two or three first years of our residence here, to be in danger of starvation from the extreme difficulty of procuring any sort of provisions in this neighbourhood and from the uncertainty of conveyances from Cobourg, our roads being few and very bad, and for some time, both in spring and autumn, our navigation being interrupted by broken or bad ice, not good for sleighing. The first year we had no potatoes until August, and were glad to gather any wild plants which we were told could be safely used as greens to make a little variety. Salt pork, pease soup, and bread being but bad food for children, sometimes for weeks together we have used tea made of the young shoots of the hemlock-pine, or burnt Indian corn for coffee. We lived so far from other settlers that we seldom heard of any opportunity of sending out for any thing we wanted. I have had three or four men working for me, and have not had provisions sufficient for the next day. I have gone out with my ox team, and a man to forage, and after travelling an entire day returned with a couple of sheep that had not a pound of fat upon them, a little pork, and a few fowls, and when crossing the river, just near my own house, have been near losing the whole cargo by the strong current.

The most interesting time had now arrived, when we saw our first crops appear above ground. I had the honour of planting and sowing the first seeds in Douro. But our troubles were not at an end, for in June, when all our crops were looking well and when we looked forward to having a reward for our patience and industry, a great fire, which began in the woods, extended into our clearing and burnt up a large portion of the young Indian corn and potatoes, and it was with the greatest exertion that we were able to save a part of our precious crops. This fire lasted for two or three days, and all hands were busily employed carrying water.

In the second year of our sojourn we lost a dear little daughter, nearly two years old, one who was most endearing to all who saw her, and who often beguiled an hour after a day of hard labour. Two days passed before we could send and procure a doctor. A short time after this my wife was confined, and I had to send fifteen miles for a nurse tender, who reached us with much difficulty, as she was obliged to walk through woods where no road had ever been cut, and to be carried sometimes across swamps, and lifted over large logs. My wife, however, recovered safely and speedily, although her confinement took place in the depth of winter; and now we have three little children, who have never been three miles from this house. Nothing unpleasant has happened within the last year or two, with the exception of the loss of some cattle by the falling of trees and other accidents. Our provisions occasionally ran short for the first three years; and at times we have literally used plain bran made into cakes, and used Indian corn boiled when we could not procure flour. In the winter of 1824 we had four Scotsmen employed; and in order to supply them with bread we were obliged to grind our wheat in a small hand-mill, which, fortunately, we had brought with us for grinding coffee, pepper, &c. Every evening, after a hard day's work, these four young men ground as much wheat as was sufficient for supplying bread for each day.

We had been nearly a year and a half living here before my wife saw a female of any description, except those of our own two families; and one day I took her down to the mill where two women were washing at the river side, when she immediately cried out, 'Oh! there are two women!' Three years passed away without any appearance of settlers coming near us. I thought, as my family were growing up, it was a pity to spend any more time in this hopeless retirement. So I had written to a friend on Cobourg to procure for me a snug little place in that neighbourhood, with about 50 acres of land. A few days after this Mr. P. Robinson came to my house and mentioned to me his intention of bring up the emigrants to these back townships. At once we gave up every idea of removing—the clouds dispersed—all our difficulties seemed over.

The plains at Scott's Mills were soon after covered with huts and shanties and inhabited by 2000 souls. All became bustle and activity; houses and stores erected; a clergyman, priest, doctor, besides various kinds of tradesmen, were soon established; in fact every thing we wanted appeared within our reach, and we had the prospect of some society. Now I would not exchange for any other part of the province. Our farm (which is now near 70 acres) will give us all the necessaries of life. Often my wife and I look back, I may say with pleasure, at our little grievances, and enjoy the retrospect. No settlers coming here now can have any idea of the difficulties of the first settlers, as they can now procure every thing they require if they have the means of purchasing it. We now have good mills both for flour and boards, thanks to our good governor, Sir Peregrine Maitland, and Mr. Robinson; a bridge over the river, roads in every direction, and a regular communication with the towns in front, so that any lady and gentleman with a small annual income, and the prospect of a family, with proper management would do well here by securing a landed property for their children. All unnecessary expenses must be avoided for some time, as labour and necessaries are high-priced—I mean clothing, provisions, &c., particularly if a man cannot work himself or if his family are not able to assist him. A settler in this country, though he may have an income, must do all he can to assist in getting on the work; and he must come here with the full determination to become a farmer to all intents and purposes. The lady must be a good economist and housekeeper; and if she is willing, contented, and reasonable she will have it in her power to save her husband many an hour of anxiety and pain.

Try to surmount all difficulties; and as there is always constant employment for both head and hands, never for a moment let your mind dwell on your apparent unpleasant situation; look forward with hope, and all will go on well, no danger.

I have now given you a short account of our sojourn of five years in this new country; and though we have had some little difficulties, and some anxieties, yet we are as happy and contented as any others in the country, or perhaps as we could be any where; we certainly regret the loss of the society of our distant friends, yet we consider the step we took in coming here was that of duty to our children. My property here will become valuable in time; and the great pleasure of still living under the protection and care of the British Government, though last, is not the least of the many blessings we enjoy.

It would be a most desirable thing to have a few thousand English and Scots settlers amongst us, particularly the latter as they are so steady, industrious, and moral. Douro settlers are at present all Irish, and though doing very well, yet, from their former indolent habits, they have not exerted themselves as much as they might, being addicted to taking a little too much whisky, and by doing so lose a great deal of time. A great improvement would arise from the settlers of the different parts of Great Britain intermarrying; and any differences which might have existed would soon wear away. The Scots have all got more or less education, and think it a disgrace not to have their children taught the common rudiments of learning. This is apt to be neglected in a new country from the excuse of want of time, for a child even of five years old may be of great use to its parents; but if the country were better settled, so as to reduce the price of labour, parents could then hire assistance and spare their children to go to school.

A thousand arguments might be produced in favour of mixing English and Scots settlers with the Irish here, not so much for their mode of farming as from the good example they would give of sobriety, regularity, morality, and steadiness; not fond of visiting, card-playing, carousing, or party spirit. As for farming, the best and only way (if settlers want to succeed in the back-woods) is to follow the methods of the Americans, as they are our masters in these matters. I am sure I speak the sentiments of all who have succeeded in those parts when I say that great benefits would arise from a number of Scots emigrants being introduced amongst the Irish. We have a few in some of the neighbouring townships. They are proverbial for good conduct in every way, and every one wishes to employ them in preference to others. For the first two years I never was without one or two, and sometimes four. I found them industrious, obliging, and honest, and free from presumption—they were very superior to the Irish or even the English. Mind, I am an Irishman myself!

I hope what I have said is something to the purpose. And believe me, my dear sir,

Yours, &c.

3. Captain Charles Rubidge (1786–1873)

Captain Rubidge, one of the early settlers of Otonabee Township, entered the Navy as a boy of nine in 1796 and served under Nelson and other commanders until 1815, narrowly escaping death in several engagements. Like many others in the Services, he was discharged at the end of the war. Finding no opportunity for further service he emigrated to Upper Canada in 1819, stayed in Cobourg over the winter with his old friend Captain Boswell, and on the 8th of May, 1820, took his wife and three children into 'the bush' of Otonabee, the second settler[1] in the township. 'During

[1]With reference to the first, George Kent, Caroline Rubidge Dunsford wrote this note in her copy of her father's *Autobiographical Sketch*: "who had a wife & one son & one daughter, John Kent & Sarah Kent." This copy of the rare booklet is in the possession of Mrs. Kathleen (Sibbald) Lloyd, Cobourg, whose husband was a great-grandson of Captain Rubidge.

my long residence in Canada I have filled many honourable situations in the County', he wrote in *An Autobiographical Sketch* (Peterborough, 1870), and among them was his capable supervision of the settling of the Peter Robinson Irish in 1825, as well as thousands of subsequent settlers in 1831 and 1839. During this period he published *A Plain Statement of the Advantages Attending Emigration to Upper Canada* (London, 1838). He died in 1873. One of his daughters, Caroline Maud (Mrs. Gartley Dunsford) wrote a number of annotations in her copy of the *Autobiographical Sketch*, among them the following: 'Died Feb^{ry} 5th 1873 . . . Had my Father lived four years longer he would have been an Admiral by Seniority'; 'Was married the 20th of Jan^{ry} 1810 to my dear Mother Margaret Clarke. . . . My mother was the handsomest woman I ever saw—she was the belle of Kensington in her youth.'; 'My mother, two little brothers, & sister came to the log house when in this state & the ladder by which they got aloft had to be pulled up at night to keep the bears out—my dear Mother's experience was something truly wonderful, for an English lady—such hardships she had to endure. My loved Father helping her in every way possible. He was a man in ten thousand.—his daughter loved him dearly, C. M. Rubidge Dunsford.'

CAPTAIN CHARLES RUBIDGE TO CAPTAIN BASIL HALL

[*Hall,* Travels in North America . . . *Vol. I, pp. 325–339*]

When I was residing near Swansea in South Wales I happened one day to be dining at the house of an esteemed friend, when the conversation commenced by some one, after dinner, speaking about the Canadas, the probable chance of mending our fortunes, providing for our families, and mode of proceeding. At the time it appeared mere conversation. However, it made such a deep impression on us all that from that day we never met without renewing the subject, reading every work we could procure, both on these Provinces and the United States of America, and gaining what information we could from every person who had ever been in Canada. My brother shortly afterwards removed to Swansea, in order to accompany my friends, who had also made up his mind to emigrate; but a severe domestic loss prevented the former from going and changed his views: but I had come to the determination to go to Canada; for I found that with a limited income of L.100 a-year it was impossible to maintain, with proper respectability, that situation in life which my profession called for. My family consisted of a wife and three children, from seven to three years old.

Thus having made my mind up, in the winter of 1818, I began to make preparations by disposing of my household furniture, reserving for myself beds, bedding, carpets, and such other things as were portable and like to be useful. I also made arrangements for borrowing the sum of L.200. Arrived at Bristol I procured a variety of tools, implements of husbandry, clothing, &c., to the amount of L.100, and laid in a good stock of provisions and every thing like to make the voyage comfortable across the Atlantic.

We sailed on the 3d of May, 1819, and after a tedious voyage to Quebec, and some detention afterwards in getting up the country, we arrived at the village of Cobourg in the district of Newcastle on the 19th of July. The whole of my expenses for voyage, provisions, and all other travelling charges amounted to L.100, 8s., so that on my arrival I had a very small sum left. However, my quarter's pay came round, I was in a cheap country, and, moreover, found a most warm and hospitable reception in the house of my old and esteemed friend. As a new township on the Rice Lake was about being surveyed, and I had not means to purchase a cleared farm near my friend, I determined to wait till the survey was finished and try the Bush—as the woods here are called. This was in the month of December of the same year. I then obtained the grant of land my rank in the naval service entitled me to. In February 1820 I contracted with two men to put me up a log-house, 28 feet by 20, and thirteen logs, or as many feet, high; to roof it with shingles, and to board up the gable ends; and to clear off one acre about the house to prevent the trees from falling on it, for all which I paid them 100 dollars. This shell of a building had merely a doorway cut out of the middle; and when my friend and the clergyman of Hamilton drove out in a single sleigh with me to see it, and we took our dinner at one end and our horse at the other on a miserably cold day in the month of March, it looked wretched enough; but as it was the first but one, so it was the last in the township. Whilst the snow and ice were good I moved all my effects, got boards sufficient to finish my house, and a six months' stock of provisions out; and on the 8th of May took my family into their pile of logs in a Canadian forest.

I will own, for a time our situation appalled me, and to my then unformed judgment in Bush matters it seemed a hopeless struggle; but I was out with my family, and as I did not want for energy I set to work in earnest. To two Americans I let a job to chop four acres and a half at six dollars an acre; and at the same time a man whom I had occasionally employed at home followed me out and came to hire. During the course of the summer he felled and chopped up three acres more: my cleared acre I planted with potatoes, a little corn, and turnips: my stock consisted of a cow and yoke of steers three years old, with the management of which I was totally unacquainted when I bought them; but if a man will give his mind to any common thing of the kind, and not think it a hardship, it is surprising what he may do, as in this case after a few days I found no difficulty.

I was now anxious to get my house made habitable as soon as possible, and a carpenter being employed not far off I endeavoured to engage him to put in the windows and door; but finding that he wished to take advantage of my situation, I determined to do it myself, and thus was forced to learn the business of a carpenter. This I considered no hardship, as I had always been fond of the use of tools, and had, previous to my leaving England, taken several lessons in turning. During the summer I got my house chinked, or filled the interstices between the logs with pieces of wood to make the inside flush or smooth, and to prevent the mud used as plaster on the outside from coming through. I then put in the windows and door, laid the floors, and partitioned off the lower part of the house into two good rooms, on wet days employing my man to dig a cellar under the house; in short, before the winter I had made the log-house comfortable within, and, with the addition of some white-wash, smart without.

In August we cut some coarse grass in a beaver meadow close by, sprinkling salt through the little stack as we made it; after this we logged up and cleared three acres of the land I had chopped, and by the latter end of September had it sown with wheat; the logging, though heavy, I did with my hired man and steers, and before the winter had it fenced with rails. Here, it may be remarked, I did not get much land cleared, but by doing little, and that partly with my own hands, I gained experience; and I would strongly advise gentlemen settling in Canada with small means to commence clearing slowly, and with as little expense as possible.

In the fall, or autumn, I put up a log-kitchen, and a shed for my cattle; during the winter I employed my man in chopping three acres more, in which I now and then assisted him and soon became very expert in the use of the axe, felling the trees to the most advantage to assist their burning and to save trouble in logging. With my beaver-meadow hay and the fir tops of the fallen trees my cattle were kept fat all the winter. In the spring three acres more were cleared, fenced, and cropped with corn, potatoes, and turnips; and where log heaps had been burnt, the ashes were hoed off, and planted with melons and cucumbers; a small patch was fenced off for a nursery and apple seeds sown—trees which are now ten and twelve feet high. I also put out several of the wild plum-trees of the country, which now bear abundance of fine fruit.

From this time about five acres yearly have been added to my farm, taking great care, in clearing off my land, never to destroy a log that would make rails, by which means the fence always came off the field cleared; and although they are small—from four to six acres—the fences are all six feet or nine rails high. Here, I will remark, it is a great fault to split rails small, an error that most new settlers persist in. In the spring of 1822 my attention was turned to making a flower and kitchen garden. Round the latter I made a straight fence with cedar posts and thirteen rails high, which is at this day stocked with every kind of fruit tree to be had in the neighbourhood, which flourish beyond my expectation. My stock of animals have been gradually increasing, and to my other stock I have added horses and sheep, with poultry of all kinds.

In the year 1825 I had repaid the money I borrowed, by leaving back a small part of my half pay every quarter, and had received a deed for 600 acres of my land, on which I had performed the settlement duty, which cost me L.30. My farm is now increasing to 36 acres. I have the deed for the remaining 200 acres of my land; also deeds for town and park lots in the rapidly-settling town of Peterborough; and as my family have increased to six, and are growing up, I am just now about building a frame-house, 36 feet by 26 in the clear, two stories high, with a commodious kitchen behind, the timber and shingles for which I have bought by disposing of a mare after using her for five years and breeding a pair of horses from her. With my own exertions—being able to do most of the carpenter's work inside—and about L.100, I expect to get it finished.

Some of my first chopped land is now nearly clear of stumps. I am planting out an orchard of apple-trees, raised from the seed sown by myself; have a good barn, and stable, with various other offices;—in short, feel that I have surmounted every difficulty. A town is growing up near me, roads are improving, bridges are built; one of the best mills in the province is just finished at Peterborough, another within three miles of me. Boards, and all descriptions of lumber, are cheap—about five dollars 1000 feet, four saw-mills being in operation. Stores, a tannery, distillery, and many other useful businesses, are established, or on the eve of being so, at Peterborough; on the road to which, through Otanabee, the Land Company, the clergy, and some private individuals, have some of the best land in the province for sale, at from 7s. 6d. to 10s. per acre. The price of land generally, except on the roads, is about 5s. per acre.

I was the first settler in the township, and almost before a tree was cut down; now there are nearly two thousand acres cleared, and 125 families, consisting of 500 souls. On parallel lines, at the distance of three quarters of a mile apart, roads, of from 33 to 66 feet wide, are cut and cleared out by the parties owning the land all through the township, which will ultimately be of the greatest benefit, and are so now to those settlers near them. They have been much cavilled at, and found fault with, by land speculators, and persons having large grants; but I never yet heard an actual settler complain of them. One great objection urged against them was, that a second growth of trees would spring up along these cleared avenues, or roads, and be worse than that removed; but, from strict observation, I find this fallacious, as the second growth is always a different wood, generally poplar, cherry, elder, &c., with sprouts from some of the old stumps, and so thick that they cannot come to any size; while every year there is destroying, by slow but sure means, stumps that will take 20 or 30 years to get rid of. . . .

Having been in the neighbourhood of the last emigrants brought out by the Honourable Peter Robinson,[1] who deserves the highest praise for his humanity, consideration, and care in settling them, and having read some of the Reports of the Committee on Emigration, I beg leave to offer an idea that strikes me on the subject. From observation, I think the Government did too much for those already out, and still the Committee propose to do too much for any that may be sent out; they are not left to find resources from their own industry and energy. While the rations last, many of the emigrants make little exertion, and dispose of food they have not been used to, such as pork, for whisky, thereby injuring their constitutions and morals, and fixing for a time habits of idleness. Let the settlers be put on their land with a shanty up; give a family of five persons, five barrels of flour and one of pork, with two axes and two hoes, and, with this assistance, let them work their way. During the time Mr. Robinson's last settlers were getting rations, labourers' wages were higher than they had ever been known except during the war. This certainly would not have been the case if they had been less lavishly supplied. An ablebodied man that is industrious, will never want for work in Upper Canada; and, if he will work, he will in a very short time get himself a cow, grain, potatoes, &c. &c. . . .

Respectable yeomen, or small farmers, having sufficient to settle themselves and support their families, if they go on wild land for two years, will, with industry, always do well. Certainly, having L.100 clear when they have paid a seventh of the purchase money for 200 acres, they will, before that sum is expended, raise sufficient for their future

[1]This is a modest statement for a man who was so diligent in settling the Peter Robinson Irish. Among those who assisted Captain Rubidge were Wesley Ritchie and Captain John Armstrong, subsequent Douro settlers. Captain Rubidge superintended the settlement of the English emigration to Dummer in 1831, and of the Irish in 1839.

maintenance; but in all cases, much of what is required depends on what persons have been used to, and the sacrifices they will make for a short time, to acquire property and become independent. Mechanics of all descriptions will do well, and indeed any one used to labour, or who will be industrious. Some of the best settlers in this township were at home weavers. But tradesmen, or shop-keepers of ruined fortune, if they do ill at home, will do worse here; and let all persons who will not put their hand to every thing, who feel discouraged at trifles, and who expect any thing like a life of idleness, beware how they make the trial of settling in a new country. My opinions are founded on observation and practical knowledge, and in giving them, though in a very homely and jumbled manner, still I have endeavoured to give the true statement, and, I trust, just recommendations; and I shall feel gratified and happy, if Captain Hall can cull any thing from what I have written that may benefit the public or a single individual, or be the means of doing even a small good to this happy and thriving province.

I remain, sir,
Yours most truly.

4. A Journey to Peterborough and the "Back Townships"

[*Letter of 'C.K.' in the* Cobourg Star, *October 9, 1833*, et seq.]

The township of Otonabie is improving rapidly and possesses 'capabilities' that would render it a rich and favorite township, did not the intervention of the Rice Lake very much tend to interrupt the communication with the front. The opening of the Trent navigation will do great things for Otonabie.

Several respectable gentlemen from the United Kingdom have purchased cultivated farms there this summer and, I learn, are highly pleased with their situations. The farms on the road between Anderson's and Peterboro' are assuming a very interesting appearance, particularly those situated on the last six miles of the route. The road for the last distance is in excellent order—quite as good as our front roads—and everything, indeed, bears the impress of great prosperity.

With the exception of Rubidge's and Connin's, two excellent houses, and all around them smiling with cultivation, I did not observe any frame buildings—they do not appear to be in vogue in Otonabie, a circumstance which to my particular taste is not to be regretted; for a good log house is far more warm, comfortable, and picturesque in the forest than a raw, gray, weather-boarded frame house, which, unpainted (as such houses commonly are), looks very cold and uncomfortable. Many of the farms are rid of the ugly-looking stumps; while the extensive

Courtesy George M. Douglas

[39] ELIZABETH AND JOHN CLAGUE
Clague was an old sailor and primitive artist, his wife "the family doctor of Dummer Township"

Courtesy George M. Douglas John Clague

[40] "THE BOY HARRY BLUFF SHOT WHEN THE COLOURS OF OLD ENGLAND HE NAILED TO THE MAST. BATTLE OF TRAFALGAR"

Photograph by George M. Douglas

[41] JOHN CLAGUE'S FORT ROYAL, STONEY LAKE
The old sea-dog filled his Fort with paintings of flags, birds, animals, and people recalled from his service on the seven seas. His cannon may be seen above the roof, but the sentries who once mounted guard were gone when this photograph was taken in 1908

Photograph by George M. Douglas

[42] THE *EMPIRE*
First government steamer on the Trent Canal

Courtesy Miss Phyllis Denne

[43] CHEMONG FLOATING BRIDGE
To avoid the long way around the lake

Courtesy Miss Phyllis Denne

[44] CHEMONG PARK BUS AND HOTEL

Photograph by George M. Douglas

[45] THE *MAJESTIC* AT YOUNG'S POINT

Courtesy Miss Phyllis Denne

[46] THE *OGEMAH,* BOBCAYGEON, 1890

Courtesy Miss Phyllis Denne

[47] THE *SUNBEAM,* Stoney Lake, 1872

Courtesy Miss Phyllis Denne

[48] THE DREDGE *McCLINTOCK,* OTONABEE RIVER

Courtesy Miss Phyllis Denne

[49] THE *WHISTLE-WING,* RICE LAKE

Courtesy of the family

Edward Caddy

[50] STONEY LAKE IN THE EIGHTEEN-FIFTIES

Courtesy Miss Phyllis Denne

[51] PETERBOROUGH COUNTY COUNCIL, 1863

Rear row: 3rd and 4th are J. J. Hall and J. A. Hall, auditors, and 6th is Stephen Norton, jailer

Middle row: Reeve P. M. Grover of Asphodel, Reeve Evans Ingram of Otonabee, Reeve Peter Pearse of Belmont (Warden of the County), Deputy Reeve Isaac Garbutt of Smith, Reeve John Walton of Smith, Reeve Cornelius Sullivan of Ennismore.

Front row: 1—Assistant County Clerk Edgcumbe Pearce, 2—Reeve George Lockie of North Monaghan, 3—unknown, 4—Registrar of Deeds Charles Rubidge, 5—County Clerk and Treasurer Walter Sheridan, 6 and 7—unknown, 8—Deputy Reeve Andrew Nelson of Otonabee, 9—Deputy Reeve R. E. Birdsall of Asphodel, 10—Mayor Charles Perry of Peterborough.

Courtesy Miss Phyllis Denne

[52] AN EARLY PETERBOROUGH FIRE BRIGADE

clearings, the large out-houses, and numerous cattle and pigs denote a degree of improvement and increase in worldly means truly gratifying. . . .

Peterborough is a fast-rising, prosperous, and very extensive village, occupying in proportion to the number of its houses a large extent of ground. It is full of bustling merchants and aptly provided stores. A rich and populous country surrounds it on every side, and the neighbouring farmers find it a ready and excellent market. . . . Last year 4,000 emigrants were sent to the Newcastle District, most of whom were settled in the back townships.

Peterborough possesses all the repulsive features incident to the new and fast-thriving towns of this country. The first arrangement which displeases the eye on walking through it is the singularly straggling position of the houses. The streets are, I am ready to believe, laid out according to some preconceived and fixed plan, but the outlines are so ill-developed that it would puzzle the penetration of La Place himself to define their contemplated direction by any calculations derived from the position of the houses. The next offence to all ideas of neatness or beauty arises from the regiments of deplorable looking pine stumps, standing like sentinels round almost every house in the out-skirts of the place. But such things are easily tolerated, and are perhaps unavoidable in a town which has sprung up, as it were, in a night, from the silence and solitude of the wilderness.

However, there is one intolerable nuisance—the more offensive because unnecessary—which gives a desolate appearance to the part of the town where it is situated—I allude to the stagnant pond near Mr. Murphy's store. It is a great eyesore, and little conducive to the health of the inhabitants; but such is the *inexplicabilis vis* of the love of mill-dams that, although this is situated in the centre of the place, no consideration on the score of beauty or healthiness can possibly lead to its removal. Oh! for a breath to utter what I think of such practices!

Most of the town is pleasantly situated, and some parts are really beautiful. The neat little villas perched on the hill above Mr. Hall's extensive establishment particularly attracted my attention, and the situation of McFadden's Tavern is still more attractive—a situation, indeed, of which a nobleman might well be proud—the broad, rapid, glittering Otonabie rolls its clear waters by the very door of the tavern, and at a short distance beyond divides to surround a thickly wooded islet—green to the water's edge. 'The world of eye and ear' is greatly narrowed by the interminable forests which literally girdle in and overshadow Peterborough. As the woods are cleared around, the prospect from the upper part of the village will be exceedingly picturesque.

The number of inhabitants are 850. Prosperity and plenty are settling among them. The accommodations at the taverns about the same as at Cobourg, if that be any commendation, and the daily demands on your pocket also the same. Everyone is very civil and obliging and apparently alive to the warmest hospitality. It is with pride and satisfaction that I hear from every person the most pleasing remark on the general tone of society here—so truly British in its feelings, habits, and manners. Long may such feelings spread and flourish among the prosperous people of Peterborough—who, by the by, are singularly proud of their village, and jealous of any remarks derogatory to its character. . . . The sudden rise of Peterboro' is truly astonishing. . . . The chief emporium of the back settlements, it promises in a few years to be one of the largest and richest towns in the province. . . .

The village of Bridgenorth is at present in *puris naturalibus*. We found there, it is true, an exceedingly neat and comfortable Tavern, but, *mirabile dictu*, it is the only house in the village. It is kept by Dore. . . . On entering we received a hearty and noisy welcome from our shrewd host, and found ourselves in the midst of a jovial party of mechanics, who were laughing and carousing around a bright fire. . . .

Our bustling hostess . . . quickly prepared us an excellent dinner, consisting of fowls (which, by-the-bye, we shot for her), warm bread, butter as yellow as butter-cups, eggs with savoury ham, and everything betokening the Land of Plenty instead of the confines of barbaric life. . . .

CHEMONG is an extensive lake lying between Ennismore and Smith (two populous and wealthy townships—the latter containing a population of a thousand souls). It is long, narrow, and shallow, with an extremely muddy bottom. The country round is hilly and varied, with several clearings on the lake shore. . . . After rowing four or five miles we came in sight of the Indian village, situated on the point of a long tongue of land that separates Buckhorn Lake from Lake Chemong. The village looks pretty and picturesque, but there are few evidences of prosperity perceivable among its red inhabitants. . . . This village was formed under the superintendence of Elder Scott, who deserves great credit for the pains he has taken in the worldly and spiritual interests of his red proteges. The number of Mud Lake Indians were about 100, but John Iron, Chief of the Mud Lake Indians, having received under his protection John Crane, Chief of about 60 Scugog Indians, has added considerably to their number.

The Indian village [Chemong] is the landmark by which to discover the channel leading to BUCKHORN LAKE, as it forms the northern bank of the entrance of that channel. The route then lies directly N.W. until you arrive at the second log house, inhabited by one Bill M'Cue, a distance of about three miles from the Indian village, and from which a second departure may be taken, observing to turn a bold point and broad channel to the north, at about the eighth of a mile from Billy's house. Here a most beautiful lake opened upon us—STURGEON LAKE. . . .

Captain Nichol's is the only house we saw or heard of in Harvey, bordering on the Lake shore, and the lots around it the only tolerable land we observed. . . . The Lake shores are rocky and covered with dwarf pines and ragged scrubby oaks—in appearance very sterile and repulsive. We were kindly treated at the Captain's; his servant, a stout, honest, simple-minded Irishman, was delighted to see us, (for visitors there, we found, were few and far between, with little to break the monotony of a backwoods-man's life—not even a cow or pig for his companion)—on a Sunday his only pleasure is to sit by the lakeshore all alone, pensively gazing o'er the lake till he is wearied, and then return to his shanty to think of the olden times and of old Ireland. We were invited to shake down our blankets in the shanty, which we did. . . .

It was one of the most beautiful evenings I have ever witnessed, and its loveliness might have challenged Windermere and her peaceful isles. The calm seclusion, the bright waters, glittering and spangling in the rays of the sun and all speckled with innumerable islands; the leafy woods, varied by the splendid countless tints of autumn, with the pine 'grouping their dark hues with every stain', formed a scene I shall never forget. . . . We kindled a fire, threw our wearied limbs on our blankets, and welcomed repose.

5. Captain George Arundel Hill (1796–1861)

To have been a man of importance in his generation and almost entirely forgotten a lifetime later was the fate of Captain Hill of Dummer Township. The son of Arundel and Catharine Hill of Limerick, Ireland, he was born in 1796 and served as an officer nineteen years later under Wellington at Waterloo. It was appropriate, consequently, that among his literary efforts was the poem 'Verses for the Twenty-fourth Anniversary of the Battle of Waterloo'. Like many another veteran, Hill had commuted his pension for land in Upper Canada, and like many another too, his farm two or three miles east of Clear Lake proved so rocky and untillable that, when his family were through with it, it was abandoned, and remains so to the present. Arriving in Dummer in 1831, he had entered with vigour into the life of the pioneer. Three years later there appeared from his hand a 56-page pamphlet with the quaint title *A Guide for Emigrants from the British Shores to the Woods of Canada.*[1] In his later years he became not only a radical in politics but an eccentric in religion, and in the Lindsey Papers, University of Toronto Library, is a lengthy manuscript in a copper-plate hand which he had apparently tried to get Charles Lindsey to publish. A hint from an old Dummer resident led to a search on his lot for his grave, and in a rail-fence enclosure, without a stone or any distinguishing mark, lie the remains of Captain Hill, veteran of Waterloo, pioneer settler and eminent official, educationist, author, and first Warden of the District of Colborne.

BUILDING THE LOG HOUSE

[*Hill,* A Guide for Emigrants from the British Shores to the Woods of Canada (*Dublin, 1834*), *pp. 25–8*]

In selecting a site for your house, do not forget that a good fall from the front will serve to carry off the melting snow in the spring; as well as the water from the heavy thunder showers which you may expect in summer. Before you lay one log over another, I remind you to have every tree felled, which, if left uncut, could afterwards reach the intended dwelling. It would be still better, if time allowed you, to get a space of the forest of forty or fifty yards square burnt off before the shanty was commenced; and then, and then only, can it be perfectly safe. This precaution, however, seems seldom attended to by new settlers; sometimes, perhaps, from impatience to see their woodland residence in progress, but still oftener from ignorance of the serious risk incurred by neglecting it. After a little dry weather the branches of the trees, if they have been cut for a few weeks, will with a very slight breeze burn most furiously, assisted by the thick coat of leaves on the surface of the ground; and, should the running fire take its course towards the newly-erected edifice, you will have something to do to save it from the devouring element. I am not myself a 'burnt child', but was too near being so not to 'dread the fire'. My shanty had been up some months when the burning of the brush and timber of my clearance was commenced, and it required the utmost exertions of four persons to prevent its being destroyed. The smoke and heat were so suffocating and intolerable that my family was obliged to take refuge for two hours in the cellar; and from the circumstance of the fire having completely sur-

[1]Published in Dublin in 1834. After years of search in Britain and America we found a copy in the Canadiana collection of J. G. Ketcheson, Richmond Hill. Photostatic copies are in the Public Archives at Ottawa and the Toronto Public Library.

rounded the premises it would have been very difficult to have removed our things to a place of safety, had it been necessary to make the attempt. I would therefore repeat the advice to new settlers, to chop down and burn off at once one acre of the forest immediately about the spot where he intends to put up his house; but should he have neglected doing so, and that he comes afterwards to enter into a contract with some person for clearing a certain quantity of his land, let him take the consequence if he does not make it a condition in their written agreement that he is to be indemnified for the loss he may sustain, should his house (or shanty) be consumed when the clearance is being burnt off.

Personal observation will give you a clearer idea of the manner in which shanties are put together than could be obtained from any detail of mine; still, I conceive, you may derive advantage from a sketch of such an operation. Your inexperience will very naturally lead you to leave a great deal to the men you have employed, and more largely so if you have good men who are used to such kind of work; but if you shut your own eyes altogether, and totally decline the suggestions of your own judgment, I will prophesy you will regret having done so.

Having decided on the extent and plan of the edifice, your men proceed to hew down such trees, convenient to the intended site, as are of a proper thickness. The straighter these are the better; and if cedars can be procured without much difficulty they should be chosen. Maples are said to decay very soon—in some cases after five or six years; but though it might be impossible to make them last for a great length of time, I suspect the true cause of the so rapid decay of the shanties alluded to was their having been constantly soaking water, whenever rain fell, from the gross laziness or neglect of the persons who occupied them.

The trees are now cut into the proper lengths and collected together. Digging for a foundation is of course never thought of. Having placed two end logs in the places where they are to remain, a man with an axe, within a few inches of the extreme ends of each, puts a kind of cut, whose breadth is the diameter of the letter V turned upside down; the under sides of a front and rere log are then cut, like the said letter V, so as to lie close on the end logs, and thus they become, as it were, locked together. A similar operation is repeated—two end and two side logs—until the wooden walls have attained the required height, when the door and window spaces are cut away. If the trees have been carefully selected, so as to be as nearly of one size and as straight as possible, there will be little trouble or difficulty in laying the logs so as almost to touch each other in every part; and though some of your men will endeavour to persuade you that this is a matter of no consequence, and that it is the easiest thing in the world to ram in a piece of basswood into the chinks, mind them not. You have now to get up the roof, which for a shanty is made by splitting the straightest basswood trees in two, and after they have been hollowed out with axes, placing them, the hollow part up, side by side, and as closely together as you can, so that the ends will rest on the upper back and front logs. To prevent rain getting through, other troughs, similarly prepared, are placed one over every joint, with the concave side under, and the roof is finished.

I strongly recommend you to have the sides of these under troughs made quite straight, which can easily be done by the assistance of a black-line. This will spare you much trouble afterwards, and render it an easy matter to make the joints impervious to the cool air of winter. Here again the workmen will exclaim against your unusual nicety; but remember that it is your own wife and your own children who are to spend the approaching winter under that roof, and be resolved to make them as comfortable as you can.

If you are anxious to have your family in their new habitation as soon as possible, they may now come into it. The weather, until the middle of November, will render a slight curtain tacked up at night, a sufficient substitute for glazed sashes; and the good behaviour of your neighbours, should you happen to have any, will cause any stronger door to be quite unnecessary.

You will then have leisure to make, or get made, by degrees, any articles of household furniture you require, and whatever you judge proper for finishing your shanty.

Under this last head your fire-places and chimneys claim the first attention. For a short time you may perhaps find it expedient to imitate a very general plan among new settlers—just to place a few large stones loosely against that part where a fire is to be made, in order to prevent the logs of the shanty from igniting; and let a square hole in the roof serve as a chimney. If, however, time and circumstances allow it, it will be better to do at once what must otherwise be shortly done, and get a stone chimney put up.

It may happen that you will be advised, as I was, to put up a wooden chimney, well plastered within and without. Such are in pretty general use, and may answer very well where a constant or strong fire is not required. Still I cannot recommend them, as, let their construction be ever so perfect, they are certainly exposed to the danger of catching fire sooner or later; and the consciousness of this danger will often come upon you, while enjoying a roaring fire of a cold night, like a bitter breeze from the north.

If you can at once burn some limestone, well and good; but you are not without an excellent substitute for lime mortar by mixing together two parts of woodashes with one of red earth, which is found by removing the surface stratum of black vegetable mould. Lime is burned here in kilns, pretty similar to those of the old country; but it is also made in a simpler manner. The stones, well broken, are placed on the top of a large heap, which is then set on fire, and if the logs are gross enough, and piled very close together, you will have plenty of excellent lime in a few hours.

Should there be no saw-mill within a reasonable distance you will find that boards can be procured by splitting basswood, cedar, or pine; they will at least make a tolerable floor, doors, &c. An adze here will be a very useful tool, as by means of it you can make such boards nearly as fair as if they had been sawn, and smooth enough to require no planing.

6. A Visit to Douro Township, 1836

[*James Logan*, Notes of a Journey through Canada, the United States, and the West Indies (*Edinburgh, 1838*), *pp. 44–6*]

Next morning, at six, we reached Coburg, which is a hundred and seventy miles distant from Brockville. The fare from Montreal to Prescott was £1, 10s., and from the latter place to Coburg £1, 5s.

Having hired a horse from Mr Strong of the American Hotel, near the pier, I joined Mr Thomson and a Mr Hickston, an Irishman, whom we met at the hotel, and started for Peterborough. About a mile from Coburg, which, like most of the places on this route, is a neat small town, is the county-hall and jail, a rather handsome stone building. We passed several well cultivated farms and saw a number of excellent fields of wheat and oats. The road, however, was very bad, there being no stones on it and numberless ruts. About eighteen miles from Coburg we came to a clearing in the forest, which is an Irish settlement, and dined at a small inn.[1] Farther on were several farms on which were good crops. Peterborough, which is thirty-five miles from Coburg, is very romantically situated on a rising ground overlooking the river Ottanabe, which runs into Rice Lake. After remaining there a few hours I crossed the river by a ferry-boat which the current carries across, it being attached to a wheel running along a rope stretched over the river, and arrived at Mr S. Cunningham's, where I staid all night.

I remained in the Newcastle district nine days, principally in the township of Duro, where several of my friends were settled. One day I called on Mr Traill, whose lady has published an account of Canada,

[1]Joseph Graham's Tavern, now Bailieboro.

and another day went with Mr Carnegie to a *logging-bee* at his neighbour F.'s. There were about six acres to log, and he had collected about twenty of his neighbours, or their servants, as those who could not work were obliged to find substitutes. There were five yokes of oxen, and generally four, but sometimes only three, men to a yoke, with a boy to drive. To the yoke over the necks of the oxen is fastened a long chain, with a hook at the end, and this chain is put round a log, which is thus dragged to the pile. Two of my friends, myself, and a servant were attached to one of the yokes, which was driven by a boy. When the logs, which vary from ten to fifteen feet in length and from one to two and a half in diameter, were brought to the pile we laid them on in a proper manner. After the first layer was arranged the rest of the logs were hoisted on with handspikes; the heaps vary from four to five feet in height, and are not made too large so as to burn with facility. This is a very laborious part of the operation, especially when the logs are heavy; and if they should slip you are in danger of getting your leg broken or even of losing your life. We worked hard all day from nine, and logged about three acres. At one we had dinner in the barn, masters and servants together without distinction. Two young Englishmen were present but did not assist, and were therefore laughed at. They disliked the country after three years' trial and were on their way home. In the evening we had a dance and were otherwise agreeably entertained until one in the morning, when we walked home, but were entangled in a wood, where we groped about for two hours although the distance we had to go was only half a mile. On another occasion I visited Lake Clear, where three of us lay out in a deserted shantie, the smallest description of log-house, resembling in shape a pig-stye, baked our bread, and roasted potatoes. The scenery of this lake is very beautiful, and its numerous wooded islands, its romantic banks, and dense forests, inhabited by woodpeckers and other gaudy birds, wolves, and squirrels, merit a more extended encomium.

7. CATHARINE PARR TRAILL (1802–1899)

The eldest of the three 'literary Stricklands'[1] who emigrated to Canada, Catharine was undoubtedly the most even-tempered and least critical of her new environment. She quickly became, in fact, a lover of nature, and as a naturalist she developed a fellow-feeling for the Indians, from whom she learned much natural and tradi-

[1]Samuel Strickland's *Twenty-Seven Years in Canada West* is not among the works from which excerpts are given in this Section, but he and his book are given adequate attention in the Introduction.

tional lore. Her botanical descriptions are consequently her greatest contribution to Canadian literature. Among her other books, *The Female Emigrant's Guide* (1854) included nature remedies, recipes, and helpful hints of various kinds to assist in adjustment to the new land.

A bibliography of Mrs. Traill's works, from 1818 when at the age of sixteen she produced a small volume of children's stories in England, to 1895 when her last book, *Cot and Cradle Stories*, appeared, would be a lengthy list complicated by numerous reprints under varied titles. She wrote some verse, most of which is interspersed among her prose compositions or in one or another of the newspapers and literary periodicals of the day. Her reputation, however, is based upon *The Backwoods of Canada* (1836) and her various nature studies such as *Canadian Wild Flowers* (1868).

In 1832, prior to emigration to Canada, she married Lieutenant Thomas Traill, and they first resided at Lakefield, where her brother Samuel was living. Suffering the various vicissitudes of pioneer life, they subsequently lived in Ashburnham and on the shores of Rice Lake, but her long life as a widow (her husband died in 1859) was spent at 'Westove', Lakefield, or at 'Minnewawa', her island in Stoney Lake. She died on August 29, 1899, 'a cultured and gifted lady' as the obituary notice in the *Peterborough Examiner* put it, and one whose life and writings did much to raise the tone of cultural and intellectual life in Canada.

(*a*) JOURNEY FROM COBOURG TO DOURO TOWNSHIP, 1832

[*Catharine Parr Traill*, The Backwoods of Canada . . ., *pp. 55* et seq.]

We left Cobourg on the afternoon of the 1st of September in a light waggon comfortably lined with buffalo robes. Our fellow-travellers consisted of three gentlemen and a young lady, all of whom proved very agreeable and willing to afford us every information respecting the country through which we were travelling. The afternoon was fine—one of those rich mellow days we often experience in the early part of September. The warm hues of autumn were already visible on the forest trees, but rather spoke of ripeness than decay. The country round Cobourg is well cultivated, a great portion of the woods having been superseded by open fields, pleasant farms, and fine flourishing orchards, with green pastures where abundance of cattle were grazing.

The county gaol and court-house at Amherst, about a mile and a half from Cobourg, is a fine stone edifice, situated on a rising ground which commands an extensive view over the lake Ontario and surrounding scenery. As you advance further up the country, in the direction of the Hamilton or Rice Lake plains, the land rises into bold sweeping hills and dales.

The outline of the country reminded me of the hilly part of Gloucestershire; you want, however, the charm with which civilization has so eminently adorned that fine county, with all its romantic villages, flourishing towns, cultivated farms, and extensive downs so thickly covered with flocks and herds. Here the bold forests of oak, beech, maple, and bass-wood, with now and then a grove of dark pine, cover the hills, only enlivened by an occasional settlement with its log-house and zig-zag fences of split timber: these fences are very offensive to my eye. I look in vain for the rich hedge-rows of my native country. Even the stone fences in the north and west of England, cold and bare as they are, are less unsightly. The settlers, however, invariably adopt whatever plan saves time, labour, and money. The great law of expediency is strictly observed—it is borne of necessity. Matters of taste appear to be little regarded, or are, at all events, after-considerations. . . .

About halfway between Cobourg and the Rice Lake there is a pretty valley between two steep hills. Here there is a good deal of cleared land and a tavern: the place is called the 'Cold Springs'. Who knows but some century or two hence this spot may become a fashionable place of resort to drink the waters. A Canadian Bath or Cheltenham may spring up where now Nature revels in her wilderness of forest trees.

We now ascended the plains—a fine elevation of land—for many miles scantily clothed with oaks, and here and there bushy pines with other trees and shrubs. The soil is in some places sandy, but varies, I am told, considerably in different parts, and is covered in large tracts with rich herbage, affording abundance of the finest pasture for cattle. A number of exquisite flowers and shrubs adorn these plains, which rival any garden in beauty during the spring and summer months. Many of these plants are peculiar to the plains, and are rarely met with in any other situation. The trees, too, though inferior in size to those in the forests, are more picturesque, growing in groups or singly at considerable intervals, giving a sort of park-like appearance to this portion of the country. The prevailing opinion seems to be that the plains laid out in grazing or dairy farms would answer the purpose of settlers well; as there is plenty of land that will grow wheat and other corn-crops and can be improved at a small expense, besides abundance of natural pasture for cattle. One great advantage seems to be that the plough can be introduced directly, and the labour of preparing the ground is necessarily much less than where it is wholly covered with wood.

There are several settlers on these plains possessing considerable farms. The situation, I should think, must be healthy and agreeable from the elevation and dryness of the land and the pleasant prospect they command of the country below them, especially where the Rice Lake, with its various islands and picturesque shores, is visible. The ground itself is pleasingly broken into hill and valley, sometimes gently sloping, at other times abrupt and almost precipitous.

An American farmer, who formed one of our party at breakfast the following morning, told me that these plains were formerly famous hunting-grounds of the Indians, who, to prevent the growth of the timbers, burned them year after year; this, in process of time, destroyed the young trees, so as to prevent them again from accumulating to the extent they formerly did. Sufficient only was left to form coverts; for the deer resort hither in great herds for the sake of a peculiar tall sort of grass with which these plains abound called deer-grass, on which they become exceedingly fat at certain seasons of the year.

Evening closed in before we reached the tavern on the shores of the Rice Lake, where we were to pass the night; so that I lost something of the beautiful scenery which this fine expanse of water presents as you descend the plains towards its shores. The glimpses I caught of it were by the faint but frequent flashes of lightning that illumined the horizon to the north, which just revealed enough to make me regret I could see no more that night. The Rice Lake is prettily diversified with small wooded islets: the north bank rises gently from the water's edge. Within sight of Sully, the tavern from which the steam-boat starts that goes up the Otanabee, you see several well-cultivated settlements; and beyond the Indian village the missionaries have a school for the education and instruction of the Indian children. Many of them can both read and write fluently, and are greatly improved in their moral and religious conduct. They are well and comfortably clothed and have houses to live in. But they are still too much attached to their wandering habits to become good and industrious settlers. During certain seasons they leave the village and encamp themselves in the woods along the borders of those lakes and rivers that present the most advantageous hunting and fishing-grounds. . . .

There are some fine settlements on the Rice Lake, but I am told the shores are not considered healthy, the inhabitants being subject to lake-fevers and ague, especially where the ground is low and swampy. These fevers and agues are supposed by some people to originate in the extensive rice-beds which cause a stagnation in the water; the constant evaporation from the surface acting on a mass of decaying vegetation must tend to have a bad effect on the constitution of those that are immediately exposed to its pernicious influence.

We left the tavern at Rice Lake, after an unusual delay, at nine o'clock. The morning was damp, and a cold wind blew over the lake, which appeared to little advantage through the drizzling rain from which I was glad to shroud my face in my warm plaid cloak, for there was no cabin or other shelter in the little steamer than an inefficient awning. This apology for a steam-boat formed a considerable contrast with the superbly-appointed vessels we had lately been passengers in on the Ontario and the St. Laurence. But the circumstances of a steamer at all on the Otanabee was a matter of surprise to us and of exultation to the first settlers along its shores, who for many years had been contented with no better mode of transport than a scow or canoe for themselves and their marketable produce, or through the worst possible roads with a waggon or sleigh.

The Otanabee is a fine broad clear stream, divided into two mouths at its entrance to the Rice Lake by a low tongue of land, too swampy to be put under cultivation. This beautiful river (for such I consider it to be) winds its way between thickly-wooded banks which rise gradually as you advance higher up the country.

Towards noon the mists cleared off, and the sun came forth in all the brilliant beauty of a September day. So completely were we sheltered from the wind by the thick wall of pines on either side that I no longer felt the least inconvenience from the cold that had chilled me on crossing the lake in the morning.

As I felt a great curiosity to see the interior of a log-house, I entered the open door-way of the tavern as the people termed it, under the pretext of buying a draught of milk. The interior of this rude dwelling presented no very inviting aspect. The walls were of rough unhewn logs, filled between the chinks with moss and irregular wedges of wood to keep out the wind and rain. The unplastered roof displayed the rafters, covered with moss and lichens, green, yellow, and grey; above which might be seen the shingles, dyed to a fine mahogany-red by the smoke which refused to ascend the wide clay and stone chimney, to curl gracefully about the roof and seek its exit in the various crannies and apertures with which the roof and sides of the building abounded.

The floor was of earth, which had become pretty hard and smooth through use. This but reminded me of the one described by the four Russian sailors that were left to winter on the island of Spitzbergen. Its furniture was of corresponding rudeness; a few stools, rough and unplaned; a deal table, which, from being manufactured from unseasoned wood, was divided by three wide open seams and was only held together by its ill-shaped legs; two or three blocks of grey granite placed beside the hearth served for seats for the children, with the addition of two beds raised a little above the ground by a frame of split cedars. On these lowly couches lay extended two poor men, suffering under the wasting effects of lake-fever. Their yellow bilious faces strangely contrasted with the gay patchwork-quilts that covered them. I felt much concerned for the poor emigrants, who told me they had not been many weeks in the country when they were seized with the fever and ague. They both had wives and small children who seemed very miserable. The wives also had been sick with ague, and had not a house or even shanty of their own up; the husbands having fallen ill were unable to do anything; and much of the little money they had brought out with them had been expended in board and lodging in this miserable place, which they dignified by the name of a tavern. I cannot say I was greatly prepossessed in favour of their hostess, a harsh, covetous woman. Besides the various emigrants, men, women, and children, that lodged within the walls, the log-house had tenants of another description. A fine calf occupied a pen in a corner; some pigs roamed grunting about in company with some half-dozen fowls. The most attractive objects were three snow-white pigeons that were meekly picking up crumbs and looking as if they were too pure and innocent to be inhabitants of such a place.

Owing to the shallowness of the river at this season, and to the rapids, the steam-boat is unable to go up the whole way to Peterborough, and a scow or row-boat, as it is sometimes termed—a huge, unwieldy, flat-bottomed machine—meets the passengers at a certain part of the river within sight of a singular pine-tree on the right bank; this is termed the 'Yankee bonnet,' from the fancied resemblance of the topmost boughs to a sort of cap worn by the Yankees, not much unlike the blue bonnet of Scotland.

Unfortunately, the steamer ran aground some four miles below the usual place of rendezvous, and we waited till near four o'clock for the scow. When it made its appearance, we found, to our discomfort, the rowers (eight in number and all Irishmen) were under the exciting influence of a cag of whiskey which they had drunk dry on the voyage. They were, moreover, exasperated by the delay on the part of the steamer, which gave them four miles additional heavy rowing. Beside a number of passengers there was an enormous load of furniture, trunks, boxes, chests, sacks of wheat, barrels of flour, salt, and pork, with many miscellaneous packages and articles, small and great, which were piled to a height that I thought very unsafe both to goods and passengers.

With a marvellous ill grace the men took up their oars when their load was completed, but declared they would go on shore and make a fire and cook their dinners, they not having eaten any food though they had taken large potations of the whiskey. This measure was opposed by some of the gentlemen and a fierce and angry scene ensued, which ended in the mutineers flinging down their oars and positively refusing to row another stroke till they had satisfied their hunger.

Perhaps I had a fellow-feeling for them, as I began to be exceedingly hungry, almost ravenous, myself, having fasted since six that morning; indeed, so faint was I that I was fain to get my husband to procure me a morsel of the coarse uninviting bread that was produced by the rowers, and which they ate with huge slices of raw pickled pork, seasoning this unseemly meal with curses 'not loud but deep,' and bitter taunts against those who prevented them from cooking their food like *Christians*.

While I was eagerly eating the bit of bread, an old farmer, who had eyed me for some time with a mixture of curiosity and compassion, said, 'Poor thing: well, you do seem hungry indeed, and I dare say are just out from the *ould* country, and so little used to such hard fare. Here are some cakes that my woman (*i.e.*, wife) put in my pocket when I left home; I care nothing for them, but they are better than that bad bread; take 'em, and welcome.' With these words he tossed some very respectable home-made seed-cakes into my lap, and truly never was anything more welcome than this seasonable refreshment.

A sullen and gloomy spirit seemed to prevail among our boatmen, which by no means diminished as the evening drew on and 'the rapids were near.' The sun had set, and the moon and stars rose brilliantly over the still waters, which gave back the reflection of this glorious multitude of heavenly bodies. A sight so passing fair might have stilled the most turbulent spirits into peace; at least so I thought as, wrapped in my cloak, I leant back against the supporting arm of my husband and, looking from the waters to the sky and from the sky to the waters, with delight and admiration. My pleasant reverie was, however, soon ended when I suddenly felt the boat touch the rocky bank, and heard the boatmen protesting they would go no further that night. We were nearly three miles below Peterborough, and how I was to walk this distance, weakened as I was by recent illness and fatigue of our long travelling, I knew not. To spend the night in an open boat, exposed to the heavy dews arising from the river, would be almost death. While we were deliberating on what to do, the rest of the passengers had made up their minds and taken the way through the woods by a road they were well acquainted with. They were soon out of sight, all but one gentleman who was bargaining with one of the rowers to take him and his dog across the river at the head of the rapids in a skiff.

Imagine our situation, at ten o'clock at night without knowing a single step of our road, put on shore to find the way to the distant town as we best could, or pass the night in the dark forest.

Almost in despair, we entreated the gentleman to be our guide as far as he went. But so many obstacles beset our path in the form of newly-chopped trees and blocks of stone scattered along the shore, that it was with the utmost difficulty we could keep him in sight. At last we came up with him at the place appointed to meet the skiff, and, with a pertinacity that at another time and in other circumstances we never should have adopted, we all but insisted on being admitted into the boat. An angry growling consent was extorted from the surly Charon, and we hastily entered the frail bark, which seemed hardly calculated to convey us in safety to the opposite shores. I could not help indulging in a feeling of indescribable fear as I listened to the torrent of profane invective that burst forth continually from the lips of the boatman. Once or twice we were in danger of being overset by the boughs of the pines and cedars which had fallen into the water near the banks. Right glad was I when we reached the opposite shores; but here a new trouble arose: there was yet more untracked wood to cross before we again met the skiff, which had to pass up a small rapid and meet us at the head of the small lake, an expansion of the Otanabee a little below Peterborough. At the distance of every few yards our path was obstructed by fallen trees, mostly hemlock, spruce, or cedar, the branches of which are so thickly interwoven that it is scarcely possible to separate them or force a passage through the tangled thicket which they form.

Had it not been for the humane assistance of our conductor, I know not how I should have surmounted these difficulties. Sometimes I was ready to sink down from very weariness. At length I hailed, with a joy I could hardly have supposed possible, the gruff voice of the Irish rower, and after considerable grumbling on his part we were again seated.

Glad enough we were to see, by the blazing light of an enormous log-heap, the house of our friend. Here we received the offer of a guide to show us the way to the town by a road cut through the wood. We partook of the welcome refreshment of tea, and having gained a little strength by a short rest we once more commenced our journey, guided by a ragged but polite Irish boy, whose frankness and good humour quite won our regards. He informed us he was one of seven orphans who had lost father and mother in the cholera. It was a sad thing, he said, to be left fatherless and motherless in a strange land; and he swept away the tears that gathered in his eyes as he told the simple but sad tale of his early bereavement; but added, cheerfully, he had met with a kind master, who had taken some of his brothers and sisters into his service as well as himself.

Just as we were emerging from the gloom of the wood we found our progress impeded by a *creek*, as the boy called it, over which he told us we must pass by a log-bridge before we could get to the town. Now the log-bridge was composed of one log, or rather a fallen tree, thrown across the stream, rendered very slippery by the heavy dew that had risen from the swamp. As the log admitted of only one person at a time I could receive no assistance from my companions; and though our little guide, with a natural politeness arising from the benevolence of his disposition, did me all the service in his power by holding the lantern close to the surface to throw all the light he could on the subject, I had the ill luck to fall in up to my knees in the water, my head turning quite giddy just as I came to the last step or two; thus was I wet as well as weary. To add to our misfortune we saw the lights disappear, one by one, in the village, till a solitary candle, glimmering from the upper chambers of one or two houses, were our only beacons. We had yet a lodging to seek, and it was near midnight before we reached the door of the principal inn; there, at least, thought I, our troubles for to-night will end; but great was our mortification on being told there was not a spare bed to be had in the house, every one being occupied by emigrants going up to one of the back townships.

I could go no further, and we petitioned for a place by the kitchen fire where we might rest, at least, if not sleep, and I might dry my wet garments. On seeing my condition the landlady took compassion on me, led me to a blazing fire, which her damsels quickly roused up; one brought a warm bath for my feet, while another provided a warm potation which, I really believe, strange and unusual to my lips as it was, did me good: in short we received every kindness and attention that we required from mine host and hostess, who relinquished their own bed for our accommodation, contenting themselves with a shake-down before the kitchen fire.

I can now smile at the disasters of *that* day, but at the time they appeared no trifles, as you may well suppose.

Farewell, my dearest Mother.

(*b*) A WALK TO RAILWAY POINT, 1853

[*'Forest Gleanings', No. XII*, Anglo-American Magazine (*Toronto*), *Vol. III, October, 1853, No. 4. By Catharine Parr Traill*]

Thirty years ago the emigrant who desired to settle himself and family in the townships north of Rice Lake, on reaching its southern shore after a weary day's journey through roads deeply cut by ruts and water-worn gullies could obtain no better mode of conveyance across its waters than what was afforded by a small skift or canoe, unless he committed himself and his worldly goods to the safer keeping of a huge, flat-bottomed ark called a scow, which usually took two whole days to perform its toilsome voyage up the long-winding Otonabee; the navigation of which in these days, and indeed for a many a long year after that time, was considerably obstructed by rapids on the spot now occupied by the fine substantial locks, which afford an easy entrance to the little lake; and may be called the key to Peterboro'.

Ten years passed on, and the wants of the traveller who was wending his way northward were met by a small steamer which plyed on Rice Lake and took passengers and goods part of the way, being met by the scow when the water was low in the river some miles below the town, at a certain part marked by a tall pine, called the *Yankee Bonnet* from its top bearing a resemblance to that article. Scanty as were the accommodations on board, the advent of this boat was hailed with infinite satisfaction, and great praise was bestowed on the spirited proprietors, gentlemen and merchants of Cobourg, who had thus met the requirements of the public and doubtlessly greatly facilitated the settlement of Peterboro' and her back country.

By degrees a better class of steamers were launched on Rice Lake. At this date no less than four are cleaving its waters and enlivening the lonely shores of the Otonabee river. And here it is but just to remark that where a public benefit is to be conferred the men of Cobourg, whatever may be their politics or private opinions, are ready to come forward heart and hand to promote the work.

Roads have been constructed to enable the traveller after crossing the winter flooring of Rice Lake to reach Peterboro' and the surrounding country by the shortest possible route, but ice is but a treacherous foundation to trust to, and moreover there are intervals in early winter before its safety has been tested, and in early spring when the sun is exerting its power over the ice-locked streams, that a total stop is put to journeys, either business or pleasure, unless by a circuitous route through the worst of roads by the head of the lake.

To meet the wants of the fast increasing population, and to enable Peterboro' to send forth her abundant stores of lumber, grain, wool, and dairy produce to a ready market, something more was required,—and lo! ere the blessing was asked it was as it were cast into her lap. No sacrifice of labour, time, or money was demanded. Let us hope that the townsmen of Peterboro' will unite in gratitude towards the enterprizing men of Cobourg, the spirited movers of this great work and national benefit—a RAILROAD AND BRIDGE ACROSS THE RICE LAKE. A work which when completed will enrich even the poorest of her backwoodsmen, and be the means of opening out a wide extent of unreclaimed forest; a field for the future labours of the industrious farmer and skilful mechanic. Will not a work like this ultimately prove more beneficial to the Colborne District than the discovery of mines of silver and gold in her vicinity?

As a lover of the picturesque I must confess that I have a great dislike to railroads. I cannot help turning with regret from the bare idea of scenes of rich rural beauty being cut up and disfigured by these intersecting veins of wrought iron, spanning the beautiful old romantic hills and rivers of my native land; but here, in this new country, there is no such objection to be made, there are no feelings connected with early associations to be rudely violated; no scenes that time has hallowed to be destroyed. Here the railroads run through dense forests where the footsteps of man have never been impressed, across swamps and morasses on which the rays of the sun have scarcely ever shone, over lonely rivers and widespread lakes that have never echoed to the dash of the oar or reflected aught on their bosoms but the varied foliage of the overhanging woods.

If little can be said in behalf of the picturesque beauty of a railway, it may be observed on the other hand that it is quite as pleasing a sight to the eye of most persons as a chaotic map of fallen pines and decaying cedars stretching across each other in wild confusion; that a rail-car is at least as sightly as an ox-cart or lumber-waggon. If its presence does not embellish, neither can it mar a country where it interferes with none of our natural beauties or ancient works of art. Nay, in future years will it not be looked upon with veneration and admiration, as were many of the public roads and viaducts of ancient Rome?

Here we have scope and verge enough to act upon, without offending the eye of taste or intruding upon any man's prejudice or taste. If the old settler be in the neighborhood of a railroad he can remove elsewhere, and dispose of his lands to great advantage: the new comer need not purchase in its vicinity if he does not value the advantages that it offers. The benefit to a new country so deficient in really good roads must be great; therefore, I say, let the work go on and prosper—let it stretch from East to West; from the shores of the Atlantic even to the Georgian Bay.

Twenty years ago the most sanguine speculator would have smiled sceptically at the suggestion of a bridge spanning the wide extent of the waters of Rice Lake,—five years ago he would have laughed at such an idea. Nay, within the last twelve months the scheme was regarded as an impossibility, and behold, it is now half completed. The difficulties have vanished before the enterprise and skill of engineers and mechanical operatives, incited by the assurance of certain remuneration from the Shareholders.

Quietly and steadily has the work progressed; the neighbourhood has not been disturbed by scenes of riot or drunkenness; there has been no bloodshed nor disorder among the hands; no man's property has been pillaged, and no one has suffered wrong; strict order has been observed, greatly to the credit of the overseers, whose respectability of conduct deserves all praise.

In a few weeks longer and the great work of pile-driving will be completed, and the shores of the Township of Hamilton and Otonabee will be linked together by an enduring monument, greatly to the credit of American ingenuity and Canadian enterprise. Were I as well skilled in the science of political economy as Miss Martineau I might have enlarged on all the advantages to be derived from the railroad, but I must leave it to wiser heads than mine to discuss such matters.

It was on a bright summer afternoon, in the early part of July, that, accompanied by my eldest daughter and some young friends with whom we were spending the day, I set out to visit the works at Railway Point, for as yet I know no other more significant name for the site of the Railway station and future village on this side the lake. We thankfully accepted of the escort of the master of the house, who graciously gave up some important out-of-door work to accompany us, a sacrifice of time for which I hope we were all sufficiently thankful.

The sun was so hot that we were glad more than once to rest under the shade of some noble butternut trees which spread their most refreshing branches across the narrow sandy road, and as I looked up among the broad-spreading leaf boughs I marvelled at the size of the trees which had been only saplings when first I passed along that very road some twenty-one years before. Near the spot where formerly stood the old inn at the landing place known as Sully the path turned abruptly in a direction parallel to the lake eastward, and we crossed a crazy log bridge over a small creek and a wilderness of the blue iris and rushes, thistles and wild camomile, and entered on a newly-cut road which had been operated by the Railway men for a more ready communication with the Sully road.

Through an old bit of marshy clearing, thick covered with rushy grass and small bushes of dwarf willow and alder, lay our path: the black sphagnous soil, owing to the long drought, was fortunately for us dry, but an hour's rain would have made our footing far from agreeable. Through this meadow ran a bright stream which was unbridged save by sundry blocks of granite and fragments of limestone which afforded a stopping place to our feet; from this point our way lay through a regular growth of forest trees, lofty pines, maple, bass, and oak, the dense thicket of leafy under-wood shutting out the lake from our sight. You might have imagined yourself in the very heart of the forest; many rare and beautiful flowers we gathered, flourishing in the rank soil and among the decaying trunks and branches that strewed the leafy ground. There, among others, was that gem of beauty, the chimaphila or shining leafed wintergreen; rheumatism weed, as some of the natives call it, its dark glossy leaves of holly-green, and corymba of peach-coloured flowers, its amethyst-coloured anthers set round the emerald green turban-shaped pistil, forming a contrast of the most perfect beauty. This elegant flower might well be called by way of distinction, the 'Gem of the Forest'. There were pink milk weeds as fragrant as beautiful, white piroles, and the dark rich crimson blossoms of the red flowering raspberry, with many others with which we quickly filled our hands; nevertheless we were not sorry when we emerged from the close sultry forest path and felt the delicious breeze from the lake blowing fresh upon us. There lay the bright waters glittering in the sunlight full before us. The ground in front sloped gently down to the shore, forming a little peninsula; on one side a deep cove wooded on its banks to the water's edge, in front the long line of piles stretching towards a small island on which a station-house is to be erected for the keeper of the gates, which are to admit of the egress and regress of boats and rafts.

Far to the eastward the shores rose, rounded with dark forest trees, forming bold capes and headlands with bays and inlets. Full in the opposite shore lay the extensive clearing of the Indian village, with the green slopes of Anderson's Point, once the memorable scene of an exterminating slaughter between the Mohawks and the Ojibbewa Indians; their bones and weapons of war, axes, arrow-heads, and scalping knives are still to be found on turning up the now peaceful soil, where the descendants of the war-chiefs now reap a harvest of golden grain and bow the knee at the bloodless altar beneath the roof of that humble village church which silently points upward to that gracious Saviour who said to his disciples: 'My peace I give unto you, not as the world giveth it'.

Many there are who can recall the time when the very men who inhabit that village knew not the Lord but wandered in the darkness of heathenism, whose hand was against every man, and every man's hand against them, but who now worship their God in spirit and in truth.

It is somewhere eastward of the church that the bridge will strike the shore, and so stretch on through the low lands which we may call the vale of the Otonabee towards Peterboro'. Further on, westward of the Indian village, are the two mouths of the river, divided by a low swampy island; and there, on the Monaghan shore, far up towards the head of the lake, are sunny clearings and pleasant farms, looking bright and cheerful in the warm beams of the afternoon sun.

Our own southern shore is the most picturesque; but to obtain a sight of it we must go out upon the water; but just now we are glad to rest on the broad bench beneath a clump of bowery basswood trees, which have been most judiciously left on the cleared space to afford a shady seat for the workmen at noon-time; and here we can sit beneath the thick foliage which shuts out the sultry summer sun, and look at the busy scene before us. The shore is all alive with workmen. From that long low shed rings the clank of the blacksmith's hammer; that column of blue smoke rising among the graceful group of silver birches and poplars points to the forge. There is a boat building at the edge of the water; there is a scow, and a small steam-engine is being fixed to move the hammer of that pile-driver; it will be the third or fourth in operation; boats, skiffs, and scows are moving to and fro, each guided by some hand who has his appointed labor in the bee-hive. On that little eminence stands a young man whose figure and bearing mark his situation to be one superior to the common mechanic. The sun's rays fall with dazzling effect upon some brass instrument that rests on a high stand. He courteously returns the greeting of one of our party, and informs us 'He is taking an observation of the level of the bridge'.

Those three principal buildings are a boarding-house for the workmen and two stores, where all the necessaries of life may be purchased in the shape of groceries, provisions, and ready-made clothing. You see no women in this temporary village: but there peeps out a sweet baby-boy, with fat-dimpled shoulders and bright curls; his gay red frock sets off the whiteness of his skin, and you are sure a mother's gentle hand has brushed those sunny locks from his broad white brow and made those hands so clean, though she herself is not visible.

The eye follows that line of posts, four abreast, which stretches its leviathan length far, far across the rippling waters of the lake. There, at the utmost limits, is the mighty machine that looks in the distance like a tall gibbet, against which a huge ladder is leaning, but that dark figure mid-way on the scaffold is no miserable felon, but a good, honest, hard-working Yankee, who directs the movements of the ton weight of iron that now slowly ascends between the sliding grooves in the tall frame; and now, at the magic word 'All right!' descends with lightning swiftness upon the head of the pile that has just been conducted to its side. It is curious to see the log of timber, some twenty-five or thirty feet in length, emerge from the depth of the lake; you do not see the rope that is fastened to it, which that man in the skiff tows it along by—it seems to come up like a huge monster of the deep, and rearing itself by degrees, climbs up the side of the frame like a living thing; then for a second swing to and fro, till steadied by the least apparent exertion on the part of the guide on the scaffold. Now it is quite upright—plumb I suppose the carpenter would say—then at the signal, clack, clack, clack, goes the little engine on the scow; slowly aloft mounts the great weight, down, down, down it comes—the first blow fixing the timber in its destined place—and sends a shower of bark flying from the pile; when the weight comes down on to the head of the pile the jerk disengages a sort of claw that is attached to it; this ascends and again comes down, seizing the ring of the weight in its own grasp and bearing it again triumphantly upwards—again to descend upon the pile with unerring aim—lower it sinks, and every fresh blow comes with accelerated force, till it is brought to the level of the others. From a quarter of an hour to twenty minutes is the time employed in sinking each of these posts—that is, if the lake is calm; but when much swell is on the water the work is carried on much slower or the pile-driving is delayed after for some days.

To obtain a near view of the process a boat was procured, and we were rowed within a few feet of the machine; and there, as we lay gently rocking to and fro, we could see the whole of the process and enjoy the delightful scenery of the southern shore, the green-wooded island, the bold hills with the sunny slopes where the grain was beginning to acquire a golden hue, the graceful trees relieving the open clearing with their refreshing verdure; even the new sheds and buildings on the little point seen among the embowering trees had a pleasing effect—so truly does 'distance lend enchantment to the view' and harmonize in nature all objects to one pleasing whole.

But the bang of the last hammer has ceased to vibrate on our ears, the little skiff is turned towards the shore, and fearing that my unartist-like description will convey but a faint idea of this great work, I will leave it to abler pens than mine, and only close my article with wishing success to Canadian enterprize and American ingenuity, and may they ever work in brotherly unity and be a mutual support to each other.

NOTE.—I was assured by the contractor that the bridge, when completed, would be a greater achievement as a work of engineering skill than the bridge over Lake Champlain, on account of the superior depth of the water. The distance from shore to shore of the Rice Lake at this point is about three miles; the average depth as far as they had hitherto sunk the piles did not exceed fifteen feet; but the deepest part was supposed to be north of Tick Island.

8. Rhoda Anne Page (1826–1863)

AN HOUR IN THE ICE[1]

[Maple Leaf (*Montreal, 1853*), *Vol. 2, pp. 130–6*]

Sleigh bells! who has not listened for their glad music, when friends or dear ones have been waited for? Who has not watched for them, perhaps hopefully, perhaps anxiously, perhaps in that agony of suspense which has made their first tone seem as if struck from the very heart? Surely, if the term 'joy bells' can ever be rightly applied, it must be to those blithesome heralds of friends approaching. The very house-dog knows his master's bells, and changes his warning bark as he recognises them, to one of joyous welcome.

One evening, the close of a March day—it matters not how long ago—that merry peal might have been heard approaching the shore of one of the fairest of these island-studded 'back lakes', which, if they cannot vie with the broad Huron and Ontario in grandeur, yield in beauty to none of their mighty rivals. The winter had been severe and protracted and the lake was still frozen over, but the ice had been for some days reckoned unsafe, and in the darkness which was now fast gathering over all things, to cross upon it seemed a perilous attempt.

The person who now appeared, however, driving rapidly towards the shore, looked like one who had braved such dangers many a time before. Every thing about him, from his own blanket coat and crimson sash, to the rough but powerful team he drove, and the shaggy, good-natured collier dog which lay at his feet in the sleigh, spoke the true back-woodsman—one of those hardy, fearless, much-enduring men, who seem made to be the pioneers of civilization, clearing away forests for others to plant cities in their room.

As the night, however, closed about him, it became evident that even to him the prospect of crossing the unsound ice in the darkness was far from welcome. 'It will be as dark as pitch', said he, half aloud, 'and the ice is rotten in a dozen places. Well, there's no help for it now, and I know the road blindfold. Once safe on the other side and I've done with the ice for this winter. I promised Mary this should be the last time.'

As the young teamster—for such he was—spoke, he urged his already tired horses to greater speed, for their hoofs were plashing in several inches of water, and the ice beneath was in a state which allowed no dallying by the way.

[1]One other short story by Rhoda Page has been located, "The Lost Boy: a Tale of the Burning Plains," in the January issue of the *Victoria Magazine* (Belleville, 1848). See Section XII, No. 7, for a biographical note and a selection from her poetical compositions.

The moon had not risen, nor could she have given him any assistance if she had, for the sky was covered with thick black clouds, and not so much as a solitary star peeped forth through the gloom. Relying, however, on his own knowledge of the track, James Gray drove on fearlessly until he was convinced that he must be nearing a point where it became necessary to make a wide *detour*, to avoid a spot where the ice was both thin and unsound. Rising to his feet in the sleigh, he peered eagerly into the darkness, to ascertain, if possible, his exact position.

Well was it for him that he did so, as by that movement he freed his limbs from the encumbrance of sundry empty bags, horse cloths, &c., which, when not required for their legitimate uses, were gathered about him as defences from the raw night air.

Even as he stood gazing wistfully forward into the black night, not daring greatly to slacken his horses' speed where the foundation on which they stood was at best so precarious, the brittle ice yielded, cracked, and finally gave way with a fearful crash, breaking into a thousand fragments, upon which the frightened animals vainly struggled to regain their footing. There were a few terrible convulsive efforts, a wild snort of terror, and then horses and sleigh disappeared in the black chasm.

As he felt the sleigh sinking under him, Gray sprang out of it, with a strong, sudden bound; but the treacherous ice again broke under him; he clung to its edge with the grasp of a drowning man, but though it supported his weight in the water, it crumbled and gave way beneath him, as often as he attempted, by its aid, to extricate himself from his terrible position. He shouted for help till his voice failed him, but no man heard or answered to his call. Then, as he literally hung there between life and death, his thoughts turned, as those of all human beings in such sore straits must, to One whose ear is never closed, and he 'cried unto the Lord in his trouble'.

'God have mercy upon me!' broke from his whitened lips, as he clutched yet closer the jagged edges of the ice which his numbed fingers now could scarcely feel. At this instant something swam by him, and a struggling and panting sound told him that his poor dog was still near him, striving, like himself, to escape from the abyss into which they had been so suddenly plunged. Even in his own utmost need the brave man could still spare a thought for his faithful friend.

Releasing, for an instant, his hold by one hand, he seized the poor creature and flung him as far as possible upon the firmer ice. He heard him shake his shaggy coat, and then, after a brief pause, as if in doubt whether to remain and share his master's fate, set off at full speed in the direction of his home. A ray of hope flashed at once through the mind of the despairing man. He well knew that Watch's appearance, alone and dripping with water, would arouse the fears of the anxious wife who awaited his return; she would probably surmise the truth, and then he felt that nothing would be left undone that human power could do, to seek for, and if possible to save him. Minute succeeded minute—time, which, to him, seemed like eternity, passed by, and still he clung with that vice-like grip to his frail support. Through his half-maddened brain all the scenes of his early boyhood, of his young, vigorous manhood, passed in rapid review; but above all rose the image of that fair, fond young wife, as he had seen her that morning standing at his side, with her baby in her arms, and forcing him to repeat, again and again, the promise that this journey across the lake should be the *last*. The last! the words seemed to ring in his ears; and as his brain whirled and his senses swam in that unutterable agony, a voice of fiendish mockery seemed to shriek them out—for the last time! for the last time!

. . . . .

Meanwhile, in the neat, cheerful, humble home on the farther shore, sat the expectant wife, awaiting the coming of her husband, listening eagerly for the first sound of his well-known bells. It was Saturday evening, and the small log house wore its neatest aspect, to welcome the return at once of the Sabbath and of its master. Everything, including Mary herself and her boy, was as neat and pleasant to the eye as hands could make it; and a fair object she was, as, seated by the cradle of her child, she plied her knitting-needles busily, or now and then interrupted her occupation to raise her head and listen.

Suddenly she started up, as a scratching and whining noise at the door caught her ear. She threw the door wide open, and poor Watch sprang over the threshold, wet, panting, and *alone*. The moon was shining feebly now, and one glance showed Mary that her husband was not there—another at the dog's dripping coat told her that her fears were but too well realized. A dizzy sickness came over her. It passed in an instant, and she stood, pale indeed as death, but with every faculty aroused, every nerve strung, to meet the need of the moment. Time enough would there be for tears and wailings, should the worst prove true; at present she must *act*—not waste, in idle sorrow, moments as precious as years.

Half-way between Mary's cottage and the lake, stood the rude cabin of an honest Irishman, who, with his 'boys', two stalwart young men, had come, not long before, to reside in the neighborhood. In less than five minutes Mary was on her way thither; her infant, warmly wrapped up, clasped even more closely than usual to her bosom, as if she feared to lose what might now be her only earthly treasure.

Great was the astonishment of honest Tim Martin and his household when Mary Gray suddenly appeared in their midst, (none of them ever knew exactly how she came there, for she had entered without knock or call), and still greater was the sympathy of their kind hearts, when, in accents of forced calmness, she told her story, expressing her belief that something (she could not bring herself to speak more plainly) had befallen her husband, and imploring them to aid her in her search for him. Gladly would they have persuaded her to remain in the cabin with the good dame while they went forth upon the search; but Mary was inflexibly determined to share in it.

'Ye can be of no use, darlin', said the good-hearted fellow, when the simple preparations for starting were completed; 'ye're better here by far; you, too, that slip about upon the ice like a cat in walnut shells.

'I shall stand as firm to-night as any of you', said Mary, as she gave her child to Mrs. Martin and stepped out of the cabin. 'It's no use talking, Mr. Martin; do you think I can sit here when James is perhaps—' She could not finish the sentence, but she was understood.

With rapid steps the little party set off, followed by the dog, which, however, they lost sight of soon after they left the shore. Mary kept her promise of standing firm upon the slippery surface of the lake, for a far deeper fear had banished all timidity for herself, and it would scarcely have been felt had her path been through burning coals. Long and carefully did they search, narrowly examining every crack and fissure in the ice where it seemed at all possible that the catastrophe they dreaded but would not name might have taken place. At length one of the young men, who was a little in advance of the rest, suddenly started back with an exclamation of surprise, and lifting the lantern he carried shewed them a yawning gulf but a few feet from where they stood.

'There was no hole here this morning', he whispered to his brother; but low as was the tone in which he had spoken, it struck like a knell upon the wife's ear. With a sudden mad impulse, she sprang towards the chasm, but was instantly stopped by a strong but kindly hand. 'Ah! thin, the crathur', said the kind Irishman; 'sure ye would n't think of it. Think of the boy at home, jewel; why should ye lave him too?' Mary felt all that these words were meant to imply; but the sinful impulse was checked, and burying her face in her hands, tears—hot, burning tears—came to relieve her breaking heart.

Suddenly a low whine caught the ear of one of the young Irishmen, and at the same instant a faint gleam of moonlight showed him the dog at a little distance, standing at the edge of the chasm and looking fixedly downwards, apparently at the black waters below. With a mute sign to the others to keep Mary back, he crept cautiously round towards the faithful animal, and there, still clinging with that desperate, straining grasp to the rough edge, he saw James Gray, speechless, motionless, and evidently almost gone.

The lost was found, but his extrication was still not easy. The ice under the brave youth's feet cracked and strained, as, creeping as near to the edge as temerity itself could dare to go, he threw round the half lifeless body the knotted rope with which he had come provided.

A few minutes more and the now rejoicing little party were on their homeward way, bearing in their arms the rescued one, while Mary walked beside, now audibly blessing her kind true-hearted friends—now, in the silent depths of her heart, offering up thanksgivings to Him who had thus given her back her husband from the very gates of death.

My simple tale is told. James Gray is now a thriving farmer, with more gray than dark hairs upon his head. Mary has become a grave but gentle matron, with many fair young faces smiling round her, but neither has ever forgotten that awful night; and still when winter comes round again and the frozen lake lies glittering in the sunbeams, 'a sea of glass like unto crystal', do the thoughts of both travel backwards—hers to that agonizing search, and his to the untold, unspeakable sensation of that fearful Hour in the Ice.

9. Thomas Need (1808?—?)

Six Years in the Bush (London, 1838) contains in abbreviated form the diary of Thomas Need, though it was published anonymously. An uncle, one of the deans of Canterbury, tried to make a clergyman out of him by paying his expenses at University College, Oxford, but he withdrew when, as he put it, he 'couldn't swallow the 39 Articles'. He travelled to Canada with a servant and plenty of money, and, being a typical Englishman of the day, had a number of the rough edges rubbed off in the process, all of which he took in the right spirit. He first travelled about looking for a favourable place, observing from the appearance of Percy Village, in Seymour, that a settlement was so called because nothing was settled. Finally he purchased 3000 acres in Verulam Township for £750 and became founder of the village of Bobcaygeon. Fond of hunting, he once appeared in Peterborough in a half-Indian Robinson Crusoe costume, followed by hooting boys. He resented the destruction of Cameron Falls and other beauty spots by commercial development just as people capable of their appreciation were beginning to arrive. In 1850 he left John Langton in charge of his Canadian affairs and returned to England, married, and lived in

Nottingham until his death. There are no direct descendants of this interesting pioneer of the district, since his daughter Mary had no children. In 1926 she and her husband, E. W. Chambers, addressed the following interesting letters to Librarian Arthur Wilgress at the Legislative Library of Ontario. They are enclosed in an envelope affixed to the Library's copy of *Six Years in the Bush*:

Woodlands House, Holford,
Bridgewater, Feb. 3rd [1926].

Dear Sir,—

I was delighted to hear from you in reference to "Six Years in the Bush". Most interesting to me. (T. N.) He was eight times across the Atlantic. He worked very hard—flour mills—after being sent to University College, Oxford by his uncle, one of the Deans of Canterbury who intended him for a parson. He passed but, as he said, he couldn't swallow the 39 articles—so Uncle said "I will do nothing for you, Tom". So he and a friend Geff. Hall—also from Notts.—went out to Canada 1832. Mr. Hall married out there and my father came home 1850, having been left some money by his Aunt Miss Welfitt. My father married 1850 and I am the sole result, 1851. I married in 1877 Ernest Chambers who is writing to you. We have no results. I have two pretty little water colors in my bed room of the flour mills.

Yours most sincerely,
"Mary E. Chambers".

I have a "Six Years in the Bush" which is an abbreviated account, a diary brought out by my father's old friend Mr. Roper, since dead. He was a College friend.

Woodlands House, Holford,
Bridgewater, Feb. 3rd, 1926.

Dear Sir,—

I have been trying to think of something to tell you about Mr. T. Need in addition to what my wife has said. He bought the Village of Bobcaygeon in 1833 from Mr. Boulton. He sold his saw mills and property to Mr. Boyd,[1] I think in 1849, who eventually paid off what

[1]Mossom Boyd came to Canada in 1834 at the age of nineteen and was the only original settler to remain in the Sturgeon Lake region. A man of great energy and persistence, he chopped his first clearing on the north shore of the lake himself. In rafting square timber to Quebec he was for a time a partner of John Langton. He was eminently successful in the lumber trade, but the Boyd Papers, Public Archives of Canada, concern largely the post-Confederation period. He died in 1883.

was still owing in 1866 or –68. He had given a piece of ground near the Church for a cemetery. The clergyman came here about 12 or 14 years ago for my wife's signature as there was no title to it, which she signed and we believe a railway ran through the land soon afterwards.

After his marriage he lived at Gannow in Derbyshire but eventually moved to Nottingham where he and Mrs. Need[2] died. He was very fond of hunting and shooting and good at both. He became very deaf—a family failing. He was great friends with the Langtons and Mr. John Langton looked after his affairs when he left Canada. I don't know what else to say, but if you care to write again we shall be very glad to answer any questions we can.

We hear Bobcaygeon has become a great holiday resort. There is a Street called Need St.

I have a very heavy old rifle of his he had in Canada, grooved bore. He could not have carried it, but probably used it when in his canoe; his dogs used to run deer into the lake.

Yours sincerely

"E. W. Chambers"

We have four good heads of Canadian Stags.

SELECTIONS FROM HIS JOURNAL

[Six Years in the Bush; or Extracts from the Journal of a Settler in Upper Canada, 1832–1838 (*London, 1838*), *pp. 40* et seq.]

The distance from Peterboro' to the [Chemong] Lake shore was about six miles, over which a friend kindly offered to transport my effects in his waggon. We started about nine o'clock in the morning; I, in my inexperience, believing that though the road through the forest was notoriously bad, a couple of hours at most would suffice for the traject: at the end of that time, however, we had scarcely accomplished half the distance when the wheels sunk so deep in a slough that two hours more were taken up in extricating them. The next two miles were accomplished with still more difficulty, for we were obliged repeatedly to make a *corduroy*, or in other words to cut stakes and lay them horizontally for the wagon to pass over; but even this scheme failed at last; and at a mile distant from the lake our teamster declared the waggon inextricably

[2]There are portraits of Mrs. Need and Mary (Need) Chambers in Anne Langton, *A Gentlewoman in Upper Canada*, facing p. 128, but if one of Need exists it is probably in the hands of the family connection in England.

fixed; our only chance was then to loosen the horses and load them with the goods, which was done; and in this manner we reached the lake at six o'clock in the evening, covered with mud, hungry, and exhausted. On regaining the waggon we made some ineffectual efforts to draw it out backwards, but in the end were compelled to abandon it for the night and make the best of our way back to the town. At day break I started again on foot, in company with three hired laborers, to rejoin the baggage at the lake side, where a boat was appointed to meet us. On reaching the shore no boat was in waiting, nor was there any appearance of one on the whole water; this was a bitter disappointment, and I fear I lost both temper and patience; but after a little time, growing more cool, I walked along the shore in the hope of falling in with some Indians and procuring a canoe: in this I was unsuccessful; but just as I was giving up the search in despair I observed something like a boat beating against a rocky headland a few hundred yards off, which indeed it proved to be, though apparently water-logged and rotten. Still it seemed a godsend; and when, with the assistance of my companions, who soon came up, we had got it on shore, it was pronounced by one of them, a carpenter, capable of being made sea-worthy in a few hours. It had evidently been ice-bound in the early part of the winter and abandoned by its owner. We all set to work immediately, the laborers to caulk the gaping seams with clay and moss; I to make a paddle to steer by, and the carpenter to fashion a pair of oars: at length we got off, but my companions were wholly unacquainted with the use of the oar, and my practise had not extended beyond an occasional pull on the still surface of the Isis, at Oxford, a very different affair from encountering a head wind and a heavy sea on a Canadian lake in a crazy old water-logged boat: still, by hugging the shore and alternately cheering and scolding the men, some little way was made; and when, at night-fall, we landed to light a fire and obtain some rest, the carpenter announced that seven miles had been accomplished. The night was very stormy, and the ensuing morning, if possible, worse; so that after an ineffectual effort to continue our voyage it was decided to remain where we were. I took my gun and wandered into the forest in quest of game, while my companions started off to visit some Indians, of whom they procured a large maskalongy or pike, which, together with a few pigeons, furnished us with an excellent supper. Towards evening the wind lulled; and the men being now less alarmed for their personal safety exerted themselves with such good will that before night-fall we brought our boat safely to anchor at Verulam, and I leapt ashore on my own territory. . . .

August 20.—Went to Peterboro'; where a rapid improvement had taken place during the summer—new houses had been built, new shops opened, and a large influx of inhabitants had arrived. I had been so many weeks absent that I had forgotten to change my half-Indian costume before I left the woods, consequently my old acquaintance recognised me with difficulty, and especially as the sun had sadly changed my complexion; even the boys in the street hooted as I passed. . . .

October 6.—A Land Surveyor arrived to-day to lay out the ground plan of a village, which some projected public works on our chain of lakes is likely to call into existence on my property. We measured several lots, and in many instances had bidders for them immediately. One person proposed to open a tavern; which, if respectably conducted, will be very useful to the infant settlement. The intention of Government, sanctioned by the Legislature, is to cut a canal between Lake Sturgeon and Pigeon Lake for the purpose of avoiding the present dangerous river and rapids and connecting the navigation of the two Lakes. Such an undertaking I had in some degree anticipated when I selected my lot of land; but I had not imagined that it would have been so soon executed, or that the interests of our rude district could so soon have attracted public attention. From this time I may fairly consider the value of my property in the market quadrupled.

24.—Yesterday two large flat-bottomed boats arrived, with the families and effects of the new settlers, at the projected village. The sound of the axe and the hammer and the mixed voices of women and children, fell strangely but delightfully on my ear as I strolled along the shore this evening: a striking contrast to the time, only a few weeks past, when on the temporary absence of the woodmen I was left alone in the howling wilderness.

27.—An Indian camp has been formed on the opposite shore of the Lake for the autumn hunt: two of the men brought me a present of a haunch of venison, with an invitation to join them in the chase: in two days we succeeded in taking three deer, one of which fell to my rifle.

30.—This morning I was favored with a visit from three Indian ladies, seemingly, however, under the vows of La Trappe, for not one word would they utter, either in English or their own language: what freak took them I cannot imagine, as I afterwards found that they could talk fast enough when they liked.

31.—Accompanied an Indian to the forest to learn the art of barking squirrels: this is performed by striking the bark of the tree with a rifle ball, just under the animal, which is thus killed by the splintered bark without injury to the fur or flesh. . . .

May 20.—Two boats, heavily laden with work people and artisans, passed up the lake to day on their way to Cameron's Falls, which have been lately purchased by two young adventurers for the site of a saw mill. Sentiment is out of place in this Colony, where for many years to come the ornamental must give place to the profitable; the 'το καλὸν' to the 'το πρεπον'; but I confess it was not without deep sorrow I learned that in a few weeks one of the loveliest scenes in the province would be destroyed. It had been a great delight, on the long evenings of the last summer, to sail up the lake in my canoe and pass a quiet hour or two at the Falls after the toils of the day were over. The Indians, whose limited vocabulary rarely admits an inappropriate appellation, have given them a name, which signifies 'listen, what a sound'. They have however but a faint idea of the sublime and beautiful, and it seemed very sad that this spot, whose loveliness has been wasted upon the heedless eyes of the savage from time immemorial, should be doomed to destruction just as beings capable of appreciating it were beginning to settle in the neighbourhood. I must believe that these master works of nature, though buried in a wilderness and unobserved or unappreciated by human eye, are not lost, any more than the countless flowers that are 'born to blush unseen'.

In the old world we should people such a spot with fairy habitants; but in this cold, dull, matter-of-fact country there is no room for imagination to work, no cherished associations or ancient recollections suited to feed and nourish it: all is too new and too real. I have sometimes attempted to trace back the records of the Indians, but they have little to impart: even the forest trees are not ancient, the 'gnarled and knotted oak' of the old world is utterly unknown. The lakes and the rivers indeed are of yesterday, and so are the beavers; but every thing else is of *to-day*, plain matter-of-fact *to-day*. . . .

June 18.—At the Rapids below the clearing I fell in to day with three Indians of the Mohawk tribe, returning from the chase with a quantity of furs. One of them was Pierre, a celebrated model of Indian symmetry. Indeed I do not think I ever witnessed so faultless a form and figure, whether for strength or beauty; I asked him if he and his companions had not been trespassing on the hunting grounds of my friends the Chippewas, to which he replied, with a scornful laugh, that 'the Chippewas were women, and dare not look a Mohawk in the face';—in fact, an ancient feud has existed for many generations between the two nations, which even Christianity has not succeeded in healing. The lake country of the district belonged of ancient right to the Chippewas, but some time since a portion of it was invaded and apparently conquered by some of the Mohawks. The Chippewas, defeated in many bloody encounters, at length gave up the struggle and retired farther back into the forest: their quiet, however, was only the lull of the winds before a storm: for one night, long after their enemy were, as they imagined, securely settled, they came down from their retreat in overwhelming numbers, surrounded the wigwams of the sleeping Mohawks, and throwing firebrands into the roofs, butchered the startled inmates as they rushed out; neither sex nor age were spared, and it is said that scarcely one of the invaders survived to tell the tale of horror or exact vengeance from their tribe. This act of terrible but scarcely unjust retribution occurred on Rice Lake, where a grass-grown mound still marks the Indians' grave. Near it the settlers turn up with the plough tomahawk blades and arrow heads, with other implements of Indian warfare. Since that dreadful night the Chippewas have never been disturbed by any aggression on their territory, unless, as in the present instance, by individuals; but nevertheless the tradition of the Mohawk's prowess in the field has come down to the present generation, heightened by the colouring of time, and I doubt whether the whole tribe could be brought to encounter my three marauding acquaintance of to day in open fight: the very name of Mohawk is a bugbear to them, and there are few that will not turn pale at the mere mention of it. . . .

July 13.—The evening being soft and still I got into my canoe and paddled up the lake to observe the progress of the works at Cameron's Falls. A very few weeks had elapsed since the purchase, but with more than the usual celerity of this wonder-working country a vast deal had been effected. A broad mill-dam was thrown across the stream at the head of the cascade to stem the current and conduct it over the wheels of the mill; the green meadow, which for countless ages had afforded the richest pasture to the wild deer, was now browsed by horses and cattle; and where the little copse of oak had stood, nothing remained but blackened stumps, interspersed by rude unsightly log houses; numbers of workmen were plying their respective trades on the ground, and everything bore the appearance of an active and rising settlement. . . .

March 9, Sunday.—A day ever to be marked with a 'white bean' in the annals of our settlement; for on it an humble building, which we had raised for the worship of God, was opened for divine service. The highly-esteemed clergyman of Peterboro' consented to officiate, and never I believe was there a more devout or attentive congregation assembled within the walls of a Christian church. Some time before the hour of service our settlers had taken their places, the women seated, and the men for the most part leaning in deep thought against the walls. Several were in tears, and all seemed much affected with the idea of being permitted once more to worship God after the manner of their fathers, in the rude wilderness; perhaps, also, they thought of friends separated from them for ever, who at the same hour were about to join in the same services with themselves, and wending their way to more costly but not more sincerely dedicated temples. They who are privileged to live within sound of the church bells, and are in the habit of attending their summons at stated seasons as a thing of course, can scarcely enter into the feelings of the exile on such an occasion as the present, for his habit and mode of life, together with his (in most cases) eternal separation from all his friends, naturally leads him to rely less upon man and more upon his Maker. His undertakings, his successes, even the daily blessings of preservation and food, seem more immediately to flow from a particular Providence and make him serious and thoughtful. We sang together the Morning Hymn, and then the service was proceeded with. Afterwards, in the presence of the whole congregation, a number of young children were admitted by baptism within the pale of the Church, who, if it please God, shall grow up to preserve the faith as well as the language of their Fathers in this distant land and add one more link to the chain which binds the colony to the mother country. . . .

10. J. W. Dunbar Moodie (1797–1869)

An officer and an author when he met Susanna Strickland, Dunbar Moodie was at once *persona grata*. His books, however, *Narrative of the Campaign in Holland in 1814* and *Ten Years in South Africa*, are dull and in no respect notable. After a series of errors and misfortunes in Upper Canada he obtained the office of Sheriff of the District of Victoria (now Hastings County), and from 1839 until his death in 1869 the Moodies resided there. Though appointed by Sir John Colborne in a period of Tory ascendancy, Moodie was a personal friend of the Honourable Robert Baldwin, to whom, as Attorney-General, he made continual complaints and requested more lucrative posts. He was actually a moderate Reformer with strong views in favour of Responsible Government.[1] Continually in financial and political trouble in Belleville, he was eventually ousted from his office by a series of lawsuits. Poverty and disappointment, as well as ill-health, followed. Like his wife, he contributed to literary journals, though frequently his articles were mere excerpts from earlier books. His best Canadian writing comprises a few sketches, in both verse and prose, of his pioneering experiences in Douro. He died in 1869.

[1]See the series of his letters, 1843–1849, in the Baldwin Correspondence, Vol. 58, in the Toronto Public Library.

THE OULD DHRAGOON

A VISIT TO THE BEAVER MEADOW, A SKETCH FROM THE BACKWOODS

[*J. W. D. Moodie*, Scenes and Adventures, as a Soldier and Settler, during Half a Century (*Montreal, 1866*), *pp. 219–29*]

Behold that man with lanky locks,
That hang in strange confusion o'er his brow;
And nicely scan his garments, rent and patched,
In colors varied like a pictured map;
And watch his restless glance—now grave, now gay—
As saddening thought or merry humour's flash
Sweeps o'er the deep marked lines, which care hath left
As when the world is steeped in blackest night,
The forked lightning flashes through the sky,
And all around leaps into life and light,
To sink again in darkness blacker still.

Yes! look upon that face, lugubrious, long,
As thoughtfully he stands with folded arms
Amid his realm of charred and spectral stumps
Which once were trees—but now, with sprawling roots,
Cling to the rocks that peep above the soil.

Aye! look again,
And say if you discern the faintest trace
Of warrior: bold, the gait erect and proud,
The steady glance that speaks the fearless soul,
Watchful and prompt to do what man can do
When duty calls? All wrecked and reckless now.

But let the trumpet's soul-inspiring sound
Wake up the brattling echoes of the woods,
Then watch his kindling eye, his eagle glance,
While thoughts of glorious fields, and battles won,
And visions bright, of joyous hopeful youth
Sweep o'er his soul. A soldier now once more
Touched by the magic sound, he rears his head,
Responsive to the well known martial note,
And stands again a hero 'mid his rags.

It is delightful to observe a feeling of contentment under adverse circumstances. We may smile at the rude and clumsy attempts of the remote and isolated backwoodsman to attain something like comfort, but happy he who with the buoyant spirits of the light hearted Irishman, contrives to make himself happy when all others would be miserable.

A certain degree of dissatisfaction with our present circumstances is necessary to stimulate us to secure future comfort; but where the delusive prospect of future happiness is too remote for any reasonable hope of ultimate attainment, then surely it is true wisdom to make the most of the present, and to cultivate a spirit of happy contentment with the lot assigned to us by Providence.

Ould Simpson, or the 'Ould Dhragoon', as he was generally called, was a good sample of this happy character; and I shall proceed to give the reader a sketch of his history and a description of his establishment. He was one of that unfortunate class of discharged soldiers who are tempted to sell their pensions, often far below their real value, for the sake of getting a lot of land in some remote settlement, where it is only rendered valuable by the labor of the settler, and where they will have the unenvied privilege of expending the last remains of their strength in clearing a patch of land for the benefit of some storekeeper who has given them credit while engaged in the work.

The Ould Dhragoon had fixed his abode on the verge of an extensive beaver-meadow which was considered a sort of natural curiosity in the neighbourhood; and where he managed, by cutting the rank grass in the summer time, to support several cows which afforded the chief subsistence of his family. He had also managed, with the assistance of his devoted partner, Judy, to clear a few acres of poor rocky land on the sloping margin of the level meadow, which he planted year after year with potatoes.

Scattered over this small clearing, here and there might be seen the but-end of some half-burnt hemlock tree which had escaped the general combustion of the log heaps, and now formed a striking contrast to the white limestone rocks which shewed their rounded surfaces above the meagre soil.

The Ould 'Dhragoon' seemed, moreover, to have some taste for the picturesque; and by way of ornament had left standing sundry tall pines and hemlocks neatly girdled to destroy their foliage, the shade of which would have been detrimental to the growth of the 'blessed praties', which he designed to grow in his clearing, but which, in the meantime, like martyrs at the stake, stretched their naked branches imploringly to the smiling heavens.

As he was a kind of hermit from choice, and far removed from other settlers whose assistance is so necessary in new settlements, old Simpson was compelled to resort to the most extraordinary contrivances while clearing his land. Thus after felling the trees, instead of chopping them into lengths for the purpose of facilitating the operation of piling them preparatory to burning, which would have cost him too much labour, he resorted to the practice of 'niggering', as it is called; which is simply laying light pieces of round timber across the trunks of the trees, and setting fire to them at the point of contact, by which means the trees are slowly burned through. It was while busily engaged in this interesting operation that I first became acquainted with the subject of this sketch.

Some twenty or thirty little fires were burning briskly in different parts of the blackened field, and the old fellow was watching the slow progress of his silent 'niggers', and replacing them from time to time as they smouldered away.

After threading my way among the uncouth logs blazing and smoking in all directions, I encountered the old man, attired in an old hood or bonnet of his wife Judy's, with his patched canvass trowsers rolled up to his knees; one foot bare, and the other furnished with an old boot, which from its appearance had once belonged to some more aristocratic foot. His person was long, straight, and sinewy, and there was a light springiness and elasticity in his step which would have suited a younger man, as he skipped along with a handspike over his shoulder. He was singing a stave from the 'Enniskillen Dhragoon' when I came up with him:

'With his silver mounted pistols and his long carbine gun,
Long life to the brave Inniskillen Dragoon'.

His face would have been one of the most lugubrious imaginable, with his long tangled hair hanging confusedly over it in a manner which has happily been compared to a 'bewitched haystack', had it not been for a certain humorous twitch or convulsive movement which affected one side of his countenance whenever any droll idea passed through his mind. It was with a twitch of this kind, and a certain indescribable twinkle of his somewhat melancholy eye, as he seemed intuitively to form a hasty conception of the oddity of his appearance to a stranger unused to the bush, that he welcomed me to his clearing. He instantly threw down his handspike, and leaving his 'niggers' to finish their work[1] at their leisure, insisted on our going to his cabin to get something to drink.

On my way I explained to him the object of my visit, which was to mark out, or 'blaze', the side lines of a lot of land I had received as part of a military grant immediately adjoining the beaver meadow, and I

[1]One settler wrote home that he had "a hundred niggers" working for him! (See Guillet. *Early Life in Upper Canada* (Toronto, 1933), p. 277.)

asked him to accompany me, as he was well acquainted with the different lots.

'Och! by all manner of manes and welcome, the dhevil a foot of the way but I know as well as my own clearing; but come into the house and get a dhrink of milk an' a bite of bread and butter, for sorrow a dhrop of the whisky has crossed my teeth for the last month; an' its' but poor intertainment for man or baste I can offer you, but shure you're heartily welcome.'

The precincts of the homestead were divided and subdivided into an infinity of enclosures, of all shapes and sizes. The outer enclosure was a bush fence, formed of trees felled on each other in a row, and the gaps filled up with brushwood. There was a large gate swung with wooden hinges, and a wooden latch to fasten it; the smaller enclosures were made with round poles tied together with basswood bark. The house was of the rudest description of 'shanty', with hollowed basswood logs fitting into each other somewhat in the manner of tiles for a roof, instead of shingles. No iron was to be seen, in the absence of which there were plenty of leathern hinges, wooden latches for locks, and bark strings instead of nails.

Here was a large fire place at one end of the shanty, with a chimney constructed of split laths, plastered with a mixture of clay and cow dung. As for windows, these were luxuries which could well be dispensed with; the open door was an excellent substitute for them in the day time, and at night none were required; when I ventured to object to this arrangement, that he would have to keep the door shut in the winter time, the old man replied in the style so characteristic of his country: 'Shure it will be time enough to think of that when the cowld weather sets in.'

Every thing about the house wore a Robinson Crusoe aspect, and though there was not any appearance of original plan or foresight, there was no lack of ingenious contrivance to meet every want as it arose. Judy dropped us a low curtsey as we entered, which was followed by a similar compliment from a stout girl of twelve and two or three more of the children, who all seemed to share the pleasure of the parents of receiving strangers in their unpretending tenement.

Many were the apologies that poor Judy offered for the homely cheer she furnished us, and great was her delight at the notice we took of the 'childer'. She set little Biddy, who was the delight of her heart, to reading the Bible; and she took down a curious machine from a shelf, which she had 'contrived out of her own head', as she said, for teaching the children to read. This was a flat box, or frame, filled with sand, which saved paper, pens, and ink. Poor Judy had evidently seen better days, but, with a humble and contented spirit, she blessed God for the food and scanty raiment their labour afforded them. Her only sorrow was the want of 'iddication' for the children.

She would have told us a long story about her trials and sufferings before they had attained their present comparative comfort and independence, but, as we had a tedious scramble before us, through cedar swamps, beaver meadows and piney ridges, the 'Ould Dhragoon' cut her short, and we straightway started on our toilsome journey.

Simpson, in spite of a certain dash of melancholy in his composition, was one of those happy fellows of the 'light heart and their pair of breeches' school, who, when they meet with difficulty and misfortune, never stop to measure its dimensions but hold in their breath and run lightly over, as in crossing a bog where to stand still is to sink.

Off then we went, with the 'Ould Dhragoon' skipping and bounding on before us over fallen trees and mossy rocks, now ducking under the low tangled branches of the white cedar, then carefully piloting us along rotten logs covered with green moss, to save us from the discomfort of wet feet. All this time he still kept one of his feet safely ensconced in the boot while the other seemed to luxuriate in the water, as if there were something amphibious in his nature.

We soon reached the beaver meadow, which extended two or three miles; sometimes contracting into a narrow gorge between wooded heights, then spreading out again into an ample field of verdure, and presenting everywhere the same unvarying level surface surrounded with rising grounds covered with the dense unbroken forest, as if its surface had formerly been covered by the waters of a lake,—which in all probability has been the case at some not very remote period.

In many places the meadow was so wet that it required a very large share of faith to support us in passing over its surface; but our friend the Dhragoon soon brought us safe through all dangers to a deep ditch, which he had dug to carry off the superfluous water from the part of the meadow which he owned. When we had obtained firm footing on the opposite side we sat down to rest ourselves before commencing the operation of 'blazing', or marking the trees with our axes, along the side-line of my lot. Here the mystery of the boot was explained. Simpson very coolly took it off from the hitherto favored foot, and drew it upon the other. He was not a bit ashamed of his poverty, and candidly owned that this was the only boot he possessed, and he was desirous of giving each of his feet fair play.

Nearly the whole of the day was occupied in completing our job, in which the 'Dhragoon' assisted us with hearty good will, enlivening us with his inexhaustible fund of good-humour and drollery.

It was nearly dark when we got back to his shanty, where the kind-hearted Judy was preparing a huge pot of potatoes and other 'combustibles', as Simpson called the other eatables, for our entertainment.

Previous to starting on our surveying expedition we had observed Judy very earnestly giving some important instructions to one of her little boys, on whom she seemed to be most seriously impressing the necessity of using the utmost diligence. The happy contentment which now beamed in poor Judy's still comely countenance bespoke the success of the messenger.

She could not 'call up spirits from the vasty deep' of the cellar, but she had procured some whisky from her next door neighbour—some five or six miles off; and there it stood somewhat ostentatiously on the table in a 'grey beard', with a 'corn cob' or ear of Indian corn stripped of its grain for a cork, smiling most benevolently on the family circle and looking a hundred welcomes to the strangers.

An indescribably enlivening influence seemed to exude from every pore of that homely earthen vessel, diffusing mirth and good-humour in all directions. The old man jumped and danced about on the rough floor of the 'shanty', and the children sat giggling and nudging each other in a corner, casting a timid look from time to time at their mother, for fear she might check them for being over 'bould'.

'Is it crazy ye are intirely, ye ould Omadhawn', said Judy, whose notions of propriety were somewhat shocked with the undignified levity of her partner: 'the likes of ye I never seed; ye are too foolidge intirely. Have done wid yer diviltries, and set the stools for the gintlemans, while I get the supper for ye's.'

Our plentiful though homely meal was soon discussed; for hunger, like a good conscience, can laugh at luxury; and the 'grey beard' made its appearance with the usual accompaniments of hot water and maple sugar, which Judy had scraped from the cake and placed in a saucer on the table before us.

The Ould Dhragoon, despising his wife's admonitions, gave way freely to his feelings and knew no bounds to his hilarity. He laughed and joked, and sung snatches of old songs picked up in the course of his service at home and abroad.

At length Judy, who looked upon him as a 'raal janius', begged him 'to sing the gentlemens the song he made when he first came to the country'. Of course we ardently seconded the motion, and nothing loth the old man, throwing himself back on his stool and stretching out his long neck, poured forth the following ditty, with which I shall conclude this hasty sketch of the 'Ould Dhragoon'.

DAN SIMPSON'S SONG.

Och! its here I'm intirely continted,
In the wild woods of swate Mericay;
God's blessing on him that invinted
Big ships for our crossing the say!

Here praties grow bigger nor turnips;
And though cruel hard is our work,
In ould Ireland we'd nothing but praties,
But here we have praties and pork.

I live on the banks of a meadow,
Now see that my maning you take;
It bates all the bogs of ould Ireland—
Six months in the year it's a lake.

Bad luck to the beavors that dammed it!
I wish them all kilt for their pains;
Fur shure though the craters are clever,
'Tis sartin they've drowned my domains.

I've built a log house of the timber
That grows on my charmin estate;
And an illegant root-house erected,
Just facing the front of my gate.

And I've made me an illegant pig-sty,
Well littered wid straw an' wid hay;
And it's there free from noise of the childer,
I sleep in the heat of the day.

It's there I'm intirely at aise, Sir,
And enjoy all the comforts of home;
I stretch out my legs as I plase, Sir,
And dhrame of the pleasures to come.

Shure, 'tis pleasant to hear the frogs croakin'
When the sun's going down in the sky,
And my Judy sits quietly smokin'
While the praties are boiled till they're dhry.

Och! thin if you love independence,
And have money your passage to pay:
You must quit the ould counthry intirely,
And start in the middle of May.

11. SUSANNA MOODIE (1803–1885)

Susanna, the prettiest of the Strickland girls—'a curly headed emotional creature, rather Keatsian in appearance'[1]—was the youngest of the six daughters of Thomas and Elizabeth Strickland of Sussex, England. She was the rebel of the high-Tory Stricklands, who were scandalized when she underwent conversion and joined the Methodist Society in a neighbouring village. She came back to the fold, however, as did her sister Sarah, piquant and unintellectual, who first married a Methodist but was subsequently able to retrieve the family's lost prestige by marrying a clergyman of the Establishment.

In 1831 Susanna married a half-pay officer, J. W. Dunbar Moodie, and the Moodies and Traills came out to Canada in 1832. They settled in Douro near Lakefield, but were unsuccessful as farmers in 'the Bush'. The exigencies of pioneer life and the birth of children prevented Mrs. Moodie from employing her gift of authorship until about 1836–37, when she contrived to write while her children slept. A number of rather artificial novels of the type common at that time were published in periodicals and in book form, chiefly in the United States. She was something of a philosopher, and soon came round to the view that the world did not owe her or her husband a living, and that the best people were those who worked hard and used their talents to the peak of their ability. While living in Belleville, in 1847–48, the Moodies ventured upon a literary enterprise, the *Victoria Magazine*, but she is best known for her *Roughing It in the Bush* (1852) and *Life in the Clearings Versus the Bush* (1853). She died in Toronto on April 8, 1885.

OUR LOGGING-BEE

[*Susanna Moodie*, Roughing It in the Bush; or Life in Canada (*London, 1852*), *Vol. II, pp. 67–83*]

There was a man in our town,
In our town, in our town—
There was a man in our town,
He made a logging-bee;

And he bought lots of whiskey,
To make the loggers frisky—

[1]Una Pope-Hennessy, *Agnes Strickland: Biographer of the Queens of England* (London, 1940), p. 20.

To make the loggers frisky
At his logging-bee.

The Devil sat on a log heap,
A log heap, a log heap—
A red-hot burning log heap—
A-grinning at the bee;

And there was lots of swearing,
Of boasting and of daring,
Of fighting and of tearing,
At that logging-bee.

J. W. D. M.[1]

A Logging-Bee followed the burning of the fallow as a matter of course. In the bush, where hands are few and labour commands an enormous rate of wages, these gatherings are considered indispensable, and much has been written in their praise; but to me they present the most disgusting picture of a bush life. They are noisy, riotous, drunken meetings, often terminating in violent quarrels, sometimes even in bloodshed. Accidents of the most serious nature often occur, and very little work is done when we consider the number of hands employed and the great consumption of food and liquor. I am certain, in our case, had we hired with the money expended in providing for the bee two or three industrious, hard-working men, we should have got through twice as much work, and have had it done well, and have been the gainers in the end.

People in the woods have a craze for giving and going to bees, and run to them with as much eagerness as a peasant runs to a race-course or a fair, plenty of strong drink and excitement making the chief attraction of the bee. In raising a house or barn a bee may be looked upon as a necessary evil, but these gatherings are generally conducted in a more orderly manner than those for logging. Fewer hands are required, and they are generally under the control of the carpenter who puts up the frame, and if they get drunk during the raising they are liable to meet with very serious accidents.

Thirty-two men, gentle and simple, were invited to our bee, and the maid and I were engaged for two days preceding the important one in baking and cooking for the entertainment of our guests. When I looked at the quantity of food we had prepared I thought that it never could

[1]J. W. Dunbar Moodie, Susanna's husband.

be all eaten, even by thirty-two men. It was a burning-hot day towards the end of July when our loggers began to come in, and the 'gee!' and 'ha!' of the oxen resounded on every side. There was my brother S——,[1] with his frank English face, a host in himself; Lieutenant—— in his blouse, wide white trousers, and red sash, his broad straw hat shading a dark manly face that would have been a splendid property for a bandit chief; the four gay, reckless, idle sons of ——, famous at any spree but incapable of the least mental or physical exertion, who considered hunting and fishing as the sole aim and object of life. These young men rendered very little assistance themselves, and their example deterred others who were inclined to work.

There were the two R——s, who came to work and to make others work; my good brother-in-law,[2] who had volunteered to be the Grog Bos, and a host of other settlers, among whom I recognized Moodie's old acquaintance, Dan Simpson, with his lank red hair and long freckled face; the Youngs, the hunters, with their round, black, curly heads and rich Irish brogue; poor C——, with his long, spare, consumptive figure, and thin, sickly face. Poor fellow, he has long since been gathered to his rest!

There was the ruffian squatter P——, from Clear Lake,—the dread of all honest men; the brutal M——, who treated oxen as if they had been logs by beating them with handspikes; and there was Old Wittals, with his low forehead and long nose, a living witness of the truth of phrenology, if his large organ of acquisitiveness and his want of conscientiousness could be taken in evidence. Yet, in spite of his derelictions from honesty, he was a hard-working, good-natured man, who, if he cheated you in a bargain, or took away some useful article in mistake from your homestead, never wronged his employer in his day's work. . . .

Monaghan was in his glory, prepared to work or fight, whichever should come uppermost; and there was old Thomas and his sons, the contractors for the clearing, to expedite whose movements the bee was called. Old Thomas was a very ambitious man in his way. Though he did not know A from B, he took it into his head that he had received a call from Heaven to convert the heathen in the wilderness; and every Sunday he held a meeting in our logger's shanty for the purpose of awakening sinners and bringing over 'Injun pagans' to the true faith. His method of accomplishing this object was very ingenious. He got his wife, Peggy—or 'my Paggy', as he called her—to read aloud for him a text from the Bible until he knew it by heart; and he had, as he said truly, 'a good remembrancer', and never heard a striking sermon but he

[1]Samuel Strickland.
[2]Thomas Traill, Catharine's husband.

retained the most important passages, and retailed them secondhand to his bush audience. . . .

There was John R——, from Smith-town, the most notorious swearer in the district; a man who esteemed himself clever, nor did he want for natural talent, but he had converted his mouth into such a sink of iniquity that it corrupted the whole man and all the weak and thoughtless of his own sex who admitted him in their company. I had tried to convince John R—— (for he often frequented the house under the pretence of borrowing books) of the great crime that he was constantly committing, and of the injurious effect it must produce upon his own family, but the mental disease had taken too deep a root to be so easily cured. Like a person labouring under some foul disease, he contaminated all he touched. Such men seem to make an ambitious display of their bad habits in such scenes, and, if they afford a little help, they are sure to get intoxicated and make a row. There was my friend, old Ned Dunn, who had been so anxious to get us out of the burning fallow. There was a whole group of Dummer Pines.[1] Levi, the little wiry, witty poacher: Cornish Bill, the honest-hearted old peasant with his stalwart figure and uncouth dialect; and David, and Ned—all good men and true; and Malachi Chroak, a queer, withered-up, monkey-man that seemed like some mischievous elf, flitting from heap to heap to make work and fun for the rest; and many others were at that bee who have since found a rest in the wilderness: Adam T——, H——, J. M——, H. N——. These, at different times, lost their lives in those bright waters in which, on such occasions as these, they used to sport and frolic to refresh themselves during the noonday heat. Alas! how many, who were then young and in their prime, that river and its lakes have swept away!

Our men worked well until dinner-time, when, after washing in the lake, they all sat down to the rude board which I had prepared for them, loaded with the best fare that could be procured in the bush. Pea-soup, legs of pork, venison, eel, and raspberry pies, garnished with plenty of potatoes, and whiskey to wash them down, besides a large iron kettle of tea. To pour out the latter, and dispense it round, devolved upon me. My brother and his friends, who were all temperance men, and consequently the best workers in the field, kept me and the maid actively employed in replenishing their cups.

The dinner passed off tolerably well; some of the lower order of the Irish settlers were pretty far gone, but they committed no outrage upon

[1]Paynes, whose descendants are widely spread throughout Canada and the United States. Many other family names could be identified from Mrs. Moodie's description, but her comments about them suggest that their descendants would prefer them to remain anonymous.

our feelings by either swearing or bad language, a few harmless jokes alone circulating among them. . . .

After the sun went down the logging-band came in to supper, which was all ready for them. Those who remained sober ate the meal in peace and quietly returned to their own homes; while the vicious and the drunken staid to brawl and fight.

After having placed the supper on the table I was so tired with the noise, and heat, and fatigue of the day that I went to bed, leaving to Mary and my husband the care of the guests.

We were obliged to endure a second and a third repetition of this odious scene before sixteen acres of land were rendered fit for the reception of our fall crop of wheat.

My hatred to these tumultuous, disorderly meetings was not in the least decreased by my husband being twice seriously hurt while attending them. After the second injury he received he seldom went to them himself, but sent his oxen and servant in his place. In these odious gatherings the sober, moral, and industrious man is more likely to suffer than the drunken and profane, as during the delirium of drink these men expose others to danger as well as themselves.

The conduct of many of the settlers, who considered themselves gentlemen and would have been very much affronted to have been called otherwise, was often more reprehensible than that of the poor Irish emigrants to whom they should have set an example of order and sobriety. The behaviour of these young men drew upon them the severe but just censures of the poorer class, whom they regarded in every way as their inferiors.

'That blackguard calls himself a gentleman. In what respect is he better than us?' was an observation too frequently made use of at these gatherings. To see a bad man in the very worst point of view, follow him to a bee; be he profane, licentious, quarrelsome, or a rogue, all his native wickedness will be fully developed there. . . .

12. Sir Richard Bonnycastle

A VISIT TO SEYMOUR TOWNSHIP, TRENT RIVER, IN 1845

[*Bonnycastle,* Canada and the Canadians in 1846 (*London, 1846*), *Vol. II, pp. 235–59*]

The River Trent is a large stream, full of shallows and rapids and beautiful lakes, taking its rise north of the township of Somerville, in the Colborne District, not very far from a chain of lakes which reach the Ottawa on the east, and the Black River, a feeder of Lake Simcoe, and a tributary of Huron and the Severn, on the west.

The river Trent is strangely tortuous, but keeps almost entirely within the Colborne district, named after Lord Seaton, and at Rice Lake afforded a site for the Colonial Office to establish a flourishing colony a few years ago at Peterborough, and to open an entirely new and very rich portion of Canada West.

This river, placed, as it were, by Nature as the connecting link of a great chain of inland navigation embracing the expanse of Huron, Ontario, and the Ottawa, opens a field of research both to the agriculturist and the forester. The woods abound with the finest kind of untouched timber; the land is fertile in the extreme; and the rivers, streams, and lakes abound with fish. In short, had the Trent Canal been finished, instead of the miserable and decaying timber-slides which now encumber that noble river, another million of inhabitants would, in ten years more, have filled up the forests which are now only penetrated by the Indian or the seeker after timber.

A private individual has, however, put a steamboat upon the centre of the river's course; and Mr. Weller, no doubt, finds that it pays him well, for the portion of Colborne district near Rice Lake is settling rapidly.

The Trent Canal, or a railroad in the same direction, would lead to the Georgian Bay of Huron, and thus render a journey to the far West easy of accomplishment, as it is the most direct route from Oswego and New York.

But I must journey on, and after resting at Brighton start by daylight and penetrate into the bowels of the land by a sandy road, which, after passing that village, stretches into the forest due north.

Away the waggon went, not at a hand-gallop, for the sand was too deep for that, and, passing through woods by a tolerably good road for so new a settlement, we, every now and then, at intervals few and far between, saw a new farm or a new log-hut.

The day was fine, and so, having carried our provision with us, we halted in the deep woods upon the muddy banks of the Cold Creek to breakfast. A Tartar camp was visited by an English traveller somewhere in the dominions of the Grand Lama, and he was treated to London porter. So were we in the deep forest of Central Canada, for London porter appears to travel everywhere; and discussing it with much relish, we fed the horses and gave them what they liked much better, clear and pure water—which, indeed, I now think would have been quite as good for us—and waggoned on until we came to a surprising new settlement in the Bush, the villages of Percy and Percy Landing, where, there being mill 'privileges', as a sharp running water-stream is called in the United States, flour and saw-mills have been established and a very thriving population is rising both in numbers and in means. Here we dined in a new inn, or rather tavern, kept by a French Canadian, and then pursued our journey for a few miles on a decent new road amidst fine settlements and good farms, and, crossing a beautiful stream, plunged into the undisturbed forest by a road in which every rut was a canal, and every stone as big as a bomb-shell at the very least. How the waggon stood it, and the roots and stumps of the trees with which these boulders were diversified, I am still unable to explain; for my part I walked the greater part of it, for the bones of my body seemed as if they were very likely, after a short trial, to part company with each other.

At length, after jolting, jumping, complaining, and comforting, we came to a bridge near Myer's Mills. Our *conducteur*, my young friend aforesaid, who was more used to the road, saw at a glance that something had gone wrong with the said bridge; for it exhibited a very disorderly, drunken sort of devil-may-care aspect.

He was too far advanced upon it to retreat, when he discovered that a beam or two had departed into the lively current below. With true backwoodsman's energy he pulled his horses up sharp, reined them well up, and then, with a tremendous shout, applied the whip, and actually leaped horses, waggon, and passengers over the chasm, the remainder of the bridge groaning and saying most plainly, 'I will not bear this any longer'. Next morning we heard that the whole structure had fallen in and disappeared.

I have been in some danger in the course of my life; but a visit afterwards to this spot convinced me that one's existence is often a sort of size-ace throw; and whether the six or the one comes up or goes down is a miracle. I never had a nearer leap for clearing Styx than this, excepting one shortly afterwards upon the timber-slides of the Trent, at Healy's Falls.

A vast timber canal or way had been constructed here by the Board of Works to convey timber down a rapid without danger, the slide being alongside of that rapid. It was an interesting work; and with my young friend and two naval officers, settled in Seymour, I went to examine it. At the sluiceway or timber-dam was a sort of bridge composed of parallel pieces of heavy square joists and a platform; we walked along this Mahomet's railway, where Azrael seemed to have established pretty much the same sentry as Cerberus, having two or three mouths ready to devour the adventurous passenger.

The parallel pieces were about two feet distant from each other; I walked on one and my companions on the other, until a good view of the whole work and the splendid rapids was attained. Under our feet at some distance was the water of the slide running on an inclined plane of woodwork, at a great angle and with enormous power and velocity into a pitch or cauldron far below.

The day was bright, and the shadow of the parallel logs left between the space no view of the water underneath. They called me suddenly to look at the rapid. I jumped, as I thought, over the space between us; but my jump was into the shadow. One of the naval officers, a powerful man six feet and more in height, saw me jump; and just as I was disappearing between the timbers caught me by the arm and, by sheer muscle and strength, held me in mid-air. The other immediately assisted him, but my young friend became deadly pale and sick. I did not visit either the slide or the cauldron; in either, instantaneous and suffocating death was inevitable. Reader, never leap in dark places, and look before you leap. My young friend looked before he leaped over the bridge with his span of horses, and, like a gallant *auriga*, guided his van without fear; but he told me afterwards that the cold sweat sat on his brow when the chasm was cleared, as much on the bridge as it did at my Quintus Curtius venture. By the by, did Quinte Curce, as the French so adroitly call him, ever leap—I doubt the fact—into the chasm which closed over him? . . .

I went to a combined fishing and shooting pic-nickery, and travelled from Rainey's mills and Falls all along the valley of the Trent to Healy's Falls.

The Trent is a beautiful and most picturesque river, rushing roaring along over a series of falls and rapids for miles together, and expanding in noble reaches and little lakes.

Rainey's Falls I have faintly sketched to show the soft beauty of some parts of this river; at Healy's Falls it is more broken.

We went to Crow Bay, just above which the Crow River, from the iron mine country of Marmora, runs into the Trent. Here we found two friends, brothers, settled in great comfort. They had been about ten years in the 'Bush' and had excellent farms and horses equal to any I have seen so far in the interior, with every comfort around them. In one of their pleasure-boats, we embarked for the junction of the rivers, on which it is intended to place a town when the country becomes more settled.

All is now forest excepting a very extensive and very flourishing settlement of twelve hundred acres, undertaken by a retired field-officer in the army, which was a grant about ten years ago for his services and is now worth two thousand pounds, or perhaps more since a bridge has been built by the provincial legislature over the Trent in order to connect the mail route between the townships of Seymour-East and Seymour-West, as both are filling up rapidly and land becomes consequently dear and scarce. . . .

The first settlers in Seymour were lumber merchants who, seeing the wealth of the country in pine, and oak, and ash, the great fertility of the soil, and the facilities afforded everywhere for erecting mills, established themselves permanently, and, before the agriculturists were induced to think of it, had removed from all land within miles of the river the only valuable timber that the township contained. Thus one source of profit, and that a very great one to the farming settler, has been destroyed, and the enterprising timber-merchant has established at convenient distances several saw-mills where his lumber is converted into plank and boards for the lower markets, and where he is at all times ready to saw whatever timber the farmer has left into boards and planks for him, receiving so many feet of timber and giving so many feet of lumber, as sawed timber is called, taking care of himself, of course, in the exchange.

The flour-mills at Percy proceed upon the same principle: a farmer brings sacks of grain and receives sacks of flour in exchange, said exchange being of course three to one, or more, against him.

Throughout Canada is this truck or barter system pursued, and very little money finds its way either into or out of the back townships, unless it be the receipts of the lumber-merchant from Quebec or the lakes. The lumber-merchant is, therefore, the lord of the Trent, or of any other great internal river whereon are new settlements; and many of them have amassed large fortunes.

Thus came timber-slides instead of canal upon this splendid river, which must, as soon as the Murray Canal on the Bay of Quinte is undertaken, be also opened to navigation, as by it the richest part of Western Canada, both in soil and in minerals, will be reached, and a direct communication had in war-time from Kingston, the great naval key of the lakes, with Penetangueshene, and Lakes Huron and Superior. . . .

It was somewhat melancholy, on reaching Healy's Falls, which are turbulent rapids of the most picturesque character with an immense timber-slide or broad wooden sloping canal alongside of them, to see the clearance in this far solitude formed by the workmen. They had built houses, shanties, and sheds, and had lived and loved together for many a month, with their families, on this charming spot. Nothing was in ruin: all was new, even to the window-glass; and when our party, after toiling away through the forest, reached the opening and saw below us the foaming rapids, the grand forest, the rugged banks, the timber-slide, and the little wooden town, we thought here at least is a well chosen hamlet at which we may rest awhile.

No smoke rose from the chimneys; not a soul appeared to greet us; the eagle soared above; the cunning fox, or the murderous wolf, the snake and the toad alone found shelter, where so many human beings had so recently congregated, where from morn till dewy eve the hum of human voices had been incessant, and where toil and labour had won support for so many.

Occasionally the rude and reckless lumberman halts here whilst his timber is passing the slide; the coarse jest and the coarser oath are alone heard at the falls of the Trent, save when the neighbouring farmer visits them to procure a day's relaxation from his toils and to view the grandeur of creation, and, we trust, to be thankful for the dispensation which has cast his lot in strange places. What must be the occasional thoughts of a man educated tenderly and luxuriously in England, when he reflects upon the changes and the chances which have brought him into contact with the domain of the bear, of the snake, and of the lumberer! Dear, dear England, thy green glades, thy peaceful villages, thy thousand comforts, the scenes of youth, the friends, the parents who have gone to the land of promise—will these memories not intrude? No where in this wonderful world do they come upon the mind with more solemn impressiveness than in the wild woods of Canada.

13. Charles Richard Weld

A VISIT TO THE PETERBOROUGH REGION, 1854

[*Weld,* A Vacation Tour in the United States and Canada (*London, 1855*)*, pp. 93–118*]

Immediately after leaving Coburg we plunged into the forest, through which the railway is carried to the [Rice] lake. Here we found a tiny steamer, with high-pressure engines, which snorted and splashed across the water to the discomfort of ducks and other birds feeding on the wild rice. This plant, which gives its name to the lake, grows in such profusion as to make the water appear in many places like green pastures. Steering through these we drew near the wooded shore and entered the mouth of the Otonabee, a lazy river about a hundred yards wide, lined by the dense and dark primeval forest. The sail up this stream is extremely wild and romantic. As the steamer puffed round each bend, flights of scared water-fowl made the river

'Vocal in its wooded walls',

and passed away into the wilderness yet undisturbed by man. For, with rare exceptions, the forest is in a state of nature; and, even where the settler has broken in, his labours have made but little impression.

'Captain', said the butter-merchant, 'be sure you put me out at Campbell Town.' Shortly after this injunction the little steamer paused abreast of a small clearing, provided with a rude landing-place constructed of unhewn logs. 'Now then, who's for Campbell Town?' exclaimed the captain, as he threw an attenuate leathern bag lettered 'Her Majesty's Mail' to a lad in waiting with a cart. At these words the butter-merchant, valise in hand, came forward and begged to know where Campbell Town was, as no houses were visible. The question was not irrelevant. Town in the shape of houses there was none; a few scattered log-huts and shanties formed the embryo of what, doubtless, will be ere long a flourishing community. Beyond these there was nothing in sight but the interminable forest. The Yankee's countenance fell as his vision of a thriving agricultural settlement was dispelled by the reality; and as he stepped on shore to seek his fortune we heard him uttering, 'Wall, I'm darn'd if I ever see sich a town'.

Near Peterborough the settlements increased in number and extent, and were of all ages, from the first stage where the prostrate trees or unsightly stumps told how fiercely war had been waged against the forest, to the period of glorious victory proclaimed by the snug house and homestead standing amidst green pastures or corn-fields, whose golden waves awaited the sickle, or stood gathered into banded sheaves,

'Like armies of prosperity'.

As the steamer drew near Peterborough, and the captain pointed to the residence of my friend, I felt strange emotions; for it had been a day-dream of many years' duration to visit him and his sister in their Canadian home. Now it was on the eve of realisation; and those who have enjoyed the warm welcome of affectionate friendship in a far distant land will conceive my feelings of joy when I passed under their roof. One purpose of my tour was accomplished; and, casting off the cares and anxieties of travel, I gave myself up for a season to quiet repose. . . .

Accompanied by two friends I left Peterborough early on a glorious morning for the backwoods. We travelled in a buggy, the vehicle generally used in Canada, which, although extremely light, successfully resists the terrible concussions arising from the wretched roads. Our destination was the township of Douro, about twelve miles from Peterborough, where I was promised a hearty welcome from Major Strickland, brother of the authoress of the 'Queens of England', who has long been settled in the above township. Our route lay up the left bank of the Otonabee, the stream not being navigable higher than Peterborough. Its dashing waters are, however, used for floating down logs for the lumber trade, and driving saw-mills. We visited the largest of these establishments, about three miles from Peterborough. The machinery is on a gigantic scale. One hundred and thirty-six saws were working with tremendous velocity, reducing huge logs to planks at the rate of nearly fifty an hour. Instead of using files to sharpen the saws, a powerful punching machine is employed, which cuts fresh faces on the teeth; a process combining greater efficiency with saving of time. . . .

Resuming our drive we entered the bush, now unenlivened by settlements, their absence being made painfully sensible to us by the terrible condition of the road. Holes masked by mud were of constant occurrence. Into these our vehicle plunged with a crash, threatening to reduce it to atoms; but, much to my surprise, it was on each occasion dragged out by the willing horses, apparently uninjured. Worse, however, than the holes, was the dreadful corduroy composed of large logs, over which we bumped with a dislocatory motion, rendering it difficult to keep one's seat. To avoid these bad places, we frequently turned aside into the bush, preferring to rough it through the tangled underwood; and occasionally drove in the bed of the river when it afforded an easier route. So bad, in short, was this road, that although we had only a dozen miles to drive, we were five hours on the way. But as our bones outlasted the jolting, the varied incidents were highly diverting. As we approached Douro, the forest gave place to clearings, affording charming views of the scenery of this favoured township. Presently we came to small houses and log-huts sown broadcast upon the land; the commencement of a town to which the name of Lakefield has been given, as the sheet of water from whence the Otonabee issues is within a short distance. Hastening onwards, for an ominous black cloud threatened a storm, we at length arrived at Major Strickland's settlement,[1] and had just time to get under shelter, when the thunder-cloud discharged its contents in torrents of rain, imparting a delicious coolness to the atmosphere. It has been said everything is on a larger scale in the New World than in the old. That the thunder is louder, and the rain heavier in Canada than in England is certain; at least, if what I heard and saw on this occasion were fair specimens of these phenomena.

Fortunately the Major was at home, and as soon as the weather permitted we crossed the yard to his house, where we received a warm welcome. Dinner was immediately ordered, and as *impromptu* repasts are of constant occurrence in the bush, where even stage-coaches are

[1]"Lakefield," says a *Directory* contemporary with Samuel Strickland's farm-school, "is a beautiful little Village in the Township of Douro, on the banks of Katchewanoc Lake. It is the residence of a number of young Englishmen, who have come to the country with the view of learning the art of farming or 'roughing it in the bush'." (*Directory of the United Counties of Peterborough and Victoria for 1858* (Peterborough, 1858), p. 32.)

unknown, we were soon seated before fare which, if a little rough, had the advantage of being highly appreciated by the zest of keen hunger. But it would have ill accorded with my expectation or desire to have found luxuries in the bush, for I had come to see the life led by the bold settler who makes his home in the wilderness. As we sat down the Major's son stepped out into the verandah and blew a long and loud blast upon a horn, which was answered by the arrival of half-a-dozen fine young men wearing loose trousers and red flannel hunting-shirts secured round the waist by a leather belt, from whence formidable knives depended. In a few minutes another party of young men made their appearance similarly attired. I was somewhat puzzled; for although I knew the Major had more than one son, I had not heard that his children were as numerous as those vouchsafed to the patriarchs of old.

The mystery was explained by the Major telling me the young gentlemen were his pupils, whom he received into his house for a term of years, and instructed in various agricultural pursuits and matters relating to a settler's life.[1] Thus a young man disposed to settle in the backwoods, by the payment of a small annual sum, has an opportunity of acquiring the information requisite for the successful pursuit of his proposed career, with the soundest practical advice in the selection of cleared or uncleared land; for Major Strickland is an old settler, and moreover agent to the Canada Land Company. And should the roughing which he has to submit to during his probation cause him to turn aside from his intention, he has the satisfaction of not losing his capital, which is too frequently sacrificed in the purchase of experience.

As my friends had to return to Peterborough, and had no desire to be permanently engulphed in a mud hole or wrecked on the ribs of a corduroy during night hours, they departed in the afternoon, leaving me in the care of my kind host. Under his guidance I took a walk through a portion of the township, and was initiated into the mysteries of clearing land, the first business of a settler's life. This is a tedious process, nine or ten years being required to get rid of most stumps. Hard wood stumps, such as beech, maple, oak, iron-wood, elm, &c., rot out in that period, but pine stumps remain sound much longer, and require to be either burnt out or extracted by the aid of oxen or horses. It is, however, when the stumps are in the ground, that the heaviest crops are

[1]A biography of Mutius V. Clementi describes his emigration from England to New York, and gives this interesting estimate of the farm-school: "Thence he proceeded direct to a so-called 'Agricultural School' at North Douro (now Lakefield), Peterborough County, operated by the late Colonel Strickland, a retired army officer. Many young Englishmen of good family learned the rudiments of practical farming as understood by the genial Colonel. They consisted chiefly in a thorough training in manly sports and a fine discrimination in the selection of liquors." (*Report* No. 41 of the Ontario Land Surveyors Association, 1926, page 103.)

obtained from the virgin soil, which for some years requires no manure. At the same time, no wise farmer will exhaust the vegetable supersoil by taxing its wonderful producing properties too severely. . . .

On our return we found the young gentlemen putting their rifles in order and eagerly planning a deer-hunt for the following morning. The woods abound with these animals, which are started by dogs and driven towards the lake; the sport consisting in either shooting them as they bound across openings in the forest, or capturing them in the water. A locality is assigned to every person joining the sport, where he is enjoined to remain until he has either the good fortune to shoot the deer, or is apprised that the game has gone off in another direction.

The necessary preliminaries having been arranged to the satisfaction of all parties, we sat down to supper, after which songs were sung with *fortissimo* choruses; for, at the time of my visit, Major Strickland's domestic establishment had not the advantage of a lady at its head. At the same time, I must say, social conviviality never degenerated to coarseness; and though the red hunting-shirts, looming through tobacco-smoke, gave the company a brigandish appearance, gentlemanly conduct was as strongly maintained as if the scene of our merriment had been a London drawing-room.

As the deer-hunt was fixed for an early hour, we soon retired to rest; and thanks to fatigue and a good bed I was in a few minutes in the land of dreams, from whence I did not emerge until roused by the hunting party. The scene of the sport was about two miles from the house. The dogs were sent into the forest, and the hunters repaired to their places. Faithful to their instructions, they remained at their post a long time with their eyes 'peel'd', as the Yankees say, and their ears alive to the faintest sound. But it was not my fortune either to shoot the deer or see it; for, although one was started, it took a course towards the interior of the bush, into which it was pursued by the dogs. The preconcerted signal, a blast from a horn, set the hunters free; but before turning homewards I could not resist the desire of penetrating alone into the forest. Carefully noting conspicuous trees, I went on until wrapped by the mazy folds of innumerable stems, between which daylight and gloom struggled for mastery. The silence, broken only by the occasional scream of a wild bird or the hum of insects, was painfully oppressive; and as the spirit of the scene grew upon me I felt how truly Goldsmith has pictured the lost wanderer in an American wilderness—

'Where beasts with man divided empire claim,
And the brown Indian takes a deadly aim;
There, while above the giddy tempest flies,
And all around distressful yells arise,

The pensive exile, bending with his wo,
To stop too fearful, and too faint to go,
Casts a fond look where England's glories shine,
And bids his bosom sympathise with mine.'

A duck-shooting and fishing expedition, on which we started after breakfast, was attended with greater success than the deer-hunt. These birds in autumn are numerous, and easy of approach, as the sportsmen are masked by the rice-beds among which they feed. It would, indeed, have been easy to shoot dozens of these fowl; but we were content with a moderate bag, and relinquishing our guns, prepared our tackle for basse fishing. Stout rods and lines are requisite for this sporting and heavy fish, which on this occasion, I am sorry to say, we captured with bait. No flies were to be had; so the tourist who may be tempted to visit the backwoods on a sporting expedition will do well to bring a supply with him.

The piscatorial wealth of the water was amazing. Standing on a raft constructed expressly for fishing, moored in favourable localities, we caught in the course of a few hours several basse weighing from two to four pounds each, besides numerous goodly perch and sun-fish, glorious in their golden splendour, which eagerly struggled for the bait with their finny brethren.

But pleasant as are my associations with Lake Clear—its beauteous wooded isles,[1] around which the basse love to lead

'A cold, sweet, silver life, wrapped in round waves,
Quickened with touches of transporting fear,'—

more undying memories attach to an excursion, on the last day of my brief sojourn at Lakefield, to visit some Indians in their lodge on an island in an upper lake.

Major Strickland paddled me in his log canoe; giving me, before starting, strict injunctions to maintain as perfect an equilibrium as possible, as the slightest swerve would in all probability result in precipitating us into the lake; a difficulty which promised to be increased, as part of our plan was to troll for maskinonge. Now as these fish are noted for their great size and strength, it was evident no small care would be requisite, should I capture one of these monsters, to keep the canoe steady; for matters were so arranged that, while half-reclined at one end, the Major, squatted on his hams, paddled at the other; and a stout

[1]At that time the western half of Stoney Lake, with its beautiful islands, was considered part of Clear Lake.

trolling-line was towed astern, one extremity of which was secured to my right arm. The bait used for maskinonge is curious; being a large spoon of polished metal, generally copper or brass, within the concavity of which a strong hook is soldered. A swivel attached to the head of the spoon allows it to rotate when drawn rapidly through the water; and whether it be that maskinonge are spoon-fed during their infancy, or other reason, I cannot say; but it is certain they have a great fondness for this glittering bait. But the reader will, perhaps, want to know what a maskinonge is like. Similar to the pike in shape (*Esox estor* of Cuvier), it is generally much larger; and though the weight of a fish is often its only title to fame, the maskinonge has the merit of being good as well as great. In common with the pickerel, which occupies a position somewhere between the trout and perch, it is peculiar to the United States and especially to the great lakes and the northern waters, where it is very abundant. This I can confirm; for we had not made much progress before I felt a sharp twitch at my arm, quickly succeeded by a pull which arrested the skiff's progress. Taking the line in my hand, I played the fish as well as I could, and succeeded eventually in drawing him alongside. To secure him was, however, quite beyond my skill, for he was of prodigious size. Handing the tackle to the Major, he dexterously swung our prize into the canoe, where he was speedily reduced to tranquillity by a well-administered blow on the back of his head from a small mallet. He weighed 22 lbs.; and those who have captured large and strong pike will conceive the exciting work it was to battle with such a fellow from the narrow confines of a log canoe. We afterwards caught two more; and might have swelled the number to almost any amount had we felt inclined. But we could not fish and visit the Indians; so we wound up our lines and paddled swiftly through the bright waters. The trip was delightful. At the head of Clear Lake, a reach, not unlike that separating the upper and middle Killarney lakes, occurs, studded by wooded islands. On one of these the Indians were camped; but there was no sign of life, nor could we detect amidst the dense foliage a landing-place.

A wild whoop from my companion was answered by an Indian, who burst through the bush and motioned us to a little creek, where we disembarked. Following our swarthy guide, we came suddenly on a small clearing, in the centre of which was the lodge. A more picturesque spot could not well be conceived. The ground, mantled by a variety of wild flowers, sloped gently towards the Lake. Lofty trees shut out the oppressive sun, and a tiny brook gurgled sweetly as it leaped into daylight from the gloom of the forest. The lodge was constructed of birch-bark, open at the top for the egress of smoke. Around were various hunting and fishing implements. Portly fish, with strips of bear-flesh and venison hanging on poles in process of curing, attested how efficiently these had been used.

Pushing aside the buffalo-skin serving as a door we entered the lodge, from which, however, I was nearly driven by the dense and acrid smoke. The family consisted of the Indian's wife, mother-in-law, and two girls, who were squatted round the fire superintending a savoury mess of boiled ducks, fish, and squirrels.

The women and girls could not speak a word of English. The excessive natural simplicity of the girls and the freedom of their limbs were remarkable. With their naked feet, which were beautifully formed, they seized fragments of wood and cast them on the fire with the same ease as we should perform the operation with our hands.

The whole scene was sufficiently wild and novel to be very interesting; and I sincerely recommend the tourist to turn aside from the beaten track to visit the Indians in the bush. He must not, however, expect to see the wild savage in this part of North America. The white man has driven him into the far west beyond the Mississippi. But though the Ojibeways residing in Upper Canada pass a considerable portion of the year in the outskirts of towns, their hunting spirit breaks forth in the autumn, when, casting off the trammels of civilisation, at all times galling and perplexing, they seek the wilderness, erect their lodges by the side of a lake or stream, and spend their days hunting and fishing; while their squaws make Indian ornaments or sew the seams of birch-bark canoes, for which they have a constant demand from settlers. The Indian whom I visited had several of these graceful boats in hand, for each of which he was to receive six dollars. . . .

We returned to Lakefield in the evening; and the following day my kind host drove me to Peterborough. On our way he frequently expatiated on the state of the road, which I thought wretched, but which he contrasted with the condition of things when it took him an entire day to journey from Peterborough to his home in the bush.

14. Colonel Samuel Strickland Presents Diplomas

["*Katchewanoonka Herald.*"]

Last Thursday Lieut Col. Strickland granted Diploma's to two of his pupils, T. B. Allen Esq and W. P. Band. The Former Gentleman passed a highly creditable Examination and as a proof of what high esteem he is held the next day he received the appointment of Steward over the Estate of the Rev. P. S. Warren. Mr Band was not so fortunate we believe, not so much from want of abilities, but from too great a con-

Courtesy of George M. Douglas

AGRICULTURAL DIPLOMA

This item from the manuscript newspaper circulated in the Lakefield district in the late eighteen-fifties makes fun of "the gallant Major" and his Agricultural School for budding Canadian backwoodsmen. The writing is by T. B. Allen, who stands behind W. P. Band as he receives his diploma. J. E. Beatty, another pupil, is the artist. The banner at the left bears the inscription DIPLOMAS FOR EVER. This unique material is reproduced by courtesy of George M. Douglas of Lakefield, in whose possession is a fragmentary file of the "Katchewanoonka Herald."

fidence in himself, and therefore not studying sufficiently; Mr Band is much cut up about it, but idleness always meets its reward; he was nearly losing an extremely advantageous situation with E. Leigh Esq. who of course could not receive him without his diploma; the unfortunate youth is now staying at the hospitable mansion of J. E. Beatty Esq., who is attempting to eradicate those pernicious seeds of idleness which have been sown on a too fertile mind.

15. Captain Horton Rhys

A VISIT TO PETERBOROUGH AND LAKEFIELD, 1860

["*Morton Price*", A Theatrical Trip for a Wager! through Canada and the United States (*London, 1861*), *pp. 60–9*]

From Port Hope we journeyed north to Peterborough. This is a portion of my journey that I look back to with much pleasure. I, by this time, began to see my way. My winning the wager was a certainty, bar accidents or ill-health. We were gradually getting into the ways of the country and the habits of the people, and, strangely enough, so it then seemed to us, the farther we got into this strange land, the more Englishified it became; at least, as far as the inhabitants were concerned.

So, be it understood, I did not go to Peterborough for the purpose of increasing my professional receipts, (though, as luck had it, I did to some extent, most unexpectedly, and as will be seen); but rather to investigate a little life amongst the backwoodsmen, and what I saw I will now relate. Peterborough, which is quite a frontier town, there being no other pretention to the term 'town' north, or beyond it, is a most eccentric-looking place. Though quite in its infancy, it appears to have grown prematurely aged—a sort of young child with an old man's face.

A few years ago its site was a wilderness. Now there's, I don't know how many, but a good lot of people there. Of course the greater number of the houses, especially the large ones, or those intended to have been large, are, and are likely to remain, in an unfinished state. . . .

At Peterborough I was destined to meet an old friend with a new face; he was at Eton with me, and was then and there a very pretty boy; and being of a retiring mild nature, I had often on more than one occasion taken his part against some juvenile bully. He had come to Canada to *learn farming*. 'Heaven save the mark!'—and was *studying* 'away out' at a place called Douro, about twelve miles off.

The pretty, retiring, mild youth, had changed into a big-bearded, brawny, bellowing back-woodsman. I never saw such a creature. (I told *him* so; so, of course, I may *you*.) If you can fancy Ben Caunt, with an enormous red beard, whiskers, and mustachios, in a Glengarry cap, a red flannel shirt, loose leather breeches, and a pair of knicker-bockers, you have (barring the nose) a good likeness of my friend (what shall I call him?)—'Blazes!'

When he discovered my 'little game', as he called it, nothing would satisfy him but that we must and should give our Entertainment in Peterborough. 'He would bring in all his friends from Douro, he would keep them and himself perfectly sober until it was all over; and if every-body in Peterborough didn't come he'd know the reason why!' *&c., &c., &c.* To such powerful arguments we could but succumb, and, much to our surprise, we discovered that there was a little amateur theatre in the town, called 'White's Room'. At this time I had just written a new enter-tainment, called *A Scene in the Highlands*, and being anxious for a re-hearsal, and having little dread of Peterborough critics, we 'concluded' to play, and did so, with such success, and to such crowded and respect-able audiences (whether owing to our friend *Blazes*' persuasion or threats I know not), that not content with *two* nights, we played four!

I thought Lucille's[1] hearers would never be satisfied with 'Ever of thee', 'Annie Laurie', and 'I'm sitting by the stile, Mary'. They *would* have her back, time after time; and I think if *I* had been exiled there I should have done the same. *Blazes* persisted in *crying* over 'I'm sitting by the stile, Mary', and said he was an Irishman, though I know he used to be a Londoner. This, however, was late in the evening.

Having thus paid our way, and a little to spare, I determined on a slight relaxation from mental labour, and ditto a little in the body. Douro, I have said, is a 'diggings' some twelve miles from Peterborough, and is a regular stronghold of sucking farmers. Suckers, and no mistake! Their powers of suction would astonish a Pitman!

Well, this Douro is right in the bush, and if any of my readers *should* journey from Peterborough to Douro they'll wonder how it ever got there; a more *villainous* road I never travelled, though my friend *Blazes* (of course), and also *his* friend (another long but not *so* rough-looking customer, who had something to do with the lumber—i.e. timber trade), declared ' 'twas nuts to what it *was*!'

I was glad that a slight cold prevented Lucille from being one of the party, though that fact prevented me from staying to see and do all that I should have wished. A deer hunt, of course, we had—that is to say, the dogs had, and having, I suppose, 'By raison of being a stranger', as a *bona fide* Irishman of the party said, been put in a 'convaynient' position—which meant that I could neither see or be seen—and told to keep my eyes and ears open and my mouth shut, I had my first and last acquaintance with a Canadian Deer Hunt. . . .

Breakfast at seven. 'Any head-ache?' 'No?' 'What do you say to fishing?'

'Why, you know', I said, '*that* was what I came here for.'

'*And* the whisky?'

'Bother the whisky!'

'Well, you *were* "tight";' and I shall tell your friends that I took care of you.'

The speaker was so utterly 'sewn up' some two hours before the party quite dispersed, that he slept where he fell, and never 'turned in' at all.

Fishing, some two or three of us went; and if I at all astonished these rough sons of Englishmen with my 'pop-gun', I did so still more with my rod. It was an ordinary trout rod, made by an old fellow named Hucklebridge, in Bath, (one that I have fished with over fifteen years), and with a few sewin flies (my friends used bait), I succeeded in landing, or rather in *boat*ing, for I fished principally from the latter, thirteen bass—a fish neither a salmon, a trout, nor a grayling, but (with a dash

[1]This was Rhys's actress-companion on the American trip.

of the porpoise) a little of all combined. They averaged three pounds apiece. But, bless you! a good old English trout of that weight would have made my ancient piece of hickory bend its back a little more than any of them did.

They were, however, good fun. There was a nice breeze, and the *thing was new*; and that goes a long way towards temporary satisfaction.

Blazes was a great hand at a canoe, and after I was tired of fishing he insisted on paddling me up a lake, I forget the name, where he said he had appointed to meet an Indian.

'What—a real live Indian?'

'I believe you, my bo-hoy!'

Now I had often wished to see an Indian, and, like most things that one wishes much to see, when I *did* see one I didn't think much of it.

The dark and almost indecent individual we were in quest of, made a sudden appearance in answer to an unearthly screech from the lungs of my Charon as we neared the shore of a thickly-wooded eyot. Paddling over the tiny waves with a marvellous rapidity in a similar unsafe looking concern to that we were in, he came alongside; and after an interchange with Blazes of a few words in French and Chinese—at least it sounded like it—and an awful lot of grimaces, he pointed at me with the spoon end of his paddle, saying, or rather shouting, 'Hi-phiz, cockonoscrummery!' or *words to that effect*, and darted off; and, much to my surprise, we after him!

'Where are you going?' I asked.

'Going! Going to introduce you to my father-in-law, that is to be!' he answered, paddling away with all his might.

'Your what?'

'Yes; it's all right! That's my wife's brother, on ahead, there!'

'Get out!' I exclaimed, forgetting I was in a çanoe, and bestowing a kick on his shins.

'By G—d!' was his reply, 'we shall both *get out* sooner than we can get in again, if you come any of those games. Sit still, man!—you are not in bed!'

Thus admonished, I collapsed.

We shortly reached a large raft moored along-side a steep bank, the bank itself being nearly hidden from view by overhanging trees and bush. Blazes here pulled up, and told *me* (this time) to 'Get out!'—a performance of no easy accomplishment. Canoes are the most slippery things in creation—our outriggers are jolly-boats to them. Out, however, I got, after a deal of wibble-wobbling; and Blazes paddled off somewhere out of sight, much to my momentary discomfiture. He, however, quickly appeared on the bank overhead, and from thence directed me to a flight of steps, or rather stones, which I had not until then perceived. I ascended, and found myself on a little green knoll with large tree stumps here and there, and studded around with huts apparently made of logs and bark of trees. Well, I never!—I was actually in an Indian encampment! There were men and women, and children and dogs; and Blazes seemed on intimate terms with all.

He presently introduced me to a venerable-looking old picture card, wrapped—although it was very hot—in a buffalo skin, and squatted on his haunches smoking a red clay pipe with a profusely ornamented stem.

'Father-in-law', he said, 'this is my friend—a mighty hunter in England—a great warrior in many lands—and a jolly good fellow!'

This correct description, being given in English, not a word, of course, the old gentleman would have understood but for the expressive pantomine with which it was accompanied. It, however, evidently impressed the aged Ojibbeway that I was somebody; and he thereupon set up a howl of welcome and beckoned me to squat. This, imagining myself tolerably secure, I did, and looked about me; and thereupon saw the retreating form of Blazes on the point of entering one of the huts. Now I had no intention of being left with this old heathen, so I *made tracks* after him, and affectionately taking his arm I requested Blazes to bear the same in mind. He looked annoyed—which, however, did not affect me in the least, and we entered together.

There were only two occupants—a frightfully plain specimen of an aged female, and a girl of about fifteen or sixteen. They were both employed in embroidering velvet with beads. Immediately the younger of the two saw my companion she sprang up, and jumped into his arms, and in (as far as I am a judge) very fair French welcomed him, said she had been expecting his visit; and it was evidently a lover's meeting. I *must* describe her. She had very little on; what she had, appearing to me to be a blue serge petticoat with some sort of embroidery round the skirt, over which was a dingy white '*cutty sark*', confined at the waist with a beadwork embroidered girdle, and over this a man's work-a-day cloth jacket with large mother-o'-pearl buttons! Her hair was jet black, with a sort of oily look about it I didn't quite like; but, lor! she had enough for a dozen women—I never saw such a magnificent mop! If she had put it *à l'Anglaise* into a net at the back of her head she would never have seen her toes again! Her complexion was brown—yes, *brown*—the brown of the ripe filbert. Her nose was perfect, if not *too* small;—her mouth a little large. But—murder! such red lips and white teeth you almost wished it larger that the vermillion and the pearl might show the more;—and her eyes—well, *there* I am beaten. Suffice it to say, that I never saw such eyes for black ones. I dreamt of them more than once afterwards. Her head was beautifully put on; and her legs, which were naked to the knee, were the *moral* of Louise Leclercq's brown silk stockings. I never *could* see any beauty in a naked foot—especially when the sole was as hard as nails—so I'll leave her *foot* alone—excepting to say it looked very small.

But I am over-spinning my yarn. These were the wife and granddaughter of the old gentleman whose society I had so rudely declined. Blazes[1] was desperately in love with the girl; it seems he had some months previously picked her out of the water as she was vainly endeavouring to right her canoe, which had topsy-turvied. They swim like corks (the women, I mean); but she was nearly exhausted with her efforts, being very young; and would most likely have been drowned but for *Blazes*' assistance. Of course, the old ones were immensely grateful for the preservation of their 'che-ild'; and would have tattoed, or otherwise ennobled Blazes upon the spot had he wished it. But he didn't: he made himself, however, a sort of godfather to the young Naiad, and had succeeded in teaching her French and a smattering of English; and I think he said she could write 'a tolerable fist'.

We stayed until our watches warned us to be off—for darkness in Canada, like the thunder-storm, comes on you *bang*—without the prelude of twilight; and I didn't care much about remaining after nightfall in this wild region, even under the wing of *Blazes*. Had there been a twin Naiad I might have been reconciled; but there wasn't.

I shall ever remember our homeward voyage through the beauty of that night. Squatted in the stern of the canoe, with a delicious pipe of tobacco in my mouth, I watched the deep shadows of the bush-covered shore as the moon rose—full, large, and red—lighting up the waters but throwing land and forest into deeper gloom. My companion paddled leisurely along, playing, as it were, with the sparkling water; and our

[1]George M. Douglas, an authority on the district, believes H. Pierce (or Pearce) is the farm student referred to by Rhys. He is frequently mentioned in the manuscript newspaper 'Kachewanoonka Herald', which the students circulated between 1855 and 1859 and of which Mr. Douglas has some copies. Among items written in satirical vein by Thomas Balguey Allen is one quipping Pierce for deserting Fanny his dog, and observing that

> *"Our Gentleman Hero no longer will take ob-*
> *Servation of any but pretty Miss Jacob";*

and the concluding verse runs

> *"If a Bride you take home of the Indian breed,*
> *Your father and mother would sorrow indeed;*
> *So repent, foolish youth, take warning, be sure*
> *That if you must marry don't marry a squaw."*

The Jacobs and Irons were among the Indians of the district, and they were at that time encamped opposite Colonel Strickland's where the Lakefield Park now is.

Courtesy J. S. Smart — Water-colour by Sier

[53] WALTON STREET, PORT HOPE, 1833

Courtesy of the Artist — Alen McCombie

[54] CAMERON LAKE

Looking northeastward towards Fenelon Falls

Courtesy of the Langton family — Anne Langton

[55] "BLYTHE," THE LANGTON HOME, STURGEON LAKE

The marquee was the dining-room

Frances Stewart, "Our Forest Home"

[56] FRANCES STEWART (1794-1872)

At the age of 72

"Our Forest Home"

[57] HON. THOMAS STEWART (1792-1847)

As a young man in Ireland

Public Archives of Canada

[58] SIR JOHN COLBORNE

Lieut.-Governor of Upper Canada, 1828-35; visited the Trent valley in 1834

Public Archives of Canada

[59] SIR PEREGRINE MAITLAND

Lieut.-Governor of Upper Canada, 1818-28; visited the Trent Valley in 1826

Toronto Public Library

[60] HON. PETER ROBINSON (1785-1838)

Supervised Irish emigration, 1825

Courtesy Mrs. Kathleen Lloyd

[61] CAPT. CHARLES RUBIDGE (1786-1873)

Prominent in settling immigrants

Archives of Ontario Anne Langton

[62] JOHN LANGTON
(1808-1894)

Fenelon Falls Library Anne Langton

[63] ANNE LANGTON
(1804?-1893)

From a miniature

[64] SUSANNA MOODIE
(1803-1885)

[65] J. W. DUNBAR MOODIE
(1797-1869)

Courtesy Miss Florence Atwood

[66] CATHARINE TRAILL
(1802-1899)

Courtesy Miss Florence Atwood

[67] CAPT. THOMAS TRAILL
(1790-1859)

Courtesy of the family

[68] ROBERT McCAULEY
MARY JANE McCAULEY

Courtesy of the family

[69] PATRICK YOUNG
The Youngs founded Young's Point

Courtesy of the family

[70] McCAULEY'S HOTEL, BURLEIGH TOWNSHIP
A Temperance house in a day of hard drinking

Courtesy of the family

[71] LEVI PAYNE (1790-1866)
SARAH PAYNE (1792-1869)
Prominent early settlers

Photograph by George M. Douglas, 1910

[72] THE ORIGINAL LEVI PAYNE LOG HOUSE, 1831
Located on the Indian River in the Township of Dummer

Courtesy Miss Florence Atwood

[73] CATHARINE PARR TRAILL
(1802-1899)

The scene is the verandah of "Minnewawa," Stoney Lake, about 1897; with the authoress are her granddaughters Katharine (left) and Caroline

Courtesy George M. Douglas

[74] SAMUEL STRICKLAND
(1804-1867)

"The gallant Major," as he was called by the pupils of his Agricultural School for training Canadian backwoodsmen

Courtesy George M. Douglas

[75] THE STRICKLAND HOME IN FULL GLORY

Courtesy of the family

[76] CAPT. CHARLES RUBIDGE
(1786-1873)
A noted pioneer in old age, 1870

Green, "Life and Times"

[77] REV. ANSON GREEN
(1801-1879)
Early Methodist circuit-rider

Public Archives of Canada

[78] SIR RICHARD BONNYCASTLE
(1791-1847)
Author who visited Seymour Township

Courtesy Miss Matthews

[79] GERALD HAYWARD
(1847-1926)
Famous as a painter of miniatures

Courtesy Ontario Land Surveyors

[80] J. W. FITZGERALD
(1828-1901)
Prominent early surveyor

Courtesy Ontario Land Surveyors

[81] EDWARD C. CADDY
(1815-1897)
Surveyor and artist

[82] ARCHIBALD LAMPMAN
(1861-1899)
Poet who spent his boyhood at Rice Lake

[83] GEORGE COPWAY
(1819-1863)
Rice Lake Indian Missionary and poet

Courtesy F. H. H. Lowe

[84] PAUL KANE
(1810-1871)
Famous Canadian artist

Courtesy Royal Ontario Museum

[85] CHARLES FOTHERGILL
(1782-1840)
Early settler, artist, and ornithologist of Port Hope and Rice Lake

Courtesy Mrs. Robert Scully

[86] ELIZABETH AGNES AND RHODA ANNE PAGE
Poets of Cobourg and Rice Lake

Courtesy Ontario Land Surveyors

[87] FREDERICK P. RUBIDGE (1806-1898)
Poet and surveyor

Courtesy of the family — Anne Langton

[88] PETERBOROUGH FROM WHITE'S TAVERN

Hall, " Forty Etchings . . . " 1829 — Basil Hall

[89] PETERBOROUGH IN 1827
Capt. Hall made this sketch with the Camera Lucida

Courtesy Royal Ontario Museum — Charles Fothergill

[90] PORT HOPE IN 1819
Looking south from Fothergill's grounds towards Lake Ontario

Courtesy of the family — Anne Langton

[91] FENELON FALLS WITH THE MILL
The Falls was a noted beauty spot before commercial development

Courtesy Miss Sheila Boyd — Miss Lowe

[92] HOME OF MOSSOM BOYD, BOBCAYGEON
In the rear at the left is the Roman Catholic Church

Courtesy Miss Sheila Boyd — Miss Lowe

[93] BOYD MILL AND FIRST LOCKS, BOBCAYGEON
Mossom Boyd bought out Thomas Need, founder of the village

Courtesy Miss Matthews

[94] ALFRED HAYWARD (1856-1939)
Famous as a painter of flowers

Courtesy F. H. H. Lowe

[95] HARRIET CLENCH
(18?-1892)
Became the wife of Paul Kane in 1853

Courtesy F. H. H. Lowe — Pencil sketch by Harriet Clench

[96] FLOWER ARRANGEMENT

Courtesy Miss Matthews — Alfred Hayward

[97] RICE LAKE TRILLIUMS

Courtesy Miss Matthews — Alfred Hayward

[98] CALIFORNIAN POPPY

Courtesy of the family Paul Kane

[99] WILLIAM WELLER
(1799-1863)

Courtesy of the family Paul Kane

[100] MERCY (WILLCOX) WELLER

Courtesy of F. H. H. Lowe Paul Kane

[101] MRS. F. S. CLENCH
Her daughter was the wife of Paul Kane

Courtesy of F. H. H. Lowe Paul Kane

[102] F. S. CLENCH
Prominent Cobourg cabinetmaker

Peterborough Public Library Paul Kane

[103] WILSON S. CONGER
(179?-1864)
Prominent in York, Cobourg, and Peterborough

Courtesy of the family Paul Kane

[104] HON. HENRY RUTTAN
(1792-1872)
Speaker of the Legislative Assembly

Photograph by James Guillet

[105] ROADBED, COBOURG AND PETERBOROUGH RAILROAD
The Hiawatha-Peterborough section

Photograph by George M. Douglas

[106] GRAVES ON THE ROGERS FARM, YOUNG'S POINT
A typical pioneer burial-place

Photograph by George M. Douglas

[107] LIMESTONE FIREPLACE
Log house of Capt. Hill, 1831

Photograph by George M. Douglas

[108] HILL BURIAL-PLACE
The abandoned farm near Clear Lake

Photograph by George M. Douglas

[109] ABANDONED FARM OF GEORGE A. HILL
Capt. Hill, veteran of Waterloo, was first Warden and the author of *A guide for Emigrants from the British Shores to the Woods of Canada* (Dublin, 1834)

little bark went bobbity-bobbity, as much as to say 'I should just like to pitch you two out, you seem so jolly lazy!'

Blazes was evidently buried in a *brown* study, and I didn't care much about interrupting him. I, too, was thinking—thinking of a picture I had somewhere seen of a very dark girl and a very fair one;—and wishing that I were an artist that I might put on canvas the darkest and the fairest beauty in creation. Heigho!

Nothing occurred to disturb the even tenur of our way; and on we went, paddling and puffing—an occasional snatch of a song on my part, and a melancholy effort at a second on his, alone mingling with the gurgling of the water at the bow of the canoe and the hum of many insects in the air. We arrived at the landing-stage, and there found a servant waiting with a trap and, what much gladdened my eyes, a bottle of whisky, for we long since finished the flask that accompanied us. We had only a few miles to go to '*Blazes' Park*'—as I termed his few acres of clearing—and whether it was the whisky or jolting I know not, but Blazes at last opened his mouth and blurted out, 'I say, old fellow, I'm going to marry that nigger lass!'

'*Marry*?' I said, putting the bowl end of my pipe in my astonishment to my lips—'the devil!'

'Nearly as black, certainly', he replied, mistaking my exclamation; 'but there's more of the angel in her than the devil—anyhow!'

'My dear man, I didn't mean that———'

'No, no; I know. Of course you'll laugh; but mark my words: if you ever come to Douro again you'll find that girl in my house—my lawful wife!'

He made his words good; for in spite of the jeers of his wild band of companions he carried her off one fine night and *married* her by book and candle (Blazes is a Roman Catholic); and, as he is next heir to many a broad acre in 'Merrie England', it is just possible I may yet again see the heroine of this little yarn, and presiding over a very different establishment to that in her Indian home.

XII. POETICAL PRODUCTIONS OF THE INHABITANTS

THERE IS a distinct difference, if often subtle and frequently arbitrary, between poetry and verse; and it is equally apparent that the beauty of either is often merely in the eye of the beholder. In the old Newcastle District there were several inhabitants who have considerable claim to the name and fame of "poet," and many others who were clever versifiers. Notable among the former is Rhoda Anne Page, whose poetical compositions, although almost unknown to modern readers, have been praised by both her contemporaries and competent critics. Forgotten in this generation is *The Ojibway Conquest*, an epic poem by the Rice Lake Indian, George Copway. That Copway, though scarcely a generation removed from savagery, should be an author is remarkable enough, but that he should produce a work with as much beauty of narrative and grace of style as this story of the Wen-di-go, Me-gi-si, and Me-Me—and still be unknown—is a reflection upon Canadians. His friendship with the poet Longfellow is not the least interesting incident in his career. In addition to those whose verse is represented here, many others contributed fugitive poems to the *Cobourg Star* and other newspapers, and to the various literary periodicals of the day. Included among them are many of merit printed anonymously or with initials only. The amount of "literary" material in the periodicals of that period is indicative of the general standard of readers' taste, though it is equally apparent that, due to restricted education, subscribers to newspapers and magazines comprised but a small proportion of the population. Like the government of the day, this enjoyment of literary and cultural excellence was predominantly aristocratic, not democratic, but it formed a solid basis for general education and intellectual advancement.

1. Frederick Preston Rubidge (1806–1898)

Frederick Rubidge was born in London, England, on March 10, 1806, one of five sons of Robert and Eleanor Rubidge and a half-brother of Captain Charles Rubidge, second settler in Otonabee Township, 1820. He came to Canada about 1825 with two younger brothers and studied surveying, probably under Major Samuel Wilmot, a prominent surveyor in the district. In 1831 he received his certificate, locating first in Peterborough but a few months later in Cobourg, where he was active also in literature and amateur dramatics, as is apparent from the columns of the *Cobourg Star* in the years 1831–1833. As a result of the successes of "The Gentlemen Amateurs of Cobourg," a similar association produced plays in Peterborough. In 1836 he married Jane Boswell of Cobourg. Among the important surveys in which he participated were the first for the Cobourg Rail Road Company, 1835, and several related to northerly townships and the Trent Canal. His verse is largely patterned after that of Pope and other eighteenth-century poets, with but little of the Romantic influence, and much of it was caustically anti-Reform.[1] In his later life he resided in Ottawa and Montreal, and died in 1898 at the age of ninety-two.

MITHER MAY PEEP

[Cobourg Star, *November 22, 1831*]

Na' gang, laddie—Mither may peep, and thee spy out,
For partin-time's past, when ye hame was to win;
Should she catch thee thus hugging me, lack! how she'd cry out;
Then hie awa', laddie, leest mither pop in.

Her e'e wi' suspicion o' somethin will glisten,
My braw gown all tumbled, and hair out o' pin.
She'll ask for my knitting, ye've stolen—Oh! listen!
Pray hie awa', laddie, 'ere mither glide in.

Na' be not sae foolish—I'll gie ye my promise,
Niest time ye shall kiss me, but don' now begin;
She'll want her wee supper, and—harkee! she come is!
O hie thee hame, laddie, 'ere mither glide in.

Slink down by the paddock, where oft ye ha' tarried,
To coax me as now—Oh, ye lads mak us sin!
Well, well then, to-morrow wi' ye I'll be married;
So gie o'er your teazing—Hush!—rin, laddie! rin!

SONNET—RIVER OTONABEE

[Cobourg Star, *September 6, 1831*]

Stream of the wilderness, at whose far source
The fierce wolf lappeth, or awaits his spoil,
Thro' ages rolling thy ignoble course,

[1]See the biography and collection of his verse, in typescript in the Toronto Public Library, compiled by Edwin C. Guillet.

But now to flow with corn, with wine, and oil.
Time was, dark river, when thy current bore
None other burthen than the frail canoe;
Or when the wild deer, snorting from the shore,
Deep plung'd him where the floating lilies grew.
Then came the Explorer from yon eastern main.
Tracking Cabotia's* streams, he looked on thine;
The Emigrant close follow'd in his train,
And other barks sail'd 'tween thy banks of pine.
Their sway the Indian Nereides now resign,
And maids from England's Thames upon thy marge recline.[1]

THE DROWNED EMIGRANT!

[Cobourg Star, *November 14, 1832*]

On the sand of the shore, a bloated corpse,
He lay where the waves had thrown him;
No wail of the widow lamented his loss,
No friend stood by to own him.

Yet was he unknown? Ah no! for his ways
Had been one wild course of error;
And some there were who remember'd the days
When his name was a name of terror.

He fled—for the life his treach'ry prolong'd,
From a hundred hands was in danger:
He was cast at the feet of the man he had wrong'd,
As tho' heav'n were that man's avenger.

Why miss'd the Atlantic-shark his prey?
Why wander'd he hither to perish?—
To yield, in the judgment which snatch'd him away,
A warning for us to cherish.

And thus when injuries prompt our hate,
When we feel with revenge excited,
Let us think of this poor drowned wretch[2] and his fate,
And look to be heav'n-requited.

*From Sebastian Cabot, the discoverer.

[1]The poet is thinking, no doubt, of the wife and daughters of his brother, Captain Charles Rubidge, who settled on the shores of the Otonabee in 1820.

[2]The subject of this poem is James Demsey, an Irish emigrant from Queen's County. In October 1832 the steamer *William IV* landed passengers at the Cobourg wharf in a heavy sea, and two men were washed overboard by huge waves as the ship was turning out into the lake. They were drowned, and the body of Demsey was found half buried in the sand about half a mile west of the harbour, on the property of James Calcutt, who had left Ireland to escape ruin at the hands of a band of marauders called White Feet, led by Demsey. It would be difficult to find a more remarkable coincidence.

2. Thomas Carr (1780–1860)

Thomas Carr, who was born in Scotland and spent ten years of his youth in the West Indies, emigrated to Upper Canada with his brother Andrew in 1819. They were among the first settlers in the following year in the Township of Otonabee, where they were the original owners of the entire site of the village of Keene, on Indian River. Soon afterwards Andrew Carr was killed by a falling tree. District councillor, postmaster, road commissioner, and justice of the peace, Thomas Carr was always a man of prominence in Otonabee. When the *Cobourg Star* was established in 1831 he became among the earliest contributors of literary material to its columns. In his latter years he became melancholy and depressed, and his death by suicide on November 1, 1860, closely paralleled that of a friend whose death had inspired an elegy thirty years earlier. Like many another worthy, he was buried on his own land, and the present owner of the property still points out, between the house and the barn, the grave of the founder of the village of Keene.

ELEGY

On the death of a favorite cat, who spent a long and apparently happy life in the faithful discharge of her humble but useful duties.

[Cobourg Star, *September 7, 1836*]

Poor Puss has paid great Nature's debt—
A debt *we* all must pay,
Howe'er we mortals toil and fret,
As fast our lives decay.

Whilst wintry blasts were howling round,
And dark'ning all the sky,
While snow's deep mantle deck'd the ground,
Poor Puss was left to die.

Her mistress, cruel and ingrate,
Sought a far-distant home,
And Puss abandoned, hapless fate,
In solitude to roam.

The mice had sought their dark retreat,
No squirrel gamboll'd round,
The birds had winged their distant flight,
And milder climates found.

Deep wand'ring through the pathless waste,
I saw her slender form;
I ran to hail my stranger guest,
And shield her from the storm.

Debarred of speech her thoughts to tell,
She, purring, shewed her bliss;
No pris'ner rescued from his cell
Could warmer thanks express.

Winters twice seven have shed their snow,
Yet still she shared my cot;
Of ev'ry pilf'ring knave the foe,
Nor sought a happier lot.

A longer life Puss could not crave;
Death dealt the fatal blow
That ends the coward and the brave,
And lays the fav'rite low.

Farewell; my humble, faithful friend,
Thy fate I need not mourn;
My years, like thine, must have an end,
My frame to dust return.

Let all who read my artless lays,
Full gently treat thy kind;
Such faithful service merits praise
From ev'ry grateful mind.

MY HAME

By a settler in Otonabee Township, probably Thomas Carr

[Cobourg Star, *December 27, 1831*]

I canna ca' this forest hame,
It is nae hame to me;
Ilk tree is suthern to my heart,
And unco to my e'e.

If I cou'd see the bonny broom
On ilka sandy know';
Or the whins in a' their gowden
pride,
That on the green hill grow:

If I cou'd see the primrose bloom
In Nora's hazel glen;
And hear the linties chirp and sing,
Far frae the haunts of men:

If I cou'd see the rising sun
Glint owre the dewy corn;
And the tunefu' lavrocks in the sky
Proclaim the coming morn:

If I cou'd see the daisy spread
Its wee flowers owre the lee;
Or the heather scent the mountain
breeze,
And the ivy climb the tree;

If I cou'd see the lane' kirk yard,
Whar' frien's lie side by side:
And think that I cou'd lay my
banes
Beside them when I died:

Then might I think this forest
hame,
And in it live and dee;
Nor feel regret at my heart's core,[1]
My native land, for thee.

3. Captain George Arundel Hill

VERSES FOR THE TWENTY-FOURTH ANNIVERSARY OF THE BATTLE OF WATERLOO[2]

[Cobourg Star, *June 19, 1839*]

This morning brings a festival to Britain's triple shore,
The mimicry of war is seen, the thund'ring cannons roar;
Her merry bells peal rapidly, gay streamers meet the view,
It is her day of triumph on the plains of Waterloo;

Around her youthful Queen are met the high-born of the land,
While there, in gorgeous warrior garb, a hundred chieftains stand;
And he, the victor-chief, is there, and starts to find how few
His eye can count, in that proud throng, who fought at Waterloo;

Where are the rest? Where should they be, but where all that live must lie?
For Time is gleaner to the sword, and takes what *it* passed by;
His path is land and ocean; and his step, though soft as dew,
Effaces all it treads upon, and will tread on Waterloo;

Twas not the weak, in heart or arm, that Britain conquered then,
But the flower of France's chivalry, well-trained and gallant men;
Then honor to the victors, and to the vanquished too,
For gallantly they struggled on the plains of Waterloo!

[1]This is the source of the title of a recent play by Robertson Davies of Peterborough.

[2]Captain Hill, who had served with Wellington at Waterloo, wrote the verses in 1838. He speaks for many veterans who had settled in the wilds of Canada, giving up their small pensions for land that sometimes proved almost useless. He himself was settled near Clear Lake on rocky land that has remained an abandoned farm to this day.

There wakens revelry tonight in many a princely hall,
Where the battle will again be fought, again will Picton fall;
The shout, the charge, the closing shock, will many a voice renew,
And wine-cups will be drained to those who fell at Waterloo.

Oh! in that hour of patriot pride, of music and of song.
Will not there be one generous heart to feel a soldier's wrong?
One tongue of honesty and zeal to bring that wrong to view,
And claim a late redress for men who bled at Waterloo?

Before thine eyes had seen the light, VICTORIA, Queen of Isles;
They bled to guard the jewelled crown that shades thy brow of smiles;
And later, when a foe appeared, to watch that crown they flew,
And its gem of Canada was kept by men of Waterloo!

O, speak the word; they look to thee to cheer their life's cold eve,
For want and age have crushed them down in the wild woods where they grieve;
O, speak, and let them have again the boon which away they threw,
And greater will be thy glory than was theirs at Waterloo!

The purest wreath the conqueror boasts is stained with earthly leaven,
The widow's shriek, the orphan's cry, go with his name to heaven;
And lovelier 'tis in heaven's sight, one generous act to do,
Than to wear the proudest medal which was won at Waterloo.

4. Dr. James Haskins (1805–1846)

Born in Dublin in 1805 and a graduate of Trinity College, Dr. Haskins emigrated to Upper Canada in 1834. He engaged in his profession first in Belleville, then at River Trent or Trent Port (later Trenton), and subsequently in the Township of Loughborough, where his young wife died in childbirth. He removed to Frankford, on the west bank of the Trent, where he lived a solitary and melancholy life until his death in 1846. In a poem "To the Memory of Dr. Haskins", Mrs. Susanna Moodie eulogized the poet:

"Neglected son of Genius! thou hast passed—
In broken-hearted loneliness—away."

TO THE RIVER TRENT[1]

Noble river! rushing on,
Deep and broad, and bright and free;
Winter's rage hath come and gone,
But no bonds he had for thee.

[1]From *The Poetical Works of James Haskins, A.B., M.B.* (Hartford, 1848.)

Strong, unfettered, bold and deep,
Here, in majesty, thy tide
Rushes with resistless sweep,
Pours along in stately pride.

Blue thy breast, with billows bright
Sparkling in the fervid ray;
Glorious is thy stream with light,
Gilt with gold of vernal day.

Green thy banks, with budding groves
Bordering the meadows fair;
Still thy shore the cedar loves,
Shoots the tam'rack high in air.

Cedars white, and alders grey,
Circling many a lordly pine;
Giant oaks their forms display,
Firs whose silv'ry leaflets shine.

Hangs the mighty maple o'er
Trunks upturned and rocks around;
Hark! I hear a sullen roar—
'Tis the rapid's thundering sound.

Boil the foaming torrents through
Rocks that fain would check their rage;
See! the monarch stream anew,
Calm, pursues his pilgrimage.

Calmly, through the forest glade,
View his peaceful current glide;
Solemn now, through deep'ning shade,
Dark, yet tranquil, is his tide.

Onward, on! the goal is nigh;
Glorious lake! thy form I view,
Blending with th'ethereal sky—
One bright tract of boundless blue.

Noble river! fare thee well!
As thy current, strong and deep,
Onward—irresistible—
May my soul its progress keep.

Heav'nward to its peaceful home,
In the world where live the blest;
Past the rocks, the rapids' foam,
Thus may speed—there gladly rest.

5. Susanna Moodie

[*Mrs. Moodie's Canadian poems are scattered through her prose works*]

THE OTONABEE

Dark, rushing, foaming river!
I love the solemn sound
That shakes thy shores around,
And hoarsely murmurs ever,
As thy waters onward bound,
Like a rash, unbridled steed
Flying madly on its course,
That shakes with thundering force
The vale and trembling mead.
So thy billows downward sweep,
Nor rock nor tree can stay
Their fierce, impetuous way;
Now in eddies whirling deep,
Now in rapids white with spray.

I love thee, lonely river!
Thy hollow, restless roar,
Thy cedar-girded shore,
The rocky isles that sever
The waves that round them pour.
Katchawanook basks in light,
But thy currents woo the shade
By thy lofty pine-trees made,
That cast a gloom like night,
Ere day's last glories fade.
Thy solitary voice
The same bold anthem sung
When Nature's frame was young;
No longer shall rejoice
The woods where erst it rung.

Lament, lament, wild river!
A hand is on thy mane
That will bind thee in a chain
No force of thine can sever.
Thy furious headlong tide,
In murmurs soft and low,
Is destined yet to glide
To meet the lake below;
And many a bark shall ride
Securely on thy breast,
To waft across the main,
Rich stores of golden grain
From the valleys of the West.

INDIAN SUMMER

By the purple haze that lies
    On the distant rocky height,
By the deep blue of the skies,
    By the smoky amber light
Through the forest arches streaming,
Where Nature on her throne sits dreaming,
And the sun is scarcely gleaming
    Through the cloudlets, snowy white,
Winter's lovely herald greets us,
'Ere the ice-crown'd tyrant meets us.

This dreary Indian Summer day
    Attunes the soul to tender sadness;
We love, but joy not in the ray;
    It is not summer's fervid gladness,
But a melancholy glory
    Hovering softly round decay,
Like swan that sings her own sad story,
    'Ere she floats in death away.

6. Catharine Traill

THE GRAVES OF THE EMIGRANTS

Here are some verses written as the thoughts occurred to me on the graves of the Emigrants. These household graves became the more interesting to me on learning that, when a farm is disposed of to a stranger, the right of burying their dead is generally stipulated for by the former possessor.—C.P.T.

They sleep not where their fathers sleep,
    In the village churchyard's bound,
They rest not 'neath the ivied wall
    That shades that holy ground;

Nor where the solemn organ's peal
    Pours music on the breeze
Through the dim aisles at evening hour,
    Or swells among the trees;

Nor where the turf is ever green,
    And flowers are blooming fair,
Upon the graves of ancient men
    Whose children rest not there;

Nor where the sound of warning bell
    Floats mournfully on high,

And tells the tale of human woe—
That all who live must die.

Where, then, may rest those hardy sons,
Who left their native shore
To seek a home in distant lands,
Beyond the Atlantic's roar?

They sleep in many a lonely spot
Where mighty forests grow;
Where stately oak and lofty pine
Their darkling shadows throw.

The wild bird pours her matin song
Above their lonely graves;
And far away in the stilly night
Is heard the voice of waves.

Fair lilies, nursed by weeping dews,
Unfold their blossoms pale;
And spotless snow-flowers lightly bend
Low to the passing gale.

The fire-fly lights her little spark
To cheer the leafy gloom,
Like Hope's blest ray that gilds the night
And darkness of the tomb.

Where moss-grown stone or simple cross
Its silent record keeps,
There, deep within the forest shade,
The lonely exile sleeps.

7. Rhoda Anne Page (1826–1863)

Thomas Page[1] of Cobourg and his two literary daughters, Elizabeth Agnes and Rhoda Anne, are among numerous cultured people of the old Newcastle District whose literary achievements were appreciated in their own day, and for a generation afterwards, but have since been neglected. Rhoda Anne's early poetical works were published in her lifetime in a small rare booklet entitled *Wild Notes from the Back Woods* (Cobourg, 1850), and by wide search in contemporary periodicals the Editor has located about a dozen of her subsequent poems. She first resided at "The Pines," a few miles northeast of Cobourg, but upon her marriage to William B. Falkner she removed to the vicinity of Rice Lake. The vicissitudes of family

[1]Thomas Page was editor of the *Newcastle Farmer* in the late eighteen-forties.

life restricted her subsequent literary work. She died on December 7, 1863, and her grave is in the small but beautiful Church of England cemetery at Gore's Landing.[1] Many of her works have a sad and melancholy tone, for she was often depressed by the trials of life and the sadness of illness and death. Sir John Macdonald was impressed by her patriotic song, "St. George's Flag," and requested a copy of it; but her "Voices from the Woods" and other nature poems have perhaps a larger share of true poetry in their composition.

VOICES FROM THE WOODS

[*Toronto* British Colonist, *November 15, 1850*]

We talk of lifeless things, and creatures dumb,
Of stocks and stones, and voiceless flowers and trees,
To me there seems strange eloquence to come
From every one of these.

One eve I wandered in the quiet wood,
The light leaves rustled in the summer gale,
Whose sighing through the forest solitude
Went like a spirit's wail.

The tall oak reared his branches to the sky,
Lordly and proud—the stately and the strong—
The type of daring thoughts and actions high
That live in memory long.

A woodland king he seemed, but near his side
Drooped gracefully a weeping willow tree;
That spake of strength and might and manhood's pride,
This of Humility.

For its green branches bent them to the sod,
And softly kissed the lowly daisy's face,
As if the humblest workmanship of God
Were worthy an embrace.

The trembling aspen quivered in the breeze,
Wavering like weakness in temptation's breath,
But the still solemn cypress grew by these,
And preached unshaken Faith.

[1]A later and more famous poet, Archibald Lampman (1861–1899), is closely connected with this beautiful village, where he spent seven years of boyhood. Gore's Landing is named after Captain Thomas Sinclair Gore, who owned 265 acres along the shore in 1840. He died in 1858. The settlement was first called Tidy's Tavern, David Tidy being "a very respectable Scotchman."

And the dark, sullen, sombre hemlock there,
Stood dull and cheerless as despondency,
But a sweet briar was blooming, fresh and fair,
    Hard by the gloomy tree.

And round his rugged trunk her branches twined,
All rich with scented leaves, and buds, and flowers,
Sweet as the gentle words and accents kind,
    That brighten grief's dark hours.

Oh! many a voice from the sequester'd wood
In the deep calm of a still summer even,
May whisper to the soul in thoughtful mood,
    Wisdom that comes from Heaven.

FLOWER FANCIES

[Cobourg Star, *June 13, 1855*]

ROSE

A crown! a crown! to grace the garden's Queen,
    A crown of dew-gems, stolen from old night;
A diamond here, and there an emerald sheen,
    And there a pale pearl with its trembling light;
But let the glowing ruby shun the sight,
    Lest it grow pale and wan with jealousy,
And sicken into dimness with despite,
    At tints that do its own outvie.
Bid her to raise her graceful head full high,
    And crown her as an Empress should be crown'd,
And call her sister flowers that cluster nigh,
    And bid them circle her and hem her round—
    Lo! Beauty's train once more their Goddess-Queen surround!

LILY OF THE VALLEY

Oh! beautiful vale Lily! sweet and sainted,
    Like a pale nun in holy cloister dress,
Thy graceful bells low-drooping, as they fainted
    Beneath the weight of their own loveliness;
Shrinking alike from Zephyr's cool caress,
    And the hot kisses of the Sun-King's ray,
In modest walk and quiet humbleness,
    Blooming unseen thy virgin life away;
The dews steal to thee at the close of day,
    (Tears that kind angels weep o'er this world's woe),
And in thy green leaf nests the weary fay,
    And cools his hot cheek on thy bosom's snow,
And sleepeth in love-dreams thy pearly domes below.

RICE LAKE BY MOONLIGHT[1]

A WINTER SCENE

Moonlight upon the frozen Lake! how radiantly smiles
The Queen of solemn midnight upon all its fair Isles,
And the starry sparkling frost-work, that, like a chain of gems,
Hangs upon each fair islet's brow in glittering diadems.

How stilly lies the sleeping lake, how still the quiet river,
As though some wizard-spell had laid their waves at rest for ever;
Murmurs abroad the hoarse night wind, waves every leafless tree,—
Yet not one ripple stirs thy breast, oh! proud Otonabee.

How strange it is, this death in life, this mute and stirless show,
While we know the prison'd waters are heaving yet below,
Like the cold calm look the strong mind may to lip and brow impart,
While ceaseless care, like canker-worm, is gnawing at the heart.

Light, but no warmth—a dancing gleam—while all is cold beneath,
Like the sweet smile that mocks us yet upon the face of death;
While yet the dead lip wears so much of beauty and of bloom,
We scarce can look on it and think of darkness and the tomb.

How quiet in the Moon's pale light the tiny islands lie,
Down-looking to the waveless lake, up-gazing to the sky,
Slumb'ring beneath her holy beam like children lull'd to rest,
Watch'd by a mother's loving eyes—upon that mother's breast.

Awake, awake, oh! sleeping Lake, at the wild wind-spirit's call,
Wake in thy summer's joyousness, shake off the Frost-king's thrall;
For back to wood, and stream, and brake, glad spring returns once more,
And thy merry waves shall break again in music on the shore.

How many changes hast thou seen, since first the sunbeam's smile,
Through the dim-twinkling forest leaves, glanc'd down on wave and isle;
Ere yet upon thy sunny banks a mortal footstep trod,
Or any eye had look'd on thee, except the eye of God.

The dusky tribes that knew thee first have vanish'd from the scene,
And scarcely left a wreck behind to tell of what hath been;
Yet still through time, and chance, and change, smile the fair lake and river,
As pure and bright and beautiful, and shadowless as ever.

Man dies, and is forgotten, his monuments decay,
His very memory passes like a dream of yesterday;
But the glorious trophies of His might that God himself hath plann'd,
Till earth and heaven pass away, unchangeable shall stand.

[1]This and the remaining three poems are reprinted from *Wild Notes from the Back Woods.*

ST. GEORGE'S FLAG

St. George for merry England, ho! up with the pennon brave!
It hath streamed o'er many a conquered land, o'er many a distant wave;
Up with the red cross banner! 'tis a glorious sight to see,
The noblest flag that ever flew, stream out so fair and free.

It floated o'er proud Acre's towers in days long passed away,
When Lion Richard led his host at the holy tomb to pray;
And still the Crescent paler waned before the hallowed sign,
That flew in triumph o'er thy fields, oh! sacred Palestine.

It cheered Old England's stalwart sons thro' Cressy's hard won fray,
It waved o'er royal Henry's head on Agincourt's proud day;
The sultry breath of sunny Spain its crimson cross has fanned,
And gallant hosts have borne it on through India's burning land.

Oh! many a flag of gaudier hue the fanning breeze may wave,
But none that bears a nobler name, more stainless or more brave;
None that hath led more dauntless hearts to battle for the right,
None that hath flown more proudly o'er the crimson field of fight.

Up with the brave old banner then! the peerless and the bold,
True hearts will rally round it yet as in the days of old;
And still on every English lip the thrilling cry shall be:
'St. George for merry England, ho! God and our own country!'

THE OLD MAN'S DEATH SONG

Nay! leave the old man to die!
All whom he loved are gone before,
They have landed alone on a brighter shore,
And earth is joyless, and cold, and dim,
It has lost its beauty and light for him,
Leave, leave the old man to die!

Call him not back to earth!
There are spirit voices that bid him come,
Would ye keep the wanderer from his home?
Would ye woo the bird to his cage again?
Would ye rivet the freed slave's broken chain?
Call him not back to earth!

Lay him down, lay him down to sleep!
Make the old grave more deep and wide,
Where long have slumbered his child and bride,
One in her youthful matron glee,
One in his joyous infancy,
Make the grave wide and deep!

Toll not the passing bell!
Mourn for the dead who have passed from earth
In manhood's glory or boyhood's mirth;
The old man hath drank from Life's cup of woe,
And his spirit is weary and glad to go,
Bid him a long farewell!

FROST ON THE WINDOW

There's not a thing that Nature's hand hath made,
However simple be its outward seeming
To careless eye or listless ear displayed,
But hath a hidden meaning.

Alike, unto the Saint's or Atheist's ear,
The anthem of the woodland choir is given;
One hears the lark, what doth the other hear?
A hymn of praise to heaven.

The glowing rainbow steals its silent march
Athwart the sky when raindrops gem the sod,
One sees three gorgeous hues in Heaven's arch,
And one the law of God.

The winter moon was shining coldly bright:
The birds and leaves had left the trees together,
Save, here and there, one that on some lone height
Still braved the bitter weather.

And o'er the window crept the hoary frost,
With many a wayward freak and curious antic,
In varied lines, that quaintly blent and crossed
In tracery romantic.

Here, bloomed a wreath of pure pale flowers,
As hueless as the faded cheek of death;
There, rose tall pinnacles and Gothic towers,
That melted with a breath.

And trees and foliage rich—the tinted oak,
The willow, wan and still, like settled grief,
The hazel, easy bent but hardly broke,
And varying maple leaf—

—That changes still its green or crimson hue
With every season, autumn, spring, or summer,
Sycophantic like, donning a livery new
To welcome each new comer.

The gentle moonbeam kissed the silvery pane
With a most sister-like and chaste caress,
As if it fain a fellowship would claim,
With such pure loveliness.

And still more beautiful the magic ray
Made all it rested on, leaf, flower, and tree,
And lingered there, like innocence at play
With stainless purity.

Oh! beautiful it was to watch them there,
Those varied forms, so gracefully fantastic,
The handiwork, so delicately fair,
Of Nature's fingers plastic.

And as I gazed, methought such sights were given
Not to our gross material senses solely,
But to the soul, like messengers from Heaven,
Prompting pure thoughts and holy.

There's not a thing that Nature's hand hath made,
However simple be its outward seeming,
To careless eye or listless ear displayed,
But hath a hidden meaning.

8. *Kah-ge-ga-gah-bowh* (George Copway, 1818–1863)

George Copway was born in the autumn of 1818 near the mouth of the Trent. His father belonged to the Crane, and his mother to the Eagle tribe. His great-grandfather is said to have been the first Chippewa to settle in the Rice Lake district, long the territory of the Hurons. His father was an hereditary chief and medicine man, and known as an excellent hunter. A Wesleyan missionary, the Reverend James Evans, taught him to read, and he was a convert to Methodism in 1830. Four years later he was serving as a missionary among the Lake Superior and Illinois tribes, where he is said to have travelled 185 miles on foot within two days to obtain food for starving companions.

In 1839 he was back at the Indian Village (Hiawatha), on Rice Lake. In 1840 he married Elizabeth Howell, daughter of an English officer in Toronto; and she and her sister suffered many hardships when they accompanied him into the Indian territories west of Lake Superior. A son was born in 1842. Copway subsequently lectured in England and Scotland, and in 1850 attended the Peace Congress in Frankfurt, Germany. In addition to the remarkable poetical work, *The Ojibway Conquest*, reprinted herewith, the

Michigan Historical Commission lists *Pa-mah-duk ke-ne-bood* (*Life and Death*) as published in Indian verse with translation, in New York, December 24, 1850. His prose works, partly autobiographical, are rambling and at times incoherent. In appearance he was tall, handsome, and muscular, and he had fine manners. He died near Pontiac, Michigan, in 1863. His Indian name, Kah-ge-ga-gah-bowh, means "He who stands forever."

The friendship between Henry Wadsworth Longfellow and George Copway, occurring as it does near the time of publication of *The Ojibway Conquest*, suggests that Longfellow may well have aided him in its composition, or at least polished the manuscript before it went to press. The references to Copway are found in Volume II, pp. 135 *et seq.*, of Samuel Longfellow's *Life of Longfellow* (Boston, 1886), though there is no listing in the index. In his Journal for February 26, 1849, Longfellow wrote; "Kah-ge-ga-gah-bowh, an Ojibway preacher and poet, came to see us. The Indian is a good looking young man. He left me a book of his, an autobiography." Elsewhere he refers to him as an Ojibway Chief, and on April 12 he attended one of Copway's lectures—"A rambling talk, gracefully delivered, with a fine various voice, and a chief's costume with little bells jangling upon it, like the bells and pomegranates of the Jewish priests." Two days later he attended a second: "He described very graphically the wild eagles teaching their young to fly from a nest overhanging a precipice on the Pictured Rocks of Lake Superior." On June 13, 1850, Longfellow's journal says that Copway came to tea. Other references thereafter are in a letter to Ferdinand Freiligrath, a German poet whom Copway visited while attending the peace conference in Germany. In the letter, dated July 16, 1851, Longfellow wrote:

> Copway returned with very grand and gracious accounts of you, and described in flowing colors the "merry night at Cologne". . . . But the precious books you sent me he has not yet delivered. I have written to him lately about them; and if they are not forthcoming I shall raise such a war-whoop that it will frighten him.

Copway is a good story-teller, and *The Ojibway Conquest* bears much resemblance to Arnold's *Sohrab and Rustum*. Following the fashion of his day, and no doubt his own inclination, he draws the characters of his epic poem in the "noble savage" tradition. If there are defects in his work there are also many beauties, and it is fitting that belated justice should be done to this Rice Lake Indian by resurrecting his poetry and bringing *The Ojibway Conquest: a Tale of the Northwest* to the attention of his fellow-Canadians a century later.

Copway dedicated the poem to his wife:

TO ELIZA ———.

I have no words to tell the loveliness
Which breathes o'er thy fair form; then how much less
The bright, the pure, the beautiful, the blest,
Which wake their harmony within thy breast.
When after weary wanderings by wood,
And lake, and stream, and mountain wilds, I stood
Upon thy island home, thy guileless heart
A healing welcome gave. When forced to part,
And the frail bark, that o'er the waters bore
Me on my way at last from thy loved shore,
Receded in the distance from thy view,
Thy lovely hand waved a most sweet adieu.
Fair daughter! accept this tribute of a breast,
Rich in thy smiles, hath been so richly blest.

NOTE TO THE READER

Of all the numerous and populous tribes of Indians found inhabiting the northern part of this continent at the time of its discovery, the Sioux and Ojibways alone retain anything like their original character.

Of these two tribes or nations the Ojibways inhabit principally the mountainous country about Lake Superior, extending south to the plains of Illinois or Wisconsin, and on the west bordering on that of the Sioux, between whom and they have had a bloody warfare [*sic*]. The Mississippi valley now forms a common boundary, with the exception of the upper or the head of the great river.

It is a well-known fact, known by all who have travelled among them or who are conversant with their past history, and, as traditions transmitted to the present races indicate, that all the country lying south and west of the head of Lake Superior once belonged to the Sioux. By a constant warfare carried on for a great many years, and a succession of misfortunes and defeats, the Sioux were at length compelled to abandon to their more fortunate enemies all of their possessions east of the Mississippi river, and even a not inconsiderable portion on the west of its more northern sources. Tradition says that the last decisive battle was fought near the islands of the south-west end of the Superior, known as the 'Apostle Islands', on a point where La Point now stands. It is on this circumstance that the following tale is founded.

This is given in a form which may be interesting to some who otherwise might not be interested in the nation,—whose ever kind intercourse with the pale faces has ever been apparent. None who have lived any length of time among us could but have observed the manner of relating historical narrations of by-gone days to the children, as the Ojibways do.

I am very glad to think that justice has been done to them by many writers in their tales, and the peculiar romance which belong to them.

A residence of Teba-koo-ne-wa-we-ne-neh, in the remote west, originated the tale which is now presented to the public.

KAH-GE-GA-GAH-BOWH,
Ojibway Nation.

New York, *April* 25, 1850.

The Ojibway Conquest*

THE ST. LOUIS

There is a stream that hath its rise
Beneath the veil of northern skies,
Where frosts and snows eternal meet
In wild array the wanderer's feet,
And all, above, beneath, around,
Is fast in icy fetters bound;
A gloomy, wild, a dreary waste
As ever the eye of man embraced;
Where shrub, if shrub perchance be there,
Blooms not as elsewhere, fresh and fair;
But stinted, bare, and small of growth,
It nestles to the earth as loath
To spread its branches where the breeze
Which passes, kisses but to freeze;
And if a flower should rear its head
From such inhospitable bed,
When thawing snows may yield a day
To summer sun's resistless sway,
It is a flower which doth not blight[1]
By frosts that clothe its leaves in white,
But smiles e'en from its bed of snow.
Like Hope upon the lap of Woe.
The reindeer there roams fleet and free,
And men as wild and fleet as he,
Though small in size, of iron mould,
No fear of storms, no thought of cold,
With limbs unchilled, unslackened pace,
They fleetly follow in the chase,
From dawn till twilight paints the west,[2]
Without a moment lent to rest,
Then stretched at length upon the snows,
Till morn they find a sweet repose.

Ah! little knows the child of ease,
Whom everything is culled to please,
To whose convenience every shore,
From North and South must yield its store,
And o'er whose well protected form
There never beats the freezing storm;

*The footnotes to this poem were numbered in the original; in most other original texts in this volume asterisks were used.

[1]In the north and north-west there is a kind of flower which matures late in the fall, and still blossoms in the dead of winter. There is a strange contrast between its snowy bed and its delicate hues. In spring it dies with the snow, and again reappears in the fall.

[2]The facility to endure long journeys and fatigues has long been the admiration of the people abroad. Those Indians who lived in the north and about the head waters of Lake Superior are an active and the most energetic race. Long journeys were performed in times of war, and with little or no rest during the day of hunting. One would hardly credit the feats they can perform in the dead of winter. Over hill and down ravines, covered with snow, they make their snow-shoe track. Through the forest-world, the trees heavily ladened with snow, they seek the game; and this is done day after day through the period of life.

Ah! little knows he of the woes
Which gather round the life of those
Who live, in nature's rudest mood,
In these deep haunts of solitude,
For though the tempest's power hath
  wrought,
To their bold minds, with danger
  fraught,
Though youth and manhood, and old
  age
Succeed in their accustomed stage,
The body bared to every wind,
The chase that leaves the deer behind,
The frequent want, the frequent fast,
Break up life's healthful flow at last,
And leave a wreck 'tis dread to see,
Of what was once so bold and free.

II. THE STREAM

Thou fair St. Louis! such the scene[3]
  From which thy waters flow;
But different far the land of green
  To which from thence they go;
For many a long, long mile they speed,
  Through fairer, brighter lands,
Tranquil and free like a noble steed
  Unchecked by rider's hands;
From their far source to where they pour
  Into bright Superior's side,
All is wild nature on thy shore,
  Man hath not curbed thy tide;
But on thou flowest in thy might
  Untainted as when God
First called thee sparkling unto light,
  At his creative nod.
The vale through which thy waters
  sweep,
The forest shade, the craggy steep,
The cataract whose thunder fills
The echoes of an hundred hills,
The deep ravine, the precious mine,
Whose ores beneath thy current shine,
Such is the path thy waters take,
Ere lost within the Ocean Lake.
O! often on thy limpid stream,
Hid from the noon tide's sultry beam
By trees whose giant branches cast
A deep shade o'er me as I passed,
Hath my light bark now danced along
To music of some carolled song,
Or floating, like the lightest bird,
It only with the current stirred,
While I have passed hour after hour,
Beneath the scene's enchanting power,
The sweetest perfume on the air
From thousand wild flowers growing
  there,
And colors of the brighest hue
On every side that met the view;
The wild rose, with its sweets beguiling
Along the shore so brightly smiling,
Whose petals falling on the wave,
Their own hue to the current gave;
The mellow light of different dyes
Which came from forest shaded skies;
The stillness over all that dwelt,
So deep it could almost be felt;
All these have held me many a day
A willing captive to their sway.
  O, who that has a heart to feel,

[3]There must ever be a peculiar interest attached to the St. Louis River, arising from the consideration that it is the proper source of that mighty chain of waters, which, after pouring their tide through more than half the extent of the western hemisphere, at last discharge themselves in the Gulf of St. Lawrence, where they mingle with and are lost in those of the Atlantic. But if it had not this fact to draw an interest around it, the character of the river itself is such as to leave an impression upon the mind of one who has glided upon its pure waters not easily to be forgotten. The variety of its scenery, the beauty of its evergreen edges, the rapid and whirling toss of its waves, and the high cliffs of rocks where it swells its maddening roar—all this can be seen in the St. Louis about the extreme west end of Lake Superior, and one can follow it up through its various windings, now narrow and then widens like a lake. The scenery about the head of Lake Superior is picturesque and grand, and a little way up, farther on, dashing with impetuous fury through some narrow and rocky passes, or over falls from whose height the beholder becomes dizzy in looking down, make the voyage one of continual excitement and delight. We might here present a more minute description of the onward windings of this river, but we forbear at present, believing none will contradict us when we say it is not less in grandeur than the scenery on the North River.

Would barter one such hour as this,
For all the gay world can reveal,
Or all it ever knew of bliss!
Pleasures! in vain the precious gem
Ye seek in fashion's heartless throng,
Ask those who seek there, ask them
Who sought the floating phantom long.
There's not a joy that throng can give,
Which does not cost a pang more deep;
There's not a pleasure it bids live,
But lulls some virtue into sleep.

III. THE DANCE

Many a year has passed away
Since at the close of summer's day
Upon a green and level side
Which overlooks St. Louis' tide
A noble band of warriors stood
Who roam at will this solitude.
The bow, the spear, the barbed dart,
Which errs not pointed at the heart,
The paint in earnest colors spread,
Not for maid's love but foeman's dread,
The plumes which in their raven hair
Waved graceful at each breath of air,
The trophies in their battles taken,
When foeman's prowess had been shaken,
Each warrior there was decked with these,[4]
Profuse as summer decks the trees.
The foremost of this hero band
A standard carried in his hand,
Which from its waving top displayed
A flag most curiously made
From feathers of the wild bird's wing,[5]
Of every shade of coloring.
He was a youth, in whom combined
All that was bright in form and mind;
The noble forehead, broad and high,
The soul that shone within his eye,
The thoughts which o'er his features played
With quick and ever varying shade,
The limbs where strength was seen to dwell
In every full and graceful swell,
Distinguished him as one of those
Where nature's fairest gifts repose—
ME-GI-SI—such the name he bore,
The Eagle of the Lonely Shore,
And as he planted in the ground
That pinion's shaft amid the sound
Of drum, and song, and echoing shout,[6]
He looked like Mars himself come out
To take, as in the day of yore,
The van upon the field of gore.
Around this shaft with measured pace
Each warrior found a ready place,
And soon the circling folds advance
And mingling in the wild war-dance,
While ever and anon a loud
And piercing whoop rose from the crowd,
Sending its accents, shrill and clear;
In answering echoes far and near;
And when they died in air away,
Each warrior in that dread array
Stood like a statue planted deep,
So still and firm their track they keep;
While at each pause a brave advanced
Within the ring, then round him glanced,
And in rude eloquence portrayed
The havoc he in war had made,

[4]There is no time in which an Indian brave adorns his person with so much care as when going to war. Here the warrior lays aside the encumbering articles of dress worn at other times, and only wears those light, and yet, often extremely ornamental, which, without confining in the least the free and easy motion of every limb, exhibits their fine forms to the best possible advantage.

[5]The feather flag is the flag which was and, in some parts, is yet used. The feathers of the rare gray eagle are knitted together over four feet long. When ready for war, this is stuck in the centre of the war-party, while now and then the standard-bearer waves it, while the rest send a piercing shout to heaven.

[6]The drum is one of the principal instruments we used in time of war preparations, and at all times, and although very unmusical to finer ears in the civilized world, is by us held in great estimation. It is made by tightly stretching a piece of deer-hide over a hoop, and somewhat resembles a tambourine. The drum-stick is a piece of wood with a short cross at one end, with which the drum is beaten.

The feats of bravery he had done,[7]
The scalps from slaughtered victims won,
As well of fallen warrior bold,
As wife and child, of these he told,
And as he held them out to view,
Some of them yet of fresh blood hue,
And raised the war whoop loud and high,
With swelling breast and flashing eye,
He seemed again amid the strife
With which his tale had been so rife,
That morn had pealed the rolling drum
Amid the cry 'They come! They come!
The Sioux! The Sioux!' And at the sound,
Each warrior's foot was on the ground,
And knife to knife, and breast to breast,
The doubtful strife they long contest;
They fought as though their blood were water,
Resumed again when ceased the slaughter,
They fought like men whose deadly hate
Nothing but death could satiate.
The Sioux at length were forced to yield
And leave to foe a hard-earned field;
Some fled and some were captive led,
Better to have been with the dead,
Better by far, for though to-night
They have from death a brief respite,
They're not deceived, for well they know
To-morrow comes the fatal blow,
It comes with all the cruel art
Hate can invent to wring the heart,
When should it quail or yield to fear,
They die without a pitying tear,
They die and meet the recreant's end,
Despised alike by foe and friend.

[7]At the public dances of our nation is the only place where any one can boast of bravery, and it is not expected a brave should boast at all times but at such places of their exploits in battle. On such occasions I have sat to listen to their bold eloquence and graphic descriptions, until my own breast irresistibly caught the passionate feelings of theirs.

IV. THE WENDIGO

The dance is o'er, the revel past,
And of that savage host the last
Hath thrown himself upon the ground
And his accustomed slumber found.
Close by their side the captives slept,
And watch or guard there none was kept,
For hand and foot securely tied,
Vain were the effort, that they tried
To shake from off their limbs the thong
Which bound them in its folds so strong;
Vain, did I say;—no, one was there,
Who, though the bands he knew to wear,
While eye of foe was on him bent,—
And to his skill a caution lent,—
When watchful eyes were sunk to rest,
And measured breathings heaved the breast,
Could tear those shackles from his flesh,
As easy as the spider's mesh.[8]

[8]I would not like to hazard the assertion, in this enlightened age, that there is such a thing as magic or supernatural agency among the Indians, but I must confess myself unable as all have done who have witnessed those exhibitions, to account for satisfactorily; one of those Indians who pretends to have an intercourse with spirits will permit himself to be bound hands and feet, then wrapped closely in a blanket or deer's hide, bound around his whole body with cords and thongs as long and as tightly as the incredulity of any one present may see fit to continue the operation, after which he is thrown into a small lodge. He begins a low, unintelligible incantation to the gods, and increases in rapidity and loudness until he works himself up into a great pitch of seeming or real frenzy, at which time, usually three or four minutes after being put in, he opens the lodge and throws out the thongs and hides with which he was bound without a single knot being untied or fold displaced, himself sitting calm and free on the ground. Carver, in his travels, gives a curious and interesting account of an exhibition of this kind, accompanied with a

The frosts of many winters sped
Had left their trace upon his head,
His life, which passed in constant wars,
Had marked him with a thousand scars,
But every iron muscle told
That vigor had not yet grown old.
He might have lost youth's spring and grace,
But strength had well supplied their place.
Whether by force or magic spell
He burst his shackles, none could tell,
Yet never, but for one brief hour,
Had they upon his limbs a power.
Among his native brethren famed
For many years he had been named
For feats of strength and wondrous art,
The WEN DI GO OF ICY HEART.[9]
In the day's strife of ancient foes,
To which this night had brought a close,
His heavy blows, which fell like rain,
Had worked his way with heaps of slain.
Through yielding ranks he held his place,
Till like a rock at whose firm base
The ocean breaks in murmurs hoarse,
ME-GI-SI checked his onward course.

prophecy, which was astonishingly fulfilled. Those who possess this art pretend that a spirit comes and relieves them from their bonds. You say this is superstition. Much of the same kind is among the pale faces. I believe the Indians had, and do have, mesmerism among them.

[9]This Wen-di-go, in the idea of the Indians, is a monster, who lives in the north: a supernatural being who roams about the earth in search of victims, for he lives on human flesh. He is represented to be as tall as the pine trees; a whirlwind's tread is heard around him wherever he is; frost and cold are his companions; he is devoid of feeling—'Icy heart.' It is believed men have become Wen-di-go's by a mysterious process, and if any one is supposed to become one he is immediately dispatched. When a Wen-di-go can be killed it is only done by men who are supposed to have a strong arm, or an array of favorites from the spirits to aid them.

As springs the tiger on his prey
When pressed by hunger, so sprang they;
Reckless of all that might oppose,
They rushed upon each other blows,
And grappled with a force they feel,
To which the grasp of vice of steel
Would be an infant's touch. The knife
Then flashes quick in deadly strife.
They fought as though on them alone
The fortunes of the day were thrown;
They fought as if they proudly felt
On no mean foe their blows were dealt;
Each nerve to its last tension wrought,
Like meeting thunder-bolts they fought.
The WEN DI GO'S superior strength
O'ercame youth's suppleness at length,
And while Me-Gi-Si freely bleeds,
He of the icy heart succeeds;
His blade is raised to strike the blow,
The last he need to strike, when lo!
His threatening arm all sudden stops,
And down as by a palsy drops;
He stood a moment fixed and still,
Then yielded at ME-GI-SI'S will;
And captive now and captor keeping,
Side by side are calmly sleeping.

Midnight had passed, and there they lay
In rest unbroke, that warrior band;
The powerful conflict of the day
Had now relaxed each iron hand.
The moon, too, now had sunk to rest
Behind the hills which skirt the west,
And damp mists from the river rose,
And o'er the banks in circles close.
A silence deep was over all
Except the noisy waterfall,
That, indistinct by distance, fell
Alternately in ebb and swell,
When hush! a careful hand is pressed
Upon the brave ME-GI-SI'S breast.
The touch awoke him quick as thought;
He sprang upon his feet and caught
Within one hand his ready blade,
The other on the foeman laid;
But when he saw in what calm mood
The WEN-DI-GO before him stood,
He did not strike, but for a space
They looked within each other's face:
ME-GI-SI with a blended feeling
Of awe and wonder o'er him stealing,
And which he could not all conceal
By the dim light the stars reveal;
Sternness and dignity alone

Upon the other's features shone.
The WEN-DI-DO the silence broke,
As scarce above his breath he spoke,
'Youth, are you brave? Then follow me';[10]
Thus saying, turning carefully,
And with a step that had no sound,
To wake the foemen sleeping round,
He passed, and striding on before,
Pursued the winding trail that bore
Through wild grass of a growth most rank
Along the river's sloping bank.
ME-GI-SI for a moment cast
His eyes upon him as he passed,
Irresolute, then quickly sped
Along the track the other led,
And now by the dim starlight they
Together hold their silent way.

V. THE CAVE

A league was passed, yet on they went,
Whate'er their thoughts, they had no vent;
But mute they still their way pursued,
Deeper within the solitude.

At length the youth impatient grown,
Paused and exclaimed in no slight tone—
'That I am brave no longer thou
Canst doubt from what thou seest now;
If thou hadst not that lesson learned
By yesterday's experience earned.
The distance now precludes all fear
Of treacherous band or listening ear;
Then tell thy wish what e'er it be,
Thou'll find no coward heart in me;
Speak! or this knife may shame to wear
Another sheath than that I bear.'
'Peace, fool', replied the WEN-DI-GO,
As quick he turned and struck a blow
That sent the spinning blade so well
They could not hear it where it fell.
'Check thy hot blood, nor deem that I
Have brought thee here for treachery.
Think you, had I desired your life,
Ere you awoke could not my knife
Have borne to your unconscious breast
The blow that brings eternal rest?
I have a tale will pierce thy heart
Worse than a foeman's barbed dart.
Doubt not, but follow me;' and then
Turned and pursued the trail again,
Nor long pursued before around
A bold and rocky point it wound,
Which sent its craggy summit high
Aloft into the dusky sky,
And terminated in a cove
Formed by the arching rocks above.
Here entered they, and on a rock
Torn from the roof by some rude shock
They took their seat. A wilder spot
Throughout the universe is not
As this which now their steps had found,
Than that by which they were surround.
Far, far away beneath the ground
There came a hoarse and gurgling sound
Of water into fury lashed,
As o'er some precipice 'twere dashed;
The owl, scared by their entrance, fled,
And screamed its notes above their head;
Lank wolves, whose den the cave had been,
Prowled round them as they entered in,
While just without the cavern's door
The waters of St. Louis roar,
As o'er the dizzy fall they flow;
And then an hundred feet below,
With deafening sound they break and boil
In endless strife and wild turmoil.
'Here in this dark and gloomy grot',
The WEN-DI-GO began,—'a spot
Where oft, 'tis said, the Manitou
Unveils himself to human view,
And smiles or frowns as he discovers
Of truth or falsehood they are lovers—
Here let me rest while I disclose
A tale may leave us no more foes,

[10] This is an expression we use in challenging one another when we desire to engage another in any enterprise which requires the exercise of this attribute of the mind. When any one is insulted by another, he immediately calls at the wigwam, and in looking through the lodge asks him this question, and if he speaks in the affirmative an appeal then is immediately made to their relative prowess. If he does not so answer he is immediately branded as an old 'woman', an appellation for all cowards; not that all women are cowards, for some deal in cowhides in civilized countries.

And the Great Spirit do by me,
As I shall deal in truth with thee.

You wonder that I brought you here,
But ah! you know not half how dear
Is this wild spot to me. Strange chance
Which brings again within my glance
The scenes where long, long winters past,
When the quiet blood of youth flowed fast,
I wandered with my bow well strung
And quiver o'er my shoulders flung,
And if my arrow rightly sped
When pointed at the wild bird's head,
Whatever fortune might betide,
My merry heart was satisfied.
Here, too, in after years I roved
In fondness with the bride I loved;
This was our home till that foul day
When the accursed Ojibway
Rushed down upon us, scattering death
Like Evil Spirit's poisoned breath,
And with false heart and bloody hand
Drove us from our paternal land.
Thou knowest well the hatred strong
Hath dwelt between our nations long,
And from this land where now you see
The curs'd Ojibway roving free,
Thou knowest by that hated race
The Sioux was torn till not a place
By stream or mountain now is left
Of which he hath not been bereft.
Strange chance! Upon that very steep
Where those we left so lately sleep,
My wigwam stood. My bride as bright
As the unclouded moon at night,
Ahpuckways from rushes wove,[11]
And sung sweet notes which spake of love,
While o'er the grass with prattling joy
Gambolled, with happy heart, our boy.
It was a bright and summer's day;
They were alone, I was away
Upon the wild deer's track. Night fell
And I returned, but who can tell
The anguish of that hour! I came
To see my wigwam in a flame—
My wife was slain—the purple tide
Was oozing yet warm from her side,
But still so sweet was that faint smile,
Which shone upon her face the while,
I could not deem her dead, but flung
Myself upon the ground and clung
To her loved side, kissing away
The crimson drops of blood that lay
Sprinkled upon her pallid cheeks;
And then in wild and broken shrieks
I fondly called upon her name;
I kissed her lips, but closed in death
Those lips from which there came no breath.
I sought my boy, but he was gone,
And I, in anguish and alone,
Stood like an oak the thunder bird
Had riven at the spirit's word.[12]
Till that day passion's fearful blast
Had never o'er my spirit passed;
No angry strife, no withering care,
No burning curse had entered there;
My bride, my boy, they were the springs
That ever moved my spirit's wings.
But as I stood and wept to view
Her own heart's blood my bride bedew,
And thought upon the hated foe
Whose arm had dealt the scathing blow,
Dark thoughts within my soul found place
In strange and lightning-like embrace.
Horror and anguish and despair

[11]Ahpuckway is a kind of mat which is made out of the blades of the rush vulgarly called 'cattail' with great skill, for the purpose of covering the wigwams of the natives. They appear at a distance light, and glisten before the sun. These, too, they make mats for their beds to repose upon in the night.

[12]Our nation believe that thunder is caused by a large bird which lives so far up in the sky as not to be visible. The noise is caused by the motion of his wings. This idea, no doubt, they received from the drumming of the pheasant, which so nearly resembles distant thunder. The lightning they imagine the opening and shutting of the bird's eye; and its fierceness is sometimes so fearful and keen as to ignite the object on which it falls. This happens when fire follows a stroke of lightning. Whenever lightning strikes an object, they think that the bird shoots from its eye a small round stone which produces the effect; and assure you that if you will dig and examine where the lightning enters the ground, this stone will be, and has been, found.

Alone at first were mingled there,
But these full soon gave place to one
Deep burning passion, which alone
Took full possession of my breast.
Revenge! Revenge! How I caressed
The darling thought! All else that life
Deems worthy of a mortal's strife
Was swallowed up in this wild thirst
For vengeance on the foe accursed.
I knelt upon the turf beside
The murdered body of my bride,
And with one hand upon her head,
The other with the warm blood red,
There, in the presence of the dead,
I vowed my first and latest breath
To hate, to vengeance, and to death!
Winters have passed, and it is now
Long since I made that fearful vow,
But never since that fatal hour
Hath it a moment lost its power.
How well it hath been kept let those
Who fell beneath my arm disclose.
Revenge! It is a powerful charm
To steel the heart and nerve the arm,
To give the foot unwonted speed,
And to the eye in hour of need
A lynx-like quickness; such I've proved
The passion that within me moved.
An hundred warriors hath this hand
Already sent to that far land
Where wander shadows of the dead
By the dim light Aurora shed;[13]
Thine would have been among the rest,
But that I marked upon thy breast
That which withheld my lifted head.
My bride had in our happy hours,
Marked, with the dyes of various flowers
Such as our tribe alone employ
Our Totem on our little boy.[14]
I saw upon thy breast that sign—
I knew it well—Yes! thou art mine!
My long lost child! Thy purple veins
No foul Ojibway blood sustains.
O'er thy bold form there is no trace
Of that despised, snake-hearted race,
Who, not contented our fair land
To desolate with knife and brand,
Must yet our very sons engage,
Contest against their sires to wage.
But theirs no more thy iron nerve;
Rather than thou that foe shouldst serve
My blade shall penetrate thy heart,
E'en though my only child thou art.
If yet a single spark remains
Of noble impulse in thy veins,
And contact with the Ojibway
Hath not extinguished the last ray
Of the proud spirit of thy sires,
Now, 'ere the waning night expires,
Swear to revenge the wrongs we bear,
And here thy murdered mother's, swear!'
The old man ceased, and had the light
Permitted him the welcome sight,
He would have seen that haughty ire
Which lent his eye its dazzling fire,
The features of the youth reveal,
As thus he answered the appeal:

'By the dread Manitou that dwells
Within these arched and craggy dells,
By her whose bright and watchful eye
Was o'er me bent in infancy,
I swear!' The echoes of the word
Along the cavern's roof was heard,
And when they died away, a sigh,
Soft as when evening winds pass by,

[13]The Indians, unable to account for the various phenomenas of nature, have associated with most of them some curious superstition. The aurora borealis they believe shines to illuminate the pastime of the disembodied spirits, when, in the shadowy land, they gather in the chase or mingle in the dances, with which they amuse themselves.

O-ge-chog means shadow, and when applied to man, we say, in reference to his soul, his shadow; the reality of such attribute they see yet cannot feel.

[14]Among the Indians each family is designated by some distinguished badge or crest, such as the figure of a swan, deer, crane, eagle, bear, otter, or moose. This emblem we call a totem. The laws relative to it are somewhat curious. It is not permitted for a male and female to intermarry whose totem happens to be the same; they are all considered as brother and sister. In adopting or inheriting their totem among the children, the boys and girls take that of their father, and sometimes the girls can only take that of their mother. This is only true as to the different other nations.

Sweet as the swan's expiring notes[15]
Upon the air around them floats.
'Hush!' said the WEN-DI-GO; 'It is
My bride come from the bower of bliss,
In the far country of the dead,
To breathe a blessing o'er thy head.
Thou shadowy spirit, for whose sake[16]
I live both when I sleep and wake,
Whose influence in rest and strife
Hath been the guide-star of my life,
And, to revenge whose wrongs, no pains,
No torture could my hand restrain,
Delay thy flight to the bright shore
Which waits thy coming, till once more,
As in that bitter day, I swear
For every tress of thy fair hair
Which decked thy head when laid so low
I'll pluck a scalp from that of foe.
Spirit! Let this thy sadness cheat,
Till shadows both again we meet.'[17]

[15]Though this is a common-place allusion, yet the lakes about the country where the scenes are we speak of are filled with wild fowl, and among which is the most graceful of all birds —the swan.

[16]Like all unenlightened nations, our nation have many extremely superstitious notions. They believe the visitation of the souls of their departed friends not often to be visible with a natural body, but they hear them in some way—by the sighing of the winds, the hum of creation, or fancy they ride on the fleecy clouds of an evening sky.

[17]Some of the ideas in reference to the immortality of the soul they represent under the idea of a shadow. Their explanation which they generally give of the reason why they bury their dead with weapons of hunting and war, food, and apparel is so curious and ingenious that we cannot help relating it. The Indian is asked why he does this. His reply is that the shadow of the body has left for the distant west; that the soul needs the shadow of these articles and not the material. The shadow of these things serves to the soul as they did to the body while living.

VI. THE COUNCIL

Upon a mountain whose high peak
The very heavens seems to seek,
Which rises on the southern shore
And looks Superior's waters o'er,
Are gathering now the few who fled,
When yesterday so illy sped.
Though the gray dawn of morn appeared,
Ere from the cave their course they steered,
And many a long mile lay between
This place and where the strife had been,
The gathered ranks already show
ME-GI-SI and the WEN-DI-GO.

Quickly they come and silent meet,
Without a word or look to greet,
But each as up the steep he wound,
Threw himself mutely on the ground,
Till of that scattered band the last
Had to his place in silence passed.
No darkly agitating trace
Could be discovered in the face
Of ardent youth or furrowed age
To tell of passion's inward rage,
But every brow was calm and stern,
Whatever smothered fires might burn.
The WEN-DI-GO, to whom the lead,
As well in council as in deed,
Had long been given as his due,
For wisdom deep, and courage true,
Slowly arose. There was no burst
Of passion in his words at first,
But calmly over each event
That marked their recent strife he went,
And e'en his voice grew sadly mild
As his words turned upon his child
Whom the great Manitou, he said,
Had now restored as from the dead,
From which the cheering hope he drew,
Although their numbers might be few,
The Manitou was still their friend,
And would not fail them, in the end,
A hallowed cause like theirs to bless
With signal and complete success.
But when he dwelt upon the wrong
Which they had now endured so long
From the foul race of Ojibway,
And pointed to the land that lay
Far as the eye around could roam,
And told them, that was once their home,

But home from which they were
expelled,
And now by hated foemen held,
The powers which in his bosom reigned,
But which till then he had restrained,
Burst forth and like Heaven's lightning
glowed,
While every working feature showed
Which passion held within his soul.
Like fire when o'er the prairies rushing,
Or torrents from a mountain gushing,
The impulse of his own was pressed
With light-like speed from breast to
breast.
No bosom there but was on fire,
No heart which did not glow with ire;
And when he ceased, in such dread yell
Upon the air their warwhoop fell,
The wild beast from his covert fled,
The wild birds screamed above their
head,
And long when from their lips it died,
It echoed down the mountain's side.

A free discussion then arose
For every warrior to propose
What to each one might seem to show
The best advantage o'er the foe.

At no great distance to the right,
And only hidden from their sight
By rocky bluffs, which ledge on ledge
Abrupt rose in the water's edge,
Within a large and quiet bay
A clustering group of islands lay.
Here, scattered o'er the banks of green
And shady groves, there might be seen
Many a lodge whose bark so white[18]
Was sending back the noonday light.
Upon these isles the Ojibway,
Since, from their homes they drove
away
The conquered Sioux, had dwelt secure,
And deeming them at once a sure
And safe retreat, had gathered all
Incessant warfare did not call,
To deeds from deeds already done,
To keep the land thus foully won.
To this fair spot each thought was
turned,
And every warrior's bosom burned
To win again those long-lost isles
And live within their quiet smiles.
Here then each heart resolved as soon
As reached to-morrow's sun its noon,
To strike a blow should free the land
From the accursed foemen's hand,
Or fighting till the last was slain,
Leave their hearts' blood upon the
plain.

VII. THE SACRIFICE

The day that dawned upon the foe,
ME-GI-SI and the WEN-DI-GO
Had left while, all unconscious, rest
Was reigning over every breast,
Awoke the encampment's busy hum,
And, at the sound of signal drum,
The warriors gathered round their chief,
Whose look was stern, whose words
were brief.
He waved his hand, and quick as
thought
A shaft of stoutest oak was brought
And planted firmly in the ground;
To this with winding thongs were
bound
The captives, whose unhappy fate
Must gratify their captors' hate.
And where is he who always bore
The foremost honors heretofore,
And where the noble captive he
Had led in their late victory?
Strange that he comes not, he, whose
hand

[18]The lodges are made by poles stuck in the ground, and these meet at the ends, which, in meeting, lap over and are tied, and these are covered with the white birch. This kind of bark is so white that when many are seen at a distance they appear as though there were more than what is really the number.

This bark is used for almost every purpose. We cover our wigwams with it, make our canoes, vessels for water, and the dishes we used to eat out of. Fancy work-boxes are made out of this material. Our songs of war, triumphs, and traditions are recorded on this bark.

One Indian family often have five thousand, six thousand, eight thousand, and ten thousand dishes to gather sap from the noble trees in the spring, and the bark holds the sugar which has been made.

Was ever first to light the brand,
And by whom were the victors tied;
None ever knew the knots to slide.
ME-GI-SI, favorite of all,
Why comes he not at comrades' call?
And why lays he the rest behind,
While other hands the victims bind?
These are the questions rapidly
From lip to lip are heard to fly.

By the Ojibway 'tis believed
That when a mortal hath received
A vigorous and fearful fast,
And day and night in watching passed,
And who hath long withdrawn his mind
From all communion with his kind,
And hath within the forest's shade
His home with evil spirits made,
Learning from them each magic art
Which their instruction can impart,
And hath his heart darkly imbued
With all of ill, and naught of good—
These do a fearful power instil
Beyond all merely human skill,
Freedom, at will the form to change,
The water, earth, or air to range,
And most of all they strangely give
Desire on human flesh to live.
Thus when an hour or more is sped,
And still no trace of either fled,
They doubt not that the haughty Sioux,
With whom ME-GI-SI had to do,
Was one of these, and deem full well
Their favorite, by his magic fell.
The unhallowed rites no longer wait,
Their thirst for blood to satiate,
But with redoubled zeal are made
Because unwillingly delayed.
Nothing their vengeance could suggest,
To daunt the heart or wring the breast,
But was prepared with savage art
In the dire scene to bear a part.
The faggots at the victim's feet,
The scourge their naked flesh to beat,
The arrows of the pine well dried,
The bow to hurl them in their side,
And as the flames around them rise,
Burning to aid their agonies;
Tortures like these they do not lack
The victim's outward sense to rack;
But more tormenting far are those
Designed to wake his inward throes—
The taunt, the gibe, the goading sneer,
The insulting charge of coward fear,
Imbecile strength the bow to bend,
And erring skill the shaft to send,
A soul which could not look on pain,
And hands which had no foeman slain,
Limbs bowed with grief and not with years,
And eyes which shone but not with tears—
Such were the taunts upon them hurled,
As o'er their forms the hot blaze curled.

What sounds are those that fill the air,
Above all others echoing there,
As doth the cataract's loud roar,
The brook which murmurs at its shore,
Or thunders bursting through the sky,
The owlet's hoarse and startled cry?
It is the victim's death-song shout
Which burst from their firm bosoms out,
Casting defiance at their foes,
And mocking at the torturing throes
Their thirsty vengeance would bestow;
The hissing flames which round them glow
To break their courage have no power,
But as exulting as in hour
When victory hath wreathed their brow,
Is the bold shout they put forth now.
The noble deeds they have performed,
The noble thoughts their hearts have warmed,
The sunset land, so bright and fair,
Which waits to bid them welcome there—
These are the burden of their song,
Which swells in such proud notes along.

Brave Sons of Nature! Ye need not,
To make you at this moment what
Hath been, will be, while time succeeds,
And hearts alive to noble deeds,
The admiration of mankind;
Ye need not in the mazes wind
Of the philosophy of schools,
To teach you the eternal rules
Of fortitude and self-control,
And all which doth exalt the soul.

Fainter and fainter, yet still clear
That death-song falls upon the ear
Of those who dance around the fires,
Where bravery such as this expires.
At length each victim's voice is still,
And vengeance now hath drank its fill.

The fires are out, the warriors gone,
And, MO-NING-WUN-AH, ere the sun
Sinks to his couch behind the west,
Their barks upon thy shores shall rest.

VIII. THE LOVERS

The sun had set, the clouds which fringed
The sky were gorgeously tinged
With gold and purple, and all dyes
Which make the summer sunset skies
So lovely, and whose rays impart
To every impulse of the heart
Such chastened, hallowed thoughts, as are
Akin to the soft light which there
Beams forth so beautifully bright,
Sweet herald of approaching night!
O'er the calm waters of the bay,
Where the Ojibway Island lay,
Those rays are glanced in many a track
To the bright clouds, which send them back
Beneath the waters where they glow,
Forming a mimic heaven below.
Oh! that such hallowed scenes as this
Should ever look on ought but bliss!
When the fond soul hath felt the power
Of this enchanting, soothing hour,
To wipe out every stain which care
Or sin hath left corroding there,—
Oh! why will it again return
To drink from the polluted urn,
With which guilty pleasures allure
The bosoms thus, once rendered pure.

This lovely scene has passed away,
And the last tints of dying day
Are fading from the western skies,
When MO-NING-WUN-AH, there arise
Along thy shores a voice's wail,
Whose accents through thy lovely vale
All sorrowful and plaintive spread:
It is the wailing for the dead.[19]
When the light barks, the rest that bore,
Passed rapidly upon thy shore,
A maiden band was there to find
If brother, lover, stayed behind;
And as they found them there, or not,
With joy or grief they left the spot,
And now when the faint twilight spreads
Its sombre veil above their heads,
The voice of mother, sister, bride,
Is mingled in the plaintive tide,
For those they may not greet again
Who sleep upon the battle plain.
But one was there from whose distressed
And deeply agitated breast
No wailings flowed; she could not weep,
Her agony was all too deep.
ME-ME, fair child of light and love![20]
Lovely and beautiful above
All earthly power to describe
In the soft language of her tribe.[21]
She had most fittingly been styled
The DOVE, so innocent and mild
The feelings nature had impressed
Upon her bright and sinless breast.
No thought which did not breathe of Heaven
Had ever to her heart been given,
No passion angels might not own
Had ever in her dark eyes shone,
But all was hallowed, pure and bright
As heaven's own celestial light.
The form that held that soul encased
So sinless, was the no less graced
With more that the rapt heart ere deemed
Of bright when it most fondly dreamed.

---

[19]The evening is always the time the friends of the deceased collect around their graves and sing a low, wailing sound of the voice. Often, by the banks of the Mississippi, we have heard the Ojibway sing the death-song, and the voice seems to creep over the distant hills, which sound, they believe, aids the soul in travelling to the distant west. When the shadows of the red races collect from the valleys of that Happy Land they send their echoing shouts to each other from hill to hill.

[20]This is one of the most harmless of birds, which you call dove. A beautiful legend is told the children of this bird, when in flocks they return from the north in the spring, in the wigwam.

[21]Travellers have found the language of the Ojibway to be very musical, and at the same time to be one of the most noble in America. This is susceptible of expressing the nicest shade of thought by endless modifications of the verb. The language of the nation has justly been called the 'Greek of America'.

She loved with all the power of such,
To love when tones from others touch
The chords which with responsive thrill
Vibrate in their own heart until
There is no power or faculty
Within the soul, all joyously,
Which doth not tremble with the weight
Of feeling which it hath in freight.
Such was the love, so pure, so deep,
ME-GI-SI from its mystic sleep
Had wakened never more to rest,
To life within her gentle breast.
They loved as mortals never should—
To stake the whole life hath of good
Upon one cast, and see that fail—
O, the sad tortures which assail
The trusting heart! and ME-ME felt
Hers with this bitter anguish melt,
When he whose smiles alone could give
All for which she would wish to live
Came not, and as she deemed no more
Would roam with her their happy shore.

There was a sweet secluded spot,
A gentle point which slightly shot
With sloping bank into the bay,
Where often at the close of day,
Apart from those whose noisy mirth
Had in it all too much of earth
For pleasures of that hallowed kind
Which love had in their hearts enshrined,
She and ME-GI-SI passed the hours
In weaving garlands of bright flowers,
And circling with love's trembling hand
Around their brows the fragrant band,
Or breathing to each other's ear
The tender words they loved to hear,
He with a deep and noble feeling
His passion's fervent strength revealing,
While she, with less of words perchance,
But with a bright enrapturing glance
From her full eyes responsive turned,
To all that in his own heart burned;
Or, leaning fondly on his breast,
She sung the dying day to rest.

Now, while with melancholy swell
The dirge upon the night air fell,
She sought this spot and, seated there,
Upon her hands she bowed her fair
And gentle face, o'er which was spread
The marble paleness of the dead.
Ah! ME-ME! none can ever know
The full extent of that deep woe
Which wrung thy heart, until the hour
When they, like thee, have felt its power.

While thus she sat a bark appeared,
And to this spot its swift course steered.
A moment, and its prow was fast
Upon the shore, and from it passed
A tall and noble youth, who went
With gentle steps and slowly bent
In saddened fondness by her side.
She saw him not; for sorrow's tide
Had swept across her heart until
Her senses sank beneath its chill.
But when her name he fondly spoke,
She raised her head—'ME-GI-SI' broke
In joyful accents, as she sprung
And round his neck in transport clung.
The sudden joy his presence brought
Upon her heart so overwrought,
Her consciousness fled with the shock,
And now like ivy to the rock
She lay in sweet unconscious rest,
Entwined around her lover's breast.
And when at length her eyes unclosed
To his, on whose breast she reposed,
The look was all so mild and sweet
With which those eyes her lover's greet,
As though their light beamed from a soul
Into which Heaven's sunshine stole.
'To what a fearful weight of grief,
Beloved, thou hast brought relief!'
Thus she began, 'I ask not what
The reasons why thou camest not
When others of our tribe returned,
From whom the fearful tale I learned
That thou hadst fall'n beneath the art
Of one of those of icy heart,
Once in the power of whose dread spell
None e'er returned his fate to tell.
It is enough for my glad heart
To know that here again thou art,
That oft in this, our loved retreat,
With gladsome hearts we yet may meet,
To tell o'er and o'er to thee
How very dear thou art to me,
And thou to fold me to thy breast,
And say "Thou art in that love blest".
O! when we meet at times like this,
It seems as though the whole of bliss
Which ever in the bright world shone,
Gathers in my poor heart alone!
To gaze in fondness on thy brow,
And feel thy heart as I do now,
Beneath my own so wildly beat,

To hear thy words, so soft and sweet,
Call me, as oft they do, thy bride,
O! what hath earth to give beside!
When will the war-cry cease to grieve
My heart because it bids thee leave;
While I an hundred times a day
Come to this lovely spot to pray,
Until it seems my heart would break,
To the Great Spirit for thy sake.
Say, must thou yet again expose
Thy life among those cruel foes,
The fearful Sioux?—But ah, love! why
Breaks from thy bosom that deep sigh?
Has thy heart any care? ah, say,
And let me kiss that care away',
She said, and with her fingers fair,
She brushed away the raven hair
Which o'er his forehead clustering strayed;
And when upon his brow she laid
Her gentle lips, ME-GI-SI felt
His purpose almost in him melt,
And for a moment he forgot
His sad, inexorable lot,
So sweet the thrill that kiss had sent
Through his sad heart; but when he bent
His eyes upon her lovely face,
And saw how deep and pure the trace
Of trusting love in every look,
His bosom heaved, and his soul shook
With the intensity of pain
Its breaking chords had to sustain,
As rushing thoughts again impress
The withering, blighting consciousness
That he no more upon that smile,
Which had such power to beguile,
Could in the bliss of former days
Fix his full soul's adoring gaze.
Alas! he knew the dream was past,
And this fond look must be his last.
He knew that should those eyes beam yet
When he was gone, as when they met,
He could not, must not, from the sight
Receive, as he had done, delight.
He knew it yet that cheek should wear
The hallowed smiles which now were there,
The thrills of rapture they impart
Must fall upon another's heart.
If those eyes beam! If that cheek glow!
Alas! He doth too sadly know,
His presence only can awake
Those smiles which beam but for his sake,
That he alone can give the light
Without which they will sink in night.
'Twas this which gave the deadliest sting
To all his soul was suffering.
If he alone might meet the blow,
And his heart only feel the woe,
If on his own the blight might rest,
And leave unscathed her tender breast,
He could sustain the scathing stroke,
And firmly meet it like the oak
Whose trunk lightning indeed might break,
But whose firm roots they could not shake,
But that the misery he knew
Should tear her heart asunder, too!
O! that was torture all too deep;
He felt these thoughts in tumult sweep
Across his brain, and when at length
A powerful effort called the strength
Into his prostrate breast again,
And he so far o'ercame its pain
As to, in broken words, relate
The tale he knew must seal their fate,
It was with accents so subdued,
In spite of all his fortitude,
As though at every word he spoke
A chord within his sad heart broke.
'Ah! ME-ME, thou hast been and art
The sparkling dew-drop of my heart,
Beneath whose brightness I have felt
In that of love all feelings melt;
O, 'twas a glorious dream that stole
So sweetly, purely o'er my soul:
I did not deem that I should wake
To see my heart with that dream break.
But, ME-ME, that bright dream is fled:
Like the cold fingers of the dead,
I feel its dead joys o'er my breast
In icy suffocation pressed.
O, what but thee and this dear spot
Would I not give could I but blot
From memory all that hath passed
Since in this bower we parted last.
I've struggled, but it is in vain;
The fire is in my heart and brain,
And will not cease its torturing strife
Until extinguished with my life.
Thou knowest the totem I have borne
Is not such as by thy tribe worn;
That we, unknowing what its name,
Have often wondered how it came
That I alone have worn a crest
Differing so strangely from the rest.
'Tis strange no more; the battle-field
Thy mystery hath at length revealed,

And thy fond lover hath his sire
Among the foe whom thy tribe's ire
Hath driven from their native land,
A scattered but unconquered band.
Yes, ME-ME, I am one of those,
Thy nation's fiercest, deadliest foes,
Whom, but a moment since, so true
Thou didst well term the fearful Sioux.
Fearful they are, and will be yet,
To those who shall their path beset.
Thou knowest between this tribe of thine
And that which henceforth must be mine
Exists a hatred strong as death,
Resigned not even with their breath.
Judge, then, if they could e'en abide
To see the dove the eagle's bride.
Alas! ME-ME, it may not be,
And were it not, my love, for thee,
I could rejoice that my firm nerve
To direful vengeance yet might serve,
For her whose soft and gentle lays
Were carolled to my infant days,
But whom the Ojibway beguiled,
And robbed at once of wife and child;
And I have sworn my soul to give
To retribution while I live;
But short the moments that remain
Before that vow will be in vain.
To-morrow's sun will see its beam
Flashed back in many a war-knife's gleam,
And yonder waters on whose breast
The moonbeams now so sweetly rest,
Shall drink before the day shall close,
The mingled blood of warring foes,
And I shall be amidst the strife,
But not, as erst, against the life
Of sire and kindred warrior, no,
My arm must find more fitting foe.
Something forewarns me that my blood
Shall mingle with to-morrow's flood;
I feel it now within my heart,
To-night, for the last time, we part;
And yonder stars which shine so bright,
When they come not another night,
Will look upon my bleeding form
No longer with life's pulses warm,
And that brow, cold, and damp in death,
So lately hallowed by thy breath.
But let it come! Why should I live
When life hath nothing now to give
But blighted hopes and vain regrets;
And every lingering sun that sets
Adds only to the bitter store
With which the heart was charged before.
Yet O, how happy! were it not
That this inexorable lot
Hath interposed its withering blight
Between my heart and all that's bright,
How happy to observe each day
Beneath thy sweet smile pass away,
To feel thy warm breath on my cheek,
To see thee, love thee, hear thee speak,
And shield thy tender heart from all
Which on it might too rudely fall.
Bright picture of our former days,
But one on which I must not gaze,
I've braved both friends' and foemen's power
For the enjoyment of this hour,
To bathe my soul once more in light,
Ere it sink into endless night.'

He paused, and closer to his breast
The maiden's form he wildly pressed,
As if that pressure could keep under
A heart which else would burst asunder.
And there they stood, that hapless pair,
The victim each of mute despair;
Yet how exalted, noble, pure,
The anguish which their souls endure!
When the full bosom swells like this
With feelings boundless, fathomless,
There's something so exalted there,
That e'en though springing from despair,
The heart would scarce desire repose
If purchased at the life of those.
Sensations vague and undefined
Had agitated ME-ME's mind
When first ME-GI-SI's word conveyed
The destiny o'er them weighed,
But when at length she knew the worst,
And the full truth upon her burst,
A pang shot through her heart and brain,
But one, and all was calm again;
But with that pang had fled all sense
Of pain or woe forever hence.
'Twas so intense no other grief
Could wake a throe, however brief,
And then a holy calmness came,
Succeeded to the passioned flame
Which had so brightly, till that hour,
Maintained within her breast its power.
It was a calmness which had birth
In the conviction that the earth
With all its pleasure, all its sweet,

Had nothing which could ever cheat—
Even for one brief moment's flight—
The sadness of her bosom's blight.
All tranquilly she raised her head,
Drooping like lily o'er its bed,
And gently loosed her from the clasp
Convulsive of her lover's grasp,
And spoke with look so calm and mild
It might almost be said she smiled,
But such a smile as one might trace
Upon the cold and marble face
Of one whose spirit had just riven
The bonds which checked its flight to heaven.
'ME-GI-SI, O how glad would I
Lay this poor body down to die,
Could it but bring again to thine
The joy that can no more be mine.
Let not thy ME-ME's broken heart
One sorrow to thine own impart;
O, no, but go, forget that we
Have ever loved so trustfully.
Thy duty calls, then be it so,
And let no thought of me e'er throw
Across thy breast a single cloud
The sunshine of its peace to shroud.
What though this fate shall blight my powers
Like early frosts the gladsome flowers,
And my poor body find its rest
Full soon upon the earth's cold breast?
My spirit still shall hover near thee,
And this, its only thought to cheer thee,
And pour most fondly into thine
The light which in itself shall shine.
Yes, go, forget that we have met,
Or if thou canst not all forget,
Think of it as a dream which stole
In night's calm hours into thy soul,
Whose memory perchance may cling
Around thy softened heart and fling
A shade of sadness which you may
Not altogether dash away,
But which thou shouldst not let control
The strength and bravery of thy soul.
No, if thou canst not banish all,
And memory will at times recall
The gladsome hours our hearts have known,
Thrilled by each other's look and tone,
There let thy fond thoughts only dwell
On this, thy ME-ME loved thee well,
And only look on those sweet hours
As thou would'st look on lovely flowers,
From which the freshness might be fled,
But which, though withered, yet would shed
Their fragrance sweet as when their hue
Was heightened by the night's soft dew.
O! let me deem that thus thy heart
Will look on me, and I can part
With one less pang from all those bright
And happy dreams which take their flight,
Till on the far-off spirit-shore
We meet again to part no more.'

O, Love! How hallowed, noble, pure,
The feeling which thou dost secure
Upon the breast where thou dost deign
To institute thy perfect reign!
When touched by thee, how all the dross
Of earthly passions, which so toss
And heave their billows o'er the soul
Before it hath felt thy control,
By thy strong alchemy expelled,
Yields up the places it hath held,
And all that finds acceptance there
Is hallowed as the breath of prayer;
And ME-ME, though despair's cold breath
Had sent the icy chill of death
Over her bosom's tender chords,
Yet even then her love found words
She fondly hoped might interpose
A power to sooth her lover's woes.
But vain! The love which thus could make
Such sacrifices for his sake
Had kindled in his heart the same
Self-sacrificing, generous flame,
And when his quick sense caught this new
And last fond proof of love so true,
And saw and felt himself how much
The purpose cost which made it such,
And gazed upon her standing there
So droopingly and yet so fair—
It was too much, he could not brook
That quiet and heart-stricken look.
He caught her up and wildly pressed
The blighted lily to his breast,
And for a moment yielded all
His heart and soul to love's fond call,
Resolved to brave scorn, torture, death,

To save that gentle heart from scath.
Fond dreamer, up! away! away!
Death and dishonor if you stay,
But death and honor if you go—
Away! to meet your country's foe!
A moment, and he felt it true,
No word broke forth to say adieu,
But one long burning kiss he gave
Upon that brow he could not save,
Then turned and wildly rushed again,
With wildered sense and maddened brain,
To where his light bark floating lay,
And o'er the waters shot his way.

IX. THE LAST BATTLE

'Tis noon again. The sun's warm beam
Is gleaming brightly o'er the stream,
Which, with a current calm and slow,
Bears on its breast the stealthy foe,
Within their light barks noiselessly;
Who now have paused a moment by
Its entrance to the crystal bay,
Opposed to where the islands lay.
A few brief words to nerve their breast,
The WEN-DI-GO to each addressed,
With promises of bravery's meed
Should they in that day's strife succeed,
And meed to warrior's heart more sweet,[22]
Which in the spirit-land should greet
Their souls, should death their path beset,
And when it came be bravely met.
These said—his bark, whose prow displayed
A feathery pennon's varying shade,
Shot from among the rest, and led
The way around a woodland head
Which had the bay and isles concealed,
And now before them lay revealed
The scenes whose memory around
Their warmest feelings long had wound,
And where so soon they must decide
If once again they shall abide
Within their quiet spell, or whether
They and this last hope die together.
As the last bark in that array
Came out upon the open bay
And caught the view, a moment's pause
Ran through the whole, while each one draws
A smothered breath and drops a prayer
For the Great Spirit's guardian care;
Then with a shout of curses dread
To gather upon foemen's head.
By their strong arms each light bark there
Sped onwards like a thing of air,
And should no foemen check their speed,
Short were the moments that they need
Ere they shall rest their glancing oar
Upon the nearest island's shore,
Where o'er the green and shady strand
The lodges of Ojibway stand,
Beneath whose shady folds repose,
Unconscious of approaching foes,
The chiefs and warriors, but with spear
And bow and war-club lying near,
Ready, upon the first alarm,
To be resumed with sturdy arm.
The foremost of the barks hath now
Almost upon the shore its prow,
When sudden from the Ojibways rang
The war-cry's blast, and, with it sprang
Each warrior there upon his feet

[22]In the idea of the Indian, bravery is the key that unlocks the entrance to the most exalted joys of the Great West, or future state. The peaceful and Christian virtue of humanity, forgiveness, and benevolence are powerless to open the gates of an Indian's Paradise.

Things have changed, and now it is otherwise. Once the Indian brave adored the man who recognized him as a noble warrior; yet however he may now admire that quality in man, it has been so refined by education, he yet loves to exhibit that manliness which exalts and ennobles man. Never will a true Indian stoop to low cunning and meanness which characterizes the higher state of pretended civilized life of other nations.

One of the greatest reasons which has made the paleface desist in his endeavors to civilize the Indian is because he could not subdue the high state of noble independence in him, as though it was necessary that his spirit was to be subdued first before he could be taught the noble spirit of Christian morals.

With answering shout, and rushed to meet,
In strife too wild and dark for name,
The foe that thus upon them came.
Then grappled each his nearest foe,
Nor yielded either till the blow
Which drank life's latest current well,
Left him all lifeless where he fell.
But vain the strife, though for each Sioux
There perished of his foemen two,
There lived but two of that brave band
To track through foes their way to land.
ME-GI-SI and the WEN-DI-GO,
Around whom fell at every blow
Victims to their resistless strength,
Had fought their bloody way at length
Upon the beach, and there they stood
Alone, unconquered, unsubdued,—
Keeping, like lions fierce, at bay
Surrounding foemen's whole array,
Or those who were upon them rushing,
In ghastly heaps around them crushing.
Maddened to see the slaughtering tide
And feel their power thus defied,
Shame to their courage adding wing,
The Ojibways upon them spring
Like famished wolves upon the prey
That chance hath thrown within their way,
And sire and son are borne beneath,
Their flesh an hundred weapons sheath;
And when the rushing crowd gave place,
Within ME-GI-SI's breast all trace
Of life with all its pains had fled,
Mangled he lay among the dead!
But from beneath their raining blows
The WEN-DI-GO again arose,
And dashing off, as things of naught,
Those who to stop his progress sought,
One thrilling yell of scorn he gave,
Then plunged beneath the blood-dyed wave.
They saw no more, and whether then
His spirit passed, or if again,
Concealed by magic from the view
He living rose, none ever knew;
Still they believe, amid the dirge
Of winter's winds and water's surge,
Or in the tempest's blasting hour,
They hear his voice and feel his power;
And even upon summer's night,
When winds are hushed and stars are bright,
They sometimes see his shadow pass
Slowly along the moon-lit grass,
And then with bloodless lips they tell
Of some mischance they know full well
To fall on whom the spirit's eye
Glanced angrily as it passed by.

THE REQUIEM

The eve that gathered o'er the water,
Yet crimson with the recent slaughter,
Came slowly, beautifully on;
And when its last faint hues were gone,
Shadowed in the embrace of night,
The moon and stars looked down as bright
As though no scenes of carnage lay
Where now their beams so sweetly stray.
Chance led at this delightful hour
A band of maidens to the bower
Where ME-ME and her lover parted
The night before so broken hearted;
And there upon a mossy bed
Lay ME-ME, silent, cold, and dead.
With the last look on lover cast,
Her gentle spirit sweetly passed,
And now she lay in cold death sleeping,
Their watch the wild flowers o'er her keeping,
And, as they waved with the soft sigh
Of the night zephyrs passing by,
Wept dewy tears o'er one so fair,
Lying like blighted rose-bud there,
And poured the fragrance of their breath
To hallow such a tristful death.
When first beheld, the maidens deemed
'Mid flowers and moonbeam's light she dreamed,
But when they gathered near and felt,
As by her side they fondly knelt,
That death's rude fingers had impressed
Their icy touch upon her breast,
Stilling each throb of bliss or pain
Beyond the power to beat again,
A wailing low, like sighing tone
Of winds when through the trees they moan,
While all around beside was hushed,
From their full bosoms sadly gushed:
'Heart of our hearts, farewell, farewell!'
Thus rose the dirge's plaintive swell,
'Thou wast the sunbeam spirit given,

But softened like the light of even,
Within our darkened bosoms stealing,
That kissed the buds of happy feeling,
And in the fragrant breath and hue
Of sweetest love to flowers drew.
O, what shall keep that hue so fair!
O, what shall keep that fragrance there?
Their warmth, and light, with thee withdrawn,
Their hue is fled, their fragrance gone.
We withered where our sister fell,
Heart of our hearts, farewell, farewell!'
Ere the sad tones had left the ear,
An airy spirit hovering near,
Caught up again the lingering strains,
And in such music as enchains
The raptured heart in childhood's dreams,
When in some fairy land it deems
'Mid bright ethereal forms it dwells,
The requiem around them swells:

'There's a bower prepared in the land of the blest,
Where the young, and the pure, and the lovely shall rest,
Who have left the sad earth, where the tempests that rushed
O'er their sensitive bosoms, forever are hushed.

O, the heart of the dead beat too warmly for earth,
Like a bird in the far sunny south that had birth,
But which wandered where winds from the northern sky passed,
Where it sung one sweet strain, then sank in the blast.

So the soul that once dwelt in that fair form of clay
Over which you now weep, that it thus passed away,
Like that bird hovered near you, then went to its rest
In the sweet spirit home, in the land of the west.

Weep not that her spirit thus early hath fled,
That spirit still lives, though the body be dead;
It lives where its joys pass no more with a sigh,
It lives where its happiness never shall die.'

INDEX

IN INDEXING this volume the Editor has kept in mind that the Table of Contents is particularly detailed, and in itself enables the reader to locate subjects in which he is interested. The following qualifications and restrictions form the basis of this index:

1. Officers' titles, and those of clergymen, doctors, and similar persons, are omitted except in instances where no first name or initial is available.

2. Indian names, which have many variants, are in general indexed only when they are still in common use.

3. Names which lie outside the old Newcastle District are omitted unless there is a special reason for their inclusion.

4. Signatures to petitions, which are often indecipherable, are not indexed.

5. Printed matter accompanying the rotogravure illustrations is not indexed.

6. For similar reasons the material in the following sections has been omitted from the index: Section III, No. 3; Section IV, Nos. 2, 3, 4, 5, and 9; Section V, No. 13; Section VI, Nos. 5 and 8; Section VII, Nos. 3 and 5; Section VIII, Nos. 1 and 2.

www.ingramcontent.com/pod-product-compliance
Lightning Source LLC
LaVergne TN
LVHW010446080826
844660LV00027B/1223

9781487599386